Communicating
Ethnic and
Cultural Identity

Communicating Ethnic and Cultural Identity

Edited by
MARY FONG
and
RUEYLING CHUANG

ROWMAN & LITTLEFIELD PUBLISHERS, INC.
Lanham • Boulder • New York • Toronto • Oxford

ROWMAN & LITTLEFIELD PUBLISHERS, INC.

Published in the United States of America
by Rowman & Littlefield Publishers, Inc.
A wholly owned subsidary of The Rowman & Littlefield Publishing Group, Inc.

4501 Forbes Boulevard, Suite 200, Lanham, MD 20706
www.rowmanlittlefield.com
P.O. Box 317, Oxford OX2 9RU, UK

British Library Cataloguing in Publication Information Available

Library of Congress Cataloging-in-Publication Data

Communicating ethnic and cultural identity / edited by Mary Fong and Rueyling Chuang.
   p. cm.
  Includes bibliographical references and index.
  ISBN 0-7425-1738-1 (cloth: alk. paper) — ISBN 0-7425-1739-X (pbk: alk. paper)
  1. Group identity. 2. Group identity—United States. 3. Ethnicity—United States.
4. Pluralism (Social sciences)—United States. I. Fong, Mary, 1959– II. Chuang, Rueyling, 1964–
HM753 .C66 2004
305.8'00973—dc21   2003011933

Printed in the United States of America

♾️™ The paper used in this publication meets the minimum requirements of American National Standard for Information Sciences—Permanence of Paper for Printed Library Materials, ANSI/NISO Z39.48-1992.

Contents

v

PART III Language, Terms, and Identity

PART IV Cultural Communities and Social Identities

PART V Negotiating Cultural Identities and the Sense of Belonging

PART VI Autoethnographies: Developing and Transforming Ethnic and Cultural Identities

Preface

In the face of the emerging awareness of cultural diversity and globalization, our sense of identities becomes multidimensional and fluid. Further, the notion of "cultural identity" is relational, contextual, and constantly evolving. It can also be ambiguous (e.g., Asian American, biracial children), fragmented (e.g., "third-culture kid," multicultural individuals), paradoxical, and problematic.

In resolving these challenges, individuals undergo self and cultural identity transformation in order to achieve understanding, harmony, and balance within themselves, their environment, and their connection with others. In this process, culture to a degree also changes according to the dynamics of historical, political, economic, and social influences that affect cultural and intercultural interactions.

It is commonly understood that cultural identities are negotiated, co-created, reinforced, and challenged through communication with one another. Identities and ethnicity are both the manifestations of socially constructed reality. Reflecting on the personal journeys that we have embarked on throughout our lives, we find ourselves wrestling with our own identity issues. Rueyling Chuang sees herself as a perpetual outsider in the United States; however, when she goes back to her home country of Taiwan, she is criticized for being too "Americanized" because she does not speak and act like a stereotypical Chinese woman. Her Chinese seems a little rusty and she seems to act too "assertive" for the Chinese culture. While in the United States she feels her deeply ingrained Chinese value of concern for others makes it difficult for her to speak her mind. She constantly has to negotiate and negate her own sense of cultural and ethnic identity.

Mary Fong, on the other hand, grew up in a predominately European American community in the United States in which she was the only Asian student in her elementary school class. Her classmates ostracized her by not playing with her, and a couple of little boys harassed her. She experienced an identity crisis to such an extent that she did not want to be Asian. Instead she wished that she were Caucasian so that her peers would not reject her. However, through this experience she became independent and accelerated in her studies and sports in order to gain approval and to feel better about herself. While she was in fifth grade, her family moved to Chinatown, Los Angeles, where she experienced reverse cultural shock in her socialization with Chinese children. Eventually, she learned a great deal about her culture and felt accepted by her Chinese immigrant classmates. She developed a healthy ethnic identity as a Chinese American.

Based on our personal and professional experiences, we feel that there is a need for a book that includes a wide variety of insightful articles pertaining to ethnic and cultural identity and various co-cultural groups. Our focus is given to diverse cultural groups and their ways of communicating that reflect, recreate, unify, and maintain their cultural identities. We seek to incorporate current literature on ethnic/cultural identity concepts, theories, and approaches and to provide refreshing research topics in this area. This book illuminates the complexity, ambiguity, and multiplicity of cultural identity and ethnicity.

Objectives of This Book

In light of the multifacetedness of ethnicity and cultural identity, our book seeks to (1) illustrate the extent to which ethnicity and cultural identity are negated, negotiated, or displaced; (2) explicate the complexity, fluidity, and ambiguity of ethnicity and cultural identity; (3) present the life world and lived experiences of various ethnic and cultural groups; and (4) shed light on cultural and intercultural interactions that influence our identity. The chapters included in this book use a wide variety of methodological approaches such as autoethnography, ethnography, narrative, textual analysis, and other interpretive research methods. This anthology aims to address ethnic groups such as African Americans, Asians, Asian Americans, Latino/as, and Native Americans, as well as different social classes, sexual orientations, and cultural communities in the United States (e.g., Deadheads, Franco Americans, interstate truckers). Chapters cover issues such as gender, race, class, media, sexual identity, and inter-/intra-ethnic identity.

In addition, this reader-friendly book aims to broaden the scope of knowledge for upper-division undergraduate and graduate students in courses that address topics such as culture, intercultural issues, or ethnicity. Not only do we integrate the conceptual and theoretical framework of ethnic and cultural diversity, but we also include chapters that provide critical examinations and discuss intercultural implications. To ensure the quality of the chapters chosen, we used a blind peer review process.

Organization of This Book

In part I of this text, we begin with five chapters that lay out the conceptual and theoretical foundations of cultural and ethnic identity. Parts II through VI extend cultural identity concepts and theories from part I. These articles illuminate our theoretical perspectives by integrating narratives of diverse cultural voices and members' life examples. These contributors incorporate description, observation, and analysis of specific cultural and intercultural contexts and events of diverse members' social interactions.

We organize this eclectic volume into six sections based on emerging themes. They are: (1) Introduction to Ethnic and Cultural Identity; (2) Artifacts and Cultural Identity; (3) Language, Terms, and Identity; (4) Cultural Communities and Social Identities; (5) Negotiating Cultural Identities and the Sense of Belonging; and (6) Autoethnographies: Developing and Transforming Ethnic and Cultural Identities.

It is our hope that this text will aid both students and scholars in their understanding of and dialogue on cultural and ethnic identity. As the twenty-first century brings increasing globalization and opportunities for cultural and intercultural interactions, may we keep in step with the dynamic times and strive to better understand one another in diverse social and cultural contexts.

Acknowledgments

This book would not have been possible without the contributors' invaluable works, efforts, and patience. We would like to express our heartfelt gratitude to our contributors, who have shared insights and expertise that will enrich our readers. We are grateful and appreciative to Rowman & Littlefield Publishers for having faith in us and publishing our first book. We would like to extend special thanks to Brenda Hadenfeldt for her continuous support, encouragement, understanding, and helpful editorial feedback in the creation of our text. Thanks are in order to Kristinn Leonhart and April Leo for their beneficial editorial assistance and to Hallie Gladden, the creative designer of our book cover. We want to thank our university, California State University, San Bernardino, for awarding us a summer research grant.

Together we would like to give our warmest thanks and appreciation to the reviewers and anonymous reviewers for their generosity, time, and valuable comments in the selection and revision stages of this anthology. They are:

Rosalind Bresnahan, California State University, San Bernardino
Ling Chen, Hong Kong Baptist University
Hui-Ching Chang, University of Illinois, Chicago
Steve Classen, California State University, Los Angeles
Jeanne Cook, St. John's University, Minnesota
Leda Cooks, University of Massachusetts, Amherst
Patricia Covarrubias, University of Montana
Robin Crabtree, Fairfield University
Lyall Crawford, Zayed University—United Arab Emirates
Rob Dechaine, California State University, Los Angeles
Margaret D'Silva, University of Louisville
Janie Harden Fritz, Duquesne University
Susan Hafen, Weber State University
Heather Hundley, California State University, San Bernardino
Fred Jandt, California State University, San Bernardino

Randy Kluver, Nanyang Technological University, Singapore
Robin Larsen, California State University, San Bernardino
Kathy Nadeau, California State University, San Bernardino
Anjali Ram, Roger Williams University
John Powers, Hong Kong Baptist University
Kristin Vonnegut, St. John's University
Mei Zhong, San Diego State University
Anonymous Reviewers

Mary: Above all, I would like to thank my loving God who has guided me from the inception of the book through the many stages toward completion of a work that required nothing less than a synergetic team effort of many gracious people. Much love to my Mom, both of my brothers, Richard and Jimmy, and my sister-in-law, Pei Li, and in memory of my Dad for their continuous loving support. Also, I am ever so appreciative of nothing less than warm times, smiles, and special memories of Troy, Charles, and Trojan for their happy enthusiasm and love that warms my spirit forever; and Hiker and Runner for their splashing, exciting energy that embraces me. Special acknowledgment to Catherine H. Peters for her love, generosity, kindness, and friendship for almost twenty years. Further thanks go to my students in the winter 2002 class, Ethnicity and Culture in Language, for their feedback on many of the chapters in this anthology. And I would like to express my thanks to my wonderful friends from near and far, with whom I have the joy of experiencing life in many dimensions. Final thanks to all colleagues and students whom I have had the pleasure of knowing and will know in the future in maintaining dear friendships.

Rueyling: Editing this book was an intellectual journey and a rewarding learning process for me. I am blessed with my parents', my brothers', and my sister's unwavering and unconditional love. My family members' steadfast support keeps me going. I am indebted to Susan Hafen, Martha Kazlo, Sister Olivia Forster, and Chris Stageberg for their altruism, encouragement, and loving-kindness. My friends' moral and emotional support enriches my life and helps me stay grounded. I would also like to extend my heartfelt gratitude to my colleagues and students for my intellectual growth.

PART I

Introduction to Ethnic and Cultural Identity

THIS SECTION is an introduction to basic concepts, theories, and research approaches to the area of ethnic and cultural identity. In the first chapter, Mary Fong surveys a variety of definitions of racial, ethnic, and cultural identity. An introduction of concepts related to the speech community such as norms, patterns, personhood, codes, and components of the Hymes S-P-E-A-K-I-N-G framework are discussed. Also, the influence and power of language and the use of labels and names are explored in relation to identity. Last, a presentation of the adaptive intercultural model (AIM) is introduced.

In the second chapter, Mary Fong further explains and illustrates the development of cultural identity and the seven properties of identity. Also, several dimensions of identity are discussed: gender, age, spiritual, class, national, regional, and personal.

In the next chapter, Mary Fong covers aspects such as surnames, physical attributes, and historical and celebratory events that people consider in determining a person's cultural and ethnic identity. Examples of surnames of several ethnic groups are included, physical attributes of a variety of ethnic groups are discussed, and many historical and celebratory events that are meaningful and significant to cultural and ethnic group members are noted.

In the fourth chapter, Rueyling Chuang discusses the theories of identity. She illustrates the fluidity and complexity of cultural and ethnic identity. Important issues that she covers are static versus fluid identity, double consciousness, dual cultural identity, cultural adaptation, and intercultural communication competence.

In chapter 5, Gust A. Yep discusses the complexity and nature of cultural identity. He further covers the major theoretical approaches to the study of cultural identity in communication and the implications of identity labels in intercultural interactions. Yep discusses various approaches such as autoethnographies, and functionalist, interpretive, critical humanist, and critical structuralist approaches.

This section provides an introduction to concepts, theories, and major research approaches of cultural and ethnic identity. These five chapters build a foundation of understanding in this growing area of identity research and application to our cultural and intercultural interactions.

Identity and the Speech Community

MARY FONG

LEARNING OBJECTIVES

After reading this chapter, students will be able to:

- discuss various definitions of racial, ethnic, and cultural identity;
- understand a variety of concepts related to the speech community (e.g., co-cultures, in/out-groups, norms/rules, patterns, speech code);
- recognize the power of language in relation to identity; and
- identify the components of the adaptive intercultural model (AIM).

When neighborhood loyalty, already something quite primordial, is reinforced by a common religion and a sense of common ethnic origins, the commitment to the neighborhood can become fierce and passionate indeed. Its streets, its markets, its meeting places, its friendships, its accepted patterns of behavior, its customs, its divisions, and even its factional feuds provide a context for life that many of its citizens are most reluctant to give up. It is curious that in a world in which the "quest for community" has become so conscious, so explicit, and so intense there is little awareness of the existence of such primordial community ties.

—A. M. Greeley (1994, p. 303)

Every speech community is layered with multiple identities of its members. And yet, these multiple identities come together at varying points to establish, affirm, and maintain identification to the speech community. There is a dynamic synergy that brings together members with multiple identities.

This chapter explores some definitions of racial, ethnic, and cultural identity. Then, it addresses several conceptual aspects related to the speech community. Next, there is a discussion of the power of language and the use of names and labels that influences and reflects our identity. Last, the chapter presents an introduction to the adaptive intercultural model (AIM).

Defining Racial, Ethnic, and Cultural Identity

In every discipline, scholars sometimes agree and other times differ in their definition of concepts. As a whole, scholars contribute a piece of the puzzle in understanding the phenomenon at hand. It is helpful to become familiar with various definitions of racial, ethnic, and cultural identity.

Racial Identity

The *Random House Webster's College Dictionary* (Costello 1995) defines **race** as "a group of persons related by common descent or heredity" and "a classification of modern humans . . . based on an arbitrary selection of physical characteristics as skin color, facial form, or eye shape, and now frequently based on such genetic markers as blood groups" (p. 1110). Orbe and Harris (2001) describe race as "a largely social—yet powerful—construction of human difference that has been used to classify human beings into separate value-based categories" (p. 6).

The study of **racial identity** in the intercultural field has "traditionally accentuated racial imparity, interracial interaction, and accommodation" (Jackson and Garner 1998, p. 39). Racial identity research may also include the sociopolitical ideologies related to race relations. Identity research in the intercultural communication field began to take on increasing importance in the late 1980s. In the 1990s, the terms *interracial communication* and *racial identity* are mentioned infrequently in communication studies (Jackson and Garner 1998).

However, *Interracial Communication: Theory into Practice* by Orbe and Harris (2001) argues that on the basis of democratic principles in the United States, we "must work through the issues related to racial differences" and "come to understand the significant role that race plays in our interactions with others" (p. 8). The authors further argue that there is a changing shift in the racial and ethnic composition of the United States that will increase the need for effective interracial communication. Using the singular term "racial/ethnic identity" rather than separating race and ethnicity, they credit Gordon's (1978) idea that "race and ethnicity represent social categories that develop during early socialization and maintain a central place in self, culture, and communication processes" (p. 74).

Orbe and Harris (2001) define **interracial communication** as a "transactional process of message exchange between individuals in a situational context where racial difference is perceived as a salient factor by at least one person" (p. 5). In other words, for an interaction to be considered interracial communication, at least one person's perceptions of racial difference need to take a central role in the exchange. If racial difference does not take a central role and only similarities exist in the interaction, it is interpersonal rather than interracial.

Ethnic Identity

The *Random House Webster's College Dictionary* (Costello 1995) defines **ethnic** as "pertaining to or characteristic of a people, especially a group sharing a common and distinctive culture, religion, language, etc." (p. 459). De Vos and Romanucci-Ross (1982) provide a general definition of **ethnicity** as "the attribute of membership in a group set off by racial, territorial, economic, religious, cultural, aesthetic, or linguistic uniqueness" (p. 3). They further define ethnicity on four levels of analysis: the social structural level, a pattern of social interaction, a subjective experience of identity, and as expressed in relatively fixed patterns of behavior and expressive emotional styles (p. xi).

Cyrus (1997) explains ethnicity:

When we identify someone as a member of an ethnic group, we mean that she or he belongs to some identifiable group within American society. This is the most important component of ethnicity: membership in a subgroup within an environment dominated by another culture. Ethnic subgroups are defined by many complex, often variable traits, such as religion, language, culture, customs, traditions, physical characteristics, and, probably most important in this country, ancestral origin. (p. 11)

Orbe and Harris (2001) define ethnicity as "a cultural marker that indicates shared traditions, heritage, and ancestral origins; ethnicity is defined psychologically and historically" (p. 7). They further differentiate ethnicity from race; for example, they note that a person's race may be Asian American, but that individual's ethnic makeup is Korean.

Edward (1979) defines **ethnic identity** as an:

allegiance to a group—large or small, socially dominant or subordinate—with which one has ancestral links. There is no necessity for a continuation, over generations, of the same socialization or cultural patterns, but some sense of a group boundary must persist. This can be sustained by shared objective characteristics (language, religion, etc.) or by more subjective contributions to the sense of "groupness," or by some combination of both. (p. 10)

De Vos and Romanucci-Ross (1982) define ethnic identity as "essentially subjective, a sense of social belonging, an ultimate loyalty" (p. 3). Collier and Thomas state that "Ethnic identity is identification with and perceived acceptance into a group with shared heritage and culture" (1988, p. 115).

Van den Berghe (1981) explains that primordialists define ethnic identity as an emotional bond that unites people together that is rooted in the past, and that people are born into such an identity. Cornell (1988) explains the emotional bond as a bond of "sentiments" that people share that originates from their past and that gives them an emotional force to claim their common historical origins.

Martin and Nakayama (2000) define ethnic identity as a:

set of ideas about one's own ethnic group membership. It typically includes several dimensions: self-identification, knowledge about the ethnic culture (traditions, customs, values, and behaviors), and feelings about belonging to a particular ethnic group. Ethnic identity often involves a shared sense of origin and history, which may link ethnic groups to distant cultures in Asia, Europe, Latin America, or other locations. (p. 122)

Eriksen (1993) defines ethnicity as:

An aspect of social relationship between agents who consider themselves as culturally distinctive from members of other groups with whom they have a minimum of regular

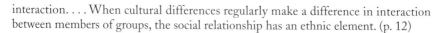

interaction. . . . When cultural differences regularly make a difference in interaction between members of groups, the social relationship has an ethnic element. (p. 12)

Eriksen (1993) identifies three important characteristics of ethnic identity. First, ethnic identity is socially enacted in interactions; and second, there is a perceived difference that is noticeable to the interactants. Third, ethnic members have a perceived common origin. Language, religion, and kinship are important aspects of ethnicity, particularly during periods of change such as migration, or in economic or demographic situations.

Since the 1990s, very little attention has been given to interracial communication in the intercultural field. Jackson and Garner's (1998) extensive literature review surmised that the terms *ethnicity* and *race* are still used but are less commonly referred to in the area of intercultural communication (p. 44). Instead, *culture* is increasingly becoming the preferred term.

Cultural Identity

Culture and cultural identity in the study of intercultural relations have become umbrella terms that subsume racial and ethnic identity. Orbe and Harris (2001) define culture as "learned and shared values, beliefs, and behaviors common to a particular group of people; culture forges a group's identity and assists in its survival. Race is culture, but a person's culture is more than her or his race" (p. 6).

Jackson and Garner (1998) provide a concise and consolidated definition of culture from a variety of sources (Ani 1994; Diop 1991; Holloway 1990; Levine 1977; Nobles 1986) as "a set of patterns, beliefs, behaviors, institutions, symbols, and practices shared and perpetuated by a consolidated group of individuals connected by an ancestral heritage and a concomitant geographical reference location" (p. 44).

Carbaugh uses both terms, *ethnic* and *culture*, together. We agree with Carbaugh's (1996) conceptualization of ethnic culture as a system of interdependent patterns of conduct and interpretations. He further explicates that "ethnic culture describes communication patterns of action and meaning that are deeply felt, commonly intelligible, and widely accessible in the process of creating, defining, and communicating identity or personhood" (Carbaugh 1988).

Cultural communication in this book is defined as a historically transmitted system of symbols, meanings, and norms (Collier and Thomas 1988; Geertz 1983; and Schneider 1976) shared by group members and passed down to the following generations of members who will maintain and modify particular aspects of the system in order to adapt to the needs of the group.

Lustig and Koester (1999) define cultural identity as a "sense of belonging to a particular culture or ethnic group. It is formed in a process that results from membership in a particular culture, and it involves learning about and accepting the traditions, heritage, language, religion, ancestry, aesthetics, thinking patterns, and social structures of culture" (p. 138).

We define **cultural identity** as the identification of communications of a shared system of symbolic verbal and nonverbal behavior that are meaningful to group members who have a sense of belonging and who share traditions, heritage, language, and similar norms of appropriate behavior. Cultural identity is a social construction.

Aspects of the Speech Community

Researchers interested in an aspect of a speech community's identity—whether it be ethnic, racial, cultural, class, or gender-related—look to cultural members' language use to discover their distinctive way of speaking that is meaningful to them in particular social interactional contexts. By exploring the culturally situated uses of norms, forms, and codes (Carbaugh 1990), we can capture and discover the communication patterns of social lives of diverse speech communities. These aspects reveal and reflect some dimension of members' ethnic and cultural identity.

Speech Community, Subculture, Micro-culture, Co-culture

Saville-Troike (1989) outlines several definitions of a **speech community,** which include such criteria as:

> Shared language use (Lyons 1970), frequency of interaction by a group of people (Bloomfield 1927; Hocket, 1958; Gumperz 1962), shared rules of speaking and interpretation of speech performance (Hymes 1972), shared attitudes and values regarding language forms and use (Labov 1972), and shared sociocultural understandings and presuppositions with regard to speech. (Sherzer 1975, p. 16)

In addition to the criteria of a speech community, Romaine (1982) points out that a speech community sharing the norms and rules of a language may not necessarily use the language in the *same* way. Romaine explains that there will probably not be a one-to-one mapping of the uses of languages for different members and groups within a speech community. She further points out that Hymes (1974) states that researchers need to discover the *uses* of language. We also agree with Romaine that a speech community may generally share the norms and rules of a language. However, it is not necessarily the case that *all* cultural members will use *all* the aspects of the language the *same* way. Our conceptualization of this allows for speech communities to be maintaining, changing, and at times, finding alternative acceptable ways in their speech uses. In this respect, we acknowledge the varying degrees in speech diversity within a speech community. Examples of speech communities are Chinatown, San Francisco; Warm Spring Indians in Oregon; African Americans in South L.A.; Mexican people in the Coachella Valley.

Subcultures are smaller cultures within a larger culture. However, the use of subcultures has been criticized to imply that a smaller culture within a larger culture is "less than" or inferior in terms of importance, value, or power as a people because of their perceived "minority" status. Instead, Hall (1959) first named these smaller cultures **micro-cultures.** Co-cultures are more commonly used in cultural and intercultural communication studies to convey the idea that one culture is not superior over another (Orbe 1998). Examples of these groups are Mexicans, Koreans, African Americans, Russians, Germans, American Indians, and Irish.

We refer to **co-cultures** as *all* cultural groups or speech communities that exist together in society but are respected as equals in terms of value and importance and are appreciated for their uniqueness and cultural ways of communicating as people who have worthy contributions to offer. However, we do acknowledge that in reality, cultural groups around the world are not equal in political power and treatment. Our definition of co-culture is merely

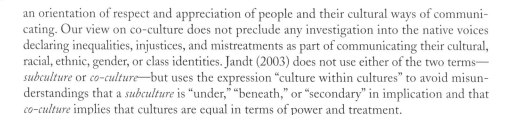

an orientation of respect and appreciation of people and their cultural ways of communicating. Our view on co-culture does not preclude any investigation into the native voices declaring inequalities, injustices, and mistreatments as part of communicating their cultural, racial, ethnic, gender, or class identities. Jandt (2003) does not use either of the two terms—*subculture* or *co-culture*—but uses the expression "culture within cultures" to avoid misunderstandings that a *subculture* is "under," "beneath," or "secondary" in implication and that *co-culture* implies that cultures are equal in terms of power and treatment.

In-group and Out-group

Within and between every speech community there are in-groups and out-groups (Tajfel 1981). **In-groups** refer to group members who identify and associate with each other. Members of the group see themselves and other members as part of their "in-group." They help each other during times of need, they care about what happens to each other, they associate with members, and they feel an emotional bond with their group. People who are kept at a physical and emotional distance are considered the **out-group** from the view of in-group members. Typically, there is very little interaction between the two groups. In some situations, a conglomerate of people who are labeled "out-group" may actually see themselves as the in-group.

The concepts of in-group and out-group also deal with power and dominance. Many times, in-group members are the majority, in a position of power and dominance, while the out-group members are considered the minority, lacking in power and feeling marginalized. Formation of in-groups and out-groups sometimes serves the function to include and exclude people for a variety of reasons. Possible reasons are perceptions of cultural differences, differing comfort, attraction, or preference levels, and prejudices. For example, athletes and cheerleaders may consider themselves as the in-group at their school and see the student government leaders as the out-group. Depending on the group's point of view, the student government leaders may think the contrary.

Norms, Rules, and Patterns

Every speech community has spoken and unspoken norms or rules of communication. Scholars in the communication field often use the terms *rule* and *norm* interchangeably (Shimanoff 1980). **Norms** or **rules** are social standards of acceptable and appropriate behavior shared by members of a speech community who expect members to conform to them. An example of a norm in the Hispanic culture is that guests never arrive to a party or fiesta at the written or spoken time. Instead it is normative and appropriate behavior for guests to arrive one, two, or three hours after the designated time.

Kroeber and Kluckhohn (1952) have stated, "culture consists of patterns . . . of and for behavior" (p.181). Essentially, **patterns** refer to reoccurrences or regularities of specific behaviors in a particular situation or interaction. When qualitative researchers establish a cultural pattern, this not only means that there is a behavioral tendency or normative behavior that exists, but there is also a small degree of deviation or exception inherent in the pattern. That is, patterns do not indicate that *all* group members will always behave in a specific way in a situation. Carbaugh (1990) states, "Cultural identity is everywhere coded in communication, but nowhere is it coded exactly the same in all contexts" (p. 157). There is a degree of variation that is seen as appropriate in every context. "**Normative behavior** is behavior that happens on the average" (Shimanoff 1980, p. 110).

Carbaugh (1990) refers to norms as "patterns for proper communication conduct that are used discursively to instruct, regulate, and evaluate routine practices. . . . Normative patterns are granted moral status within identifiable speech situations as 'the right thing to do' . . . to the practical 'thing to do'" (pp. 161–62). He further states the guiding criterion is appropriateness of speaking and behaving in a specific context within a speech community.

Schneider (1976) explains that a pattern of behavior is a norm; and norms are patterns that shape our action and are "patterns for action" (p. 200). Schneider (1976) further elaborates on the nature of norms:

> Action means that norms entail the clear mandate of legitimacy, propriety, appropriateness, moral authority. Some norms may be obligatory, some preferential, some allowable, some acceptable, but none can be morally wrong in any absolute and unqualified sense . . . . The point about norms being like patterns and templates is that they are more or less complete, detailed, and specific instructions for how the culturally significant parts of the act are to be performed, as well as the contexts in which they are proper. (pp. 200–201).

Forms of Communication and Speech Codes

Cultural and intercultural researchers are interested in discovering and articulating the cultural patterns within a speech community. **Forms of communication** exist in every speech community that emanates unique contours and characteristics in its types of expression. Examples of forms of talk are: the Teamsterville male who speaks "like a man" (Philipsen 1975), the Israeli Sabra culture engaging in *Dugri* speaking, also known as talking straight (Katriel 1986), the Chinese from Hong Kong using "Luck Talk" during their celebration of the Chinese New Year (Fong 2000), and African Americans interacting through their call/response form between the preacher and the church members (Daniel and Smitherman 1990) and in interpersonal conversations.

Carbaugh explains that a cultural model of personhood is one aspect of cultural identity that is interactionally coded (1990). He further explains, "the cultural model for being a person focuses attention on the sense that constitute personhood, or the concepts and premises for being a cultural agent that are marked for communication performance" (p. 157). Essentially, a model person in a speech community is one who is recognizable to its members through the communicative performances that are enacted and observed.

A model person and members of a speech community know the speech code. Carbaugh (1990) refers to a speech code as a "semantic system-in-use that renders communal ways intelligible" (p. 9). A **speech code** is a system of symbols, signs, meanings, and rules shared by group members who are competent in appropriate speech conduct in a specific situation, interaction, or act.

The Hymes S-P-E-A-K-I-N-G Framework

The ethnography of communication is one qualitative approach that offers researchers the Hymes (1972) **S-P-E-A-K-I-N-G framework** to discover the communication patterns of a cultural or ethnic speech community. Hymes's mnemonic framework represents several components in which an ethnographer can discover and describe how cultural/ethnic members of a speech community communicate their speech code to one another.

The components of the Hymes S-P-E-A-K-I-N-G framework begin with the **speech community** discussed above. "S" also represents the **scenes**, which are the physical and psychological settings where the communication takes place. Scenes are similar to the different settings found in a play or a movie. For example, the Oscar-winning best picture, *The Titanic*, had the love-making scene between Leonardo DiCaprio and Kate Winslet, the sinking of the *Titanic* when everyone was on the top deck, and the sentimental exchange of words between DiCaprio and Winslet at the end of the movie when holding on to a remnant of the ship in the ocean.

Participants are members of the speech community. Ethnographers are interested in identifying the relationship of participants to one another in interaction, and also their age, gender, ethnicity, social status, and generation. Examples of participants are American Indians on the San Manuel reservation in California, first-generation Vietnamese living in Little Saigon, Orange County, California, and Jehovah's Witnesses in Little Rock, Arkansas.

"E" represents **ends** that refer to the goal or intent of the verbal or nonverbal communication act. For example, Fong and Philipsen (2000/2001) found that parents sent indirect messages through implied statements, comparisons, questions, and the use of intermediaries for the ends or intent to persuade their adult child on various concerns such as marriage and caring for them. **Event** is also a component characterized by having the same purpose for communicating, the same general topic, involving the same participants, and generally using the same language and the same rules for interaction in the same setting. An event terminates whenever there is a change in the major participants, their role-relationships, or the focus of attention. Within an event there can be scenes and situations (Saville-Troike 1989).

Act is a single interactional function that is either verbal or nonverbal. A **verbal act** is also known as a speech act, such as a statement, a request, a command, compliment, compliment response, or apology. A **nonverbal act** refers to cultural members perceiving the gesture or movement to have a meaningful intent in a specific situation. For instance, a person is grocery shopping and recognizes an acquaintance and waves from a distance with the intent to nonverbally say "hi." But the other person quickly looks away and ducks behind the pastry counter with the intent to hide from the other. The **act sequence** is also another important component that refers to stages or chronological order of acts that a participant performs. For example, a person is interested in asking someone to go out on a date. The first act in the sequence is to engage in positive chitchat with the other. The second act may involve finding out if the person is busy that weekend. If the person is not busy, the third act would be asking the person out, the fourth act is the obtaining of the phone number, and lastly mentioning that one will call tonight to talk more about the date plans.

Key deals with the tone or mood of how something is said or done. For example, when a person apologizes, he or she should show seriousness and some degree of remorse or regret comparable to the seriousness of the infringement.

Instrumentalities refer to the means or channel by which the act is conveyed. This includes the physical means used to perform the act and the style in which it is performed. For example, a parent who gives the "evil eye" and crosses both arms at the child is using eye contact and arm gesturing to communicate a displeased manner so the child will behave without being told in public.

Interactional rules (Saville-Troike 1989) involve explanations of the rules for the use of speech that are applicable to the communication event. **Rules of speaking** deal with speaking conduct. Cultural members know what is considered appropriate and inappropriate speaking behavior within a situation and with particular relationships. Ethnographers wish to discover what should and should not be said, how it should be said, when to say or not to say, who to say and not to say, where it should and should not be said. An example of a rule of speaking is during class when a teacher is talking, students should not be talking, but listening. Also, **rules of interaction** refer to how a person should and should not act toward others, and when, and where. A description of how a person should and should not interact with others is important in understanding the code of a group. For example, in an elevator with strangers, exchange of words is at a minimum, except for the floor request and excusing oneself on or off the elevator. Also, minimal eye contact is made when entering the elevator, just enough to position oneself, allowing as much space as possible and no bodily contact.

Norms of interpretation deal with common knowledge, the relevant cultural presuppositions, or shared understandings and meanings of the participants of a speech community. An example in both the Chinese and Japanese culture is when one is offered some food at a friend's home during an occasional visit, refusal of food is normative. The offerer interprets the refusal of food as a polite gesture and makes an offer again. Another polite refusal of food is likely to occur, and then a third offer is made again, but showing more insistence. Then the guest accepts graciously with a smile. The common knowledge shared in both cultures is to show politeness by refusing so that the guest does not appear to be a "hungry pig."

Lastly is **genre** that involves the type of event or act, like telling a joke, a story, a lecture, a greeting, or a conversation. All of Hymes's components help the cultural and intercultural researcher bring to light the shared coding system of a group in their communicative rituals, interactions, and activities in their daily lives.

Power of Language and Identity

The power of language and the use of names and labels influences, reflects, and sometimes misrepresents our identity. The use of a language functions not only as a means of communicative expression, but often it is a **marker** or indicator of the speaker's ethnic or cultural identity. Hecht and Ribeau (1987) posit that identity is communicated through messages during interaction. Scott (2000) found that *girl* and *look* are two **discourse markers** used by a group of Black women. The use of *girl* indicates solidarity between Black women. The discourse marker *look* calls attention to differences in identity of those who are not Black and female. The Black women in the study used *look* when discussing interactions in predominantly Caucasian environments. Scott (2000) reported that the Black participants do not feel recognized or understood. The **linguistic marker** *look* appears to distance "self" from "the other" in order to call attention to self and to assert an identity that is different from that of the other person.

Language seems to have a life of its own, or does it? When a person expresses a favorable or unfavorable comment, do the words have an impact on you? We have heard the expression, "Sticks and stones may break my bones but words can never hurt me." Do you agree with this expression or not? It just may depend on what is said and by whom, and on how secure we are. At times, names and labels have a powerful impact on us, especially if we allow the words to influence our being. If we have a good sense of who we are and we have good reasoning skills, we can lessen the impact of names and labels on us, especially if they are negative and undeserved.

We often use **labels** and **names** to refer to ourselves and other people. Researchers have examined racial or ethnic identity labels and the meanings associated with them according to the ethnic members. Labels for various ethnic groups have been examined, such as *African American, Black, Afro American* (Hecht, Collier, Ribeau 1993), *Hispanic, Latina/Latino, Chicana/Chicano, Mexican American* (Tanno 2003), *Whiteness* (Nakayama and Krizek 1995), and hyphenated and dehyphenated identity (Chen 2003).

The politically correct term *Native American* is commonly used. Many, however, identify themselves as American Indians, Indians, Nations, and Tribes. All the tribes are as diverse as other pan-ethnic groups such as Asian (e.g., Chinese, Japanese, Korean, Vietnamese, Thai) and Hispanic/Latino (e.g., Argentine, Colombian, Nicaraguan, Mexican). There is not one shared language among each pan-ethnic group such as the Asians, the Tribes, and European cultures (e.g., Swedish, Hungarian, Polish) (Futch 2003).

The term *Asian American* is preferred and often used and has replaced the label *Oriental*, which has been rejected by Asian Americans. *Oriental* conjures up stereotypical images of "the sexy Susie Wong, the wily Charlie Chan, and the evil Fu Manchu" (Weiss 1974, p. 234) and connotes exotic submissive women and the martial arts experts Bruce Lee and Jackie Chan. *Asian Americans* stands for Americans of Asian descent.

Labels and names are communicative devices to express a dimension of our own identity (Carbaugh 1996) or another's social identity. In October 2002, Chief Charles Moose was in charge of catching the serial sniper in the Washington, D.C., area. At a press conference, a news reporter asked him why he was speaking so nicely to the snipers. Chief Moose did not raise his voice, show any anger, make any threats, or call the snipers any disrespectful or demeaning names such as cowards, low-life scum, or criminals. Chief Moose responded to press questions that he was raised in a way to speak respectfully and courteously toward everyone. A day after the suspected snipers were arrested, a press conference was held. Community leaders spoke highly of Chief Moose, praising him for his leadership and handling of the situation with the utmost professionalism, in spite of the great pressures he was under to find the snipers and the criticism he received. The words we use and how we carry ourselves speak volumes and communicate our self-worth and how we regard the worth of others too.

Difficulties arise when names and labels are used inappropriately in a social context or we feel they do not accurately describe who we are. I recall an interaction I had in my freshman year in college. I was in a children's musical play and was practicing the choreography with two other cast members. One fellow was a Japanese American who asked me where my parents were from. I told him that they were born and raised in Mainland China. He asked what part of China? I said Canton.

Then he made a jesting comment, "Oh, they're peasants." I did not say anything to him, but he certainly could see that I was not pleased by his comment. After a silence, he said, "I'm only joking."

I said, "Well, that wasn't funny. I don't appreciate the way you put my parents down. Who do you think you are?" He apologized. In this instance, his comment was hurtful because he offended my parents. His comment was insensitive, immature, and ignorant—and it reflected an aspect of his character.

The use of labels and names can create inclusion or exclusion depending on the socio-cultural context and relationships. Labels are one way to communicate a concept for cognitive and/or emotional identification or nonidentification with a real or imagined community of people (Carbaugh 1996). In many Asian cultures, such as Filipino, Chinese, Korean, Japanese, and Thai, close friends of the family are referred to as aunts and uncles who are a part of the extended family. Often we create inclusion when we use terms of endearment to express affection toward our parents, children, romantic significant others, or just good friends. A friend from Hong Kong had told me that in very traditional Chinese culture, some families who have newly born infants call them a particular animal such as a "little piggy," "little doggy," and so forth. This practice is meant both as a term of endearment and to protect the infant from evil spirits that wish to prey on the vulnerable. Calling it by an animal name is meant to trick the evil spirits into thinking that it is an animal or it is an ugly newborn. Some traditional people who choose to practice this believe that complimenting a newborn would attract evil spirits who want to take the baby's life.

When people use labels and names to exclude others, often it is an expression of separation, discrimination, or prejudice. For example, in the final part of this book, there are autoethnographies by Jerry Pinkney and Peter Chhuor, who write about their multiethnic identity experiences. They write about the discrimination they have experienced from some members of various ethnic groups. The discriminators used name calling to make Jerry and Peter feel ostracized and that they did not belong.

Adaptive Intercultural Model (AIM)

We define **intercultural communication** as an area of research that studies the interactional processes of participants who have culturally different communication styles where differing patterns of communication exist. The **adaptive intercultural model (AIM)** simplifies the complex intercultural process and illustrates the essence of this communication phenomenon. (See fig. 1.1.) The emphasis of AIM is to provide choices in adapting to cultural differences in order to achieve balance or **homeostasis** to both cultural interactants and as an intercultural communication system.

For intercultural communications to occur, two culturally different members interact where differences occur. **Cultural difference** is a primary component that emerges from the intercultural interaction. Any culturally different nonverbal and verbal communication messages—eye contact, gestures, pauses, turn-taking, touch, use of time, and rituals—are some potential sources of creating intercultural communication clash or conflict. Frustration, confusion, tension, and embarrassment are feelings that occur during an intercultural communication clash. During this clash, often interactants cannot put their finger exactly on the cultural difference but only have feelings that something is not right. It is not until one or both of the interactants reflect, analyze, and collect more data on the interaction that clarity of the cultural differences begins to be understood.

At this juncture of clashing cultural differences, both cultural interactants may choose an approach to deal with this. They can either take a **functional approach**—positive and nurturing—or a **dysfunctional approach**—negative and hostile. An **attitude** is a favorable or unfavorable predisposition toward a person, thing, or an idea. The functional approach further carries an attitude of openness, acceptance, and trust. The dysfunctional approach leads to

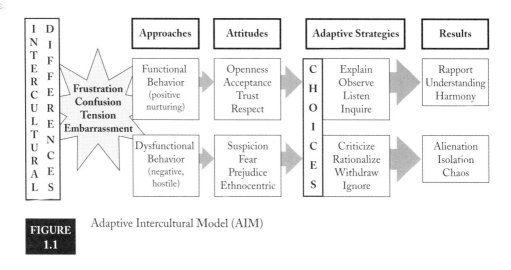

FIGURE 1.1 Adaptive Intercultural Model (AIM)

an attitude of suspicion, fear, ethnocentrism, and prejudice. **Ethnocentrism** is a person's attitude of superiority over another cultural person or group. It involves negatively judging another culture by the standards of one's own culture.

Both cultural interactants make choices in using adaptive strategies to cope with the cultural difference in the intercultural interaction. The participant who selects the functional approach has further choices of **adaptive strategies** such as explaining or inquiring about cultural behavior in a discussion with the other cultural interactant. Also, observing and listening enables participants to collect more information to figure out what is occurring. The participant who chooses the dysfunctional approach displays negative adaptive strategies—criticizing, rationalizing, withdrawing, and ignoring—toward the other cultural interactant. As a **result,** the dysfunctional approach leads to eventual alienation and isolation of both cultural interactants. However, the functional approach results in a favorable way such as rapport building and understanding between the two intercultural participants.

Summary

This chapter explored some definitions of racial, ethnic, and cultural identity. *Culture* and *cultural identity* are the umbrella terms that subsume racial and ethnic identity. *Racial identity* deals with physical characteristics such as skin color, facial form, and eye shape. Further, racial identity research may also include the sociopolitical ideologies related to race relations. *Ethnic identity* includes several dimensions—self-identification, knowledge about ethnic culture (e.g., traditions, customs, values, and behaviors), and feelings about belonging to a group. *Cultural identity* is the identification of communications of a shared system of symbolic verbal and nonverbal behavior that are meaningful to group members who have a sense of belonging and who share traditions, heritage, language, and similar norms of behavior.

There was also a discussion of aspects of the speech community. *Subculture, micro-culture,* and *co-culture* are synonymous and refer to a culture within a culture. *In-groups* and *out-groups* are found in every speech community. In-group refers to a group whose members identify and associate with each other. Out-group pertains to people who are kept at a physical and emotional distance from in-groups. Distinctions of in-groups and out-groups show inclusion and exclusion in communications. Power and dominance are involved. *Norms* and *rules* are used interchangeably; they are social standards of acceptable and appropriate behavior shared by members of a speech community who expect members to conform to them. *Patterns* refer to reoccurrences and regularities of specific behaviors in a particular situation or interaction.

In the Hymes S-P-E-A-K-I-N-G framework, "S" stands for *speech community,* a culture of members who share language use and have shared socio-cultural understandings regarding speech. "P" represents *participants* who are members of the speech community. "E" refers to *ends,* the goal or intent of the communication act. "E" can also mean *event,* which is characterized by having the same purpose for communicating, the same general topic, involving the same participants, and the same rules for interaction in the same setting. "A" represents act. It is a single interactional function that is either verbal or nonverbal. "K" is *key,* that means tone or mood in how something is said or done. "I" refers to *instrumentalities,* the means or channel by which the act is conveyed. "I" also includes *rules of speaking, rules of interaction,* and *norms of interpretation. Rules of speaking* deal with speaking conduct. *Rules of interaction* refer to how a person should act, and how a person should and should not act toward whom, and when, and where. *Norms* ("N") *of interpretation* pertain to common knowledge and shared understandings and meanings of group members. Lastly, "G" represents *genre,* a type of event like telling a joke, a greeting, or a conversation.

This chapter examined the power of language and how the use of names and labels influences, reflects, and sometimes misrepresents our identity. The use of labels and names can create inclusion or exclusion depending on the sociocultural context and relationships. Labels are one way to communicate a concept for cognitive and/or emotional identification or non-identification with a real or imagined community of people. When people use labels and names to exclude others, often it is an expression of separation, discrimination, or prejudice.

The adaptive intercultural model (AIM) was introduced. Essentially, two culturally different interactants exchange verbal and nonverbal messages displaying intercultural differences. A clash occurs where frustration, confusion, and tension are felt by at least one of the interactants. They have a choice to take a functional approach—positive and nurturing—or a dysfunctional approach—negative and hostile. The functional approach further carries an attitude of openness, acceptance, and trust. The dysfunctional approach leads to an attitude of suspicion, fear, and prejudice.

Both cultural interactants make choices in using adaptive strategies to cope with the cultural differences in the intercultural interaction. As a **result,** the dysfunctional approach leads to eventual alienation and isolation of both cultural interactants. However, the functional approach results in a favorable way, such as rapport building and understanding.

References

Ani, M. 1994. *Yurugu.* Trenton, N.J.: Africa World Press.

Bloomfield, L. 1927. Literate and illiterate speech. *American Speech* 10: 432–39. (Reprinted in Hymes 1964, pp. 391–96.)

Carbaugh, D. 1988. Comments on "culture" in communication inquiry. *Communication Reports* 1: 38-41.

———. 1990. *Cultural communication and intercultural contact.* Hillsdale, N.J.: Lawrence Erlbaum Associates.

———. 1996. *Situating selves: The communication of social identities in American scenes.* Albany, N.Y.: SUNY Press.

Chen, V. 2003. (De)hyphenated Identity: The double voice in the woman warrior. In A. Gonzalez, M. Houston, and V. Chen (Eds.), *Our voices* (pp. 25–28). Los Angeles, Calif.: Roxbury Publishing Co.

Collier, M. J., and M. Thomas. 1988. Cultural identity: An interpretive perspective. In Y. Y. Kim and W. B. Gudykunst (Eds.): *Theories in intercultural communication* (pp. 99–120). Newbury Park, Calif.: Sage.

Cornell, S. E. 1988. *The return of the native: American Indian political resurgence.* New York: Oxford University Press.

Costello, R. 1995. *Random House Webster's College Dictionary.* New York: Random House.

Cyrus, V. 1997. *Experiencing race, class, and gender in the United States* (2nd ed.). Mountain View, Calif.: Mayfield Publishing Co.

Daniel, J. L., and G. Smitherman. 1990. How I got over communication: Dynamics in the Black community. In Donal Carbaugh (Ed.), *Cultural communication and intercultural contact* (pp. 27–40). Hillsdale, N.J.: Lawrence Erlbaum Associates.

De Vos, G., and L. Romanucci-Ross. 1982. *Ethnic identity: Cultural continuities and change.* Chicago: University of Chicago Press.

Diop, C. A. 1991. *Civilization or barbarism: An authentic anthropology.* Chicago: Lawrence Hill.

Edward, A. D. 1979. *Language in culture and class.* London: Heinemann.

Eriksen, T. H. 1993. *Ethnicity and nationalism: Anthropological perspectives.* Boulder, Colo.: Pluto Press.

Fong, M. 2000. "Luck talk" in celebrating the Chinese new year. *Journal of Pragmatics* 32: 219–37.

Fong, M., and G. Philipsen. 2000/2001. A Chinese American way of speaking: The persuasive function. *Intercultural Communication Studies* 10 (2): 65–83.

Futch, J. 2003, January. Interview with Director John Futch, California State University, San Bernardino.

Geertz, C. 1983. *Local knowledge: Further essays in interpretive anthropology.* New York: Basic Books.

Gordon, M. M. 1978. *Human nature, class, and ethnicity.* New York: Oxford University Press.

Greeley, A. M. 1994. Social turf. In J. Zaitchik, W. Roberts, H. Zaitchik (Eds.), *Face to face: Readings on confrontation and accommodation in America* (pp. 300–304). Palo Alto, Calif.: Houghton Mifflin.

Gumperz, J. 1962. Types of linguistic communities. *Anthropological Linguistics* 4 (1): 28–40.

Hall, E. T. 1959. *The silent language.* Garden City, N.Y.: Anchor Press/Doubleday.

Hecht, M. L., M. J. Collier, and S. A. Ribeau. 1993. *African American communication: Ethnic identity and cultural interpretation.* Newbury Park, Calif.: Sage.

Hecht, M. L., and S. Ribeau. 1987. Afro-American identity labels and communicative effectiveness. *Journal of Language and Social Psychology* 6: 319–26.

Hockett, C. F. 1958. *A course in modern linguistics.* New York: Macmillan.

Holloway, J. E. 1990. Introduction. In J. E. Holloway (Ed.), *Africanisms.* Bloomington: Indiana University Press.

Hymes, D. 1972. Models of the interaction of language and social life. In John J. Gumperz and D. Hymes (Eds.), *Directions in sociolinguistics: Ethnography of communication* (pp. 35–71). New York: Holt, Rinehart and Winston.

———. 1974. *Foundations in sociolinguistics: An ethnographic approach.* Philadelphia: University of Pennsylvania Press.

Jackson, R. L., II. 1999. *The negotiation of cultural identity: Perceptions of Europeans and African Americans.* Westport, Conn.: Praeger.

Jackson, R. L., II, and T. Garner. 1998. Tracing the evolution of "race," "ethnicity," and "culture" in communication studies. *The Howard Journal of Communications* 9: 41–55.

Jandt, F. 2003. *Intercultural communication: An introduction* (4th ed.). Thousand Oaks, Calif.: Sage.

Katriel, T. 1986. *Talking straight: "Dugri" speech in Israeli Sabra culture.* Cambridge: Cambridge University Press.

Kroeber, A., and C. Kluckhohn. 1952. Culture: A critical review of concepts and definitions. 47 (1), Papers of the Peabody Museum, Harvard University.

Labov, W. 1972. On the mechanism of linguistic change. In John J. Gumperz and D. Hymes (Eds.), *Directions of sociolinguistics: The ethnography of communication* (pp. 512–38). New York: Holt, Rinehart and Winston.

Levine, L. 1977. *Black culture and Black consciousness.* New York: Oxford University Press.

Lustig, M. W., and J. Koester. 1999. *Intercultural competence: Interpersonal communication across cultures* (3rd ed.). Menlo Park, Calif.: Addison Wesley Longman, Inc.

Lyons, J. 1970. *New horizons in linguistics.* Harmondsworth: Penguin.

Martin, J., and T. Nakayama. 2000. *Intercultural communication in contexts.* Mountain View, Calif.: Mayfield.

Nakayama, T., and R. Krizek. 1995. Whiteness: A strategic rhetoric. *Quarterly Journal of Speech* 81: 291–309.

Nobles, W. 1986. Ancient Egyptian thought and the development of an African (Black) psychology. In M. Karenga and J. Carruthers (Eds.), *Kemet and the African world view.* Los Angeles: University of Sankone Press.

Orbe, M. P. 1998. *Constructing co-cultural theory: An explication of culture, power, and communication.* Thousand Oaks, Calif.: Sage.

Orbe, M. P., and T. M. Harris. 2001. *Interracial communication: Theory into practice.* Belmont, Calif.: Wadsworth/Thomson Learning.

Philipsen, G. 1975. Speaking "like a man" in Teamsterville; Culture patterns of role enactment in an urban neighborhood. *Quarterly Journal of Speech* 61: 13–22.

Romaine, S. 1982. What is a speech community? In Suzanne Romaine (Ed.), *Sociolinguistic variation in speech communities* (pp. 13–24). London: Arnold.

Saville-Troike, M. 1989. The ethnography of communication (2nd ed.). New York: Basil Blackwell.

Schneider, D. M. 1976. Notes toward a theory of culture. In K. R. Basso and H. A. Selby (Eds.), *Meaning in anthropology* (pp. 197–219). Albuquerque: University of New Mexico Press.

Scott, K. 2000. Crossing cultural borders: "Girl" and "look" as markers of identity in Black women's language use. *Discourse and Society* 11 (2): 237–49.

Sherzer, J. 1975. Ethnography of speaking. Manuscript, University of Texas at Austin.

Shimanoff, S. B. 1980. *Communication rules: Theory and research.* Beverly Hills, Calif.: Sage.

Tajfel, H. 1981. *Human groups and social categories.* Cambridge: Cambridge University Press.

Tanno, D. 2003. Names, narratives, and the evolution of ethnic identity. In A. Gonzalez, M. Houston, and V. Chen (Eds.), *Our voices* (pp. 25–28). Los Angeles: Roxbury.

Van den Berghe, P. 1981. *The ethnic phenomenon.* New York: Elsevier.

Weiss, M. S. 1974. *Valley City: A Chinese community in America.* Cambridge, Mass.: Schenkman.

KEY TERMS

act

act sequence

adaptive intercultural model (AIM)

adaptive strategies

attitude

clash

co-culture

cultural communication

cultural difference

cultural identity

culture

discourse markers

dysfunctional approach

ends

ethnic

ethnic identity

ethnicity

ethnocentrism

event

forms of communication

functional approach

genre

homeostasis

in-group

instrumentalities

interactional rules

intercultural communication

interracial communication

interracial identity

key

labels

linguistic marker

marker

micro-culture

names

nonverbal act

normative behavior

norms

norms of interpretation

out-group

participants

patterns

race

racial identity

result

rules

rules of interaction

rules of speaking

scene

S-P-E-A-K-I-N-G framework

speech code

speech community

subculture

verbal act

REVIEW AND DISCUSSION QUESTIONS

1. Discuss the definitions of *racial, ethnic,* and *cultural identity*. Which definition do you like the most for each concept and why? How are these concepts similar to and different from one another?
2. Define *cultural communication*.
3. Explain what *norms/rules, patterns,* and *normative behavior* are.
4. Identify, explain, and provide an example of each component of Hymes's mnemonic S-P-E-A-K-I-N-G framework.
5. Define intercultural communication. Explain the adaptive intercultural model (AIM).
6. Do you agree or disagree with the expression, "Sticks and stones may break my bones, but words will never hurt me"? Why?
7. Discuss the power of language and its relation to cultural identity.

Multiple Dimensions
of Identity

MARY FONG

Hearing classmates express contempt and hatred toward people who did not come from the right backgrounds shocked me. . . . To survive in this new world of divided classes, I had to take a stand to get clear my own class affiliations.

—bell hooks (2000, p. B16)

The plethora of available "I's" throws into relief the multiple ways people present themselves and their identities in particular situations. You are not an "I" untouched by context, rather you are defined by the context. . . . Boundaries between self and other are fluid and constantly changing depending on context and on the social positioning people adopt in particular situations. . . . These multiple, relationally defined selves offer culturally specific possibilities for human fulfillment in the intertwinings of deep feeling and the inextricable connectedness of selves.

—Dorinne Kondo (1990, pp. 29, 31–32)

Every person has multiple "I's": multiple dimensions of identities, of who we are, communicated accordingly as we enter the fluid boundaries of scenes in daily interactions. Within these scenes we create, affirm, and negotiate our "I's" with people who are similar to and dissimilar from us. Our racial, ethnic, or cultural identity is also developed in our social interactions. Frequently our ways of manifesting our identities reflect patterns of communication that are shared with like identities. Other times aspects of our identity come in direct conflict with unlike identities.

In this chapter we first look at the development of cultural identity. Next, we discuss the properties of cultural identity. Last, we explain social and cultural identities.

Development of Cultural Identity

Drawing from Phinney's (1993) model, cultural identity development involves three stages: unexamined cultural identity, cultural identity search, and cultural identity achievement. During the **unexamined cultural identity** stage, young children do not typically examine or question their cultural, ethnic, or racial identity. Instead they tend to take their cultural values, norms, beliefs, customs, and other characteristics for granted and are not aware of ethnic, cultural, or racial differences between themselves and others. They rarely show any interest in discovering their backgrounds.

However, there comes a time when children are confronted with cultural, ethnic, and racial conflict that creates difficulty and confusion in their lives. At this time, they begin their **cultural identity search** regarding self and others. Children may experience a personal event, hear a comment made—by a friend, a bully, parents, relatives, or neighbors—or see a message on television, the internet, a newspaper, a magazine, or a billboard that triggers a question about their ethnic, cultural, or racial identity. They become aware of cultural, ethnic, and racial differences and begin to explore and discover aspects of identity. They may pursue social interaction with cultural and ethnic groups they identify with; they may read nonfiction books and take classes pertaining to cultural, ethnic, and racial topics; they may participate in ethnic, cultural, social, and service organizations. In this continuous process, they also reflect and evaluate themselves, others, the world, and how they fit within the various groups. The individual's values, morals, ethics, and beliefs are being influenced and shaped. He or she may encounter discrimination and unfairness and may perceive potential difficulties in attaining and maintaining personal goals, educational aspirations, and career objectives.

In extending Phinney's second phase of cultural identity development, some people experience an identity crisis that involves a conflict between their subjective and objective identities. **Subjective identity** refers to how one perceives oneself, particularly in regard to ethnic, cultural, or racial terms. **Objective identity** involves how others perceive a person to belong to a particular cultural, ethnic, or racial group(s) based on observable characteristics, including physical and behavioral manifestations. People struggling with an identity crisis often perceive themselves as belonging to a particular ethnic, cultural, or racial group, but their peers are communicating to them that they do not belong to their group because they do not have similar physical and behavioral characteristics.

Children and teenagers are vulnerable to peer pressure, especially if their peers are ostracizing them through ridicule antics, prejudicial comments, physical attacks, and social isolation. When a person is one of the few members of a ethnic, cultural, or racial subgroup (e.g.,

Caucasian, Filipino, African American) in a dominant group (in terms of quantity), the minority person will often desire to identify with the dominant group. The minority person wants to feel accepted rather than rejected by his or her peers. Whether the minority person is well treated or mistreated in the dominant group, the need to belong and to feel accepted is a powerful influencing factor. A minority person in a dominant group who denies his or her ethnic, cultural, or racial identity is known to have an **identity crisis.** A minority person who has an identity crisis sometimes does not admit that he or she is experiencing a psychological struggle.

An identity crisis can be short term, but oftentimes a minority person may experience an identity struggle for years. If a minority person has a support system (e.g., psychologist, parents, teachers, siblings, friends), these supporters can help clarify and make sense of what he or she is experiencing. This can help create psychological balance for the individual. If the minority person is exposed to cultural events, activities, educational material, and friendships from the same cultural/ethnic group, this will help him or her to develop a healthy ethnic/cultural identity.

I recall when I lived and maintained ties in Chinatown, Los Angeles, from the late 1960s through the late 1970s, presentations on cultural pride emerged in the schools for students. In the fifth grade, our class participated in the P.I.E. program (partnership intercultural education). Our class of Chinese immigrant children and some Mexican children went on field trips with African American children from South Los Angeles to experience intercultural friendships throughout the year.

If a minority person does not have exposure to his or her people and culture or does not have a support system, it will prolong the person's identity struggle. Many students tell me that it was not until they took a college class involving culture, ethnicity, or race that they began to understand and come to terms with their ethnic or cultural identity. People experiencing an identity struggle can also receive help from people who share or understand the same type of predicament.

The final phase is **cultural identity achievement,** where individuals have developed a fairly solid grasp of their own cultural identity. They have reached a state of clarity, confidence, understanding, appreciation, and acceptance of that identity. If they are confronted with discrimination and stereotypical comments, these individuals are able to avoid internalizing the negative communications. This does not mean that negative comments by others are not hurtful to the individual, but that he or she does not question his or her cultural identity.

Properties of Cultural Identity

Collier (1997) discusses seven properties of cultural identity, as follows: avowal and ascription; modes of expression; individual, relational, and communal forms; enduring and changing aspects of identity; affective, cognitive, and behavioral components of identity; content and relationship levels; and salience or prominence. Researchers analyze, understand, and write about these seven properties in order to bring to light how members of a speech community communicate their cultural identity.

Avowal and Ascription

The first property involves the avowal and ascription processes of self-perception as a person enacts identities in different everyday contexts. **Avowal** involves the presentation of self in demonstrating the "who I am" to others. **Ascription** is what others perceive and communicate about a person's identity, which may involve attributions and stereotypes.

For example, Keshishian's (2000) autobiography discusses how the mass media presented negative images of Iranians during and after the Iranian hostage crisis that began November 4, 1979, when some student followers of Ayatollah Ruhollah Khomeini (the religious leader of the country following the revolution) took fifty-three Americans hostage in Tehran. Keshishian describes the negative ascription in the news media and the anti-Iranian feelings much of the United States public developed as a result. She writes, "These negative perceptions were further intensified by references to Iranian leaders as 'anti-modern,' 'fundamentalist,' and 'irrational'; and referred to the people in Iran as 'religious fanatics,' 'leftist-backed,' and 'backward'" (p. 99).

Modes of Expression

The second property of cultural identity contains the **modes of expression** that include core symbols, names and labels, and norms. **Core symbols** are expressions of group members' cultural beliefs and theories about the universe, people, living creatures, and the functioning of society. Members' use of their cultural symbols, ideas, and everyday behaviors characterizes their membership in a group(s).

Names and **labels** are a category of core symbols. For example, Basso's (1988) ethnography examines the Western Apaches in Cibecue, Arizona. He observed the Western Apaches' use of **place names** to engage in the communicative ritual of **"speaking with names."** In this ritual, place names are core symbols that Western Apache speakers use to serve the function of registering "claims about their own moral worth, aspects of their social relationships with other people on hand, and a particular way of attending to the local landscape that is avowed to produce a beneficial form of heightened self-awareness" (p. 106). "Speaking with names" is an intense activity of thinking, in which the Western Apaches visualize sites that in turn serve specific needs. Some examples of functions fulfilled this way might include comforting another, recalling ancestral wisdom and applying it to matters of concern, expressing simple daily chores to indicate where one is going, announcing where the person has been, planning for an upcoming hunt, and helping others to know the latest happenings.

In understanding how **norms** are related to cultural identity, Collier (1997) explains,

> Cultural groups create and reinforce standards for "performing the culture" appropriately and effectively. Norms for conduct are based upon core symbols and how they are interpreted. Defining who you are tells you what you should be doing. Norms of appropriate and acceptable behavior, moral standards, expectations for conduct, and criteria to decide to what degree another is behaving in a competent manner from the prescriptive or evaluative aspects of cultural identity. An individual is successful at enacting identity when one is accepted as a competent member of the group. (p. 41)

A norm in the Athabaskan culture is not making predictions about the future in everyday talk. Scollon and Scollon (1990) found that Athabaskans feel it is bad luck to speak in a way that foretells the future. For example, if Athabaskans enjoyed a conversation with someone it is bad luck to say so and express the hope that it would happen again. "I'll see you later" or "I'll see you tomorrow" are closing comments of a conversation that predict the future and Athabaskans would avoid this. Athabaskans' way of speaking is to enter and exit gatherings and conversations unobtrusively. However, in many cultures—American, Latino, Asian—it is a norm to have a departure comment that speaks well of the interactions and expresses that the interactants hope to have more conversation in the future. For example, "Hey, it was great talking with you. We'll have to do it again soon," "Hasta mañana" (See you tomorrow), and "Joi Gin" (See you again) are norms that guide people to behave appropriately to fulfill cultural expectations. Members performing the expected norms of a culture are demonstrating a cultural identity that is shared.

Individual, Relational, and Communal Identity

A third property of cultural identity includes individual, relational, and communal forms of identity. **Individual identity** refers to the individual's interpretation of his or her cultural identity based on his or her experiences. This lends a valuable voice in understanding varying degrees of differences and similarities among members of a group. At the end of this book are two autoethnographies of individual identity. In one, Jerry Pinkney writes about his multiethnic and multicultural identity as a Cuban, African American, and German.

Intercultural researchers who investigate groups are particularly interested in the relational aspect between friends, colleagues, neighbors, coworkers, and others in specific types of interactions, situations, and topics. How the various relationships in a culture are played out in terms of appropriate behavior is known as **relational identity**.

Philipsen (1987) defines **communal identity** as the "cultural function of communication, the use of communication in the creation, affirmation, and negotiation of shared identity" (p. 249). Understanding group members' knowledge and use of shared discursive forms—such as interactional sequences, stories, and aligning actions—helps us to see that their communal practices reflect their identity.

Researchers are able to identify and examine a group's cultural identity by observing everyday situations and communal activities, rituals, rites of passage, and holiday celebrations. Collier (1997) states that such activities show how group members "use cultural membership to establish community with one another" (p. 42). Philipsen (1987) defines **ritual** as "a structured sequence of actions the correct performance of which pays homage to a sacred object" (p. 250). Rituals are performed in an organized sequential fashion that is recognizable and meaningful to speech community members.

We identify members to perform rituals that are recognizable on a continuum from formal ceremonies to informal conventions. **Formal ceremonies** are rituals that are performed on occasions such as a wedding, baptism, graduation, or inauguration into office. At the other end of the continuum are the **informal conventions** such as greetings, compliments, leave-taking, and gift exchanges. One example of an informal conventional ritual is an experience I have had in the Chinese culture. One evening, two of my friends from Hong Kong and I went out to eat at a Chinese restaurant in Chinatown, Seattle, Washington. We were celebrating the completion of years of studies, and we knew we would soon go our separate ways. After eating our delicious Chinese meal, the waiter brought our bill. Siu Ling told the waiter to give her the bill; then both Shun Yee and I said we wanted it. The waiter knew a "struggle" was imminent, so he held the bill out and all three of us grabbed for it. Siu Ling was able to grab it the quickest. The "struggle" proceeded with Shun Yee and me trying to grab the bill out of Siu Ling's hands, saying:

"Siu Ling, let me pay the bill."

"No, don't worry, it is my treat."

"No, I want to treat."

"Come on, I want to treat."

Suddenly, Shun Yee grabbed the bill from Siu Ling, who was reaching into her purse. A chase ensued; we were all running around the table yelling back and forth, trying to get the bill. The waiter, chef, and kitchen workers came out from the kitchen and looked on, amused. Shun Yee wrestled with Siu Ling just enough for me to grab the bill and we sat down at the table (fortunately, we were the only customers in the Chinatown restaurant after 9 P.M.). Both Siu Ling and Shun Yee tried to persuade me to give it back to them. Shun Yee insisted she wanted to treat her good friends. I told her it was thoughtful of her, but I'd pay the bill since I had it and was the eldest of the three. A few more persuasive words were exchanged before we concluded that they would pay the next time. As we left the restaurant, both thanked me for the dinner. I must say I found it quite entertaining—as much as karaoke singing.

This experience demonstrates a Chinese ritual with structured sequential moves and actions. Essentially, one or more people "commands" the waiter to give them the bill; then the waiter either gives the bill to someone or puts it in the center and backs off to allow the struggle to occur. Several verbal and physical exchanges occur, in which everyone involved tries to persuade the other to hand over the bill. Hall (2002) explains that in the structured sequence of moves there is room for great creativity among the participants. For example, it is not typical that participants run around the table. I have commonly observed men standing and eventually sitting while motioning to the person who grabbed the check to hand it over. They too would go back and forth with persuasive comments.

Our struggle was serious at times, quite comical at others. The "I'll pay the bill" ritual pays homage to a sacred object or ideal—to save one's "face" by a show of generosity toward others; and, at the same time, it is considered an honor to pay the dinner bill. I have observed the "I'll pay the bill" ritual in the Chinese culture since I was a child, seeing my father "fight" over the dinner bill with his friends and relatives. I have performed this ritual at least a handful of times with my friends. It is not practiced every time there is a meal; rather, it is done occasionally in particular situations.

Enduring and Changing Aspects of Identity

The fourth cultural identity property presented by Collier (1997) features the **enduring** and **changing** aspects of identity. Naturally, over time, cultural identities change and endure due to the demands of economic, political, social, psychological, and contextual factors that influence group members. For example, China has undergone drastic changes in its history, and cultural changes have resulted. Zhong (2003) discusses historical and cultural changes in China in five main eras. She provides an example from the New China Era that began in 1949 and extended over a decade, in which Mao Zedong gained power through military actions and established the People's Republic of China (PRC). Mao used military terms during the political movements that still influence aspects of the interpersonal relationships of the Chinese people. Zhong writes,

Interpersonal relationships were changed by the blanket use of "comrade," replacing the traditional "Mr." "Mrs.," and "Miss." Thus, in a traditionally hierarchical society, suddenly everyone was equal in title—"revolutionary comrade," with the exception of the "class enemy." "Comrade" was used commonly in plural form as well, for instance, "worker comrades," "farmer comrades," "teacher comrades," "men comrades," "women comrades," and so on. Intimate terms, such as "husband" and "wife," were replaced by "lover" (ai ren) in order to diminish the status differences associated with the traditional male-dominated language connotations. A husband may have introduced his wife as: "This is my lover, Comrade Chen." These terms were the only way to address anyone formally during those years, and "comrade" and "lover" are still used habitually by some people in China today. (p. 208)

The military address *comrade* was conventionally used by people to address one another on a daily basis, recreating an identity for the Chinese people in which everyone is equal in title and "we are one." Thus, a dimension of Chinese peoples' identity changed during the New China Era. Today, some Chinese still use *comrade* in addressing one another, which demonstrates the enduring aspect of cultural identity.

Affective, Cognitive, and Behavioral Components

The fifth property of cultural identity contains the affective, cognitive, and behavioral components of identities. The **affective** component involves emotions and feelings that are attached to cultural/ethnic/racial identities in particular situations, interactions, and roles that are played out. The **cognitive** component refers to members identifying with a particular cultural group who share common beliefs and cultural understandings in relation to their identity. The **behavioral** component is made up of the group members' verbal and nonverbal actions, performed in specific situations and interactions that they identify as representing their cultural identity.

Fong (1994a, 1994b) conducted an ethnographic study on Chinese immigrants' adaptation in interactions when receiving a compliment from a Caucasian American. She explains the affective, cognitive, and behavioral components of one of the orientations that Chinese immigrants may have in their adaptation to receiving a compliment. Compliments in the Chinese culture are not commonly used in comparison to American culture. Chinese compliment on significant matters that are meaningful for both participants, such as excellent work, outstanding beauty, and great generosity—to express appreciation and recognition for its worth. If Chinese immigrants are in the intercultural shock state, they will affectively be in a state of discomfort, uneasiness, or nervousness, feeling stressed, embarrassed, surprised, shocked, or afraid. Cognitively, Chinese immigrants in the intercultural shock state will have minimum knowledge of intercultural communication differences regarding compliment exchanges between Caucasian Americans. They will not know Caucasian Americans' generous way in giving (1) compliments, (2) compliments containing strong positive adjectives, (3) compliments intended to encourage a person after an unsatisfactory performance, and (4) compliments on a wide variety of topics; and they are unfamiliar with (5) accepting compliments and (6) face-to-face compliments in all types of relationships. One example of a behavioral response is in the following interaction between a driving instructor and the trainee:

Male instructor: You did a good job (driving).
Female student: No, I drove so dangerously.

The Chinese student is rejecting the compliment with a disagreement. These three components—affective, cognitive, and behavioral—provide one consistent framework that researchers can use to examine the nature of ethnic/cultural identity manifested in interactions.

Content and Relationship Levels

Another property of cultural identities according to Collier (1997) includes the content and relationship levels of interpretation. Messages exchanged between interactants carry not only the information, or **content**, but also the **relational** aspect implied in the message by *how* a person says it. Interactants interpret the choice and meanings of words used based on their own cultural and intercultural experiences. The relational level of a message can imply and signal a cultural interpretation of who is in control, how close the interactants are, how they feel about each other, how much trust they share, or how much inclusion or exclusion they feel.

An example of the content and relationship property of identities is Basso's (1979) *Portraits of the Whiteman,* an ethnographic research on Western Apaches in Cibecue, Arizona. Basso examined the Western Apaches' use of humor and wit in their imitations of the white man's way of social interaction. In performing imitations, a Western Apache is the designated "butt" of the joke—typically not a favorable position because of the subordination to the white man. The social significance of joking imitations of the white man among Western Apaches is likened to the analogy of a deer hide or a buckskin in the development of solidarity in interpersonal relationships. In order for the joking imitator to be successful, the content needs to have humor and wit within a "safe" boundary toward the "butt," depending on the closeness or "pliability" of their relationship. Jokers need to be careful to keep their bogus slurs and criticism within appropriately playful limits in relation to the resiliency of their relationship, or the joker's imitations may be interpreted as an expression that veils genuine hostility. Basso reports Western Apaches' metaphorical use of "stiff" relationships is like untanned hides that can be easily "cracked" and are often difficult to mend, whereas "soft" relationships like supple buckskins have flexibility but may tear, but they can be mended without excessive effort. Friends who share a "supple" relationship have known each other for a long time and have established solid bonds of mutual confidence and affection that allow them to take certain liberties.

Salience, Prominence, and Intensity

The final property of cultural identity, according to Collier, takes into account that identities differ in their salience or prominence and intensity in situations. **Salience** or **prominence** involve how much a person's cultural identity stands out and attracts attention. **Intensity** refers to the degree to which an identity is performed in a situation. Collier (1997) states, "intensities provide markers of strong involvement, and investment in the identity" (p. 43). An excerpt from Dorinne Kondo's (1990) ethnography, *Crafting Selves*, describes a situation in Japan in which her Japanese and Japanese American identities were salient and intense in a formal ritual. She describes,

> At a tea ceremony class, I performed a basic "thin tea" ceremony flawlessly, without
> need for prompting or correction of my movements. My teacher said in tones of

approval, "You know, when you first started, I was so worried. The way you moved, the way you walked, was so clumsy! But now, you're just like an *ojosan*, a nice young lady." Part of me was inordinately pleased that my awkward, exaggerated Western movements had finally been replaced by the disciplined grace that makes the tea ceremony so seemingly natural and beautiful to watch. But another voice cried out in considerable alarm, "Let me escape before I'm completely transformed!" And not too many weeks later, leave I did. (p. 24)

As a Japanese American woman, dimensions of Kondo's identity became particularly salient when her teacher spoke of her transformation from being clumsy in her walk to behaving now as a nice young lady, *ojosan*, in performing the basic "thin tea" ceremony. Admittedly, Kondo was delighted to rid herself of an awkward, exaggerated Western carriage. Through her months of "intense" involvement—investment of time and practice—she transformed her identity into a disciplined and graceful performer. She realized, however, that she did not want completely to give up her identity as a Japanese American woman because it was almost time for her to return to the United States.

Social and Cultural Identities

We have familiarized ourselves with the nature of racial, ethnic, and cultural identity. We now turn to identifying with a variety of groups that connect to the multifaceted dimensions of our identity—gender, age, spiritual, class, national, regional, and personal or self-identity.

Gender Identity

How our parents, family, relatives, friends, and neighbors have treated us since childhood influences our perception of our **gender identity.** Within each culture, there are communications of what is considered feminine, masculine, and androgynous behaviors. In the American culture often we are dressed in designated colors such as pink and pastel colors for girls and dark colors like blue, green, and brown for boys. The toys typically given to girls are dolls, tea sets, kitchen cookware, and nurse, mother, and teacher paraphernalia. Boys are commonly introduced to trucks, tractors, hardware tools, and doctor and combat gear.

Although many children play with toys that equate to cultural expectations of thinking and behaving in feminine or masculine ways, it seems that today, children have opportunities that go beyond the traditional gender expectations. Toys, games, videos, books, sports, computers, and musical instruments are alternatives to help develop youths' intelligence and physical abilities that are less considered culturally feminine or masculine, but more androgynous. People who have both masculine and feminine characteristics of their gender identity are known as **androgynous.**

The media also influence our identity of what is considered feminine, masculine, androgynous, gay, and lesbian. Increasingly over the past decade, androgynous qualities have become more acceptable because both genders have opportunities to participate in sports, such as basketball, soccer, swimming, golf, biking, gymnastics, and ice skating. This is also influenced by the portrayals in the media depicting both males and females playing roles such as doctors, lawyers, judges, teachers, sports reporters, and others. The hit sitcom *Will and Grace* includes two gay men who invite their viewers to expand their comfort zone to see that gay men are just as human and "okay" as everyone else.

All of these influences—colors, toys, music, books, technology, media, sports—affect how we learn, contribute, and socialize according to cultural norms pertaining to gender. As our cultural milieu changes, so will our perception of what characteristics are considered acceptable in regard to femininity, masculinity, androgyny, and homosexuality.

Age Identity

Age is relative for each individual, and it is an aspect of our identity. Some people feel old when they are actually young in age, and some people who are in their senior years feel vivacious and so alive. Various cultures view and treat people who are in their senior years in different ways.

In most Asian cultures, getting on in your senior years is viewed as positive. The Asian elderly are respected, they are seen as wise, and their children care for them. In some United States cultures, there are more possibilities that the elderly are less respected, cared for in a nursing or rest home, and seen as living in an antiquated generation that does not have much to offer to the younger generation. When it comes to your parents' senior years, how will they be treated? And when it comes to your retirement years, how will your children and the younger generation treat you? No matter what cultural group we belong to, how we treat one another will influence how we see ourselves as youths, middle aged, and seniors.

Age and appearance in the United States seem to go hand in hand. Commercials and advertisements on problems with balding, graying, wrinkling, and weight gain are money-making concerns that tie not only directly to our appearance but reveal our age identity. Solutions like hair transplants, Rogaine, botox, crèmes, fad diets, exercise equipment—all are used to defy our identity of aging, which is seen in an unfavorable way. Sooner or later, if we live to our senior years, people will communicate to us in a way that makes clear that we are the older generation. How will we handle our **age identity**, especially when people see us as old?

Spiritual Identity

Depending on the context, **spiritual identity** is salient particularly in the church, temple, and any fellowship gathering. Typically in everyday secular activities in the United States spiritual identity is not apparent. In countries like the Middle East to Northern Ireland, and from India and Pakistan to Bosnia, spiritual differences are at the forefront of conflict and strife in which people have waged war and are willing to die for their spiritual beliefs. In some interpersonal relationships, spiritual identity becomes salient if both parties have the same spiritual commitment in their lives. In other relationships, when one party is spiritually oriented, and the other does not believe in the same God or does not believe in a God, their differences in their spiritual identities have many times created a wedge between both parties. People's spiritual identity can also be a source of conflict, especially among those who are not open-minded and are judgmental of other spiritual faiths.

People who truly understand and love God strive to live a godly life. These people who take on a serious spiritual identity, either private or public, no matter what race, ethnicity, and culture, will practice their spirituality to help them to live and to communicate toward others according to godly principles. Some people who are serious about their spirituality will look to their faith to help them during difficult times to resolve issues, to become more solid in character, to be stronger in their faith, and to serve others, especially people who are in need.

Class Identity

Our **class identity** influences how we communicate toward others and how others perceive us based on our communication competence, our material possessions, and how we conduct ourselves with "class" or a "lack of class," which is reflected in how we demonstrate our character and show respect and politeness toward others.

A person's class identity is typically not noticed until he or she encounters people who are of another class. Writer bell hooks was born and raised in the South. She writes about the experience of race and class differences she encountered when she attended Stanford University between 1969 and 1973. She writes,

> At the university where the founder Leland Stanford had imagined different classes meeting on common ground, I learned how deeply individuals with class privilege feared and hated the working classes. Hearing classmates express contempt and hatred toward people who did not come from the right backgrounds shocked me. . . . To survive in this new world of divided classes, this world where I was also encountering for the first time a black bourgeois elite that was as contemptuous of working people as their white counterparts were, I had to take a stand to get clear my own class affiliations. This was the most difficult truth to face. Having been taught all my life to believe that black people were inextricably bound in solidarity by our struggles to end racism, I did not know how to respond to elitist black people who were full of contempt for anyone who did not share their class, their way of life. . . . Despite this rude awakening my disappointment at finding myself estranged from the group of students I thought would understand I still looked for connections. I met an older black male graduate student who also came from a working-class background. Even though he had gone to the right high school, a California school for gifted students, and then to Princeton as an undergraduate, he understood intimately the intersections of race and class. . . . He became my mentor, comrade, and companion. (p. B16)

Thirty years later, it remains to be seen if such noticeable attitudes of classism exist in higher education. Another researcher, Basil Bernstein (1964) is known for his observations of middle-class and working-class boys in England's schools and their communities. Bernstein conducted this research to find out why working-class children were not doing well in school and were dropping out. Essentially, he found that children from working-class families used the **restricted code** of communications that is characterized to have low-level and limiting syntactic organization. He further described the restricted code to have speech that is typically fast, fluent, with minimal self-editing, and relatively unpaused. Also, ideas that are both written and spoken are not explicit and the intent is not verbalized. Bernstein also observed logical gaps in the flow of meaning and little or no use of verbal planning that required careful selection and fine discriminations in communications. He also found that the restricted code user is likely to incorporate concrete, narrative, and descriptive content.

Bernstein's (1964) investigation also found that middle-class children are capable of using the restricted code, but they often use the elaborated code. The **elaborated code** users have a relatively higher level of structural organization and vocabulary selection. Further characteristics are verbal elaborations, intent explicitness, self-edits, or self-monitors. Also frequent pauses, longer hesitations, and more analysis and reasoning in their communications are used than by a restricted code user.

Bernstein connects how parents from both classes communicate with their children to their children's performance in speaking and writing in school. He argues that the academic institution teaches and expects children to use the elaborated code. Consequently, children from working-class families who use the restricted code are at a disadvantage in school. He clearly states that neither one of the codes is better than the other; they are simply different language codes. The use of the elaborated or the restricted code is dependent on the demands of the situation. For example, in the military culture, the most appropriate form of communication is the restricted code. Military superiors barking commands and questions at subordinate soldiers during boot camp or formally addressing one another around the compound demands the use of the restricted code. Concise answers and formal address are the expectations of communication between the superior and the lower-ranked soldiers. The use of the elaborated code in the military, unless officers are asked to explain in detail, would be considered inappropriate.

National Identity

A person's legal status or citizenship in relation to a nation is referred to as **national identity.** Many people who identify with their ethnic origins—Asia, Latin America, Europe, Russia, or Africa—but who are born in the United States have a national identity as a United States citizen. Depending on the context, people may have a stronger sense of their national identity as opposed to their ethnic or cultural identity, and vice versa. For instance, men and women who serve in their country's military tend to have a stronger sense of national identity when they are called to duty and are defending their country. Another example is observed during the summer or winter Olympics. Spectators who enjoy the various sports most likely root and cheer for the country they nationally identify with—Russia, China, Spain, Korea, United States, Uganda, Britain, or another country. For instance, I have a Korean American friend and a Latina American friend who both were enjoying the recent World Cup Soccer series. Both friends were first cheering for the American soccer team until it lost and was no longer in the series. However, both friends continued intensely to watch the series, but they had switched their allegiance from the team of their national identity to those of their ethnic identities— Korea's and Mexico's soccer teams.

At times a person's ethnic and national identity are the same. For instance, a Japanese person born and raised in Japan has the same ethnic and national identity. Other times, a person's national identity is more salient than his or her ethnic identity, and vice versa. In all instances, it all depends on the situation.

Regional Identity

Throughout every country, there are many regions that people identify with themselves and with others. These **regional identities** may also carry positive, negative, real or not real generalizations about people. When one of our candidates from back East came for an on-campus interview for a teaching position, he was asked during lunch, "what part of this area would you like to see in Southern California?" He responded that it was his first time in California, and he always had this image of L.A. filled with movie stars, Hollywood, expensive homes, backyard pools, beaches, and sunny weather. Other regions of the United States include New York, Boston, Texas, back East, and down South. Oftentimes what comes with a regional identity is an accent that other people notice and use to try to assess what area one is from.

In other countries there are regional identities such as North and South Korea, North and South Vietnam, and East and West Berlin. In Mainland China, examples of regional areas are Shanghai, Canton, Beijing, and Northern and Southern China. Although the national language in China is Mandarin, the Cantonese language is the second most common dialect among several dialects of the Chinese language. However, the Chinese do share one common written language throughout their country.

Personal Identity

Our unique characteristics as people are the basis of our personal identities. Our **personal identity** is a self-perception of who we think we are. Our personal identity is important to us, and we try to communicate it, especially if other people communicate an unfavorable view of us that is not fair or true. For example, Michael Jackson spoke on television to try to clear his image. He had a Michael Jackson special that showed his nurturing interactions with his children, his career, and his works of service to help people in need. All of this was for the purpose of defending his self-identity from the bad publicity and news reports that he allegedly molested a child and dangled his own child from a balcony.

Each of us has multiple dimensions to our personal identity, and depending on the situation, one dimension of our personal identity may be more salient than other aspects. For example, when the fall season is here, anyone who calls me at home or asks if I am available on Saturday afternoons will find out that I am a college football enthusiast. At work, some of my male colleagues and I share a personal identity as football fans and basketball fans. We do our sports talk, even though at times we may root for different teams. Recently, the department secretary overheard me talking about an upcoming football game. She commented, "I didn't know you're into football, I wouldn't have known by looking at you." A female colleague walked by and said, "Oh, she's a big fan of football. Every Saturday." Then the secretary also disclosed that she used to watch the Pittsburgh Steelers—an aspect of her personal identity.

Summary

In this chapter, we covered the three stages of development of cultural identity—unexamined cultural identity, cultural identity search, and cultural identity achievement. *Unexamined cultural identity* is the phase in which children are not aware of ethnic, cultural, or racial differences

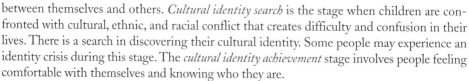

between themselves and others. *Cultural identity search* is the stage when children are confronted with cultural, ethnic, and racial conflict that creates difficulty and confusion in their lives. There is a search in discovering their cultural identity. Some people may experience an identity crisis during this stage. The *cultural identity achievement* stage involves people feeling comfortable with themselves and knowing who they are.

Next we discussed the seven properties of cultural identity—avowal and ascription; modes of expression; individual, relational, and communal forms; enduring and changing aspects of identity; affective, cognitive, and behavioral components of identity; content and relationship levels; and salience or prominence. *Avowal* involves the presentation of self in demonstrating "who I am" to others. *Ascription* is what others perceive and communicate about a person's identity, which may involve attributions and stereotypes.

Modes of expression include core symbols, labels, and norms. Core symbols are expressions of group members' cultural beliefs and theories about the universe, people, living creatures, and the functioning of society. The third property—*individual, relational, and communal forms*—covers aspects of examining cultural identity. The individual's point of view shows the uniqueness of one's experience shaped by culture and how the individual sees culture. Relational forms involves how people in relationships appropriately communicate toward one another in different cultural contexts. Communal identity is the cultural function of communication that creates, affirms, and negotiates shared identity.

Enduring and changing aspects of cultural identity are maintained and evolve according to the demands of economic, political, social, psychological, and contextual factors influencing group members. The fifth property—*affective, cognitive, and behavioral*—are components of identity. *Affective* refers to the feelings that a group member attributes to his or her cultural identity in examining self in situations. *Cognitive* refers to the thought processes and knowledge that a member holds in relation to identity. *Behavioral* refers to the communication of verbal and nonverbal messages and strategies that are cultural.

The next property—*content and relationship levels of a message*—reflects a cultural identity. The content of a message is the information. The relationship level of a message involves *how* an interactant says the message in terms of the tone of voice, the choice of words, and in what style. The relational level of message can imply and signal a cultural interpretation of who is in control, how close the interactants are, how they feel about each other, how much trust they share, or how much inclusion or exclusion they feel.

How identities differ in *salience or prominence and intensity* is the final property. *Salience or prominence* refers to how much an aspect of a person's identity stands out. *Intensity* in which an identity is performed in a particular situation refers to the strong involvement and investment of energy in an identity.

Finally, this chapter introduced a variety of social and cultural identities—gender, age, class, spiritual, national, regional, and personal identities. *Gender identity* deals with the feminine, masculine, androgynous, gay, or lesbian aspect of identity. *Age* is the dimension where interactants may identify themselves as young, middle-aged, and old based on actual age, appearance, and how they feel. *Class identity* looks at different socioeconomic classes and how one communicates based on his or her environmental upbringing. *Spiritual identity* is salient particularly in the church, temple, and any fellowship gathering. *National identity* refers to a person's legal status or citizenship in relation to a nation and how this is communicated. *Regional identity* pertains to areas of a country, and how a person communicates the discourse markers that are recognizably of this region. *Personal identity* is the self-perception of who we think we are.

References

Basso, K. 1988. "Speaking with names": Language and landscape among the Western Apache. *Cultural Anthropology* 3 (2): 99–130.

———. 1979. *Portraits of "The Whiteman."* New York: Cambridge University Press.

Bernstein, B. 1964. Elaborated and restricted codes: Their social origins and some consequences. In J. J. Gumperz and D. Hymes (Eds.), *The Ethnography of Communication, American Anthropologist special publication* 66 (2): 55–69.

Collier, M. J. 1997. Cultural identity and intercultural communication. In L. Samovar and R. Porter (Eds.), *Intercultural communication: A reader* (pp. 36–44). Belmont, Calif.: Wadsworth.

Fong, M. 1994a. Chinese immigrants' interpretations of their intercultural compliment interactions with European-Americans. Unpublished doctoral dissertation, University of Washington.

———. 1994b. Patterns of occurrence of Chinese immigrant compliment response types to European American compliments. Paper presented at the annual meeting of the National Communication Association, New Orleans, November.

Hall, B. 2002. How can we learn about our own and others' cultures? In Bradford J. Hall (Ed.), *Among cultures,* pp. 61–96. San Diego, Calif.: Harcourt College Publishers.

hooks, b. 2000. Learning in the shadow of race and class. *Chronicle of Higher Education,* B14-16, November 17.

Keshishian, F. 2000. Acculturation, communication, and the U.S. mass media: The experience of an Iranian immigrant. *The Howard Journal of Communications* 11: 93–106.

Kondo, D. 1990. *Crafting selves: Power, gender, and discourses of identity in a Japanese workplace.* Chicago: University of Chicago Press.

Philipsen, G. 1987. The prospect for cultural communication. In D. L. Kincaid (Ed.), *Communication theory: Eastern and western perspectives* (pp. 245–54). San Diego, Calif.: Academic Press.

Phinney, J. S. 1993. A three-stage model of ethnic identity development in adolescence. In M. E. Bernal and G. Knight (Eds.), *Ethnic identity* (pp. 61–79). Albany: State University of New York Press.

Scollon, R., and S. Wong-Scollon. 1990. Athabaskans-English interethnic communications. In D. Carbaugh (Ed.), *Cultural communication and intercultural contact* (pp. 259–86). Hillsdale, N.J.: Lawrence Erlbaum Associates.

Zhong, M. 2003. Contemporary social and political movements and their imprints on the Chinese language. In L. Samovar and R. Porter (Eds.), *Intercultural communication: A reader* (pp. 206–16). Belmont, Calif.: Wadsworth.

KEY TERMS

affective
age identity
androgynous
ascription
avowal
behavioral
class identity
cognitive
communal identity
content and relationship levels
core symbols
cultural identity achievement
cultural identity search
elaborated code
enduring and changing
formal ceremonies
gender identity
identity crisis
individual identity

informal conventions
intensity
modes of expression
names and labels
national identity
norms
objective identity
personal identity
place names
regional identity
relational identity
restricted code
ritual
salience or prominence
speaking with names
spiritual identity
subjective identity
unexamined cultural identity

REVIEW AND DISCUSSION QUESTIONS

1. Explain the three stages of cultural identity development according to Phinney.
2. Identify and explain the first three of seven properties of cultural identity according to Collier.
3. Identify and explain the last four of seven properties of cultural identity according to Collier.
4. Discuss the following dimensions of identity: gender, age, and class.
5. Explain the following dimensions of identity: spiritual, national, regional, and personal.

Ethnic and Cultural Identity: Distinguishing Features

MARY FONG

There is no good reason why we do not all drop our pretensions of being like everyone else, and attempt instead to enlarge the range of our sympathies, so as to delight in every observed cultural difference and to understand each cultural cue correctly and in its own historical context. . . . Each culture has its own traditions of emotional repression and expressiveness.

—Michael Novak (1994)

Speech community members identify with each other on various dimensions. These can include elements of ethnicity, culture, gender, race, or socioeconomic class, as we discussed in the first chapter. Members of a speech community share distinguishing features that help create a sense of belonging, including: language and discourse accents, family names, physical features, historical struggles, significant events and celebrations, and communication patterns. With this sense of community, there can also be a perception of common fate or destiny. For example, American citizens often share a common sense of fate or destiny in the sense that they live in a country that generally honors freedom, democracy, and individualism. In contrast, people residing in East Asian countries have a shared fate of living in a group-oriented way, with less freedom of expression and human rights as compared to the United States.

This chapter discusses some of these distinguishing features that are referenced throughout this book. Later chapters further discuss and illustrate communication patterns in a variety of ethnic and cultural speech communities. Here, we turn to language as one of the distinguishing features of ethnic and cultural identity.

Identifying through Language and Discourse Accents

Members of cultural and ethnic groups share a common spoken language and **discourse accent.** A group's discourse accent is recognized by its language features such as: syntax (sentence structure), grammar, lexicon (vocabulary), and phonology. Also, members' topic choices, style of talking, information presentation, and conduct of particular speech acts (e.g., greetings, apologies, requests) are aspects of members' discourse accent. People can recognize a variety of regional accents of speech members belonging to various communities, such as Boston, New York, California, and Texas, for example. At times, when international students, travelers, professionals, and others visit various countries, they can recognize a person's native language by hearing various languages and accents, such as French, German, Russian, Norwegian, Scandinavian, Filipino, Thai, Japanese, and English. Inside and outside our communities, nationwide, and internationally, we encounter people of various ethnic and cultural groups using their rich languages of communication. Many times, but not always, language is a distinguishing feature that may identify and reflect a person's ethnic identity. Here are some examples of various languages:[1]

1. Spanish: *¿La familia está bien?* (Is your family doing well?) (Syntax: Family is well?)
2. Mandarin dialect, Chinese: *Ni dao tu shu guan qi ma?* (Are you going to the library?) (syntax: You to library go?)
3. German: *Ich kaufe ein Buch.* (I buy a book.)
4. Japanese: *A ri ga to u, go za i ma shi ta.* (Thank you, very much.)
5. Russian: *Russkiy yazik trudno uchit.* (Russian is hard to learn.) (Syntax: Russian language hard learn.)
6. Vietnamese: *Tôi thich hoc dai hoc tai My.* (I like studying in college in America.) (Syntax: I like study college in America.)
7. Korean: *Aneong ha sayo?* (literally, Are you safe? However, it is a greeting meaning "How are you?")
8. Ibo dialect/Nigeria: *Chioma.* (God is good.)

At times, languages differ not only in phonology, but also in syntax, grammar, lexicon, and semantics, and in how words and expressions are appropriately used in a particular context. For instance, the Chinese and Russian languages do not have a form of "be" verbs or verb tense. However, tense is indicated by words such as today, yesterday, tomorrow, and now, and by clock time. Also, German, Spanish, and Russian languages require conjugation of verbs that correlate with the singular or plural subject such as I, you, we, and they.

Kramsch (1998) states that "culture both liberates and constrains" (p. 10). It is also widely accepted that language and communication both liberate and constrain. Through language, people are able to express themselves, but language also constrains them to conform to the features of the cultural discourse accent and the shared cultural standards of appropriate communication in context.

The **Sapir-Whorf hypothesis** is one of the first theories to identify a relationship between language and culture. One aspect of the Sapir-Whorf hypothesis is the deterministic view that language structure is necessary in order to produce thought. That is, language and its categories—grammar, syntax, and vocabulary—are some aspects through which we can experience the world. Essentially, language influences and shapes how people perceive their world, their culture.

The Sapir-Whorf hypothesis also posits that language and thought co-vary, which is the aspect called **linguistic relativity.** As language categories and structure differ from language to language, then cultural differences in thought and perceptions of the world change accordingly. Sapir (1951) and his protégé, Whorf (1956), believed that people who speak different languages segment their world differently. Any language such as Russian, Korean, or Spanish structures "Russian," "Korean," or "Spanish" -colored glasses that focus and screen what these cultural members pay attention to and how they interpret the world around them.

For example, in the Chinese culture, *feng shui* is a practice most members have heard of and they may choose to integrate this philosophy into their lives. *Feng shui* is the arrangement of one's surroundings in order to increase the good luck and decrease the bad luck in one's life in regard to health, relationships, career, wealth, family, and so forth. *Feng* means "wind," *shui* refers to "water" (Too 1996). The ancient and contemporary experts have observed over hundreds of years that the wind and water that circulate in our environment influence our well-being. Oftentimes when Chinese people talk about starting a business or buying a home, the consideration of *feng shui* is practiced. *Feng shui* consultants conduct assessments and provide advice. People who believe in the ideology of *feng shui* are looking through the same lens and share a common sense of fate and reality. They believe that if they practice the proper arrangement of objects in their environment, this will increase their good luck and decrease the bad.

Another distinguishing feature that people use to identify themselves and others as belonging to a particular ethnic group(s) is a **surname.** Many people, however, are not familiar with surnames from a variety of backgrounds.

Identifying through Family Names

Family names provide a possible indication that a person is of a particular ethnicity or descent. Can you tell the differences among European American last names that are Italian, Irish, Scottish, German, or Polish? Can you distinguish the differences among Asian last names that are Chinese, Japanese, Korean, Filipino, Vietnamese, Cambodian, Laotian, Indian, Thai, or Hmong? Do you recognize Russian, Armenian, Iranian, and Persian surnames? Do you know the differences between Hawaiian and Samoan surnames?

There are hundreds and hundreds of surnames of various ethnicities, and just a few examples are provided in the following tables.[2] Can you add to the list of surnames in the various ethnic groups? There are some clues in a person's surname that can possibly help us at times to distinguish a person's ethnicity or part of their ancestral descent. Other times, surnames are not accurate indicators of a person's ethnicity, especially if a married woman takes her husband's name and that differs from those of her ethnicity, or in the case of an interracial adoption, or if surnames are shared in more than one ethnic group.

In Europe, family names go back almost six hundred years, when it became legally required to take surnames. The thirteenth and fourteenth centuries in Italy were when people began to adopt a last name. Preceding this era, people generally had only a first name (www.arduini.net/names/names02.htm). Examples from a website on Italian surnames (www.arduini.net/names/names02.htm) show that, for example, two people with the same name generally required some additional description such as "Francesco with the big nose," "Leonardo from Vinci," or "Benidetto's son, Salvatore." Many **Italian surnames** end in *ini, ino, etti, etto, ello,* and *illo*—all of which mean "little." In contrast, *accio* may mean either "big" or "bad." People's professions, personalities, appearance, and their faiths became embedded in their names. Riccio or Rizzo had curly hair, Cesario had considerable body hair, and Luna had no hair at all. Mancini, Mangini, or Mancuso referred to being left-handed. Capone, Caputo, and Testa each had a big head, and Malatesta had a bad, ugly, or malformed head. The name of a great medieval storyteller, Boccaccio, meant "a big mouth." Allegretti referred to cheerfulness, and Amato was a good friend or a beloved person. Any variation of Bon or Buono in their names (Bonomo, Bonanno, Bonaminio, Bongiorno) indicated people known for their goodness. A few names are associated with days and months such as di Maggio and Sabatino for Sunday, and Mercolino after Wednesday (www.arduini.net/names/names02.htm).

The prefixes of *O', Mc,* and *Mac* are common in **Irish surnames**. However, *Mac* and *Mc* are widely used in both Irish and **Scottish surnames**.

Italian	Irish	Scottish	German
Amuzzini	Barry	Beattie	Knecht
Ciderella	Byrne	Bennett	Knopf
Cuzzupali	Donohue	Blair	Kuche
DeAugustino	Fitzpatrick	Campbell	Natzel
Fizzarotti	Kennedy	Cunningham	Neuberger
Mittino	McKinley	Low	Neuman(n)
Muzzupappa	Murphy	MacDonald	Pflaume
Romano	O'Brien	McAllister	Reichmann
Ruzzolini	Reilly	Shimmin	Schroeder
Spinelli	Ryan	Sillars	Weiss

German surnames have prefixes such as *Sch, Neu, Kn, Pf,* and *Str,* for example: *Schaefer, Schulz, Schneider, Schumacher, Schwar(t)z, Schneider, Neuman(n), Nieman(n), Knopf, Knecht, Knefler, Pfrommer, Pfister, Pfizer,* and *Stroh*. Many names with *ei* such as *Reichmann, Reimann, Reimers, Eisenhower, Heilemann, Klein, Weimer,* and *Weiss* are mostly German surnames. Surnames ending in *mann, burg, berg, lich, stein,* or *t(h)al,* are likely indications that the names are German. However, in certain settlement areas, these suffixes could also be found in surnames of people with Swedish and Russian Jewish backgrounds. Other German place names end in *burg* (castle), *bruck* (bridge), *furt* (ford), *berg* (mountain), *reuth,* and *rode* (clearing in woods) (www.serve.com/shea/germusa/surnames.htm).

Polish surnames oftentimes have suffixes like *ski, ki, yko, wicz,* and *zko*. Jewish surnames frequently have suffixes such as *son, man, stein*. The Dutch did not have surnames when they came to America. In the 1600s when the Dutch came to America, they created **Dutch surnames** for their children by using the father's first name as their child's last name. Many times a suffix was added to the father's first name to indicate "son of" or "daughter of." Females often were given feminine forms of suffixes such as *s, se, sd, sdr,* and *sen* which implied the full suffix of *sdochter,* meaning "daughter of." For example, a daughter named Janet whose father was named Dirk might be named "Janet Dirksdr." Males would have suffixes *s, se,* and *sen.* A father named Hendrick might have a son named "Jan Hendricksen" (www.ristenbatt.com/genealogy). Norwegian surnames many times have the suffix *sen,* but it is not exclusive to this ethnic group because Danish surnames also have this suffix as well.

Polish	Jewish	Dutch	Norwegian
Bem	Adler	Hendricksen	Andersen
Copernicus	Baker	Jansen	Berg
Domeyko	Benson	Pouwelse	Borkman
Dzweiki	Bernstein	Romeyn	Christensen
Kosciuszko	Cohen	Stevense	Grieg
Lukasiewicz	Coleman	Van Ness	Horn
Malinowski	Diamond	Van Nuys	Lund
Polanski	Good	Van Voorhees	Nielsen
Puchalski	Grossman	Van Winkle	Skjölsvold
Strezelecki	Weiner	Westervelt	Skovgaard

Greek surnames oftentimes have suffixes like *ous, is, os,* and have as many as five syllables. Some **Swedish** last names, like **Norwegian surnames,** have *jö* as an affix. Many Norwegian and Swedish surnames also have *lund* and *berg,* among other affixes. *Lindberg* is the most common last name that does not end with the suffix *sson.* The suffix *sson* is very common in Swedish last names. *Johansson* is the most common surname, *Andersson* is the second most common, and *Karlsson* comes in third as the most popular Swedish last name. Many **French surnames** can be recognized by suffixes such as *eaux, lion, sonne,* and *eau.* Also prefixes like *De, La,* and *Le* may indicate a French surname. Some of the most common **African American surnames** are listed below. Because of the history of slavery in the United States, the surnames were assigned based on white slave owners' last names.

Greek	Swedish	French	African American
Adamolpolous	Andersson	Caubarreaux	Campbell
Apogremiotis	Bergsjö	Chatelain	Henderson
Bairachtaris	Funk	Couvillion	Jackson
Cacavitsti	Johansson	De Lavallade	Jenkins
Coutoumanos	Karlsson	DeBellevue	Johnson
Demetrious	Lindberg	Haas	Lee
Hatziyiannakis	Lindgren	Jeansonne	Smith
Kappos	Lindkvist	LaCour	Sullivan
Lefki	Sjögren	Lemoine	Washington
Xeroteres	Swanberg	Rousseau	Wilson

Chinese and **Korean surnames** are typically one syllable. Both Chinese and Koreans share the last name *Lee*. While **Japanese** and **Filipino surnames** have two to four syllables, some Filipinos and **Latinos** share last names like *Valencia, Perez, Martinez, Hernandez*, and so forth. A majority of Filipinos are a mix of Chinese and Hispanic ancestry. Therefore, many Filipinos have **Spanish** last names. However, there are some Filipinos who have Chinese surnames like *Go, Chan, Ho, Ong,* and so on. According to the 1990 U.S. census, the last name *Kim* is the most common Korean surname in the United States. *Tran* is a common Vietnamese last name.

Chinese	Japanese	Korean	Filipino
Chang	Akiyama	Bahk	Bañez
Chen	Fujimoto	Bok	De La Cruz
Dang	Kunitomi	Chai	Dizon
Gong	Kawasaki	Cho	Gubatan
Kwan	Fukuda	Kim	Mercado
Lee	Matsumoto	Kyung	Palalay
Lim	Miyamoto	Lee	Perez
Mar	Matsuura	Paik	Samonte
Yee	Omori	Park	Tujngol
Zhong	Shirai	Sang	Valencia

Laotian surnames commonly have three to four syllables and suffixes like *xay, ong*, and others. **Cambodian surnames** typically consist of one syllable. Some Cambodian surnames are the same as Chinese surnames such as *Sun* and *Lim* and the same as Korean surnames like *Kim*. According to the 1990 U.S. census, the most common **Vietnamese surname** is *Nguyen* and 50 percent of Vietnamese have this surname. *Tran* and *Nguyen* are common Vietnamese last names. Examples of common Vietnamese names are below (www.thingsasian.com/go_article/article.630.html). Vietnamese last names are commonly one syllable also. In contrast, both Laotian and **Thai surnames** are long in spelling; and Thai last names can extend up to six syllables.

Laotian	Cambodian	Vietnamese	Thai
Aphayvong	Chey	Dang	Amatyakul
Kenemixay	Im	Dao	Bisalyaputra
Nilakout	Kim	Dinh	Krairiksha
Phimposouk	Lim	Do	Nathabhakdi
Saesavannah	Mao	Duong	Punyaratabandhu
Sanaxay	Ouch	Hynh	Sadhanabongse
Santhavisouk	Oum	Le	Simnkim
Saysavong	Seng	Ngo	Skulkan
Sisombath	Soeur	Nguyen	Talapat
Thavixay	Sun	Tran	Yindikekosont

Persian or **Iranian surnames** have suffixes such as *zadah* and *pur*. People of Persia referred to themselves as Persians, until Persia was formally renamed Iran. Today, people of this country use the ethnic identity labels Persian and Iranian interchangeably. This is similar to using ethnic identity labels such as white, Caucasian, or American interchangeably. There are also compound Persian surnames, a few examples of which are listed below. Ethnic identity labels *Latino* and *Hispanic* are used interchangeably. **Latino surnames** commonly consist of at least two to five syllables. The most common Latino surname is *Garcia. Fernandez, Lopez, Martinez,* and *Gonzalez* are the next most popular Latino surnames in descending order (www.pdom.com/spanish_names.htm). **Indian surnames** generally range from one to four syllables. Originally, Indians from India did not have family names. Common methods of creating last names involved caste names, religions, and town names. **Armenian surnames** range from two to five syllables. The suffix *ian* is commonly an affix on Armenian last names.

Persian/Iranian	Latino	Indian	Armenian
Aryanpur	Alvarez	Gandhi	Abrahamian
Bahramzadah	Castillo	Krishnamurthy	Bagaybagayan
Basiri	De La Garza	Kumar	Chirkianian
Darya Bandari	Echavarria	Lal	Der Goulisdian
Khajavi	Hernandez	Mahavajapuram	Deukmejian
Kiyanfar	Herrera	Narayan	O'Hanian
Mohamadi	Mendoza	Nehru	Peretzian
Mushfiq Kashani	Mercado	Singh	Rezian
Shariat Panahi	Rodriguez	Tilak	Soulkhanian
Vaziri	Tapia	Visweswaran	Tchalakian

Polynesians and Hawaiians use either ethnic term interchangeably. **Hawaiian surnames** commonly have at least four to seven syllables consisting of many vowels. Some Hawaiian and Samoan surnames use apostrophes within the last name. **Samoan surnames** typically have two to four syllables.

Hawaiian	Samoan	Hmong	Russian
Aikanaka	Fale	Cha	Fedorov
Alapa'iwahine	Masi	Fang	Ivanova
Halualani	Papali'I	Her	Kyznetsov
Ka'ahumanu	Siliva	Lor	Mikhailov
Ka'eokulani	Tala	Moua	Pavlova
Lahilahi	Tama	Pha	Petrov
Leleiohoku	Tasi	Vang	Smirnov
Likelike	Tautolo	Vue	Sokolova
Pauahi	Vaifale	Xiong	Vasilev

Hmong surnames are commonly one syllable like Chinese and Korean last names. **Russian surnames** typically have a suffix of *ov* to designate masculine and *ova* to indicate feminine. The surnames listed above are the ten most common Russian last names (www.pdom.com/ russian_names.htm).

Besides surnames, physical features can sometimes distinguish one's ethnicity. At times, however, it is not easy to distinguish a person's ancestry based only on their appearance. The following section looks at possible distinctions among various ethnic groups based on physical features.

Identifying through Physical Features

Many times when I converse with people belonging to general ethnic groups such as Asians, Middle Easterners, Latinos, or African Americans, they have said they can usually identify peoples' ethnic origins with some accuracy. In these cases, then, what are the physical features common among members of a particular ethnicity and the general conglomerate group?

Which ethnic groups will have blond, red, brunette, or black hair? It is very unlikely that Asians would have naturally blond or red hair. Which ethnic groups will have members with blue, green, black, or brown eyes? Asian people do not have naturally blue or green eyes. Are particular shapes of eyes seen more often in one ethnic group as opposed to another? There are single and double folded eyelids. Eyes come in all shapes—big, round, small, almond. How about the various types of noses and their features? Noses can be high bridge to low bridge. Some noses are slender, and some are wide. Other facial features include high cheekbones and varying lip shapes. The stature and body build also helps us differentiate the identity of persons from particular ethnic groups. There are tall, short, stocky, petite, small, medium, and large people. In every ethnic group we see many features and types of statures. We know that a person's physical features give us clues as to which ethnic/cultural groups they may belong to. And at other times, we may be completely inaccurate in our assumptions.

Recently, at the airport, I met a professor from my university named Nena. She was on her way to the same diversity conference I was. She has red long hair, a fair complexion with freckles, green eyes, and a slender bridged nose, and she is in her fifties. I identified her as a Caucasian American. Shortly after our meeting, she saw her Latina colleague, who was waiting to board another plane. I noticed that Nena had an interesting style of talking, and I could not pinpoint her accent. Matching her appearance with the rural region where we teach, I was getting a sense that she was not a city person. As we chatted, she used Spanish words now and then, mixed with mostly English. I was quite surprised when she eventually revealed to me that she was of Hispanic descent. In every ethnic group there may be one, two, or three predominate patterns of how members may physically look, but at times there are some ethnic members who will not fit any of our observed predominate patterns. Such was the case with Nena. Her parents, grandparents, and relatives are Hispanic. I mentioned this in one of my classes, and the Latino students said that there are many Hispanic people who have green eyes and red hair. Although I have lived in Southern California for most of my life and have gone to multicultural schools and colleges, I had never seen a Hispanic person with red hair and green eyes. This was definitely an eye opener for me.

On a daily basis, especially with new people and situations that we encounter, we are constantly making sense of who others are based on our field of experiences. In the process of adapting and making sense of the thousands of stimuli around us, our brain automatically undergoes a **perceptual selection** process, selecting what stimuli are important and what comes to the forefront to catch our attention. As humans we receive first impressions of people and situations that are fundamentally initial stereotypes based on our field of experience.

Especially when we are in new situations and unfamiliar environments we need to make quick assessments in order to adapt accordingly. Essentially, **stereotyping** is a natural human survival mechanism that is a generalization based on limited information, limited interaction, and limited experience with a person, group, or situation. Stereotypes are simplified categorizations of a person, group, or situation. Many times stereotypes of people are negative or positive conceptions or images that are resorted to because of convenience.

As our brain picks up additional information about the environment from our senses, we can modify our impressions of people and the situation in order to adapt appropriately and more accurately to the situation and to those with whom we interact. It is important, however, to be flexible and open to changing our initial impressions and stereotypes by modifying them as more data are gathered. This healthy adaptation provides a more fair, accurate, and ethical treatment of people.

Stereotypes are hurtful to people because the stereotyped person is not treated as a person with unique qualities. When we continue to hold to fixed stereotypes this can manifest itself in negative ways through our decision making and our superficial interactions with others. Oftentimes, when a person maintains rigid negative stereotypes they are meant to discriminate and to keep a person or a group at a distance. This may occur because the perpetrator feels intimidation, fear, and lack of security and self-confidence, or simply holds prejudicial biases. Several researchers (Allport 1954; Ashmore 1970; Duckitt 1992; Secord and Backman 1964; Simpson and Yinger 1985; van Dijk 1984) agree on two fundamental characteristics in their definition of **prejudice:** (a) a rigid attitude that is based on group membership and that (b) predisposes an individual to feel, think, or act in a negative way toward another person or group of persons.

At times, stereotypes can be positive, but the effects are potentially hurtful. Many times, the media and people stereotype Asians as the "model minority." A person who has a positive stereotype of someone or a group is not treating the recipient in a fair manner. An excerpt from my autoethnography demonstrates this idea.

> One day I was at the supermarket filling my water bottles at the water machine. As I was waiting for one of my bottles to fill up with water, a Hispanic woman and her two-year-old child were in close proximity to me. The child was running around and mischievously wanting to touch the water that flowed into my water bottle. When the child reached up to try to touch my water, I nudged him lightly on the shoulder and said, "excuse me," so that he would not contaminate my water. Then he ran about. Meanwhile, his mother did nothing but stood there looking elsewhere with her arms crossed. Again, the child mischievously attempted to touch the flowing water two more times, but I nudged him on the shoulder once again and said, "excuse me." His mother stood by and said nothing, but looked at me. Then suddenly, out of nowhere, his mother yelled at the top of her voice at me, "We can't all be like you Orientals!" I stood there totally astonished and embarrassed by her public shout at me. I responded defensively, but not angrily by saying, "He was trying to touch my water." She said nothing. I quickly finished filling up my water bottles and carried them to my car. (Fong 1999/2000, p. 150)

I interpreted her comment, "We can't all be like you Orientals!" to mean that she and her child cannot measure up to the positive image of Asians. Positive stereotypes of one group can be hurtful to another group if they are compared to them and they feel "less than." In such cases, members of a group who feel "less than" may show their frustrations toward members of the group whom they are compared to, as evidenced in the above scenario. Further, people who hold fixed positive stereotypes of a particular group will hold such expectations toward these members. If a person in the group does not match up to the positive stereotype, that person will be looked down on.

It is also important to realize that stereotypes and generalizations are not the same as patterns. As discussed in the first chapter, cultural patterns refer to the norms or recurrent behaviors that are established based on academic, systematic, and sufficient data collection and research methods. In contrast, stereotypes and generalizations do not undergo such rigor.

In the next section, we'll explore some of the historical events and struggles that are meaningful to various ethnic and cultural groups. Many members who experienced particular historical events and struggles—or who have learned of and identify with them—often feel an ethnic or cultural bond and an understanding that is shared among them.

Identifying through Historical Events and Struggles

Ethnic and cultural members may identify with one another because of common **historical events** or **political struggles**, holiday and event celebrations, and a sense of a common fate. Many members share an interest in and concern with what happens to fellow members. Throughout the world's history, every country and its people have suffered some historical or political event in which people have had to struggle together against some opposition. Several ethnic groups have experienced horrific historical and political struggles of power and human rights. History books and movies—such as Steven Spielberg's Academy Award–winning *Schindler's List* and Roman Polanski's Oscar-winning movie *The Pianist*—teach, remind, and relive the tragedy of the Holocaust of the Jewish people in the 1940s. Globally, many Jewish people identify with one another because of the historical event of the genocide of their people by the dictator Adolf Hitler and his accomplices. Another historical and political struggle was that between communism and democracy in East and West Germany, and the 1961 erection and the 1989 fall of the Berlin Wall—also called the Iron Curtain by Winston Churchill (Lagasse 2000; http://members.aol.com/johball/berllinwl.htm). For twenty-eight years, the Berlin Wall separated the people of Germany, families and friends. The Germans and many people worldwide rejoiced when the East German communist regime lost power in November 1989. Travel restrictions were then lifted and the dismantling of the Berlin Wall began (Lagasse 2000). In China, a human rights struggle occurred on June 4, 1989. The Chinese government massacred several thousand peaceful student and scholar demonstrators at Tiananmen Square in Beijing. These protestors were demonstrating against government corruption and lack of human freedoms (Jin and Zhou 1989).

The many wars that have been fought over the centuries in every country—WWI, WWII, Korean War, Vietnam War, Iraq War, and others—are major historical events of struggle that people talk about and refer to in identifying with one another, especially those who have witnessed such times. For example, on December 7, 1941, Japan attacked Pearl Harbor in Hawai'i, killing almost 2,500 Americans. Franklin D. Roosevelt declared war against Japan soon after. Two months later President Roosevelt signed Executive Order 9066 to relocate more than 110,000 Japanese Americans living on the West Coast to concentration camps for more than three years (Healey 1998). Japanese Americans lost their homes, businesses, freedom, and rights.

From the 1960s Watts Riots to the early 1990s Rodney King beating and the South L.A. Riots, these struggles have dealt with injustice, discrimination, and violence experienced by the people living in this vicinity of California. Over two hundred years of dehumanization and lynchings of Black slaves is a painful part of American history. The day-to-day struggles of African Americans in the 1960s are described in an excerpt from a letter written by Martin Luther King Jr. from a Birmingham jail in Alabama on April 16, 1963. He writes:

> We still creep at horse-and-buggy pace toward gaining a cup of coffee at a lunch counter. . . . But when you have seen vicious mobs lynch your mothers and fathers at will and drown your sisters and brothers at whim; when you have seen hate-filled policemen curse, kick and even kill your black brothers and sisters; when you see the vast majority of your twenty million Negro brothers smothering in an airtight cage of poverty in the midst of an affluent society; when you suddenly find your tongue twisted and your speech stammering as you seek to explain to your six-year-old daughter why she can't go to the public amusement park that has just been advertised on television, and see tears welling up in her eyes when she is told that Funtown is closed to colored children, and see ominous clouds of inferiority beginning to form in her little mental sky, and see her beginning to distort her personality by developing an unconscious bitterness toward white people; when you have to concoct an answer for a five-year-old son who is asking: "Daddy, why do white people treat colored people so mean?"; when you take a cross-country drive and find it necessary to sleep night after night in the uncomfortable corners of your automobile because no motel will accept you; when you are humiliated day in and day out by nagging signs reading "white" and "colored," when your first name becomes "nigger," your middle name becomes "boy" (however old you are) and your last name becomes "John," and your wife and mother are never given the respected title "Mrs."; when you are harried by day and haunted by night by the fact that you are a Negro, living constantly at tiptoe stance, never quite knowing what to expect next, and are plagued with inner fears and outer resentments; when you are forever fighting a degenerating sense of "nobodiness"—then you will understand why we find it difficult to wait. (1994, pp. 170–71)

Perhaps some people will feel removed from Martin Luther King Jr.'s depiction of yesteryear. Yet some may hear remembrances of this era from their parents, relatives, and the media. Although time has brought some changes, we need to understand the daily lives of Black Americans, and ask curiously and listen openly to their depiction of day-to-day struggles and how they perceive the world and people. Perhaps one will hear the echo of truth in the words of Martin Luther King Jr. What are these truths? **Black consciousness** is an important awareness for many Black Americans today. It is an understanding of who they are, their past history, and the experience and knowledge of their daily lives.

In the multicultural United States, members of diverse ethnic co-cultures were affected by the tragedy of September 11, 2001. The United States suffered terrorist attacks at the World Trade Center Towers in New York City and the Pentagon in Washington, D.C.; four hijacked planes killed thousands of American people (abcnews.com). The 9/11 terrorist attacks created a sense that people from all ethnic and cultural backgrounds who were citizens of the United States identified with one another and united as Americans. People made monetary and blood donations to aid the injured and to feed and help people who no longer had shelter. Many displayed the American flag on their homes and cars. American citizens identified with each other through actions, demonstrating a love for people and a wish to help rebuild what was lost. Every cultural and ethnic group has a history of events and struggles that leaves an imprint on the memories of many of its ethnic and cultural members. Members of ethnic and cultural groups identify with particular historical events because of their meaningful significance. Participants' acts of remembrance are expressions that they will not forget those who sacrificed and endured such times.

Exposure to films, books, exhibits, travels, and discussions help educate and promote understanding and empathy of members culturally and in intercultural contexts. In some cases, particular historical and political struggles can create intercultural friction and animosities—for example, the Chinese-Japanese war during WWII when the Japanese invaded China. Some Chinese parents who experienced the horrors of this war discourage interrelations with Japanese and Japanese Americans. Another instance is the political struggle between the People's Republic of China and Taiwan. The people of Taiwan want to remain independent from Mainland China and do not wish to have their government and way of life changed. Many people from Taiwan identify themselves as Taiwanese, and not Chinese.

Identifying through Celebrations

As much as there are historical and political events and struggles, there are also **holidays** and celebratory events in every culture. Almost every culture celebrates the New Year in which differing communication rituals, customs, and foods are enjoyed. Particular Asian cultures (e.g., Chinese, Korean, Vietnamese) celebrate their New Year by the lunar calendar, whereas Americans, Japanese, and many others celebrate it according to the solar calendar (Dresser 1996). Ethnic groups such as the Cambodians, Iranians, Laotians, and Thai celebrate their New Year in April (Dresser 1996). The Jewish celebration Rosh Hashanah, meaning "Head of the Year," takes place in September in some years and October in others, according to the Jewish calendar (Dresser 1996). Most members of each ethnic group participate in the festivities and partake in the understood expected cultural behaviors that may cleanse the self, forgive others, increase good luck, and help them avoid bad luck—all designed to improve their future lives (Dresser 1996).

Another cultural event, the large urban powwow, endorses pan American Indian values (Young 1981). A variety of tribes come together to enjoy dance, music, food, one another, cash prizes, give-aways, craftspeople, and traders (Moore 1999). The simple give-aways at powwows in small American Indian communities in central and western Oklahoma, for example, are frequently held to commemorate occasions like a death of a family member, a one-year anniversary ending the mourning period (when the family can appear at public functions), the return of a son from the military, or a graduation from high school or college. The significance of give-aways is to acknowledge people who have been good friends—who have been helpful toward the family in need and can be counted on in the future (Moore 1999).

Birthday **celebrations** vary across ethnic groups. Many Chinese and Japanese eat a bowl of long noodles, which symbolize longevity. In the Latino culture, a *quinceañera* is the fifteenth birthday of a young woman in which many family and friends are invited to mark her "coming of age" transition from girlhood to womanhood. The word *quinceañera* comes from the Spanish words *quince* for fifteen, and *años,* which is years (www.velocity.net/~yanqui1/quinceanera.htm). It is a daylong celebration that involves a rehearsal, the Mass, the dance, and the escort. Many of these activities mirror those of a wedding. In both the wedding and the *quinceañera* the girl is in white, there is food and dancing, and the father gives the girl away and introduces her into society. Originally the tradition was initiated to signify the virginity of the girl and her readiness for marriage. The girl would have spent her childhood developing the necessary skills for becoming a mother. This event indicated that the girl was willing, ready, and able to become a wife and mother. Also, it presented the opportunity for potential suitors to be introduced.

In Nicaragua, San Sebastian Day is celebrated on January 20th. People celebrate the patron saint with a spiritual emphasis in communal prayers and a parade of the statue throughout the town, reminding all the people of the miracles the saint has granted them. St. Patrick's Day may be celebrated by anyone wearing green so as not to be pinched, but Irish folks especially lay claim to the day to identify that they are of Irish descent. These are just some examples of holidays and celebrations that cultural members share in their identification with one another as they interact to foster a bond of belongingness.

Summary

This chapter discusses language and discourse accents that are distinguishing features that may identify people as belonging to a particular ethnic or cultural group. A group's discourse accent is recognized by its language features, such as syntax, grammar, lexicon, and phonology. The Sapir-Whorf hypothesis states that language and its categories—grammar, syntax, and vocabulary—are some of the categories through which we can experience the world. Essentially, language influences and shapes how people perceive their world, their culture. Further, the Sapir-Whorf hypothesis also posits that language and thought co-vary, which is known as linguistic relativity.

A family name is another feature that may provide a possible indication that a person is of a particular ethnicity or descent. Many family names of various ethnic groups are surveyed here and the origin of surnames explored. The chapter also includes a discussion of physical features of several ethnic groups, especially facial features and body types.

Historical and political struggles, significant celebrations, and a sense of common fate or destiny are distinguishing features that we consider in identifying people as belonging to a particular ethnic or cultural group. *Historical* and *political struggles*—the Holocaust of the Jewish people in the 1940s, the erection and fall of the Berlin Wall, the Tiananmen Square massacre in Beijing, the Pearl Harbor attack in Hawai'i, Watts Riots of the 1960s, the Rodney King beating and the South L.A. Riots in the 1990s, the 9/11 terrorist attack in New York City and the Pentagon—are significant events discussed in this chapter. The meanings and the variety of ways of celebrating ethnic and cultural events are examined, such as New Year, the Jewish Rosh Hashanah, American Indian powwows, birthdays, Nicaragua's San Sebastian Day, and the Irish Saint Patrick's Day. Members from a variety of groups feel an identification and commonality with each other through their shared experience of and education about these historical political struggles and celebratory events.

Notes

1. I received assistance from the following people in writing a sentence and translation in their native language. Raphael Correa, a Spanish professor at CSU, San Bernardino, was consulted on August 20, 2002; James Cheng, IT consultant for CSU, San Bernardino, International Student Services, is a Taiwanese native and was consulted on August 20, 2002. Rueyling Chuang, assistant professor at CSU, San Bernardino, has a degree in German and has taught it and was consulted on July 10, 2002; Urara

Shirai, a native of Japan, is a junior at CSU, San Bernardino, majoring in computer science, and was consulted on July 10, 2002. Alexey Zabolotskikh is a senior in economics at CSU, San Bernardino, who is a native of Russia and was consulted on August 20, 2002. Tuyen Dao, master's graduate student at CSU, San Bernardino, in educational administration, is a native of Vietnam and was consulted on August 20, 2002. Kathy Nadeau, assistant professor of anthropology, who studied the Korean language in Seoul, Korea, was consulted on August 19, 2002. Chioma Okpara, a sophomore undergraduate at CSU, San Bernardino, and a Nigerian American, was consulted on August 20, 2002.

2. The following people provided examples of last names. Khalil Daneshuvar, a native of Iran, is a staff analyst at the Program in Enrollment Services at CSU, San Bernardino, and provided examples of Iranian last names. M. Teuíla is a native of Hawai'i and was interviewed on Hawaiian-Polynesian surnames. She owns Teuíla's Polynesian Bakery in Grand Terrace, California, and was consulted in July 2002. I spoke to an assistant at the Laos Cultural Center, San Diego, on Laotian last names. Oung Pichara is a social worker at the Asian American Resource Center, San Bernardino, and assisted in Hmong and Cambodian surnames in June 2002.

References

ABC News. Retrieved March 23, 2003, from abcnews.com.

Allport, G. W. 1954. *The nature of prejudice.* Reading, Mass.: Addison-Wesley.

Ashmore, R. 1970. The problem of intergroup prejudice. In B. Collins (Ed.), *Social psychology* (pp. 245–96). Reading, Mass.: Addison-Wesley.

Decarlo, J., Jr., and A. Kanter. The Berlin wall. Retrieved December 15, 2002, from www.members .aol.com/johball/berllinwl.htm.

Dresser, N. 1996. *Multicultural manners.* New York: John Wiley and Sons, Inc.

Duckitt, J. 1992. *The social psychology of prejudice.* New York: Praeger.

Fong, M. 1999/2000. Autoethnography: Chinese conflict management of prejudice in intercultural interactions. *Intercultural communication studies* 9 (2): 145–62.

Global Directions Inc. 2001. Explore the cultures of Asia: Vietnamese names. Retrieved July 2002, from www.thingsasian.com/goto_article.630.html.

Healey, J. F. 1998. Asian Americans: Modes of incorporation. Chapter 10 in *Race, ethnicity, gender, and class* (pp. 415–71). Thousand Oaks, Calif.: Pine Forge Press.

Jin, Z., and Q. Zhou. 1989. *June four* (translation). London: University of Arkansas Press.

King, M. L. 1994. Letter from Birmingham jail. In J. Zaitchik, W. Roberts, and H. Zaitchik (Eds.), *Face to face: Readings on confrontation and accommodation in America* (pp. 166–80). Palo Alto, Calif.: Houghton Mifflin Publishing Co.

Kramsch, C. 1998. *Language and culture.* London: Oxford University Press.

Lagasse, P. 2000. *Berlin wall.* New York: Columbia University Press.

Moore, J. H. 1999. How giveaways and pow-wows redistribute the means of subsistence. In C. G. Ellison and W. A. Martin (Eds.), *The political economy of North American Indians* (pp. 176–83). Los Angeles, Calif.: Roxbury Publishing Co.

No author. Chinese names and their symbols/characters. Retrieved August 18, 2002, from www.pdom.com/ chinese_names.htm.

No author. Indian names—baby names and surnames. Retrieved August 18, 2002, from www.pdom.com/ indian_names.htm.

No author. Japanese names/symbols/kanji characters. Retrieved August 18, 2002, from www.pdom.com/ japanese_names.htm.

No author. Quinceanera. Retrieved February 23, 2003, from www.velocity.net/~yanqui1/quinceanera.htm.

No author. Russian names—surnames and baby names. Retrieved August 18, 2002, from www.pdom.com/ russian_names.htm.

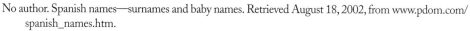

No author. Spanish names—surnames and baby names. Retrieved August 18, 2002, from www.pdom.com/spanish_names.htm.

No author. 1999, July 25. The origins of Italian surnames. Retrieved August 18, 2002, from www.arduini.net/names/names02.htm.

No author. 1996, September 22. German names in America. Retrieved August 18, 2002, from www.serve.com/shea/germusa/surnames.htm.

Novak, M. 1994. How American are you? In J. Zaitchik, W. Roberts, and H. Zaitchik (Eds.), *Face to face: Readings on confrontation and accommodation in America* (pp. 166–80). Palo Alto, Calif.: Houghton Mifflin.

Ristenbatt, D. S. 2001. On the trail of our ancestors. Retrieved August 18, 2002, from www.ristenbatt.com/genealogy.

Sapir, E. 1951. The status of linguistics as a science. In D. Mandelbaum (Ed.), *Selected writings.* Berkeley: University of California Press.

Secord, P. F., and C. Backman. 1964. *Social psychology.* New York: McGraw-Hill.

Simpson, G., and J. M. Yinger. 1985. *Racial and cultural minorities* (5th ed.). New York: Plenum Press.

Too, L. 1996. *The complete illustrated guide to feng shui.* New York: Barnes and Noble.

van Dijk, T. A. 1984. *Prejudice in discourse.* Amsterdam: John Benjamins.

Whorf, B. L. 1940/1956. In J. B. Carroll (Ed.), *Language, thought, and reality: Selected writings of Benjamin Lee Whorf.* Cambridge, Mass.: MIT Press.

Young, G. A. 1981. Pow-wow power: Perspectives on historic and contemporary intertribalism. Ph.D. dissertation, Indiana University, Bloomington.

KEY TERMS

African American surname	Italian surname
Armenian surname	Japanese surname
Black consciousness	Jewish surname
Cambodian surname	Korean surname
celebrations	Laotian surname
Chinese surname	Latino surname
discourse accent	linguistic relativity
Dutch surname	Norwegian surname
Feng shui	perceptual selection
Filipino surname	Persian surname
French surname	Polish surname
German surname	political struggles
Greek surname	prejudice
Hawaiian surname	Samoan surname
historical events	Sapir-Whorf hypothesis
Hmong surname	Scottish surname
holiday	stereotyping
Indian surname	Swedish surname
Iranian surname	Thai surname
Irish surname	Vietnamese surname

REVIEW AND DISCUSSION QUESTIONS

1. What additional surnames can you add to the tables of surnames of the various ethnic groups?
2. From your experience how do you tell the physical difference (face, hair, skin, and stature) between the various ethnic subgroups within a general ethnic group such as: Asians, Latinos, Middle Easterners, Blacks, Tribes, and so forth?
3. Describe our perceptual selection process; and how is stereotyping involved?
4. Discuss and provide examples of both positive and negative stereotyping and their effects.
5. From your ethnic background, what historical events and struggles are meaningful to you in which you feel a sense of commonality and identification with your ethnic group members?
6. Name celebrations and festivities that you share and identify with your ethnic group members.

Theoretical Perspectives: Fluidity and Complexity of Cultural and Ethnic Identity

RUEYLING CHUANG

LEARNING OBJECTIVES

After reading this chapter, students will be able to:

- understand the fluidity and complexity of cultural and ethnic identity;
- discuss the dialectical nature of cultural identity;
- recognize the characteristics of cultural identity as being dynamic, fluid, dialectical, and multifaceted; and
- identify four major theories pertinent to cultural identity.

A telemarketer called her, assuming she spoke Spanish since she had a common Mexican last name similar to Martinez or Lopez. She tried to tell the telemarketer that she couldn't speak Spanish. At first, the telemarketer didn't hear her and kept on speaking Spanish. When the telemarketer finally realized that she couldn't speak Spanish, the telemarketer reacted angrily and told her that she was not a real Mexican *since she couldn't speak Spanish.*

This chapter illustrates the fluidity and complexity of cultural and ethnic identity. Important issues include static versus fluid identity, double consciousness, dual cultural identity, cultural adaptation, and intercultural communication competence.

Locus of Cultural Identity

According to Johnson (2000), the **locus of cultural identity** can be national, regional, or sometimes racially or ethnically based. Other dimensions of our cultural identities can arise from regions, in the sense that "Midwest culture" differs from "southern culture" and "New England culture" (p. 53). The locus of other cultures can be community based, such as Little Italy in New York City or Chinatown in San Francisco. Other loci for culture include race (e.g., Asian Americans); ethnicity (German, Norwegian, Danish); or spiritual identity (Muslim, Mormon, Buddhist). Cultural identity also resides in gender, lifestyle choices, organizations, age, class, and group membership (e.g., fraternity, deaf culture).

Cultural and ethnic identities are dynamic and constantly in flux. The identity process is fluid, dynamic, and dialectical, and sometimes it can be problematic (Hecht, Collier, and Ribeau 1993). Increasing numbers of communication scholars are paying close attention to the **dialectical** nature of a person's identity (see for example, Hecht 1993; Hecht, Collier, and Ribeau 1993; Martin and Nakayama 2000). A person may encounter the dialectical tension and contradictory tension (e.g., dependence and independence; inclusiveness and exclusiveness) of one's own identity. The prominence of our identity rises and falls relationally, depending on the context. Our identity is dependent on the relationships we have with other people. For example, a young African American woman may use Black vernacular when she speaks to her close friends who are also African Americans to solidify their cultural identity. However, when she is conducting business meetings she may choose to speak Standard English to present her professional image. As Hecht (1993) notes, "the establishment and maintenance of identity are problematic" due to the competing and paradoxical forces that move toward different directions of identities (p. 52). An ethnic minority member can feel that she is an American when she is talking to an international student who just came to the United States a few weeks ago. At the same time, she may also feel that she does not fit into mainstream White America when she notices the lack of an ethnic minority presence in hit TV shows such as *Friends*.

Many communication scholars hold that cultural identities are neither stable nor fixed and cannot be conceptualized as self-contained. They are relational and negotiated through a communication process (Hecht, Collier, and Ribeau 1993; Hedge 1998; Jackson 1999; Martin and Nakayama 2000). Identity is shaped and reshaped in interaction and thus it has an "emergent quality" (Collier and Thomas 1988; Hecht 1993). A young European American boy who lives in Kenya for many years may find himself acting more and more like a Kenyan as each year passes by and he befriends many Africans. A new sense of identity starts to emerge that may transcend national and racial boundaries. This emerging identity is not static and ascribed to predetermined group membership. For example, a young man from Morocco who was sent to a boarding school in the United States and stayed in the United States all through his college years may identify more with White middle-class students than with his Muslim friends back home. Another situation can also be true: he can feel very relaxed with and close to his American friends when he is in the United States, and still feel a sense of closeness and bonding with Muslim and Arabic-speaking friends in Morocco when he goes back to his country for a visit. He not only does code switching but also identity shifting.

Hecht, Collier, and Ribeau (1993) and Lian (1983) caution that **bicultural** people who occupy two worlds, such as Arab Americans, switch and alter identity as they move back and forth between social worlds. This alternation of identity may lead to **displacement** or fragmented identity. There is a strong connection between identity and social interaction. Identity is shaped and formed through social interaction. The **fluid nature of identity** is an important element in understanding immigrants' experience, because their identities are continuously renegotiated in their attempt to adapt to and integrate with the host culture (Hedge 1998).

For example, an Afghani who has lived in the United States for more than ten years and has never visited his hometown after he fled Afghanistan in the late 1980s could be just as proud of the American culture as he is of Afghani culture, even though he is a Muslim and speaks Arabic. The notion of "American" becomes increasingly blurry amid globalization and border crossing. An "American" can be someone who was born in Taiwan and speaks English with a Chinese accent. This same person may be proud of being a (naturalized) "American" and may, for instance, have felt as shaken and violated by the September 11 terrorist attack on the World Trade Center as any other U.S. citizen.

The relationship between culture and identity is complex. Our identities are constructed through an integral connection of language, social structures, gender orientation, and cultural patterns (e.g., the use of an intermediary to deal with conflict or the lack thereof). Thus, Fitzgerald (1993) contends that we do not see our self-identity passively but through active selection and reconstruction. We select our identity and pick which ethnic name we prefer to be called. For example, certain people from South America feel more comfortable being associated with the ethnic label *Latino* or *Latina*, while other people from the same region identify themselves as *Hispanic*. Yet there are some people who find the term *Hispanic* offensive. Collier (1998) notes that one of the major premises of the cultural identity theory is that cultural identities are "historical, contextual, and relational constructions" (p. 131). Cultural identity can be enduring, ephemeral, and constantly changing (Hecht, Collier, and Ribeau 1993; Martin and Nakayama 2000). Certain parts of our cultural identity may be permanent, such as our national origin and mother tongue. It can also be ephemeral and transient. As we go through changes in life, such as moving from one place to another, we may adapt to the new environment and take on a whole new identity.

For example, in greater China areas (Mainland China, Hong Kong, and Taiwan), we see the prevalent influence of **Confucianism.** The deeply rooted cultural values instilled by Confucianism, such as interdependence, reciprocity, righteousness, responsibility, and loyalty to friends and leaders, remain a significant part of Chinese cultural values. To be a Chinese is to be a person who understands the importance of being considerate and respectful to one's elders and leaders. In another sense, the emergence of capitalism and globalization propels the Chinese people into becoming extremely mutable. They embrace changes probably faster than, say, Americans who live in a small town in Minnesota. In Taiwan, different persons may see terms or words, for example, in different ways, symbolizing the rapid change of cultural identity. The term *e-generation*—short for electronic generation—indicates a cultural group vastly affected by the impact of electronic technology, such as e-mail and the World Wide Web. In another example, the coastal areas in China have changed so speedily that the whole cityscape looks radically different from just one year to another. The economic boom in places such as Shanghai, Canton province, and Xiamen City has transformed local

Chinese people's cultural identity. They may perceive wealth, fashion, and luxurious materials as being more desirable than communist ideology.

Metaphors of Cultural Identity

Various **metaphors** can be used to describe the essence of cultural identity. For example, Fitzgerald (1993) uses the "**conductor**" **metaphor** to capture the orchestration of identity through coordinating cultural rules and cultural codes and communicative action (p. 60). For example, to maintain the harmony of a Lebanese immigrant's cultural identity amid adaptation to American culture, he may choose to speak English and conform to American mainstream culture in public, while he speaks Arabic and eats traditional Lebanese cuisine at home. Code and rule switching become important actions in navigating one's self and social identity.

Fitzgerald (1993) states that identity provides a "frame of reference" for perceiving one's lived experience (p. 60). Using the **compass as a metaphor** for identity, Fitzgerald suggests that it helps to point out the directional path. Cultural varieties, such as high-context culture (implicit communication, subtle hint) and low-context culture (explicit verbal communication, straightforward) and individualism (self-orientation, focuses on self-interests) and collectivism (group orientation, focuses on group interests), offer a psychological process of how one mediates identity (Gudykunst and Ting-Toomey 1988; Fitzgerald 1993). Our **self-identity** affects how we perceive, interpret, and negate cultural knowledge and norms. For example, a middle-class European American may perceive a forty-year-old man who still lives in his parents' basement as a "loser," whereas a traditional Chinese person may interpret the person's behavior as being "caring" and "cost effective."

Hecht, Collier, and Ribeau (1993) discuss the association between **sense of belonging** and ethnic culture as "ethnic identity." **Ethnic identity** is related to how meaning is socially constructed. Jackson (1999) argues that ethnic identity not only involves group membership but also is an interactive dynamic process. He further argues that identity is a fluid process, which involves constant redefinition and reconstruction.

Blurry Boundary of Cultural Identity

In addition to the idea that cultural identity is contextual, relational, and dialectical, this identity has also become increasingly ambiguous and **multifaceted** in postmodern society. Gergen (1991) holds that in the postmodern era the boundaries between self and other become blurry. The categories of race, gender, nationality, religion, and age deteriorate and the assumptions of self-identity become problematic. We no longer have a clear sense of self; what we have now is relational self. Who we are and our identity are dependent on our relationship with others and "the web of interdependencies" (p. 158). As Gergen concluded, when the clear distinction of self-identity starts to erode, we form our self-identity through various social groups and contexts.

In light of our **relational self**, our gender and cultural identity become much more hazy and complex. We see more people who do not conform to the socially expected or stereotypical gender roles. Not only does a transgender and transsexual movement emerge, but also people frequently take on both traditionally masculine and feminine gender roles. For example, a straight man may be comfortable in admitting that he enjoys doing gardening work, while a straight woman may be just as interested in stock investment as many men are. Women can be just as competitive as men, while increasingly more young men feel comfortable marrying women who have higher educational degrees than they and make more money. The change of gender roles and gender identity confront the recent assertions scholars have generated (see, for example, Wood 1996).

Double Consciousness and Multifaceted Cultural Identity

Double consciousness and fluid identity coincide with Gergen's notion of blurred self-identity and the relational self. DuBois (1982) argues that Blackness and Black consciousness were and are significant components of Black reality—they were and are the essence of being Black in America. DuBois defines **double consciousness** as the myopia of a dual or bipolar consciousness or identity which produces a fundamental alienation in Black people; double consciousness causes Black people (and, one could claim, members of any "minority" group) to view themselves both through their own eyes and through the eyes of people from the dominant culture. This self-consciousness of alienation is problematic because it embodies both self-disregard and self-liberation. The result is a self in search of its own identity and fulfillment through the presence of the other. To DuBois, double consciousness not only accounts for the double bind and ethnic identity of African Americans, but it can also be extended to other minority groups (e.g., Asian Indian immigrants) and other outsiders (e.g., see Starosta 2000).

Immigrants' experience of **border crossing** and cultural adaptation illustrates that cultural identities are relational and not necessarily dichotomous. A person's dual identity or multiple identity is no longer perceived as an "either/or" choice but "both/and" (see Chen 2000; Tanno 2000). Chen uses "double vision" to describe an Asian American's lived experience and dual identity in the United States. In a similar vein, Tanno (2000) associates many labels with her cultural identity. She sees herself as Spanish, Mexican, Latina, and Chicana. Each name represents a different dimension and layer of cultural identity. Tanno (2000) notes that it is sometimes difficult for people to apprehend her "both/and" simultaneous existence (p. 27). In a recent article to describe his experience of being a Taiwanese immigrant in the United States, whose parents migrated from Mainland China to the United States, Ma (2000) even goes so far as to argue that his identity is a combination of both/and and neither/nor. He is both a Taiwanese Chinese and a naturalized American. However, he can never quite feel like he is a true "American" in the White-dominant society, nor does he feel like he is the Chinese person he used to be when he goes back to Taiwan or visits Mainland China.

Passing

Moon (1998) uses the notion of "passing" to illustrate that identity is not constrained by static national, racial, and sexual boundaries. Identities transcend class, age, race, ethnicity, and gender orientation. **Passing** can be performed to achieve different purposes—to become a member of another cultural group, to be accepted, to gain personal benefits, to avoid persecution. Passing can be done through undergoing plastic surgery to pass as a younger person. Passing's direction can be upward or downward. Rapper Eminem dresses and acts in a certain way so he can be part of and accepted by the hip-hop culture. Passing can be passive or active. For example, a Euroasian, whose mother is Korean and whose father is European American, may not actively reveal her identity while listening to someone else's criticism of Asians. Thus, she is passively being passed as a member of the dominant group. Passing can be permanent or temporary. For example, to protect herself from an unwanted admirer on the airplane, a single woman may wear a wedding ring to "pass" for someone who is married. To cross over to American culture, artists who are Latin Americans may color their hair blonde (e.g., Jennifer Lopez) and change their last name to an Anglo-sounding name (e.g., Ricky Martin) so they can be accepted by mainstream Americans.

The muddled cultural identity is even more apparent with biracial children. As Harris (2000) comments, American mainstream society uses a "dichotomous approach" to cultural diversity and identity (p. 184). This dichotomous approach puts everybody into a clearly defined either-or category. Cultural identity is polarized in such a way that everything seems to be black and white and there is no gray area. What about those people who do not fit in either way? The dilemma becomes even more confusing when individuals possess biracial or multiracial lineage. For Harris and people like her who come from biracial or multiracial backgrounds, a search for a cultural identity may be a "tumultuous journey" (p. 185).

In addition to the aforementioned cultural identity theory, the following sections delineate three major concepts that are intertwined with cultural identity theory.

Communication Accommodation Theory

Language is pivotal to the identity formation process. It can help solidify cultural identity, whereas linguistic distinctiveness can be used to differentiate the ingroup and outgroup members. It is important for ensuring within-group cohesion and identity. The use of language is strongly tied to the feelings of ethnic identity and belonging. According to the **communication accommodation theory** (CAT), individuals are "motivated to use language in different ways to achieve a desired level of social distance between ourselves and our listener. Each of us often accommodates verbally and nonverbally to others" (Giles and Noels 1998, p. 141). The essential concepts of CAT are convergence, divergence, and maintenance, which are also called **approximation strategies** (Gallois, Giles, Jones, Cargile, and Ota 1995; Giles 1973; Giles, Mulac, Bradac, and Johnson 1986).

Communication convergence is a strategy or tactic where individuals adapt their communicative behavior to become more similar to their interlocutor's behavior. The convergence can be done through changing accent, modifying word choice, using similar expressions, or adjusting nonverbal behaviors to create a sense of similarity between two people. The convergence behaviors include modifying language and dialects, speech rate, pauses, utterance length, phonological variations, smiling, gaze, and any other kind of nonverbal gestures. In **communication divergence,** the speakers accentuate speech and nonverbal differences between themselves and others. Giles and Noels (1998) describe the tendency to enlarge linguistic difference as speech divergence. They assert that speakers move through their linguistic repertoire to converge and to gain social approval and identity, or to diverge to show distinctiveness. Convergence or divergence motives are adopted to maintain a "clearer and smoother communication" (Gallois, Giles, Jones, Cargile, and Ota 1995, p. 117).

We may find that, to create a sense of being part of Southern California identity, new-comers in Southern California may pick up phrases such as "my bad" for "my fault" and "4 sho" for "for sure" when they are talking to young native Californians. A newcomer in Minnesota may learn to adapt speech patterns such as "you betcha" or "you bet" to either indicate agreement or to respond to utterances such as "thank you." By adapting to these linguistic features, individuals strengthen their cultural identity. Even among friends we see individuals accommodate each other's idiosyncratic ways of expression to solidify their group identity. If someone uses the phrase "that's not my speed" to show that "that's not my style," we may see that gradually his or her friends also use similar expressions. If a college campus is prone to acronyms, such as FAR for Faculty Activity Report, for most of its daily operations, then we see employees of this campus converge to use these linguistic features.

Conversely, an example of divergence can be found in a Chinese couple who may choose to speak Mandarin Chinese in the face of their American son-in-law, whom they don't perceive as their ingroup member. By speaking a different language in front of their son-in-law, the Chinese parents accentuate their difference and identity disassociation. Another common example of divergence encountered by some Mexican Americans who do not speak Spanish well or at all is people looking down on them for not being able to speak Spanish. One student described her personal experience: A telemarketer called her, assuming she spoke Spanish since she had a common Mexican last name similar to Martinez or Lopez. She tried to tell the telemarketer that she couldn't speak Spanish. At first, the telemarketer didn't hear her and kept on speaking Spanish to her; when the telemarketer finally did realize that she couldn't speak Spanish, the telemarketer reacted angrily and told her that she was not a *real Mexican* since she couldn't speak Spanish. Clearly language helps determine cultural identity or the lack thereof.

Nonapproximation Strategies

In addition to convergence, divergence, and maintenance, which is done to achieve smoother communication, Gallois, Giles, Jones, Cargile, and Ota (1995) add three different **nonapproximation strategies.** They are interpretability, discourse management, and interpersonal control. The first nonapproximation strategy is **interpretability**, leading to the speaker's relying on the skills of the partner or on stereotypes about the other person to whom he or she is speaking. One person assumes the other person is not a native speaker of the language and purposely slows down and simplifies the conversation. A person who speaks with a heavy Appalachian accent is often stereotypically perceived as slow and as not educated. The second nonapproximation strategy is **discourse management**, where a speaker focuses on her partner's conversational needs. This will then affect the choice of conversational topics and the depth versus superficiality of the conversation. For example, an immigrant who does not watch sports games may find it frustrating to conduct an in-depth conversation with her American colleagues who are sports fans. Their conversation on sports or athletic celebrities may not be as fruitful as those on other topics, say in the job related area. The third nonapproximation strategy is **interpersonal control,** which may include the use of interruptions and more polite forms of talking such as honorifics to maintain role expectations or allow the other person "the freedom to change roles" (Gallois et al. 1995, 118). An honorific is a polite or grammatical form used in speaking to show respect. For example, in the Japanese language there are very strict grammatical rules with regard to the honorifics used in a conversation between men and women, a talk between men and their male counterparts, and a chat between a younger person and an older person. These honorifics clearly define gender role expectations and social status. These nonapproximation strategies can be used to increase closeness and solidify cultural identity (convergence, or accommodating) or to accentuate cultural differences (divergence, or nonaccommodating).

In answering the question of why language is so important for interethnic relations and cultural identity, Giles and Noels (1998) state that (1) language serves to classify people as members of a particular ethnic group; (2) language is believed to be an important element of ethnic identity, probably more so than cultural background for many ethnic groups; (3) language can be used to enhance solidarity between ingroup members and to exclude outgroup members from interacting with people who belong to the ingroup.

Consider the social phenomenon in Taiwan where students and teachers were once mandated to speak Mandarin Chinese, the official language in Taiwan and China, in the classroom. Mandarin Chinese was the only acceptable language to use when conducting public event speeches. However, in the late 1980s and throughout the 1990s, during a big political transformation, political candidates purposely used the Taiwanese dialect (Southern Min) to separate themselves from people who were inclined to advocate reunification with Mainland China. By speaking the Taiwanese dialect, the candidates made a political and cultural statement that they wanted to reclaim their local identity. By refusing to speak Mandarin Chinese, some residents in Taiwan have intentionally claimed their marginalized status, especially in the early 1990s when the political environment was less open to nonmainstream political voices.

Ethnolinguistic Vitality

Another important concept of CAT is **ethnolinguistic vitality.** It concerns the importance and the vitality of language identity within a cultural group. Ethnolinguistic vitality involves a cultural group's social status, such as whether it is a dominant group or marginalized group in a specific community. It also deals with the economic, social, and language status of a particular social group. Gallois et al. (1995) assert that the higher a group's social status, the greater its vitality. The institutional support or oppression affects the status of a particular cultural group's language or dialect. As the previous example shows, the institutional support of Mandarin Chinese in China and Taiwan strengthens the cultural values and identity of *Han,* the largest of all Chinese ethnic groups. In fact, in China, Mandarin Chinese (the official language of China) is called *Hanyu,* which literally means the language of Han ethnicity. In China, Mandarin Chinese is also called *Putong Hua,* which can be literally translated as "the common language." The term *Putong Hua* suggests that the Han ethnic group's language is the common language, while other ethnic groups' (e.g., Hmong or Yao) languages or other regions' dialects (e.g., Cantonese) are not the standard language. In a similar vein, amid the political climate change, the indigenous tribes in Taiwan also sought

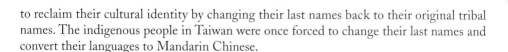

to reclaim their cultural identity by changing their last names back to their original tribal names. The indigenous people in Taiwan were once forced to change their last names and convert their languages to Mandarin Chinese.

Cultural Adaptation

Another important communication theory, closely related to the fluidity of cultural identity, is the **cross-cultural adaptation theory.** Using a holistic open-systems approach, communication scholar Kim (1995) contends that human beings are adaptive. Kim asserts that the cultural adaptation process is dynamic, multidimensional, and interdependent. The cultural adaptation process also includes **enculturation**, acculturation, and deculturation. The process of **socialization** instills children with an understanding of the modus operandi, the way things work and the modes of operation. Children learn by following members of their cultural group and cultural milieu. Children are enculturated in the home culture by observing their family members' or significant others' culturally patterned behaviors. For example, Chinese children learn Chinese New Year's Eve rituals and traditions such as eating dumplings for good luck by watching how their parents and relatives interact. As individuals move away from their familiar cultural environment to a brand new and unfamiliar culture, they begin the process of resocialization or acculturation (Gudykunst and Kim 1992). The process of **acculturation** involves acquiring the elements and cultural patterns of a new host culture. For example, a person who came from a country where a public transit system is readily available may find it almost impossible to get around in the greater Los Angeles area without a car. To survive in the so-called Inland Empire area, which covers a wide range of geographical territories in inland Southern California such as San Bernardino and Riverside counties, the person would need to learn not only the complex and congested freeway system but also how to drive aggressively. Kim (1995) notes that this secondary process may not occur as smoothly as the childhood enculturation "because of the distinct cultural identity" previously internalized by the sojourners traveling to and staying in a different country (p. 176). Simultaneously, the process of unlearning the original home culture is called **deculturation**. For example, many Chinese students find that the longer they stay in the United States, the more difficult it is for them to speak Chinese without mixing English words or grammar in their sentences. They may even forget how to write certain Chinese characters. They take on the deculturation process as they act less like a traditional Chinese would and become more "Americanized."

The process of enculturation, acculturation, and deculturation is dynamic. Kim (1995) observes that sojourners may cope with this state of flux through defense mechanisms, such as denial, hostility, avoidance, and withdrawal. However, the stress the sojourners experience may also work as the impetus for their cultural adaptation and transformation of a new cultural identity. The sojourners undergo a progressive intercultural transformation process that includes change of habitual cognitive (knowledge of the host language and culture), affective (emotional sensibilities), and behavioral (expression) responses. Kim further depicts three aspects of cultural identity transformation: functional fitness, psychological health, and an emergent new cultural identity. **Functional fitness** is gained through repeated activities and internal reorganization. Increased functional fitness creates a sense of equilibrium between internal adjustment and external demands in the new culture. It helps individuals to establish a proficiency and competency in communicating with members of the host culture. Subsequently, increased **psychological health** enhances the immigrants' or sojourners' ability to communicate and "the accompanying functional fitness in the host society" (Kim 1995, p. 179). Psychological well-being reduces the level of stress and disturbance in dealing with the new culture. Kim further theorizes that the increased functional fitness and psychological health deteriorates the original cultural identity while a new cultural identity starts to emerge. The cultural boundary becomes more ambiguous and flexible. The emergent identity is not completely a part of the new culture nor detached from the old culture.

The **emergent cultural identity** can be seen in recent new immigrants from the Hong Kong and Taiwan areas. Many affluent Chinese families send their children to the United States or Canada to receive their high school and higher education. As these young immigrants began the journey of cultural adaptation, they encounter the enculturation they acquired in their home countries, the acculturation process in North America, and the deculturation stage of being less and less attached to their home culture. Therefore, we may see Asian-looking new immigrants who speak English as fluently as the native speakers. They may behave "more American than the Americans" by immersing themselves in high fashions, technology, and other materialism, which is one of the dominant cultural patterns of the United States (see, for example, Jandt 2001). However, they may still prefer Chinese food to other kinds of cuisines in North America. Their cultural boundary becomes multidimensional and contextual.

Intercultural Communication Competence

Intercultural communication competence is another important theory pertinent to cultural identity. **Communication competence** refers to individuals' abilities to formulate objectives and achieve goals in a socially appropriate and personally effective manner. It has two major concepts: effectiveness and appropriateness. **Effectiveness** relates to "an individual's ability to produce intended effects through interaction with the environment" (Chen and Starosta 1996, p. 356). Effectiveness relates to the ability to control and manipulate one's environment to attain personal goals and to accurately predict other's responses. Effectiveness may include individuals' ability to act assertively to get what they want. For example, individuals who came from countries where a subtle hint is a preferred way of communicating may find that the only way a person gets around in the United States is to speak up and make direct requests, or else the other people may assume "if you don't say anything, then it must be okay with you." The so-called squeaky wheel gets the oil. On the other hand, **appropriateness** is the ability to recognize how context constrains communication, to avoid inappropriate responses, and to adhere to appropriate communication functions such as sharing feelings and sympathizing (Chen and Starosta 1996).

The seven types of communication competence include fundamental competence, social competence, social skills competence, interpersonal competence, linguistic competence, communicative competence, and relational competence (Spitzberg and Cupach 1984). Chen and Starosta (1996) explained that **fundamental competence** includes the ability to adapt

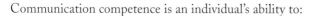

Communication competence is an individual's ability to:

- Formulate and achieve objectives

- Collaborate effectively with others, and to adapt to situational variations

- Form an impression based on perception

- Choose among available communicative behaviors to successfully accomplish "interpersonal goals during an encounter . . ." (Wiemann 1977, p. 198)

FIGURE 4.1   Intercultural Communication Competence (Chen and Starosta 1996)

to a new environment in an effective manner. For example, for a person who lives in a tropical area to move to Michigan and to survive in the area, he or she will need to learn how to drive in the snow and deal with the harsh winter. **Social competence** includes skills of empathy, role taking, cognitive complexity, and interaction management (p. 359). Social competence requires a person to be able to act effectively and appropriately in social settings. For example, learning what to say to other people at the time of their profound loss such as at a funeral involves a person's social competence. **Interpersonal competence** refers to how individuals perform communication skills to control their environments to accomplish goals. For example, it includes how to interact with colleagues after work. In certain workplaces it is expected that co-workers socialize after work much like a family, whereas in other workplaces co-workers almost never mingle after they get off work. **Linguistic and communicative competence** both deal with the ability to use language effectively and appropriately. The competent individual learns how to speak the language and knows how to use the language in a socially appropriate manner. For example, someone who did not grow up in the United States may find it hard to understand English jokes because so many of them rely on wordplay and double entendres. **Relational competence** emphasizes the independent and reciprocal process of interactions. For example, in the Chinese culture, reciprocity is a key element of social interactions. It is expected that a person at the receiving end of the social favor would try to find a way to repay the other person somehow. Chinese may not go Dutch when they go to restaurants; however, it is an unwritten rule that a person who didn't pay last time would pick up the bill the next time. Chen and Starosta conclude that individuals must maintain a certain degree of relationship with others before goals can be achieved. Relational competence comprises multiple dimensions of language, ethnicity, and cultural identity.

Chen and Starosta summarize Collier's (1989) four approaches to intercultural communication competence as ethnography of speaking, cross-cultural attitude, behavioral skills, and cultural identity. The **ethnography of speaking approach** assumes that meaning, conduct, and cultural memberships are interdependent and communication competence is contextually and relationally defined. The **cross-cultural attitude approach** advocates understanding

Dinges (1983) identifies six approaches:

- Overseasmanship: have the ability to convert lessons from a variety of foreign experiences into effective job-related skills

- Subjective culture: to understand the causes of interactants' behavior

- Multicultural person: adapt to difficult circumstances by adjusting to different contexts and keeping coherence in various situations

- Social behaviorism: individual's predeparture experiences, such as training and sojourning in another country

- Typology: nonethnocentrism and nonprejudicial judgments are the most valuable attitudes for effective intercultural communication

- Intercultural communicator: establish interpersonal relationships by understanding others through exchange of verbal and nonverbal behaviors

FIGURE 4.2   Approaches to the Study of Intercultural Communication Competence

the culture of those with whom one is communicating and stresses the importance of developing a positive attitude toward another culture. The **behavioral skills** approach focuses on the ability to identify and adopt effective communication skills in intercultural interaction. Finally, the **cultural identity approach** to communication competence suggests that intercultural communication competence is a dynamic and emergent process. It is important to recognize the existence of each other's cultural identities. Thus, cultural identity is pivotal in adaptation to a new culture.

Holistic Model of Intercultural Communication Competence

Chen and Starosta (1996) advocate a holistic model of intercultural communication competence. It represents a "transformational process of symmetrical interdependence" that ties to three perspectives: "(a) affective, or intercultural sensitivity; (b) cognitive, or intercultural awareness; and (c) behavioral, or intercultural adroitness" (p. 362). Intercultural adroitness "refers to the ability to get the job done and attain communication goals in intercultural interactions" (p. 367). The **affective process** focuses on intercultural sensitivity, a nonjudgmental attitude, and open-mindedness. **Cognitive perspective** deals with cultural awareness, self-awareness, and understanding of others. Intercultural communication competence relies on the knowledge of dimensions in cultural variability (e.g., individualism versus collectivism), cultural value orientation (use of intermediaries), and cultural patterns. Finally, the **behavioral perspective** deals with message skills, social skills, and identity maintenance. Specifically, identity maintenance deals with the ability "to maintain one's counterpart's identity in interaction" (Chen and Starosta 1996, p. 367).

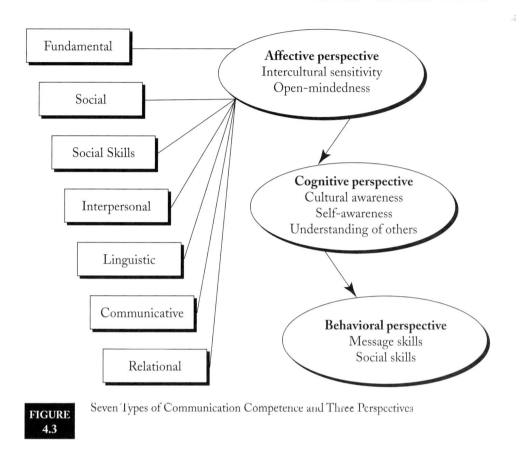

Fundamental

Social

Social Skills

Interpersonal

Linguistic

Communicative

Relational

Affective perspective
Intercultural sensitivity
Open-mindedness

Cognitive perspective
Cultural awareness
Self-awareness
Understanding of others

Behavioral perspective
Message skills
Social skills

FIGURE 4.3   Seven Types of Communication Competence and Three Perspectives

Third Culture Building

Third culture building is relevant to bicultural identity, cultural adaptation, and intercultural communication competence. The dynamic process of cultural adaptation and intercultural communication competence may lead to third culture building. As Casmir and Asuncion-Lande (1989) note, after going through the initial contrasting cultural perceptions and behaviors, two interlocutors create a unique pattern for their interaction. "In the conjoining of their separate cultures, a third culture, more inclusive than the original ones, is created, which both of them now share" (p. 294). Casmir and Asuncion-Lande further explain that this third culture is not only the result of "fusion of two or more separate entities, but also the product of the 'harmonization' of composite parts into a coherent whole" (p. 294). A third culture can only be created through interaction and it cannot be understood without the influence of two individuals' original cultures. Casmir and Asuncion-Lande summarize four fundamental approaches to third culture building:

(1) It is "open-ended." It has the potential for absorbing additional information and continuous growth. (2) It is expansive. Its contextual boundaries include individual, organizational, institutional, and mediated communication situations. (3) "It is responsive to new demands emerging from constant adjustments and readjustments" (p. 294). And finally, (4) it focuses on the future. The third culture helps individuals embark on a new journey of a joint venture that evolves over time. The third culture includes three interwoven levels: the individual (philosophical and psychological outlooks), organizational/institutional structures (e.g., family, workplace), and mediated communication (the influence of new technology and new media).

The Third Culture Development Model

Third culture building recognizes intercultural communication and cultural identity and involves multiple levels, ranging from "micro (individual) to macro (societal) level" (Jackson 1999, p. 55). The third culture development model encompasses the following five chronological and cyclic phases and levels: (1) intrapersonal intracultural communication, (2) interpersonal intercultural communication, (3) rhetorical intercultural communication, (4) metacultural communication, and (5) intracultural communication. According to Chen and Starosta (1998), in the early phases of intrapersonal intracultural communication all intercultural interactions begin at the unilateral awareness stage. In this phase, individuals are motivated to interact with one another to fulfill mutual needs; this process involves information sharing, friendship, and cooperation toward a mutual goal (p. 134). This is a cognitive process, which allows the initiators of the intercultural interaction to size things up. The subsequent action of this awareness is unilateral presentation in which the initiator makes himself or herself known to the recipient of the intercultural interaction.

The second phase of the third culture building model is **interpersonal intercultural communication**, which begins with inquiry, or information seeking. This further develops into reciprocation and mutual adjustment between interlocutors. Chen and Starosta note that during the mutual adjustment stage any intent of exploitation or colonization may end the progress toward third culture building. The **mutual adjustment** stage marks the identification of mutual purposes to maintain efforts of interaction, and this process then leads to convergence. Both parties modify their behaviors, values, mores, and beliefs to better adjust to each other. Convergence and reconfiguration indicate the stage of rhetorical intercultural communication. Both parties realize that cultural differences are "simply alternative perspectives, not to be judged in terms of their own respective cultures" (Chen and Starosta 1998, p. 136). Reconfiguration involves the process of two intercultural participants integrating new and modifying their own attitudes, behaviors, and values. The readjustment/reinforcement process embarks on the "**metacultural communication**" phase (Jackson 1999, p. 58). In this metacultural communication stage the third culture begins to construct and rearrange itself to fit both parties' needs. The interdependent parties seek to maintain balance through self-regulation. In the mutual assimilation part of the metacultural communication, certain elements of the new third culture are constructed and perpetuated. Upon completion of all the aforementioned stages, individuals begin to separate from their primary culture. This stage is marked as the "**primary culture abandonment**" process. The newly established primary culture is maintained through a mutually agreed-upon reality adhered to by both parties. In the final stage of the third culture building model both intercultural communication parties "adopt the revised identity as their primary identity and transmit their new identity to a subsequent generation" (Jackson 1999, p. 56).

Summary

This chapter examined the loci of cultural identity. They include nationality, race, ethnicity, gender, lifestyle choices, organizations, age, class, group membership, regional identity, and spiritual identity. The author emphasized the characteristics of cultural identity as being dynamic, fluid, dialectical, relational, contextual, and multifaceted. Cultural identity becomes blurry in the midst of cultural integration, bicultural interactions, interracial marriages, and the mutual adaptation process. The concept of double consciousness and double vision is prevalent in those people who are bicultural. People who are crossing cultural boundaries and borders and going through cultural identity transformation may also find this notion of double consciousness relevant. The essence of cultural identity can be manifested through metaphors such as "conductor," which illustrates the idea of integrating and harmonizing various cultural identities, and "compass," which indicates that identity provides a mental and social guideline for our daily conduct.

This chapter delineated four major theories pertinent to cultural identity. They are communication accommodation theory, cultural adaptation theory, intercultural communication competence, and third culture building. Communication accommodation theory addresses the importance of language on cultural identity formation and transformation. The approximation strategies of convergence, divergence, and maintenance are pivotal to individuals' choice of cultural identity adaptation through language. Ethnolinguistic vitality suggests the importance of language identity, institutional support, and social status. These factors affect individuals' or a particular cultural group's decision to prefer one language over the other, maintaining a language, or abandoning a language.

The second theory, which is relevant to cultural identity and closely related to communication accommodation theory, is cultural adaptation theory. Taking an open systems perspective, this chapter highlighted the cultural adaptation process as multidimensional and interdependent. This process includes the enculturation, acculturation, and deculturation processes. The intercultural transformation includes changes in cognitive (knowledge of new cultural patterns), affective (emotional closeness and connection), and behavioral (expression) responses. Subsequently, this involves three aspects of cultural identity transformation: functional fitness, psychological health, and an emergent new cultural identity.

The intercultural communication competence model addresses the importance of appropriateness and effectiveness in intercultural communication and cultural identity transformation. Collier's (1989) four approaches to intercultural communication competence are: ethnography of speaking, cross-cultural attitude, behavioral skills, and cultural identity. Chen and Starosta's (1996) holistic intercultural communication competence model is closely related to the cultural adaptation theory because it also addresses cognitive, affective, and behavioral dimensions of communication interaction and cultural identity.

The third culture building model illustrates how the dynamic process of cultural adaptation and intercultural communication competence may lead to third culture building. The four fundamental approaches to third culture building, according to Casmir and Asuncion-Lande (1989) are open-ended, expansive, responsive to new changes, and future-oriented. The third culture building model involves multiple levels of cultural identification processes, ranging from the individual (micro) level to the society (macro) level. The third culture building model includes five progressive and cyclic phases: intrapersonal intracultural communication, interpersonal intercultural communication, rhetorical intercultural communication, metacultural communication, and intracultural communication.

By explicating these four essential theories of cultural identity, this chapter sought to demonstrate our creation of identity as a complex process. These four theories interconnect with the loci of cultural identity and the fluid nature of identity. Cultural identity is multi-directional, multidimensional, and multifaceted, which can be at times ambiguous and blurry. Our cultural identity is dynamic and constantly evolving.

References

Casmir, F. L., and N. Asuncion-Lande. 1989. Intercultural communication revisited: Conceptualization, paradigm building, and methodological approaches. *Communication Yearbook* 12: 278–309.

Chen, G. M., and W. Starosta 1998. *Foundations of intercultural communication*. Boston: Allyn and Bacon.

Chen, V. 2000. (De)hyphenated identity: The double voice in *The woman warrior*. In A. Gonzalez, M. Houston, and V. Chen (Eds.), *Our voices: Essays in culture, ethnicity, and communication* (pp. 3–12). Los Angeles, Calif.: Roxbury.

———. 1996. Intercultural communication competence: A synthesis. *Communication Yearbook* 19: 353–85.

Collier, M. J. 1989. Cultural and intercultural communication competence: Current approaches and directions for future research. *International Journal of Intercultural Relations* 13: 287–302.

———. 1998. Researching cultural identity: Reconciling interpretive and postcolonial perspectives. In D. V. Tanno and A. Gonzalez (Eds.), *Communication and identity across cultures* (pp. 122–47). Thousand Oaks, Calif.: Sage.

Collier, M. J., and M. Thomas. 1988. Cultural identity in inter-cultural communication: An interpretive perspective. In W. B. Gudykunst and Y. Y. Kim (Eds.), Theorizing intercultural communication. *International and intercultural communication annual* 12 (pp. 94–120). Newbury Park, Calif.: Sage.

Dinges, N. 1983. Intercultural competence. In D. Landis and R. W. Brislin (Eds.), *Handbook of intercultural training: Vol. 1. Issues in theory and design* (pp. 176–202). Elmsford, N.Y.: Pergamon.

DuBois, W. E. B. 1982. *The souls of Black folk*. New York: Dodd, Mead.

Fitzgerald, T. K. 1993. *Metaphors of identity: A culture-communication dialogue*. Albany: State University of New York Press.

Gallois, C., H. Giles, E. Jones, A. Cargile, and H. Ota. 1995. Accommodating intercultural encounters: Elaborations and extensions. In R. Wiseman (Ed.), *Intercultural communication theory* (pp. 115–47). Thousand Oaks, Calif.: Sage.

Gergen, K. J. 1991. *The saturated self: Dilemmas of identity in contemporary life*. New York: Basic Books.

Giles, H. 1973. Accent mobility. *Anthropological Linguistics* 15: 87–105.

Giles, H., A. Mulac, J. Bradac, and P. Johnson. 1986. Speech accommodation theory. In M. McLaughlin (Ed.), *Communication yearbook* 10 (pp. 13–48). Newbury Park, Calif.: Sage.

Giles, H., and K. Noels. 1998. Communication accommodation in intercultural encounters. In J. Martin, T. Nakayama, and L. Flores (Eds.), *Readings in cultural contexts* (pp. 139–47). New York: The Pilgrim Press.

Gudykunst, W. B., and Y. Y. Kim. 1992. *Communicating with strangers: An approach to intercultural communication* (2nd ed.). New York: McGraw-Hill.

Gudykunst, W. B, and S. Ting-Toomey. 1988. *Culture and interpersonal communication.* Newbury Park, Calif.: Sage.

Harris, T. 2000. "I know it was the blood": Defining the biracial self in a Euro-American society. In A. Gonzalez, M. Houston, and V. Chen (Eds.), *Our voices: Essays in culture, ethnicity, and communication* (3rd ed., pp. 184–89). Los Angeles, Calif.: Roxbury.

Hecht, M. 1993. 2002—A research odyssey: Toward the development of a communication theory of identity. *Communication Monograph* 60 (1): 76–82.

Hecht, M. L., M. J. Collier, and S. Ribeau (Eds.). 1993. *African American communication.* Newbury Park, Calif.: Sage.

Hecht, M., S. Ribeau, and J. Alberts. 1989. *African American communication: Ethnic identity and cultural interpretation.* Newbury Park, Calif.: Sage.

Hegde, R. S. 1998. Swinging the trapeze: The negotiation of identity among Asian Indian immigrant women in the United States. In D. V. Tanno and A. G. Gonzalez (Eds.), *Communication and identity across cultures* (pp. 34–55). Thousand Oaks, Calif.: Sage.

Jackson, R. L. 1999. *The negotiation of cultural identity: Perceptions of Europeans and African Americans.* Westport, Conn.: Praeger.

Jandt, F. 2001. *Intercultural Communication: An Introduction* (3rd ed.). Thousand Oaks, Calif.: Sage.

Johnson, F. L. 2000. *Speaking culturally: Language diversity in the United States.* Thousand Oaks, Calif.: Sage.

Kim, Y. Y. 1995. Cross-cultural adaptation: An integrative theory. In R. Wiseman (Ed.), *Intercultural communication theory* (pp. 170–93). Thousand Oaks, Calif.: Sage.

Lian, K. F. 1982. Identity in minority group relations. *Ethnic and Racial Studies* 5: 42–52.

Ma, R. 2000. "Both-and" and "neither-nor": My intercultural experience. In M. W. Lustig and J. Koester (Eds.), *Among us: Essays on identity, belonging, and intercultural competence* (pp. 100–106). New York: Longman.

Martin, J. N., and T. Nakayama. 2000. *Intercultural communication in contexts* (2nd ed.). Mountain View, Calif.: Mayfield.

Moon, D. 1998. Performed identities: "Passing" as an inter/cultural discourse. In J. N. Martin, T. K. Nakayama, and L. Flores (Eds.), *Readings in cultural contexts* (pp. 322–30). Mountain View, Calif.: Mayfield.

Spitzberg, B. H., and W. R. Cupach. 1984. *Interpersonal communication competence.* Beverly Hills, Calif.: Sage.

Starosta, W. 2000. Dual_consciousness@USAmerican.white.male. In M. Lustig and J. Loester (Eds.), *Among us: Essays on identity, belonging, and intercultural competence* (pp. 107–18). New York: Longman.

Tanno, D. 2000. Names, narratives, and the evolution of ethnic identity. In A. Gonzalez, M. Houston, and V. Chen (Eds.), *Our voices: Essays in culture, ethnicity, and communication* (3rd ed., pp. 25–30). Los Angeles, Calif.: Roxbury.

Wiemann, J. M. 1977. Explication and test of a model of communicative competence. *Human Communication Research* 3: 195–213.

Wood, J. 1996. Gender, relationships, and communication. In J. Wood (Ed.), *Gendered relationships* (pp. 3–19). Mountain View, Calif.: Mayfield.

KEY TERMS

acculturation
affective process
appropriateness
approximation strategies
behavioral perspective
behavioral skills
bicultural
border crossing
cognitive perspective
communication accommodation
    theory
communication competence
communication convergence
communication divergence
compass as a metaphor
"conductor" metaphor
Confucianism
cross-cultural adaptation theory
cross-cultural attitude approach
cultural identity approach
deculturation
dialectical
discourse management
displacement
double consciousness
effectiveness
emergent cultural identity
enculturation
ethnic identity

ethnography of speaking approach
ethnolinguistic vitality
fluid nature of identity
functional fitness
fundamental competence
intercultural communication competence
interpersonal competence
interpersonal control
interpersonal intercultural
    communication
interpretability
language
linguistic competence
locus of cultural identity
metacultural communication
metaphors
multifaceted
mutual adjustment
nonapproximation strategies
passing
primary culture abandonment
psychological health
relational competence
relational self
self-identity
sense of belonging
social competence
socialization
third culture building

REVIEW AND DISCUSSION QUESTIONS

1. Discuss the locus of your cultural identity.
2. Reflect on situations where you feel the dialectical nature of your identity. Describe the contradictory tension of identity.
3. Create a metaphor that best describes your sense of cultural and ethnic identity.
4. What is the relationship between "passing" and cultural identity, based on Moon's assertions of passing? Have you ever tried to pass for someone else? Give personal examples.
5. Compare those essential theories outlined in this chapter and discuss which theory pertaining to cultural identity you like the best and which theory you like the least.

Approaches to Cultural Identity: Personal Notes from an Autoethnographical Journey

GUST A. YEP

LEARNING OBJECTIVES

After reading this chapter, students will be able to:

- understand the complexity of cultural identity;
- learn about autoethnography as a concept and a method;
- describe the nature of cultural identity;
- identify the major theoretical approaches to cultural identity in communication; and
- understand the implications of identity labels in intercultural interactions.

We live in a world where identity matters. It matters both as a concept, theoretically, and as a contested fact of contemporary political life. The word itself has acquired a huge contemporary resonance.

—Paul Gilroy (1997, p. 301)

Just now everybody wants to talk about "identity." As a keyword in contemporary politics it has taken on so many different connotations that sometimes it is obvious that people are not even talking about the same thing. One thing at least is clear—identity only becomes an issue when it is in crisis.

—Kobena Mercer (1990, p. 43)

Cultural identity is a vibrant, complex, and highly controversial concept in our increasingly diverse and fragmented postmodern world (Tanno and González 1998). Although some might argue that we need to find our "true identities" while others maintain that we are in an era of "identity crises," we experience cultural identity at the global, national, local, and personal levels in very "real" ways. For example, people have gone to war because of their cultural identity (e.g., the Serbs and the Croats in former Yugoslavia) while others have created cohesive communities through the unifying power of their identity (e.g., Chinese immigrants in San Francisco's Chinatown). However, the very notion of cultural identity invokes different meanings and experiences for people (Mercer 1990; Woodward 1997), and communication scholars and other researchers tend to study this concept from a variety of perspectives (Appiah and Gates 1995; Martin and Nakayama 2000; Tanno and González 1998). To enhance our understanding of this complex concept, different approaches to cultural identity are examined in this chapter. First, how autoethnography can provide rich and embodied insights into cultural identity is explored. Second, the nature of cultural identity is examined. Third, the current approaches to cultural identity in communication are identified, and how such approaches address identity is illustrated by using some personal ethnographical notes. Finally, these diverse approaches to identity, which can be potentially integrated, are explored and reflected upon in this chapter.

Autoethnography and the Study of Cultural Identity

Before I discuss autoethnography, let me introduce myself with a personal narrative. I am multicultural and use the label **Asianlatinoamerican** (Yep 1998, p. 79) to describe myself culturally and ethnically. I speak three languages (English, Spanish, and Chinese)—all of them with a slight accent. The fact that I "look Asian American" and speak English with what I call a "Spanese" (combination of Spanish and Chinese) accent has proven to be both funny and perplexing for many people I have met. I am a permanent member of the speech and communication studies and human sexuality studies faculty at San Francisco State University, and my teaching and research focus is on communication at the "busy intersections" (Rosaldo 1989, p. 17) of culture, race, class, gender, and sexuality. I live in a "mixed" (racially, ethnically, and socioeconomically) neighborhood in San Francisco with my two fluffy and effervescent Pomeranians, Tyler and Dino, and fairly near Lance, Soo Kin, Petals, Jerika, Tulip, Emma, Beth, Karen, and Mark, my "family of choice" in California. My neighborhood is predominantly African American, Asian American, and Latino, and one of my neighbors (although not quite accurately) describes herself as "the last White woman on the block." In my neighborhood, the intersections of culture, race, class, gender, and sexual identities are not simply academic activities but facets of my daily "encounters with 'difference'" (Rosaldo 1989, p. 28). It is in this neighborhood, this zone of difference, that I have become more intensely mindful, inquisitive, and reflective about my own assumptions about what it means to be a middle-class, educated, liberal, multicultural person.

What is autoethnography? According to Ellis and Bochner (2000), **autoethnography** is an autobiographical form of writing and research that seeks to connect the personal to the cultural. It is a self-report of personal experiences in the cultural borderlands (Conquergood 1991; Crawford 1996). Reed-Danahay (1997) notes that the term "autoethnography" has a double sense, "referring either to the ethnography of one's own group or to the autobiographical writing that has ethnographic interest" (p. 2). Autoethnographic texts can appear in a variety of forms including personal narratives, journals, short stories, poetry, photographic essays, and social science prose, among others (Ellis and Bochner 2000). There are different types of autoethnography (Ellis and Bochner 2000; Reed-Danahay 1997). For example, Ellis and Bochner (2000) identify five different types or exemplars of autoethnography: reflexive ethnographies, native ethnographies, "complete-member-researchers," literary autoethnographies, and personal narratives. In **reflexive ethnographies,** researchers use and reflect on their own experiences in a culture to understand the interactions in that culture. In **native ethnographies**, researchers are natives of cultures that have been marginalized or exoticized, and these native researchers present their own interpretations of their culture. As the description indicates, **complete-member-researchers** are those who are, or have become, full members of a culture they are interpreting and reporting. In **literary autoethnographies,** the author can be both an autobiographical writer and a researcher interpreting his or her culture for an audience that is not necessarily familiar with the writer's culture. Finally, in **personal narratives,** researchers use their academic and personal identities to tell autobiographical stories about some aspect of their lived experiences.

As a method, text, and concept, autoethnography has been used for over two decades (Ellis and Bochner 2000; Reed-Danahay 1997). As an attempt to, "quite literally, *come to terms* [italics added] with sustaining questions of self and culture" (Neumann 1996, p. 193), autoethnography has been used in communication (e.g., Allen, Orbe, and Olivas 1999; Goodall 1991, 1999; Payne 1996; Tillmann-Healy 1996; Trujillo 1993) and other disciplines (e.g., Driessen 1997; Ellis 1995; Herzfeld 1997; Jaffe 1997; Kideckel 1997; Svensson 1997) in recent years. Because autoethnography, including personal narratives, is concerned with identity, selfhood, voice, and authenticity (Reed-Danahay 1997), I propose that it can be a particularly useful method for understanding cultural identity. This method can provide us with a productive, deeply contextual, and more personal glimpse of how an individual experiences cultural life, negotiates meaning, and attempts to create continuity and coherence in a fragmented world. I now turn my discussion to the nature of cultural identity.

The Nature of Cultural Identity

Cultural identity, according to Yep (1998), "is a **social construction** that gives the individual an ontological status (a sense of 'being') and expectations for social behavior (ways of 'acting')" (p. 79). It is the many changing faces of "I" in the cultural borderlands. Trinh (1989) reminds us that the "I" is "not a unified subject, a fixed identity, or that solid mass covered with layers of superficialities one has gradually to peel off before one can see its true face. 'I' is, itself, *infinite layers*" (p. 94, emphasis in the original). How do we get to know and learn these many layers of the "I"? Autoethnography as an embodied research practice and an "intensely sensuous way of knowing" in which the "embodied researcher is the instrument" (Conquergood 1991, p. 180) is, in my view, an ideal way to learn, know, and understand the complexities of cultural identity in the postmodern world.

Cultural identities are **political,** fluid, nonsummative, and paradoxical (Yep 1998; Yep, Lovaas, and Pagonis, 2002). These identities are categories based on socially constructed differences (e.g., ethnicity, race, class, gender, sexuality) and social exclusion (e.g., undocumented "aliens"[1] do not have rights and privileges that U.S. citizens take for granted) that create insider/outsider status separating individuals and groups within a hierarchical political system (Batstone and Mendieta 1999; Hall 1997a). Bornstein (1998) calls this hierarchy the "gender/identity/power system" (p. 42) which looks like a pyramid with few people on top and many in various lower positions. Bornstein lists a number of qualities of the individual at the top of her metaphorical power system: European American; U.S. citizen; Protestant-defined Christian; middle-aged; middle- to upper-class; heterosexual; monogamous; able-bodied; tall, trim, and reasonably muscled; attractive, according to cultural standards; right-handed; well-educated; well-mannered; professional or executive; capitalist; self-defining and self-measuring; physically healthy and with access to health care; in possession of all rights available under the law; free and safe access to all private and public areas as allowed by the law; property-owning; rational and logical; and virile, among others. According to Bornstein's assertion, the aforementioned attributes are considered the center that all U.S. cultural values are evaluated upon or measured against, which is perpetuated by institutions, media, and mainstream society. People who do not conform to or reflect the aforementioned attributes are considered marginalized. Although some progress have been made, there are still challenges yet to be overcome (e.g., underrepresentation, gender and racial inequalities, etc.).

Cultural identities are also **fluid**, evolving, growing, and ever changing and individuals can, to some degree, move within the power hierarchy (Yep 1998). As an Asianlatinoamerican, I have experienced numerous changes in my **multicultural identity.** After reading Amy Tan's (1989) *The Joy Luck Club* and subsequently viewing the film, I felt a strong sense of joy, pride, sadness, and anger about many aspects of my multicultural identity. I felt joy to see so many Asian faces on the screen; these were people who looked like me. I felt proud of my own Chinese cultural heritage as I reminisced about my family history. I felt sad when I thought about how underrepresented and invisible Asian Americans are in the media and in many spheres of public life. I also felt anger when I was reminded of the subtle and not-so-subtle prejudices that others have expressed toward Asian Americans.

Cultural identities are **nonsummative** (hooks 1990; Takagi 1996; Trinh 1989; Yep 1998). I cannot simply quantify and separate which aspects of my identity are due to culture, race, class, gender, or sexuality. My experience of self as a multicultural "hybrid" person is the sum total of all of these elements, or I communicate and relate to people from the point of intersection of my culture, race, class, gender, and sexuality. To dispel the popular myth that identity can be cleanly dissected and compartmentalized into separate display windows, Takagi (1996), in her essay on sexuality and identity politics in Asian America, writes,

> While many minority women speak of "triple jeopardy" oppression—as if class, race, and gender could be disentangled into discrete additive parts—some Asian American lesbians could rightfully claim quadruple jeopardy oppression—class, race, gender, and sexuality. Enough counting. Marginalization is not as much about the *quantities* of experiences as it is about *qualities* of experience. (pp. 22–23, italics added)

Qualities of experience rooted in the multiplicity of overlapping, contingent, conflicting, and colliding social categories like racial origins, class roots, gender identification, or sexual desire are certainly not additive or quantifiable.

Finally, cultural identities are **paradoxical** (Yep, Lovaas, and Pagonis, 2002). When we express who we are in terms of our cultural identity, it appears that we belong to a distinct category with shared beliefs, behavioral norms, and cultural practices. In fact, individual differences as well as our various belongings and the social responsibilities attached to them pull us toward many, sometimes conflicting trajectories. For example, in my family, there is an unspoken expectation that I, as a son who is not married, should live with my aging parents (cultural expectations), yet I value my own sense of space and freedom (individual wishes). Although I have chosen the latter, this choice is not without internal tensions and guilt. "Am I being a dutiful Chinese son?" and "Am I being a good Asianlatinoamerican family member?" are questions that I often ponder and I have diverse reactions to them at different times.

Approaches to Cultural Identity

Based on Burrell and Morgan's (1979) typology of schools of social science research and Rosengren's (1989) subsequent adaptation of this typology to the communication discipline, Martin and associates (Martin and Nakayama 1999, 2000; Martin, Nakayama, and Flores 1998) identify several distinct approaches to the study of culture and communication. They are: functionalist, interpretive, critical humanist, and critical structuralist (Martin and Nakayama 1999). This typology integrates previous attempts to classify theories of culture and communication proposed by Kim (1988) and Gudykunst and Nishida (1989). In this section, I first present an overview of three approaches to the study of culture and communication.[2] Next, I discuss how functionalist, interpretive, and critical approaches examine cultural identity using some of my personal ethnographical notes as illustrations.

Functionalist Approach

Based on the assumption that reality is objective, external, and describable, this approach to culture and communication became dominant in the 1980s (Martin and Nakayama 1999, 2000). It assumes that human behavior is predictable and the goal of research is to describe and predict behavior. Culture is generally viewed as a stable and transhistorical set of attributes and characteristics and treated as a variable like national group membership. Likewise, ethnicity is generally treated as a categorical (e.g., African American, Asian American, European American, Latino, Native American, etc.) or continuous variable (e.g., strength of ethnic affiliation). This approach assumes that culture is stable and fairly harmonious, and the political and ideological dimensions of social and cultural relationships are not examined. It assumes that society is more or less integrated and the current social hierarchy and status quo should be maintained. Research follows the **"etic"** (outsider) perspective in which the conceptual and theoretical framework is externally imposed by the researcher who seeks generalizations from the data (Alasuutari 1995; Gudykunst and Nishida 1989; Headland, Pike, and Harris 1990; Martin and Nakayama 1999).

The **functionalist approach** posits that cultural identity is created in part by the self and in part by membership in a larger group (Martin and Nakayama 2000). This perspective recognizes multiple identities within a cultural context through group memberships based on nationality, race, ethnicity, class, gender, sexual orientation, and religion, among others (Tajfel 1982).

One of the ways to understand cultural identity, according to this approach, is to examine a person's group memberships and his or her degree of identification with those groups.

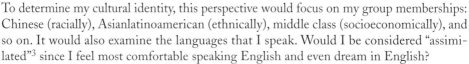

To determine my cultural identity, this perspective would focus on my group memberships: Chinese (racially), Asianlatinoamerican (ethnically), middle class (socioeconomically), and so on. It would also examine the languages that I speak. Would I be considered "assimilated"[3] since I feel most comfortable speaking English and even dream in English?

To further understand cultural identity, this approach examines the degree of emotional significance that people attach to their group memberships (Tajfel 1978). Some (e.g., Gudykunst 1988) have used the term **ethnolinguistic identity** to refer to the extent to which language and ethnicity come together to create a social identity and group membership. When I go to a Mexican restaurant, I usually speak Spanish with some of the staff members who speak Spanish. This typically creates an immediate cultural bond between us after some of the Spanish-speaking staff members recover from the initial surprise that an "Asian looking person" can speak Spanish fluently. The degree to which I and the restaurant staff members feel comfortable to speak Spanish in this and other communication settings has been referred to as **ethnolinguistic vitality** (Gallois, Giles, Jones, Cargile, and Ota 1995).

In sum, the functionalist approach views cultural identity as a social categorization process based on the relationship between the individual and the community or communities to which this person belongs. To assess a person's cultural identity, this approach examines group memberships, the strength of such affiliations, and the extent of identification with the values, norms, and language of the group, among other variables.

Interpretive Approach

This approach to culture and communication became prominent in the late 1980s and operates under the assumption that reality is subjective, internal, and describable (Martin and Nakayama 1999, 2000). Human behavior is creative and voluntary and the goal of research is to describe and understand behavior. Culture is created and maintained through communicative practices. This approach assumes that culture is subjective and fairly harmonious, and the political and ideological contexts of society and culture are generally not examined. With a focus on social order and the status quo, the interpretive perspective is similar to the functionalist approach, and ethnicity is typically examined from the perspective of the subjective experiences of individuals who belong to specific pre-established social categories. Research follows the **"emic"** (insider) perspective in which the conceptual framework and meanings emerge from the cultural community and "thick," contextually based descriptions are sought (Alasuutari 1995; Dublin 1996; Gudykunst and Nishida 1989; Headland, Pike, and Harris 1990; Martin and Nakayama 1999).

The **interpretive approach** maintains that cultural identity is not created by the self alone but is co-created through interaction with others (Martin and Nakayama 2000). It is through communication and the exchange of messages between people that identities are co-created, negotiated, reinforced, and changed (Hecht, Collier, and Ribeau 1993).

This perspective identifies both **ascribed** and **avowed identities** in communication (Martin and Nakayama 2000). For example, when I talk with others, some of my identities are ascribed, that is, others attribute identities to me. Others are avowed, that is, I portray myself and present my own identity. Because of my physical characteristics, many people assume that I am Asian American until they hear my "Spanese" accent. Others attribute a middle-class identity to me on the basis of my personal appearance and clothing. When people see the onyx cross that I wear, they immediately give me a certain religious identity and interact with me based on that assumption. In one situation, a student who identified herself as a fundamentalist Christian came to my office to share her religious beliefs and moral judgments. When I inquired about her motivation for sharing, she looked surprised and said: "I thought that you were a fellow Christian and would understand about the moral problems in this country today." I told her that I, too, reflect on these issues but from a very different perspective and went on to share my own perspective on religion. She appeared uncomfortable and for the remainder of the term, she never visited me to discuss religious matters again. In this incident, my ascribed and avowed identities did not match and in our conversation, I negotiated and challenged my ascribed identity.

The interpretive perspective also focuses on **core symbols** (Hecht, Collier, and Ribeau 1993). Core symbols refer to the constellation of meanings that members of a particular cultural group use to differentiate themselves from constituents of another cultural community (Collier and Thomas 1988). For example, individual accomplishment might be considered a U.S. American core symbol. Since I highly value individual achievement, my cultural identity, according to this approach, would be characterized as highly U.S. American.

Cultural identities, according to Collier and Thomas (1988), differ in regard to several dimensions. These are scope, salience, and intensity. **Scope** refers to the breadth of one's cultural identity. For example, my multicultural identity is very broad while my caretaker identity only becomes evident when I am with my dogs at home. **Salience** is the degree of importance of an identity in a particular communication setting. When I have members of my "family of choice" visiting, I talk to my dogs; in this instance, my identity as caretaker is most salient. Finally, **intensity** refers to the strength with which one's identity is communicated. When I attend the Chinese New Year Parade and cheer for specific groups, my Chinese identity is strongly communicated.

To summarize, the interpretive approach views cultural identity as more dynamic and fluid than the functionalist perspective. Cultural identities are contextual as they get enacted, maintained, and challenged through specific communication encounters. To assess cultural identity, this approach would examine ascribed and avowed identities, core symbols, and scope, salience, and intensity of identities communicated during interaction with others.

Critical Approach

Based on the premise that reality is subjective and changeable, this approach has recently become a force in culture and communication scholarship (Collier, Hedge, Lee, Nakayama, and Yep, 2001; Martin and Nakayama 1999, 2000). It assumes that human behavior is malleable, and the goal of research is to change behavior and to emancipate cultural constituents from domination and oppression. Culture is generally viewed as a fluid and contested zone of differences where power struggles are enacted and meanings are challenged. This approach assumes that culture is unstable and deeply seated conflicts exist; therefore, the political and ideological dimensions of social and cultural relationships become the focus of theory and research. Ethnicity is viewed as a social and historical construction with specific sociological, political, and economic consequences (Stanfield 1993a, b). Research typically focuses on analysis of textual and mass media products and artifacts.

The **critical approach** postulates that cultural identities are always formed, produced, reproduced, and challenged in symbolic, historical, socioeconomic, and political contexts. Woodward (1997) identifies several features associated with identity. Identity is relational and marked by difference; for example, to be a Latino is to be "not a European American"; to be a woman is to be "not a man." Identity constructions are both symbolic and social, for example, a button with a pink triangle to indicate gay and lesbian rights has both symbolic and social significance for the wearer. Identity is maintained through social and material conditions; for example, a U.S. passport allows its holder rights and legal protection under U.S. law as well as unimpeded entry to this country. The conceptualization of identity involves the creation and reproduction of classificatory systems that show social organization and division; for example, to be a working-class person means to be separated from and below middle-class individuals in the social order. The critical perspective is therefore interested in how and why individuals identify with some groups and not others as well as the choices available to them. The critical perspective brings to light the political and ideological nature of cultural identity that is embedded in the deep structure and power imbalance of sociocultural praxis.

Hall (1990) offers two ways of thinking about cultural identity. The first position, he argues, conceptualizes cultural identity based on

> one, shared culture, a sort of collective "one true self," hiding inside the many other, more superficial or artificially imposed "selves," which people with a shared history and ancestry hold in common. Within the terms of this definition, our cultural identities reflect the common historical experiences and shared cultural codes which provide us, as "one people," with stable, unchanging and continuous frames of reference and meaning, beneath the shifting divisions and vicissitudes of our actual history. (p. 223)

This definition homogenizes and reduces members of a group to one "true essence." Hall goes on to suggest a second view of cultural identity. This position recognizes both points of similarity and significant difference. He writes,

> Cultural identity . . . is a matter of "becoming" as well as "being." It belongs to the future as much as to the past. It is not something which already exists, transcending place, time, history and culture. Cultural identities . . . have histories. But, like everything which is historical, they undergo constant transformation. Far from being eternally fixed in some essentialized past, they are subject to the continuous "play" of history, culture and power. Far from being grounded in a mere "recovery" of the past, which is waiting to be found, and which, when found, will secure our sense of ourselves into eternity, identities are the names we give to the different ways we are positioned by, and position ourselves within, the narratives of the past. (p. 225)

Hall's (1990) second definition reflects the focus of the critical approach to cultural identity: To understand the process of identity and representation as a regime of power/knowledge with multiple histories that do not proceed from a fixed, unbroken, straight line. Discourse, or the ways in which language is used by particular groups of people for specific reasons in particular contexts, and representation, or the production of meaning through language, are key concepts for understanding cultural identity (Hall 1997b).

The critical perspective focuses on "identity politics" (Weeks 1990, p. 88) which are now at the center of contemporary political life. **Identity politics** refers to the process of claiming one's identity as a member of a marginalized group as a political point of departure and political mobilization. These politics involve celebration of a group's uniqueness as well as examination of its particular oppression. Woodward (1997) notes that the celebration of a group's uniqueness, which constitutes the basis of its political solidarity, can be translated into **essentialist** and biologically given (i.e., fixed essences and inherent qualities) features of identity. For example, racial separatists might argue for the celebration of that race based on the argument that different races possess inherently different qualities. On the other hand, some groups have adopted a **nonessentialist** approach to identity, that is, identities are regarded as fluid cultural categories rather than absolute, fixed essences. For example, radical women of color have resisted the singular category of "woman" to address the intersections of gender with race, class, and sexuality.

In sum, the critical approach places identity in the middle of contemporary politics. This approach focuses on the symbolic, discursive, historical, and economic conditions surrounding the creation, production, reproduction, and dispute over identities in contemporary culture. Cultural identities are political and struggles over representation are constantly played out interpersonally and in the media.

A Dialectical Integration of Approaches to Cultural Identity?

In this chapter I outline three approaches to cultural identity. Such approaches offer different conceptualizations, insights, and ways of looking at identity. They also make different assumptions about society, social order, and the status quo. The functionalist and interpretive approaches do not focus on social inequality and power differences between groups. The critical perspective, on the other hand, examines how individuals and groups negotiate their identities on an uneven power field.

I also propose that autoethnography is an ideal way of knowing and understanding the complexities of cultural identity. As a method, Crawford (1996) reminds us, "autoethnography orchestrates fragments of awareness—apprehended/projected and recalled/reconstructed— into narratives and alternative text forms which (re)present events and other social actors as they are evoked from a changeable and contestable self" (p. 167). Thus, it allows us to narrate the different changing faces of the "I" by epitomizing "the reflexive turn of fieldwork for human study by (re)positioning the researcher as an object of inquiry who depicts a site of interest in terms of personal awareness and experience" (Crawford 1996, p. 167) through the celebration of what Conquergood (1991, p. 180) calls active "open air" research (as opposed to less active "arm chair" methods).

Can the aforementioned approaches to cultural identity be integrated? Martin and associates (Martin and Nakayama 1999, 2000; Martin, Nakayama, and Flores 1998) propose a **dialectical approach** in which contradictory assumptions and different ways of examining cultural identity can coexist to yield a more complete picture of this complex concept. As we can see from the previous section, each approach offers a different view of cultural identity. Together, these perspectives can provide us with a more thorough examination of a contemporary concept that appears to be in crisis today.

To conclude, I would like to reflect on the implications of the labels that I use to describe myself here in my autoethnographical notes. I use various terms to describe my cultural identity throughout this essay: I describe my experiences as a Chinese American, Asian American, Latino, and Asianlatinoamerican. These are self-prescribed labels; therefore, they are my avowed identities. Such identities are contextual and strategic, and they are important in intra/intercultural encounters. Labels, like social locations, matter. They have social and material consequences: A label can give us political representation and power, just like a label can disenfranchise and ostracize. I created this new term, *Asianlatinoamerican,* to call attention to my multicultural experience (Yep 1998), to highlight the increasing number of multicultural and multiracial identities in the United States today (Root 1996), and to invite others to celebrate these identities in our diverse and fragmented society.

Notes

1. By using quotation marks around this label, I am calling attention to the negative connotations and underlying ideological assumptions surrounding this term. An alien represents the ultimate "other": exiled, deviant, undesirable, marginalized, disenfranchised, and dispossessed.

2. Although there are important differences between the critical humanist and critical structuralist approaches, I follow the original formulation proposed by Martin and associates (Martin and Nakayama 2000; Martin, Nakayama, and Flores 1998) and describe these two approaches as "critical." For a discussion of the differences between them, see Martin and Nakayama (1999) and Rosengren (1989).

3. Once again, I use quotation marks around this term to highlight the beliefs and assumptions associated with it. To assimilate means to give up one's cultural heritage so that one can adapt to the mainstream hegemonic cultural system, namely, European American culture.

References

Alasuutari, P. 1995. *Researching culture: Qualitative method and cultural studies.* London: Sage.

Allen, B. J., M. P. Orbe, and M. R. Olivas. 1999. The complexity of our tears: Dis/enchantment and (in)difference in the academy. *Communication Theory* 9: 402–29.

Appiah, K. A., and H. L. Gates. 1995. Multiplying identities. In K. A. Appiah and H. L. Gates (Eds.), *Identities* (pp. 1–6). Chicago: University of Chicago Press.

Batstone, D., and E. Mendieta. 1999. What does it mean to be an American? In D. Batstone and E. Mendieta (Eds.), *The good citizen* (pp. 1–4). New York: Routledge.

Bornstein, K. 1998. *My gender workbook.* New York: Routledge.

Burrell, G., and G. Morgan. 1979. *Sociological paradigms and organisational analysis.* London: Heinemann.

Collier, M. J., R. Hedge, W. Lee, T. K. Nakayama, and G. A. Yep. 2001. Ferment on the edges: Dialogue on communication and culture. In M. J. Collier (Ed.), *Transforming communication about culture: Critical new directions* (pp. 219–80). Thousand Oaks, Calif.: Sage.

Collier, M. J., and M. Thomas. 1988. Cultural identity: An interpretive perspective. In Y. Y. Kim and W. B. Gudykunst (Eds.), *Theories of intercultural communication* (pp. 99–120). Newbury Park, Calif.: Sage.

Conquergood, D. 1991. Rethinking ethnography: Towards a critical cultural politics. *Communication Monographs* 58: 179–94.

Crawford, L. 1996. Personal ethnography. *Communication Monographs* 63: 158–70.

Driessen, H. 1997. Lives writ large: Kabyle self-portraits and the question of identity. In D. E. Reed-Danahay (Ed.), *Auto/Ethnography: Rewriting the self and the social* (pp. 107–21). Oxford, U.K.: Berg.

Dublin, T. (Ed.). 1996. *Becoming American, becoming ethnic: College students explore their roots.* Philadelphia: Temple University Press.

Ellis, C. 1995. *Final negotiations: A story of love, loss, and chronic illness.* Philadelphia: Temple University Press.

Ellis, C., and A. Bochner. 2000. Autoethnography, personal narrative, reflexivity: Researcher as subject. In N. K. Denzin and Y. S. Lincoln (Eds.), *Handbook of qualitative research* (2nd ed., pp. 733–68). Thousand Oaks, Calif.: Sage.

Gallois, C., H. Giles, E. Jones, A. C. Cargile, and H. Ota. 1995. Accommodating intercultural encounters: Elaborations and extensions. In R. Wiseman (Ed.), *Intercultural communication theory* (pp. 115–47). Thousand Oaks, Calif.: Sage.

Gilroy, P. 1997. Diaspora and the detours of identity. In K. Woodward (Ed.), *Identity and difference* (pp. 299–343). London: Sage.

Goodall, H. L. 1991. *Living in the rock n roll mystery: Reading context, self, and others as clues.* Carbondale: Southern Illinois University Press.

———. 1999. Casing the academy for community. *Communication Theory* 9: 465–94.

Gudykunst, W. B. 1988. Uncertainty and anxiety. In Y. Y. Kim and W. B. Gudykunst (Eds.), *Theories of intercultural communication* (pp. 123–56). Newbury Park, Calif.: Sage.

Gudykunst, W. B., and T. Nishida. 1989. Theoretical perspectives for studying intercultural communication. In M. K. Asante and W. B. Gudykunst (Eds.), *Handbook of international and intercultural communication* (pp. 17–46). Newbury Park, Calif.: Sage.

Hall, S. 1990. Cultural identity and diaspora. In J. Rutherford (Ed.), *Identity: Community, culture, difference* (pp. 222–37). London: Lawrence and Wishart.

———. 1997a. The spectacle of the "other." In S. Hall (Ed.), *Representation: Cultural representations and signifying practices* (pp. 223–79). London: Sage.

———. 1997b. The work of representation. In S. Hall (Ed.), *Representation: Cultural representations and signifying practices* (pp. 13–74). London: Sage.

Headland, T., K. Pike, and M. Harris (Eds.). 1990. *Emics and etics: The insider/outsider debate.* Newbury Park, Calif.: Sage.

Hecht, M., M. J. Collier, and S. A. Ribeau. 1993. *African American communication: Ethnic identity and cultural interpretation.* Newbury Park, Calif.: Sage.

Herzfeld, M. 1997. The taming of revolution: Intense paradoxes of the self. In D. E. Reed-Danahay (Ed.), *Auto/Ethnography: Rewriting the self and the social* (pp. 169–94). Oxford, U.K.: Berg.

hooks, b. 1990. *Yearning: Race, gender, and cultural politics.* Boston: South End Press.

Jaffe, A. 1997. Narrating the "I" versus narrating the "isle": Life histories and the problem of representation on Corsica. In D. E. Reed-Danahay (Ed.), *Auto/Ethnography: Rewriting the self and the social* (pp. 145–65). Oxford, U.K.: Berg.

Kideckel, D. A. 1997. Autoethnography as political resistance: A case from socialist Romania. In D. E. Reed-Danahay (Ed.), *Auto/Ethnography: Rewriting the self and the social* (pp. 47–70). Oxford, U.K.: Berg.

Kim, Y. Y. 1988. On theorizing intercultural communication. In Y. Y. Kim and W. B. Gudykunst (Eds.), *Theories of intercultural communication* (pp. 11–21). Newbury Park, Calif.: Sage.

Martin, J. N., and T. K. Nakayama. 1999. Thinking dialectically about culture and communication. *Communication Theory* 9: 1–25.

———. 2000. *Intercultural communication in contexts* (2nd ed.). Mountain View, Calif.: Mayfield.

Martin, J. N., T. K. Nakayama, and L. A. Flores. 1998. A dialectical approach to intercultural communication. In J. N. Martin, T. K. Nakayama, and L. A. Flores (Eds.), *Readings in cultural contexts* (pp. 5–15). Mountain View, Calif.: Mayfield.

Mercer, K. 1990. Welcome to the jungle: Identity and diversity in postmodern politics. In J. Rutherford (Ed.), *Identity: Community, culture, difference* (pp. 43–71). London: Lawrence and Wishart.

Neumann, M. 1996. Collecting ourselves at the end of the century. In C. Ellis and A. P. Bochner (Eds.), *Composing ethnography: Alternative forms of qualitative writing* (pp. 172–98). Walnut Creek, Calif.: AltaMira Press.

Payne, D. 1996. Autobiology. In C. Ellis and A. P. Bochner (Eds.), *Composing ethnography: Alternative forms of qualitative writing* (pp. 49–75). Walnut Creek, Calif.: AltaMira Press.

Reed-Danahay, D. E. 1997. Introduction. In D. E. Reed-Danahay (Ed.), *Auto/Ethnography: Rewriting the self and the social* (pp. 1–17). Oxford, U.K.: Berg.

Root, M. P. P. 1996. The multiracial experience: Racial borders as a significant frontier in race relations. In M. P. P. Root (Ed.), *The multiracial experience: Racial borders as the new frontier* (pp. xiii–xxviii). Thousand Oaks, Calif.: Sage.

Rosaldo, R. 1989. *Culture and truth: The remaking of social analysis.* Boston: Beacon Press.

Rosengren, K. E. 1989. Paradigms lost and regained. In B. Dervin, L. Grossberg, B. J. O'Keefe, and E. Wartella (Eds.), *Rethinking communication: Paradigm issues* (pp. 21–39). Newbury Park, Calif.: Sage.

Stanfield, J. H. 1993a. Methodological reflections: An introduction. In J. H. Stanfield and R. M. Dennis (Eds.), *Race and ethnicity in research methods* (pp. 3–15). Newbury Park, Calif: Sage.

———. 1993b. Epistemological considerations. In J. H. Stanfield and R. M. Dennis (Eds.), *Race and ethnicity in research methods* (pp. 16–36). Newbury Park, Calif.: Sage.

Svensson, B. 1997. The power of biography: Criminal policy, prison life, and the formation of criminal identities in the Swedish welfare state. In D. E. Reed-Danahay (Ed.), *Auto/Ethnography: Rewriting the self and the social* (pp. 71–104). Oxford, U.K.: Berg.

Tajfel, H. 1978. Social categorization, social identity, and social comparisons. In H. Tajfel (Ed.), *Differentiation between groups* (pp. 61–76). London: Academic Press.

——— (Ed.). 1982. *Social identity and intergroup relations.* Cambridge, U.K.: Cambridge University Press.

Takagi, D. Y. 1996. Maiden voyage: Excursion into sexuality and identity politics in Asian America. In R. Leong (Ed.), *Asian American sexualities: Dimensions of the gay and lesbian experience* (pp. 21–35). New York: Routledge.

Tan, A. 1989. *The joy luck club.* New York: G. P. Putnam's Sons.

Tanno, D. V., and A. González. 1998. Sites of identity in communication and culture. In D. V. Tanno and A. González (Eds.), *Communication and identity across cultures* (pp. 3–7). Thousand Oaks, Calif.: Sage.

Tillmann-Healy, L. M. 1996. A secret life in a culture of thinness: Reflections on body, food, and bulimia. In C. Ellis and A. P. Bochner (Eds.), *Composing ethnography: Alternative forms of qualitative writing* (pp. 76–108). Walnut Creek, Calif.: AltaMira Press.

Trinh, T. M. 1989. *Woman, native, other.* Bloomington: Indiana University Press.

Trujillo, N. 1993. Interpreting November 22: A critical ethnography of an assassination site. *Quarterly Journal of Speech* 79: 447–66.

Weeks, J. 1990. The value of difference. In J. Rutherford (Ed.), *Identity: Community, culture, difference* (pp. 88–100). London: Lawrence and Wishart.

Woodward, K. 1997. Concepts of identity and difference. In K. Woodward (Ed.), *Identity and difference* (pp. 8–50). London: Sage.

Yep, G. A. 1998. My three cultures: Navigating the multicultural identity landscape. In J. N. Martin, T. K. Nakayama, and L. A. Flores (Eds.), *Readings in cultural contexts* (pp. 79–85). Mountain View, Calif.: Mayfield.

Yep, G. A., K. E. Lovaas, and A. V. Pagonis. 2002 . The case of "riding bareback": Sexual practices and the paradoxes of identity in the era of AIDS. *Journal of Homosexuality* 42 (4): 1–14.

KEY TERMS

ascribed identity
Asianlatinoamerican
autoethnography
avowed identity
core symbols
critical approach
cultural identity
dialectical approach
emic
essentialist view
ethnolinguistic identity
etic
fluidity of identity

functionalist approach
identity politics
intensity
interpretive approach
multicultural identity
nonessentialist view
nonsummative
paradoxical
power
salience
scope
socially constructed view

REVIEW AND DISCUSSION QUESTIONS

1. When you think of the term *identity*, what comes to mind? How are your conceptions of identity similar to or different from the ideas presented in this chapter?

2. Without judging whether they are desirable or undesirable characteristics, make a list of statements about yourself ("I am . . ."). Write as many statements about yourself as you can possibly think of in 15–20 minutes. What do these statements reveal about your cultural identity?

3. Can you think of personal examples that illustrate the political, fluid, nonsummative, and paradoxical nature of cultural identities?

4. Select one of your favorite films and describe how the identities of the main characters are presented. Imagine how functionalist, interpretive, and critical scholars would investigate and research the cultural identities of these characters. Be specific.

5. In your opinion, can the above three approaches to cultural identity be integrated? Explain why or why not.

6. Based on what you learned in this chapter, do you see any implications for intercultural communication? Can you think of an example that might illustrate your position?

Artifacts and Cultural Identity

THE CHAPTERS in part II illustrate how artifacts communicate various ethnic groups' cultural identities. Artifacts under investigation include a Japanese American's photo album, the image of Our Lady of Guadalupe, Indian cinema, and the planning and actual displays of intercultural weddings.

Fay Yokomizo Akindes's chapter focuses on a collection of family photographs selected and presented by her grandma, a *nisei* (second-generation) American Japanese woman in Hawai'i. These alternative texts speak to each other, communicating how Grandma negotiated her Japanese and American cultural identities through her life and the lives of her two oldest daughters. Particular attention is paid to clothing as symbolic representations of acculturation to U.S. American life after World War II. What results from this study is not only a deepened understanding of *nisei* and *sansei* (third-generation American Japanese) women in Hawai'i, but an appreciation for alternative archival texts that speak for the historically silenced.

Robert Westerfelhaus examines how sixteenth-century Aztecs reinvented Catholicism's Blessed Virgin, as Our Lady of Guadalupe, in ways that incorporated and affirmed important features of their own cultural and religious traditions. Westerfelhaus explains how one sign— in this case, the image of Our Lady of Guadalupe—can function simultaneously as an index, icon, and a complex collection of symbols. He explores how this image lends itself to different interpretations based upon codes imposed upon it by two competing religious traditions through the processes of resistive appropriation and co-optation. His study points out how, over time, the codes governing these traditions have blended together to form a new code.

Anjali Ram examines how popular cinema mediates collective and personal memories in the Asian Indian diaspora and how such mediated memories give us clues to how Asian Indian immigrants negotiate their identity. In both cases, Ram specifically explores how Indian cinema is activated to mediate memory and thereby reconstitute questions related to home, community, nation, and gender. Using ethnography to uncover some of the ways in which collective and personal memories are deployed to construct and communicate identity, she analyzes both a community gathering of Indian immigrants and the personal recollections of Indian diasporic women. She concludes by arguing that we need to rethink our traditional notions of acculturation and assimilation as new immigrants forge ways of simultaneously belonging to different cultural worlds.

Wendy Leeds-Hurwitz's chapter briefly outlines a long-term research study on the topic, describes the research methodology followed, and provides a case study of one intercultural wedding. Her study shows that intercultural weddings are an excellent example of a communication event between members of different cultural groups, and yet this topic has never been a site of research. The conclusion makes recommendations for future research into real interaction between members of different cultures.

Grandma's Photo Album: Clothing as Symbolic Representations of Identity

FAY YOKOMIZO AKINDES

LEARNING OBJECTIVES

After reading this chapter, students will be able to:

- understand the acculturation process of Japanese American women in Hawai'i through the experiences of a nisei woman and her sansei daughters;
- consider alternative archival material, such as family photo albums and oral history interviews, in understanding intercultural communication;
- reflect on their own families; and
- seek out their own family photo albums to "read" stories of cultural and ethnic identity.

The next few pages further document Shigechan's acculturation (or assimilation) into "mainland" life. There are photos of her posing with her haole *housemates on the front lawn, front stoop, and in the living room. There's a photo of her driving a tractor at a friend's farm, eating a caramelized apple, and standing at the entrance to a summer camp. Behind one group photo of Shigechan and five friends (four haole, one Japanese), she writes: "Front row: recognize me?"*

My grandma, Ineyo Kanda Fukumoto, died in her sleep on Sunday, May 21, 1995, at Kuakini Medical Center in Honolulu. She was eighty-eight years old. Alzheimer's disease made it impossible to communicate with her for the last ten years of her life. Grandma was extraordinary in her ordinariness. She recycled glass, metal, and paper years before it was the socially responsible thing to do. When she was in her mid-fifties, she learned how to drive a Volkswagen stick-shift Bug, the only car she ever felt comfortable driving, and one she continued to drive through her seventies. Among her senior-citizen friends, she was the only person with a car and a valid driver's license. On Wednesdays she would taxi them to Chinatown for fresh fish and *choi sum*. Her day started at sunrise with yoga exercises; she often vacuumed the bedrooms in the afternoon heat wearing only a pair of shorts. When she was in her mid-seventies, she performed solo before an audience of strangers. It was evening and she was singing, "Oh, What a Beautiful Morning." My grandma was not a famous woman. There are no newspaper accounts of her life; nor did she leave any personal journals or letters worth note. The remains of her days are pressed in the photo albums she kept that chronicle the life of her family.

Sontag (1977, p. 71) describes a photograph as a quotation, which "makes a book of photographs like a book of quotations." Consequently the manner in which people dress for a photograph constitutes the message behind the quotation. In other words, **clothing** is a system of signs or codes that communicates meaning (Barthes 1967/1983). Photographs are ideal artifacts for studying families and especially **women**'s positions and functions within them, areas not traditionally documented in written form and, therefore, not often a subject of historical inquiry. Family photographs are nontraditional academic texts that serve as a feminist alternative to traditional narrative-interview-based archival historiography. This historiographical work analyzed feminist principles based on the assumptions that knowledge is a human construction, that domestic spheres of life are legitimate sites for scholarship, and that point of view is consequential to experience (Nelson 1990; Spigel 2000).

Informed by cultural studies, this chapter particularizes the acculturation of Japanese American women in Hawai'i after **World War II**. The **photo album**'s meaning is reconstructed through supplemental primary texts, including an oral-history interview transcript and phone conversations. My grandma, Ineyo, a *nisei* woman from Hawai'i, assembled the photo album, which is central to this study.[1] The transcript is based on an oral history interview conducted by a University of Hawai'i graduate student in 1979 when Ineyo maintained an independent life. The telephone conversations were with my mother, Kachan, the oldest of grandma's five children.[2] Before I begin my analysis and interpretation of the photographic texts, I explore photography and clothing/fashion through the lens of cultural studies and provide a brief history of the Americanization movement in **Hawai'i**.

Double Portrait

Kotkin (1978) identifies four communicative modes of family folklore: (1) verbal, (2) written, (3) behavioral, and (4) visual. My primary text for this study is **photography**, what Kotkin calls "the visual counterparts of family stories," and which constitutes the fourth mode of family folklore. A photo album is not only a portrait of the family it represents but also a portrait of the person who assembles it. As such, the photo album not only portrays Ineyo's family, but Ineyo herself. Kotkin (1978, p. 5) writes: "We tend to take photos according to how we want to preserve, remember, and be remembered . . . family photos represent a stylized reality." She further quotes psychologist Steward Albert who observes that "The resulting pseudo-narrative high-lights all that is life-affirming while it systematically suppresses life's pains" (Kotkin 1978, p. 7). As Mavor (1997, p. 126) writes, "all family pictures are masked: they assume the mask of the familial." This tendency to produce a "stylized reality" of family life in photos is radically disrupted by photographer Nan Goldin in *The Ballad of Sexual Dependency* (1986, p. 6), a "visual diary" for public gaze with pictures that "show exactly what my world looks like, without glamorization, without glorification." Goldin's collection of photos, including the photographer with a bruised eye (abuse from her lover), are uncharacteristic of most family photo albums, which are carefully edited and masked (Mavor 1997). Jacobs (1981, p. 98) explains that snapshots are usually taken during extraordinary moments and affect the behavior of photo subjects and that we "are not wholly 'natural' at such moments; rather we project images of ourselves, poses that sometimes harden into postures." Moreover, the romanticized image of the happy family in advertising con-tributes to the attempted replication of advertising's myth of domestic bliss in personal pho-tographs (Benjamin 1993). This was particularly true during the early days of popular photography when the affordability and accessibility of cameras transformed ordinary people into photographers. Advertising thus became a source of instruction, naturalizing the unnatural.

Chalfen (1991) provides the best theoretical framework for family photo albums. In his book *Turning Leaves*, Chalfen analyzes the photographic collections of two *nisei* families living on the U.S. continent. He considers the photographs cultural symbols of **identity** and ethnicity, and traces the continuity or transformation of these symbols, or values, through the pages of the albums. Chalfen observes how the Japanese Americans in his study construct their identities in relation to other family members, as well as institutions of learning, religion, sports, and work. Similarly, Motz (1989, p. 73), in her study of photograph albums by turn-of-the-century Midwestern women, contends that the "meaning of the albums arises in large part from the rela-tionship of the photographs to one another, and each photograph itself takes its meaning in part from its juxtaposition with other photographs." **Intertextuality**, the idea that meaning derives from our engagement with multiple texts, is an important concept in analyzing and interpreting photo albums. Albums are not isolated texts but part of familial and social structures. When read-ing meaning in albums, therefore, the selection and placement of photographs within an album must be contextualized within and beyond the borders of the photo, the page, and the album.

Form Precedes Word

Clothing is a visible form of acculturation; it constructs what Bourdieu calls a **habitus** or "structured structures" that "function as structuring structures" (Bourdieu 1993, p. 480). In other words, clothing functions as a structure that, in turn, structures to some degree the life of the person wearing the clothing. As Craik (1994, p. 5) writes, "We use the way we wear our bodies to present ourselves to our social environment, mapping out our codes of conduct." These codes are used in constructing the self we choose to present to others. As such, cloth-ing "creates a 'face' which positively constructs an identity rather than disguising a 'natural' body or 'real' identity." This is evident among many immigrants to the United States who shed their native clothing for American dress, even before they master the language or learn to negotiate cultural codes. Similarly, subcultures, such as punk or hip-hop, gain their personae through the hyper-display of codes such as Doc Marten boots or Tommy Hilfiger clothing (Hebdige 1979; Rubinstein 1995). Thus, *form precedes word*.

Old clothing as objects of nostalgia, as opposed to clothing that is worn, is explored by Mavor (1997) who poignantly stitches together old clothing and photographs, subject and object, life and death, by studying (as I did), her grandma's photo album in relation to other memorabilia. What emerges in her study is an understanding of saved objects as filling in a sense of loss. Mavor (1997, p. 121–22) writes, "Objects keep death away by helping us to remember. . . . I am so afraid of forgetting." Mavor fetishizes clothing and photographs and draws on Christian Boltanski's (Gumpert 1994, p. 110) provocative observation that "What they [clothing and photographs] have in common is that they are simultaneously presence and absence. They are both an object and a souvenir of a subject, exactly as a cadaver is both an object and a souvenir of a subject." Clothing and photographs are both/and, negating and projecting, which explains their powerful hold on our sense of belonging.

Current fashion discourse by contemporary critical scholars emphasizes racialization (Kondo 1997), **semiotics** (Barthes 1983; Leeds-Hurwitz 1993; Rubenstein 1995), cultural studies (Craik 1994; David 1992; Mukerji and Schudson 1991), and the political economy of fashion (Wark 1991). Literature on fashion as an artifactual text in studying the acculturation process of immigrants also exists, although it is more limited (Gordon 1995). Exhibition materials and the review of *Becoming American Women: Clothing and the Jewish Immigrant Experience, 1880–1920*, sponsored by the Chicago Historical Society in 1994, are the most relevant studies. The exhibition displayed the acculturation process of Jewish women through their dress, yet, as Gordon (1995) notes, the exhibition ultimately failed to explore the meaning of Americanization. She writes: "Does 'becoming American' simply involve adopting or conforming to external forms or styles? Does it mean obliterating all ethnic distinctions, or casting oneself into the proverbial melting pot?" (p. 129). In *Adapting to Abundance: Jewish Immigrants, Mass Consumption, and the Search for American Identity*, Heinze (1990, p. 9) includes a chapter on "The Clothing of an American." He explicates the role of clothing as a signifier of American identity and as "an important symbol of cultural transformation." Similarly, Kawakami (1995) focuses on fashion in her book, *Japanese Immigrant Clothing in Hawai'i 1885–1941*, by studying the clothing of *issei* men and women in Hawai'i. Although she does not explicitly address acculturation as a theme, her rich collection of archival photographs illustrates how *issei* adopted, adapted, and transformed Western and Hawaiian clothing during that historic epoch.

This chapter intersects clothing with the acculturation process by approaching articles of clothing as signifiers or **symbolic representations** of identity. Therefore, when analyzing and interpreting photographs in Grandma's album, much of my contextualization includes clothing as signs or symbols of culturally specific meaning.

Americanization Crusade in Hawai'i

Tamura (1994, p. 52) defines *Americanization* as the "organized effort during and following World War I to compel immigrants and their children to adopt certain Anglo-American ways while remaining at the bottom socioeconomic strata of American society." The Americanization movement on the U.S. continent, at its height from the late 1910s to 1920s, was spearheaded by such groups as the Daughters of the American Revolution and the American Legion, which sponsored education programs "to indoctrinate the adult foreigner with loyalty to America" (Tamura 1994, p. 53). The Americanization crusade in Hawai'i differed from that on the U.S.

continent in two significant ways: first, the majority of immigrants in Hawai'i were Asian, not European; and second, the Americanization movement in the U.S. Territory of Hawai'i continued after World War I (when the campaign on the continental U.S. ended) and through World War II. When discussing the experience of **Japanese Americans**, particularly the *nisei* in Hawai'i, Tamura prefers the term **acculturation** (rather than assimilation or Americanization), which implies a "persistence of ethnic identity." In other words, Japanese Americans in Hawai'i did not experience the unidirectional process most European immigrants experienced but maintained dual identities of Japanese *and* American.

Although European Americans on the U.S. continent may also maintain dual identities, the degree to which this occurred among Asian Americans, specifically the Japanese Americans, was much more pronounced. Physiological differences created a basis for *haoles*'[3] racial prejudice against the Japanese, who comprised 37.2 to 42.7 percent of Hawai'i's population for the first four decades of the twentieth century. A growing number of this population were *nisei*, born in Hawai'i, thereby making them U.S. citizens. This large population base triggered a wave of fear among the island's *haole* oligarchy who envisaged the "Japanization" of Hawai'i. Americanizers in Hawai'i, therefore, demanded the eradication of Japanese practices and values as signs of absolute loyalty to the United States and, in the process, contradicted the meaning of "democracy." For example, Japanese were expected to discard their cultural identity by speaking Standard English (as opposed to Japanese or **Pidgin English,** a hybrid language of Asian, English, and Hawaiian words that evolved from the multicultural work environment of the sugar plantations) and by converting from **Buddhism** to Christianity. At the same time, the Japanese were *excluded* from basic American privileges, such as fair legal hearings and equity in education (Okihiro 1991; Tamura 1994). There were political efforts to halt the publication of newspapers written in the Japanese language, to prevent the naturalization of Japanese immigrants, and to restrict future Japanese immigration to the United States. Such legal maneuvers hindered Japanese acculturation by alienating Japanese from *haole*s and underscoring their marginal existence as Americans. Thus, as Tamura notes, many Japanese retained their cultural identity "partly because pride in their cultural heritage gave them the self-respect denied them in the American setting" (Tamura 1994, p. 67).

This drive to Americanize the Japanese people was further motivated by fear of Japan's growing military power in China and its possible threat to the future of Hawai'i. Consequently, the Americanization campaign culminated in a situation of cultural ambiguity for Japanese Americans in Hawai'i. Were they Japanese or American? What were the possibilities of hybridization? How did they negotiate their Japanese and American identities in their everyday lives? How did this negotiation manifest itself in material terms?

The Americanization crusade in Hawai'i, with its questions of acculturation and assimilation, is instructive when analyzing, interpreting, and contextualizing Grandma's photo album. The album consists of photographs taken in Hawai'i in the 1950s and early 1960s; this post–World War II period represents a dramatic shift in Hawai'i's political and socioeconomic landscape. Politically it signaled a transfer of power from the *haole* Republican oligarchy of the plantation era to the Japanese American and working-class Democratic Party. This period also represents the development of multinational corporations, which had a significant impact on Hawai'i's economy. As a result of external investors, agriculture was soon replaced by **tourism** as the state's dominant industry. These historical shifts provide the contextual backdrop for Grandma's album—in itself a chronicle of change.

Grandma's Album

Printed on the cover of Grandma's photo album is the word *Photographs.* There is no other inscription or personalization. The album contains a single color photo and 314 black-and-white photos of various sizes mounted on seventy-eight black pages, the edges of which are now brittle. The photos were taken by various people, including Ineyo, during the 1950s and 1960s, and are assembled chronologically in cycles. More specifically, the photo album begins in the early 1950s and continues chronologically to 1963 when Ineyo and her husband Hisaji sold their business in **Pahala**, Hawai'i, and moved to a modern home in Honolulu, Oahu. There are a series of photos documenting the move, followed by photos that return to earlier years in Pahala. There are no annotations. A few of the photos have handwritten captions written in blue ink on the white borders of the photos. Other photos, given to Ineyo by her children, have captions handwritten behind them.

The photographs positioned on the first page of Ineyo's photo album seem to shout "American!" The dominant image is a group photo of the Ka'u softball team with her youngest son Clyde sitting in the front row. There are also photos of Clyde leading the Pahala School J.P.O. (Junior Police Officers) in a Hilo parade (see fig. 6.1) and a Boy Scout troop with Clyde in the front row. Situated in the bottom corners of this front page are two small

FIGURE 6.1   Ineyo's youngest son, Clyde (front right), is one of two Junior Police Officers carrying the Pahala School Banner in a Hilo parade. The indoctrination into American life was important, particularly after WWII when Japanese Americans' patriotism to the United States was questioned and denied.

 FIGURE 6.2 Ineyo rests on a wooden deck chair aboard the U.S. *Lurline* with her youngest son Clyde, who wears an aloha shirt like a tourist. Sitting to Grandma's right, oblivious to the camera, is a man who bears a striking resemblance to Grandpa.

photos: one shows the façade of a small building with a sign that reads: "KANDA'S GIFT HOUSE—GRAND OPENING." The second photo features Ineyo and Clyde, wearing a touristy aloha shirt, sitting on wooden deck lounge chairs on what appears to be the *Lurline* cruise liner. (See fig. 6.2.) The right half of the photo is overexposed, a strip of light obliterating a man who resembles Ineyo's husband Hisaji. He is facing another direction, oblivious to the camera.

The second page of Ineyo's photo album illustrates the dual identity of **Japanese American** women living in Hawai'i during the post–World War II period. The photographs on this page chronicle the young adult life of her oldest daughter Kachan (my mother). In one photo she is wearing a Western version of a kimono, in another, also taken around 1954, Kachan models a Western dress with a fitted waistline and flared skirt (see figs. 6.3 and 6.4). Both photos position Kachan as "up-to-date" (as she says), and distance her from the dusty menial labor of Pahala's sugarcane fields. In the third photo, Kachan kneels next to her daughter, Lei, who is sitting in a stroller. This photo was taken about four years after the other two; she is now married and living on the rural island of Molokai where she is a housewife and mother of two girls. Coconut and *kiawe* (algaroba) trees frame the background.

These first two pages are representative of the photo album. At first they seem haphazard, with no underlying theme connecting them. The oral history interview with Ineyo and phone conversations with Kachan, however, help construct an understanding of Ineyo's selection

FIGURE 6.3 Kachan models a Westernized version of a Japanese kimono without the multiple layers of fabric and waist-constricting *obi* (belt). She gazes into the distance, coy to the camera.

process. The prominent photos on the first page honor her sons and their American identities as symbolized by the uniforms they wear. Her youngest son, Clyde, is represented as a softball player, a Boy Scout, and junior police officer (see fig. 6.5). In the fourth picture he is dressed in an aloha shirt, signifier of Hawaii's shift from sugar plantation to tourist plantation (see fig. 6.6). The photograph of the Kanda's Gift House, the family business where Ineyo worked as a teenager, anchors Ineyo to the past. The photo of Ineyo and Clyde on the *Lurline* is a promise of the future: a life far removed from the dusty sugar plantation, a life where even Ineyo is a tourist of the leisure class. The pictures of Kachan on the second page represent a balancing of two cultures—not necessarily Japanese or American, but Japanese *and* American—and, ultimately, privilege her role as mother.

The absence of captions suggests that the purpose of the album is for those, including Ineyo, who understand the context behind the photographs. The images she selected for inclusion in the album clearly define her as a mother. There are group and individual photographs of her with her children. The few photographs of Ineyo's husband, however, identify him with groups other than the family. This is not unusual considering the traditional Japanese roles of women in the private *(uchi)* sphere and men in the public *(soto)* sphere. Indeed, the group photos in which Hisaji appears commemorate public events: in the Buddhist temple; as coach of the Aces baseball team in which their oldest son Juchan is a player; and a photo of Hisaji taken in front of an inter-island Aloha Airlines airplane with a group of golfers. Besides these posed group photos of Hisaji, there are a few candid shots of him in social settings. In one photo he is sitting on the floor with a few other men. The table in the center of the men holds a plate of fresh fruit, bowls of food, a container of *sake* (rice wine), and *sake* cups. The women sit in the

 FIGURE 6.4

Kachan's direct gaze into the camera is consistent with her smart Western A-line dress, which she designed and sewed.

FIGURE 6.5

Ineyo's two sons, Juchan and Clyde, in Boy Scout and Cub Scout uniforms. Their rolled-up slacks and chunky sneakers resonate of the emerging American teenager.

Ineyo, her two sons, and two neighborhood boys all sport aloha shirts made popular as leisure wear for tourists after WWII.

background outside the circle. This particular scene is not an uncommon one in Japanese culture: men situate themselves in the center while the women and children fill the periphery.

Lacking in prominence are photographs of Hisaji in his role as father, and photographs of his parents in their role as grandparents to the children. These are significant omissions considering that the grandparents lived in the same household and that the grandmother took on the role of primary caregiver to Ineyo's three youngest children (Eichan, Juchan, and Clyde), as well as preparing the family meals and managing the housework while Ineyo assisted Hisaji in the family's service station business. Two possible explanations for these omissions are: (1) Hisaji is the photographer of the featured pictures, or (2) no photographs exist of him alone or his parents. The first explanation is a possibility, although Kachan claims he was often too busy with his business and civic activities to spend time with the family. The second explanation is proved false by other family albums, which feature photos of Hisaji and his parents—both studio-posed photos and candid family shots. This evidence makes Ineyo's selection of photographs in her album all the more significant and meaningful: she has *chosen* to exclude him and his parents from her field of representation.

Throughout the photo album there is an abundance of photographs chronicling the lives of Kachan and Shigechan, Ineyo's oldest and second-oldest daughters. In studying the photos of these two daughters, one gains a strong sense of their individual personalities and the significance these identities may have had in the life of Ineyo. Kachan is often photographed in stylish dress as a young woman; and after she is married there are many photos of her new life as mother and housewife. The pages of photographs devoted to Shigechan portray her as a university student on the U.S. continent, dressed in "mainland" accessories, such as gloves, a scarf, and hat (see fig. 6.7).

Chalfen (1991) writes that the selection of photographs displayed in a family album represents the "preferred patterns of belonging." In analyzing the relationships in George Nagano's photo album, Chalfen observes how the sons and mother are acknowledged and honored while the daughter is ignored through her absence from the photo album. Conversely, Ineyo's assemblage of photographs privileges the lives of her two oldest daughters. This emphasis speaks against the grain of traditional Japanese thinking, which privileges the patriarchy (father and oldest sons) and elders (grandparents). Ineyo rejected not only the superficial aspects of Japanese patriarchy but also its implications for the development of her Japanese American daughters.

The function of education in the lives of plantation children was not of concern, however, to those with economic and political power. Pahala plantation manager James C. Campsie, for example, is quoted as saying, "Public education beyond the fourth grade is not only a waste, it is a menace. We spend to educate them and they will destroy us" (Fuchs 1961, p. 263). This sentiment was reflected in the poor educational quality of the school, which ignored the dual-identity needs of its Japanese students, including Kachan. "I was a whiz at math, but I had difficulty understanding English because we used to speak Japanese at home," she says (E. Shinsato, personal communication 1995).

FIGURE 6.7   Shigechan (Caroline), a co-ed at a Midwestern university, accents her suit with white shoes, gloves, and a hat—accessories that unmake her Asianness.

After her junior year at Pahala High School, Ineyo enrolled Kachan in the Mid-Pacific Institute (M.P.I.), a private Christian boarding school in Honolulu, where Kachan repeated her junior year and graduated a year later. Ineyo continued to guide her oldest daughter's life beyond high school, enrolling her in the Style Center, a fashion design center in Honolulu. When asked how she learned what was fashionable, Kachan replies, "It really wasn't my choice to go to sewing school" (E. Shinsato, personal communication, March 2000). Her seemingly indirect answer suggests that it was Ineyo who valued style and the ability to invent oneself through fashion. In this sense, Kachan's life was being directed by Ineyo, just as Ineyo's life decisions had been determined by her mother, brother, and husband. Kachan thrived at the Style Center, often receiving compliments for her fine work designing and sewing clothing ranging from play wear to formal evening gowns, Japanese-inspired clothing to Western dresses (see fig. 6.8). This duality was evident in other areas of her life. During World War II, for example, when Buddhist churches in Hawai'i (and on the U.S. continent) were closed down (and Buddhist priests from Hawai'i were relocated to the U.S. continent where they were placed in concentration camps), Kachan was asked to play the organ during Sunday services at the Methodist Church. Although she became active in church activities, she still considered herself foremost a Buddhist and, at home, her grandmother prayed and chanted in Japanese every day before a *butsudan* (ancestral shrine). Similarly, as a student at M.P.I., Kachan was required to attend Christian services. This "Americanization" process was not something Kachan was conscious of; she simply accepted it as "the way things were."

 Kachan's aloha shirt, rolled-up jeans, and rubber slippers combine Hawaiian and American identities.

The dual identity of being Japanese American was naturalized into everyday life, particularly in the area of education. Every day after English-language school, Kachan and her siblings would attend Japanese-language school for lessons in penmanship, reading, and history. On Saturdays they would clean the Japanese-language schoolyard and take classes in sewing. The importance that her parents placed on the Japanese school made it seem more important than English-language school, according to Kachan, although she says she always understood she was a U.S. citizen. She remembers watching war movies, such as *Iwo Jima,* and recalls how "everyone would cheer for the American side by clapping and shouting." In remembering the war she says, "Whenever one of the boys in Pahala got drafted the parents [of the boy] would come around and have us make a French knot in a piece of fabric for them [the boys] to wear around their waist for strength." Thus, the community reinforced its American affiliation and identity through collectivist acts that also served as sources of strength and hope.

In the early 1950s, while attending the Style Center, Kachan answered a newspaper advertisement offering free room and board in exchange for light housekeeping. This was a common occupation for Japanese women, some of whom chose such work for the opportunity to learn the *haole* (white) lifestyle (Geschwender and Argiro 1993). In exchange for her room, meals, and $25 a week, Kachan assisted the full-time housekeeper in performing such chores as polishing silver, cleaning the refrigerator, and washing the laundry. She was also responsible for frying the breakfast eggs and broiling steaks for Mr. and Mrs. Doolittle's dinner. Living in this *haole* household introduced her to a different diet; steak was a novelty in her family where vegetables and rice were more common, although she says, "Our favorite food, what we had on our birthday, was hamburger, peas and corn, and mashed potatoes" (E. Shinsato, personal communication, April 25, 2000). Less than a year after moving in with the Doolittles, Kachan returned to Pahala to marry.

Ineyo's second daughter followed a different path. Shigechan was the "brain" in the family, as Kachan put it. Because of this she was *not* enrolled in M.P.I., and this created a deep-rooted resentment toward Ineyo who, Shigechan believed, prevented her from experiencing boarding school in the city. After graduating from Pahala High School, however, Shigechan attended college in the Midwest where she eventually enrolled in graduate school, married a *haole* graduate student, and earned a Ph.D in psychology. During this time, she made a conscious decision to break all ties with her Hawai'i family and has not communicated with her parents or siblings for more than thirty years. While in graduate school, I located a copy of her doctoral dissertation, which begins with an epitaph, a line from Robert Frost's "The Road Not Taken": "Two roads diverged in a yellow wood, And sorry I could not travel both."

Knowing this course of events illuminates the meaning in the series of photographs displayed in Ineyo's album. A full page of photographs is devoted to Shigechan's departure from the Honolulu Airport on September 15, 1951. (See fig. 6.9.) There are four group photos of Shigechan, Ineyo, Eichan, Ineyo's brother Stephen, his wife Myrtle, and their three children. Hisaji does not appear in any of the photographs; he is either the photographer or, perhaps, absent from the event. Subsequent pages feature a series of photographs documenting Shigechan's college life in Michigan. Situated in the center of the page is a photo of a Japanese woman dressed in a traditional kimono, the U.S. Capitol building looming behind her (see fig. 6.10). The handwritten caption on the back reads: "Amy Takase from Japan with Capitol in back. Feb. 1952." The photos next to this one show Shigechan in Western clothes—short-sleeved blouse with scarf at neckline tucked into an A-line skirt. There is an implicit

FIGURE 6.9 Grandma, whose education ended after the eighth grade, bids farewell to her daughter Shigechan, who is leaving for college in the Midwest.

negation of Shigechan's Japaneseness in the juxtaposition of her photograph with Amy's. The contrast of Amy's constricting kimono next to an architectural icon of Americanism, and Shigechan in American dress, is striking.

The next few pages further document Shigechan's **acculturation** (or assimilation) into "mainland" life. There are photos of her posing with her *haole* housemates on the front lawn, front stoop, and in the living room. There's a photo of her driving a tractor at a friend's farm, eating a caramelized apple, and standing at the entrance to a summer camp. Behind one group photo of Shigechan and five friends (four *haole*, one Japanese), she writes: "Front row: recognize me?"

To understand the lives of Kachan and Shigechan beneath the photographic surface, it is instructive to revisit Ineyo's earlier life. Her formal schooling ended after the eighth grade because of family circumstances: she cared for her father, who had a stroke, while her mother traveled to Japan. At thirteen, Ineyo worked in the Kanda family store while her older siblings attended college; her older sister became a pharmacist and her older brother a teacher who became the education superintendent for the State of Hawai'i. He was also "the first non-Caucasian as well as the first Japanese American principal of Farrington High School" in Honolulu (Tamura 1994, p. 242). Ineyo's marriage to Hisaji was arranged by a *shimpai* (matchmaker), a common practice among Japanese families. They were married in February 1928 but

FIGURE 6.10 The juxtaposition of traditional Japanese kimono and the U.S. Capitol in Washington, D.C., suggests a collision of cultures on the continental United States. This photograph is positioned in Grandma's photo album next to photographs of Shigechan in American dress.

did not live together until September of that year. After her husband opened his automobile service station, a business venture that she encouraged him to pursue, Ineyo assisted him in the business (see fig. 6.11). Ineyo says:

> I had to run up when no cars, run home and cook and run [back]—run home wash clothes. Sometimes he's busy with cars and people came for gas. He came home and says, "Stay down there!" because he cannot be filling gas and work on the cars. I used to run up and down. (Taketa 1979)

Ineyo negotiated her responsibilities in business and domestic spheres until the arrival of her in-laws, specifically her mother-in-law (my *Obabasan*) who assumed care for the children and household matters.

Years later, as a grandmother and widow, Ineyo expressed her regret at not being able to raise her children. She says, "One thing business not good for children. You cannot stay with children. . . . Good though, the wife stay home with the children. That's why they have grandmother picture in wallet—not my picture" (Taketa 1979). This poignant statement suggests the place and function of Ineyo's photo album in her life—a space of resistance for reliving and reinventing herself. The images she deliberately chose to include and exclude in her field of representation inform her self-construction as a mother, wife, and woman. (See fig. 6.12.) As Barthes (1981, p. 34) writes, "Photography cannot signify (aim at a generality) except by assuming a mask." Grandma's album of photographs is her *masked* self.

FIGURE 6.11   Pumping gas was a gendered task for women, as pictured here by Grandma. Grandpa (standing next to her) was the auto mechanic who got his hands greasy in repair work.

Intercultural Implications

What emerges from "Grandma's Photo Album: Clothing as Symbolic Representations of Identity" is an understanding of how *nisei* and **sansei** women in Hawai'i negotiated their U.S. American and Japanese identities after World War II. Grandma's two oldest daughters sought different directions in their adult lives, both embodying the dreams of their mother who had limited choices as a *nisei* woman. One daughter was an at-home mother to five children, while the other daughter pursued a doctoral degree on the U.S. mainland, eventually relinquishing all ties with the family and, assumably, her Japanese heritage.

Findings from the study suggest four key intercultural implications. First, cultural and ethnic identities are situated in historical contexts. The experiences of Grandma's two oldest daughters, for example, were subject to post–World War II expectations of American Japanese to prove their loyalty and citizenship to the United States. In the process of acculturating to American culture, some Japanese cultural and ethnic practices were suppressed. Intercultural implications, then, are closely related to power and who controls it. Second, cultural and ethnic identities are situated in social contexts, including gender, race, and class. Gendered expectations, such as bearing and raising children, were central to a woman's identity in the Japanese community. "Race" and ethnicity were also social markers of class in Hawai'i's stratified plantation industry. Third, cultural and ethnic identities are not fixed, but open to new interpretations. The generational shifts in lifestyles between Grandma and her two daughters, for example,

FIGURE
6.12

Grandma (happily) wears a housewife's apron after retirement. Here she examines the shiny stove in her new house in Honolulu, islands away from the dusty sugar plantation of Pahala.

are illustrative of this idea. Finally, cultural and ethnic identities are complex and, at times, dialectical. The way that Grandma's second oldest daughter negotiated her Japanese and U.S. American identities, ultimately choosing between the two, represents the dialectical tension in Asian American cultural and ethnic identities.

Summary

When I first started analyzing Grandma's photo album, I was interested in clothing as symbolic representations of identity in the context of Japanese women's acculturation to an Americanized Hawai'i. In the process of analyzing the photographs, however, I found that my grandma's story as a *nisei* whose life was a string of sacrifices resonated in the lives of her children. In particular, the implicit privileging of her two oldest daughters suggests an embracing of their lived experiences as symbolized in their clothing. Kachan's production and consumption of "up-to-date" fashion and her eventual domestic role of mother, and Shigechan's adoption of *haole* clothing and accessories that mirrored her academic pursuits on the mainland, signified what Ineyo yearned for herself.

Clothing was an important signifier of class status, communicating the successful acculturation into American life (Rubinstein 1995, Veblen 1953). It was a visible measurement of one's distance from the manual field labor of the *issei* and signaled the modern civility of post–World War II life. Just as Kachan rejected wedding pictures taken in the church by the plantation photographer ("they yellowed"), and chose instead modern photographs in a Hilo studio, Ineyo distanced her children from plantation life. She dressed their feet in store-bought shoes.

Writing this chapter subverted traditional research practices by privileging **alternative archival historiography** as a means of listening to ordinary people and opening a space for them to enter history. As such, it applied feminist principles to communication historiography. Grandma's photo album was foreground as a primary archival text—a text traditionally not considered a legitimate historical source—supplemented by an oral-history interview and personal conversations. Textual analysis and interpretation were informed by concepts of clothing as symbolic representations of identity, photography, and American acculturation.

Communication often occurs in oblique, indirect ways, as Grandma's album demonstrates. What she chose to make visible through photography—subject positionings of mother—as well as what she chose to render invisible—subject positionings of wife and daughter-in-law—represents her resistance to patriarchy. While her life was a series of self-sacrifices, her photo album gave her agency to reconstruct her life for future reading, to have others (her children, grandchildren) remember her as she wished. As Martinsons (1996) writes, "I construct photographs according to the set of discourses that I am familiar with, am drawn by, feel connections to: I use who I am, my several selves, to construct and to enter into dialogue about and with an image." In this sense, Ineyo constructed a photographic discourse of her idealized life as a mother whose children embodied all that she wished to experience. Epistemologically, Grandma's album represents an alternative site for understanding how ordinary people make meaning of their lives. The message inscribed in Grandma's album is that the silenced are not silent.

Notes

I wish to thank Jenny L. Nelson, Judith Yaross Lee, and Wendy Leeds-Hurwitz for their insightful comments on earlier drafts of this chapter. I also thank Don Lintner for his help with photography.

1. Chalfen (1991) posits that Japanese Americans are the only ethnic group in the United States that has distinct classifications for each generation, beginning with the first immigrant group. *Issei* are the first generation to live in the United States; *nisei* are the second generation (first generation to be born in the states); *sansei* are the third generation; and *yonsei* are the fourth generation. Kiefer (1974) explores the cultural process of three generations of Japanese American *(issei, nisei, sansei)* in *Changing Cultures, Changing Lives.*

2. Ineyo had five children, all with English first names and Japanese middle names. At home, all of the children—except the youngest son Clyde—were identified by derivations of their Japanese names. The children's names were: Kachan (*Evelyn*), Shigechan (*Caroline*), Eichan (*Corinne*) and Juchan (*Alvin*). The "chan" suffix is an affectionate term for children still used among adult family members today. For example, Kachan, a derivation of Katsuko, is in her late sixties and is still called by her childhood name by aunts, uncles, and brothers.

3. *Haole* is a Hawaiian term that literally means "without breath." It refers to white Western foreigners who, upon arrival in Hawai'i, could not speak the native language. Today *haole* refers to whites.

References

Barthes, R. 1981. *Camera lucida*. (R. Howard, trans.) New York: Hill and Wang. (Original work published 1980.)

————. 1983. *The fashion system.* (M. Ward and R. Howard, trans.) New York: Hill and Wang. (Original work published 1967.)

Benjamin, M. 1993, June 25. Picturing the silences. *New Statesman and Society* 6 (258): 32–33.

Bourdieu, P. 1993. Structures, habitus, practices. In C. Lemert (Ed.), *Social theory: The multicultural and classic readings.* San Francisco: Westview.

Chalfen, R. 1991. *Turning leaves.* Albuquerque: University of New Mexico Press.

Craik, J. 1994. *The face of fashion: Cultural studies in fashion.* London: Routledge.

David, F. 1992. *Fashion, culture and identity.* Chicago: University of Chicago Press.

Fuchs, L. H. 1961. *Hawai'i pono: A social history.* New York: Harcourt, Brace, and World.

Geschwender, J. A., and R. Argiro. 1993. *Social movements, conflicts and change* 15: 29–53.

Goldin, N. 1986. *The ballad of sexual dependency.* New York: Aperture.

Gordon, B. 1995. Becoming American women: Clothing and the Jewish immigrant experience, 1880–1920, in an exhibition review, "They don't wear wigs here": Issues and complexities in the development of an exhibition. *American Quarterly* 47 (1): 116–39.

Gumpert, L. 1994. *Christian Boltanski.* Paris: Flammarion, p. 10.

Hebdige, D. 1979. *Subculture: The meaning of style.* London: Methuen.

Heinze, A. R. 1990. *Adapting to abundance: Jewish immigrants, mass consumption, and the search for American identity.* New York: Columbia University Press.

Jacobs, D. 1981. Domestic snapshots: Toward a grammar of motives. *Journal of American Culture* 5 (1).

Kawakami, B. 1995. *Japanese immigrant clothing in Hawai'i, 1885–1941.* Honolulu: University of Hawai'i at Manoa.

Kiefer, C. W. 1974. *Changing cultures, changing lives.* San Francisco: Jossey-Bass.

Kondo, D. 1997. *About face: Performing race in fashion and theater.* London: Routledge.

Kotkin, A. 1978. The family photo album as a form of folklore. *Exposure* 16 (1): 4–8.

Leeds-Hurwitz, W. 1993. *Semiotics and communication: Signs, codes, cultures.* Hillsdale, N.J.: Lawrence Erlbaum Associates.

Martinsons, B. 1996. The possibility of agency for photographic subjects. In S. Aronowitz, B. Martinsons, M. Menser, and J. Rich (Eds.), *Technoscience and cyberculture,* pp. 231–53. New York: Routledge.

Mavor, C. 1997. Collecting loss. *Cultural Studies* 11 (1): 111–37.

Motz, M. F. 1989. Visual autobiography: Photograph albums of turn-of-the-century midwestern women. *American Quarterly* 41 (3): 63–92.

Mukerji, C., and M. Schudson. 1991. *Rethinking popular culture.* Berkeley: University of California Press.

Nelson, J. L. 1990. Phenomenology as feminist methodology: Explicating interviews. In K. Carter and C. Spitzack (Eds.), *Doing research on women's communication: Perspectives on theory and method.* Norwood, N.J.: Ablex.

Okihiro, G. 1991. *Cane fires: The anti-Japanese movement in Hawai'i, 1865–1945.* Philadelphia: Temple University Press.

Rubenstein, R. P. 1995. *Dress codes: Meanings and messages in American culture.* Boulder, Colo.: Westview.

Sontag, S. 1977. *On photography.* New York: Farrar, Straus and Giroux.

Spigel, L. 2000. Women's work. In H. Newcomb (Ed.), *Television: The critical view* (2nd ed., pp. 73–99). New York: Oxford University Press.

Taketa, C. 1979. Mrs. Ineyo Kanda Fukumoto. Unpublished manuscript and oral-history interview transcription, University of Hawai'i at Manoa.

Tamura, E. 1994. *Americanization, acculturation, and ethnic identity: The nisei generation in Hawai'i.* Urbana: University of Illinois Press.

Veblen, T. 1953. *Theory of the leisure class.* Boston: Houghton Mifflin.

Wark, M. 1991. Fashioning the future: Fashion, clothing, and the manufacturing of post-Fordist culture. *Cultural Studies* 5 (1): 61–76.

KEY TERMS

acculturation	Pahala
alternative archival historiography	photo album
Buddhism	photography
habitus	Pidgin English
haole	*sansei*
Hawai'i	semiotics
identity	symbolic representation
intertextuality	tourism
issei	women
Japanese American	World War II
nisei	

REVIEW AND DISCUSSION QUESTIONS

1. What was the significance of Grandma's photo album to Grandma herself?
2. How does clothing represent cultural identity? How does the clothing you wear communicate your cultural identity? How would you describe the cultural identity of your classmates?
3. How did Grandma's daughters negotiate their cultural identities as U.S. American Japanese?
4. Why is a family photo album an alternative archival text? Can you name other alternative historical texts for studying intercultural communication?
5. Assignment: Select one of your family's photo albums and analyze it in a 3–5-page paper. What photographs are included (and excluded)? How are the photographs positioned? Who produced the photo album? Who "consumes" the photo album? What stories do the photographs tell about your family?

She Speaks to Us, for Us, and of Us: Our Lady of Guadalupe as a Semiotic Site of Struggle and Identity

ROBERT WESTERFELHAUS

LEARNING OBJECTIVES

After reading this chapter, students will be able to:

- identify the basic elements and terminology of semiotic theory;
- understand the three primary types of signs;
- know how codes guide the use and interpretation of signs;
- comprehend how competing cultures use the processes of oppositional appropriation and co-optation to impose their own codes upon contested signs;
- identify how the imposition of different codes upon the same sign can produce multiple, and sometimes contradictory, meanings;
- explain how syncretism creates new codes by drawing upon and mixing the signs and rules of two or more codes;
- articulate how narrative can serve as a powerful tool of resistance.

She is everywhere. On T-shirts, tattooed on biceps and chests, etched into the back windows or lacquer enameled on the back trunks of low riders, on murals, on tiles and medals. Even on cowboy boots.

—Corona (1996, p. 18)

I n 1519, Hernán Cortés led a small expedition of Spanish soldiers and Roman Catholic missionaries into the heart of central Mexico. The twin goals of Cortés's expedition were the political conquest and the religious conversion of the **Aztecs**. In attempting to accomplish the second of these goals, the Spanish seized sites sacred to the Aztecs, destroyed the religious objects associated with them, and inserted Christian objects in their place. Among these sites was a hillside shrine devoted to the popular Aztec goddess Tonantzin. In an effort to Christianize the shrine, the Spanish destroyed the idol of the goddess they found there and replaced it with an image of the **Virgin Mary** they had brought with them from Spain (Gonzalez-Crussi 1996).

The Aztecs did not passively accept the Roman Catholic **religion** their Spanish conquerors sought to impose upon them, however, nor did they outright reject it. Instead, they transformed **Catholicism** even as they converted to it. The Aztecs accomplished this transformation by appropriating Catholicism's most popular saint, the Virgin Mary, and giving Her a new name, a new history, and new religious meanings that reflected their own unique cultural needs and historical experience. The product of this appropriation is an Aztec **reinvention** of the Virgin Mary that draws upon, and yet departs from, the religious traditions of both the Aztecs and the Europeans. This chapter examines how sixteenth-century Aztecs reinvented Catholicism's Blessed Virgin, as **Our Lady of Guadalupe**,[1] in ways that incorporated and affirmed important features of their own cultural and religious traditions. It also explores how this process has provided contemporary Meso-Americans with a powerful marker of **cultural identity**. A communication-based body of theory called semiotics guides this chapter's treatment of these issues.

Semiotics

Semiotics traces its origin to the work of American philosopher Charles Sanders Peirce and Swiss linguist Ferdinand de Saussure. Working independently of one another during the late nineteenth and early twentieth centuries, these two thinkers laid the foundations for a field of communication inquiry that focuses upon how meaning is produced, shared, and sometimes contested.

Signs

According to semiotic theory, the smallest unit of meaning is the **sign**, defined as anything that can be used to represent something else (Eco 1976). Some signs, called **icons**, signify (are meaningful) because of a resemblance they have to what they represent. A portrait is an icon that represents the person whose image is pictured. Other signs, called indices (plural for **index**), signify because they have some kind of natural connection with what they represent. Smoke is an index that suggests the presence of fire. **Symbols**, yet another kind of sign, acquire meaning through shared cultural convention. A red light at an intersection is a symbol that means *stop* only because our culture says it does. We could just as easily have assigned the same meaning to green, yellow, or any other color. Other examples of symbols include company trademarks, brand logos, **religious images**, the alphabet we use in writing, and the words we use in speaking.

Unlike icons and indices, which have relatively fixed meanings in relationship to the things they represent, the culturally determined meanings assigned to symbols are arbitrary and subject to change. Often, change occurs as a natural response to the evolving needs of a culture. For example, the emerging importance of computers has resulted in additional meanings being assigned to such English words as *click, drag, icon,* and *mouse*. At other times, signs acquire additional meanings through a process called **appropriation**.

Appropriation

As defined by Leeds-Hurwitz (1993), "Appropriation refers to the taking of a sign in use by one culture for use in another culture, giving it new meaning in the process" (p. 168). Examples of appropriation are plentiful. The use of brightly colored eggs to celebrate Easter is a practice appropriated by ancient Christians from a Roman-era Mediterranean fertility cult. The bunnies associated with Easter were appropriated by Christians from a Germanic fertility cult. When Christianity supplanted these fertility cults, Christians did not eliminate the eggs and bunnies that had played a popular role in their spring celebrations. Instead, they appropriated these signs, incorporating them into their own spring celebration of Easter and assigning them new meanings.

Two kinds of appropriation are relevant to this chapter. Oppositional, or resistive, appropriation provides marginalized groups a way of offering **resistance** to, and commentary upon, the broader sociocultural processes that affect their lives. A classic example of such appropriation is the recoding by 1970s British punks of the innocuous safety pin as a fashion accessory and form of body adornment (Hebdige 1979). **Co-optation**, on the other hand, is a form of appropriation used by a **dominant** or **mainstream culture** as a means of containing and taming expressions of resistance and opposition. A good example is the mainstreaming of fashion and music that originated as forms of protest by members of such marginalized groups as gays and African Americans. Through appropriation, signs often come to mean many different things. The capacity of signs to carry multiple, and even conflicting, meanings is referred to in semiotic terms as **polysemy** (Barthes 1983; Gottdiener 1995). Polysemy is made possible by introducing additional codes to govern an existing sign.

Codes

According to semiotic theory, much of a sign's meaning is derived from its relationship to other signs. Such relationships are governed by **codes.** As defined by Fiske (1987), "A code is a rule-governed system of signs, whose rules and conventions are shared amongst members of a culture, and which is used to generate and circulate meanings in and for that culture" (p. 4). Each code has its own set of signs and a body of rules that define the meaning of those signs and govern their use. The language we use is a good example of a semiotic code. Its vocabulary constitutes the code's content, its grammar the code's set of rules.

Cultures are composed of numerous codes that govern the use of, give meaning to, and guide **readings (interpretations)** of such things as the food we eat and the way we dress. According to our culture's culinary code, for example, food has symbolic as well as nutritional value. This code assigns meaning to food and to the circumstances in which it is consumed,

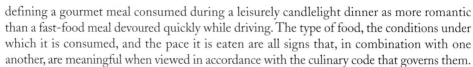

defining a gourmet meal consumed during a leisurely candlelight dinner as more romantic than a fast-food meal devoured quickly while driving. The type of food, the conditions under which it is consumed, and the pace it is eaten are all signs that, in combination with one another, are meaningful when viewed in accordance with the culinary code that governs them.

In what follows, we see how **narrative** can serve as a powerful tool of appropriation capable of redefining a sacred place and reinventing the spiritual entity associated with it. We look at how a religious image associated with a spiritual entity—a Meso-American **reinvention** of the Catholic Church's universal Virgin, the Blessed Virgin Mary—functions as a complex sign that is simultaneously index, icon, and a complex collection of symbols. We examine how this image is coded differently by two competing religious traditions through the processes of resistive appropriation and co-optation. We point out how, over time, the codes governing these traditions have blended together to form a new code. And we explore how this image has come to function as an iconic sign that not only speaks to, but speaks for and of, the peoples of Meso-America. In order to explore the iconic dimension of the image, and the sense of identification it fosters, Mexican pilgrims to the Basilica of Our Lady of Guadalupe were interviewed under the direction of this author immediately prior to, during, and after Her annual feast day (December 12).[2]

Narrative as a Tool of Appropriation: The Story of Juan Diego

The appropriation of the Virgin Mary by the Aztecs, and their reinvention of Her as Our Lady of Guadalupe, has its origin in 1531 when a poor Aztec farmer named Juan Diego claimed to have had a series of visions in which he encountered a woman who called Herself the Mother of God. According to the *Nican Mopohua* (Barber 1996),[3] the earliest account of Juan Diego's visionary encounters, the woman spoke to him in his native tongue, Nahuatl, and instructed him to tell the local bishop that She wanted a church built in Her honor upon the site where She had appeared to him. The site, a small hill called Tepeyac, is located on the outskirts of Mexico City. This hill was of special spiritual significance to the Aztecs because it was the site of the shrine of Tonantzin, which had been seized by the Spanish. Dutifully, Juan Diego went to the local bishop, told him about the vision, and informed him that a woman referring to Herself as the Mother of God wished to have a church built in Her honor upon Tepeyac. Skeptical, the bishop dismissed both Juan Diego and his story. The woman, however, continued to appear to Juan Diego, who in turn continued to prod the bishop about building the church.

In response to Juan Diego's persistence, the bishop asked him to produce some tangible proof that he was indeed meeting with the Blessed Virgin Mary. The bishop assumed Juan Diego had been speaking of the Virgin Mary, since Juan Diego was a recent convert to Catholicism and Catholics use the title "Mother of God" exclusively in reference to Her. The Aztecs, however, also used this same title in reference to their goddess Tonantzin. When informed of the bishop's request, the woman directed Juan Diego to pick some nearby flowers. Since it was early December, Juan Diego saw the flowers as the kind of proof the bishop required because they were miraculously blooming out of season. He gathered some of the flowers, wrapped them carefully in his cloak, and took them to the bishop. When he was once again in the presence of the bishop, Juan Diego opened his cloak and let the miraculous flowers cascade toward the ground. To his delight and the surprise of all present, mysteriously imprinted upon the cloak was an image of the woman he had encountered in his visions (see fig. 7.1).

FIGURE 7.1   Our Lady of Guadalupe

This story supplied a narrative rationale that made possible an Aztec response to, and their reinvention of, the Virgin the Spaniards had brought with them. The story redefined Tepeyac's sacredness by once again associating the site with an indigenous version of the Mother of God rather than the imported Virgin brought by the Spanish. In asserting that he had spoken with the Mother of God, Juan Diego claimed for himself—and by extension, for the Aztecs in general—spiritual equality with, if not superiority to, the Spanish. He did so, however, in a way that simultaneously affirmed and challenged the authority of the Catholic Church. By petitioning the bishop, he publicly deferred to the authority of the bishop and the Church. And yet, in claiming to have had visionary encounters with the Mother of God, Juan Diego also suggested he had direct access to Her through a channel of spiritual communication not under the control of the bishop or the Church. Although the Church rarely extends official recognition to such visions, it could not outright reject the possibility that Juan Diego had spoken with the Mother of God since the Church itself teaches that such visionary encounters occasionally occur. In approaching the bishop, Juan Diego claimed to speak not for himself, nor for the Aztecs, but rather on behalf of the Mother of God. If true, any request made by the Mother of God had to be taken seriously by Church officials, as was the person She found worthy to serve as Her messenger.

The story of Juan Diego's visions thus provided the Aztecs with the spiritual authority to shape their religious experience in ways that appealed to them and not their European oppressors. The story also offered a miraculous explanation that legitimized the image of this indigenous Virgin—whose language, physical features, and mode of dress were those of the Aztecs and not their conquerors—and inscribed the image with special spiritual significance. This new Virgin offered the Aztecs, and continues to offer their modern Meso-American heirs, a powerful female spiritual entity with whom they could identify. In part, this identification is due to Our Lady of Guadalupe's indexical ties to central Mexico; in part, to the presence of Aztec symbolism in Her image; and in part, to Her iconic resemblance to the indigenous peoples of Mexico.

(Re)Appropriation of Place

The seizure of shrines associated with Aztec deities was a regular feature of the conquistadors' campaign to convert the Aztecs (Gonzalez-Crussi 1996). This practice was in keeping with a long-standing policy of the Roman Catholic Church regarding the use of co-option as a tool in dealing with recent and potential converts. This policy was explicitly expressed in a letter written in 601 by Pope Gregory the Great, in which the pope offered advice to missionaries who were attempting to convert the English. The pope counseled that, whenever possible, the missionaries should appropriate places sacred to local peoples and incorporate indigenous religious customs into the institutional practices of the Church (Bede 1990).[4] In keeping with Pope Gregory's advice, those missionaries who expanded the sphere of Church influence beyond the boundaries of the old Roman empire replaced local deities with Catholic saints, gave Christian meanings to the rituals and symbols of indigenous religions, and erected churches on the sites of pre-Christian shrines. Evidence of such appropriation can still be seen today. Irish Catholics pray to the patron saints who have replaced older Celtic gods and goddesses; the evergreen trees formerly used by Nordic peoples to observe the winter solstice are now used by American and German Catholics to celebrate the birth of Jesus; and the Cathedral of Mexico City stands on a site once dominated by an Aztec temple.

As noted above, one of the shrines the Spanish seized in central Mexico is that of the Aztec mother goddess, Tonantzin, located at Tepeyac. In claiming to have encountered the Mother of God atop Tepeyac, the narrative of Juan Diego's visions redefined the hill's spiritual importance. Tepeyac's sacredness was no longer defined solely in terms of long-standing Aztec tradition, nor was it deemed sacred because of its forced connection with the European Madonna. Instead, the hill was defined as sacred because of a new episode in the spiritual history of the Aztecs: it was the place where the Mother of God had spoken directly to an Aztec. This provided the Aztecs with justification for exiling the European Virgin the Spanish had placed there and replacing Her with an indigenous Virgin who had more in common with them than with their oppressors.

Tepeyac was thus once again defined as the center of a sacred geography with physical and spiritual ties to central Mexico. Since the sixteenth century, a series of shrines have been erected on and near the hill in honor of this local version of the Virgin. The site's main shrine is the modern basilica (a special church). Currently, this shrine attracts over twenty million religious pilgrims annually. This shrine is deemed sacred because it is located near the place where the Virgin is reported to have spoken with Juan Diego. It is defined thus because of its indexical connection with Her. In addition, the site is also regarded as sacred because it is the place where the image that Our Lady of Guadalupe is said to have left behind is now displayed.

Appropriating the Virgin: The Image of Our Lady of Guadalupe as Codex

To this day, there is some dispute as to whether the image of Our Lady of Guadalupe on display in Mexico City is the product of natural or supernatural processes. There is no dispute, however, regarding its influence. News of the miraculous image spread quickly throughout central Mexico. In less than a decade after Juan Diego first showed the image to the bishop, ten million Aztecs and related peoples converted to Catholicism; in the previous decade, there were fewer than a million converts (Father Maximilian 1997). This rapid and widespread embrace of Catholicism, the fastest and largest unforced conversion in the history of Christianity, was not an embrace of the Catholic faith per se, but rather a conversion to a particular version of the faith, one associated in the popular mind with the woman depicted in the image.

The image depicts a brown-skinned woman with her hands joined, head tilted, and eyes partly closed and slightly averted. Supported by a winged child, She stands upon a crescent-shaped sliver of moon. She is clothed in a cloak studded with stars and framed by the golden rays of a hidden sun. Unlike the image of the Blessed Virgin Mary that the Spanish had brought with them from Europe, the woman depicted in the image of Our Lady of Guadalupe possesses Meso-American rather than European facial features. The image is much more, however, than a mere depiction of the woman Juan Diego claimed to have seen in his visions. It is also a complex collection of floral symbols, astronomical imagery, and other signs that are distinctively Aztec (Ascheman 1997; Barber 1997a, 1997b; Castillo 1996; Gonzalez-Crussi 1996; Guerrero 1996).

Floral Symbolism

The floral designs that adorn Our Lady of Guadalupe's tunic serve more than a decorative purpose. The pre-Christian Aztec religious code regarded flowers as symbolic vehicles capable of conveying profound spiritual truths (Barber 1997a, 1997b; Guerrero 1996). In accordance with the conventions of Aztec glyphs (standardized pictographic designs used by the Aztecs to convey symbolic meanings), the flowers are rendered with a flatness that allows viewers to see them in full. One of the flowers that adorns the Virgin's cloak is the quincunx, which is positioned over the Virgin's womb. According to the Aztec floral code, as explained by Barber (1997b), this flower represented:

> the four compass directions of the world, with heaven and the underworld vertically encountering earth in the center, in the "navel" of the world, or, to use the metaphor, in the navel of the moon, as they call the Valley of Mexico. (p. 72)

The placement of this flower over the woman's womb thus signified to the Aztecs that She is bearing an important child with strong ties to the cultural and geographic center of their world. That the woman depicted in the image is pregnant is also indicated by another Aztec symbol of pregnancy, the black sash She is wearing around Her waist (Castillo 1996; Gonzalez-Crussi 1996). (The depiction of a pregnant Mother of God differs from the European tradition, which typically represents their version of the Virgin postpartum.)

Other flowers that adorn the Virgin's cloak are also part of the Aztec's symbolic repertoire. For example, the nine large, triangular, heart-shaped flowers—the Mexican magnolia—were traditionally used to represent the nine levels of the Aztec underworld. In Nahuatl, the language of the Aztecs, the name for these flowers is *yolloxochitl*. As explained by Barber (1997a), "Yolloxochitl was an Aztec metaphor for the palpitating heart torn from the body of sacrificial victims" (p.76). Human sacrifice played a prominent role in the pre-Christian Aztec religion (Harris 1978). Barber notes that this same glyph was also used to represent "*tepetl*, hill, and precisely, Tepeyac Hill" (p. 76), the site where Our Lady of Guadalupe is said to have appeared to Juan Diego and the location of the shrine of Tonantzin that had been appropriated by the Spanish missionaries. Such floral symbolism reaffirmed the Virgin's connection to the people of central Mexico and Her ties to the religious traditions of the Aztecs.

Astronomical Symbolism

In addition to floral symbolism, the image of Our Lady of Guadalupe also includes solar, lunar, and stellar symbols derived from the Aztec's astronomical code. For example, the cloak the Virgin wears is bedecked by stars that are symbolic as well as decorative. According to Barber (1997b), "the stars on Mary's mantle are indeed the ones present over Mexico City just before sunrise on December 21, 1531, the morning of the winter solstice, which occurred that morning at 10:40, probably just when Juan Diego was opening the tilma [i.e., cloak] before Bishop Zumárraga" (p. 69). The winter solstice, which plays an important role in many religions, was of great religious importance to the astronomically obsessed Aztecs. That Our Lady of Guadalupe is said to have appeared on that special day reinforced for the Aztecs Her spiritual significance. Another key element of the image's astronomical symbolism is the crescent moon upon which the Virgin stands. According to the astronomical code of the Aztecs, this symbol represents the Valley of Mexico, their geographical, cultural, and spiritual center. Read in this way, the placement of Our Lady of Guadalupe upon this crescent moon suggests that She is rooted in, and has arisen from, the Aztec's culture, geography, and spiritual traditions. The symbolism is yet another indication of the Virgin's connection to the Aztecs and their culture.

(Re)Appropriating the Virgin: The Image of Our Lady of Guadalupe as Religious Icon

Understandably, the Church was not passive regarding this new Meso-American Virgin and the large following She attracted. Initially, Juan Diego's claims, as well as the beliefs and practices that developed in response to them, were met with much resistance on the part of the institutional Church (Ascheman 1997). According to Brother Francis Mary (1997), the Spanish missionaries working in central Mexico "were very cautious about supporting any devotion . . . which might be misinterpreted as a carry-over from worship of one of their pagan deities" (p. 173). This caution was echoed by the Vatican. Juan Diego reported his visions in 1531. It was not until 1666, 135 years later, that Church officials in Rome began their investigation. Another eighty-eight years passed before the Vatican, in 1754, deemed Juan Diego's visions worthy of faith.

This delayed acceptance served as a means of Church resistance. In the face of Our Lady of Guadalupe's continued popularity, the Church was compelled to respond. It finally extended its official recognition to Juan Diego's vision. This approval defined the woman of Juan Diego's visions as a local manifestation of the Blessed Virgin Mary, the Church's universal mother. This definition provided a mechanism for co-opting the indigenous Virgin and the religious beliefs and practices that had developed around Her. In this way, the Church could attempt to impose upon Her its own code, one rooted in the Church's long and—at that time—primarily European history.

Initially, the Spanish missionaries and Church officials based in Europe were largely unaware of the meanings the Aztecs ascribed to the floral and astronomical symbols that adorn the image of Our Lady of Guadalupe (Guerrero 1996). As Catholic scholars became aware of these signs and their meaning, some came to regard them as a new way of conveying traditional Christian concepts (Barber 1997a, 1997b; Guerrero 1996). This has led to these signs being read in accordance with Catholic codes. For example, Catholic scholars argue that the flowers the image includes that are associated with the Aztec god *Quetzalcoatl*—who according to the Aztec myths died and then arose from the dead—can be interpreted as signifying Jesus Christ, who the Church likewise teaches was resurrected from the dead.

In contrast to the Aztecs, who regarded the image of Our Lady of Guadalupe as a codex (the Scriptures), the Catholic Church codes the image as a religious icon. In the Christian tradition, a religious icon is a stylized work of art that conveys spiritual truths through the use of traditional symbols. (Note: this definition of the term *icon* differs from the semiotic definition.) Defined in this way, the image yields a very different reading than that of the Aztecs. In part, this is because some of the same elements of the image are seen differently, and in part, because this coding emphasizes different elements.

One emphasis of the Christian coding is color. Traditionally, blue is the color Catholics associate with the Virgin Mary (Hawkins 1997). In all likelihood, however, the historical Mary, a working-class woman who was a member of a subjugated people living in an obscure province on the fringes of the Roman Empire, did not wear blue clothing. In Her time, such clothing was reserved for people whose status permitted them to wear it and whose wealth enabled them to buy it. The association of the Virgin Mary with the color blue is the product of a fourth century co-optation. At that time Athanasius, bishop of Alexandria, Egypt, suggested that blue be used in depictions of the Virgin Mary as a way of co-opting the color's use from the then popular cult of the goddess Isis. The color of Our Lady of Guadalupe's robe, however, is turquoise, the color worn by Aztec nobility. And yet, a Roman Catholic analysis of the image of Our Lady of Guadalupe offered by Hawkins (1997) makes much of the Guadalupan Virgin's blue tunic. This illustrates the powerful influence codes have upon us. They shape not only what, but how we see. In this case, the Catholic code literally colored Hawkins's vision.

Another example of how the European-based Catholic tradition codes the elements of the image differently than the Aztecs did is the symbolic meaning it ascribes to the placement of Our Lady of Guadalupe upon the image's crescent moon. According to conventions of the Catholic code, this kind of image, a figure representing the Virgin Mary standing atop a moon, is commonly interpreted as a symbol of Her triumph over some local mother goddess. In many religious traditions, mother goddesses are frequently associated with the moon because of the indexical connection between the lunar cycle and the female menstrual cycle. A Catholic reading of the Guadalupan image sees Her position in relation to the crescent moon as symbolizing the Virgin Mary's dominion and victory over the Aztec moon goddess Tonantzin, whom She ostensibly replaced. This reading, of course, differs sharply from the Aztec one discussed above, in which the same lunar imagery is coded as an affirmation rather than negation of indigenous traditions.

Blending the Codes

Codes are living things that evolve over time and change in response to contact with codes from other cultures. In this way, for example, the English language as it is spoken today differs from the English of Shakespeare's time. The religious codes that are the focus of this chapter have also changed. Over the past four hundred years, the Aztec and Catholic codes have blended to form a new code that now governs the beliefs and practices associated with Our Lady of Guadalupe. Such blending, which draws upon and mixes the signs and rules of two or more codes, is referred to as **syncretism**.

Although the Spanish had tried to eradicate Aztec religious practices, many of these have continued under the guise of quasi-Catholic devotional practices devoted to Our Lady of Guadalupe. One such practice is that of religious dance. To those viewing the Virgin's image from the perspective of the Catholic code, She appears to be in an attitude of static prayer, with Her hands joined, Her eyes averted, and Her head slightly bowed. However, these same postures, as Barber suggests (1997a), could also be read as representing gestures associated with Aztec religious dances rather than those of traditional European habits of prayer. Dancing remains a part of the religious practices that have developed around devotion to Our Lady of Guadalupe. These dances incorporate Aztec and Catholic imagery and music (see fig. 7.2).

**FIGURE
7.2** A dance combining Aztec and Catholic elements.

The inclusion of ritual dance in devotional practices directed toward the Virgin is yet another way the Aztecs, and their contemporary Meso-American heirs, have been able to incorporate practices from the region's pre-Christian religious traditions within the context of Catholicism. This is a good illustration of syncretism. Because it is done in connection with a version of the Virgin that has the Church's stamp of approval, the dancing associated with Our Lady of Guadalupe is now coded as a Catholic devotional practice, even though dancing as a formal religious ritual is not part of Catholicism's prayer repertoire. Indeed, the use of dancing as a religious ritual is actually banned in many parts of the Catholic world.

Our Lady of Guadalupe as Cultural Icon: Identifying with the Virgin

Another important custom associated with Our Lady of Guadalupe is the practice of making pilgrimages to the basilica in Mexico City in which the original image of the Virgin is displayed. This site is where a team of researchers working under the author's direction conducted interviews with contemporary devotees of the Virgin. Interestingly, few pilgrims expressed interest in or awareness of the Aztec and Catholic readings of the Virgin's image we have discussed. This should not be surprising, however, as the average American, for example, would be hard-pressed to give a detailed description of the history and meanings of many of the Christmas decorations that adorn shopping malls and other places during the December holidays. People tend to focus on those aspects of a code that emphasize what is most important to them.

Most of the Mexican pilgrims our research team interviewed emphasized that, for them, the most important feature of the image of Our Lady of Guadalupe is the Virgin's dark skin and the iconic resemblance that skin has to their own. The following comments are typical:

- She's very beautiful. She's dark-skinned just like us, like a little Indian, like us.
- She is dark-skinned, *morena,* She has long black hair. And Her eyes are brown.
- She's a vision who is sort of dark-skinned.
- She's dark-skinned and She's just beautiful to us.

The importance of the Virgin's dark skin was explained by one pilgrim in his mid-twenties, who had this to say when asked what Our Lady of Guadalupe looked like:

Well, just the way we see Her: dark-skinned, beautiful, just the way we see Her. There's no other way to see Her. Like the priest says, She represents us. She has to be dark-skinned; She cannot be White, because She represents us.

This iconic connection engenders a close, intimate relationship with Our Lady of Guadalupe on the part of those Meso-Americans who are devoted to Her. Indeed, one pilgrim—a man in his early thirties—described his relationship with the Virgin in this way:

I treat Her as *tu* instead of *usted* because, I don't know, it's the way I feel I should talk to Her, in a friendly way, because that's what She is to us, not only a Mother but also a friend.

In Spanish, *tu* is the familiar form of the pronoun you, *usted* the formal. *Tu* connotes a close relationship. *Usted* is more formal than *tu;* it is a respectful way of addressing elderly people, those with status, and the like. The warm, familiar way this pilgrim speaks of and to the Virgin reflects an intimate relationship that would be less likely with a Virgin whose image looked less like him and more like the European Spanish who had imposed themselves upon his land several centuries earlier.

"Our" Lady of Guadalupe

Because of Her indexical ties with Meso-America and Her iconic resemblance to its people, Our Lady of Guadalupe has played an important role in the development of a distinctively Mexican cultural and national identity (Corona 1996; Gebara and Bingemer 1989; Zimdars-Swartz 1991). Today, images of the Virgin are present throughout Mexico and in places where Mexicans have emigrated (DePalma 1996). As one observer puts it:

She is everywhere. On T-shirts, tattooed on biceps and chests, etched into the back windows or lacquer enameled on the back trunks of low riders, on murals, on tiles and medals. Even on cowboy boots. (Corona 1996, p. 18)

These images do more than simply provide a focus for devotional attention, however; they also offer a marker of Meso-American cultural identity removed from distinctively Roman Catholic concerns. Indeed, as Vara notes (2000), there are Protestant churches in Houston, Texas, with predominantly Hispanic congregations that contain images of the Virgin, even though Protestant theology does not support this Catholic practice. The use of the Virgin as a cultural marker divorced from Her connection to Catholicism is made possible by Her indexical connection to Mexico, Her long history with that country, and Her iconic resemblance to its peoples.

Our Lady of Guadalupe has become a major entity throughout the Catholic world. Today, shrines have been erected, and devotion directed, to Her in places as geographically and culturally removed from one another as France, Ethiopia, Japan, Kenya, Korea, Poland, Spain, Sweden, and, of course, the United States (Corona 1996). Devotees that dwell in such places do not physically resemble the Virgin; nor do they have any historical or cultural tie to Her. Instead, they see Her as a manifestation of the universal Mother of God, the Blessed Virgin Mary. In calling Her "Our" Lady of Guadalupe, devotees claim Her as theirs. As the popularity of Our Lady of Guadalupe spreads, it is likely that Her new devotees will draw upon different culturally based codes than the ones discussed in this chapter as they attempt to interpret Her image in light of what She might mean for them. In the process, no doubt, She will be reinvented in accordance with new codes and the cultural needs that those codes serve, codes that depart from, challenge, and incorporate those of the Aztecs, the Church, and the Cult of the Virgin.

Intercultural Implications

In today's world, cultures are coming into more frequent contact, and sometimes conflict, with one another. These intercultural encounters occur through emigration and immigration, as a by-product of the booming tourist trade, as a result of the international climate in which business is now conducted, and through the shrinking of the world due to the modern media. Some intercultural encounters between competing cultures give rise to contested meanings. Others result in blendings that draw and mix elements from two or more cultures. This chapter provides students with a communication-based theory with which to identify, make sense of, and respond to the processes of appropriation (e.g., resistance), co-optation, polysemy (multiple meanings), and syncretism (blending of two codes) that play an increasingly important role in shaping their personal and professional lives.

Notes

1. This is in keeping with the Roman Catholic practice of referring to local versions of the Virgin Mary with titles that begin with "Our Lady of," as is this chapter's capitalization of the pronouns *She* and *Her*. In this chapter, the terms *Virgin* and *Mother of God* are used interchangeably to refer to the Virgin Mary and Our Lady of Guadalupe.

2. Interviews were conducted with pilgrims in the vicinity of the Basilica of Our Lady of Guadalupe immediately prior to, during, and after the Virgin's annual feast day (December 12). Six days were spent at the research site. The primary interviewer was Rafael Obregon. The other interviewers were Carmen Rosiles Arrendondo, Jannet Velencia Flores, Veronica Mondragon, Marissa Hernandez Perez, and Yolanda Uresti. The interviews were conducted in Spanish. Rafael Obregon translated them into English. The research team conducted 41 interviews with 75 pilgrims: 45 men and 30 women. Twelve interviews were conducted with groups of pilgrims, 5 with couples, and 24 with individuals.

3. Authorship of the *Nican Mopohua* is traditionally ascribed to Antonio Valeriano, a well-educated Aztec nobleman. It was written in Nahuatl (the language of the Aztec people) sometime between 1548 and 1560, seventeen to twenty-nine years after Juan Diego's visions are alleged to have occurred (Wahlig 1997).

4. The letter, which is included in Bede's (1990) classic *Ecclesiastical History of the English People*, was written in 601. Bede's history was written in 731.

References

Ascheman, T. J. 1997. Guadalupe: Good news for all people. In *A handbook on Guadalupe* (pp. 116–20). New Bedford, Mass.: Franciscan Friars of the Immaculate.

Barber, J. (Trans.) 1996. *Nican mopohua.* In Our Lady of Guadalupe, symposium conducted at Pontifical College Josephenum, Columbus, Ohio, December.

———. 1997a. The codex that breathes life. In *A handbook on Guadalupe* (pp. 75–80). New Bedford, Mass.: Franciscan Friars of the Immaculate.

———. 1997b. The sacred image is a divine codex. In *A handbook on Guadalupe* (pp. 68–73). New Bedford, Mass.: Franciscan Friars of the Immaculate.

Barthes, R. 1983. *The fashion system.* New York: Hill and Wang.

Bede. 1990. *Ecclesiastical history of the English people.* New York: Penguin. (Original work written 731.)

Castillo, A. 1996. Introduction. In A. Castillo (Ed.), *Goddess of the Americas/La Diosa de las Américas: Writings on the Virgin of Guadalupe* (pp. xv–xxiii). New York: Riverhead Books.

Corona, I. 1996. Guadalupismo: Popular religiosity and cultural identity. In Our Lady of Guadalupe, symposium conducted at Pontifical College Josephenum, Columbus, Ohio, December.

DePalma, A. 1996. Let heavens fall, Mexicans will revere Virgin. *New York Times*, June 21, p. 4.

Eco, U. 1976. *A theory of semiotics.* Bloomington: Indiana University Press.

Fiske, J. 1987. *Television culture.* New York: Methuen.

(Brother) Francis Mary. 1997. What the Church . . . [*sic*] has to say about Guadalupe. In *A handbook on Guadalupe* (pp. 172–78). New Bedford, Mass.: Franciscan Friars of the Immaculate.

Gebara, I., and M. Bingemer. 1989. *Mary: Mother of God, mother of the poor.* Maryknoll, N.Y.: Orbis Books.

Gonzalez-Crussi, F. 1996. The anatomy of a Virgin. In *A handbook on Guadalupe* (pp. 1–14). New Bedford, Mass.: Franciscan Friars of the Immaculate.

Gottdiener, M. 1995. *Postmodern semiotics: Material culture and the forms of postmodern life.* Cambridge, Mass.: Basil Blackwell Inc.

Guerrero, J. L. 1996. The "Nican Mopohua": A magnificent example of inculturation. In Our Lady of Guadalupe, symposium conducted at Pontifical College Josephenum, Columbus, Ohio, December.

Harris, M. 1978. *Cannibals and kings: The origins of cultures.* London: Collins.

Hawkins, C. 1997. The iconography of Guadalupe. In *A handbook on Guadalupe* (pp. 63–67). New Bedford, Mass.: Franciscan Friars of the Immaculate.

Hebdige, D. 1979. *Subculture: The meaning of style.* London: Methuen.

Leeds-Hurwitz, W. 1993. *Semiotics and communication: Signs, codes, and cultures.* Hillsdale, N.J.: Lawrence Erlbaum Associates.

(Father) Maximilian. 1997. Our Lady of Guadalupe—Model of prayer and holiness. In *A handbook on Guadalupe* (p. 80). New Bedford, Mass.: Franciscan Friars of the Immaculate.

Vara, R. 2000. The Lady of Guadalupe: From Mexican shrine to Houston autoshop, tributes to Mary abound. *Houston Chronicle,* December 9, pp. 1E, 3E.

Wahlig, C. 1997. First author of historic account on Guadalupe: Don Antonio Valeriano. In *A handbook on Guadalupe* (pp. 51–54). New Bedford, Mass.: Franciscan Friars of the Immaculate.

Zimdars-Swartz, S. L. 1991. *Encountering Mary: From La Salette to Medjugorje.* Princeton, N.J.: Princeton University Press.

KEY TERMS

appropriation	polysemy
Aztec	reading
Catholicism	reinvention
code	religion
co-optation	religious image
cultural identity	resistance
icon	semiotics
index	sign
interpretation	symbol
mainstream culture	syncretism
narrative	Virgin Mary
Our Lady of Guadalupe	

REVIEW AND DISCUSSION QUESTIONS

1. What elements of Juan Diego's narrative do you think made it an effective means of promoting an indigenous Virgin? How did these promote distinctively Aztec interests? Can you think of another way that Juan Diego or his Aztec contemporaries could have successfully introduced a reinvented version of the Virgin Mary that would have met with Church approval?

2. Why do you think the Church delayed extending its formal recognition to Juan Diego's visions? Could this have been a successful strategy if circumstances had been different? Why did the Church eventually affirm the visions?

3. What does it mean to say that the image of Our Lady of Guadalupe can be "read" in different ways? Why is this the case? How can Santa Claus, for example—or any other such figure you can think of—be read differently by different people?

4. Hawaiian pizzas, kosher burritos, and Tex-Mex food are examples of culinary syncretism (the blending of two or more codes related to food). Can you think of other examples? What cultures' foods are mixed? Why do you think this has occurred?

5. Contemporary hip-hop artists have fashioned a new form of music by appropriating and then mixing samples from such disparate musical traditions as rhythm and blues, rock-n-roll, country, and classical. How has mainstream society attempted to co-opt these artists and their music?

6. What cultures—ethnic, linguistic, religious, etc.—do you claim as your own? What markers proclaim your cultural identity? What items serve as cultural markers for your friends and neighbors?

Memory, Cinema, and the Reconstitution of Cultural Identities in the Asian Indian Diaspora

ANJALI RAM

LEARNING OBJECTIVES

After reading this chapter, students will be able to:

- learn the role of collective and personal memory in constructing cultural identity;
- understand the role of media in filtering, translating, and reconstituting memory; and
- comprehend the notion of the diaspora and how it forces us to rethink traditional notions of acculturation.

[Hindi cinema allows] our children to be educated in their own culture, to know about our own childhood, how we grow up—children get to understand about our own culture and that in reality we are foreigners here.

Contemporary or what has been termed "new" immigrants can no longer be characterized as uprooted, alienated individuals who move from a state of cultural differentiation to cultural assimilation. Rather, bridging two or more cultures involves new ways of understanding self and other. Recently, scholars across the humanities and the social sciences have begun to consider these new immigrants to be living in transnational, diasporic spaces (Glick Schiller, Basch, Blanc 1995; Tö,löyan 1996). The term **diaspora** originally described Jewish communities living outside Palestine. In its current usage, it encompasses communities of any ethnicity composed of exiles, refugees, and immigrants. In his comprehensive explanation of the term, Töyan (1996) describes diasporas as communities that actively maintain links with their culture of origin, including creating and maintaining their own religious institutions, language schools, community centers, newspapers, radio stations, and so on. Similarly, Glick Schiller et al. (1995) refer to new immigrants as being "transnational" as they "forge and sustain simultaneous multi-stranded social relations that link together their societies of origin and settlement" (p. 48).

Belonging to such transnational, diasporic groups inevitably results in what Smith (1994, p. 17) calls "cultural bifocality." Such cultural bifocality is further heightened today as we experience an emergence of new media and communication technologies. The emergence and extensiveness of electronic innovations raise important questions with regard to the construction and reconstruction of **cultural identity** in transnational, diasporic contexts. For example, today immigrants can quite easily consume media from their cultures of origin and construct digital communication bridges between cultures.

The **Asian Indian** community in America is one such immigrant community, which has attempted to mark out a space in what Soyini Madison (1994) calls "between and betwixt the American dream" (p. 2). The Indian diaspora in the United States is considered to be among the fastest-growing Asian communities in the United States and currently is close to two million people (U.S. Census 2000). Like many other contemporary diasporas, communication about identity continuously changes as Asian Indian immigrants attempt to cope simultaneously with the separations and upheavals of displacement *and* the prejudices and racialized stereotypes aimed at them in the United States (Ganguly 1992; Grewal and Johnston 1994; Hegde 1998; Radhakrishnan 1991). Given such new, unstable, and shifting realities, Asian immigrants like many others draw on collective and personal memories as they construct their identity. To be an immigrant means to shift between an unfamiliar yet very real present and the memories of the past. My present is foreign, claims celebrated writer Salman Rushdie (1992), "the past is home, albeit a lost home in a lost city in the mists of lost time" (p. 9).

One of the most important vehicles of memory, both collective and personal, are **mass media**. As Kaes (1990) argues, "the past cannot be recovered and 're-experienced,' since it is not 'out there' to be visited . . . the past has to be reconstructed and reconstituted" (p. 117). In our increasingly mediated world, photography, popular music, radio, print media, television, and **cinema** become crucial repositories for such reconstructions of the past. The study of memory has shifted from being analyzed exclusively as an individual, cognitive process to exploring its collective and social dimensions. Such a move indicates that acts of remembering can be related both to identity formation and to cultural reproductions (Zelizer 1995). By drawing upon the past, we give shape and form to our present understanding of self and other.

In this chapter, I explore how acts of collective and personal remembering preserve selective constructions of national and gendered identities while muting others in the Asian Indian diaspora. In order to uncover some of the ways in which collective and personal memories are deployed to construct and communicate identity, I analyze both a community gathering of Indian immigrants and the personal recollections of Indian diasporic women. In both cases, I specifically explore how **Indian cinema** is activated to mediate memory and thereby reconstitute questions related to home, community, nation, and gender.

This study derives from a larger project where I focused on local practices, cultural texts, and oral narratives to build a picture of how Indian women in the diaspora negotiate with nationalist and gendered representations inherent in popular Indian cinema.[1] I spent two years gathering ethnographic data including in-depth interviews and participant observation. To accomplish a dialogue with the women participants, I avoided a prepared questionnaire in favor of a topical protocol that included both questions and topics for discussion and attempted to develop a collaborative interaction as advocated by several feminist scholars (Brown 1989; Langellier and Hall 1989; Minister 1991; Nelson 1989). I interviewed fourteen women who were all part of the second wave of Indian immigration to the United States living in central Massachusetts; these women had immigrated as wives of Indian professionals, and their ages ranged from twenty-five to fifty-five.[2] I situate my analysis within the interpretative paradigm (Bohman, Hiley, and Shusterman 1991) and emphasize cultural particularities, contradictions, and concurrences in the social construction of meaning. As Fiske (1991, p. 451) explains, data in interpretative and critical traditions are not statistically and proportionately "representative." Instead, they must be considered as "instances of a system in practice" whereby analysis provides insights and clues into the larger social, cultural, and political structures within which they are instituted.

Diwali: The Gendered Nature of Commemoration

Every year immigrant Indians participate in events that help build and sustain their community. These celebratory instances range from major religious festivals such as *Diwali*[3] to secular and national holidays like Independence Day. The Indian immigrant community where I conducted my research is no exception. The local Indian association actively hosts several community gatherings throughout the year. Although I have attended several events during the course of my research, I concentrate here on one specific event to show how **collective memory** is actively nourished by Indian cinema and how it contributes to the communication of identity.

Throughout my extended observation and participation in community events, I noticed the predominant role played by women in organizing and performing "cultural" events. Additionally, many of the women I interviewed commented with pride on their daughters' participation in such shows. In this section, I demonstrate how the past is recollected through the bodies of the daughters of Indian immigrants, who perform song and dance sequences inspired by popular Indian cinema[4] at public community gatherings. To understand the gendered nature of such commemoration, I draw upon my observations in 1997 of **Diwali,** one of the most popular, annually recurring events marked by the Hindu religious calendar.

The *Diwali* celebrations included a "cultural show" to commemorate the event. In the program pamphlet, the president of the Indian association welcomed the community and announced:

> We are so proud to have come together as one ISW family and be able [sic] to continue with our traditions and heritage and share the richness of it with our other local community friends although we are so far away from our homeland.[5]

Before the show began, he similarly wished the audience of about seven hundred immigrant Indians a happy *Diwali* and declared that the impending performance had been designed to "promote and preserve our culture."

Scholars on social memory argue that all beginnings contain elements of recollection. In other words, the present is embedded in the past (Connerton 1989; Fentress and Wickham 1992; Hallbawachs 1992). Connerton (1989) argues that commemorative ceremonies function as effective mnemonic devices. By engaging in what he calls the "rhetoric of re-enactment," commemorations use calendrical, verbal, and gestural ways of expressing memory (p. 65). Such re-enactments literally embody the past through sacred rituals or the recitation of sacred verses so that we can achieve what Connerton calls "a re-presenting, as causing to reappear that which has disappeared" (p. 69). So, for instance, when nations sing their national anthem on the day designated as their national day, they are reinvoking specific historical events in order to reaffirm patriotic pride and a sense of national identity. The central argument that runs through Connerton's theory of memory is that, if there is anything like social memory, we are likely to find it in commemorative ceremonies.

By collectively participating in the annual ritual of *Diwali*, the Indian immigrant community is observing much more than a religious day. Indeed, *Diwali* serves as an occasion for establishing continuity between the past and the present and for publicly and collectively affirming the heritage of the community. According to Lowenthal (1994), the notion of heritage denotes our inescapable dependence on the past, as it "distills the past into icons of identity, bonding us with precursors and progenitors, with our own earlier selves, and with our promised successors" (p. 43). The invocation of heritage is clearly articulated in the president's welcome statements. Heritage is crucial to the construction of national identity as it is used rhetorically to distinguish one group of people from another, which is important because acts of delineating a heritage signify the uniqueness of a given community. This brief example reveals all the rhetorical power of "heritage" in securing group identity, which becomes imperative for dislocated groups. From the use of "we" to the explicit statement of pride in the richness of "our traditions and heritage," as well as the need to "preserve and promote" it, this short declaration captures the past, links it to the present, and looks forward to the future.

The cultural performance that ensued after the president's message almost exclusively and predictably relied on Hindi cinema to enact this "heritage" and to preserve linkages to the past. Social memories need vehicles in order to be collected and shared within a community. Zelizer (1995) argues that the materiality of collective memory externalizes it and places it outside the individual human mind. Memory thus becomes stored and embodied in various vessels, of which one of the most powerful is the media. Within the context of the *Diwali* celebrations, collective memory becomes doubly embodied. If Hindi cinema provides texts for activating social memory, then the singers and dancers, by re-enacting, representing, and recalling the "richness" of "our traditions," provide live bodies to capture and contain these memories. For the most part, these are the bodies of young girls and women. By serving as a repository for collective memory, the female body is transformed into a signifier for culture, tradition, heritage, and the nation.

The predominant role played by women in organizing the cultural events was evident in all the community events I attended. However, on the occasion of *Diwali*, the gendered nature of the commemoration was particularly apparent. In my efforts to understand the contexts in which Indian immigrant women consume Hindi film, I participated as a volunteer for the event. From decorating hallways and podiums and setting the tables for the community dinner to choreographing and organizing the various cultural performances, women participated with great enthusiasm and vigor. Men were enlisted primarily for the purposes of carrying furniture and selling sweets and tickets for the cultural show. The cultural performance itself was entirely choreographed by women, with young girls and women composing the majority of the performers. In the opening dance and song sequence, young boys ranging from the ages of five to seven also participated. Additionally, in two of the dance sequences there were two young male performers about the age of eighteen, and in the Hindi film song sequence the keyboard player was male. However, the rest of the performers, fifty-two in all, were all young girls and women ranging from the ages of ten to twenty.

The conspicuous centrality of young women as performers, encoding "heritage" through their twirling bodies and mimicking popular cinema dance sequences, clearly establishes the gendered nature of this commemoration. Not coincidentally, Hindi cinema lends itself easily to such conflations where **gender** becomes the discursive terrain for inscribing "Indian" tradition and culture. Deploying women to stage narratives of nations has been and continues to be a dominant theme in Indian cinema. From the legendary movie *Mother India* (1957) to contemporary box office successes such as *Dilwale Dhulhania Le Jayange* (1995) and *Pardes* (1997),[6] portrayals of Indian women are suffused with the rhetoric of **nationalism.** In a pamphlet designed to introduce the film *Mother India* to Western audiences, the cultural values that frame Indian womanhood are clearly stated. The Indian woman is described as "an altar in India," and the same pamphlet points out that "Indians measure the virtue of their race by the chastity of their women" and that the Indian mother is "the nucleus around which revolves the tradition and the culture of ages" (Thomas 1989, p. 21).

Hindi cinema frequently employs notions like *izzat* and *amanat* to describe the role of women. *Izzat* refers to one's reputation and social esteem, and in relation to women designates them as embodying the honor of the clan. Similarly, *amanat*, which means charge or trust, positions the woman as precious, precarious property requiring protection and guardianship, for she symbolizes the wealth or the heritage of the family and larger kinship networks.

Given such cultural framing, the *Diwali* cultural show, performed by the young daughters of the community, can be read as a site where discourses of Indian womanhood and nationalism intersect. Hindi cinema, with its heavily symbolic images of Indian women, provides ample material for such gendered performances of the nation. The culmination of the cultural show blatantly demonstrated the convergence of gender and the nation in a dance sequence inspired by a popular song from the film *Purab aur Paschim* (East and West, 1970). In the program brochure it was referred to as "A Grand Finale: A Surprise," and in the quarterly report that followed a few months later, it was hailed as carrying over the theme of the previously celebrated Indian Independence Day, by adding "a touch of patriotism" to the celebration of *Diwali*.[7]

The film *Purab aur Paschim* is an overtly nationalistic film and it portrays its patriotic theme by aggressively counterposing the "degeneration" of the West against the "purity and tradition" of Indian culture. Written, produced, and directed by Manoj Kumar, well-known for making patriotic films in the 1970s and the 1980s, *Purab aur Paschim* was a box office hit. The male protagonist, in Pygmalion fashion, transforms the heroine, a British-born Indian woman, from her Westernized self into the ideal Indian woman. This change is effected symbolically by the heroine abandoning her miniskirts and coming to understand the meaning of *sharam* or shame. She emerges transformed at the end of the movie, demurely clad in a red and gold silk *sari*, her head appropriately covered to signify her compliance to traditional Indian precepts of femininity. *Dhulan chali* (The Bride Walks), the song from the film that inspired the "Grand Finale" during the *Diwali* celebration, invokes such feminine iconography to laud the nation. The lyrics narrate the nation as a young bride, clad in the colors of the Indian flag. This is an English translation of selected verses of the song:

> The bride walks, wearing the tri-color/In her arms the *Ganga* and the *Jamuna* ripple and fill the watching world with blissful joy/ Her face is like the Taj Mahal / She is the walking embodiment of the Ajanta sculptures / She wears the *mehendi* of love and togetherness / . . . the bride walks/ . . . our bride of independence /Our neighbor's (Pakistan) intentions are dishonorable /O husband(s) save her / Our bride is very innocent . . .

These lyrics clearly demonstrate the gendered construction of nationhood. Moreover, the metaphors employed suggest that women are the bearers of tradition and heritage and the patriotic duty of the Indian male is to preserve and protect both the nation and by association its women. The Indian audience, familiar with the film and the song, applauded resoundingly as the group of young women, wearing a generic interpretation of Indian folk dress (not unlike the ones generally used in Hindi cinema), emblazoned with the saffron, white, and green of the Indian flag, danced to strains of *Dhulhan chali*.

Facilitated by images from Indian cinema, the *Diwali* celebration accomplished a commemoration that used a religious occasion to mark a secular one and explicitly included gender in this collective remembering of the nation. Such bodily performances of the nation indicate some of the cultural discourses available in the Indian immigrant community for the construction of gender identity. Consider as well an incident reported by Bhattacharjee (1992), where a prominent Indian women's organization, *Sakhi*, which focuses on domestic violence, was not allowed to participate in the annual *Diwali* celebrations of the New York Indian immigrant community. The play that *Sakhi* wished to stage was considered by the organizers of the commemoration as "too political and [having] no place in this exclusively cultural celebration" (p. 29). Bhattacharjee goes on to comment, "*Sakhi's* presence is a continual reminder of the presence of the historical self behind the mythical Indian women" (p. 31). Similarly, in the *Diwali* celebration that I witnessed, ideal, mythified notions of Indian womanhood are carefully preserved, thereby inhibiting any representation of the more complex, contradictory, and multifaceted experiences of actual Indian immigrant women. Further, such representations are kept alive mainly by the use of Hindi cinema, which serves the community's need to "preserve and promote" heritage. However, I do not wish to argue that such ideological frames are uncontested and that Indian immigrant women are passively bound by its discourse.[8] Rather, my aim here is to illustrate how the need to imagine and remember the nation involves gender, thereby creating cultural representations that display and objectify the Indian woman.

Sites of Recollection: Personal Memory and Indian Cinema

So far, I have focused on how Indian film is used in a public commemoration to inscribe social memory and consolidate cultural identities. In this section, I draw upon the voices of the Indian immigrant women I interviewed to articulate how cinema provides texts for recollection, whereby memories of the past can be reconstructed within more personal, everyday contexts. By bringing distant events into everyday consciousness, as Giddens (1991) argues, popular media allow for reflexive projects of the self. Such self-reflexivity consists of sustaining coherent, yet continuously revised, narratives about one's identity, facilitated by our media experiences. Contemporary memory studies likewise view remembering as a process, as ongoing acts through which people constantly transform their recollections in order to construct stable narratives of the self (Zelizer 1995).

The Indian immigrant women I interviewed consistently explained the pleasures of viewing Indian cinema in terms of recollecting the past. As one woman narrator explained, "you cannot really part with" Hindi movies, "because that is how you grow up." She went on to comment that Hindi cinema was "like your own." Another participant, Meera,[9] referred to her engagement with Hindi cinema by explaining how she herself is inserted into the narrative:

> Maybe, maybe you kind of look at a Hindi movie . . . more subjectively as though you are a part of it . . . you know like it could happen to you or you may you know if it is set in Madras or Bombay I mean you know it maybe brings up certain . . . you know.

Although Meera struggles to complete her statement, it is clear that for her the pleasures of viewing are bound up intimately with nostalgic identification. Some of the participants I interviewed referenced specific film texts and rendered autobiographical sketches that employed Hindi cinema to structure and organize their recollections. So, for instance, Jayshree used the movie *Nishant*, a powerful depiction of the oppressive, feudal system that still exists in villages in India, to frame her own story:

> Like *Nishant* was one of the movies, that is a good one, that way you don't like miss Indian life you see it like . . . say this family's history is going on . . . you feel like. . . . See I am from a very poor family, as I, like, sometimes I had a pair of shoes that I must have worn for the entire year, must have worn the same one, did not have a choice, so I think I am in India when I watch those things, so it gives kind of like it happens.

Similarly for Nita, the film *Hum Aapke Hai Kaun* captured how "things happened" in her family:

> *Hum Aapke Hai Kaun* was more—you see—more family, what's going on, especially *Hum Aap*, was more like our family, it was done by Rajasthani guys so the story was almost how we have the weddings in Rajasthani. . . .

For some participants, Hindi cinema was used to maintain a continuity with the past, serving as constant reminders of their origins. Lamenting the loss of what she termed the "social aspects" among Indian immigrants, Jayshree asserted that by getting together with friends, "we make like we are in India . . . like watching movies," and she emphatically added, "we don't forget the past . . . we don't!" Jayshree went on to say that despite being in the United States fifteen years, she misses India, and that Hindi cinema figures prominently in her efforts to counter feelings of loss and dislocation. In fact, she confided that she named her eldest daughter as a reminder of her favorite Hindi film heroine, Rekha.

The theme of continuity through recollection was underscored in Shailaja's discourse, where she vehemently claimed that Hindi cinema is extremely important to the Indian immigrant community. According to her, it allows:

> our children to be educated in their own culture, to know about our own childhood, how we grow up—children get to understand about our own culture and that in reality we are foreigners here.[10]

Film texts for Shailaja serve a very special purpose, for they permit her to reconstruct her origins, relay the past to the next generation, and mark the boundaries of cultural identity.

In all these accounts, Hindi cinema provides narrative slates that can be erased, rewritten, and interpreted through recollections of the past, in order to secure stable scripts of selfhood. Such self-reflexive projects are crucial for immigrants, for whom feelings of displacement and disjuncture are paramount. Reliving and reinventing the past through film establish a sense of continuity and certainty. Such rhetorical revivals produced in joint collaboration with Indian cinema allow these women narrators to deal with the inevitable breaks between the past and present that are caused by migrancy.

According to Ganguly (1992), the past is vital to the negotiation of identity for the Indian immigrant community:

> The authority of the past depends on people's present subjectivity and vice versa; the stories people tell about their past have more to do with the continuing shoring up of self-understanding than with historical "truth." (p. 28)

The women I talked with were not necessarily conveying "historical truths" about their pasts or about the India they left behind. After all, it is well known that popular Indian film rarely follows conventions of realism. The unrealistic portrayals in Hindi cinema have always been a cause for much denigration. In other words, the film texts themselves make no pretense of presenting "historical truths." Indian cinematic tradition has always rejected Aristotelian recommendations for mimesis in favor of grand, melodramatic, hyperbolic, metaphoric, mythologized, heroic tales that require suspensions of disbelief, which are freely given by Indian audiences. Chakravarty (1989) places the aesthetic traditions of Indian commercial cinema within the context of the classical Sanskrit view of art, which uses character types and patterned emotions. She quotes a well-known director, Bimal Roy, who argues that the goal of realism within the context of Indian aesthetics is not "scientific understanding," but a creation of a mood, or *rasa* (p. 35). Chakravarty's argument that popular Indian cinema relies more on Sanskrit views of aesthetics than Western notions of realism provides a useful context for interpreting how Indian immigrant women use film to remember their past.

The theory of ***rasa*** attempts to explain how spectators experience a performance and is very much a theory of reading as opposed to a theory of textuality. For a performance to be judged successful from the point of view of *rasa* theory, it must employ a range of feelings and emotions or *bhava* to evoke a certain dominant mood or *rasa* in the spectator. *Rasa* also means flavor, which has prompted theorists to compare the performance experience to a gastronomic one (Janji 1978; Richmond 1990). Extending the theory of *rasa* to Indian immigrant women's engagement with film helps us understand how the pleasures of Hindi cinema lie in its power to evoke certain sentiments and emotions, which in turn create a nostalgic mood by capturing the flavor of the past. Many of the women I talked with maintained that they do not necessarily think that Hindi films are "good," with the standard for "good" here being films that strictly adhere to realist aesthetics. Yet, their reasons for choosing a popular Hindi film over any other had more to do with the emotional response that it could evoke by allowing them to reminisce. For instance, one participant, Rita, emphatically declared:

> I like the drama, it feels so familiar, it kind of strikes a chord . . . it actually feels like being at home. There is something very raw in Hindi film and that kind of appeal (emotional), that very intense kind where they take it to the hilt to the full . . . I get my money's worth (laughs).

From the point of view of contemporary theories of memory, the issue is not how accurately a recollection adheres to some past reality, but why and how socially and historically situated actors construct memories "in a particular way at a particular time" (Thelan 1989, p. 1125, cited in Zelizer 1995, p. 217). From the discourse of the women I interviewed, it is clear that Hindi cinema functions as much more than entertainment. Rather, it facilitates and shapes recollections, it allows the past to be reconstructed within the present context, and it provides an emotionally charged, technicolor medium through which the past can be shared and communicated about with others, both in everyday contexts and in public commemorative events.

Sites for Forgetting

If remembering and reconstructing the past enable the consolidation and affirmation of cultural subjectivities, then the very same process involves elisions, selections, and denials, so that coherent, stable, continuous narratives of the present can be maintained. So far, I have attempted to establish the role of popular Indian cinema in activating and sustaining recollections and commemorations. However, these gestures of social and personal remembering, which are facilitated by Hindi film, retain certain constructions of the past while discarding others. Middleton and Edwards (1990) call this process "the rhetorical organization of remembering and forgetting," whereby the "right kind of story is told" (p. 9). Zelizer (1995) argues that collective memories "help us fabricate, rearrange, or omit details from the past we thought we knew" (p. 217).

Such selectiveness acquires an added salience for members of the Indian immigrant community, who actively use memory within both public and private contexts to construct narratives of the self. One of the most crucial ways in which Hindi cinema assists in acts of forgetting is in its portrayal of Indian identity as Hindu identity. A striking example of such collapsing occurs when the *Diwali* event, which is a Hindu religious festival, is turned into a display of nationalism. Here we witness what Zelizer (1995) terms "retrospective nominalism," whereby certain older events are renamed and reassigned to serve additional functions that fit with the needs of the present (p. 222). For the Indian immigrant community, the present seems to need an assertive display of national identity, and the occasion of *Diwali* is used to serve such a purpose. However, by rewriting national identity through a specifically Hindu ritual, the lines between "Hindu-ness" and "Indian-ness" get blurred and start to overlap. With such renaming and rerouting of identity, it becomes easy to "forget" that any understanding and celebration of Indian-ness must be cast in secular terms, so as to avoid the erasure of diverse religious communities, such as Indian Muslims, Indian Christians, Indian Parsis, Indian Buddhists, and Indian Jains.

Rethinking Acculturation:
Implications of Intercultural Communication

In this article, I examine how popular cinema mediates collective and personal memories in the Asian Indian diaspora and how such mediated memories give us clues to how Asian Indian immigrants negotiate their identity. I also explore how gender is implicated in the community's need to imagine and recollect its collective heritage. Additionally, by including interviews with Asian Indian immigrant women, I demonstrate how they use cinema as a resource to deal with the stresses of dislocation and displacement.

Questions about migration and the construction of identity are paramount today as the rate of immigration into the United States rapidly increased in the 1990s to nearly a million a year (Suárez-Orozco and Suárez-Orozco 2001, p. 55). These "new" immigrants present a dramatically different demographic portrait from the previous great wave of immigration at the turn of the last century. In 1890, over 90 percent of immigrants were European, whereas in 1990 only 25 percent were European, with 25 percent being Asian and 43 percent being from Latin America (Rong and Preissle 1998). For older immigrants the desire to melt into the American pot was viewed as appropriate and implied that cultural differences should be minimized or erased. We now recognize that even if an immigrant wanted to slough off his or her cultural identity and become reincarnated as an "American" (whatever that might mean), he or she may not be allowed to do so. For instance, many second- and third-generation Asian American citizens are still assumed to be "foreigners" or are asked "where they come from" or if they plan to return home. The melting pot notion of **acculturation** is increasingly irrelevant to many of the new immigrants who are non-European and non-White. Further, the rapid advances in communication technology and global media have enabled new immigrants to keep alive their sense of belonging to two or more cultural worlds. Acculturation, then, for these new immigrants can no longer be thought of as a series of linear phases where one goes from being different to being assimilated. Rather, we need more dynamic, fluid understandings of acculturation that allow us to see it as a process that is continuous and not viewed as a static, finite end product.

Traditional notions of acculturation also imply that it is primarily the immigrants who change and not the host culture. On the contrary, with regard to the new immigrants, society and culture in the United States are being inexorably affected. Expressing both the rewriting of immigrant identity and conversely the impact that the diaspora has on Western urban societies, Salman Rushdie (1992) ventriloquizes through Dr. Simba, a fictional character in his novel *The Satanic Verses,* "African, Caribbean, Indian, Pakistani, Bangladesh, Cypriot, Chinese, we are other than what we would have been if we had not crossed the oceans, . . . we have been made again: but I say we shall also be the ones to remake this society, to shape it from the bottom to the top" (p. 414).

By uncovering how Indian cinema is used to recollect the past and to construct identity, I wish to draw attention to how new immigrants are constantly shuttling between cultures. Rather than moving inevitably toward assimilation, **popular culture** assists in what Hermans and Kempens (1998, p. 1117) call the "moving and mixing of cultures." Traditionally, intercultural communication has paid scant attention to the role of media in constructing cultural identities. Given the pervasiveness of both mass media and new media such as the Internet and the world wide web, it is imperative that we explore how culture is being reconfigured, remembered, reimagined, and reinvented through media. Incorporating the study of mediated communication will give us invaluable insights into the complex interplay of cultural influences that emerge as immigrants traverse multiple geographies and redraw cultural topographies.

Notes

1. This chapter emerged out of my dissertation research where I examined how Indian women in the diaspora read the gendered and nationalist representations in popular Indian cinema. The dissertation concluded by drawing upon Bourdieu's notions of "field" and "habitus" to demonstrate the political, economic, and social contexts within which texts and readers' readings circulate and to develop the idea of the diaspora as habitus.

2. The changes in U.S. immigration policy after 1965 allowed entry to non-European professionals and their families from the "Third World." Initially most entering Indian immigrants were young males, but after 1970 they were joined by their Indian brides. According to Bhardwaj and Rao (1995, p. 199), "the reasons for Asian-Indian immigration of the post-1965 era have probably more to do with the American pull than with the Indian push factors." Most Indian immigrants in the United States, therefore, tend to belong to the educated professional elite rather than the unskilled working class. Although in the 1990s Indian immigration patterns were slowly changing, lending a more diverse complexion to the Indian diaspora in the United States, the majority is still composed of middle-class professionals and their families. Given this predominance, I sought to interview women who belonged to such a socioeconomic context, and who came to the states as wives, in order to make meaningful connections among texts, readers, and contexts.

3. *Diwali,* the festival of lights, commemorates the return of the Hindu god Rama from his exile in the forest. The celebrations connote renewal and the onset of a new year.

4. In this chapter, I refer to the Hindi-language cinema produced by the Bombay film industry. Although there are strong regional language film industries in India, the Hindi films produced in Bombay or "Bollywood" form the national cinema. I use the terms *Indian cinema, Bombay cinema,* and *Hindi cinema* interchangeably.

5. *India Society of Worcester Presents Diwali - 97* (Worcester, Mass.: India Society of Worcester, 1997).

6. *Dilwale, Dhulhaniya Le Jayenge* (He who follows his heart will win the bride); *Pardes* (Foreign Land).

7. *Sandesh:* The Quarterly Magazine of the India Society of Worcester (Worcester, Mass.: India Society of Worcester, 1998), 11.

8. See Ram (2002), where I argue how Indian immigrant women simultaneously comply with and resist the dominant patriarchal representations that saturate Indian cinema.

9. To maintain confidentiality I have assigned a pseudonym to identify each participant.

10. Translated from Hindi.

References

Bhardwaj, S. M., and M. N. Rao. 1995. Asian Indians in the United States: A geographic appraisal. In C. Clarke, C. Peach, and S. Vertovec (Eds.), *South Asians overseas: Migration and ethnicity* (pp. 197–219). New York: Cambridge University Press.

Bhattacharjee, A. 1992. The habit of ex-nomination: Nation, woman and the Indian immigrant bourgeoisie. *Public Culture* 5 (1): 19–44.

Bohman, J., D. R. Hiley, and R. Shusterman. 1991. Introduction: The interpretative turn. In J. Bohman, D. R. Hiley, and R. Shusterman (Eds.), *The interpretive turn: Philosophy, science, culture* (pp. 1–14). Ithaca, N.Y.: Cornell University Press.

Brown, M. E. 1989. Soap opera and women's culture: Politics and the popular. In K. Carter and C. Spitzack (Eds.), *Doing research on women's communication: Perspectives on theory and method* (pp. 161–90). Norwood, N.J.: Ablex.

Chakravarty, S. 1989. National identity and the realist aesthetic. *Quarterly Journal of Film and Video* 11 (3): 31–50.

Chambers, I. 1994. *Migrancy, culture, identity*. London: Routledge.

Connerton, P. 1989. *How societies remember*. Cambridge, U.K.: Cambridge University Press.

Fentress, J., and C. Wickham. 1992. *Social memory*. Oxford, U.K.: Blackwell.

Fiske, J. 1991. For cultural interpretations: A study of the culture of homelessness. *Critical Studies in Mass Communication* 8 (4): 455–74.

Ganguly, K. 1992. Migrant identities: Personal memory and the constructions of selfhood. *Cultural Studies* 6 (1): 27–50.

Giddens, A. 1991. *Modernity and self-identity: Self and society in the late modern age*. Stanford, Calif.: Stanford University Press.

Glick Schiller, N., L. Basch, and C. S. Blanc. 1995. From immigrant to transmigrant: Theorizing transnational migration. *Anthropological Quarterly* 68: 48–63.

Grewal, I. 1994. The postcolonial ethnic studies and the diaspora. *Socialist Review* 24 (4): 45–74.

Hallbawachs, M. 1992. *On collective memory*. Trans. Lewis A. Coser. Chicago: University of Chicago Press.

Hegde, R. S. 1998. Swinging the trapeze: The negotiation of identity among Asian Indian immigrant women in the United States. In D. V. Tanno and A. Gonzalez (Eds.), *Communication and identity across cultures* (pp. 34–55). Thousand Oaks, Calif.: Sage.

Hermans, J. M., and H. J. G. Kempens. 1998. Moving cultures: The perilous problems of cultural dichotomies in a globalizing society. *American Psychologist* 53: 1111–20.

India Society of Worcester. 1997. *India Society of Worcester Presents Diwali – 97*. Worcester, Mass.

———. 1998. *Sandesh:* The Quarterly Magazine of the India Society of Worcester. Worcester, Mass.

Janji, R. 1978. *Bharata* on aesthetic emotions. *British Journal of Aesthetics* 18 (1): 66–69.

Kaes, A. 1990. History and film: Public memory in the age of electronic dissemination. *History and Memory* 2 (1): 111–29.

Langellier, K., and D. L. Hall. 1989. Interviewing women: A phenomenological approach to feminist communication. In K. Carter and C. Spitzack (Eds.), *Doing research on women's communication: Perspectives on theory and method* (pp. 193–220). Norwood, N.J.: Ablex.

Lowenthal, D. 1994. Identity, heritage, and history. In J. Gillis (Ed.), *Commemorations: The politics of national identity*. Princeton, N.J.: Princeton University Press.

Madison, S. 1994. Introduction. In S. Madison (Ed.), *The woman that I am: The literature and culture of contemporary women of color* (pp. 1–18). New York: St. Martin's Press.

Middleton, D., and D. Edwards. 1990. Introduction. In D. Middleton and D. Edwards (Eds.), *Collective remembering* (pp. 1–22). New York: Sage.

Minister, K. 1991. A feminist frame for the oral history interview. In S. B. Gluck and D. Patai (Eds.), *Women's words: The feminist practice of oral history* (pp. 27–42). New York: Routledge.

Nelson, J. 1989. Phenomenology as feminist methodology: Explicating interviews. In K. Carter and C. Spitzack (Eds.), *Doing research on women's communication: Perspectives on theory and method* (pp. 221–41). Norwood: Ablex.

Radhakrishnan, R. 1991. *Diasporic mediations: Between home and location*. Minneapolis: University of Minnesota Press.

Ram, A. 2002. Framing the feminine: Diasporic reading of gender in popular Indian cinema. *Women's Studies in Communication* 25 (1): 25–53.

Richmond, F. P. 1990. Characteristics of Sanskrit theater and drama. In D. L. Swann and P. B. Zarrilli (Eds.), *Indian theater: Traditions of performance* (pp. 80–81). Honolulu: University of Hawaii Press.

Rong, X. L., and J. Prissele. 1998. *Educating immigrant students: What we need to know to meet the challenge*. Thousands Oaks, Calif.: Corwin Press.

Rushdie, S. 1991. *Imaginary homelands: Essays and criticism 1981–1991*. New York: Penguin.

———. 1992. *The Satanic verses*. Dover, Del.: The Consortium.

Smith, M. P. 1994. Can you imagine? Transnational migrations and the globalization of grassroots politics. *Social Text* 39: 15–35.

Suárez-Orozco, M., and C. Suárez-Orozco. 2001. *Children of immigration*. Cambridge, Mass.: Harvard University Press.

Thelen, D. 1989. Memory and American history. *Journal of American History* 75 (4): 1117–29.

Thomas, R. 1989. Sanctity and scandal: The mythologization of Mother India. *Quarterly Review of Film and Video* 11 (3): 11–30.

Tölöyan, K. 1996. Rethinking diaspora(s): Stateless power in the transnational moment. *Diaspora* 5: 3–35.

U.S. Census Bureau. 2000. Census 2000 Summary File 1, Matrices P3, P4, PCT4, PCT5, PCT8, and PCT 11.

Zelizer, B. 1995. Reading the past against the grain: The shape of memory studies. *Critical Studies of Mass Communication* 12 (2): 214–39.

KEY TERMS

acculturation

Asian Indian cinema

collective memory

cultural identity

diaspora

gender

immigrant identity

Indian cinema

mass media

nationalism

popular culture

rasa

REVIEW AND DISCUSSION QUESTIONS

1. Do you agree with the argument that our memories are mediated? In other words, what role do media play in filtering, giving shape to, and constructing our memories of the past? Can you think of examples from your own life where your remembrance of a certain event or a past era has been shaped by the media?

2. Alternatively, do certain media texts (e.g. a popular song, television serial, movie, etc.) evoke certain memories for you? How do you know if those memories are real or if they have been shaped by the media?

3. What is "heritage"? In what ways does the cultural community you belong to maintain and communicate its heritage?

4. Reflect on the ways in which you recollect your past and how that recollection and remembering affect your sense of self.

5. Do you think that various media have led to the collapsing of national boundaries and the development of a globalized culture?

6. Why does the author conclude by arguing that we need to rethink our standard notions of acculturation?

7. Do you or anyone you know belong to a diasporic community? What does it mean for someone to belong to a diaspora? Research the origin of the term *diaspora*. What does this term tell you about cultural identity?

Intercultural Weddings and the Simultaneous Display of Multiple Identities

Wendy Leeds-Hurwitz

Learning Objectives

After reading this chapter, students will be able to:

- understand why intercultural weddings are an interesting research site; and
- explain how couples combine cultural identities in new ways, so as to display multiple identities simultaneously.

The Chinese groom reported: "Ever since my mother knew I was a boy, even probably before I was born, she'd been saving these little trinkets or jade things, just for the purpose of giving them to the bride, her son's wife. They were in little red envelopes, good luck envelopes."

When two people of different cultural backgrounds decide to get married, they encounter the problem of simultaneously displaying multiple identities. Sometimes the issue is so difficult that they decide not to get married; other times, they choose one of several alternatives that avoid the problem entirely. If they do manage to make it through the wedding ceremony, they have successfully navigated the difficulties and should serve well as models for interethnic couples, including those who only have to cope with intercultural differences more sporadically, and in less intimate contexts.

Over the past ten years, I have investigated five types of intercultural weddings: inter-racial (for example, African American–Caucasian), interethnic (as in Polish American–Irish American), interfaith (as in Christian–Jewish), international (such as American–French), and interclass (for example, upper class–working class). It seems to me that the central problem is the same, regardless of the exact type of cultural difference involved for each couple: they must find some way to overcome the differences. Intercultural weddings exemplify a social location where meanings come into conflict and serve as particularly fruitful sites of analysis, for they involve the voluntary crossing of symbolic boundaries. There is no chance that all cultural boundaries will disappear, but they are likely to continue becoming more permeable—so it is important to study occasions on which they are stretched thin or torn down entirely. Intercultural weddings display all of the issues available for study, magnified: the joining of families, the resolution of conflicts, the fulfilling of expectations, the integration of the past with the present and potential future; all come to the fore. As a result, intercultural weddings are a good starting point for research into how intercultural communication is handled on an individual level.

Intercultural weddings are the least frequent type of wedding held in the United States, since most people marry persons who are similar to them in most ways. However, there is extensive evidence showing that intercultural marriages of all types are increasing. Therefore, this is a significant issue to study, both because more and more couples will face the problem in the future, and because of what we can learn that will apply to other contexts of intercultural interaction.

The modern United States is a plural, multiethnic society, with a wide variety of cultural groups together making up the whole. Root (2001) points out, "As structured barriers to equality between race and gender continue to be challenged, the matrix of gender and race changes. The result will be more interracial marriage" (p. 75). It is important to ask how such diversity is socially articulated and, equally, how diverse expectations can be fruitfully combined. Since the major participants in intercultural weddings can be assumed to have the effective combination of multiple traditions as a goal, studying this one ritual event may throw light on other sorts of cultural conflict and their potential solutions. Participants in a wedding epitomize high motivation: the new couple has greater incentive to overcome cultural conflicts of any sort than many others do. Thus, studying the design of intercultural weddings should demonstrate what forms of creativity in combining different cultures are possible, given sufficient motivation.

The logic of studying only the wedding ceremony, and not the marriage or the relationship underlying it, is simple. A wedding is a uniquely public event, unlike most of a marriage (or other long-term relationship), and one of the few events where the presence of legal witnesses is essential to the validity of the ceremony. It is also relatively short-lived (although a few wedding ceremonies may last for days, most are only a few hours in length), which makes it easier to gather data on the entire event and analyze its significance for the participants; marriages, at least ideally, last decades or more. It is also designed by and for the participants, not the researcher, and so the major decisions are made without the influence of the researcher's concerns. And weddings are particularly well-documented, again at the request of the major participants rather than the researcher, so they are accessible to description and analysis, unlike more private moments.

Briefly, then, the basic question can be phrased as follows: How is it possible to present multiple identity statements (which are often contradictory) simultaneously in a single event? This is an issue to which I did not have a clear answer, and so this became a "genuine" question; because I was studying people who identified *themselves* as members of particular groups (rather than my identifying them as such, on a temporary basis), this was a study of "bona fide" groups.[1] With a genuine question, there is no hypothesis to prove, just a problem to investigate. With a bona fide group, the answer to the genuine question comes from those who have actually faced, and resolved, the matter for themselves.

Even among those planning intercultural weddings, clearly many couples manage to avoid the difficulties inherent in the simultaneous display of multiple identities. There are four basic designs serving as possible resolutions to the issue: the couple can choose to display only one identity, ignoring all potentially relevant others; they can display different identities in separate events, often holding one wedding for each side of the family, in multiple but distinct ceremonies; they can display no cultural identity at all by either having a judge conduct a brief legal ceremony that forgoes all ritual elements, or by adopting the mainstream American tradition of a wedding (the wedding evident in popular culture sources such as films, which is largely White, Christian, and middle class), or they can figure out how to combine the display of disparate cultural traditions into a single ceremony. It is this last category that most interested me, as it most directly confronts the issue of cultural difference.

Method

Over the course of ten years, I gradually came to study a total of 112 couples, covering a wide range of identities.[2] The couples included have at least one member who is from the United States, or they live in the United States and held their wedding here.[3]

My training is in the **ethnography of communication,** which involves participant observation and interviews. When possible, I attended weddings. Mostly these observations and interviews were face to face (and with a tape recorder), with as many of the original participants as possible (bride, groom, parents, children, officiants), but occasionally they were by telephone or e-mail. Most of the time we reviewed photo albums, videotapes, and objects from the ceremony to keep the discussion close to the actual details of what occurred during the wedding.[4] During several semesters I encouraged my students to describe intercultural weddings they had attended and to interview intercultural couples they knew; in these cases, they were given a clear set of topics to discuss, and they recorded these interviews for me using either audio or videotape; I then followed up with the couples myself to confirm the accuracy of the original reports and my summaries.[5]

Due to the fact that I was not present at all weddings included in the study, it made sense to focus on specific material culture elements (clothing, food, objects) that were clearly visible in the photographic evidence and that held a position of prominence in the couple's memories. When Chinese tradition calls for a red dress, but American tradition calls for it to be white, this is no minor matter for a Chinese American couple to negotiate. Whatever choice the couple makes will be visible to all the guests and assumed to have significance as a statement about the identities of the participants.

Case Study

What follows is a presentation of one wedding in some detail as a case study, to illustrate how individual preference, family tradition, ethnicity, religion, and mainstream expectations were successfully combined by one couple into a coherent whole. The exact domains that proved of greatest significance for each couple varied (for one, it might be geographic location, while for another, it might be religion), but the fact of reasonable accommodation of difference is the focus here, not which particular elements a given couple integrates into a whole.

Traditional Chinese wedding invitations are printed on red paper, with gold ink, and in Chinese characters. Traditional American wedding invitations are printed on white paper, in black ink, using the Roman alphabet. Clearly an invitation both in Chinese and in English indicates a wedding between members of both cultures. The bride in this case was Italian American and Catholic; the groom was Chinese American (Cantonese), raised Christian, and converted to Catholicism prior to the wedding (couple 10).[6] They wanted a "contemporary American wedding," yet incorporating some of their own traditions as well remained an important consideration for them.

The invitations were ordered from a Chinese printer in San Francisco, printed on red paper with gold ink, and the bride explained that they "opened backwards, according to us [Americans]" (see fig. 9.1).

There was Chinese calligraphy on the cover, including the *shuang-hsi* (the double happiness symbol commonly integrated into Chinese wedding celebrations) drawn inside a heart (traditional American symbol for love), as well as phoenix and dragon motifs, which signify eternal life and strength as well as the bride and groom, respectively (Costa 1997, p. 42). Specifically, for a wedding, the phoenix and dragon motifs are understood to represent "eternal" happiness in marriage and good karma.[7] On the inside right was the announcement of the marriage and an invitation to attend in Chinese calligraphy; the same announcement and invitation were printed in English on the left side (see fig. 9.2). (They used the groom's Chinese name but had to make one up for the bride.) The back has additional Chinese calligraphy, repeating the image of the phoenix and dragon, as well as the *shuang-hsi*. Thus were both traditions incorporated into a single object.[8]

The same printing company produced place cards of the same red paper with gold printing (the bride and groom chose the guests' seats at the reception to reduce potential language barriers), and thank you notes (also red with gold). They also had a red silk banner, 37 inches by 29 inches, with a large Chinese character (the *shuang-hsi* again) embroidered on it in the shape of a heart (in lieu of the explicit heart drawn around it), as well as another dragon and phoenix, very large and extremely colorful, at the reception (see fig. 9.3).

This banner was placed on a table with black markers so guests could sign it. Next to it was the more traditional American guest book, thus inviting people to sign either or both, as was most comfortable (most guests appear to have signed both).

At the wedding ceremony, guests were provided a program on blue paper with black ink, with an image of doves at the top (see fig. 9.4). This was printed only in English and resembles the programs provided by other couples at this church at their weddings.

Cantonese Chinese tradition requires that the groom give the bride's family a roast pig at the engagement. Since the bride's family did not expect this, instead, the groom's family served roast pig the morning of the wedding to their own family members. Also during that morning, the eldest male of his family (the groom's great-uncle) cut the groom's hair to symbolize his coming of age, now that he was to be married.

At the wedding, the bride wore a variant of the traditional American white bridal gown, long, and with lace. She held white and red flowers, red to match the traditional Chinese red of happiness, and white to match her dress. The bridesmaids wore royal blue, tea-length gowns, and held white and blue flowers. The groom wore a dark tux with a white and red boutonniere, to match the bride's bouquet. The groomsmen wore matching tuxes with white shirts. (Thus, in addition to the colors indicating both Chinese and American wedding traditions, the combination of the red and white with blue referenced the American flag, since they are both citizens of the United States.)

A tea ceremony was held between the wedding and the reception in a convent near the church. The bride was introduced to her new relatives; she served them tea and called them by

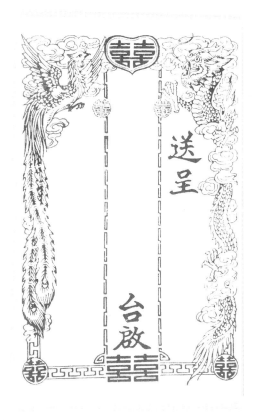

FIGURE 9.1   Wedding Invitation (Cover)

name in Cantonese (a language she does not speak, so she was coached for this performance). The guests, in turn, gave her gifts of money and jewelry, which she immediately wore.

The groom reported: "Ever since my mother knew I was a boy, even probably before I was born, she'd been saving these little trinkets or jade things, just for the purpose of giving them to the bride, her son's wife. They were in little red envelopes, good luck envelopes" (with gold writing, like the wedding invitations, red and gold being associated with happiness and good luck for the Chinese; see fig. 9.5).

Although this ceremony would normally not include the bride's family, they were invited along to watch, since it was a new and unusual experience for them.

At the reception, guests were served one variant of the standard American wedding foods: filet mignon, peas and carrots, baked potato, mushrooms, cake, along with "the little Italian cookies my [the bride's] aunt made." The cake had blue frosting on it, to match the bridesmaids' dresses and flowers, and "there were two doves with rings in their mouths" as

| FIGURE 9.2 | Wedding Invitation (Inside) |

a cake topper, matching the napkins and matchbooks that were on the tables at the reception, as well as the wedding programs, in a typically American wedding design. The napkins and matchbooks were white and blue, also matching the bridesmaids' dresses and flowers. Matching of colors across social codes (from clothing to flowers to objects such as matchbooks, napkins, and programs) frequently marks formality at mainstream American rituals such as weddings.

During the reception at a Cantonese Chinese wedding, the bride normally changes into a *cheung sam,* which this bride described as being "a long gown which is a very fancy, embroidered dress, with usually a tiger or a dragon down the whole front, the length of the dress."[9] Traditionally, the bride and groom's mothers would also wear a *cheung sam.* At this wedding, the groom's mother changed into a version of this dress (in Cantonese tradition, either or both the mother of the bride and the mother of the groom may choose to change into these dresses; the groom's mother reported it is "up to you"). The bride did not change. As the bride said, "that makes sense because I'm not Chinese," and she would not have been comfortable wearing that style of dress. In this way the tradition was upheld by the one to whom it was most important and meaningful.

FIGURE 9.3 Silk Banner

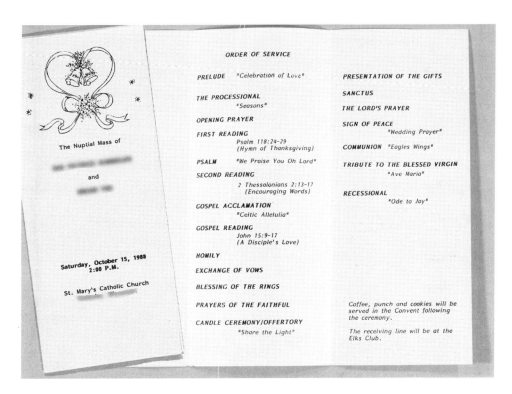

ORDER OF SERVICE

PRELUDE   *"Celebration of Love"*

THE PROCESSIONAL
            "Seasons"

OPENING PRAYER

FIRST READING
            Psalm 118:24-29
            (Hymn of Thanksgiving)

PSALM   *"We Praise You Oh Lord"*

SECOND READING
            2 Thessalonians 2:13-17
            (Encouraging Words)

GOSPEL ACCLAMATION
            "Celtic Alleluia"

GOSPEL READING
            John 15:9-17
            (A Disciple's Love)

HOMILY

EXCHANGE OF VOWS

BLESSING OF THE RINGS

PRAYERS OF THE FAITHFUL

CANDLE CEREMONY/OFFERTORY
            "Share the Light"

PRESENTATION OF THE GIFTS

SANCTUS

THE LORD'S PRAYER

SIGN OF PEACE
            "Wedding Prayer"

COMMUNION   *"Eagles Wings"*

TRIBUTE TO THE BLESSED VIRGIN
            "Ave Maria"

RECESSIONAL
            "Ode to Joy"

*Coffee, punch and cookies will be
served in the Convent following
the ceremony.*

*The receiving line will be at the
Elks Club.*

The Nuptial Mass of

and

Saturday, October 15, 1988
2:00 P.M.

St. Mary's Catholic Church

FIGURE 9.4 Wedding Program

    Good Luck Envelope

During the meal at a mainstream American wedding, guests often tap their spoons on their glasses as a request that the new couple kiss; in recent weddings, bells are provided for the guests to ring. In Chinese America this has been revised; one frequent version is that chopsticks will be used in lieu of spoons (since they are generally the utensils provided). This couple used a related tradition of providing small Chinese tea cups (no handles), filled with Jordan almonds, covered with netting, and tied with a red ribbon (to signify good luck and happiness) to guests at their places; these could be shaken, and served as a very quiet sort of bell, requesting that the couple kiss (see fig. 9.6).

After the meal at the reception, the Chinese guests left, as the groom explained, "because during Chinese receptions all they have is just a large feast and then they leave." The band played "Top 40" kind of music. The bride reported that this part of the event was "more for our friends and the American-born people." In keeping with the mainstream American audience present at that point, there was a bouquet toss and a garter toss.

Analysis

Rituals are a vehicle used to combine selected symbols into meaningful patterns (Firth 1973). Weddings are one form of ritual. In any wedding, but especially visible in intercultural weddings, the ritual serves as a vehicle for the performance of identity (among other functions). Intercultural weddings are especially valuable as sites of identity statements, for any one culture increases in visibility when contrasted with a second. Not all weddings are equally revealing. My research emphasizes intercultural weddings for a reason: the conveyance of identity in the presence of others equally concerned to simultaneously convey different identities is especially difficult and, therefore, worthy of extended investigation. It is through the design of particular combinations of cultural identities in a wedding ritual that the new couple not only displays their intentions (the performance aspect) but makes them true (the constitutive element). This harks back to the concept of **social construction:** we construct (constitute, or make real) our identities, making them visibly manifest, both for ourselves and so that we may share them with others. This is one part of what Goffman (1959) named **"identity management,"** referring to the element of deliberate control evident in identity displays.[10] We make choices about what to present in a ritual such as a wedding, thus we can be seen managing the presentation of our identities, our selves. We know who we are, but when others with different identities are present, we are more likely to *mark* our identities visibly.

The wedding examined as my primary case study in this chapter successfully combined mainstream elements, with a small nod to the bride's Italian identity, and a large nod to the groom's Chinese identity. Partly because they were both Catholic, the wedding ceremony itself was essentially governed by religious conventions, but many of the peripheral elements followed traditional Chinese expectations. Some parts were clearly intended to make the Chinese family members comfortable (the hair cutting, pig roast, tea ceremony, banner); there was an acknowledgment of the bride's Italian heritage (the cookies); and other parts of the event met the expectations of the mainstream American guests (everyone's clothing during the ceremony, the program, cake, topper, napkins, matchbooks, and guest book). At several points traditions needed to be modified to fit the specific circumstances: the traditional Chinese invitation incorporated an English translation, as well as placing the traditional double happiness symbol into an American heart; the groom's mother wore the type of dress the bride would usually be expected to change into for the reception; the double

 FIGURE 9.6   Wedding Favor

happiness symbol was designed as a heart on the silk banner; and the favor was adapted so that the Chinese tea cup given to guests at the reception was used in requesting a kiss. By all reports, this combination of cultural identities into a full day of events made everyone happy.

A series of metaphors have been used by researchers to discuss the ways different cultures combine. The old standby is the **melting pot,** where all cultures enter as unique but quickly lose what makes them different.[11] The melting pot depends upon intermarriage as the standard way to combine originally separate "ingredients," or members of different groups (Spickard 1989). A midrange metaphor is the **mosaic** (or, alternatively, "salad," "quilt," "rainbow," "kaleidoscope," "coat of many colors"), where each culture is placed near others in successful combination, but none influences the shape of others in any noticeable way (Hannerz 1992; Tuleja 1997). And so researchers needed still another metaphor, one falling somewhere between the melting pot (where no original elements are maintained) and the mosaic (where no group influences others) to describe current acculturation norms. The most recent metaphor of a "tapestry" allows for some influence yet also some ability to maintain what makes each unique (Deegan 1998).

A **tapestry** is a piece of fabric created by joining differently colored threads together, combining to create a picture more complex than any of them could display alone. This successfully conveys the image of meshing different traditions into a single whole, and so manages the conflict between maintaining differences while establishing similarities better than the other metaphors. It also suggests viewing the completed tapestry as a new and unique creation, of far greater value than its constituent threads alone would suggest (the whole being greater than the sum of its parts). The tapestry metaphor explicitly intends to refer positively to **cultural pluralism** (the state of multiple ethnic/racial/religious groups co-existing peacefully, aware of differences but not fighting as a result of them). The image of weaving together different lives makes particular sense to intercultural couples. Of these metaphors (although none is perfect, and more suggestions will no doubt be offered in the future), the tapestry is the most sophisticated and thus the most useful image to keep in mind for how different cultures can appropriately maintain their own traditions yet also successfully blend into a larger society. It also has the advantage of subtly referencing the metaphor of social life as "fabric," which is frequently used by many who study interaction (more common perhaps in sociology than communication, but a significant visual image nonetheless).[12]

In my database, there are multiple examples of all of these metaphors, showing how they explain cultural identity as displayed in rituals. Having a mainstream wedding serves as a good example of a melting pot, since the only **cultural identity marker** is generic American. This is often the solution for couples when there are so many different expectations that they cannot find an easy resolution. One example I observed of how a couple can end up conveying little of either of their cultures in opting for a traditional mainstream American wedding involved an Italian American Catholic bride who married a Greek American, Greek Orthodox groom (couple 68). They were married in a Catholic church (mainstream American weddings are nearly always Christian, so this did not constitute a significant deviation from the pattern). Because the groom had wanted to hold it in his Greek Orthodox church, he refused to participate in the planning, so the bride and the groom's mother planned it together, reportedly with little conflict (attributed by the participants to the fact that the groom's mother was a professional party planner with extensive knowledge of such events, and the bride was happy to let her make the major decisions).

The groom had given the bride a white rose on their first date, so white and roses served as the main color and theme; the bride described the result as just "too perfect." The church was heavily decorated with white roses, and white and teal (the second color chosen) carnations (flowers on each pew, and on the altar). The bride's gown was white, the bridesmaids' gowns were teal, matched to the teal flowers and teal ink on the wedding invitations. During the service the bride and groom handed each other's mothers a white rose, then lit candles from their mothers' candles, and then jointly lit the unity candle on the altar, where it was surrounded by white rose petals. The rings they exchanged were white gold with white diamonds. As guests entered the reception, they walked under an arbor with white roses and baby's breath, and a photographer took a picture of each guest. Every table had a centerpiece with two white roses in the middle, and the buffet table was scattered with white rose petals. The food was elaborate, including multiple types of seafood for appetizers, two pigs cooked on a spit, and more. The food was served on china with silver, and the servers all wore white gloves and had white roses in their lapels. By using the accepted standards for high formality within a mainstream wedding, this couple avoided the issue of whose background would be given favor; in the end, neither side's ethnic traditions or religions were even represented in most of the choices (although social class certainly was—and the bride had no objection to the groom's family taking charge of the decisions, as they were the ones who knew how it should be done and were willing to pay for it to be done "right").

Having two ceremonies, one after the other or on successive days or in different locations, exemplifies the mosaic, since the various cultural traditions exert no influence upon one another in the ritual aside from proximity. Couple 85 utilized this solution: a Hindu bride and Jewish groom, they planned two major ceremonies, incorporating a variety of contingent events, with many guests participating in both ceremonies. As the bride reported: "it was a way we found to negotiate all the different components." This solution is most common when the requirements of the bride and groom simply seem incompatible, and was the favored choice for Hindu, Buddhist, and Moslem marriages with Christians or Jews.

The weddings that seem most unique and creative are those that exemplify tapestries: permitting each cultural group to maintain a coherent set of characteristics, they also allow for the change that inevitably follows significant cultural contact between groups. For example, couple 74 joined an African American groom and a White Jewish bride under a huppah (Jewish wedding canopy) made of cloth they bought on a trip to Africa to explore his roots. The Jews in the audience recognized it as a huppah, although of unusual fabric and color (most are blue and white, representing the colors of the Israeli flag); the African Americans recognized the traditional colors signifying Africa (red, green, yellow, black) in the fabric, although they did not recognize its traditional use as a canopy. Thus both sides were able to make something of the artifact, although what they understood from it was distinctly different.[13]

These then are the various ways cultural identity can be displayed through wedding rituals. The wedding described as the primary case study here displays elements of all three metaphors: there are some mainstream traditions (the white wedding dress, the cake topper, the program), some unique cultural markers (the banner sitting next to the guest book is a perfect example), and also some influence of one culture on the other (the invitation printed in both Chinese and English, but following Chinese design and colors; the double happiness symbol in the shape of a heart on the banner; the Chinese tea cup as favor, to be pressed into service as a bell calling for a kiss, something that traditional Chinese would never do in public).[14]

Conclusion

Intercultural weddings turn out to be an excellent research site in large part because intercultural couples are particularly committed to their relationship (if they were not, they would not go so far as to marry in the face of what is often considerable opposition from family members and friends); they are unusually able to verbalize their logic (since these were generally the result of extensive discussion); and they are especially happy to discuss their choices (they generally know they are unusual, having become accustomed to answering questions; they are often willing to share whatever they have learned with others, especially if their resolutions can be of use to others facing the same complex situation).

An emphasis on material elements of wedding rituals makes sense because they are well-documented (in photographs, videotapes) and often maintained after the wedding (most people wear wedding rings, most preserve some elements of the wedding in addition to photographs or videotapes, as when the cake topper is put out for display, or the wedding dress preserved). In addition, material culture is more immediately visible and harder to modify when moving between the bride's and groom's families and friends. Although it is possible for the bride to wear multiple dresses during different parts of an event (and many Asian Americans do just that—in couple 94, the Vietnamese American bride marrying a Chinese American groom wore four different dresses during their ceremony and reception), only one can be worn while saying the all-important wedding vows (the most central element of American Christian weddings, and so Americans take special note of what is worn at that point).

Studying intercultural weddings is but one of many ways to demonstrate the extent to which cultural identity is socially constructed. Identity is never so visible as when it is placed into immediate contrast with one or more different identities. It is well understood by now that everyone chooses particular aspects of their own multiple identities (e.g., age, gender, ethnicity, nationality) to display at various moments. But what has not been studied or described often is the display of multiple cultural identities simultaneously. For this purpose, intercultural weddings are an ideal example as participants tend to have many assumptions about appropriate choices, even when these are not explicit. Weddings are complex rituals made up of many symbols; therefore, they allow enormous room for following old traditions and creating new ones, all in the same event.

As the world becomes an increasingly multicultural place, the older assumption that each country holds a single culture is contradicted by reality; more and more people are combining their different cultural expectations into a single, coherent reality. Our subjects have moved beyond us, and intercultural researchers must hurry to follow.

Notes

1. See Penman (2000) for further discussion of the nature and value of asking genuine questions; see Putnam and Stohl (1990) on bona fide groups.

2. The implication is *not* that it took ten years of full-time effort to find this many couples; I was busy with other projects as well over this time period. Rather, the implication is that some research

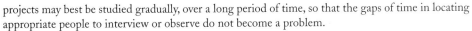

projects may best be studied gradually, over a long period of time, so that the gaps of time in locating appropriate people to interview or observe do not become a problem.

3. Other countries have their own issues as far as weddings are concerned, notably that religious leaders usually proscribe wedding rituals, and so it seemed reasonable to assign clear geographic limits to the study.

4. My definition of the wedding expanded to include not only the reception that generally followed, but also some consideration of additional events (from showers to honeymoons), as these turned out to be relevant.

5. When questions arose, my students and I interviewed secular wedding professionals (jewelers, florists, wedding planners, etc.), as well as ritual specialists (the officiants: priests, ministers, rabbis, etc.). In addition we viewed television shows and films depicting weddings, read fiction, newspapers, and popular magazines describing weddings, as well as exploring wedding-related web sites.

6. In order to protect the identities of the participants, they will not be named. Each couple has been given a number, based only on the order in which I transcribed notes and/or interviews about their event, and the participants are identified by their role rather than their names. This particular couple was initially interviewed by one of my students, Susan Glanz, as part of an independent study project in 1992.

7. Personal correspondence, Rueyling Chuang, January 4, 2002.

8. Costa (1997) documents the difficulties of second- or third-generation Chinese Americans who try hard to do the right thing without sufficient cultural knowledge to always be sure just what that is. For example, she describes a couple who "sent out invitations printed in red ink, only to have a relative inform that red ink—which looks like blood—was not appropriate" (p. 33).

9. The *cheung sam* would be called a *qi pao* in Mandarin (personal correspondence, Rueyling Chuang, January 4, 2002).

10. See Cupach and Imahori (1993) for an example of how to apply Goffman's ideas to intercultural communication.

11. Interestingly, although the United States has largely rejected the melting pot as a metaphor, it is still used elsewhere, as documented in an article about Australia (Arndt 2000); equally interesting, it is used by this author in exactly the same way it was formerly used in the United States: this is an article about how intermarriage in Australia is creating a melting pot.

12. One variant of this appears in Rieff (1964, p. xiii): "The social order does swiftly clothe the actors born into it in the self-understandings they are, thereafter, reluctant to shed even for the rare privilege of a glimpse of themselves in their nothingness."

13. This wedding, and the other examples described here only briefly, are presented in greater detail in Leeds-Hurwitz (in press).

14. Weddings exemplifying the tapestry metaphor are highlighted in Leeds-Hurwitz (2002), although extensive examples of a wide variety of resolutions, including illustrations of all of these metaphors, are also provided there.

References

Arndt, B. 2000. Aborigines lead way as mixed marriages create melting pot. Sydney *Morning Herald* (March 23). Retrieved from www.smh.com.au/0003/23/text/pageone6.html.

Costa, S. S. 1997. *Wild geese and tea: An Asian-American wedding planner*. New York: Riverhead Books.

Cupach, W. R., and T. T. Imahori. 1993. Identity management theory: Communication competence in intercultural episodes and relationships. In R. L. Wiseman and J. Koester (Eds.), *Intercultural communication competence* (pp. 112–31). Newbury Park, Calif.: Sage.

Deegan, M. J. 1998. Weaving the American ritual tapestry. In M. J. Deegan (Ed.), *The American ritual tapestry: Social rules and cultural meanings* (pp. 3–17). Westport, Conn.: Greenwood Press.

Firth, R. 1973. *Symbols: Public and private.* Ithaca, N.Y.: Cornell University Press.

Goffman, E. 1959. *The presentation of self in everyday life.* New York: Doubleday Anchor.

Hannerz, U. 1992. *Cultural complexity: Studies in the social organization of meaning.* New York: Columbia University Press.

Leeds-Hurwitz, W. 2002. *Wedding as text: Communicating cultural identities through ritual.* Mahwah, N.J.: Lawrence Erlbaum Associates.

Penman, R. 2000. *Reconstructing communication: Looking to a future.* Mahwah, N.J.: Lawrence Erlbaum Associates.

Putnam, L. L., and C. Stohl. 1990. Bona fide groups: A reconceptualization of groups in context. *Communication Studies* 41 (3): 248–65.

Rieff, P. 1964. Introduction. In C. H. Cooley (Ed.), *Human nature and the social order* (pp. ix–xx). New York: Schocken Books.

Root, M. P. P. 2001. *Love's revolution: Interracial marriage.* Philadelphia: Temple University Press.

Spickard, P. R. 1989. *Mixed blood: Intermarriage and ethnic identity in twentieth-century America.* Madison: University of Wisconsin Press.

Tuleja, T. 1997. Introduction: Makings ourselves up: On the manipulation of tradition in small groups. In T. Tuleja (Ed.), *Usable pasts: Traditions and group expressions in North America* (pp. 1–20). Logan: Utah State University Press.

KEY TERMS

cultural identity marker

cultural pluralism

ethnography of communication

identity management

melting pot

mosaic

social construction

tapestry

REVIEW AND DISCUSSION QUESTIONS

1. Why are intercultural weddings proposed as an appropriate research site for the study of intercultural communication and cultural identity?

2. What are the types of cultural differences considered in this study?

3. What are the various wedding designs available to an intercultural couple?

4. What are the different metaphors for cultural contact provided in this chapter? Provide one example of each of these metaphors as described in the data.

5. How do the couples described in this chapter use material culture elements as symbols to display cultural identity?

6. What are the larger implications of this study for intercultural communication research?

Language, Terms, and Identity

THE FOUR CHAPTERS in this section focus on language and terms that are used among ethnic and cultural members that reflect their identity. Cultural and ethnic groups discussed here include: Filipino Americans, African Americans, lesbians, and interstate truckers.

S. Lily Mendoza examines indirect verbal and nonverbal communications within the Filipino American culture. Her chapter also demonstrates the differing assumptions, values, and interpretations associated with indirect communications among Filipino Americans. She incorporates an important factor regarding the power context when making sense of communication behavior.

Mary Fong and Keturah D. McEwen investigate why some African Americans use or refrain from using the term *nigga* in their social interactions within their ethnic group. Fong and McEwen also present various contextual uses and meanings of the cultural term in cultural and intercultural interactions.

Susan Hafen discusses the etymology of the word *lesbian,* the theories of lesbian identity development, and the evolution of lesbian subcultures. She further discusses how feminism and critical queer theory have created divisions.

Debra-L Sequeira and Timothy J. Anderson research how interstate truckers comprise two speech communities, Chicken Haulers and High Liners. They investigate their social dialects, communication rituals, and how technology impacts the communication among members of the speech community of interstate truckers.

Pahiwatig: The Role of "Ambiguity" in Filipino American Communication Patterns

S. Lily Mendoza

LEARNING OBJECTIVES

After reading this chapter, students will be able to:

- understand a pattern of cultural communication that involves indirect verbal and nonverbal skills that differ from mainstream North American culture;

- develop a more complex awareness of the differing assumptions and values associated with differing forms of communication and be able to interpret accordingly; and

- consider power context as an important factor in making sense of communication behavior different from one's own, and helping promote mutually empowering intercultural relations between individuals and groups coming from different cultural backgrounds.

Filipino–English dictionaries generally give the words "both" and "fellow-being" as translations of kapwa *(Panganiban 1972; Enriquez 1979; Odulio de Guzman 1968; Calderon 1957). It should be noted, however, that when asked for the closest English equivalent of* kapwa, *one word that comes to mind is the English word "others." However, the Filipino word* kapwa *is very different from the English word "others." In Filipino,*

> kapwa *is the unity of the "self" and "others." The English "others" is actually used in opposition to the "self," and implies the recognition of the self as a separate identity. In contrast,* kapwa *is a recognition of shared identity, an inner self shared with others.*
>
> —Enriquez (1992, p. 43)

P*ahiwatig* or *pakiramdaman* (roughly, sensing or feeling each other out) consists of the whole complex of indirect verbal and nonverbal patterns of communication among Filipinos. A huge concept in Philippine culture, it has myriad ramifications in relational development, the handling of conflict, and the maintenance of social relationships in general. This chapter examines the experiences of first-generation **Filipino Americans** with regard to this specific element of *intentional* ambiguity in their sedimented patterns of communication as they navigate their way through mainstream North American culture. Using interviews, the study focuses on the informants' perceptions of the common contexts of enactment of this indirect form of communication, the kinds of adjustments they have had to make given the difference in their communicative practices from that of the U.S. mainstream, and the impact (if any) that such adjustment experience might have on their sense of ethnic identification.

When Words Don't Mean What They Say

A story is told of a seventeen-year-old Filipino exchange student named Tony. It was Tony's first time to visit the United States. The Thompsons, his host family, were quite eager to meet him. His flight came in around eight o'clock in the evening. After the usual obligatory introductions and pleasantries, Mrs. Thompson asks Tony if he would care for some dinner. Tony sheepishly casts his eyes to the floor and mumbles, "It's alright, Mrs. Thompson, I'm not hungry." Taking his word for it, Mrs. Thompson proceeds to show Tony his room, the bathroom, and some towels and asks him to make himself comfortable. That night, Tony goes to bed famished. It proves to be quite a long night as he is kept awake by a growling stomach. It turns out he hasn't had dinner and is indeed feeling quite hungry.

"Say what you mean and mean what you say" is a commonplace truism in typical North American culture. But confronted with a situation like the one above, how is one to respond when other rules seem to apply? Was Tony merely being shy, too embarrassed to really say what he meant and therefore deserving of such treatment until he learned to speak more honestly? Or should the Thompsons have been more sensitive and read between the lines instead of taking Tony's words at face value? But how could they have known? Is it possible something else was going on?

Consider another incident: A well-meaning White North American missionary assigned to the Philippines is noted to have made the remark that Filipinos generally "can't be trained for leadership." Why? Because, according to him, their *yes* is never a yes and their *no* is not a no, "so how can you trust them?" The missionary's sad conclusion was that "not until Filipinos learn to speak more truthfully will they ever be fit for leadership and become role models of candor and honesty."

These responses, with the negative ascriptions assigned to the communication, are not uncommon among those from other cultures encountering Filipinos for the first time. The problem is particularly dramatic because language in this case is not the usual source of the barrier (the Philippines being well-known for its facade of westernization and proficiency in English). Rather, something else inexplicable in the culture tends to be seen as the culprit. As one scholar (Maggay 1999) notes, "This intractability of the Filipino's interactive patterns tends to be misinterpreted by those used to starkly direct forms of communicating as rather roundabout if not downright devious" (p. 11). The result therefore is a mixture of frustration and exasperation, if not blanket condemnation of the whole culture as being "inefficient," "confusing," and simply, "duplicitous."

A well-documented phenomenon among scholars of culture, this peculiar pattern of "indirect" communication is known as making *pahiwatig* (roughly, "sensing" or attempting to send a message indirectly by putting out feelers). Another Filipino word for it is *pakiramdaman* (feeling each other out). In Philippine psychological and anthropological literature, one finds the phenomenon being linked to a complex cultural logic ordering human relationships based on a constellation of core beliefs and values that have to do with *pakikipagkapwa-tao* (a way of being human with another) (cf. Alejo 1990; Alegre 1993; Enriquez 1992; Maggay 1993; among others).

Denaturalizing Culture

While the phenomenon of *pahiwatig* has been extensively studied within the homeland context, a similar investigation has yet to be conducted in the context of Filipinos who have migrated to the United States. Here then is an exploratory study meant to develop some beginning understanding of the phenomenon as enacted among first-generation Filipino Americans. An interesting question to ask in this regard is: To what extent do Filipino Americans who have been in the United States for a period of time continue to use *pahiwatig* or *pakiramdaman* in their communication with others? And, relatedly, to what extent is such communicative practice deemed to be expressive of their sense of ethnic identity as Filipinos?

Culture, as anthropologists over the centuries have noted, operates mostly in the realm of the unconscious, that is, **cultural insiders** are mostly unaware of the sea of assumptions, values, beliefs, and practices they've been socialized to embrace growing up. The usual default position is to regard one's learned habit patterns and received beliefs and ways of looking at the world as not just one among many, but as the only logical (reasonable) response to a world believed to be of a certain given nature (Geertz 1973). Hence, it is but "natural," for example, that if you want to say something, you should say it unequivocally (read: directly without hedging, in verbal terms). Not until one encounters a different cultural system than one's own (either by going abroad, meeting others from a different culture, or undergoing life experiences that seem to defy logic and all the normative rules one has come to hold) does one's taken-for-granted world begin to get denaturalized and become visible as perhaps only one of many other ways of being and doing. We therefore begin to think consciously about the patterns of our own culture only in comparison with something quite different.

In the case of Filipinos, cultural self-awareness has been prompted mostly via the experience of colonization under Europe and the West (i.e., under Spain for more than three centuries, and under the United States for half a century; as a U.S. neocolony for much longer). The resulting clash of cultures, along with the racist denigration and attempted erasure of the local indigenous culture by the colonizers, caused Filipinos to suffer a crisis of identity that inevitably led to a passionate search for their own culture.[1] In this struggle for

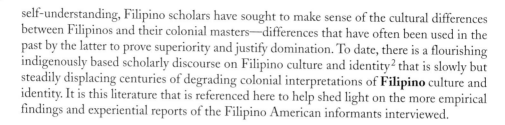

self-understanding, Filipino scholars have sought to make sense of the cultural differences between Filipinos and their colonial masters—differences that have often been used in the past by the latter to prove superiority and justify domination. To date, there is a flourishing indigenously based scholarly discourse on Filipino culture and identity[2] that is slowly but steadily displacing centuries of degrading colonial interpretations of **Filipino** culture and identity. It is this literature that is referenced here to help shed light on the more empirical findings and experiential reports of the Filipino American informants interviewed.

Participants

For this research project, ten informants were asked to share their experiences with regard to the Filipino communicative practice of *pahiwatig*. The informants were randomly selected from among this author's contacts based on their willingness to take part in the study. All the informants selected are first-generation Filipino American immigrants, thereby representing most vividly the sorts of changes and cultural adjustments Filipino Americans have had to make in the course of immigrating. A set of loosely structured, open-ended questions were asked of each of the participants, with interviews conducted either via telephone or e-mail. Where needed, followup phone calls were made to clarify certain points or to ask for elaboration.

Because this was not intended to be a systematic survey using a large number of samples, findings may not be generalized to the whole Filipino American community. The goal of the study, to reiterate, is a beginning exploration of the phenomenon of *pahiwatig* among Filipino Americans mainly by taking a look at the experiences of a selected number of informants in this regard and, one hopes, gaining insight to be used as a takeoff point for further study. Once again, given that cultural insiders are often unaware of the hidden or underlying logic of their own habitual behaviors, it becomes necessary to complement analysis of the data by referencing other scholarly literature on the subject.

Contexts of *Pahiwatig*

From the responses of various informants, several contexts may be identified as instances where **pahiwatig** is enacted as a communicative practice. Among the most salient that emerged from the interviews are the following: *pahiwatig* as (1) a way of maintaining social relations; (2) a finely calibrated response to differing power relations; and (3) an indication of distance or closeness of social relations.

"Ambiguity" as Social Maintenance

Asked whether they were familiar with the practice of *pahiwatig* or **pakiramdaman,** all ten respondents answered "yes." They were then asked to identify general contexts or situations in which they find themselves (or other Filipino Americans) resorting to the practice. Sunny, a freelance writer and editor, writes, "I think we Filipinos resort to this type of communication (i.e., *pakiramdaman*) in our attempt to accommodate the people we are talking with, not to offend or displease them, or not to reveal our shortcomings or ignorance about something." She adds, "It is especially true if we have to impart negative news or make inquiries." Likewise, Kristin, a computer analyst in Detroit, notes that Filipinos tend to use *pahiwatig* or *pakiramdaman* "when they try to avoid arguments or confrontations." Leny, a writer and professor, observes, "We use *pahiwatig* to avoid embarrassing someone; to save face, not wanting to appear demanding, not wanting to put others in a position of discomfort if they are not (yet) able or willing to meet the other's need." She adds, "There is also the wish not to offend or hurt the person's feelings because to hurt her is to hurt our relationship." The same sentiment is shared by Mae, a university researcher, who says, "We do it because we do not want to offend the other party." She further explains: "This is already part of Filipino culture; we tend to be overly sensitive to the feelings of others so we're careful not to hurt them (in the same way that we don't want to be hurt by them either)" (as translated from the Filipino original).

In all of these cases, one finds a delicate concern for the feelings of others, and conversely, a similar expectation that others would be equally sensitive toward oneself. Jesse, a thirty-year resident of New York, reiterates the notion of "saving face" (for oneself or someone else) by saying, "We resort to *pahiwatig* when we are too shy or embarrassed to say what we have in mind or to avoid an outright rejection. By making *pahiwatig,* we avoid getting an instant 'no' for an answer while at the same time, saving the other person from having to respond right away."

Several explanations have been offered by social scientists for this seeming sensitivity and over-concern for the feelings of others. Filipino psychologist Bulatao (1992) locates the underlying logic in the differing senses of self or identity between (typical North) Americans and Filipinos. He offers the analogy of Filipinos as being so many fried eggs in a pan whose experience of the self consists of a "core" (the yolk) but with the outer core (the egg white) blurring into/with the outer cores of other eggs in a coterminous fashion. Americans, on the other hand, are likened to so many hard-boiled eggs whose individual shells protect their autonomy and who then exercise the option to either open themselves (or part of themselves) to others or not at all. Thus, it is concluded from this that for Filipinos, the "other" is part of oneself also and therefore care must be taken not to hurt, offend, or cause distress or embarrassment to someone since doing such would be tantamount to doing it to oneself.

Among Filipino psychologists, this notion of a collective or communal self finds expression in the core concept of **kapwa** (roughly, shared inner self). Enriquez (1992) explains:

> Filipino-English dictionaries generally give the words "both" and "fellow-being" as translations of *kapwa* (Panganiban 1972; Enriquez 1979; Odulio de Guzman 1968; Calderon 1957). It should be noted, however, that when asked for the closest English equivalent of *kapwa,* one word that comes to mind is the English word "others." However, the Filipino word *kapwa* is very different from the English word "others." In Filipino, *kapwa* is the unity of the "self" and "others." The English "others" is actually used in opposition to the "self," and implies the recognition of the self as a separate identity. In contrast, *kapwa* is a recognition of shared identity, an inner self shared with others. (p. 43)

The use of *pahiwatig* then, within this context, is consistent with a desire to treat the other with the same regard and consideration as one would care to be treated since the other is not really a separate being but actually part of oneself. Particularly in cases involving delicate situations, Maggay (1999) finds it to be a "way of easing difficult interactive transactions" thereby enabling the culture to maintain *mabuting pagtutunguhan sa lipunan* (good, wholesome social relations). Indeed, as Maggay underscores in this regard, it is "a way of confronting painful aspects of our social relations while maintaining maximum concern for the *kapwa tao* (fellow human), that sense of the 'other' whose inner self one shares and identifies with" (p. 22). She warns, however, that this should not be mistaken for a shallow concern for "smooth interpersonal relations,"[3] of surrendering one's deeply-held conviction *(paninindigan)* for the sake of maintaining "surface harmony" or "saving face" (p. 23). Rather, she clarifies:

> Given the Filipino's wholistic orientation, which sees the part as also the whole, "face" is more than just one's public image or social standing; it is the seat of one's integrity of being, one's *dangal* [honor] or *pagkatao* (personhood). In this sense, to expose someone to public shame, or *ipahiya*, as with a good dressing-down or a no-holds-barred verbal fireworks, is not only to violate social boundaries; it is to cross that invisible line where personhood suffers degradation and demands redress. (p. 24)[4]

Indeed, it is when that line is crossed that one begins to encounter other lesser-known aspects of Filipino culture, namely, its **confrontative** values.[5] The section that follows describes situations when accommodative values give way to resistance.

A Calibrated Response to Differing Power Relations

Another context where the use of *pahiwatig* or the "indirect" form of communication has been noted by the study informants is in situations involving perceived differential power positionings of participants in a communicative interaction. Take for example the following observation from Sunny: "I think Filipinos tend to resort to this type of communication depending on who they're speaking with and based on the following factors: seniority in age and/or social status, familiarity and personal relationships, gender difference, etc." She relates, for example, how she tends to (unconsciously) modify her language and communication depending on whom she's speaking with. Kristin, for her part, notes that she tends to become more indirect in her communication "when intimidated [by someone in a more powerful position] and kept from speaking out." An interesting incident narrated by Joy, a senior student adviser, is the following:

> A co-worker who is my senior did something which humiliated me in public. [Because I didn't want any trouble] I just went to the restroom [and cried in secret]. [Then I went back to my work] as if nothing happened. But she can feel the animosity from then on because [I'm no longer the usual *pa*-sweetums towards her], just very civil. . . . [She will really feel the brunt of my] cold-shoulder treatment without [my] telling her. [with partial translation from the Filipino original]

Sunny ventures an explanation for this kind of accommodative response in the face of authority, saying, "This may be a legacy of colonialism, the hundreds of years that we've had to survive under several different 'masters,' when the wrong answer or action could lead to negative consequences or even sanctions where there are persons of authority or of higher status present, etc." Maggay (1993), concurring with such an explanation, deems it important to draw a careful distinction between what she terms "core values," which she considers integral to the culture, on one hand, and "survival values" developed as mere coping strategies in the face of domination, oppression, and marginalization, on the other. Scott (1990), in his volume, *Domination and the Arts of Resistance: Hidden Transcripts,* warns that surface compliance (often in the form of silence or outward acquiescence) in the face of authority must never be taken at face value; instead, one must learn to look for the "hidden script" of resistance within the official script often wrought by the strong and powerful.[6] An example of such a combination of acquiescence and resistance is noted by Maggay (1999) in the case of Filipino seamen who "stolidly suffer verbal abuse by their superiors." She notes, "Beneath the display of docility is cunning recalcitrance: Filipino seamen have been known to spit or boil socks for soup when preparing food for their high-handed officers." She concludes, "The lack of verbal protest is no guarantee of submission or capitulation" (p. 33).

There is, then, in the face of unequal power relations, a noted careful measuring out or calibrating of one's response where the greater the disparity in power and the greater the threat of reprisal, the greater the employment of strategies of **ambiguity** or *pahiwatig*. Again, we gain much from Maggay's (1999) elucidation in this regard:

> Expressiveness is suppressed, and as with one's dealings with outsiders, interaction is characterized by extreme formality and tentativeness, this time with the added factor of intense control where the rank and status differential requires rigid courtesies even in the face of emotional tension. (p. 33)

Such "intense control," of course, is acknowledged to have its limits. As Enriquez (1992) points out in "The Confrontative Filipino," there is a point at which a Filipino reaches the limits of tolerance and begins to invoke "*Bahala na!*" (roughly, "God's will be done"),[7] finds her *lakas ng loob* (strength of the heart), and finally launches into *pakikibaka* (cooperative resistance through concerted struggle). Indeed, the history of Filipinos in America is not lacking in such accounts of heroic struggle against racism and discrimination (cf. Bulosan 1946; Cordova 1983; Resource Development and Publications, UCLA Asian American Studies Center 1976; De Castro 1994, among others).

An Indicator of Relational Distance

Related to the earlier context of *pahiwatig* as a means of **social maintenance** is *pahiwatig*'s functioning as an indicator of relational distance. MC, a San Francisco-based social activist and educator, offers a complex explanation of this. He says,

> *Pahiwatig* is a different way of expressing one's *niloloob* [inner feelings] indirectly, but actually it can be pretty direct when both know the code. The usual assumption is that people have expectations *na alam na ng isa* [that the other knows already]. Hence, the expression, "You should already know [my meaning] by now, how come you still don't get it?" That is why there is resulting *tampo* [delicate feeling of hurt] when one's *pahiwatig* is not understood by the other [as translated from the Filipino original].

Here, the starting logic, MC points out, lies in the concept of ***kita*** (no English equivalent, but roughly, "you" and "me" taken as one). In the Filipino equivalent of the statement "I love you," for example, that is, *Mahal kita,* there is no separation between the subject doing the loving and the object being the target of the action "love." MC says that once someone says *mahal kita* to someone, there are already compounded expectations based on the declaration of the two ("you" and "I") as one ("*kita*"). He gives the illustration, "If you say *mahal kita* and then go off somewhere to eat and fail to invite your wife who would have eagerly come along, the assumption is, 'I'm your wife, how come you just left without inviting me?'" (as translated from the Filipino original). So in marriage, MC opines, *pahiwatig* is a "verification of *kita*."

MC explains that the context of *kita* assumes an established relation between two parties: the greater the sense of identification, the greater the expectation that implicit expression is sufficient and understood. As in the case of high-context situations where much of the meaning is presumed already encoded in the context, a relationship defined by *kita* assumes a lot of pre-encoded shared meanings resulting from the dynamic of the relationship itself. MC cites an actual experience in the office where he works involving both White Americans and Filipino personnel:

> You, a director, gave a card inviting your staff to an office party you're hosting. But outside the formal invitation, you never mention it—that is, when you meet them in the corridor or bump into them in the cafeteria. When the time comes, you're surprised that only a few of your staff show up and you wonder, "I did invite everybody, didn't I? How come only a few came?" [as translated from Filipino original]

The boss in this case, says MC, was relying mainly on direct, formal, and explicit communication. His staff, mostly Filipinos, on the other hand, were wondering, "Does he really want us to come, or is it just an obligatory invitation? How come he never said anything about it outside the formal invitation?" MC interprets this particular staff-director relationship as having a low level of *kita,* and consequently, a low level of shared codes of meaning. Apparently, there is, in this case, a distinction between a formal invitation that may be interpreted merely as *pabalat bunga* (lit. "skin of a fruit," that is, surface, merely obligatory, not really sincere or from the heart) and, *"Huwag kang mawawala"* ("I'm counting on you to be there"). MC suspects that in an all-Filipino office setting, one doesn't even need cards (explicit, formal invitation). Cards are only used for "others" (i.e., those with whom one doesn't have any connection other than a formal, official relationship). Without the context of *kita*, a staff member may very well think, "Even if I don't go, *hindi naman ako ma-mimiss* [I won't be missed]."

Contrary then to the accommodative use of *pahiwatig* in the two previous contexts mentioned above (i.e., within the context of social maintenance and the context of unequal power relations), here the system is deemed to fail when employed outside the context of a close personal relationship or shared identification (i.e., the context of *kita*). In other words, within the intimate context of *kita*, it is presumed that *pahiwatig* is all that's needed to send (what should be a direct, clear-enough) message to the other. This is because of the assumption of a high level of shared meanings and expectations. On the other hand, when relating with *ibang tao* (stranger, outsider), the use of *pahiwatig* would only mean ambiguity, confusion, if not downright failure of communication. MC concludes, "There is no [making] *pahiwatig* to a stranger; it just doesn't work." Even if one were to attempt to use it in a spirit of accommodation, the other, more often than not, just doesn't get the meaning.

Indeed, it is this (outsider) context that often causes conflict or misunderstanding in the interactions between Filipino Americans (at least for those who still operate within the system) and most North Americans, who are used to more direct forms of communication. MC mentions in this regard that there exists in Filipino culture a finely graduated scale of levels of social relationships that are governed by strict rules of engagement, that is, from being regarded as a total stranger or *taga-labas* (outsider) to being welcomed as a *kapwa-tao* (a spiritual kin or fellow human being) (cf. Enriquez 1992). On the level of *hindi na iba* (no longer an "other"), MC mentions the interpersonal transaction of *pakikitungo* (building good relations) and *pagpapalagayang loob* (learning to feel at ease with each other's inner selves). Within this scale of relations, *kita* indicates the highest attainment of a level of oneness.

What happens, then, when two interactants operate from differing worlds of cultural and communicative assumptions? MC's experience is instructive in this regard. As part of his combined social advocacy orientation and Filipino socialization, MC doesn't measure time in a miserly way when he conducts his work in the office. Most of the time, he stays extra hours without additional compensation out of his own free will. Operating within the system of *pahiwatig*, he mistakenly assumes that his boss, a White American, will notice the hard work he puts in every day beyond the call of duty, so when he has an emergency call, the same consideration and magnanimity that he gives will be shown to him. Yet, when his family (who resides only part of the year in the United States and part of the year in the Philippines) visits and he happens to come in to work a little later than usual, he is immediately called on his lateness by the boss and asked to account for the amount of time lost and to schedule a makeup. Instead of a more confrontational approach, MC, as in the case of Joy, described above, decides to send out feelers of hurt and displeasure to his boss. He does this by not being as close, friendly, and enthusiastic toward the latter as usual. Unfortunately the boss, untrained to read such implicit signals, fails to catch his drift. However, the boss's secretary does notice and takes initiative in conveying to the boss her sense that MC seems to have some concerns. Happily, MC reports, as a result of the secretary's intervention, his boss now wants to understand Filipinos more and learn to practice greater cultural sensitivity toward them.

MC takes a slightly different approach toward the framing of the interview questions when he clarifies that a distinction should be made between *pahiwatig* on the one hand, and mere "ambiguity" on the other. He notes that *pahiwatig* has a definite goal, and that goal is to send a clear message through the use of a variety of communicative strategies (e.g., anything from temporary withdrawal, silence, or the breaking of an ongoing pattern of relating in order to communicate displeasure, to the use of facial and other nonverbal gestures and, on occasion, the use of third-person intermediaries). Ambiguity, on the other hand, typically connotes vagueness, the lack of any clearly defined goal. But perhaps one way of resolving the difference is by indicating that to one who shares the code, *pahiwatig* can be as clear as daylight, but to someone else who stands outside it, it is as inscrutable and undecipherable as a poker-faced expression. *Pahiwatig,* then, as a communicative practice, is ambiguous only to **cultural outsiders,** who, like it or not, are forced to rely on very explicit, low-context messages to guide them in their understanding.

Pahiwatig and the Communication of Ethnic Identity

A question asked of all the informants is to what extent this form of communication is expressive of their Filipino identity. From the responses, almost all indicated that they consider it part of the core of their Filipino-ness,[8] that is, it continues to serve as a defining characteristic of Filipinos who remain culture-bearers. One informant, however, qualifies that such indirect communication may not be the sole prerogative of Filipinos, given that other cultures (e.g., most Asian cultures) have likewise been noted to have their own equivalent practice of indirect communication. Nonetheless, when it comes to its particular forms, timing, and contexts of use, those interviewed believe that Filipinos have developed their own unique way of employing such an indirect pattern of communication for specific purposes.

Asked whether they've had to make adjustments in their communication patterns since coming to the United States, the study informants all invariably acknowledged having had to make some changes in their way of communicating, with the qualifier, "depending on the situation." One, for example, shares:

> I never presume. I spell out everything. For instance, if a classmate invites my 13-year-old son to sleep over in his house, I talk to the Mom. "What time would you like me to bring Casey over to your house?" Answer: 7:00 p.m. My next response is, "Okay, so I'll have Casey eat dinner first before I bring him over to your house." If the mother says, "No, I would like him to have dinner here," that tells me that the invitation included dinner. I never presume lest I have one hungry boy who goes to a sleep-over without being fed dinner.

Dingkoy, a woman married to a White American, responded to the same question in the following manner:

> Yes and no. Since my husband and I believe in "give and take," I have changed my pattern of communication and he has, too. I tend to be more direct in communicating, as my husband (who's Caucasian . . . White as White can be) always says that he "cannot read minds." I'm sure he said this because he's also well aware of our cultural differences and therefore tries everything he can to make things work. However, no matter how much I try, I still sometimes catch myself revert[ing] back to my "old self," using the *pahiwatig* form of communication, even if I don't mean to. I guess it's just that part of me being a Filipino. However, sometimes I catch him doing that (the *pahiwatig* form of communication) too, because before we got married, I gave him a book entitled, *Understanding the Filipino,* which talked about this. And believe me, he knows almost everything that's written there by heart. In fact, when I say "No, thank you" when being asked to eat, he would try to persuade me to say "yes" by asking me over and over. It had become a joke between us because sometimes I have to tell him, "It's an American NO, honey!" before he would stop bugging me about something.

There are, however, those who feel the burden of adjustment falling more heavily on their shoulders. Kristin, who is only in her second year in the United States and is working for a predominantly White corporation, has this to say about her own experience: "I have become more direct/up front, because I know that is what they want and that is what's best for me here. It takes away a lot of complications." Whether or not someone like Kristin will eventually find other ways of negotiating the cultural difference given more years of experience to negotiate a more reciprocal adjustment with her White employers is a matter of speculation at this point. It appears, though, that adjustment (either of the newcomer to the culture or the host culture to the former's culture) is a function of a number of factors. Such factors may include years of residence in the United States, personality characteristics (e.g., whether rigid or flexible), level of security and confidence, the strength of numbers relative to the other (e.g., whether there are more Filipinos relative to Whites), positioning in the power hierarchy, and, ultimately, overall communicative skill. MC's example (of being able to lead his White boss to take an interest in his culture without employing explicit means to confront him and even while at a disadvantage in terms of his positioning in the power hierarchy) proves that adjustment need not be one-way (i.e., the minority adjusting to the majority, the weaker to the more powerful) but may be complexly negotiated into a two-way process with both parties learning from one another and being stretched in their capacities to understand the other. Ability to navigate that process so that one is able to shift easily according to the demands of any given context is not easy and can take long years of practice. Sunny attests to this when she notes:

> My husband says that he notes a distinct (and possibly an unconscious) change in my language when I'm talking with other Filipinos, as opposed to when I'm with Westerners. I'm more straightforward and frank in my speech when I'm with Westerners, whereas I tend to be less direct and more "circuitous" in my statements when I'm speaking with other Filipinos (as evidenced, for example, by my use of Taglish [Tagalog-English] and Filipino pronunciation of English words). However, there are also varying but subtle degrees of change even in my dealings with other Filipinos, depending on my familiarity with them, the age difference between us, whether I'm among all-girl friends or not, whether there are persons of authority or higher status present, etc.

Sunny has also been in the United States for about ten years now and has traveled extensively, with years of living abroad in places as divergent as Mexico and China.

With regard to whether they feel "less Filipino" when adopting more direct forms of communication, a unanimous reply is "No, it's just part of what I have to do." In Joy's own words:

> Yeah, I think it [communicating by *pahiwatig*] is very much a part of me—a trait ingrained in my being. But I don't feel any less Filipino when I have to adjust my way of expressing myself in a more direct manner to convey the meaning of things. To me it's just an effective communication strategy—no more than that!

Others expressed a similar view: "Adjustment is just a matter of being ready and open to mingle with different kinds of people: that—I don't have problems with" (Ellen, analyst programmer); "No, I just think I am sensitive enough to know that people all over the world are different. We have different values, different cultures and different ways of expressing ourselves" (Theresa, another Filipina married to a White American); and "I don't feel any less Filipino by the changes I've made in my way of communicating. Perhaps more than just a manifestation of cultural differences and values, the differences in the ways of communication may also be seen from the perspective of gender differences and the socialization process that goes with that" (Sunny).

It appears then that even while most of the informants see *pahiwatig* as a core Filipino value, it doesn't make them feel any less Filipino should they find themselves compelled to make changes in order to adjust or negotiate power at any given time within the demands of their particular contexts. A way to understand the seeming contradiction is by looking at the issue in terms of "strategic" adjustment. But that such "strategic" adjustment is not as simple as it seems is illustrated in Mae's response to the question (on whether adjusting her communication pattern makes her feel any less Filipino). She says, "No, *kaya lang* [but then] during my recent trips to the Philippines, *napapagsabihan ako lagi ng: 'O ikaw, Amerkana ka na talaga!'* ["I always get told: 'You there, you've already become an American!'"]. It is possible, then, that even while avowing Filipino identity, one may be ascribed a different identity based on cultural changes that others observe in one's communicative behavior.

Intercultural Implications

Delving into the intricacies of Filipino Americans' communicative patterns illustrates the complexities of what E. T. Hall (1973) dubbed "the silent language," that is, "the many ways people 'talk' to one another without the use of words" (Erich Fromm, in Hall, review on back cover). Despite the analysis offered here, however, it is necessary also to offer a word of caution. Cultural codes that remain unaltered in the process of interaction with another culture can be extremely frustrating in their seeming ambiguity and undecipherability to a cultural outsider. Often, the tendency is to judge such from an ethnocentric view, using one's own culturally biased lenses and ultimately ending up negatively evaluating the unfamiliar practice or behavior, thereby encouraging prejudice and ethnocentrism even more. However, there is still hope for cross-cultural understanding. By cultivating openness to knowing other ways of being and doing than our own, and by taking time to understand the deeper logic undergirding what seems to us culturally "strange" behavior, we may yet realize what Bateson (1993) envisions for multiculturalism, which is that we be given "access to a very wide range of experiences" (p. 119), thereby expanding our canon of what is deemed "human" and redeeming.

Notes

1. Fanon (1963) notes that under colonization, the self is always being constituted as "other" and therefore colonized peoples are constantly kept from becoming/being themselves.

2. Used in the singular when employed within the context of speaking with others but plural when speaking with fellow Filipino cultural insiders. It must be noted that the Philippines itself is a multicultural society, comprised of an estimated eighty ethnolinguistic communities with their own distinctive cultures and traditions. Ethnic differences notwithstanding, however, a shared culture that includes a common pattern of communication seems evident—a function either of inherent closeness or similarity of cultural characteristics or a result of centuries of shared history and interethnic interaction.

3. The classic SIR syndrome is prominent in colonial writings on Filipino social traits and characteristics. This reading has since been rejected as distorted for mistakenly locating the logic of explanation on the mere surface characteristics of the culture instead of its deep structure.

4. For a contrastive view of the notion of "face" as it relates to the performance of "self," "personhood," and "identity" in social interactions, see Brown and Levinson 1978; Goffman 1967; Ting-Toomey 1985, 1988; and Ting-Toomey, Gao, Trubisky, Yang, Kim and Nishida 1991.

5. Cf. Enriquez's (1992) discussion on "The Confrontative Filipino" in his volume, *From Colonial to Liberation Psychology*, pp. 69–77.

6. An Ethiopian proverb provides an excellent example of this: "When the great lord passes, the wise peasant bows and silently farts."

7. Read by colonial scholars as nothing more than "fatalism," indigenization scholars instead translate it as "determination in the face of uncertainty" (Enriquez 1992 pp. 75, 77).

8. Only one remarked that she's not sure if it is indeed part of being Filipino, but then she went on to say, "but it certainly is part of my personality and character" (Sunny).

References

Alegre, E. 1993. *Pinoy forever: Essays on culture and language.* Pasig, Metro Manila: Anvil.

Alejo, A. 1990. *Tao po! Tuloy! Isang landas ng pag-unawa sa loob ng tao.* Quezon City: Office of Research and Publications, Ateneo de Manila University.

Bateson, M. C. 1993. Joint performance across cultures: Improvisation in a Persian garden. *Text and Performance Quarterly* 13: 113–21.

Brown, P., and S. Levinson. 1978. Universals in language usage: Politeness phenomena. In E. Goody (Ed.), *Questions and politeness: Strategies in social interaction* (pp. 56–310). Cambridge: Cambridge University Press.

Bulatao, J. 1992. *Phenomena and their interpretation: Landmark essays 1957–1989.* Manila: Ateneo de Manila University Press.

Bulosan, C. 1946. *America is in the heart: A personal history.* New York: Harcourt, Brace and Co.

Calderon, S. G. 1957. *Talasalitaan ng Inang Wika.* Manila: Inang Wika Publication.

Cordova, F. 1983. *Filipinos: Forgotten Asian Americans.* Seattle: Demonstration Project for Asian Americans.

De Castro, S. 1994. Identity in action: A Filipino American's perspective. In K. Aguilar-San Juan (Ed.), *The state of Asian America* (pp. 295–320). Boston, Mass.: South End Press.

Enriquez, V. G. 1979. Pagkataong Pilipino: Kahulugan at pananaliksik [Filipino personality/person-hood: Significance and research.] *Sangguni* 2 (1): 112–21.

———. 1992. *From colonial to liberation psychology: The Philippine experience.* Dilliman, Quezon City: University of the Philippines Press.

Fanon, F. 1963. *The wretched of the earth.* New York: Grove Press, Inc.

Geertz, C. 1973. *The interpretation of cultures.* New York: Basic Books, Inc.

Goffman, E. 1967. *Interaction ritual: Essays on face-to-face behavior.* Garden City, N.Y.: Anchor Books.

Hall, E. T. 1973. *The silent language.* New York: Doubleday.

Maggay, M. P. 1993. *Pagbabalik-loob: A second look at the moral recovery program.* Quezon City: Akademya ng Kultura at Sikolohiyang Pilipino.

———. 1999. *Understanding ambiguity in Filipino communication patterns.* Quezon City: Institute for Studies in Asian Church and Culture.

Odulio de Guzman, M. 1968. *The new Filipino-English, English-Filipino dictionary.* Manila, Philippines: National Book Store.

Panganiban, J. V. 1972. *Comparative semantics of synonyms and homonyms in Philippine languages, involving basic words that have to do with the physical world and its larger aspects in Pilipino, Tagalog, Bikol, Kapampangan, Hiligaynon, Ibanag, Ilokano, Ivatan, Maranaw, Magindanaw, Pangasinan, Sibuhanon, Samar-Leyte, Tau Sug and Indonesia, Melayu.* San Juan, Pilipinas: Limbagang Pilipino.

Resource Development and Publications, UCLA Asian American Studies Center. 1976. *Letters in Exile: An introductory reader on the history of Filipinos in America.* Los Angeles: The Regents of the University of California.

Scott, J. C. 1990. *Domination and the arts of resistance: Hidden transcripts.* New Haven: Yale University Press.

Ting-Toomey, S. 1985. Toward a theory of conflict and culture. In W. Gudykunst, L. Stewart, and S. Ting-Toomey (Eds.), *Communication, culture, and organizational processes* (pp. 71–85). Beverly Hills, Calif.: Sage.

———. 1988. Intercultural conflict styles: A face-negotiation theory. In Y. Y. Kim and W. B. Gudykunst (Eds.), *Theories in intercultural communication* (pp. 213–38). Newbury Park, Calif.: Sage.

Ting-Toomey, S., G. Gao, P. Trubisky, Z. Yang, H. S. Kim, S. Lin, and T. Nishida. 1991. Culture, face maintenance, and styles of handling interpersonal conflict: A study in five cultures. *International Journal of Conflict Management* 2: 275–96.

KEY TERMS	
ambiguity	*kapwa*
confrontative	*kita*
cultural insider	*pahiwatig*
cultural outsider	*pakiramdaman*
Filipino	social maintenance
Filipino Americans	

REVIEW AND DISCUSSION QUESTIONS

1. Have you ever encountered the form of indirect communication discussed in the chapter? If so, how did you respond to it? Describe your thoughts, feelings, and reactions toward it, if any.

2. What did you learn about the differing assumptions behind the two patterns of communication being contrasted here, *direct* versus *indirect?* Although set up as comprising two different systems of communication here, do you find any parallelisms or equivalent concept (of *pahiwatig*) in your own cultural background in the situations being described?

3. Distinguish between and among the differing sets of values mentioned here (i.e., core/survival, accommodative/confrontative). How useful are these distinctions in terms of helping us gain a more adequate understanding of other cultures?

4. Differentiate between the *intentional* ambiguity in *pahiwatig* versus ambiguity as often understood. How does the outsider/insider distinction help nuance our understanding of ambiguity as we're likely to encounter it in most intercultural encounters?

5. Revisit the saying, "When in Rome, do as the Romans do." Do the adjustment experiences of the study participants offer you other ways of thinking about cultural adjustment in intercultural situations? In what way can this insight encourage greater mutual transformation for both newcomer and member of host community?

6. Related to the foregoing question, think for a moment about the implications of a one-way adjustment in the intercultural process (e.g., from minority to the majority; the weaker to the more powerful; newcomer expected to adjust to the culture of the host community, etc.). What potential consequences might there be for the person(s) in the disadvantaged position (i.e., those expected to assimilate to the cultural norms of the privileged party) in terms of their sense of self and the value/worth of their ethnic culture and identity?

Cultural and Intercultural Speech Uses and Meanings of the Term *Nigga*

Mary Fong and Keturah D. McEwen

LEARNING OBJECTIVES

After reading this chapter, students will be able to:

- explain why some African Americans choose to use or not use the term nigga in their communication interactions within their cultural group;
- understand the various contextual uses and meanings of the use of nigga; and
- recognize possible consequences and meanings when non-Blacks use nigga in intercultural interactions with African Americans.

Basically what I gather is that we as a people have taken the negative word and used it as a positive when we relate to one another. So when other people . . . who aren't Black refer to us as niggas, then it's looked at as very, very serious.

—Participant F

Two African American men greet one another with a soul shake and naturally and acceptingly say to one another, "What's up nigga?" To an outsider of the African American culture, this use of the term would likely seem quite puzzling. When the term is used by Whites and other non-Blacks, historically it has been used in a negative sense, as a racial epithet, and has been pronounced nigger, not nigga (Smitherman 1994). Then why do some African Americans use this term as a greeting and in conversation? This study explores this inquiry and some of the vernacular uses and meanings of the term nigga in everyday talk among African Americans who choose to use this word. Depending on who is using such slang, nigga (NA) and nigger (NR)[1] are potentially loaded and sensitive terms. These terms are examined here to understand how powerfully charged words unite or separate people through meaningful identification or nonidentification. Watts (2000) expressed, "We must convert the terror and anger we experience when confronted with the 'N-word' into a passion for confronting and comforting its speaker" (p. 175). Typically, the "N-words" elicit fear, confusion, and avoidance on the part of people who do not understand the use of them. Rather than avoiding these potentially highly charged terms, nigga and nigger, this study examines the African American point of view that provides an insider's understanding of these slangs. Much of people's ignorance and conscious and unconscious prejudices about various cultural groups are simply based on little knowledge of and social interaction with others.

Cultural and Ethnic Identity

Collier and Thomas (1988) define **cultural identity** as "identification with and perceived acceptance into a group that has shared systems of symbols and meanings as well as norms/rules for conduct" (p. 113). They posit further that cultural identity is dynamic and created in communication and symbolic interaction. Moreover, they argue that a person has **multiple identities,** and one of the identities will tend to be most salient in a given situation.

In acceptance of Thomas and Collier's position of multiple identities, we argue that multiple identities exist among members who identify themselves as belonging to the same particular cultural or ethnic group. Romaine (1982) has observed that sociolinguistic studies (Irvine 1978; Romaine 1978) "reveal that a number of linguistic changes seem to be accomplished by competing pressures from two social groups in the speech community which *do not use* the language in the *same* way" (p. 22). In any given cultural or ethnic group, members may vary in the degrees of their intensity of identification with the group's use of symbols, signs, and meanings. That is, members who identify with the same ethnic/cultural group may generally share a similar system of symbols, signs, and meanings but may differ at times in the meanings and use of particular symbols, signs, or other communication conduct. Cultural identity elicits different meanings and experiences for people (Mercer 1990; Woodward 1997). Some members will identify with particular communicative cultural practices, while other members may choose not to partake and identify themselves as enacting the same expressions, rituals, and so forth because of differing preferences, values, attitudes, beliefs, and so on.

The cultural term *nigga* is one such symbol that is used and not used, shared and not shared, preferred and not preferred by people who identify themselves as African Americans or Blacks. Three main areas are discussed here: cultural meanings and contextual uses of African Americans who choose to use the term *nigga*, cultural meanings and contextual uses of African Americans who choose not to use the slang, and the intercultural contextual uses and meanings of the term when used by non-Blacks.

Participants

Twelve participants who identified themselves as African American or Black (seven women and five men), ranging from twenty to twenty-six years old, were interviewed. Five of the participants were undergraduate students; three participants had some college education; and four participants have received bachelor's degrees. All of the participants have lived most of their lives in the Southern California area, from South Central Los Angeles (a predominately Black community) to Fontana (a mixed Caucasian, African American, and Latino community). Participants range from lower to middle socioeconomic classes.

An additional ten African American college students (five males, five females), ranging in ages from nineteen to twenty-nine, were asked to read the findings of an initial paper and to answer a questionnaire regarding the accuracy of them. This helped refine and validate initial findings. Thus, a total of twenty-two participants were involved in this study.

Cultural Meanings and Uses of *Nigga*

African Americans who use the term **nigga** in exchanging greetings with cultural members are participating in a shared ritual. Philipsen (1987) defines **ritual** as "a structured sequence of actions the correct performance of which pays homage to a sacred object" (p. 250). The structured sequence of actions is a brief exchange of greeting one another that pays homage to the ideal of both acknowledging and culturally identifying one another as belonging to the same group.

The term *nigga* is particularly used among African American men. In the greeting, mentioned above, between two African American males, the shared meaning of "What's up nigga?" is explained by participant A: "'Hello nigga'—you say it basically to your friends. It has to be to Black friends. The situation is hello . . . 'Hi, how are you doing?'" Participant C also reported, "I have only known a Black guy to come up to another Black guy like, 'What's up nigga,' like, 'What's up partner,' or 'What's up homeboy'; that means we're cool." Similarly, participants explained that the slang terms *homeboy* and *homegirl* are conversationally used to refer to a friend or significant other within the appropriate context.

The term *nigga* is normatively used among Black friends, rather than with Black and non-Black strangers. Participant D said, "Everybody has their own [terms] in every race, something that they are allowed to call each other and not be disrespected. It's not that you can call every Black person that because I wouldn't go up to a Black person I don't know and say, 'what's up nigga.' It's a personal level that you only can call somebody nigga." Participant B also said, "That's the difference with *nigga* as opposed to *nigger* that I think in the in-group, they say **nigger** as degrading, but the *nigga* is more used as only amongst themselves."

The term also signifies close friendship, cultural awareness, or fearlessness (Smitherman 1994). Participant C said, "*Nigga* means like a close friend. You know, someone that you're cool with. Or I mean to say positively, 'oh that's my *nigga*'— meaning that's my real cool close friend, or he's cool, she's cool." The use of the slang *nigga* is the language of the cool (Varner and Kugiya 1998). Participant D said, "It's used as a term of friendship. I guess only a real friend can call somebody a nigga without somebody getting mad . . . 'What's up nigga?

How are ya doing today?'" *Nigga* refers to a Black friend or significant other, depending on various relationships.

Participants reported that African Americans from all walks of life use the term *nigga,* and it is used in a variety of ways. However, all the participants said they have observed most commonly Black males using the term. The "N-word is used in private in-house dialogues between the 'fellas'" (Watts 2000). For example, Participant A said, "Normally it is guys-to- guys, but I have heard some girls who have said it. 'Oh that is my nigga over there.' She could mean her boyfriend or her friend, or it could be towards another female, like a good friend." Participants reported that they emphasized the use of the pronoun "my" in express-ing "*my* nigga" to indicate that there is a closeness between them. "She *my* main nigga," means that she is my close friend, my backup (Smitherman 1994).

Some of the participants made a point that the level of formal education does not determine whether or not an African American person will choose to use the slang. Participant G said,

> People in my family still use it. . . . Like my aunt has a master's degree—she teaches and everything. I think it's more for the males. There are a few girls like the tomboys; they might use it a lot. . . . My uncles, none of them really have middle class jobs. They don't even use it, and that's why it was weird to me how my aunt the one who was edu-cated and has a master's degree [uses it].

The derogatory label, *nigger,* historically has been used to socially degrade and dehu-manize African Americans for over four hundred years since the beginning of slavery in America. Participant D said, "*Nigger* is offensive. *Nigger* is the White man's word to disgrace us; White males brought up that word to talk about us, so that's why they refer to us as nig-gers. *Nigger* is a bad word to me." Watts (2000) stated, "being called a nigger means being subjected to White supremacist hatred and violence. . . . Nigger has only one meaning—it means worthlessness" (p. 173).

Participants also explained that most Blacks may interpret the use of the term *nigger* in an offensive way if said in a negative manner, or it can be seen as not offensive if said in a neutral to positive manner. For example, Participant F elaborated on possible negative use of the slang.

> Normally that's when people use it as an attack like, "*You* nigger." You never direct it like that when you're talking amongst family and friends. Like when I said, "nigger please, like get out of here." But, if you go, "*You* nigger," directing the word towards someone, that's when all hell breaks loose. You're just sitting here like, "What did you call me?" And that's when you defensively get up, and you get upset and you might start fighting. It depends on the way it's being used or like the tone in your voice. . . . [M]aybe two people are arguing, and if one person says something really out of line, the other person kind of raises his voice; and it's like "what nigga?"—you know like "what did you just say?" Then, it's about to get heated.

Watts (2000) expressed, "If nigga is the flip side of racist oppression, civil rights history is not erased, but kept intact as the underbelly" (p. 174). African American participants in our study who use the term *nigga* explain why they do. Participant F said,

Normally, I think it's used primarily as a term of endearment amongst Blacks when they speak to each other . . . a friend, a homey. . . . *Nigger* (even though *nigga* was derived from *nigger*) was given by Whites to indicate that we're inferior and punish us and degrade us. When Blacks use the word *nigga*, none of that is in the meaning. That's not what we mean by it.

All African American participants explained the strategy used in their communication and meaning of the slang *nigga* used among themselves. Ting-Toomey (1993) posits that one's identity is enacted and negotiated through the process of communication. She further writes, "Effective identity negotiation refers to the smooth coordination between interactants concerning salient identity issues, and the process of engaging in responsive identity conformation and positive identity enhancement" (p. 73).

Participant G said, "To me, I think a lot of them [African Americans] look at it like we changed something negative into something that is cool for us. . . . Because we are Black we can do that, but they [non-Black] can't." Moreover, participant C also agrees, "I guess Black people just do it for conversation or beginning of a conversation. We're cool. We can call each other that.'" Participant F formulated similar thoughts:

Basically what I gather is that we as a people have taken the negative word and used it as a positive when we relate to one another, so when other people outside of those who aren't Black refer to us as niggas, then it's looked at as very, very serious.

Participant B concurred:

I'm sure it's not uncommon. They [Blacks] are just turning something that is thrown at them commonly and making it acceptable. . . . You take derogatory words and use it in the in-group and joke around. Calling them that name changes the meaning. The word changes meaning. It doesn't carry the meaning like before. It's more like joking around.

African Americans who choose to use the term see it as a way to empower themselves by using and interpreting the slang in a positive manner, rather than in a negative sense, and that their own people are reclaiming and redefining the term. "The use of 'nigga(h)' among African Americans . . . also helps illustrate the idea of cultural ownership. Some argue that among African Americans, the term reflects the positivity and unity of in-group relations" (Brown 1993, p. 138). There are different contextual uses of the term *nigga*. Participant F explained,

If I'm referring to someone who's close to me, I'd say "that's my nigga," which means "he's a close friend of mine." If I'm just narrating a story or maybe if I'm just repeating what happened with someone else, I may [say], "what this nigga did," which isn't necessarily a bad thing. It's just making a reference to another person. [Another example is] "I just [saw] these two guys get into a fight, and this one nigga just hauled off and . . ."

Contextual use of the slang can also be found in the example, "That party was live; it was wall-to-wall niggas there." This usage carries a generic, neutral use of the term, meaning that many African Americans were present at the party (Smitherman 1994).

Participants explain the tone of the voice when saying *nigga* in conversational expressions. Participant H said, "It just means, 'hey what's up' towards another Black person. It's not in a vulgar way. 'Yo nigga', and it was like 'yeah that Black dude' or 'she was like way too crazy nigga.'" Participant F said, "Niggas do this, niggas do that. It's like a soft spoken or soft tone behind it. But, then it's like he or she, a stupid nigger, then it's just like total emphasis on the negative behind it."

In other situations, some African American participants use the term *nigga* in in-group interactions without being perceived as offensive. Participant I explains,

> Some people have called me *a niggerette;* that's the female version of nigger. Normally, it's a playful word. We play around with it. Like when you're joking you go, "nigger please.". . . Normally, I use it when it's in a playful matter. But it's still like a love towards your own people.

Participant H explains that the term can be used for "affection; it can be used for comedy release; it can be used when you're mad. It can be used in the Black culture, and it's appropriate." Brown (1993) spoke of his experience with the slang, "I have heard the word 'nigga(h)' all of my life. Many of my elders and friends use it with phenomenal eloquence. They say it to express amusement, incredulity, disgust, or affection. These people are very much being themselves—proudly, intensely, sometimes loudly (p. 138).

Specialized vocabulary of cultural groups, **argot,** serves the functions of maintaining group identity and keeping outsiders on the peripheral boundaries as nonmembers (Maurer 1981). Participants explained that *nigga* serves to maintain group identity by its use only among Black friends. Participant M stated, "It is used to somewhat rebuild the African American culture, and it distinguishes our culture from the European culture." Moreover, *nigga* is a statement and establishment of brotherhood among Black males and, for some Black females, of sisterhood. Participant H said, "You use *nigga* for bonding purposes, to have group affiliation, create some camaraderie."

In some cases, Black women use the slang term to express dissatisfaction with Black men in their relationships. For example, Participant I said, "When African American women talk negatively towards African American men, the 'N' word may be used." Moreover, Participant G explained, "He's [brother] the only male in the family, mostly female, and they talk something, when you want to put down Black men, they usually [say], 'That no good nigga, he just trapeze that old lady'. . . . 'That nigga did this and that,' that's when they use [it] a lot."

Participants emphasized that there are times in which any version of the "N" word is not used because it is inappropriate. For example, all participants reported that it would be inappropriate to call any mothers the "N" word in order to avoid showing disrespect. Also, in intercultural interactions, the use of any renditions of the "N" word is typically perceived unfavorably to African Americans.

Opposition to the Term *Nigga*

There are some African Americans who oppose the use of the slang *nigga* and find it offensive even when it is used by their in-group members. Six of the twenty-two African American participants expressed their discomfort with the term. Participant M said, "I believe that the term *nigga* is very oppressive. It should not be used to refer to the African Americans. Our ancestors have worked too hard." Two of the participants at an earlier age used the slang in their everyday talk with their fellow members but no longer choose to use the term. Participant O stated,

> The term refers to a possession. . . . And it is degrading. I am trying to stop using the word. I have chosen not to use it because I have researched the term and its use in other languages and they are all negative. . . . How can you take the word *ass* and turn it into a positive word? It still means stupid, dumb.

Participant N also used the slang quite often in the past—with her young peers in the military. She reported that she no longer uses the slang. She said, "I do think there is some connection between education and not using it. . . . Why must we call ourselves a degrading name?" Participant R reported, "I oppose the use of both words; they are too close to distinguish one from the other. Regardless of the context in which it is used, the negative connotation remains." Participant J sees no difference between the terms *nigga* and *nigger*. She said, "It's too close. It's the same word to me. I don't like to use it or to be called it because of the history. It's an insult. I feel hostile or enraged with it. I don't like that word. My little cousin, Cameron, heard that word from a video, and I'm trying to teach him, you don't use that word; that's a bad word." Participant G reported arguments with her aunt regarding the use of the slang. She stated her aunt consistently says, "Look at that little nigga out there playing" and "Oh look at that little nigga." Participant G responded to her aunt by saying:

> "That little boy is not a little nigga. He's a little boy, a little Black boy, a little African American boy. Take your pick. Just not nigga, nigger, or negro or colored," and it was like, "Oh, look at little Miss college student," and "Oh, look at little Miss socio-major, here," or "Quit being so stuck up. It's no big deal, we're all family." I said, "it's not a fact of being stuck up, but to me that's not a positive term no matter who's using it—White, Black, green, orange. It's not positive. It has nothing to do with going to college. I don't think that it is positive."

Participant J agreed, and said, "The only time I've heard it used appropriately is when you're putting down someone, when you want to spark a fire. That's when it's used appropriately, and I hear people use it inappropriately like greeting each other. The history of that word, it shouldn't be used as greeting anyone at all . . . they're ignorant, and they have no respect for themselves. If they just sat down and thought about the way that word is being used, you would never want to be called that again."

Two participants reported that although they understand the meaning and practice of the argot term *nigga,* they voiced their preference to use it sparingly and to use other alternative terms. Participant H said, "It's almost like a positive term we can use towards other Black people in our conversation with each other. There's some Black people who will say, 'oh no, don't say that; that's a bad word, don't say that.' But normally, it's just a way for everyone in the African American culture to use it and it's not even a problem." For example, instead of saying "What's up nigga?" participant G says she uses, "Hey girl, what's up?" Another alternative greeting to "What's up nigga?" is reported by participant I. She said,

Well, I've seen Black guys do it when they approach each other, they say, "what's up Black," instead of saying, "yo, what's up nigga,"— that's more like a street term, but when you're more educated, I think it's, "what's up Black?" . . . it's way more positive.

Participant O agrees with Participant I in that he is trying to eliminate the use of the slang by substituting the term *Black*. Although two African American participants objected to all uses of the term *nigga*, all the participants expressed their objection to non-Blacks using the slang in a greeting or in any conversation with Blacks. However, some African Americans stated that interculturally there are exceptions to this rule for particular non-Blacks.

Intercultural Meanings and Uses of *Nigga*

When a non-Black person uses the term *nigga* in an **intercultural interaction,** our data suggest, most African Americans perceive this unfavorably. Twenty of the twenty-two participants reported that if non-Black persons used the term *nigga* in a greeting or conversation, non-Blacks would be perceived unfavorably. Both terms, *nigga* and *nigger,* carry negative meanings when interculturally used by non-Black **out-group** people. An **in-group** non-Black member's use of the slang term is only considered acceptable by some in-group Blacks in certain instances and is often dependent on the relationship of the intercultural interactants. In most intercultural instances, both terms create friction or conflict when used by an out-group person. "Other African Americans argue that any form of the word, given its negative history should not be used. Regardless of where individuals fall within the debate of in-group use, clearly it represents a word extremely offensive when used by non-African Americans" (Brown 1993, p. 138). Participant I reported,

Well, it's a frightful word, and when it's used, it's not nice; and I think it's only used to put you in your place, to degrade you. Because people know that throughout history, Black people have always been [treated as] inferior to White people. So when the word is used, it's like they are setting you back in your place like, "Oh, you're nothing but a nigger. So shut up, and whatever I say, I can do." But it's not like that today. If you use the word, it's like you're going to get hurt, if you use it in the wrong way.

Participant A also explained that when someone else [White] who is outside of the in-group circle says,

"What's up nigga?" then tempers will flare and things of that nature. Unless it was a White boy that you knew. Even though you know him and he's cool to you and everything, you still don't expect him to say that. That's exclusively for Black people.

Participants have reported that they have observed a non-Black person using the term *nigga* to try to gain entry and acceptance in a social circle of African American friends. Participants reported that *wigger* is a term for Whites who "act Black," and Watts (2000) also mentioned that this slang refers to "White niggers." Participant G said,

When we were in high school, this boy was White and he wanted to act Black. He took it to the extreme. He wore pants sagged to his knees and he tried his hardest. And then one day, he came in and [said to me],

> "What's up nigga?"
> I was like, "what did you say?"
> "I'm sorry homegirl, you know, I was . . ."
> "I don't know what you're saying. Can you talk a little clearer for me?"
> "Why you know the homeys."
> "Your homeys let you call on that?"
> "You know that's all good. It's cool with them."
> "Then go on with your bad self."

Turner (1980) would describe this interactional episode as a social drama that is a "spontaneous unit of social process and a fact of everyone's experience in every human society" (p. 149). Turner (1980) has observed **social dramas** that can be studied as having four phases: breach, crisis, redress, and either reintegration or recognition of schism.

A **breach** is an infraction of a norm or a rule of morality, law, custom, or etiquette in a public arena. According to Turner's model, in the above episode, the non-Black interactant makes a breach by saying, "What's up nigga?" to the Black interactant. This breach is evident when participant G questions the White outsider's use of the term *nigga* by asking, "what did you say?" The White outsider perceptually noticed that participant G was questioning his use of *nigga* in his greeting as a **rule violation** of speaking or a breach.

The **crisis** stage of this social drama immediately begins with participant G interrogating the White outsider. The crisis phase is a "momentous juncture or turning point" in the relations between interactants where "overt conflict and covert antagonisms become visible" (Turner 1980, p.150). She continues to press the White outsider by making a direct statement, "I don't know what you're saying." The crisis continues with participant G making the point to the White outsider that his greeting is inappropriate by firmly interrogating him two more times with disapproving questions like "Can you talk a little clearer for me?" and "Your homeys let you call on that?"

Early in the crisis stage, the **redressive** stage begins and both of these phases virtually overlap one another. The redressive phase involves making amends, to set right, to adjust, to repair, to remedy. The redressive stage is initiated by the White outsider who tries to make amends by apologizing, "I'm sorry homegirl, you know, I was. . . ." The White outsider continues to respond to the interrogation by trying to repair the breach by explaining how other Blacks find his use of the slang to be acceptable by stating, "Why, you know the homeys" and "You know that's all good. It's cool with them."

The final stage is the **reintegration** or **recognition of schism.** In this intercultural social drama, it involves the "social recognition of irreparable breach between the contesting parties, sometimes leading to their spatial separation" (Turner 1980, p. 151). Participant G signals the White outsider to "go on with your bad self," essentially waving him off.

Twenty of the twenty-two participants stated that they would feel displeased if a non-Black person used the term *nigga* in a conversational manner. For instance, Participant E said, "I think I would be upset. I think I would be a little disturbed with that because he doesn't know what it means, where it came from. Here you take a White guy using the term *nigga* and you want to go back to slavery." This participant said it would be appropriate for a Black person to use the term toward another Black person, but it is inappropriate for a non-Black to use it in interaction with a Black person.

A non-Black out-group interactant seeking acceptance within an African American social group might use the slang to gain entry. Participant I explained that a non-Black out-group interactant will find it difficult to gain social acceptance by using the term within an African American group because,

> [Outsiders] don't truly understand the word. It's just because you can't relate. If you grew up with Black people, understanding their ways—our hardships, our culture, understanding almost being Black, not even a want to be, it's like you are Black conscious; you can use the term, and we know if you were raised with Black people. We will know. But if you're not Black, not Black conscious at all, we can detect it and that's when you can get hurt, by just throwing that term around.

Participants explained the various ways they would handle a non-Black person's violation of the rule of the use of the term *nigga*. Participant C explained that if a non-Black outsider uses the slang to gain entry to a group, and if the in-group Black members perceive the non-Black outsider's behavior to be not acceptable, it should be handled in a mature way, rather than with hostility. She explained,

> I think that if the person was really cool from the ghetto, I think that a Black person would maybe call him to the side and express to him that, from a White person, you don't want to use *nigga*. But if [both people] were immature, he will get knocked out or pushed around. But I know the mature thing would be maybe just call him on it.

Participant H suggests another response to an out-group non-Black person's use of the term. She said,

> It's according to how certain people in the group . . . make a quick personal judgment like "yeah, he's cool" or they may say like "what are you talking about? Do you understand what you're saying?" It could be according to the situation; they may just ignore it and just accept the person—it's a quick judgment call.

Participant F described a current situation involving a non-Black friend who socialized in the same circle of Black friends. She further said,

> Actually some of my weight lifting buddies, one is Black and the other is Mexican. We hang out and we talk a lot of shit. I've noticed that the Mexican, he's a little youngster. I think he's like 20. The Mexican seems to have gotten so comfortable with how we talk and how we interact that now he's starting to say the word *nigga* just in stories making references to us because he's kind of become part of the little group. We don't really trip . . . he's kind of one of the boys, he means it the same way we mean it. It is a little weird hearing someone non-Black say it. But if you get used to it, I don't think it's that big of a deal. I think it's how people use it. For example, one of my

friends is running late. He'd be like "where is that nigga Brad?" or "that nigga was late last week too. He late again today." I've noticed that a little more. Not a whole lot more, just over time.

All the participants agreed that there are exceptions to the rule for some non-Blacks who can use the term without experiencing difficult confrontations. For example, Participant I said, "Only if you were raised with Black people, that's an exception. Other than that you can't use the term." Participant D said,

> It makes me feel uncomfortable [if a non-Black person uses the term *nigga*]. Unless I know that person and see where they've come from and see how their background is . . . see how they were raised around Black people and how they talk and they can't help it. But if it's a person that's just for the time being want to be down and want to use that word just because they're around people, I don't think that's right.

All participants reported that the non-Black who chooses to conversationally use the term must be considered a part of the in-group and have at least a relational level of being fairly good friends. Thus, if a non-Black is defined as "'in' the community, the use of nigga can even transgress racial lines" (Watts 2000, p. 174).

To this effect, Participant F said, "If somebody non-Black is gonna say it, it can spark some tension, so the fact that he's into the same thing we're into, listens to hip-hop like we do, listens to R & B like we do, he's around us a lot. It's still kind of a little weird. Because he's part of us and because you know he has those interests and because he fits all those things . . . we just laugh with him."

Only two of the twenty-two participants reported that they do not feel any discomfort when a non-Black person uses the term *nigga* in a conversational way toward them. Participant V said, "I have friends who are White or biracial who use *nigga* around me. It doesn't bother me at all because we don't mean any harm by using it." Participant U also is very accepting of non-Blacks using the slang. He explained,

> *Nigga* is not for all Blacks or restricted from non-Blacks. It is an identity, but not by color. . . . *Nigga* is a personality. Anyone from any race can have a *nigga* personality. Niggas know who niggas are just like gays know other gays, and so forth. My opinion is that *nigga* is: street smart, rebellious, capable of making something out of nothing, able to keep composure in all situations, true to themselves and others, strong-willed, and wild-hearted. Not all Black males are this. Therefore, they aren't *niggas*. But my Arabian friends and my Mexican, White homeys are *niggas*. I feel that Blacks misuse this term [in knowing] what a real nigga is. I don't feel that *nigga* is a term to unite against the White man because those who are Black and not a real *nigga* demean the true strength and identity (personality) behind the word.

Some participants reported that they have observed occasionally that non-Blacks use the slang among their diverse group of friends because they are accepted into the group. Both participants' use of this slang suggests that this term has begun to evolve and take on additional meaning and usage. For the two Black participants, they see the use of *nigga* among friends as representing and identifying with a particular persona. On the contrary, twenty of the twenty-two participants made reference to its use based on race. Romaine (1982) observes the variation within a speech community and states, "these sorts of competing changes represent cases in which norms of speaking associated with different groups in the same community are crucial in providing an account of differentiation and change in the system" (pp. 22). Further research is necessary to understand this transformation of meaning and this display of degrees of differentiation within a speech community.

Conclusion: Intercultural Implications

The use of the term *nigga* is a powerful vernacular word that is used by Black people who choose to use the term in its various contexts to enhance cohesive in-group identity and Black consciousness. Alternatively, the term *nigger* when used among Black members is also potent, but in a negative sense, in that typically it is used when a Black member is angry toward another. This study also found that there are some African American members who oppose the use of the slang because of its historically negative connotation and implications. Further, the majority of the African American participants reported that when the term *nigga* was used interculturally by a non-Black, it created an unfavorable impression and a rule violation had occurred. Two of the participants were open to non-Blacks using the slang interculturally and perceived the use and meaning of the term in a positive manner.

This study also found that people who identify themselves as African American or Black will differ at times in their contextual uses and meanings of the term *nigga*. Hall (1990) clearly sums up the differing and dynamic cultural practices and meanings of a term used by members who identify themselves in the same ethnic or cultural group:

> Cultural identities . . . have histories. But, like everything that is historical, they undergo constant transformation. Far from being eternally fixed in some essentialized past, they are subject to the continuous "play" of history, culture, and power . . . identities are the names we give to the different ways we are positioned by, and position ourselves within, the narratives of the past. (p. 225)

As qualitative researchers, we shall continue to bring forth the untold narratives of the past and the evolving narratives of the future. Through this we hope to facilitate in the conceptualization of dimensions of identity that are touched by history, culture, power, language, and people inside and outside the group in day-to-day social interactions.

Note

1. Since both *nigga* and *nigger* are sensitive terms, readers may have differing comfort levels in saying them during discussion. Therefore, readers may or may not prefer to say these terms but can make reference to them by abbreviation of "NA" and "NR," respectively.

References

Brown, J. C. 1993. In defense of the N word. *Essence* (June): 138.

Collier, M. J., and M. Thomas. 1988. Cultural identity: An interpretive perspective. In Y. Y. Kim and W. B. Gudykunst (Eds.), *Theories of intercultural communication* (pp. 99–120). Newbury Park, Calif.: Sage.

Hall, S. 1990. Cultural identity and diaspora. In J. Rutherford (Ed.), *Identity: Community, culture, difference* (pp. 17–46). London: Lawrence and Wishart.

Irvine, P., and J. Steiner. 1978. Women's verbal images and associations. *International Journal of the Sociology of Language* 17: 103–14.

Maurer, D. W. 1981. *Language of the underworld.* Lexington: University Press of Kentucky.

Mercer, K. 1990. Welcome to the jungle: Identity and diversity in postmodern politics. In J. Rutherford (Ed.), *Identity: Community, culture, difference* (pp. 43–71). London: Lawrence and Wishart.

Philipsen, G. 1987. The prospect for cultural communication. In D. L. Kincaid (Ed.), *Communication theory: Eastern and western perspectives* (p. 250). San Diego, Calif.: Academic Press.

Romaine, S. 1978. Postvocalic /r/ in Scottish English: Sound change in progress? In P. Trudgill (Ed.), *Sociolinguistic patterns in British English* (pp. 144–57). Baltimore: University Park Press.

———. 1982. What is a speech community? In Suzanne Romaine (Ed.), *Sociolinguistic variation in speech communities* (chap. 1, pp. 13–24). London: Arnold.

Smitherman, G. 1994. *Black talk: Words and phrases from the hood to amen corner.* Boston: Houghton Mifflin.

Ting-Toomey, S. 1993. Communicative resourcefulness: An identity negotiation perspective. In R. I. Wiseman and J. Koester (Eds.), *Intercultural communication competence* (pp. 72–111). Thousand Oaks, Calif.: Sage.

Turner, V. 1980. Social dramas and stories about them. *Critical Inquiry* 7 (1): 141–68.

Varner, L. K., and H. Kugiya. 1998. What's in a name?—a hated racial slur finds new currency—and controversy—in popular culture. *The Seattle Times,* July 6, E1.

Watts, E. K. 2000. Confessions of a thirty-something hip-hop (old) head. In A. Gonzalez, M. Houston, and V. Chen (Eds.), *Our voices* (3rd ed., pp.171–76). Los Angeles: Roxbury Publishing Co.

Woodward, K. 1997. Concepts of identity and difference. In K. Woodward (Ed.), *Identity and difference* (pp. 8–50). London: Sage.

KEY TERMS

argot	nigger
breach	out-group
crisis	recognition of schism
cultural identity	redressive
in-group	reintegration
intercultural interaction	ritual
multiple identities	rule violation
nigga	social drama

REVIEW AND DISCUSSION QUESTIONS

1. What are some examples of greetings among African Americans?
2. Who normatively can use the term *nigga* and what are the functions/purposes of using it?
3. What is the difference between the meanings of *nigga* (NA) and *nigger* (NR)?
4. Why do some African Americans oppose the use of *nigga?* Do you agree or disagree?
5. Explain at least three contextual uses of *nigga.*
6. When do African Americans use the term *nigger* toward one another?
7. Explain why African Americans have a negative response when *nigga* is used interculturally. What responsive strategies are used by African Americans who initially hear a non-Black using the term?
8. Explain the "exception to the rule" when a non-Black person uses *nigga* with Blacks.

Lesbian History and Politics of Identities

SUSAN HAFEN

LEARNING OBJECTIVES

After reading this chapter, students will be able to:

- articulate the etymology of the word lesbian, and explain what early sexologists believed about female homosexuality;
- discuss the theories of identity and lesbian identity development; and
- understand the evolution of lesbian subcultures within the United States, and the divisions created by feminism and critical queer theory.

Ann emphatically said, "The choice you are making is not a lifestyle." Darla agreed, "I don't have a lifestyle; my life is like anybody else's life. . . . [L]iving with a woman rather than a man didn't change anything about my day to day life."

A student in a women's studies class, upon reading an assigned article about gay/lesbian culture, complained that the article unnecessarily displayed the word *lesbian,* flaunting it, paragraph after paragraph, "lesbian, lesbian, lesbian." Another student reminded him that if the article were about African Americans or Asians, for example, those words would be in every paragraph too. What, she asked ingenuously, is the difference? He didn't answer, but his flinching discomfort at the mere word (not to mention the referent itself) signified the power of the lesbian sign. Would *gay* have produced the same anxiety? *Homosexual? Queer?* Not likely. The first has too many definitions; the

179

second is medical nomenclature; the third is a pejorative term used by grade schoolers and only recently recuperated by some in the gay community. But *lesbian,* as Merkin, a self-described irrevocably heterosexual woman, lovingly uses it, "the slow-moving sound of it, that long first syllable-*lez*-ending on an enclosure, *bian*" (1996, p. 109), is a word that is not easily shamed, its proud etymology elided but not entirely erased. *Lesbian* evokes the island of Lesbos and long-repressed memories of a time when women were free in their bodies—"with its thousand and one thresholds of ardor"—and were no longer the dark and dangerous labyrinths of flowing blood, but were unashamed and "laughing Medusas" (Cixous 1975/1993, p. 342).

A **lesbian** by one definition is a woman "who in a particular moment feels completely authentic and whole only in a relationship that is sexual and emotional with another woman. This is not to exclude that she may find self-expression in relationships with men both sexual and emotional, but that only with another woman does she feel completely at one with herself" (Langer 1994, p. 307). Such a woman, however, might instead call herself **bisexual** because, despite a preference for women, she is still attracted to and has relationships with men. Another woman, for whom Langer's definition also applies, might call herself *gay,* rejecting the name of *lesbian* or *bisexual.* Still others might use *dyke, queer, woman-identified-woman, womanist,* or more generally, *homosexual,* or more specifically, *lesbian **feminist*** (emphasis on feminist). Finally, a woman might refuse any label at all, declaring that her identity is in no way tied to her sexuality, that she is simply a person who happens to be in love with another person who happens to be a woman.

Only a few decades ago, to identify publicly as a *woman* and to ask others to use that descriptor versus *lady* or *girl* was a political act; *gal* was often the innocuous compromise. The politics of identity that underlie words used as labels has only increased, as marginalized and stigmatized groups have found their voices, claimed their own identities, and then splintered in disagreements among themselves. To speak of one's identity is to reference one's self (or, more reflexively, one's identities and selves). Scholarship on identity/self spans the social sciences, literature, cultural studies, and philosophy. Esterberg (1997) does not exaggerate when she says the body of research on identity "is so large that it nearly defies categorization" (p. 14). The meaning of identity for lesbians is pertinent because it affects how they make sense of who they are—whether shaped by nature or by their social worlds—and what roles and labels they try on, keep, and discard.

The purpose of this study is to index the meanings of *lesbian* and how those meanings are incorporated into the individual and collective identities of particular lesbians as they interact with and view their "communities" (social circles often seen as lesbian subcultures). This study involves one (partial) lesbian community in a small Midwestern city in which the identity sense-making of these lesbians is compared with the politics of identity in lesbian feminist and lesbian queer discourses.

Focus Groups

To conduct this study, two focus groups with ten lesbians each were solicited from a social network of women I knew, some as friends and others as brief acquaintances. Their discussions about common labels and common issues related to lesbian identities were tape recorded and later transcribed. The intent of this chapter is not to reproduce the conversation, but rather to link how these women see themselves—demographically situated in 2001—with the historical and theoretical stakes of identity politics. Because the literature—historical, scientific, theoretical, auto/biographical (published accounts of lesbians who have written or been interviewed elsewhere about identity)—is so immense and yet might still be unknown to readers of this anthology, much background is necessary as context for this study. Therefore, this chapter is organized into five sections. First is a short history of lesbianism; second, a brief review of literature on identity theories; and third, a discussion on the politics of identities. Fourth, the identities of twenty lesbian participants are described as they respond to the question, "How do you label yourself and what labels do you feel comfortable with?" Finally, the conclusion summarizes what can be learned from this study. The reason for beginning with an etymology and brief history of the word *lesbian* is that there is no origin for lesbians or lesbianism, but only for the periods in time that society took special note of them, named them, and judged them.

Etymological and Historical Background of *Lesbian*

The **etymology** of *lesbian* begins with the island of Lesbos near Crete, which in the seventh century B.C.E. was "one of the jewels of early Hellenic civilization . . . a center of trade and culture" (Roche 1991, p. 30). It became notorious as the home of Sappho, who was acclaimed by 1,200 years of testimony as the greatest woman poet in the world—praised by Ovid, Cicero, Horace, Socrates, Maximus of Tyre, and countless others who had access to her books of songs and poetry before they were almost entirely destroyed by the early Christian Church. (Many resurfaced in 1879 on first century C.E. Egyptian papyrus that was unearthed.) The women of Lesbos appear to have had a higher, more autonomous social standing than the women of mainland Hellas. They cultivated the deities of Aphrodite and the Muses and were known for their "refinement and songs" (p. 33). Although scholars disagree about whether the young women who came to be taught by Sappho were simply part of aristocratic social circles or were students at an academy, what is certain is that these earliest "Lesbians" were in no way shamed or denigrated by the passions they sang for each other and Sappho put into poetry. Playwrights of the third and fourth centuries praised Sappho for her brilliance; not until the first century C.E. do Horace and Ovid turn her literary into sexual celebrity by speaking of "lesbianism" to refer to the professed love among the women of Lesbos. Their writings, almost six hundred years after her death, do not reflect the admiration and respect she had during her time as a poet, teacher, and influential wife of a wealthy merchant with children. (See also Barnstone and Barnstone 1980; Cavin 1985.)

The modern word *lesbian* is credited to Havelock Ellis, a German sexologist, in his 1897 book, *Sexual Inversion;* he was quoting an entry on Sappho in the 1890 edition of the *Encyclopedia Britannica*, which included "Sapphism" ("unnatural sexual relations between women") (Wolfe and Penelope 1993, p. 13). Krafft-Ebing was one of the first physicians to research lesbianism, naming it **"uranism"** and concluding in 1884 that it was a genetic disease of the nervous system leading to insanity and could be detected in women who had nontraditional interests and activities, such as science and sports, rather than the arts (Ponse 1978; see also Dynes 1990). In 1936 Ellis suggested that environmental factors could also influence the development of lesbianism where there was a congenital base, such as seduction by women or engaging in masturbation. While early sexologists like Ellis actually served gay men by breaking down the stereotypes that they were effeminate, writing in a more sympathetic tone than was reflected in the politics of the time, their "scientific" descriptions of lesbians were the opposite (Wolfe and Penelope 1993). Ellis—whose wife, according to Weeks (1996, p. 57), was a lesbian—wrote that lesbians did in fact appear to be more like men, moving energetically, using masculine directness and straightforward speech, and displaying freedom from shyness, which suggested a psychic abnormality. They also liked smoking, disliked needlework, and had a capacity for athletics.

Sexologists' theories of masculine, independent women being inverted men and not true women came right at the point in the nineteenth century when women began to have opportunities to live independently of men, which threatened the institution of marriage since, if women "gained all the freedoms feminists agitated for, what would attract them to marriage?" (Faderman 1981, p. 237; see also Calhoun 1996). Earlier in the 1800s, women's "romantic friendships" (e.g., the "Boston marriages" of single, educated women in New England who were usually financially independent of men through inheritance or careers) were viewed benignly, particularly when the women were respectable middle and upper class, until a growing feminist movement caused social uproar (Faderman 1981; see also Card 1995). Women with all the freedoms that the feminists demanded might not be attracted to marriage: "For the first time, love between women became threatening to the social structure" (Faderman 1981, p. 238). The sexologists' theories were politically strategic, presenting a woman's agitation for equality and independence as a sign that she was not a real woman and women's romantic friendships as dangerous perversions.

Freud, however, did not consider lesbianism to be a disease or a perversion; instead, he viewed it as arrested, immature development that was extremely difficult, if not impossible, to reverse. Not until nonmedical researchers such as Kinsey, whose 1950s studies were not based on patients but on healthy people, began to treat homosexuality as human activity rather than deviance, did the view of lesbianism begin to shift from pathological to a normal variation. Even then, in 1969 Dr. Reuben wrote, "One vagina plus another vagina equals zero," which was to say that female sexuality does not exist without a man (Whisman 1993, p. 50). Finally in 1973 in a much-disputed move, the American Psychiatric Association removed homosexuality from its list of "disorders." (For longer historical accounts, see Adam 1987; Browning 1984; Ponse 1978.)

Identity Theories

The notion of **identity** "wound its way through various sociological 'feeder streams,' including role theory, reference-group theory, and symbolic interactionism" (Epstein 1992, p. 265). Epstein defines identities as "phenomena that permit people to become acting 'subjects' who define who they are in the world, but at the same time identities 'subject' those people to the controlling power of external categorization." For Esterberg (1997), identity is "a sense of oneself belonging to a group or having group membership" and can be "something essential, tangible, and real, inherent in the self" or "shifting, constructed, a matter of creating meaning from social categories and coming to attach labels to oneself" (p. 14). For sociologists, identities are not located deep within the person but instead located within interactions between the individual and society. Identities are not products, but always in process. Identities have been theoretically delineated as social, role, or personal (Stets and Burke

2000). One's **social identity** is group-based, "seeing things from the group's perspective"; one's **role identity** is based on fulfilling "the expectations of the role, coordinating and negotiating interaction with role partners"; one's **personal identity** is more diffuse, an overarching view of the self that "may pervade all membership groups to which one belongs" (pp. 226–29). Lesbians exemplify all three distinctions: Their social identities reflect ascriptions of what they have heard, read, or believe about lesbians; their role identities are evident in how they perform, resist, or twist hetero-normative gender roles in interactions with other lesbians; and their personal identities are found in their stories as they interpret their lives and experiences loving women.

Their interpretations are revealed in the narratives they tell, which represent "a self in conversation with itself and with its world over time . . . that makes sense out of the chaotic mass of perceptions and experiences of a life," and those narratives are "reshaped and rebalanced as the life course progresses" (Josselson 1995, p. 33). Personal narratives are essential in both psychoanalytic theories of homosexual identity development, which emphasize internal or intrapsychic factors; and sociological theories, which consider how some individuals come to identify as homosexuals and others do not (Burch 1993). Blumer's (1969) symbolic interactionism—that we develop by taking on roles and labels through social interactions— is the grounding for current sociological theories of homosexual identity development. Theories of homosexuality identity development cited specifically for lesbians vary a great deal in their approaches. They are reviewed briefly below to illustrate how the development of lesbian identity can be conceptualized in terms of "steps," "stages," "elements," or "phases." Altogether, these theories witness the differing views of lesbian identity construction.

Cass's (1979) theory of homosexual identity development, based on studies of gay men, has six steps of development that have been criticized for their rigidity; "if one stops at any stage prior to identity pride and synthesis, one's identity is never fully developed" (Morris et al. 1995, p. 37; see also Bringaze and White 2001; Degges-White et al. 2000). Plummer's (1996) theory views homosexual development as analogous to three "career stages," with roles that one can adopt, build up, modify, sustain, commit to, stabilize, and discard, based on turning point decisions. Some women reach stage three ("coming out") by junior high; others only after marriage and raising a family. Still others, presumably, linger at stage two or even one. Ponse (1978, p. 125) outlines five elements of the "gay trajectory"; her elements are neither steps nor stages and can occur in any sequence. Two early models of exclusively lesbian identity development are Sophie (1987) and Chapman and Brannock (1987). McCarn and Fassinger (1996) develop a lesbian identity model based on four phases, which downplays the importance of "coming out," based on its societal stigma. Tompkins (2001) outlines a seven-step theory of identity formation that emphasizes the importance of community. Although her theory is written for lesbian identity, it can be used for any stigmatized identity, since it omits same-sex attraction as a step.

Dealing with **stigma**, as Goffman (1963) spells out in his book on stigma and "spoiled identity," requires that the stigmatized person hammer out a code to handle certain standard matters, including "how and when to reveal and conceal, formulas for dealing with ticklish situations, the support he [sic] should give to his own," and so on (p. 109). Kaufman and Raphael (1995) list some scripts that develop in response to the shame of being stigmatized—"rage, contempt, perfectionism, striving for power, transferring blame, internal withdrawal, humor, denial" (pp. 141–42; see Montini 2000, for a personal account of stigmatized disclosure). The mental juggling that maintaining this code requires helps to explain why some lesbians, like members of other stigmatized groups, reject group identity.

The ambiguity of lesbian developmental steps, stages, or elements can be illustrated by Rothblum's (1999) study of "close, passionate, and nonsexual relationships" of female adolescents that display "romantic love, idealization, obsession, exclusivity, possessiveness, and sexual desire," but are depicted by the young women and those around them as simply preludes to a future marriage. She interviewed Laura about a romantic but nonsexual relationship with her heterosexual ("straight") college roommate Violet. They had heart-shaped tattoos with each other's names, but Violet refused to become lovers with Laura. Laura later referred to their ambiguous relationship as "when we were whatever we were—whatever it was that we had" (p. 81). In terms of lesbian identity models, Plummer might posit that Violet was stuck at stage two; Ponse might explain that two of the five elements (identity and community) were missing from Violet's gay trajectory; and McCarn and Fassinger might see Violet in a phase not likely to develop into full lesbian identity.

In another study based on Ponse's gay trajectory, Grammick (1984) presents data from ninety-seven lesbians interviewed in 1979. She disagrees with Ponse's positioning of sexual relationships as less important than emotional and sexual attractions in the social construction of lesbian identity. Grammick argues that sexual behavior plays a larger and more important role than gay trajectory theory allows: "Although other social factors undoubtedly come into play, those interactions that are most explicitly sexual in nature directly influence a homosexual self-conception. Sexual attachments and sexual commitments confirm increasing suspicions of a lesbian identity" (p. 35). Her thesis would be confirmed by Laura's story, above, about her roommate who could commit to a romantic but not sexual involvement because she did not want to embrace a lesbian identity. One's identity is created by stories that one tells oneself (and others, sometimes retrospectively, making sense of past events), and their narrative logic into a coherent biography. Giddens (1991) says, "The existential question of self-identity is bound up with the fragile nature of the biography which the individual supplies about herself" (p. 54). Self-identity is both "robust and fragile"; fragile because the individual selects only one of many potential stories to tell, and robust because that story is held tightly "to weather major tensions or transitions in the social environments within which the person moves" (p. 55). Lesbians tell themselves and each other two competing narratives of origin ("when I knew about myself")—essentialist or socially constructed tales.

Identity Politics

The debate between the social constructionists and the essentialists goes back to the argument between the Sophists and Plato (Pearce 1994). Plato won, establishing a long reign of essentialist, reductionist rationality, until more recently when the postmodern turn reintroduced a different kind of logic based on knowledge of things local and inherently temporary, mutable, multiple, fragmented, and indeterminate. The politics of lesbian identities pivot on how unified and committed lesbian communities can be, given the mixtures of race and ethnicity, gender (e.g., the inclusion of male-to-female or m2f), class, sexual orientation (versus preference), age, religion, physical and mental abilities, and lifestyles (sado-

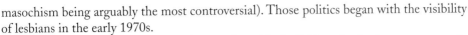

masochism being arguably the most controversial). Those politics began with the visibility of lesbians in the early 1970s.

Prior to the 1970s, in the "pre-feminist" world, the "old gay" subcultures were semi-secret societies in urban areas where the idea prevailed, among lesbians themselves, that lesbians were failed women, fixed inversions of gender (Stein 1993, 1998; see also Roof 1998). Radclyffe Hall's 1928 novel, *The Well of Loneliness,* was a landmark in its depiction of the secretive lives of lesbians who perceived themselves as a kind of third sex, neither man nor woman. Kennedy (1996) describes working-class lesbian cultures in the 1930s–1950s, and their custom of never talking about it, even among other lesbians; life-long couples were offended at being called lesbians. (See also Cruikshank 1981; Gershick 1998; for stories of older lesbians.) Simone de Beauvoir, in *The Second Sex* (1952), was the groundbreaker for gyn-affectional women, claiming as a nonlesbian that "lesbianism is a mode of resistance to male domination" (quoted in Langer 1994, p. 317). Then came women's liberation and lesbian feminism. The group **Radicalesbians** in 1973 defined lesbians as rebels—"women-identified-women, unable to accept the limitations and oppressions of society," rather than as women born into a special, homosexual category (Phelan 1993, p. 771; see also Darty and Potter 1984). The "old gay girls" called these feminist lesbians "political lesbians" or "false lesbians," contrasting them with "real lesbians," who grew up struggling with feelings of being different, as opposed to finding in their difference a common struggle against patriarchal oppression. The 1970s radical motto was "feminism is the theory; lesbianism is the practice" (Stein 1993, 1998, p. 555). Adrienne Rich (1980) made the phrase **"compulsory heterosexuality"** a feminist by-word, by turning the question of what makes women lesbians to the question of what societal forces make heterosexuality compulsory, based on the assumption that women [or men] are innately **heterosexual.** Rich shows how "lesbian existence has been written out of history or catalogued under disease . . . treated as exceptional rather than intrinsic . . . heterosexuality may not be a preference at all but something that has had to be imposed, managed, organized, propagandized, and maintained by force" (p. 133).

In the 1970s the two camps sympathetic to intimacy between women were divided between the liberal humanists and the radical feminists. **Liberal humanism** offered the "true love" ideology based on the notion that "one falls in love with a person not a gender" (Kitzinger 1989, p. 89). It should not matter what people do in their beds; what's important is what is right for each person. This discourse privatized sexuality to the personal, erasing the political. Adam (1987, p. 94) notes that this camp included women in the bar community who often found themselves rejected as "male identified." The label, **"male-identified,"** came from Mary Daly (1978), who drew a sharp line between lesbians, whom she defined as "having rejected false loyalties to men on all levels" and gay women (especially "butches"), who "although they related genitally to women, give their allegiance to men and male myths, ideologies, styles, practices, institutions, and professions" (p. 26). **Radical feminists** like Mary Daly wanted women ("wimmin"), and lesbians in particular, to have their own space, to be able to separate from time to time from patriarchy. Penelope (1992) believes such spaces are necessary because the "L-word continually disappears into the labels 'gay' and 'woman,' along with our energy, our money, our hope" (p. 49). Lesbian accounts of their sexuality also differ from gay men in that they are more likely to use a "chosen account" experiencing "sexual desires as more firmly under their control than do men, who are encouraged to experience their sexuality as a barely containable drive" (Whisman 1996, p. 116).

These **identity politics** both created and foreclosed at least three possibilities for women: First, women loving women was normalized as a political choice for female bonding rather than a genetic defect; but, as a "preference" rather than an "orientation." It was also more threatening to "malestream" society and could not be forgiven as a "sexual handicap" (see Van Gelder 1991, for her reaction to the political exigency of being "born that way"). Second, while constructing more fluidity for lesbianism (any woman can join the club), it then restricted lesbians from being too butch or too femme, or evoking heterosexuality or patriarchy in any way (Whisman 1993, p. 55; for more arguments on the pressure not to be too butch/femme, see Allen 1997; Auerbach and Bradley 1998; Halberstam 1998; Inness 1997; Loulan 1995; Morgan 1993; Peper 1994; Penelope 1992; Weston 1995). Third, by focusing on male oppression and female bonding, feminist lesbians retreated from alliances with gay male activists, who had ignored women's needs from the beginning, with the early national gay organizations focused on sexual freedoms, not child custody, rape, reproductive rights, or economic equality.

The reaction to these restrictions was a **generational rebellion** in the mid-1980s, as the lesbian cultural wars made, in Solomon's (1993) view, the female body into a "battleground" where women were judged "who dress too flannelly or too flouncy; who are too hairy or too sleek; who eat meat and drink wine or won't; whose erotic practices involve role-playing, porn, sex toys, or even men—all are subject to censure, and may even find themselves harangued at lesbian events" (p. 212). After all, dykes are rebels, and why wouldn't the new generation rebel against the older generation's rules? The upheaval within lesbian communities has been called the "sex wars," with cultural feminists on one side emphasizing the dangers of sexuality, porn, and violence; and the sex radical feminists on the other side labeling such political correctness as "antisex" and "vanilla" lesbian feminism (Taylor and Rupp 1994, p. 33). Lines were drawn by the very titles of the periodicals of each camp: *Off Our Backs* was the traditional radical feminist newspaper, and *On Our Backs* was the sexual "bad girl" newspaper (p. 46). The media joined the fray, ascribing the differences between the "old" lesbians (ugly, dowdy, poor) and the "new" (young, attractive, fashionable, employed) and coining a new term, "lipstick lesbians" (Ainsley 1995, p. 97).

The **academic lesbian** community also took sides, theorizing the distinctions. Roof (1991) applauds the new focus on difference:

> Most lesbians know quite well that lesbians are a widely divergent group, organized only loosely in their exclusions from the privileges of heterosexuality. A lesbian student easily listed for me one day the different categories of lesbians on the campus complete with their ideological positions: "style queens," "nature crunchies," "jocks," "new age," and "politicos." These categories, which have more to do with "life-style," coexist with other already evident differences such as race, class, age, physical appearance, sexual preference (bisexual, s/m, into sexual devices, no sexual devices), whose relative importance may shift depending upon the community or subgroup. (p. 251)

The list of communities or subgroups goes on and on, usually in reference to "the **visible lesbians** who are connected with lesbian institutions; bars, newspapers, bookstores, sports teams, 12-step groups, political groups, or whatever" (Hall 1993, p. 225); for in-depth analyses of lesbian communities, see Franzen 1993; Irvine 1994/1998; Krieger 1983; Lewin 1996; Wolf 1980). Hall continues with her own list, which eliminates the differences of race, class, religion, geography, disabilities, and so on, and still has differences of "bar dykes, sports dykes, women who aren't into roles, radical politicos, butches, separatists, s/m leather girls, those who aren't lesbians but are just in love with 'X,' believers in the Lesbian Nation, femme tops, Young Republicans, assimilationists, and piercing queens. And that's just for starters" (p. 225).

This diversity of young lesbian **"postfeminists"** signals their participation in the dominant culture while visibly locating themselves in the margins, committing simultaneously to feminist and queer projects (Stein 1993, 1998). What has not changed is that lesbians continue to be on the front lines as advocates for women's issues such as abortion, sexual harassment, and pay equity, "only this time they will be out as lesbians" (562). "As *lesbians*," however, presumes a common understanding of a word that has been further complicated by postmodern arguments over what "women" are. As early as 1980 Wittig shocked feminist academics by writing that lesbians are not women, since women are made and not born, and lesbians have refused to be naturalized as slaves by their "refusal of the economic, ideological, and political power of a man" (p. 13). Roof (1994) criticizes Wittig for her presumption of a "utopian, presocial, ungendered world of equality and lesbian identity" (i.e., women are made by society; lesbians are born whole) and unveils the unspoken but ever present "desire for identity, legitimation, and community" (59). What queer theorists such as Roof (see also Burack 1997; Butler 1991, 1997, 1999; Cohen 1991; Phelan 1997; Sedgwick 1993; Seidman 1996; Shugar 1999; Young 1997) offer is the use of **queer** as a verb:

> To queer identity, nation, or theory is to subvert expectations, open up possibilities for multiplicity, erase lines of division by repositioning the debate. No more ownership of identities or discourses. No borders. No ethnic models of identity as a basis for formulating a coherent politics. No coherence. No utopias. Bi? Trans? Straight? Gay? Lesbian? Whatever, queer theory responds. Get over categories. (Goldstein 1997, p. 267)

Identities are merely categories that are inherently problematic because, as Sedgwick (1993) states: "To identify *as* must always include multiple processes of identification *with*. It also involves identification *as against;* but even did it not, the relations implicit in *identifying with* are, as psychoanalysis suggests, in themselves quite sufficiently fraught with intensities of incorporation, diminishment, inflation, threat, loss, reparation, and disavowal" (p. 264).

One identity that is always in question, "diminishment, inflation, threat, loss" (etc.), is that of **bisexuality.** Young (1997) dislikes sexual categories because they are "representational fictions" that falsely simplify the complexities of sexual behaviors and desires, forcing people to discipline themselves in order to fit into the appearance of a stable, binary world; and bisexuals are the touch-point of that complexity (p. 59). She mentions a gay man who called himself bisexual until it became clear that he would have to choose since "nobody likes bisexuals" (p. 60). **"Biphobia"** is experienced by many bisexuals as coming from the lesbian and gay as well as heterosexual communities, which have "created the myths that bisexuals are oversexed, can't choose, want the best of both worlds and, in the age of AIDS, are responsible for the spread of HIV to the heterosexual and/or lesbian communities" (George 1993, p. 187; see also Ainsley 1995; Seif 1993; Stein 1993; Young 1997). In Butler's

(1999) preface to her second edition of *Gender Trouble,* a queer theory primer, she writes that what she ultimately hopes for is to "transcend the simple categories of identity, that will refuse the erasure of bisexuality." She refuses to "use, and be used by, identity" (p. xxvi). Stein and Plummer (1996) state that we need to "make theory queer and not just to have a theory about queers" (139). An example of **queering theory** is Butler's (1991) pondering whether homosexuality is in fact the original and heterosexuality the inverted copy, deciding that it is impossible to know, but noting that what gay identities work to do is "to expose heterosexuality as an incessant and *panicked* imitation of its own naturalized idealization" (p. 23). Even Butler acknowledges here some usefulness of gay identities for queer theory.

If Butler fears the erasure of bisexuality by identity categories, other writers fear the erasure of lesbian communities. Identity politics has been essential for lesbians to build solidarity as women-identified-women, and Goldstein worries that "lesbians especially get lost in the gay muscle boy shuffle of queer theory" (Goldstein 1997, p. 266), precisely the fear of Jeffreys in her (1994/1997) essay, "The Queer Disappearance of Lesbians." **Queer theory** is "cast as either the savior of lesbian sexuality because of its ability to endlessly expand the definitions of what it means to be a sexual lesbian . . . or as the demise of lesbians and lesbianism altogether" (Tyler 1991, p. 16). Seidman (1996) takes a middle road. While he asserts that identity constructions inevitably work to privilege and exclude, queer theory should nevertheless not be "anti-identity," nor abandon identity as a category of knowledge, but instead "render it permanently open and contestable as to its meaning and political role" (p. 12). Shugar agrees, albeit reluctantly: "Despite my misgivings about its efficacy for lesbian community, I do think queer theory shows us one path to broader coalitions and alliances" (1999, p. 19). And in one Midwestern lesbian community, however splintered, monthly potlucks are another path to coalitions and alliances. The two focus groups gathered to talk about their identities were solicited mainly from those potlucks.

The "Identities" of Twenty Lesbian Narrators

For several hours on two evenings, twenty women (ten each night) sat around a kitchen table, eating pizza and responding to questions about their identities, including what they called themselves, how they saw themselves, and why. Some of the women were long-time close friends, partners, and ex-lovers; others were new to the community. Ages twenty-nine to sixty-five, they are students, professors, nurses, counselors, administrators, small business owners, social workers, teachers, ministers, army sergeants, and dental technicians. While all of them currently reside in the Midwest, many grew up elsewhere, from the East Coast to the West Coast to the South. What they had in common besides race (all are White) was voluntary, sporadic attendance at lesbian potlucks (three women had attended only once), which marked them as "lesbian-identified" in some way. Determining precisely what that **identification marker** meant to them was the point of the focus groups. Although lesbian identities, as discussed both by the narrators and the literature, can be only partially (re)presented in one short chapter, the situatedness of these twenty voices may help nonlesbians to know "who we are and what to call us." Pseudonyms are used instead of "real" names, appropriate given the flux and changeableness of these women's "real" identities.

The focus groups began with the simple question, "How do you label yourself and what labels do you feel comfortable with?" Eleven of the twenty used the word *lesbian,* although they did not necessarily prefer it. Several stated that *lesbian* meant women, whereas *gay* referred to men. *Lesbian* also had the connotation of a feminist and political activist. Hannah said that she came to "honor and feel comfortable with it" because it she had "chosen *lesbian* out of feminist roots and realizing that gay women were second class in the [male] gay community and feeling a need to separate and identify ourselves as different." Betty agreed. Ann said that when she came out, feminism made it clear that "I wasn't gay, I was a lesbian." Jackie said that all her "politically aware" friends used *lesbian;* the others used *gay;* and it had taken her awhile to get used to *lesbian* herself. Connie, who at midlife is having her first lesbian relationship with Ann, said she liked the word because it is "beautiful." Lana is reminded "of the Isle of Lesbos where I would have loved to live." Sharon disagreed, because the word "always kinda reminded me of movies for men or something." Jill agreed with Sharon; it reminded her of porno films advertising "hot lesbian sex." The word felt "slimy" to Mary, who thought of "lizards/lesbian . . . it's just something about the sound of the word; it just bothers me." Sally said the word just made her "uncomfortable." Debbie said, "*Lesbian* sounds so clinical, so serious." Janet said that although she felt fine about using the word *lesbian* for herself and her friends, she wouldn't use it around her relatives: "They'll say this is my Aunt Janet, she's gay; they won't say, this is my Aunt Janet, she's a lesbian." Others agreed with her: *Gay* as a descriptor did not have the same shock value as *lesbian.*

While only five women *preferred* the word *gay,* there were less hostile responses to it than *lesbian.* Jessica definitely preferred *gay* because "if I say I am gay, then that's just one of many things I am; to me that's my preference because I am not just *"A"* lesbian, I am many things." *Gay* seemed more diffuse, less punctuated and constrained, than *lesbian.* Mary liked *gay* because "something about the word is just sort of non-threatening." Although many agreed that gay signified "male" more than "female," it mattered differently for them. *Gay* still conveyed a positive connotation for Lana, who observed that gay men in popular culture are portrayed as, for example, "fun hairdressers," or just guys "cracking jokes," like Jack in television's *Will and Grace.* Janet and Trish, on the other hand, did not like *gay* because it didn't include them. Trish preferred "women-identified," and Janet laughed and said that she preferred to be called simply "The Supreme/Wonderful." Several suggested that *gay* was more likely to be used by older lesbians (unless, Janet interrupted, they were older lesbian feminists from the 1970s). Hannah introduced **dyke,** saying it was used more than *gay* in her crowd back in the 1950s. Altogether, three preferred *dyke,* although many didn't mind it, but others hated it. Janet, noting that this particular focus group didn't reflect the "softball culture," said that they were more likely to call themselves *dykes* or *gay.* Bridget quite liked *dyke* because it reminded her of "someone who is fun and strong and wearing big boots or something." Lana and Jill said they liked to tell people, "I'm a dyke." Mary disagreed; the word sounded too "aggressive" to her. Sally was very uncomfortable with *dyke;* it made her "cringe." Connie agreed: "It conjures up pictures I am really uncomfortable with." Sally and Jackie, who both served in the military, had bad memories of being called "dykes" by other soldiers. Jackie told a story of being called a "bulldagger" by another female soldier in the army—a word she had "never heard before"—and Dana informed her it was a derivative of "bulldyke." Nancy connected *dyke* with *butch* and the "softball culture," not something she wanted to be identified with; "it's too butch an image for me." Sharon, on the other hand, liked *dyke* because it reminded her of "a powerful kind of woman with confidence in herself." She was not, however, "crazy about *queer.*"

Only Debbie preferred *queer;* for most of the other women, the word was too pejorative, except, as Lana, a professor, explained, for "those who encounter it in critical discourse . . . people outside of that world who don't read critical theory are probably less comfortable with it." Another professor, Darla agreed; she was comfortable with the word in a university setting but "would never think of calling myself queer . . . it's like taking the worst word you could be called and then taking it back for yourself," like Blacks using *nigger*. Jill thought acceptance was generational, like the younger crowd who touted "we're here, we're queer, get used to it." For her "queer was something you used on the playground to insult somebody . . . smear the queer." Connie remembered, as a child, taunting other children, "You're a queer!" and she still hates the word. Ann cautioned that you couldn't generalize by age: When her fifteen-year-old daughter (clearly part of the "younger crowd") was making signs for the Pride Parade with her friends, they all agreed that they did *not* want to use the word *queer*. Hannah, a minister, sees many reasons for using queer: "You don't have to say *LGBTQ* [lesbian, gay, bisexual, transgendered, or questioning] or all of that alphabet stew, and I am also comfortable calling myself a homosexual and a sexual minority; those are terms I use from the pulpit." Which turned the discussion to the word *homosexual*.

Trish declared that **homosexual** was the "hardest word for me to claim." Sarah explained that was because it was a "medical term." Sally was emphatic in her hatred of the word: "I think of Jerry Falwell . . . and those right wing cretin assholes." Ann, on the other hand, self-described as a fundamentalist Christian, said she used the word in a Christian community "to convince them of certain things that the Bible says and doesn't say." Mary said *homosexual* sounded "too formal . . . not something you would use in casual conversation." Jill, who has not been out at work, described a situation when one of her colleagues asked when she had realized that she was a homosexual: "I kinda looked at her like, 'Huh? What do you mean?' Although I figured it out somewhat through the conversation, I was uncomfortable with being called that." Ann had only heard the word used about her in a derogatory sense. Dana, when asked what she *preferred,* said she had a problem using labels, period: "Heterosexuals don't walk around saying, 'Hi I'm a heterosexual.'" Hannah argued that "they don't have to because we all assume everyone is." Dana rebelled, "I don't!" And Christine stepped in to make peace, "I think it's too bad we have to be labeled." Christine herself preferred *gay* but felt comfortable calling herself a "perfectly normal, well-adjusted, female homosexual." Resistance to any kind of labels was particularly an issue when women were first coming out to themselves and others.

Betty had been married twice, and when her second husband asked her if she was gay, she said, "No, no, no. I'm not gay! I just love women, I like being with them. I want to live with them." Her husband responded, "You're gay"; but she denied it again, explaining, "I couldn't say the word. I couldn't have him label me. He'd had so much control over me forever, I couldn't have him have that." She tried to explain her resistance to being labeled: "They have all of these assumptions that come with it. And we are so much more than assumptions." Sarah, also a divorced mother, felt differently about labeling herself to her exhusband, calling herself both *gay* and *lesbian:* "I wanted to be the one to label myself first." Trish, an ex-nun at age sixty-five, said that when she first came out to herself, there were no labels, she just knew she was attracted to women. Janet said she had always thought in labeling terms: "I remember reading *Time* or a newspaper and reading about Stonewall . . . and it occurred to me that's what I am. I'm a lesbian. So it's like an automatic label and then everything sort of fell into place. Of course I had a few years of denial." Hannah mentioned a friend who had always refused any labels: "She said that she identified herself as being partnered with a woman. And later on, and earlier, she had been partnered with a man . . . she just didn't identify herself as bisexual or heterosexual or homosexual . . . there was a real fluidity in her sexuality." Whether or not to call oneself bisexual when you sleep with men, have slept with men, or are attracted to men was a controversial topic.

Three of the women said that they considered themselves "bisexual" although they also used *lesbian* and/or *gay* for themselves; others said they had gone through "bisexual stages." Darla, married twice with two children, did not consider lesbianism until her late thirties and believes that she is bisexual, but "being with a woman and being in a community with women is my affectional preference." Mary would prefer to just say, "I fell in love with this person, and oh, by the way, she's a woman." She said that she could find a man physically but not emotionally attractive and had once told a lesbian friend (divorced with a kid but now with a woman partner) that she was bisexual, but her friend reacted very negatively, like she was no longer trustworthy. Mary concluded: "I just said okay, I can't refer to myself as bisexual anymore because I don't want anyone to feel any hint of doubt that I am comfortable with where I am . . . a lot of people within our community are very distrustful of people who label themselves as bisexual." Others chimed in with their opinions of bisexuals: "toying"; "relapsed"; "a transitional phase"; and "LUG (lesbian until graduation)." Ann, whose current relationships with both her husband and a woman she had also "married" in a commitment ceremony were probably the most unusual, believed that bisexuals were ostracized, "particularly lesbian women who are still in marital relationships with a man" (even when the man had agreed to the triad). Connie, Ann's female partner, also considered herself to be bisexual and wasn't certain whether, should Ann die, she would go back to another woman or man. She explained, "It's gotta be an emotional thing." The conflict and biphobia these bisexual women addressed appears pervasive, as described in the research literature.

Discussing bisexuality, Stein (1993) says: "Lesbians who sleep with men (termed 'hasbians' by the feminist publication *Off Our Backs*) are often seen as turncoats, betraying their lesbian sisters and unable to deal with their 'true' desires . . . because bisexuality may call into question the notion of sexual identity as necessarily being fixed, consistent, and either homosexual or heterosexual, it makes some lesbians uneasy" (p. 29). On the other hand, perhaps lesbians having sex with men "doesn't make you bisexual, it makes you adventurous" (Ainsley 1995, p. 97). In a study of 142 bisexual women (George 1993), several said that men were more accepting than women because heterosexual women were afraid that the friendship might become sexual and lesbians reacted in a "patronizing or hostile way" (p. 105). Of the 142 women, 108 identified as bisexual, 13 refused any label, 10 gave a variety of responses such as "confused," "not sure," "fluid sexuality," and so on; the remainder chose dual sexualities: hetero/bi or hetero/lesbian, or bi/lesbian (p. 159). Said one woman, "Sexually, I am bisexual with a strong lesbian identity; politically, I identify as gay/lesbian." Another said, "While I would be fairly happy with the word *lesbian,* and often use it to define myself, I think it's important to describe my potential to love men and women by the word *bisexual.* Rather than jumping from one closet to the other, I want to keep the door open and identify with all bisexual people, whatever their sex or exact orientation" (p. 164). Said another, "I'm a lesbian who sleeps with men" (p. 165).

Conclusion: Intercultural Implications

Clearly who we are and what we call ourselves is contested territory, so how is the heterosexual ("straight") friend, roommate, sibling, parent, co-worker, or neighbor to know what labels, if any, to use? To begin with, avoid the word *lifestyle* and think of *lives*. Both focus groups agreed that *lifestyle* was, as Lana put it, "a ridiculous expression . . . my life doesn't have as much style as I would like it to." Ann was emphatic: "The choice you are making is *not* a lifestyle." Darla agreed, "I don't have a lifestyle; my life is like anybody else's life. . . . [L]iving with a woman rather than a man didn't change anything about my day to day life." The idea that heterosexuals have lives, and homosexuals only have lifestyles, is insulting.

The names and labels we give to ourselves and each other are important identity markers by what they make visible, suppress, and privilege. Although Shakespeare's Romeo declared to Juliet that "a rose by any other name would smell as sweet," the names used to identify us have distinctly different fragrances for each of us. Had Juliet told her own story, she might have populated the plot with her own girl friends, not just Romeo and his boy pals and enemies. She might even have looked longingly at one of those girls, and killed herself not because she thought Romeo had died by poison, but because she was afraid that she might be lesbian and that would really disgrace the Capulet family. What we claim as our identities are only, according to social constructionists like O'Brien and Kollock (1997), masks that index roles we inhabit temporarily and vary across contexts and interactions. Within these interactions "humans have a deep commitment to support each other's identities, even the identities of strangers" (p. 165). O'Brien and Kollock explicate how that occurs through tact, repair work, the offering and acceptance of accounts, and framing scenes with tacit negotiation of shared social scripts.

Those social scripts are often assumed to be, or presented as, heterosexual; and so the insertion of words like *gay* and *lesbian* are seen as disruptions, "flaunting" as it were. Rather than presumptions of sexual identities, we can begin with a question mark in our interpersonal probes. "So, what is the name of your boy- or girl-friend?" And, should the name refer to someone of the same sex, "Do you like to be called lesbian-gay-queer-bisexual-or no label at all?" What matters ultimately is not the label, but how we communicate in relationships where all of us can be who we are, whoever that is, and however much we may change over time.

References

Adam, B. D. 1987. *The rise of a gay and lesbian movement.* Boston, Mass.: Twayne.

Ainsley, R. 1995. *What is she like? Lesbian identities from the 1950s to the 1990s.* New York: Cassell.

Allen, L. 1997. *The lesbian idol: Martina, k.d., and the consumption of lesbian masculinity.* New York: Cassell.

Auerbach, S., and R. Bradley. 1998. Resistance and reinscription: Sexual identity and body image among lesbian and bisexual women. In D. Atkins (Ed.), *Looking queer: Body image and identity in lesbian, bisexual, gay, and transgender communities* (pp. 27–36). New York: Harrington Park Press.

Barnstone, A., and W. Barnstone (Eds.). 1980. *A book of women poets from antiquity to now.* New York: Schocken Books.

de Beauvoir, S. 1952. *The second sex.* New York: Vintage Books.

Blumer, H. 1969. *Symbolic interactionism: Perspectives and method.* Englewood Cliffs, N.J.: Prentice-Hall.

Bringaze, T. R., and L. R. White. 2001. Living out proud: Factors contributing to healthy identity development in lesbian leaders. *Journal of Mental Health Counseling* 23: 162–73.

Browning, C. 1984. Changing theories of lesbianism: Challenging the stereotypes. In T. Darty and S. Potter (Eds.), *Women-identified women* (pp. 11–30). Palo Alto, Calif.: Mayfield.

Burack, C. 1997. True or false: The self in radical lesbian feminist theory. In S. Phelan (Ed.), *Playing with fire: Queer politics, queer theories* (pp. 31–50). New York: Routledge.

Burch, B. 1993. *On intimate terms: The psychology of difference in lesbian relationships.* Chicago: University of Illinois Press.

Butler, J. 1991. Imitation and gender insubordination. In D. Fuss (Ed.), *Inside/out: Lesbian theories, gay theories* (pp. 13–31). New York: Routledge.

———. 1997. Critically queer. In S. Phelan (Ed.), *Playing with fire: Queer politics, queer theories* (pp. 11–29). New York: Routledge.

———. 1999. *Gender trouble: Feminism and the subversion of identity.* New York: Routledge.

Calhoun, C. 1996. The gender closet: Lesbian disappearance under the sign "women." In M. Vicinus (Ed.), *Lesbian subjects: A feminist studies reader.* Bloomington: Indiana University Press.

Card, C. 1995. *Lesbian choices.* New York: Columbia University Press.

Cass, V. C. 1979. Homosexual identity formation: A theoretical model. *Journal of Homosexuality* 4: 219–35.

Cavin, S. 1985. *Lesbian origins.* San Francisco: ism Press.

Chapman, B. E., and B. C. Brannock. 1987. Proposed model of lesbian identity development: An empirical examination. *Journal of Homosexuality* 14: 69–80.

Cixous, H. 1993. The laugh of the medusa. In R. R. Warhol and D. P. Herndl (Eds.), *Feminisms: An anthology of literary theory and criticism.* New Brunswick, N.J.: Rutgers University Press. (Original work published 1975.)

Cohen, E. 1991. Who are "we"? Gay "identity" as political (e)motion (a theoretical rumination). In D. Fuss (Ed.), *Inside/out: Lesbian theories, gay theories* (pp. 71–92). New York: Routledge.

Cruikshank, M. (Ed.). 1981. *The lesbian path.* Tallahassee, Fla.: Naiad Books.

Daly, M. 1978. *Gyn/Ecology: The metaethics of radical feminism.* Boston: Beacon Press.

Darty, T., and S. Potter (Eds.). 1984. *Women-identified women.* Palo Alto, Calif.: Mayfield.

Degges-White, S., B. Rice, and J. E. Myers. 2000. Revisiting Cass' theory of sexual identity formation: A study of lesbian development. *Journal of Mental Health Counseling* 22 (4): 318–33.

Dynes, W. (Ed.) 1990. *Encyclopedia of homosexuality,* vol. A-Z (2). New York: Garland Publishing.

Ellis, H. and J. A. Symons. 1897. *Sexual inversion.* London: Wilson and MacMillian.

Epstein, S. 1992. Gay politics, ethnic identity: The limits of social constructionism. In E. Stein (Ed.), *Forms of desire: Sexual orientation and the social constructionist controversy* (pp. 239–94). New York: Routledge. (Original work published 1987.)

Esterberg, K. G. 1997. *Lesbian and bisexual identities: Constructing communities, constructing selves.* Philadelphia: Temple University Press.

Faderman, L. 1981. *Surpassing the love of men.* New York: Quality Paperback Book Club.

Franzen, T. 1993. Differences and identities. *Signs: Journal of Women in Culture and Society* 18: 891–906.

George, S. 1993. *Women and bisexuality.* London: Scarlet Press.

Gershick, Z. 1998. *Gay old girls.* Los Angeles: Alyson.

Giddens, A. 1991. *Modernity and self-identity: Self and society in the late modern age.* Cambridge: Polity Press.

Goffman, E. 1963. *Stigma: Notes on the management of spoiled identity.* Englewood Cliffs, N.J.: Prentice-Hall.

Goldstein, L. 1997. Queer theory: The monster that is destroying lesbianville. In B. Mintz and E. Rothblum (Eds.), *Lesbians in academia: Degrees of freedom* (pp. 261–68). New York: Routledge.

Grammick, J. 1984. Developing a lesbian identity. In T. Darty and S. Potter (Eds.), *Women-identified women* (pp. 31–44). Palo Alto, Calif.: Mayfield.

Halberstam, J. 1998. *Female masculinity*. Durham, N.C.: Duke University Press.

Hall, L. K. C. 1993. Bitches in solitude: Identity politics and lesbian community. In A. Stein (Ed.), *Sisters, sexperts, queers: Beyond the lesbian nation* (pp. 13–34). New York: Penguin Books.

Hall, R. 1966. *The well of loneliness*. New York: Penguin Books. (Original work published 1928.)

Inness, S. A. 1997. *The lesbian menace: Ideology, identity, and the representation of lesbian life*. Amherst: University of Massachusetts Press.

Irvine, J. M. 1998. A place in the rainbow: Theorizing lesbian and gay culture. In P. M. Nardi and B. E. Schneider (Eds.), *Social perspectives in lesbian and gay studies* (pp. 573–85). (Original work published 1994.)

Jeffreys, S. 1997. The queer disappearance of lesbians. In B. Mintz and E. D. Rothblum (Eds.), *Lesbians in academia: Degrees of freedom* (pp. 269–78). New York: Routledge. (Original work published 1994.)

Josselson, R. 1995. Imagining the real: Empathy, narrative, and the dialogic self. In R. Josselson and A. Lieblich (Eds.), *Interpreting experience: The narrative study of lives, vol. 1* (pp. 27–44). Thousand Oaks, Calif.: Sage.

Kaufman, G., and L. Raphael. 1996. *Coming out of shame: Transforming gay and lesbian lives*. New York: Doubleday.

Kennedy, E. L. 1996. "But we would never talk about it": The structures of lesbian discretion in South Dakota 1940–1975. In E. Lewin (Ed.), *Inventing lesbian cultures in America* (pp. 15–39). Boston: Beacon Press.

Kitzinger, C. 1989. Liberal humanism as an ideology of social control: The regulation of lesbian identities. In J. Shotter and K. Gergen (Eds.), *Texts of identity* (pp. 82–98). London: Sage.

Krieger, S. 1983. *The mirror dance: Identity in a women's community*. Philadelphia: Temple University Press.

Langer, C. L. 1994. Transgressing *le droit du seigneur:* The lesbian feminist defining herself in art history. In J. Frueh, C. L. Langer, and A. Raven (Eds.), *New feminist criticism: Art, identity, action* (pp. 306–26). New York: HarperCollins.

Lewin, E. 1996. Why in the world would you want to do that? Claiming community in lesbian commitment ceremonies. In E. Lewin (Ed.), *Inventing lesbian cultures in America* (pp. 105–30). Boston: Beacon Press.

Loulan, L. 1995. Butch mothers, femme bull dykes: Dismantling our own stereotypes. In K. Jay (Ed.), *Dyke life: A celebration of the lesbian experience* (pp. 247–56). New York: Basic Books.

McCarn, S. R., and R. E. Fassinger. 1996. Revisioning sexual minority identity formation: A new model of lesbian identity and its implications for counseling and research. *The Counseling Psychologist* 24: 508–34.

Merkin, D. 1996. A closet of one's own: On not becoming a lesbian. In M. Daly (Ed.), *Surface tension: Love, sex, and politics between lesbians and straight women* (pp. 99–110). New York: Touchstone Books.

Montini, T. 2000. Compulsory closets and the social context of disclosure. *Sociological Perspectives* 43: 121–32.

Morgan, T. 1993. Butch-femme and the politics of identity. In A. Stein (Ed.), *Sisters, sexperts, queers: Beyond the lesbian nation* (pp. 218–29). New York: Penguin Books.

Morris, J. F., A. J. Ojerholm, T. M. Brooks, D. M. Osowiecki, and E. D. Rothblum. 1995. Finding a word for myself: Themes in lesbian coming out stories. In K. Jay (Ed.), *Dyke life: A celebration of lesbian experience* (pp. 36–44). New York: Basic Books.

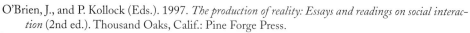

O'Brien, J., and P. Kollock (Eds.). 1997. *The production of reality: Essays and readings on social interaction* (2nd ed.). Thousand Oaks, Calif.: Pine Forge Press.

Pearce, W. B. 1994. Recovering agency. *Communication Yearbook* 17: 34–41.

Penelope, J. 1992. *Call me lesbian: Lesbian lives, lesbian theory.* Freedom, Calif.: The Crossing Press.

Peper, K. 1994. Female athlete=lesbian: A myth constructed from gender role expectations and lesbiphobia. In R. J. Ringer (Ed.), *Queer words, queer images: Communication and the construction of homosexuality* (pp. 193–208). New York: New York University Press.

Phelan, S. 1993. (Be)Coming out: Lesbian identity and politics. *Signs: Journal of Women in Culture and Society* 18: 765–90.

———. 1997. Lesbians and mestizas: Appropriation and equivalence. In S. Phelan (Ed.), *Playing with fire: Queer politics, queer theories* (pp. 75–98). New York: Routledge.

Plummer, K. 1996. Symbolic interactionism and the forms of homosexuality. In S. Seidman (Ed.), *Queer theory/sociology* (pp. 64–82). Cambridge, Mass.: Blackwell.

Ponse, B. 1978. *Identities in the lesbian world.* Westport, Conn.: Greenwood.

Rich, A. 1980. Compulsory heterosexuality and lesbian experience. *Signs* 5 (summer): 631–60.

Roche, P. (Trans.) 1991. *The love songs of Sappho.* New York: Penguin Books.

Roof, J. 1991. *A lure of knowledge: Lesbian sexuality and theory.* New York: Columbia University Press.

———. 1994. Lesbians and Lyotard: Legitimation and the politics of the name. In L. Doan (Ed.), *The lesbian postmodern* (pp. 47–66). New York: Columbia University Press.

———. 1998. 1970s Lesbian feminism meets 1990s butch-femme. In S. R. Munt (Ed.), *Butch/femme: Inside lesbian gender* (pp. 27–36). Herndon, Vir.: Cassell.

Rothblum, E. 1999. Poly-friendships. In M. Munson and J. P. Stelboum (Eds.), *Lesbian polyamory reader* (pp. 71–84). New York: Harrington Park Press.

Sedgwick, E. K. 1993. Axiomatic. In S. During (Ed.), *The cultural studies reader* (pp. 243–68). New York: Routledge.

Seidman, S. (Ed.) 1996. *Queer theory/sociology.* Cambridge, Mass.: Blackwell.

Seif, H. 1999. To love women, or to not love men: Chronicles of lesbian identification. In D. Atkins (Ed.), *Lesbian sex scandals: Sexual practices, identities, and politics* (pp. 33–44). Binghamton, N.Y.: Harrington Park Press.

Shugar, D. R. 1999. To(o) queer or not? Queer theory, lesbian community, and the functions of sexual identities. In D. Atkins (Ed.), *Lesbian sex scandals: Sexual practices, identities, and politics* (pp. 11–20). Binghamton, N.Y.: Harrington Park Press.

Soloman, A. 1993. Dykotomies: Scents and sensibility. In A. Stein (Ed.), *Sisters, sexperts, queers: Beyond the lesbian nation* (pp. 210–17). New York: Penguin Books.

Sophie, J. 1987. Internalized homophobia and lesbian identity. *Journal of Homosexuality* 14: 53–64.

Stein, A. 1993. The year of the lustful lesbian. In A. Stein (Ed.), *Sisters, sexperts, queers: Beyond the lesbian nation* (pp. 13–34). New York: Penguin Books.

———. 1998. Sisters and queers: The decentering of lesbian feminism. In P. M. Nardi and B. E. Schneider (Eds.), *Social perspectives in lesbian and gay studies* (pp. 553–63). (Original work published 1992.)

Stein, A., and K. Plummer. 1996. "I can't even think straight": "Queer" theory and the missing sexual revolution in sociology. In S. Seidman (Ed.), *Queer theory/sociology* (pp. 129–44). Cambridge, Mass.: Blackwell.

Stets, J. E., and P. J. Burke. 2000. Identity theory and social identity theory. *Social Psychology Quarterly* 63 (3): 224–37.

Taylor, V., and L. J. Rupp. 1994. Women's culture and lesbian feminist activism: A reconsideration of cultural feminism. *Signs* 19 (summer): 32–61.

Tompkins, A. B. 2001. The lesbian subculture's and communities' roles in developing and performing lesbian identity. Unpublished manuscript, University of Wisconsin, Eau Claire.

Tyler, C. 1991. Boys will be girls: The politics of gay drag. In D. Fuss (Ed.), *Inside/out: Lesbian theories, gay theories*. New York: Routledge.

Van Gelder, L. 1991. The "born that way" trap. *Ms.* (May/June): 86–87.

Walker, L. M. 1993. How to recognize a lesbian: The cultural politics of looking like what you are. *Signs: Journal of Women in Culture and Society* 18: 866–90.

Weeks, J. 1996. The construction of homosexuality. In S. Seidman (Ed.), *Queer theory/sociology* (pp. 41–63). Cambridge, Mass.: Blackwell.

———. 1997. Sexual identification is a strange thing. In J. O'Brien and P. Kollock (Eds.), *The production of reality: Essays and readings on social interaction* (pp. 495–98). Thousand Oaks, Calif.: Pine Forge Press. (Original work published 1991.)

Weston, K. 1995. Guessing games. In K. Jay (Ed.), *Dyke life: A celebration of the lesbian experience* (pp. 221–27). New York: Basic Books.

Whisman, V. 1993. Identity Crises: Who is a lesbian anyway? In A. Stein (Ed.), *Sisters, sexperts, queers: Beyond the lesbian nation* (pp. 47–60). New York: Penguin Books.

———. 1996. *Queer by choice: Lesbians, gay men, and the politics of identity.* New York: Routledge.

Wittig, M. 1980. *The straight mind and other essays.* New York: Harvester/Wheatsheaf.

Wolf, D. G. 1980. *The lesbian community.* Berkeley: University of California Press.

Wolfe, S. J., and J. Penelope. 1993. Sexual identity/textual politics: Lesbian {de/com} positions. In S. J. Wolfe and J. Penelope (Eds.), *Sexual practice/textual theory: Lesbian cultural criticism.* Cambridge, Mass.: Blackwell.

Young, S. 1997. Dichotomies and displacement: Bisexuality in queer theory and politics. In S. Phelan (Ed.), *Playing with fire: Queer politics, queer theories* (pp. 51–74). New York: Routledge.

KEY TERMS

academic lesbian	liberal humanism
biphobia	male-identified
bisexual/bisexuality	personal identity
compulsory heterosexuality	postfeminists
dyke	queer
etymology	queering theory
feminist	queer theory
gay	radical feminists
generational rebellion	radicalesbians
heterosexual	role identity
homosexual	sexologists' theories
identification marker	social identity
identity	stigma
identity politics	uranism
lesbian	visible lesbians

REVIEW AND DISCUSSION QUESTIONS

1. What does *identity* mean to you? What words do you use to describe yourself? Is your sexuality a part of your identity? Why or why not?

2. Reflect on the identity labels in your life. What categories to which you belong do you have an uneasy relationship with? Explain. (For example, deciding whether to call yourself *Indian, Native American*, or just *American*. Or struggling with both positive and negative connotations of *athlete* or *intellectual*.)

3. What did you know about the history of the word *lesbian*—historical, scientific, and theoretical? Did any of this history surprise you or change the way you thought about the word?

4. With which group(s) discussed in this chapter do you feel the most/least sympathy? Liberal humanists? Cultural feminists? 1970s radical lesbian feminists? 1990s sex-radical post-feminists? Queer theorists? Explain why.

5. Discuss Goldstein's (1997) quote: "To queer identity, nation, or theory is to subvert expectations, open up possibilities for multiplicity, erase lines of division by repositioning the debate. No more ownership of identities or discourses. No borders. No ethnic models of identity as a basis for formulating a coherent politics. No coherence. No utopias. Bi? Trans? Straight? Gay? Lesbian? Whatever, queer theory responds. Get over categories." How do you feel about using *queer* as a verb—"to queer identities and nations" and just "get over categories"? Explain.

6. Name one of the focus group members whose opinions and ideas you most agreed with and one you least agreed with. Explain.

7. In conversations about lesbian and bisexual women among heterosexual (straight) college students, which group is likely to be viewed the most positively—or least negatively? How do you view bisexuals "as benefiting by not declaring themselves homosexual, with all its stigma, or as suffering because they have not 'chosen sides'"?

The Chicken Haulers and the High Liners: CB Talk among Interstate Truckers

Debra-L Sequeira
and Timothy J. Anderson

LEARNING OBJECTIVES

After reading this chapter, students will be able to:

- realize that there are speech communities or microcultures within the United States unrecognized by mainstream culture;
- understand that speech communities are based on geography, social dialects, and communication rituals;
- explain how interstate truckers comprise a speech community and how the trucking routes they serve divide them culturally; and
- discover how technology affects the communication among members of the speech community of interstate truckers.

Driver 1: *Afternoon Westbound. If you are heading over Lookout Pass and Fourth of July Pass, you will find just a little compact snow and ice over the summit, but you shouldn't have to throw any iron as it is well sanded. The scales are open at the port of entry but they didn't appear to be doing any inspections.*

Driver 2: *Okay. Copy the dry and dusty. You look good back that way. All your scales were locked up and we haven't seen any cops since yesterday in Minnesota. You have a good trip.*

Driver 1: *You too. Drive safe.*

—High Liner CB Talk[1]

Driver 3: *Hey Eastbound, what did you leave behind you?*

Driver 4: *Well, you look good back that way. There was a dot man at the bug station but they were just rolling you across. Arizona was open but the super coops weren't looking at your comic books or nothing. Saw Evil Knievel at the 102 with a customer; a comedian in the median at the 149. Back on the other side of Flag it was greasy and a stick hauler, a parking lot, and a rooster cruiser shut it down just before Williams*

Driver 3: *'Preciate it. You look good back that way. Got two four wheelers pulled over at the 39 with a bunch of disco lights. Probably caught with go fast or something. Other than that, you look clean back to Albuquerque. Hey, if you're gonna get your sleeper time in at the TA in Albuquerque don't expect to get any z's. Had lot lizards banging on the door all night and one of them followed me into the choke and puke claiming she was the best commercial company I was ever gonna find. I told her, momma probably wouldn't appreciate her following me around. Okay, I'm losing you. You have a safe one.*

Driver 4: *Later.*

—Chicken Hauler CB Dialect[2]

Cultural communication scholars investigating American speech communities have provided invaluable insights into human interaction and American culture. One groundbreaking study, "Speaking Like a Man in Teamsterville: Cultural Patterns of Role Enactment in an Urban Neighborhood" (Philipsen 1975), opened the door for the consideration of new speech communities within American culture and broadened academic sensitivity to previously unrecognized groups. **Speech communities** are not constituted by geography alone, but by use of language: the rules, conduct, and interpretation of that language, which implicate both social norms and linguistic forms. Prior to Philipsen's work, cultural scholars were most concerned with exotic speech communities located outside the United States. Philipsen claimed that each community has its own cultural values about "talk"; these values are linked to perceptions and judgments about the use of language. Such rules and values concerning talk and other forms of communication can be found throughout the United States, even in a neighborhood of blue-collar, low-income Caucasians on the south side of Chicago, Philipsen's "Teamsterville."

A speech community that so far has escaped the attention of cultural communication scholars is that of interstate truckers. Rolling across the interstate highways, this community has developed its own distinct communication within the electronic framework of the Citizens Band (CB) Radio and, in recent years, the increasing use of real-time technologies such as two-way satellite communication and portable notebook computers. In this distinct speech community almost all communication occurs by way of electronic technology, and the language is so highly specialized that trucking company managers find themselves having to learn it in order to communicate effectively with their subordinates. Moreover, this electronic culture is not limited to a specific lexicon but includes rituals, voice inflections, and regional differences and customs.

Unfortunately, the "over the road" community escapes attention because of its closed nature and the limited access outsiders have to its language. Wary of nontruckers, truck drivers immediately differentiate between members and nonmembers of their speech community. And as Philipsen (1975) found, even within a distinct speech community not all communication is equally valued. While their CB talk separates truck drivers from the general public and thus constitutes them as a distinct speech community, various forms of this language occur; in particular, a prominent **dialect** exists that is not equally esteemed among the truckers who are familiar with it.

Background

The amount of truck traffic on the nation's highways has increased dramatically since the development of the interstate highway system. Commerce flows twenty-four hours a day, seven days a week on these economic arteries that nourish the nation. Although the importance of trucking to the nation is a fairly recent phenomenon, it now represents a large sector of the economy. As many as one out of every eleven American jobs is tied to the trucking industry (Schauerte 1999). Ironically, as the trucking industry has come to comprise a larger portion of the economy, a parallel development has largely escaped the attention of those outside of the industry.

The general public has probably glimpsed the world of trucking only briefly through Hollywood movies such as the popular *Smokey and the Bandit* films or the 1970s country western music hit, *Convoy*. Most Americans remain largely unaware that a new language is spoken all over the country, one that in recent years has evolved variant forms, including one identifiable regional dialect. Today's truck drivers, especially those operating in teams, often traverse one or more time zones in a twenty-four-hour period. Therefore, these forms of CB talk seem to reflect more than just a driver's "home 20" (permanent residence) but are related to the type of freight hauled, the equipment driven, and the parts of the country in which a driver operates. It is not uncommon for drivers to stay on the road for up to a month at a time; for the majority of that period, they roll from one new place to another. Moreover, large segments of the trucking industry are composed of irregular route carriers. This guarantees that many drivers rarely see the same scenery twice in a given run or during their time away from home.

The hours are long and the loneliness drivers experience is well documented by family therapists and the emergence of nationwide support groups such as LOADS (Loved Ones and Drivers Support).[3] Many relationships, bonds, and friendships formed on the road are hit-or-miss and fly-by-night. Strangers may meet and then never cross paths again. With so many strangers interacting through faceless CB radio conversations, it was only a matter of time before a language, a culture, and a series of rituals emerged, all transmitted almost entirely through electronic means.

The existence of this language is amply documented in the micropopulation(s) surrounding the trucking industry through editorial coverage in trade publications such as *Overdrive, Roadstar, Truckers News,* and *RPM;* but specific CB talk and associated regional variations do not receive the same attention. While the rest of the motoring public and the general population are aware that truckers communicate among themselves via CB, the accuracy of their perceptions is dubious. Hollywood frequently portrays truck drivers using the CB specifically to avoid law enforcement. Films such as *Black Dog* and *Breakdown,* as well as a *Touched by an Angel* television episode, reinforce this image that the truckers' electronic language is limited and that this population communicates only to avoid "speed cops." Much more can be learned from studying the actual communication that occurs among drivers.

This study investigates the distinctive communication that occurs among truckers, as well as a regional, dialectical difference that has emerged within a particular "rolling" community. Results suggest that CB talk along the southern transcontinental route of Interstate 40 is distinct from the communication that occurs elsewhere, for example, on the northerly Interstate 90. Further, our data support the conclusion that drivers hold two distinct attitudes toward the communication competence of the subculture surrounding the Interstate 40 route.

Due to lack of access to this community, little research has been conducted on the five million members of the trucking industry who hold commercial drivers' licenses. Johnson (1997) addresses the electronic nature of truckers' communication; Stenfield (1990) and Hiltz (1984) also reference the importance of electronic means of communication in the workplace. But these authors do not address the distinct speech community that has developed among those for whom electronics provides the sole means of communication. Just as there are rules in every culture that direct language and determine appropriate speech, rule-governed behavior exists in the trucking industry. For example, drivers understand that the mode of communication is electronic and that different CB channels are used in different parts of the country. Furthermore, cooperation must exist between participants because in CB communication, only one person can talk at a time. In spite of all the chaos, transience, and geographical barriers, this community somehow has managed to organize and follow a recognized system of meanings and behaviors.

Perhaps the **electronic medium** that drivers must use for communication, coupled with the transitory nature of their world, necessitated the development of standard practices. There are no written rules for this communication, yet the standard vocabulary of this speech is consistent nationwide. The development of a language that originates electronically and then filters into other areas of life, including a set of cultural values and the establishment of various rituals, presents a fascinating phenomenon.

The Chicken Haulers and the High Liners

The United States is traversed by a series of four interstate highways that run east to west from the Atlantic seaboard to the Pacific coastal region. The southernmost of these routes, Interstate 10 (I-10) begins in Jacksonville, Florida, and terminates in Los Angeles, California. Then, in order from south to north, one finds: I-40, running from North Carolina to California; I-80, with New York City and San Francisco as its terminal points; and I-90, beginning in Massachusetts and ending in Washington state. Two other east-west interstate highways stretch across most of the country: I-20, running from eastern South Carolina to west Texas (where it joins I-10); and I-70, which begins in Baltimore, Maryland, and ends in western Utah (intersecting I-15, a major north-south route). This study focuses on the different characteristics of the CB talk of truck drivers associated with I-40 and I-90.

Interstate 40 (I-40) stretches from Wilmington, North Carolina, on the Atlantic coast, to Barstow, California (where it joins I-15 for the final 120 miles into Los Angeles). The highway runs almost directly east-west through Tennessee, Arkansas, Oklahoma, the Texas

**FIGURE
13.1**

panhandle, New Mexico, Arizona, and into California. Drivers often refer to I-40 as "Sesame Street" or "The Boulevard." A distinct class of truck drivers is associated with this highway. Known specifically in the industry as "Chicken Haulers," they are easily identified. These drivers operate primarily on I-40 and I-10, transporting frozen poultry products, as well as other temperature-controlled freight. Preferring to run "large cars" or "hoods,"[4] these drivers proudly operate "old school" trucks. Their ride of choice is either an extended hood Kenworth or Peterbilt preferably powered by a high horsepower, ungoverned engine.[5] Such trucks defy aerodynamic advancements and are custom built to order (see figs. 13.1 and 13.2). Many Chicken Hauler rigs have CB aerials mounted to resemble bug antennas. Chicken Haulers are so ubiquitous within the trucking industry that companies have emerged that specifically market decals, T-shirts, and other items to members of this group (Garber 1998). Most Chicken Haulers call southern and border states such as Oklahoma, Arkansas, Missouri, or Tennessee home, and they haul loads that originate and terminate in these areas. Chicken Haulers approach their lives on the highway and utilize the CB radio very differently than do drivers in other parts of the country.

Interstate 90 (I-90), also known as the "High Line," has less traffic and, for much of the country, serves as the northernmost east-west interstate highway. It runs from Boston, Massachusetts, through New York state, around the Great Lakes, passing through Cleveland, Ohio, and Chicago, Illinois. Then the highway breaks through to the open country of

FIGURE 13.2

southern Minnesota, South Dakota, Wyoming, Montana, and the Idaho panhandle. After passing through Spokane and eastern Washington, it ends in Seattle. Road conditions on the High Line are extreme, especially in the winter months, and the areas through which much of this highway runs are sparsely populated. The trucking industry does not employ a specific term to refer to the drivers on the I-90 route. However, in order to distinguish them from the Chicken Haulers, we will dub this group of drivers the "High Liners."

In contrast to I-90, I-40 is one of the most heavily traveled interstate highways in the United States, the primary route connecting the two coasts, the Midwest, and parts of the South. Because it is the "great American melting pot" of highways, more drivers are familiar with I-40 and its language practices than any other North American route, even though the Chicken Hauler dialect represents a marked departure from the standard CB talk of the typical High Liner.

Interpretive Analysis

This study was designed as a **qualitative/interpretive analysis** examining the structure and function of the distinct speech community formed by interstate truck drivers. Our approach seeks to identify patterns of meaning as they are revealed through words and symbols in participants' responses (Braithwaite 1995; Kelley and Sequeira 1997; Sequeira 1994). The primary method of data collection was to interview drivers about their communication with one another; a specific goal was to determine drivers' attitudes toward the dialect peculiar to the Chicken Haulers of I-40. Preliminary data in the previously mentioned trade publications suggests that I-40 has an established reputation among drivers. The second author, Timothy J. Anderson, has been a trucker for sixteen years and collected the data for this study.[6]

The truckers interviewed represent a broad range of drivers. Interviews were conducted with driver acquaintances and through referrals. Seventy-five percent of the interviews were conducted using real-time technology over the Internet. Drivers were sent a questionnaire via e-mail and the respondents filled out the questionnaire and returned it. Subsequent information was generated over chat lines on the Internet. The other 25 percent of the interviews were conducted via telephone; these interviews lasted fifteen to twenty minutes each.

The entire data collection process took three months. Twenty-eight male truck drivers and 1 female truck driver were participants. Their ages ranged from 21 to 57 years, with a mean of 35.7 years. The drivers had from less than 1 year of experience to 31 years of experience, with a mean of 7.5 years of experience. Their education ranged from completion of less than 3 years of primary school to one driver holding a Ph.D. All of the drivers surveyed operated over the road, or "long haul," driving in all 48 states and Canada. Participants from both countries were surveyed. For our purposes, the most important difference is the one between the CB talk of truckers who frequent either I-40 or I-90, the Chicken Haulers with their distinctive subculture and dialect and the High Liners.

The Boys in the Hood Drive "Hoods"

CB talk and culture not only incorporate what language is being spoken but how it is being spoken. Some drivers try to sound larger than life as their voices echo and are amplified through various devices. "Large and in charge" is an adequate description of this phenomenon, as one Chicken Hauler (DR) puts it; to listen to their voices, one would almost assume that the people driving the big rigs are as large as their trucks. Electronic gadgetry fills the airwaves as drivers constantly key up tunes such as the theme from *The Good, the Bad, and the Ugly*. Much of what Chicken Haulers do on the radio is intended to further their "bad boy" image. While truckers participating in this subculture may be in the minority nationwide, all drivers know exactly what kind of electronic gadgets tend to be used by the Chicken Haulers. The electronics are as much a part of the subculture as the voice inflections and the vocabulary. The High Liners, on the other hand, use amplification for practical purposes, such as learning the road conditions from other truckers who are traveling in the same region but are some distance away.

Further questioning reveals that only one of the drivers (3 percent) utilizes a linear[7] to boost the power on a CB radio. But twelve drivers (41 percent) use "Talk Back"[8] amplifiers to monitor how they sound over the radio. And four (13 percent) use "Roger Beep" electronic gadgets attached to their CB microphones. These are small, high-pitched electronic noises that occur at the end of a transmission, and they make sounds similar to those that NASA utilizes in its communications between astronauts and ground control. In addition, four drivers acknowledge that they use other electronic "toys" on their radios, such as echo boxes and various noisemakers.

Each respondent answered questions about the way they spent their time on the CB radio. All of the drivers note that they use the CB to monitor traffic conditions and weather. Less frequently, drivers respond that they also utilize the CB to discover the location of law enforcement (17=59 percent), "scale activity" where truckloads are weighed (17=59 percent), or to find a parking place in a crowded truck stop (15=52 percent). The least frequent responses indicate that drivers use the CB to ease boredom (14=48 percent) or engage in conversation (13=45 percent).

Drivers were asked whether their CB radio communication extended into general conversation or other forms of electronic media. Almost all of the drivers questioned claim that their conversation is different over the CB radio than it is at a truck stop (26=90 percent), loading dock (26=90 percent), on the cell phone (26=90 percent), or while at home (28=97 percent). This feedback strongly suggests that CB talk is unique and that it exists only in certain environments.

The interview data demonstrate that drivers do communicate through electronic means and that this communication is highly organized. Drivers have given themselves names; they have purchased various forms of equipment to enable them to communicate; and they have enhanced this communication through sophisticated electronic means. While not every driver utilizes every gadget, they all own a CB radio and know of its importance in establishing and maintaining channels of interaction. Furthermore, every driver recognizes that utilizing certain gadgets over the CB radio instantly signifies membership in a distinct subculture within the trucking industry. In other words, it is by way of CB talk that "a Chicken Hauler is born," as one driver puts it.

To Be a Chicken Hauler or Not to Be a Chicken Hauler

The second section of the interview concentrated on each driver's perception of the "scene" on I-40 and I-90 and their attitudes toward language and communicative performance. The questions were of a general nature so as not to lead the answers; but they were also focused sufficiently to convey to individual drivers the type of information being sought. For example, questions such as the following were posed: "Do you think that truckers have their own language that they use on the CB? Do you think that most nontruckers would understand your CB conversations? Do you think truckers speak and use the CB radio differently depending on which part of the country they are traveling in?"

To establish whether they were universally understood, several common CB terms were listed and drivers were encouraged to note if they knew what each term meant. The terms listed were *hammer down* (driving fast; 29=100 percent reported knowing its meaning), *Radio Rambo* (an aggressive, overmodulated truck stop user; 25=86 percent), *Chicken Hauler* (a type of trucker; 29=100 percent), *Smokey Bear* (law enforcement; 29=100 percent), *lot lizard* (truck stop prostitutes; 29=100 percent), *brake check* (stopped traffic ahead; 29=100 percent), and *chicken house/chicken coop* (scale house or weigh station; 29=100 percent). With only one exception, all of the terms were familiar to all of the drivers. Four drivers (13 percent) had not heard or used the term *Radio Rambo* before.

Drivers were asked if they thought truckers use their own language on the CB and 26=90 percent feel that truckers have their own language. Yet the drivers are almost evenly split (17=59 percent yes, 11=38 percent no, and 1=3 percent undecided) when it comes to judging whether or not outsiders, or nontruckers (known in the industry as "Four Wheelers"), would understand their CB language.

This contradiction stems from the fact that most truckers, as a result of the isolation of their careers and weeks that are spent on the road surrounded only by other truckers and support personnel, suffer from a lack of contact with people outside the industry. Eventually, some drivers begin to assume that everyone speaks their unique language. Moreover, due to the difficulty of operating trucks in "non-truck friendly areas" there is little opportunity to interact with those who "don't speak the language."

Over two-thirds of the drivers (20=69 percent) acknowledge that their actual speech patterns, pronunciation, and style of speaking change depending upon the geographical region of the country in which they are operating, even if it is not speech that is naturally their own. Most drivers had difficulty answering why they changed their speech habits. Many of the truckers had never consciously considered this issue before. Drivers simply adapt to the community in which they find themselves. As one Midwest driver (AR) explains:

> I never considered how I talk too much but I suppose that the further south I get the more beat up my language is. Sometimes I call home and they swear I'm from Georgia. I don't think some people are as affected by it as others. The more time you spend in the south the more pronounced your radio talk becomes. I mean, when have you ever heard a Canadian driver talking Chicken Hauler or trash talking on the radio? It is a regional thing and the southern states seem to set the language. I guess there are just more of them out on the road than hands that hail from Minnesota or Alberta.

The most interesting findings are the responses generated from the drivers who drive I-40 on a regular basis. These drivers believe that the speech they use on that route represents the norm throughout the country, even though many have never had the occasion to haul freight in other areas, especially across I-90. These drivers tend to view their CB language as the one that is universally spoken and that this CB speech is the same everywhere. They believe that the dialect evident on I-40 is common across the country and that to be a driver means using this form of speech. Drivers who "haul" on I-40 are consistently more likely to respond that only one type of language is spoken on the radio and that it is "theirs": to be a "true" trucker means speaking fluent Chicken Hauler.

This regional dialect seems to be a combination of Southern slang along with new forms and elements that have been passed down, modified, and assimilated from one driver to the next. Words are stressed differently and there is a series of grunts, whistles, heavy breathing, raspy pronunciations, and unique vocabularies that distinguish Chicken Haulers from other drivers.

Drivers who come from other parts of the nation, especially those who drive across I-90, experience a significantly different form of CB speech than that of the Chicken Haulers. A High Liner (BD) describes I-90 as "peacefully quiet." "You can actually have a conversation up there and people are respectful. They take their personal stuff to another channel. The information you get is reliable and no one is trying to outdo anyone else. It's the way trucking used to be." Drivers have very strong opinions about the existence of a regional dialect of CB language, especially when asked if I-90 drivers practice different speech from I-40 drivers.

One Northwest driver (SW) states: "I don't want to sound like some nasty pickle park [rest area] door bell. I am not that ignorant and unfortunately that is what Chicken Haulers are. They are just ignorant! I try to be a professional out here and I try not to act like this is all some big party. Or that I am preparing to go to war!"

Yet he is completely contradicted by a Midwest driver (CJ) who says, "I think there ain't no feeling like chicken haulin' mobilin' to quote the T-shirts. Hell, when people are rolling down the road and someone stirs up some hate and discontent [truck stop arguments], it makes the miles go by. Sometimes for kicks I like to pretend I am a good buddy [a homosexual] or that I voted for Clinton. Now that will get some serious shit started!" These quotes suggest that there are stereotypes connected to these different forms of talk and that truckers have their own hierarchy concerning appropriate communicative conduct when on the road.

Specific attention was also directed toward drivers with more experience to try to understand how quickly the Chicken Hauler dialect has evolved from the standard CB speech represented by the High Liners. Drivers were surveyed to determine whether they believe that these emerging speech patterns are ones they use in their daily lives. The younger the driver, the more supportive they are of the Chicken Hauler language and the ongoing celebration of that community's rituals. These novice drivers do not experience the old "pre-deregulation" camaraderie, nor do they have any appreciation for the difficulties that truckers once faced and the loyalties that such challenges create among drivers.

However, the distinctions among drivers become most prominent and stereotypical when the members of one group distinguish themselves from the other group. Typically, the drivers on the I-40 route consider the title of Chicken Hauler to be a compliment, reflecting a rich and proud heritage, while other drivers on the I-90 route consider the title to be an insult and a status that is demeaning. These findings are similar to debates experienced in Southern states where terms such as *yankee* and *rebel* are launched at opposing camps with nationalistic gusto.

Chicken Haulers are outlandish, loud, and, as one High Liner (PO) puts it, "They seem to be in a contest among themselves to see who can appear to be the most ignorant." Another driver (BT), refers to them as "Crackerheads, who never shut up! You can run with them for four hundred miles and during that time they haven't stopped talking. Yet they haven't said a damn thing in that entire time either." However, Chicken Haulers appear to delight in their culture and its rituals. A Chicken Hauler from Arkansas (SA) notes that one of his favorite activities is to start fights in truck stops using his CB. He admits that soon after initiating the conflicts he will put his CB microphone back down and just listen, "grinning at the hate and discontent I've started."

The honesty of this admission is timely, for the issue of CB etiquette has been hotly debated in industry trade publications (Cullen 1998–1999; Pieratt 1999). Almost every driver quoted or questioned claims to be against such activities. The practices of starting radio wars, soliciting sexual favors, and engaging in endless, meaningless jabber defines these trucking taboos; many drivers cannot understand how in such a short time so much chaos has come to define "radio speak." This frustration is emphasized by one veteran driver (DW) who complains, "I am tired of not only feeling but knowing, that I am surrounded by a bunch of illiterate cretins." Although he may echo the sentiments of many of the drivers surveyed, there are others who not only enjoy the aggressive "radio wars" but actively contribute to them.

Other Voices; Other Radios

Respondents seemed inclined to suggest that the more over-the-road experience a driver has, the less tolerance they have for this sort of negative ritualistic activity. They consider the Chicken Hauler subculture's speech, rituals, and customs ignorant and unprofessional. Partially blaming these "new" attitudes for the decline of the truck driver's former reputations as the knight of the highway, DW, who has twenty years' experience, says, "It's no wonder we are having so many problems in this industry. Those guys [referring to Chicken Haulers], I mean, you are talking an average I.Q. test score of 54 . . . especially if they are from Arkansas. To them, being out here is all about having one big party and getting as much shit stirred up as possible. It is a miracle some of them can drive and that they get any of their loads delivered right side up and in one piece. I think some routes are getting worse and they are all getting noisier. You get tired of it."

Another High Liner (TJ) likens the language spoken over the CB on some of his wilder trips across I-40 to "all the levels of Dante's Inferno combined on one channel. Sometimes it's just pure chaos."

A Southwest driver (LD) seems to concur. "I consider the CB Radio in my truck to be a necessary evil and I use it as little as possible. I am not the least bit interested in other drivers' reports and instructions. I do *not* [his emphasis] drive by committee and I don't take advice from people I don't consider qualified to give it. When I do hear information about adverse traffic/weather conditions, I don't pay attention to it unless I can get some kind of confirmation of the accuracy of the report."

His sentiments are echoed by a driver from the Northwest (SW) who says, "I rarely find a driver that wants to talk about something other than trucks, drivers, dispatchers etc. When I do, we go to another channel to talk."

Nevertheless, both groups of CB users, Chicken Haulers and non-Chicken Haulers, often must share the same highways. The interviews demonstrate that these groups have very different expectations concerning the role electronic means of communication should play in their day-to-day communication. The veteran driver from the Northwest (DW) sums up his opinion of the changing nature of radio conduct on the nation's highways, saying, "The South is different from the Northeast and the Northeast is very different from the Northwest. Everyone comes from a different culture and the CB radio provides a certain amount of anonymity. The more people that you have congregating in one area, the more problems you will have. I think I-90 is quieter because there are fewer people up there. You can't be as anonymous and so there is this expectation that people are going to act a certain way. There is another expectation on I-40 because of a lot of different factors. People come from a different culture; they are anonymous; and they may not be as well educated. There is a different language spoken up on I-90. But it is changing too. There are more and more trucks up there all the time. Maybe someday the two won't be so different." At this point in time, the I-90 High Liners can be identified in contrast to the Chicken Haulers. Among the former, there is also a notable lack of electronic noises and "Radio Rambo" behavior. Although truckers universally understand their performance of CB language, their style of speaking is worlds apart from the Chicken Haulers. High Liners consider their interaction predominantly "courteous and professional" (TJ).

A novice driver (RJ) who primarily drives in the Southwest, but who is familiar with the customs on I-90, echoes these sentiments. "Yeah, I-90 is a different world. It's really quiet but that's until midnight, when suddenly it's 'yackity-yack' as drivers will do anything to stay awake." These examples from various respondents reveal the different attitudes drivers have concerning the language and rituals associated with the two different interstate routes.

Studying the communication of a rapidly changing industry is a challenge. The unique factors contributing to the methods drivers must utilize in order to communicate are recent trends, quickly changing and subject to new technology. What was common in the industry five years ago is hardly the rule now. Yet in spite of all of this rapid change, the original mode of communication, the CB radio, remains very popular.

Conclusion

Language Limited by Forty Channels of Radio

The data suggest the existence of a unique language that survives almost entirely through electronic means and that this language, while fluid, does not move from CB technology across to a driver's cellular phone, satellite hookup, or to a laptop computer, although much of the vocabulary associated with "CB talk" does. Most of the distinctive communication that occurs between drivers is **verbal** and not only occurs in the words that are spoken over the airwaves, but in how those words are pronounced and articulated. **Nonverbal** aspects of inflection, tone of voice, pitch, and speed of the words affect the meaning of the language. Furthermore, the geographical location where the conversation occurs seems to be almost as important as the actual speech itself. One Southwest driver (LD) is very adamant about this, saying, "I know this is a different language. I mean, I don't say '10-4' in a normal conversation or end every other sentence with 'Copy that.' It's only when I am talking on the radio." However, seventeen drivers (59 percent) admit that they do change their language whether or not they are talking on the CB radio. The others, typically on the High Line (12=41 percent), seem to modify their speech or even choose not to participate in certain speech acts when the cultural behavior of a particular route is not to their liking or when traveling in areas where they do not fit the local profile.

The most important finding, however, is that not all drivers view their distinct speech in the same way. While many recognize the existence of their special mode of communication, they are divided as to the merits of the particular Chicken Hauler dialect commonly found along the I-40 route, compared to the standard CB language represented by High Liner talk occurring on the northerly I-90 route. Moreover, truckers differ as to whether all drivers speak the same way in all circumstances, or whether different drivers speak variations of the same language. Many drivers, especially those from the southern states, seem to retain a particular language style no matter where they operate. The drivers who drive I-40 on a regular basis believe that the speech they use on that route represents the norm throughout the country. These Chicken Haulers tend to view their CB language as the one that is universally spoken and that this CB speech is the same everywhere. Drivers who come from other parts of the nation, especially those who drive across I-90, experience a significantly different form of CB speech from that of the Chicken Haulers. These drivers consider their speech to be more professional and respectful. Clearly, there are stereotypes connected to these different forms of talk; the drivers on the I-40 route consider the title of Chicken Hauler to be a compliment, reflecting a rich and proud heritage, while other drivers on the I-90 route consider the title to be an insult and to indicate a status that is demeaning.

The Future

Will technology change the presence and use of the **electronic means of communication** distinctive of truckers? In just a few short years, laptop computers and cellular phones have been gaining popularity in the industry. Many drivers indicate that their use of the CB is on the decline. Instead of sitting in their trucks and conversing on the CB, they are escaping from the truck stop radio wars, plugging into the Internet and surfing the web. As additional truckers acquire this technology, the traditional role that the CB radio has played in the trucking industry could diminish in importance.

Will the new technology swallow up "The Last of the American Cowboys" culture of the trucker? Will tomorrow's American truck drivers roll into the information age, still animated by the same transient spirit and nomadic leanings as the drivers who came before them? Or will they be haunted and chased into that future by the ghosts of an invisible language from another era that has gone into silent extinction?

The role of the CB radio in the trucking industry remains debatable. But as long as there are independent drivers rolling to the beat of their own drummer, it seems likely that they will continue to communicate among themselves in a language distinctive of their speech community—one that only they can fully understand and appreciate. As a Southeast driver (KT) says, "Truck drivers don't realize how much they change their language to avoid the public. We *are* a subculture. And, most drivers like it that way."

Notes

1. Translation: Afternoon, Westbound. If you are heading over Lookout Pass and Fourth of July Pass [in western Montana and Idaho], you will find just a little compact snow and ice over the summit, but you shouldn't have to throw any iron [put on chains] as it is well sanded. The scales [weigh station] are open at the port of entry [into Idaho] but they didn't appear to be doing any inspections. Okay. Copy the dry and dusty [acknowledge the bare pavement]. You look good back that way. All your scales [weigh station] were locked up [was closed] and we haven't seen any cops since yesterday in Minnesota. You have a good trip. You too. Drive safe.

2. Translation: Hey Eastbound, what did you leave behind you? [Can you give me a general traffic report?] Well, you look good back that way. There was a dot [Department of Transportation/law enforcement] man at the bug station [agriculture checkpoint] but they were just rolling you across [agriculture checkpoint was closed]. Arizona was open [weigh station open] but the super coops [full service weigh station with inspection] weren't looking at your comic books [inspection log books] or nothing. Saw Evil Knievel [motorcycle law enforcer] at the 102 [mile post] with a customer [someone pulled over for questioning], a comedian [officer] in the median [radar trap] at the 149 [mile post]. Back on the other side of Flag [Flagstaff, Arizona] it was greasy [icy] and a stick hauler [logging truck], a parking lot [car

hauler], and a rooster cruiser [large car Chicken Hauler] shut it down [closed the road due to an accident] just before Williams [Williams, Arizona]. 'Preciate it. You look good back that way. Got two four wheelers [automobiles] pulled over at the 39 [mile post] with a bunch of disco lights [law enforcement flashing lights and sirens]. Probably caught with go fast or something [drugs: crystal methamphetamine]. Other than that, you look clean [no law enforcement in view] back to Albuquerque. Hey, if you're gonna get your sleeper time [rest] in at the TA [Truckstops of America Truck Stop] in Albuquerque don't expect to get any z's [sleep]. Had lot lizards [prostitutes] banging on the door all night and one of them followed me into the choke and puke [restaurant] claiming she was the best commercial company [paid sex] I was ever gonna find. I told her, momma [my wife] probably wouldn't appreciate her following me around. Okay, I'm losing you [getting out of CB range]. You have a safe one. Later.

3. LOADS is one of many organizations that provide drivers and their families emotional support and marriage counseling, as well as advocacy in relation to trucking company management.

4. These traditionally styled class eight trucks can be identified by their noticeably larger radiator grills, protruding and exposed headlights, and unique paint styles.

5. Ungoverned engines are widely utilized by owner operators and smaller companies. Most drivers prefer these types of engines, while larger companies would rather operate trucks with more fuel-efficient, computer-controlled engines. Ungoverned engines can operate at high speeds and are known for climbing hills faster than governed engines.

6. Anderson has been a member of the Kenworth Driver's Board, is a six-year participant in the Trucker's Buddy Program, and is a member of the Overdrive's Driver Roundtable organization. He also maintains a popular website devoted to trucking issues.

7. A linear is an amplified CB radio that exaggerates a driver's voice and extends the range or area the radio covers. A typical nonamplified CB radio has only a few miles of coverage.

8. Talk Back is a device reverberating the driver's voice internally through the CB radio. It also provides an echo to the voice.

References

Braithwaite, D. O. 1995. Ritualized embarrassment at "coed" wedding and baby showers. *Communication Reports* 8: 145–57.

Cullen, P. 1998–1999. Washington insider. *Land Line* 24 (December–January): 16.

Garber, B. 1998. Chicken hauler t-shirt line keeps cluckin: Former trucker adds new designs, music cassettes. *North American Truck Stop Operators.* Irvine, Calif.: Newport Communications Group.

Hiltz, S. R. 1984. *Online communities: A case study of the office of the future.* Norwood, N.J.: Ablex.

Johnson, S. 1997. *Interface culture: How new technology transforms the way we create and communicate.* San Francisco, Calif.: Harper Edge.

Kelley, D. L., and D-L. Sequeira. 1997. Understanding family functioning in a changing America. *Communication Studies* 48: 93–108.

Philipsen, G. 1975. Speaking like a man in Teamsterville: Cultural patterns of role enactment in an urban neighborhood. *Quarterly Journal of Speech* 61: 13–22.

Pieratt, J. P. 1999. Communication technology. *RPM* 8 (January): 76–80.

Schauerte, M. 1999. Bill in Illinois calls for spot tests on trucks. *St. Louis Post Dispatch,* February 11, p. A6.

Sequeira, D-L. 1994. Gifts of tongues and healing: The performance of charismatic renewal. *Text and Performance Quarterly* 14 (2): 126–42.

Stenfield, C. 1990. *Computer mediated communication in the organization: Using electronic mail at Xerox.* New York: Guilford Press.

KEY TERMS

dialect
electronic communication/medium
nonverbal

qualitative/interpretive analysis
speech community
verbal

GLOSSARY OF ADDITIONAL CB TERMS
USED BY TRUCK DRIVERS

Alligator: separated tire recap
Back Door: traffic behind the truck
Big Word: an upcoming scale house (weigh station) is closed
Bull Wagon: cattle hauler
Castrated: a governed engine
Chicken Fried Everything: the menu of a truck stop
Contact: a radar detector alarm
Dispatcher Brains: driving with no freight
Eye in the Sky: satellite tracking
Front Door: traffic in front of the truck
Go Go Juice: fuel
Hammer Lane: the fast lane
Meat Wagon: an ambulance
Pecker Wrecker: prostitute
Protection: radar detectors and police scanners
Road Candy: amphetamines
Rocking Chair: driving between two truckers traveling in the same direction
Sailboat Fuel: driving on empty
Seat Covers: women drivers
Taking Pictures: radar guns
Tire Check: stopping to urinate
Tyco Slot Car Racing: right lane grooves caused by sun melting the asphalt

REVIEW AND DISCUSSION QUESTIONS

1. Can you name other speech communities or microcultures that go unstudied? If so, what do you think accounts for this lack of investigation?
2. What functions do rituals serve among Chicken Haulers? Would this community be any different without rituals?

3. Do you think there should be standard rules of communication competence for interstate truckers? If so, what would these rules be?

4. Part of living in any culture is managing the tension between wanting to be an individual and wanting to belong to a community. Do the Chicken Haulers and High Liners manage these opposing needs? How?

5. To many Americans, the United States is egalitarian and classless. Do we have class distinctions in the United States? Do issues of class impact the communication between the High Liners and the Chicken Haulers?

6. What do you predict will happen to interstate trucker communication? What will happen if the CB radio becomes obsolete?

Cultural Communities and Social Identities

THE CHAPTERS in part IV explore the extent to which cultural communities form and solidify social identities. Communities under examination include an African American–owned beauty salon, a Latina sorority, the Deadhead speech community, Osage American Indians, and bi-communal groups of Turkish Cypriots and Greek Cypriots.

Curtiss L. Bailey and John Oetzel's study describes the everyday interactions at an African American–owned beauty salon (the "Hair Emporium"). They bring to light the extent to which ethnic identity is reflected and maintained in everyday interactions at the "Hair Emporium." They reveal two key themes: (a) the importance of belonging to the "Hair Emporium" family and feeling connected to other members of the community; and (b) ethnic identity is reflected and maintained through unique expressions of beauty, language, and time.

Margarita Refugia Olivas's study shows that Latina sorority members struggle with many contradictions as they work to reconstruct, yet maintain, a distinct Latina identity within predominately White institutions of higher learning. She reveals that the communicative practices rooted in the cultural value of *familia* (family), *respeto* (respect), and the symbolic representation of Greek letters significantly contribute to the maintenance of a distinct Latina identity within the Greek system. Her findings indicate that Latina sorority women formed their "own sororities" out of a direct and collective need "to belong to a family," to "learn who I am," "to preserve our culture," and "to survive in the White man's world," while resisting the stereotype of being like a "sorority girl."

Natalie J. Dollar explores *membering* within the Deadhead speech community, a community held together by their passion for Grateful Dead music. Her study suggests that Deadhead members employ their speech code as instances of *cultural communication*

(Carbaugh 1988), enacting and displaying cultural identity. In her chapter, she explores three elements of the Deadhead *speech code* members call upon to communicate cultural identity: (1) nonverbal communication, (2) the pre-"show" [concert] speech event, and (3) Grateful Dead lyrics.

Steven B. Pratt and Merry C. Buchanan's study of Osage Indians investigates the communicative practice of a particular community that functions to communicate the speaker's cultural identity. The attention is focused upon occasions of formalized speaking of Osage American Indians. This is an ethnographic study of the Osage Indian tribe focusing upon the speech event of "talking for another." This ethnography of communication utilizes Hymes's (1962, 1972, 1974) schema of components that include speech community, speech situation, speech event, speech act, participants, and ways of speaking.

Benjamin J. Broome's chapter describes the identity issues that have helped create and maintain the Cyprus conflict, impeding its resolution and clouding the prospects for sustainable peace. From a series of workshops and seminars conducted with bi-communal groups of Turkish Cypriots and Greek Cypriots, he examines the dimensions on which each groups defines itself—connection to motherland, attachment to Cyprus, burden of the conflict, relation to the other community, cultural characteristics, and connection to the international community. Emphasis is placed on the interaction between each community's self-definition and on the interdependence between identities.

Tighten Me Up: Reflecting and Maintaining Ethnic Identity through Daily Interactions in an African American–Owned Beauty Salon

Curtiss L. Bailey and John Oetzel

Learning Objectives

After reading this chapter, students will be able to:

- recognize ethnic identity salience and ethnic identity content;
- articulate core symbols of African American ethnic identity; and
- identify how everyday interactions reflect and maintain African American ethnic identity.

At other salons [i.e., predominantly European American] you don't get the same feeling as being around your own people. Also, [here] you don't feel scrutinized, and you can just be yourself. At work, or in society in general, you always have to watch what you say and how you act. You do not want to use too much slang, or come off as unintelligent. Some times you just want to relax. In the [African American] salon, you are around your own people, and no one looks at you in a certain way—everyone talks like you.

—Patron

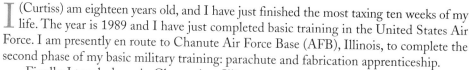

I (Curtiss) am eighteen years old, and I have just finished the most taxing ten weeks of my life. The year is 1989 and I have just completed basic training in the United States Air Force. I am presently en route to Chanute Air Force Base (AFB), Illinois, to complete the second phase of my basic military training: parachute and fabrication apprenticeship.

Finally, I touch down in Champaign, Illinois. As soon as the doors to the small prop aircraft opened, the Illinois chill that I have heard so much about becomes a reality. During the drive to Chanute AFB, I am taken aback by the vast nothingness of the landscape—it is the corn belt, and I have never seen anything like it before in my life. For miles and miles, there is nothing; just a few houses before the backdrop of alabaster skies, which exude a moderately gothic effect. Over the horizon, Chanute AFB appears. It is not the metropolis I had envisioned, but it will be my home for the next three and a half months. When I finish with the preliminaries of "in-processing" and receive my room assignment, I proceed to my room with duffel bags in tow.

I arrive at my room and unpack my belongings. I empty all of my personal belongings out of the duffel bags onto the bed, and I notice that my hair care products are missing. I think to myself, "this is a perfect opportunity for me to acquaint myself with Chanute AFB and find the main exchange." I go to the Chanute AFB main exchange to buy some toiletries and African American hair care products. I arrive at the main exchange and I immediately feel uneasiness—I feel different. There are no familiar faces around me—everything is different, or is it just me? I try to shake my feeling of uneasiness and proceed to look for my hair care products. However, aisle after aisle produces no products specifically tailored for African Americans. My dismay is compounded by the apparent lack of African American workers at the main exchange who might be able to help me. The only items that have a tinge of African American culture are the token *Jet* and *Ebony* magazines ubiquitous in all convenience stores. In this particular moment, I realize I am different.

In New York City where I was raised, there was always a wide array of persons from different ethnic groups. The exposure I had to the divergent views and cultures that exist in New York had a profound impact on my identity, which is bicultural. For example, I use code-switching between American mainstream English and African American vernacular English. I rarely thought of myself in the context of being different; I was just one of the kids on the block who was African American. My hairstyle and hair texture may have been different from some of the kids of different ancestry but, in my estimation, I was the sum product of the amalgamation of cultures in my neighborhood. Whether we were Puerto Rican, Italian, Irish, Asian American, or African American, we all played together and lived in relative harmony. I could walk down the street and go to the Spanish *bodega* for groceries, or I could walk a little further and eat at the Italian pizzeria. The way I speak has a distinct New York flair, which is composed of various jargons from other nationalities. Additionally, in New York I could always find my hair care products.

This is not to suggest that I know nothing of African American history. The civil rights movement and the struggles of the past were common knowledge in my household. My parents were from the South (North Carolina). Although they did not have stories about lynchings and segregation, they always stressed that "everyone knew their place" in the South, and very rarely did anyone venture outside of it. Furthermore, my parents told me, "there will be a time in your life when you are all alone; there will be a time when there are no other 'Black people' around you. When that time comes, be 'cognizant of your actions,' for everything you do will be scrutinized." On that peculiar day in the main exchange, all those things my parents stressed became a reality, and I have since been very cognizant of my actions. The feeling of constant scrutiny can be an unnerving experience for anyone to endure.

Until that moment in the main exchange, those struggles seemed so distant to me. This moment was the one my parents talked about; I was in mainstream U.S. America. An event that may seem trivial to others can trigger or evoke a profound thought about oneself—more importantly, make a person take heed of his or her place in the world.

My feelings are common to many African Americans. African Americans have to deal with the "cruel reality of life in racially segregated America" (Hecht, Collier, and Ribeau 1993, p. 4). African Americans live in a country where they are a numerical minority, where their voices are not always heard, where they have not achieved economic equality, and where they do not always feel they belong (Hecht et al. 1993; Spellers 1998). These struggles may affect individuals in myriad ways, causing some to look for belonging and strive for positive relationships that support ethnic identity and foster community.

Throughout my military career, I have lived in countless locations around the world and currently find myself in Albuquerque, New Mexico. Albuquerque is a culturally diverse city, but with a small African American population (less than 3 percent of the total population according to the 2000 U.S. census). I, and many other African Americans in Albuquerque, seek out locations and organizations where we can bond with other African Americans and share experiences with each other. One such location is the "Hair Emporium," an African American–owned beauty salon.

In this chapter , we describe the everyday interactions at the "Hair Emporium" and focus on the role of communication in reflecting and maintaining ethnic identity. We begin by defining ethnic identity and briefly discuss previous research describing the role of communication in the construction and maintenance of **ethnic identity.** We then note the methods used to collect data for our examination of ethnic identity at the "Hair Emporium." Finally, we describe the everyday interactions at the beauty salon framed by past research on communication and ethnic identity.

Communication and Ethnic Identity

Identity is "a person's conception of self within a particular social, geographical, cultural, and political context" (Yep 1998, p. 79). Identity is a sense of self, a sense of who we are in a specific situation. People have multiple identities that are composed of personal and cultural (or social) aspects (Cupach and Imahori 1993). Personal identities are unique qualities of ourselves such as personality and relationships, whereas cultural identities are aspects we share with other individuals such as gender, national culture, religion, and ethnicity. We focus on ethnicity and ethnic identity.

Ethnicity is a self-perceived community of people with a shared heritage (Hecht et al. 1993). Shared heritage involves aspects such as religious practices, language use, traditions, orientation to the past, ancestry, values, economics, and aesthetics. Ethnic groups have origins that are distinct from nation and race, although nation and race can be a part of ethnicity (e.g., race for African Americans). **Ethnic identity** is the "perceived membership in an ethnic culture that is enacted in the appropriate and effective use of symbols and cultural narratives, similar interpretations and meanings, and common ancestry and traditions" (Hecht et al. 1993, p. 30). In essence, ethnic identity reflects a sense of **belonging** to an ethnic group, such as African American.

Ethnic identity is composed of two key aspects: ethnic identity salience and ethnic identity content (Ting-Toomey et al., 2000). **Ethnic identity salience** refers to the degree of importance of ethnic identity, whereas **ethnic identity content** involves the values and core issues to which individuals subscribe and practice. Ethnic identity salience varies on a continuum from strong to weak (Phinney 1991). Individuals with a strong ethnic identity evaluate their group positively, enjoy their membership in the group, and are involved in ethnic practices. Individuals with a weak ethnic identity have little ethnic interest, tend to identify with the larger national culture, and have little involvement in ethnic practices (Phinney 1991). A recent study found that African Americans have a stronger ethnic identity than Asian Americans, European Americans, and Latin Americans (Ting-Toomey et al. 2000).

The content of African American ethnic identity revolves around a number of core symbols. **Core symbols** are messages that signify the central issues of identity (Hecht et al. 1993). Five core symbols of African American identity have been identified: sharing, uniqueness, positivity, realism, and assertiveness (Hecht et al. 1993). **Sharing** reflects collectivism (Triandis 1995) or the valuing of the group, whereas **uniqueness** reflects individualism (Triandis 1995) or the valuing of individual difference. African American identity is a process of managing the dialectic (i.e., finding balance between two seemingly opposite factors) of paying homage both to the group (e.g., family) and to the individual person. Further, African American identity stresses a positive and emotional outlook on life (i.e., **positivity**) juxtaposed with a strong grounding in reality (i.e., **realism**). Finally, **assertiveness** involves standing up for oneself in the face of oppression.

Ethnic identity is socially constructed (Collier and Thomas 1988; Hecht et al. 1993; Nance and Foeman 1998; Spellers 1998; Yep 1998). A social construction is created over time and is subjective, rather than fixed and objective. A social construction is given meaning through interaction with others. Ethnic identity is complex, multidimensional, and fluid. Ethnic identity is not assigned or concrete, rather it is created, reflected, and maintained through interactions between people (Yep 1998). "We create our identities with those individuals with whom we interact and in the context of specific communication episodes and encounters" (Yep 1998, p. 81). For example, an identity such as African American does not have a fixed meaning. Rather, what it means to be African American is created through interactions with others (both African Americans and non-African Americans). Once this identity is created, it does not stay fixed, but it is re-created, changed, and maintained via everyday interactions. Fluid ethnic identity explains, in part, why some individuals have a strong ethnic identity and why others have a weak ethnic identity.

Method

The research referenced in the previous section frames the current study of ethnic identity at the "Hair Emporium." Specifically, we sought to answer the following research question:

How is ethnic identity reflected and maintained in everyday interactions at the "Hair Emporium"?

In order to answer this question, we employed a combination of interviewing and participant observations. The first author interviewed twenty members of this community. Ten of the participants (four men and six women) were employees or owners of the "Hair Emporium" and ten of the participants (four men and six women) were patrons. The interviews were conducted at the beauty salon and lasted from fifteen to thirty minutes. The interview format was unstructured so as to capture the fluid nature of conversations at the salon. The interviewer took notes during the interviews and rewrote the notes as soon as possible after the interview (immediately after the interview or occasionally after several interviews).

A Day at the "Hair Emporium"

The "Hair Emporium" (the names of the business and of all the employees are pseudonyms) was opened in 1976. The salon has been in its current location for the past five years. The salon is located in an area of the city where ethnic minorities are the majority population. The area's population predominantly includes African Americans and Latin Americans (e.g., Cubans, Hispanics, Mexicans, and Mexican Americans).

There are ten principal workers: Cassandra, Henry, John, Jack, Kim, Martha, Jennifer, Earl, Mary, and Malik. The owners are Martha and Jennifer. There is a manicurist (Kim) and eight hair stylists (including Martha and Jennifer). Earl is Jennifer's husband and works around the store doing odd jobs as they are needed, such as cleaning the floors or performing repairs. He works as a supervisor at a factory and helps out in his spare time. Each of the other workers rents booth space from Martha and Jennifer and works independently. All of the workers are African American except for Jack who is European American. The salon caters to both male and female clients. The clientele is predominately African American (approximately 70 percent) or Afro Cuban (approximately 20 percent) with smaller percentages of Mexican Americans, Mexicans, and European Americans.

A typical day at the "Hair Emporium" might proceed as follows. (All of the events described here do not necessarily occur in a single day, but they do happen on a regular basis.) Today, like most days, the day starts at 9:00 A.M. Jennifer and Henry arrived at 8:30 to prepare for 9:00 appointments. Jennifer's appointment is for an aunt and her two nieces, while Henry is waiting for Bill, an older gentleman, who is scheduled for a haircut. The aunt and her two nieces enter, and Jennifer asks how they are doing. The light conversation continues for a few minutes, and Jennifer asks what they want done today. The aunt replies, "We need to get their hair permed and take care of the kitchen." A perm signifies that the girls will be getting their hair straightened and "taking care of the kitchen" refers to cleaning up the hair on the back of the neck. Jennifer begins to work on the girls' hair while the aunt sits close by and continues to talk with Jennifer.

At this time, Bill comes in for his appointment. He and Henry exchange greetings and talk about life for awhile. Bill sits down and says, "I need to get tightened up." Henry replies, "You know I'm gonna hook you up" and begins to cut his hair. The phone rings and the aunt picks it up (without being asked) because Jennifer and Henry are busy. The phone is for Henry and he takes the call. Henry talks for about ten minutes, and Bill patiently waits for Henry to finish. The smile on his face demonstrates that he is not bothered by the delay.

A new customer comes in and says she has an appointment with Martha and sits down. She waits for about fifteen minutes after her scheduled time. The phone rings and Jennifer answers it. It is Martha and she is calling to say she cannot come in today because she has to take care of her child. Jennifer tells the customer that Martha will not be able to come in today and the customer says, "That's okay, I'll just come back tomorrow." Her demeanor (soft tone of voice and smile) demonstrates that she is not upset.

Henry finishes up Bill's hair and Bill states, "Let me see the mirror and see if I'm as beautiful as I was before." Henry chides, "Now, you know all your cuts are tight; I don't know why you even ask for the mirror." Bill laughs and replies, "You know I'm just messin' with you."

Two more customers arrive, one waiting for Malik and one waiting for John. Jennifer tells the customer waiting for Malik that he is running fifteen minutes late and the customer responds, "I guess we're on CP [colored people's] time today" and sits down. The customer waiting for John is early and begins to play a game of dominoes with Bill. It is a pleasant game that Bill wins, and then the **jonesing** (high-spirited teasing with friendly barbs) begins. Bill exhorts, "Man, you can't play with me. I usually charge people for the lessons I give. Just admit it; I'm better than you." The others in the shop start teasing the loser as well: "We know you didn't let him beat you. You better play him again." They play again even though John is ready for his appointment.

By this time it is after lunch, and a couple of customers have been there two to three hours. Cassandra has arrived for her appointment with a woman who wants braids. Cassandra brought in her young child today. Cassandra is washing the customer's hair, and her child is about to get in the chemical bin (a bin with relaxers and other hair-care products). One of the customers playing dominoes notices the child, grabs him, and directs him toward his mother. Cassandra says, "Just give him a gentle pat next time he gets in there." The customer stops the child three more times.

Across the room, Malik and one of his customers are debating about sports. They are talking about the NBA championship. The customer is from New York and is rooting for the Knicks, but Malik says they do not have a chance. The customer is not getting his hair done today; he just came in to "hang out." Kim has arrived for a few nail appointments. She is painting a customer's nails in bright reds, oranges, and yellows.

The early afternoon finds a lull in the day. No customers are there so Cassandra, Kim, Malik, and John are hanging out talking. Jennifer and Henry have gone home for the day. The lull lasts for almost an hour when a customer for John enters. Soon after, Tamika, Cassandra's sister, comes in to talk. She has a mark on her arm, and she is trying to figure out what it is. A couple of patrons who have recently entered the salon join the conversation. Tamika thinks it is ringworm, but one of the patrons says it is a spider bite. Satisfied with the explanation, Tamika and Cassandra continue to talk while the patrons go to Kim and Malik for their appointments.

An hour later, Earl comes in to fix up a few things around the salon. He is quick to engage in conversation with the patrons and workers. He begins talking about the old days, about how he worked on a farm and how his family stuck together. The patrons and stylists listen with respect, as Earl has an enormous amount of life experience and represents the paternal figure of the salon. Work and conversations continue for the next couple of hours.

It is now almost five, and everyone is getting ready to go home and be with their families. Tomorrow is another day.

Communication and Ethnic Identity at the "Hair Emporium"

In examining the day's events at the "Hair Emporium," we can see how communication functions to reflect and maintain identity. We organize our analysis of the day around the importance of belonging to the "Hair Emporium" family and maintaining ethnic identity. As we analyze the events, we weave quotes from participants in and out to help illustrate our points.

Belonging to the "Hair Emporium" Family

The first apparent aspect of identity is the importance of belonging to the salon and feeling connected to the other members. The patrons and workers at the "Hair Emporium" all feel that they belong and stress the importance of belonging as one reason why they patronize or work at the salon. It is a common occurrence for patrons to "hang out" at the salon long after their appointment is completed, as Bill, for example, plays dominoes. Patrons often play games (dominoes and chess) with other patrons or stylists or simply talk about life. As one patron stated, "The reason I come to the "Hair Emporium" is the feeling of being at ease and at a comfortable environment; it gives me the feeling as if I were 'at home.'" It is also common for patrons to come in and talk even when they do not have an appointment.

The stylists also feel a sense of belonging. They can bring in their children when they need to, and can count on each other to help out. The workers are very supportive of each other and compliment each other's work, especially new stylists such as Jack. Jack (the only European American stylist) also feels the belonging: "I feel like part of the family and we are all like family."

The feeling of being part of the family is illustrated by the patrons' behaviors in the day's events. It is common for customers to answer the phone to help out the stylists when they are busy. This behavior reflects a sense of community and connectedness among the patrons and workers. Similarly, the customers help the workers in other ways, such as the customer who kept Cassandra's child out of trouble. The performance of these "small" tasks helps to keep the salon running smoothly and reflects that the participants in this community feel connected. That is, they feel like it is their responsibility to help out. In these cases, the nonverbal communication of the patrons (e.g., playing games, hanging out, and helping) demonstrates that the members are connected and serves as a means to maintain a sense of identity in the salon.

Reflecting and Maintaining Ethnic Identity

When we examine further, we can see that identity is more than just a group of people who have a common bond, but rather ethnicity is the shaping force. Several factors illustrate the reflection and maintenance of ethnic identity. First, the very purpose of the salon—**beauty**—demonstrates the uniqueness of the African American culture. During the day, two common African American hairstyles were discussed—perms and braids. The uniqueness of African American beauty ends up connecting individuals. Earl explains, "Our styles reflect African American heritage. Our textures of hair are different than other nationalities, so it is more of a community type of situation." A patron also noted, "Our skin and hair care products are very different from other nationalities. . . . I feel this bonds people together because there were not (in the past) a lot of representation in the public [the media]." Hairstyles and fingernail styles often are emotive and reflective of the positivity of African American culture (Hecht et al. 1993). As Cassandra states, "Black people like to express themselves in their nails, clothes, and hair." Thus the physical styles of beauty bring African Americans a common identity but also allow for a personal expression of self.

Second, the **language** of the salon is reflective of African American culture and identity. The members of this community utilize a style of language that is not mainstream, standard English. They utilize slang such as "take care of the kitchen" and "tighten me up" and communicative rituals such as "jonesing," "**playing the dozens**" (similar to jonesing), or boasting. These rituals are ways to gain recognition in the group as a skillful orator but also allow community members to promote community stability through expressions that are consistent with community norms (Garner 1983). Language is one of the most important factors in the maintenance of a strong ethnic identity (Ting-Toomey 1989). Language helps to make an ethnic group a collective unit during interactions with other group members and within the group (Giles and Franklyn-Stokes 1989). The unique aspects of the language in the salon help this group to maintain a strong sense of ethnic identity by distinguishing themselves from others, as well as bonding the group in common understanding.

Third, the sense of belonging is reflective of being Black and "fitting in" within mainstream U. S. America from this community's perspective. As a patron expressed,

> At other salons [i.e., predominantly European American] you don't get the same feeling as being around your own people. Also, [here] you don't feel scrutinized, and you can just be yourself. At work, or in society in general, you always have to watch what you say and how you act. You do not want to use too much slang, or come off as unintelligent. Some times you just want to relax. In the salon, you are around your own people, and no one looks at you in a certain way—everyone talks like you.

Another patron expressed this feeling as well when she said, "There is a natural instinct to come here and hang out—be Black without people judging you." One woman pointed out, "People come to the salon to get their 'Black fix.'" Working or coexisting in mainstream America, individuals of marginalized groups, such as African Americans, have to put up a corporate or social facade if they want to be successful or accepted. In the beauty salon, they can just be themselves without the reprisal of superiors or risking social censure through public scrutiny. This situation is illustrative of Goffman's (1959) **public** and **private** domains of **self**. Goffman explains that individuals perform on a public stage in a manner that is expected based on the situation. The public performance places stress on individuals and, thus, every person needs a place where he or she can escape performance demands. This place is the backstage or private domain. For the members, the "Hair Emporium" provides the private domain where they can escape from the public performance of mainstream society and simply "be themselves."

The comfort felt by the members also is simply in being understood. A patron illustrated the importance of understanding when he stated,

> At the salon, when you are around your own people, you can talk the way you want to talk, and you don't have to explain everything to other "individuals" who may not understand where you are coming from. Your people just get what you are saying the first time around. A lot of times people who do not have the same life experiences as you, really cannot see where you are coming from, so you have to stop and explain things to them. When you are around people who you can identify with, they understand where you are coming from—they just get what you are saying.

When patrons come in for haircuts, immediately one of the stylists asks how they are doing. The response may be "all right," "not so good," or "just making it." Hidden within those statements is a verbal shorthand. The person may have lost their job; times may be hard; or a host of other different factors may be plaguing that individual at that particular moment. The stylist may just say, "Man, I know where you are coming from; times are hard; and I'm just making it myself." Common understanding of daily events and common interaction styles help maintain ethnic identity.

A final important aspect of African American identity is reflected through the orientation toward time. Time is often constructed as either fixed or fluid. These two types of time are referred to as **monochronic-time** (M-time) and **polychronic-time** (P-time) (Hall 1976). People who follow M-time pay attention to actual time and do one thing at a time. They adhere to linear schedules and compartmentalize the day. The schedule may take on a priority above all else and be treated as unalterable. People who follow P-time pay attention to relational time and may be involved in simultaneous activities. P-time is characterized by a great involvement with people, and with completing human interactions rather than adhering to schedules. The culture of the "Hair Emporium" is consistent with P-time. In the day at the salon, we can see that Bill was not bothered by his stylist stopping his haircut to take a phone call. Another patron was not upset in the least when her stylist would not be keeping the appointment she had set up. A third patron commented about CP time when her stylist was running late.

The African American community has it roots from West Africa (most African Americans are descendants from tribes of West Africa vis-à-vis the slave trade), where time orientation recognizes only the past and the present, not the future (Cox 1993). Time is elastic, and relatively little consideration is given toward time. Rather, activities and people are important. This orientation toward time in the African American community is indicated by the colloquialism *CP time*. **CP time** is used to describe flexibility during the scheduling and arrival of events. When a person schedules an event, there is a great deal of leeway used for beginning and ending of ceremonies. If the ceremony is to start at 8:00 P.M., invitations might say it would start at 7:30 P.M. Moreover, in certain instances, it is vogue to arrive late to an event. In essence, African Americans, through age-old traditions that have been passed down from generation to generation, transmuted the way in which they do business in the mainstream United States to fit their own historical way of doing business—less rigidly and with an air of flexibility. However, it is important to note that not all African

Americans follow CP time, and in fact, a few customers are upset by the loose time schedules of the salon.

The orientation toward time at the salon helps the members maintain an ethnic identity that balances the dialectical tension between the core symbols of sharing and uniqueness. Earlier, we explained that patrons often remain at the salon to play games or just talk.
Time is flexible to these patrons, which allows them to maintain interpersonal relationships
and be with their "Black brothers and sisters," as one patron explains. At the same time, flexibility with time allows other individuals to maintain their uniqueness. The fact that most
of the patrons do not get upset with lateness or missed appointments reflects the attitude
that people have to do what they have to do. It enables people to "do their own thing," but
to do so in a way that reinforces African American identity.

In summary, examining the everyday activities at the salon, we can see several examples of how communication reflects and maintains a strong ethnic identity. Patrons come to
the "Hair Emporium" to feel good about themselves and be with people like them. Stylists
work at the salon not only to make a living, but because they feel comfortable there. Their
daily interactions reflect and reinforce strong, positive ethnic identities. In addition, the daily
interactions reinforce several of the core symbols of African American identity identified
by previous research (Hecht, Collier, and Ribeau 1993). Sharing is evidenced by the time
spent with each other and the common feelings and bonds expressed there. Interestingly,
there is a balance of sharing with uniqueness. The members of the salon community share
their individuality with each other and grow closer by being individuals within the community. **Positivity** is expressed in the hairstyles and nail styles—they are expressions of the
self and ways to feel good about oneself. In addition, jonesing is an example of positive,
emotional expressions to express self and to bond with one another. Overall, the everyday
activities represent the very essence of African American identity for the members of the
"Hair Emporium."

Intercultural Implications

There are several implications of the findings for intercultural interactions. First, the study
helps to illustrate the difficulty that some African Americans face in trying to "fit in" to
the mainstream United States. The interactions at the "Hair Emporium" help these individuals be comfortable and be themselves. Second, the study helps to illustrate that many
African Americans are bicultural. They are able to switch codes to communicate with
members of the mainstream United States as well as with their own ethnic group. Third,
despite the bicultural nature of many African Americans, misunderstandings and conflicts are likely to be frequent when African Americans communicate with members of
other ethnic groups. Cox (1993) explains that conflict and tensions increase because the
communication styles of one ethnic group do not necessarily fit with those of other ethnic groups. Because ethnic groups do not "practice" identity in the same way, the interactions will not fit and thus misunderstandings result. Fourth, while misunderstandings are
likely to occur, there is also commonality that can be emphasized as a way to bridge these
differences. The commonality may be found in the core symbols of African American
identity: sharing, positivity, realism, uniqueness, and assertiveness. Some of these symbols

are likely to be present in other ethnic groups (although they may be reflected in different rituals).

A final important implication is the caution with which readers should interpret the findings of the current chapter. It is possible to read the chapter and believe that African Americans are a homogeneous group; in fact, African American culture includes a heterogeneous population. It is important to realize that the group described here is a specific community that has some overlap with African American culture, but also some unique features. Effective intercultural interaction occurs when we support the cultural values and identities of a group and we respect and support individual differences.

Conclusion

Going to the "Hair Emporium" means much more to me than receiving a satisfying haircut: it is a place where I feel comfortable, and it is that little part of home for someone like me who is far away from their home. One thing that has always stood out for me as indicative of "our culture" is that we have always tried to make people feel at home. The conversations, life experiences, and certain little nuances of the daily interactions with persons who work at or patronize the salon help maintain and foster a sense of community through the age-old tradition of telling stories (some more embellished than others) and light jesting (jonesing).

Ethnic identity is created in daily interactions and rituals that demonstrate common understanding and shared experiences. The language, use of time, and communication styles may be unique to this community, but the reflection and maintenance of ethnic identity through communication is an important process for all ethnic groups.

This fact may be more true for ethnic minority groups (e.g., Asian American, Latinos, Native American) than the ethnic majority group (i.e., European American) in the United States. Ting-Toomey et al. (2000) found that European Americans have a weaker ethnic identity than African Americans, Asian Americans, and Latino Americans. Living in mainstream U.S. society is a difficult public performance for many members of ethnic minority groups because the mainstream employs a variety of rules and communication styles that are not consistent with ethnic minority cultures. Investigating other communities and businesses like the "Hair Emporium" will likely reveal similar evidence of ethnic identity maintenance that can help us learn about these communities and cultures and the construction of ethnic identity in general.

References

Collier, M. J., and M. Thomas. 1988. Cultural identity: An interpretive perspective. In Y. Y. Kim and W. B. Gudykunst (Eds.), *Theories in intercultural communication* (pp. 99–120). Newbury Park, Calif.: Sage.

Cox, T. 1993. *Cultural diversity in organizations: Theory, research, and practice.* San Francisco: Berrett-Koehler.

Cupach, W. R., and T. T. Imahori. 1993. Identity management theory: Communication competence in intercultural episodes and relationships. In R. L. Wiseman and J. Koester (Eds.), *Intercultural communication competence* (pp. 112–31). Newbury Park, Calif.: Sage.

Garner, T. 1983. Playing the dozens: Folklore as strategies for living. *Quarterly Journal of Speech* 69: 47–57.

Giles, H., and A. Franklyn-Stokes. 1989. Communicator characteristics. In M. K. Asante and W. B. Gudykunst (Eds.), *Handbook of international and intercultural communication* (pp. 117–44). Newbury Park, Calif.: Sage.

Goffman, E. 1959. *The presentation of self in everyday life.* Garden City, N.Y.: Doubleday.

Hall, E. T. 1976. *Beyond culture.* New York: Doubleday.

Hecht, M. L., M. J. Collier, and S. A. Ribeau. 1993. *African American communication: Ethnic identity and cultural interpretation.* Newbury Park, Calif.: Sage.

Lindlof, T. R. 1995. *Qualitative communication research methods.* Thousand Oaks, Calif.: Sage.

Nance, T. A., and A. K. Foeman. 1998. On being biracial in the United States. In J. M. Martin, T. K. Nakayama, and L. A. Flores (Eds.), *Readings in cultural contexts* (pp. 53–62). Mountain View, Calif.: Mayfield.

Phinney, J. 1991. Ethnic identity and self-esteem: A review and integration. *Hispanic Journal of Behavioral Sciences* 13: 193–208.

Spellers, R. E. 1998. Happy to be nappy! Embracing an Afrocentric aesthetic for beauty. In J. M. Martin, T. K. Nakayama, and L. A. Flores (Eds.), *Readings in cultural contexts* (pp. 70–78). Mountain View, Calif.: Mayfield.

Ting-Toomey, S. 1989. Identity and interpersonal bonding. In M. K. Asante and W. B. Gudykunst (Eds.), *Handbook of international and intercultural communication* (pp. 351–73). Newbury Park, Calif.: Sage.

Ting-Toomey, S., K. K. Yee-Jung, R. B. Shapiro, W. Garcia, T. J. Wright, and J. G. Oetzel. 2000. Ethnic/cultural identity salience and conflict styles in four U.S. ethnic groups. *International Journal of Intercultural Relations* 24: 47–81.

Triandis, H. C. 1995. *Individualism and collectivism.* Boulder, Colo.: Westview.

Yep, G. A. 1998. My three cultures: Navigating the multicultural identity landscape. In J. M. Martin, T. K. Nakayama, and L. A. Flores (Eds.), *Readings in cultural contexts* (pp. 79–85). Mountain View, Calif.: Mayfield.

KEY TERMS

assertiveness	jonesing
beauty	language
belonging	monochronic-time
core symbols	playing the dozens
CP time	polychronic-time
ethnic identity	positivity
ethnic identity content	public/private self
ethnic identity salience	realism
ethnicity	sharing
identity	uniqueness

REVIEW AND DISCUSSION QUESTIONS

1. What is ethnic identity salience? Ethnic identity content?
2. What are some core symbols of African American ethnic identity?
3. What are the key themes regarding everyday interactions at the "Hair Emporium"?
4. How are the daily interactions at the "Hair Emporium" reflective of the core symbols?
5. In what ways are the ethnic identity practices at the "Hair Emporium" similar to and different from ethnic identity practices of other groups (e.g., Asian Americans, European Americans, Latin Americans, Native Americans, other African American groups)?
6. What role does ethnic identity play during interactions with people from other ethnic groups (i.e., intercultural interactions)?

Communicating a Latina Identity: Becoming Different, Doing Difference, and Being Different

Margarita Refugia Olivas

LEARNING OBJECTIVES

After reading this chapter, students will be able to:

- gain a deeper understanding of the micro and macro processes that work to segregate the Greek system;
- receive a new and different perspective of the Greek system;
- expand their knowledge of the communicative practices of Latina sorority members that promote (re)construction of individual and group identities within a highly gender- and race/ethnic-segregated Greek system;
- increase their knowledge of Latina sorority formation and cultural values, norms, and belief systems that may enhance their intercultural communication skills; and
- understand Latinas' communicative practices that may hinder or enhance their intercultural and intracultural communication.

The salient issue is that each of us approaches the world and orders our perceptions from the standpoint of our group's culture. Through direct or vicarious group participation, we internalize the group's perspective, as well as external phenomena, to define ourselves.

—B. J. Risman (1982, p. 231)

Ryan Booth, a member of Alabama's Delta Kappa Epsilon house . . . [stated] if I had to vote right now on whether to bring a black member into my fraternity, I'd probably vote no. . . . But it is not that I am a racist. It is just that white fraternities and black fraternities have always been separate, and nobody wants to be the first to change that.

—E. Hoover (2001, p. A36)

Beginning in elementary school, U.S. American girls are socialized to identify with other children who hold similar cultural norms, values, and beliefs. This socialization occurs mainly through participation in groups that provide members with a sense of belonging that "isolates them from other environments and **value systems** that may not be compatible" (Peterson, Altback, Skinner, and Trainor 1976, p. 110). In a Burkean (1969) sense, this need to identify with others serves as the motivation to engage in certain activities or to join certain organizations. Since concepts of self are socially constructed through everyday interaction (Goffman 1959; Burke 1969; Berger and Luckmann 1966), such group affiliations serve as the basis for identity formation and intergroup identification. In line with Goffman, Risman, as cited above, notes that "through direct or vicarious group participation, we internalize the group's perspective, as well as external phenomena, to define ourselves" (1982, p. 231).

As with elementary school-age girls, young college women tend to engage in activities and join organizations that are gender specific, such as cheerleader groups and women's basketball. However, because athletics is not as accessible to women in college as it may have been in formative years, college women tend to join social organizations, such as Greek sororities. For more than two centuries, the Greek system has attracted mostly affluent White men and women who were, and continue to be, highly homogenous (Peterson et al. 1976) and who tend to place a great emphasis on **history** and tradition (Keller and Hart 1982). Rose and Elton (1971) have found that sororities have historically recruited members who conform to existing traditional roles and relationships based on economic and social compatibility. As a result, Greek organizational members tend to form strong intergroup identification due to similarities in sex, age, education, interests, and socioeconomic background (Giddan 1988).

Organizational communication research reveals that the more intimate a social network is, the more similar the individuals are to one another (Stohl 1995) and the more comfortable they are communicating with one another (Gudykunst 1991). Because one's "sex is associated with a variety of sources of dissimilarity, including differences in interests, norms of self-disclosure and content of humor" (Martin 1994, p. 411), men and women tend to not socialize as much with one another as do women with women and men with men. These studies suggest that individuals orient themselves toward associating with others who are more like them, while shying away from those who are more dissimilar. Such associations within the Greek system have resulted in predominately sex- and race/ethnic-segregated Greek fraternities and sororities. These organizations are cultural sites that manifested as a result of "historically transmitted systems of symbols and meanings, and norms" (Collier 1988, p. 102).

However, due to the development of coed Greek organizations, sex segregation is beginning to ease, while racial/ethnic discrimination continues to perpetuate a predominately race-segregated Greek system (Hoover 2001). Scholars have found that traditional **White**

Greek organization (WGO) members tend to be more prejudiced toward minorities than White non-Greeks (Muir 1991). White Greek members also tend to be more opposed to interracial marriages and less concerned about racial prejudices. They also tend to have less interest in the rise of hate groups than do non-Greek Whites (Morris 1991). Other studies reveal that although it may not be intentional, traditional WGOs tend to covertly exclude minority students via the Rush process (Keller and Hart 1982; Mongell and Roth 1991; Schmitz and Forbes 1994; Hoover 2001).

Through **Rush** and the ensuing pledging process, WGO members create deep-rooted intergroup identification that has historically contributed to race/ethnic minority exclusion, forced segregation, and ultimately self-segregation within the Greek system. From past research we know that self-identification "reflects and in turn shapes racial understanding and dynamics" (Omi and Winant 1986, p. 3). Consequently, as members are forced to segregate, or voluntarily choose to self-segregate, communication becomes increasingly limited between individuals who perceive themselves as different from each other. So, as individuals perpetuate segregation, the potential for "true" diversity diminishes within the Greek system.

In order for administrators and Greek leaders to better understand the differences that limit "true" integration of the Greek system, there is a need for research that explores the various socialization processes of *all* Greek organizations. To date, such studies have largely focused on WGOs (e.g., Lottes and Kuriloff 1994) and most scholars have limited their investigation to the social construction of gender roles and sexism (e.g. Risman 1982; Stombler 1994; Stombler and Martin 1994). To help fill the gap in literature, utilizing ethnographic methods of analysis this study explores the most prominent communicative practices of two Latina sororities and reports findings of how such practices promote (re)construction of their cultural group identities within a predominately race/ethnic-segregated Greek system. This study expands the existing literature that largely focuses on traditional WGOs and **Black Greek** organizations (BGOs), while answering the question, "What are the shared cultural communicative practices of Latina Greek sorority members that reflect a Latina cultural identity within a predominately race/ethnic-segregated Greek system?"

As humans we tend to stereotype and generalize. Thus, the reader should be cautious to not view the interpretations and observations extracted from this study as universal characteristics of all Latinas nor of all Latina sororities, although these findings suggest that Latina sororities in general hold similar cultural values regarding *familia* and *respeto*. The reader should also be aware that there are other types of Greek organizations not mentioned in this study. For example, one can find Jewish, Asian, and even multicultural Greek organizations. Unfortunately, due to space and time, this study was limited to reporting a brief description of the historical development of the **Latina Greek** sororities and only the most pronounced **communicative practices** of Latina Greek members. I am confident that other studies exploring various ethnic Greek organizations will follow.

Method

Data collection included consulting twenty-four participants who were each interviewed for forty-five minutes to one hour. Twenty-one participants were either active or alumnae sorority members. Three were student life administrators. Fifteen of the twenty-one participants are first-generation college bound and six of the twenty-one participants are second-generation college bound. Twenty participants ranged from nineteen to twenty-six years of age. Of the twenty-one sorority members, four are immigrants. Twenty of the twenty-one claimed a Mexican heritage, one claimed a Spanish heritage, and eleven are from a lower socioeconomic background (their parents worked in the service industry, as field hands, or as homemakers). Ten participants are from a middle- or upper-middle-class socioeconomic background. One of the twenty-one participants is a sorority adviser who is in her thirties. Other written text for analysis was obtained from various Latina sorority websites. Also, thirty hours of observation were conducted over a three-week period during sorority members' lunch breaks, cultural events, organizational meetings, and community service projects.

The Development of Latina Greek Organizations

Up until the 1970s, and even through today, United States institutions of higher learning were largely segregated by race; in particular, such institutions were Black or White. With the advent of the Chicano civil rights movement, affirmative action programs were established to integrate young Latinos/as into academic environments throughout the Southwest. Over the last couple of decades, scholars have investigated Latinos/as in such settings. Scholarly findings reflect that Latinos/as who attend predominately White institutions of higher learning have reported experiencing higher levels of feeling alienated than students who attend more diverse institutions. The most common factors contributing to such alienation are culture shock (Cardoza 1991; Loo and Rolison 1986; Vasquez 1982), perceived or blatant racism (Davidson 1996; Hurtado 1992; Nieves-Squires 1991; Thurston 1994), and a lack of sociocultural support systems (Davidson 1996; Loo and Rolison 1986; Solberg, Valdez, and Villarreal 1994). Moreover, as a result of feeling alienated due to perceptions of not belonging in such institutions, Latinos have a tendency to drop out of college (Kraft 1991; Lunneborg and Lunneborg 1986).

Combined, this literature shows that U.S. institutions of higher learning have not been conducive to the academic and career advancement of Latino/a students. As early as 1982, researchers found that Latinos/as perceived predominately White colleges as foreign and hostile (Vasquez). Considering that college campuses of the 1970s were likely to seem non-receptive of Latino/a college students, understandably Latinos/as began to create support systems for themselves, such as **Latino Greek** fraternities and sororities. Such organizations could help members gain feelings of belonging, while providing a safe place to (re)construct a sense of self.

Sorority membership would especially be desirable for those Latinas experiencing alienation, academic challenges, and the challenges of changing traditional gender roles. The following excerpt extracted from a website detailing the historical development of *Lambda Theta Alpha, Latin Sorority, Inc.*, the first U.S. Latina sorority, reveals that these organizations emerged as a response to feelings of alienation and a need to (re)construct a Latina identity within predominately White institutions.

> Traditionally, the role of the Latina woman was that of maintaining the family institution. . . . In the early '70s colleges and universities experienced an influx of female

enrollment. With this growth, the need for support groups and outreach programs was at an all-time high. This was true for all women and especially for the low percentage of Latina women in higher education. . . . In 1975, 30 women convened to discuss the formation of a sorority for Latina women. This sorority's main purpose was to create a support group for women of color in a predominately White society. . . . This allowed the independent Latina woman of a new era to have a sense of belonging and with that, achieve her highest potential.

(Re)Constructing a Latina Identity through Sisterhood: "Becoming Different"

The excerpt quoted above, like those extracted from the interviews conducted for this study, reflects that many Latinas are consciously working toward **(re)constructing** their identities as independent Latinas through sorority **sisterhood.** Through exploration of how Latina sorority members "do" the "being" of their cultural identities (Collier 1996), it is evident that such efforts to (re)construct their cultural identity create contradictions and internal conflict in the process of **"becoming different."** This is particularly true for first-generation college students who are striving to break free of traditional gender roles (Rodriguez 1988; Grebler, Moore, and Guzman 1970).

Historically, Latinas have been expected to marry young and bear children by the age of twenty (Grebler et al. 1970). The notion of Latinas attending college therefore defies traditional gender roles within traditional Latino communities (Cardoza 1991; Keefe, Padilla, and Carlos 1978; Nieves-Squires 1991). Education has historically been reserved for Latinos who support wives who, in turn, give birth to their children and care for the home. Thus, traditional value systems tend typically to keep Latinas from gaining education or entering the workforce.

In contradiction to such cultural beliefs, many Latinas believe that economic independence can be achieved through higher education. Like the undergraduate Latinas in a study conducted by Cardoza (1991), all the Latina sorority members in this study who come from lower socioeconomic backgrounds view education as a means of escaping the impoverished lifestyles of their parents. They also view their potential success as a means of assisting their parents financially. The excerpt below exemplifies such sentiments.

> My mother works cleaning rooms. Right now my father is unemployed. But usually he works in the fields. They work very hard. They didn't want me to come; they were sad. My cousin helped me convince them. They realized that I would be better able to help them and myself if I had a career. (07, Set 1)

Additionally, interviewees view their respective sororities as a way to (re)construct their identities as Latinas. A review of Latina sorority websites reveals a high degree of racial/ethnic diversity within each sorority, including Euro-American and African American members. Although the majority of the interviewees reported being of Mexican descent, the founding mothers of the two sororities participating in this study were also of Nicaraguan, Costa Rican, Guatemalan, Cuban, and El Salvadoran heritage, with a few of the women being biracial with one parent Latino/a. According to these websites and all the interviewees, Latina sororities welcome all women, as long as they are willing to accept Latino values and ways of being.

> Anyone who wants to be in this Latina sorority can. Whether they are Latino or not, whether they're gorgeous or not, whether they have enough money or not. . . .
> So again, it's a real diverse group of girls. Some are first generation. . . . Some have been in the United States for generations and generations. That's definitely an advantage, in that they are able to meet girls at different levels as far as dealing with identity issues and things like that here in the U.S. (alumni, Set 02)

Becoming fully accepted as a Latina is very important to those who are biracial Latinas but do not look Latina. For example, one White and Mexican American interviewee stated that throughout her life, people, including Latinos/as, have mistaken her for being White. Not being viewed as Latina, she claimed, was "really painful to me." For her, sorority membership provides an opportunity to "learn more about my **culture,** to be around people of my culture, and to learn more about who I am." Another way the sorority serves to legitimize her Latina identity is through performing community service, which makes her "feel proud." It's like, "Hey okay, good job, you're doing something for your people" (01, Set 1).

Although Latina sorority members are actively and consciously working to (re)construct a Latina identity within the Greek system, they are paradoxically both consciously and subconsciously resisting traditional gendered Latina identities. In the sorority it is

> safe to be assertive. . . .Your father, your brother aren't here threatening you. In the sorority there's no gender roles in the sense of you're here to wait on people. One woman, her mother blatantly told her, if you go into this field no one will want to marry you. But in our organization no one thinks she's weird because she's in a technical field. No one makes fun of her. . . . They're free to be who they are, whatever it may be, they're not playing those roles in the family. (Administrator, Set 1)

It is evident from the passage above that while the organization serves to promote a female identity that is free of male dominance, deeply embedded cultural values serve paradoxically to tie these women to traditional gender expectations. In particular, the cultural value is rooted in the concept of *respeto* as it relates to one's sexuality.

The Role of *Respeto* in (Re)Constructing Gendered Identities: "Doing Difference"

Historically, *respeto* has been at the core of one's **Latino** identity and plays a vital role in dictating appropriate behaviors, interactions, and decision-making processes (Blea 1992; Covarrubias 2002). Generally speaking, Latinos are very strict with their female children. In fact, the women tend to be as strict, if not stricter than the males in the culture. For Latinos, *respeto* is a cultural value that serves as the root of traditional Latino gender roles, particularly of female sexuality. The socialization process of female (self) *respeto*, like any other cultural value, begins at a very young age and is influenced by a history of Catholicism (Castillo 1995). One form of *respeto* specifically instilled in girls is protection of, and the holding sacred of, one's virginity and the notion of monogamy (Castillo 1995; Sabogal, Perez-Stable, Otero-Sabogal, and Hiatt 1995). To do otherwise would result in the women being viewed "as *malcriad(as)* or *sin crianza* (both terms meaning 'poorly trained at home by the parents')" (Gangotena 2000, p. 75) and would bring *verguenza* (shame) and the threat of isolation from *la familia* and *la comunidad* (Marsiglia and Holleran 1999).

As a result of *respeto* being a cultural value, women are often viewed as objects of ownership, which are

> always susceptible to being "conquered" by someone outside the family. For this reason, "good girls," (while they may not wear veils or be covered from head to foot on the street) must not behave so as to elicit aggressive male behavior that would jeopardize family honor, or as more popularly put today: "get them in trouble." (Castillo 1995, p. 79)

The deep-rooted ideology of *respeto* associated with traditionally ascribed gender role expectations manifests in Latina sorority members' perceptions of traditional Greek sorority women as "sorority girls" or "party girls." When asked why they viewed White Greek sorority women as "party girls," respondents stated that their perceptions were shaped by television, movies, and personal observations. Such stereotypes are perpetuated even by scholars who have labeled their subjects as "'buddies' or 'slutties'" (Stombler 1994). The responses to the question, "What do you like least about being in a sorority?" reflects the strong resistance Latina sorority women have to being stereotyped in the same ways in which White sorority members are stereotyped.

> The stereotypes you get are "Oh, you're a sorority girl." I really don't feel we're like that . . . . We have a lot of restrictions in our lives; the respect kind of thing. (04, Set 1)
>
> Right away it's "you guys are party girls, that's all there is to it." . . . We wanted our organization to be known as respecting a women's culture and who they are as a person, what they are academically, and what they want to achieve. (10, Set 2)
>
> We don't want to be tied up with being like a social little club. . . . We want to be known as "family girls" not "party girls." (11, Set 2)
>
> But what I had heard was that it was a lot of "Güeras" (White women) partying . . . [who] sleep around. [And, my family would say] that's not for you, you know, 'cause I come from a strict family. (01, Set 1)
>
> Some people can get out of hand with that (partying). They don't know when to stop and get control of their lives. But I feel like I was okay because my parents really taught me right from wrong. . . . My dad was a very strict enforcer of respect and we got punished. (02, Set 1)

Notably, interviewees strongly resist being stereotyped as behaving like White Greek sorority women. In fact, they perceive themselves as "different" than, thus **"doing difference"** from, White "sorority girls" who belong to a "social club." Instead, they perceive themselves as women who work in the community, who work on academics, and who were "raised with respect" by either a "strict family" or a "strict father." As Latinas, they **"do difference"** by not "partying" and by adhering to what it means to be "family girls." Consequently, to behave like a "sorority girl" runs counter to the traditional way of **"doing identity"** within the Latino community. Hence, as suggested in the excerpts above, if sorority members were to conform to such perceived Greek norms, they would confirm the stereo-type attributed to them as "party girls" who "sleep around," "get drunk," and have "no con-trol in their lives."

As with most communal **culture**s, such as with Japanese cultures (Ting-Toomey 1988), the Latino's view of "the 'self' is a situational and relationally based concept" (p. 215). So, in order to save face or to maintain "face-respect" (Ting-Toomey, p. 217), Latina sorority members must (re)construct what it means to be in a sorority. To conform to the stereotype of "party girl" would mean a loss of face, a loss of self-respect, and the possibility of sham-ing one's family. Conforming to such a stereotype would disrespect both their individual families and their sororities. This is not to say that Latina sorority women do not drink or party. In fact, I attended social gatherings at clubs where the women were observed drink-ing. However, I never observed a Latina sorority member falling down drunk or behaving in ways that reflected promiscuousness. Additionally, when socializing in places where alco-hol is served, the women do not wear their Greek letters, which they claim is done out of *respeto* for their sorority.

Communicating Identity through Symbolic Representation: "Doing Difference"

As with the concept of family, the Spanish language is an important element of what it means to be Latina. In fact, ethnic identity is based not only on symbolic themes such as rituals and shared world views, but on language as well (Tanno 2000). Moreover, "[L]anguage is the very essence of identity, self-worth and dignity. When language is lost, a part of a peo-ple's humanity is forever lost" (Ipola 1996, cited in Pratt and Buchanan 2000). Interview data reflects a strong desire among the majority of Latina sororities to regain or preserve their Spanish language use. Many of the women in these interviews told of how they were never taught to speak Spanish by their Spanish-speaking parents. The loss of the Spanish language was particularly disheartening to one interviewee, who sadly spoke of how her mother "tried to teach it to me when I was little, but I just lost it because nobody (outside the home) really reinforced it" (01, Set 1).

For some of the interviewees, getting "back to my roots" (04, Set 1) and wanting "to be around people of my culture and learn" (01, Set 1) has had a great deal to do with regain-ing the Spanish language lost to them through assimilation processes. For these women, not speaking the Spanish language has resulted in their being disconnected from *familia* in that they are viewed as "doing difference" from beloved family members. It also means missing out on learning from elders about the Latino culture, as evidenced in the statement below.

> I felt like I missed out on getting to know my grandmother better. I started getting to know her better as I started taking Spanish classes. My grandfather I didn't know at all because he passed away before I got to learn enough Spanish. So, I really wish they would've taught me more about my culture. I really feel like I've missed a lot of what my culture is about. (04, Set 1)

According to this interviewee, in an attempt to establish them as being "real" Latinas, soror-ity members consciously work at teaching each other Spanish through daily interactions.

Furthermore, their desire to preserve their identity as Latinas is reflected in the **Greek letters** that represent their Latina Greek organizations. In the two sets of interviews, members claimed that their founding mothers chose Greek letters that represent a Latina identity. According to one interviewee (01, Set 2), the most used Greek letter is *Lambda*, which tends to stand for Latina or Latino. In support of this claim, an Internet search found a variety of ways Latina sororities (and some Latino fraternities) utilize Spanish language symbolic representation. For example, members of Lambda Pi Chi have taken the *L, P, C* to stand for *Latinas Promoviendo Comunidad* (Latinas Promoting Community). Similarly, Sigma Lambda Upsilon has incorporated itself using the name *Senoritas Latinas Unidas* (United Young Latina women) *Sorority Inc.* Other LGOs incorporate both the word *Latina, Latin,* or *Hispano* into the formal name of the organization to stand for a Latina identity. For example, Chi Upsilon Sigma Latin Sorority, Inc., not only utilizes the word *Latin* in its title but also transforms the *C, U, S* to read *Corazones Unidos Siempre* (United Hearts Forever).

Maintaining a Latina Identity through the Concept of *Familia:* "Being Like a Family"

Familism is one of the most important cultural values in the Latino culture (Blea 1992; Covarrubias 2002; Gangotena 2000; Sabogal, Marin, and Otero-Sabogal 1987). "It is usually described as including a strong identification and attachment of individuals with their *familias* (nuclear and extended), and strong feelings of loyalty, reciprocity, and solidarity among members of the same family" (Sabogal et al. 1987, pp. 397–98). Similarly, Gangotena (2000) claims that the Mexican American valuation of *familia* often produces positive attributes of "community, solidarity, respect, and discipline" (p. 72). When taking into consideration this definition of *familia,* one can better understand why so many of the interviewees spoke of their organizations as "being like **family**" or as being "a family away from home," or of their wanting to be viewed as "a family girl."

However, as in "true" families, membership in the sorority can become problematic. At times people are "jealous" of one another due to individuals "doing difference" and hence **being different** from others in the Latina sorority. Discontent comes from some members having money and investing time outside the sorority that draws them away from *la familia,* while others do not. One interviewee summed it up by saying that there was

> jealousy of personality and jealousy of money. These stem mostly from sight. . . . You see a person and you see how they act. If you don't take time to open your ears and listen in order find out the inside of them, then the jealousy just immediately jumps in and prevents you from really ever wanting to get to know the inside. (03, Set 2)

Despite the tension and distance "differences" create among members due to jealousy, they are expected to "respect each other and their differences" (09, Set 2). In Latino culture, *respeto* is something that all individuals are born with, especially family members; it is not something that is earned, as is typically the case in Euro-American culture (Blea 1992; Covarrubias 2002). The cultural understanding is that their sisters are "*personas,* (who) must be treated with dignity, courtesy, and deference" (Gangotena 2000, p. 79).

Instead of viewing these women as **"sellouts"** or *"tio tacos"* who have bought into the dominant culture, sorority sisters work to overcome jealousy and negative feelings through recognizing that the sorority is "like a family."

Say you live with dad and step-mom, and stepbrother. . . . A lot of times you're frustrated with the environment and you don't want to be there. And you love them, in your heart you'll always give to your little brother . . . but you don't want to be there. So, I guess I see it like a family and I feel like a family member. (03, Set 2)

So sisterhood . . . also means having a family away from home. . . . Although you don't make the connection with everyone, you still maintain a certain degree of respect and you just keep trying. (01, Set 2)

Like some people might not get along in the sorority, like they might have had differences at the beginning but they respect each other as a sibling. (08, Set 2)

As with "true" families, the sorority is "a support group in that we're like sisters . . . in the sense of how would you treat your blood sister" (04, Set 1). To be a part of the family unit you must "know how to communicate" and "work out problems" like "blood sisters." Being a sister implies being "really close," "comforting," "loving," "sharing," and "there for each other," including monetarily. An example of such support was revealed by one interviewee who told of being evicted from her home due to her roommate not paying her portion of the rent. Knowing she did not have a place to live, two of her sorority sisters who already shared a room insisted she stay with them until she could find another place to live. Such assistance, she claimed, kept her from dropping out of school.

Intercultural Implications

There are at least three implications in this study for intercultural communication. First, as a source for classroom instruction, this study assists in not only familiarizing students with Latino cultural norms but provides insights into some of the history, beliefs, and cultural values of some Latinas/os in academic environments. In becoming familiar with Latina/o characteristics reported in this study, members of other ethnic groups may become more comfortable and willing to interact with Latinas/os whom they perceive as different from themselves. Similarly, Latinas/os may feel more comfortable to engage in intercultural communication with peers as findings may promote a degree of understanding that would allow for less of a need to explain the communicative practices, beliefs, values, and history reported.

Second, this study allows for students from the various Greek organizations to "see" themselves in ways they may not typically view themselves. In order for individuals to engage in effective intercultural communication, they first must understand how they communicate **difference** and be willing to accept difference. In so doing, it is possible to bring students of different races and ethnicities together to discuss perceived differences, which in turn will allow for realizing their commonalities, be they Greek or non-Greek. Such discussions can also assist in eliminating or clarifying stereotypes and stereotyping that otherwise hinder intercultural understanding and **communication.**

Finally, the findings herein reported can assist Greek administrators and Greek members in better understanding how the Greek system might be reformed in order to realize true diversity within the Greek system, thus, in turn, creating an atmosphere for increased and effective intercultural communication between the current predominately race/ethnic segregated Greek organizations. Moreover, findings may help to ease the intercultural tension that exists between Chicano scholars and Chicano students who view Latina sorority members as "sell-outs" to what they perceive to be a racist White Greek system. Through better understanding of how Latina sororities "do difference" within the Greek system, such tension may ease, allowing for increased intracultural communication and cultural unity.

Conclusion

Higher education has traditionally not been available and supportive to any group of people other than the eighteen-to-twenty-five-year-old White males. However, due to cultural commonalties in the ways White women and White men "do difference," White females have been able to fit into the academic environment with greater ease than members of most minority groups, despite the sexism they have historically encountered in institutions of higher learning. With the advent of the civil rights movement and forced desegregation came academic programs and services to help meet the needs of women and minorities. In fact, such programs were mostly attempts to meet academic needs, not cultural ones.

As a direct result of racism, of feelings of alienation, and of a need to belong, in 1975 Latina Greek organizations began to be established at predominately White colleges. Through these Greek organizations, members have (re)constructed not only *la familia,* but their Latina cultural identities by "becoming," "doing," and "being" different. As noted by Collier (1996), "cultural identities emerge out of class differences, ethnic differences, regional differences, sex differences and the intersections among them" (p. 16).

This study suggests that many Latina/o students may not be willing to give up their cultural heritage in order to succeed in academia or in their chosen careers. According to Vento (1998), resistance to assimilation has historically been very strong in U.S. Latino communities. The movement to diversify the workplace suggests that corporate leaders realize minorities are not willing to "check" their ethnic identities at the door. Unfortunately, the traditional Greek system has not learned from the corporate world. Judging from an interview conducted by Hoover (2001) for an article on "bigotry in fraternities and sororities" published in *The Chronicle of Higher Education,* the Greek system will have a very difficult time truly diversifying, if it is even possible to do so. According to Hoover,

> Ryan Booth, a member of Alabama's Delta Kappa Epsilon house . . . [stated] if I had to vote right now on whether to bring a black member into my fraternity, I'd probably vote no. . . . But it is not that I am a racist. It is just that white fraternities and black fraternities have always been separate, and nobody wants to be the first to change that. (p. A36)

This statement reflects a profound, deeply rooted segregationist ideology within the Greek system that hinders true reform of that system. To overcome segregation within the system, individuals such as Greek liaisons and advisers must be willing to accept, not just tolerate, difference. Nonetheless, one of the biggest obstacles to creating desegregation within the Greek system are alumni who do not want to see the fraternal order changed (Hoover 2001). In fact, attempts to reform the Greek system have failed at such institutions as Dartmouth College where such efforts "sparked a series of angry rallies . . . and a deluge of letters from Greek alumni, many of whom threatened to withhold donations to the college" (p. A37). Nevertheless, only when Greek organizations accept difference, which would mean overhauling or eliminating the antiquated practice of Rush, can individuals begin to see the commonalities that make them more alike than different. The fact that these women belong to organizations that are recognized by university Greek liaison officials allows for a sense of identification with the university, while improving the members' mental well-being and chances for academic success.

Although some feminists might argue that cultural values such as *respeto* are rooted in sexism and thus are oppressive, the concept of *respeto* plays a crucial role in the identity (re)construction of Latina sorority women. As indicated earlier, *respeto* is at the core of Latino culture, including the concept of family (Blea 1992; Covarrubias 2002; Gangotena 2000). Naturally, "being like family" would mean "once a sorority member, always a sorority member, for life." As such, "doing difference" becomes even more deeply embedded in everyday performances of cultural beliefs, values, and social norms. These communicative behaviors in turn play a significant role in fulfilling a need to preserve the Latino culture within a predominately segregated Greek system, while striving to integrate into mainstream society as a whole. In the process, Latinas deny being like White sorority women, thus avoiding assimilation and adaptation to cultural norms that are viewed as foreign and distasteful. Additionally, membership in Latina sororities is viewed as being empowering, a notion that runs counter to Stombler and Martin's (1994) findings that predominately White Greek organizations with "little sisters" encourage dependence and powerlessness.

Finally, findings demonstrate that while Latina sorority members actively seek to (re)construct a unified Latina cultural identity within the Greek system, they are also encouraged to explore their individual ethnic identities within the broader category of Latina. Furthermore, as they resist traditional gender roles of mother and subservient wife, they simultaneously embrace the traditional cultural value of *respeto,* which serves to perpetuate traditional gendered expectations related to sexuality.

There is no doubt that more studies are necessary to refute or substantiate the findings herein reported, as well as to establish the generalizability of these findings. Other studies might incorporate ethnographic comparative studies of White sororities, Black sororities, Latina sororities, Asian sororities, gay/lesbian, and even multicultural sororities, in order to ascertain if perceptions of "doing difference" align with actual organizational communicative practices. Such studies might provide insights as to the degree that these organizations might serve as retention mechanisms. Studies are also necessary to ascertain what the long-term impact of identity (re)construction is on Latina women who re-enter their respective social environments. And finally, longitudinal studies of Latina sorority women in general are necessary in order to determine how successful they become in their chosen professional careers and whether or not they actively assist each other to integrate into the U.S. corporate world.

References

Berger, P. L., and T. Luckmann. 1966. *The social construction of reality: A treatise in the sociology of knowledge*. New York: Anchor Books.

Blea, I. I. 1992. *La Chicana and the intersections of race, class, and gender*. New York: Praeger Publishers.

Burke, K. 1969. *A rhetoric of motives*. Berkeley: University of California Press.

Cardoza, D. 1991. College attendance and persistence among Hispanic women: An examination of some contributing factors. *Sex Roles* 24 (3/4): 133–47.

Castillo, A. 1995. *Massacre of the dreamers: Essays on Xicansima*. New York: Penguin Books USA Inc.

Collier, M. J. 1988. Cultural identity: an interpretive perspective. In Y. Y. Kim and W. B. Gudykunst (Eds.), *Theories in intercultural communication* (pp. 99–122). Newbury Park, Calif.: Sage.

———. 1996. Researching cultural identity: Reconciling interpretive and post-colonial perspectives. Paper presented at the Speech Communication Association conference, San Diego, Calif.

Covarrubias, P. 2002. *Culture, communication, and cooperation: Interpersonal relations and pronominal address in a Mexican organization*. Lanham, Md.: Rowman & Littlefield.

Davidson, A. L. 1996. *Making and molding identity in schools: Student narratives on race, gender, and academic engagement*. New York: State University of New York Press.

Gangotena, M. 2000. The rhetoric of *la familia* among Mexican Americans. In A. González, M. Houston, and V. Chen (Eds.), *Our voices: Essays in culture, ethnicity, and communication* (pp. 72–83). Los Angeles, Calif.: Roxbury.

Giddan, N. S. 1988. *Community and social support for college students*. Springfield, Ill.: Charles C. Thomas.

Goffman, E. 1959. *The presentation of self in everyday life*. New York: Anchor Books, Doubleday.

Grebler, L., J. W. Moore, and R. C. Guzman. 1970. *The Mexican American people*. New York: The Free Press.

Gudykunst, W. 1991. *Bridging differences: Effective intergroup communication*. Newbury Park, Calif.: Sage.

Hoover, E. 2001. New scrutiny for powerful Greek systems: Incidents force Dartmouth and the U. of Alabama to confront legacy of bigotry in fraternities and sororities. *The Chronicle of Higher Education* 47 (39), June 8: A35–A37.

Hurtado, S. 1992. The campus racial climate: Contexts for conflict. *Journal of Higher Education* 63 (5): 539–69.

Keefe, S. E., A. M. Padilla, and M. L. Carlos. 1978. The Mexican American extended family as an emotional support system. In J. M. Casas and S. E. Keefe (Eds.), *Family and mental health in the Mexican American community*, Monograph No. 7. Los Angeles: Spanish Speaking Mental Health Research Center, UCLA.

Keller, M. J., and D. Hart. 1982. The effects of sorority and fraternity rush on students' self-images. *Journal of College Student Personnel* 23 (3): 257–61.

Kraft, C. L. 1991. What makes a successful Black student on a predominantly White campus? *American Education Journal* 28 (2): 423–43.

Lamdba Theta Alpha Sorority, Inc. Historical perspectives. Retrieved March 20, 2001, from www.lambdalady.org/history.htm.

Loo, C. M., and G. Rolison. 1986. Alienation of ethnic minority students at a predominantly White university. *Journal of Higher Education* 57 (1): 58–77.

Lottes, I. L., and P. J. Kuriloff. 1994. Sexual socialization differences by gender, Greek membership, ethnicity, and religious background. *Psychology of Women Quarterly* 18: 203–19.

Lunneborg, C. E., and P. W. Lunneborg. 1986. Beyond prediction: The challenge of minority achievement in higher education. *Journal of Multicultural Counseling and Development* (April): 77–94.

Marsiglia, F. F., and L. Holleran. 1999. I've learned so much from my mother: Narratives from a group of Chicana high school students. *Social Work in Education* 21 (4): 220–37.

Martin, J. 1994. The organization of exclusion: Institutionalization of sex inequality, gendered faculty jobs and gendered knowledge in organizational theory and research. In J. Martin (Ed.), *Organization articles* (pp. 401–31). Newbury Park, Calif.: Sage.

Mongell, S., and A. E. Roth. 1991. Sorority rush as a two-sided matching mechanism. *The American Economic Review* 81 (3): 441–55.

Morris, J. R. 1991. Racial attitudes of undergraduates in Greek housing. *College Student Journal* 25 (1): 501–5.

Muir, D. E. 1991. "White" fraternity and sorority attitudes toward "Blacks" on a deep-South campus. *Sociological Spectrum* 11 (1).

Nieves-Squires, S. 1991. *Hispanic women making their presence on campus less tenuous.* Boulder: University of Colorado, Boulder—Project on the Status of Education of Women.

Omi, M., and H. Winant. 1986. *Racial Formation in the United States: From the 1960's to the 1980's.* New York: Routledge.

Peterson, H., P. Altbach, E. Skinner, and K. Trainor. 1976. A Greek revival: Sorority pledges at a large university. *Journal of College Student Personnel* 17 (2): 109–15.

Pratt, S. B., and M. C. Buchanan. 2000. Wa-zha-zhe i-e: Notions on a dying ancestral language. In A. González, M. Houston, and V. Chen (Eds.), *Our voices: Essays in culture, ethnicity, and communication* (pp. 155–63). Los Angeles, Calif.: Roxbury.

Risman, B. J. 1982. College women and sororities: The social construction of reaffirmation of gender roles. *Urban Life* 11 (2): 231–52.

Rodriguez, M. 1988. Do Blacks and Hispanics evaluate assertive male and female characters differently? *The Howard Journal of Communication* 1 (1): 101–7.

Rose, H., and C. Elton. 1971. Sorority dropout. *Journal of College Student Personnel* (November): 460–63.

Sabogal, F., G. Marin, and R. Otero-Sabogal. 1987. Hispanic familism and acculturation: What changes and what doesn't? *Hispanic Journal of Behavioral Sciences* 9 (4): 397–412.

Sabogal, F., E. J. Pérez-Stable, R. Otero-Sabogal, and R. A. Hiatt. 1995. Gender, ethnic, and acculturation differences in sexual behaviors: Hispanic and non-Hispanic White adults. *Journal of Behavioral Sciences* 17 (2): 139–59.

Schmitz, S., and S. A. Forbes. 1994. Choices in a no-choice system: Motives and biases in sorority segregation. *Journal of College Student Development* 35 (2): 103–8.

Solberg, V. S., J. Valdez, and P. Villarreal. 1994. Social support, stress, and Hispanic college adjustment: Test of a diathesis-stress model. *Hispanic Journal of Behavioral Sciences* 16 (3): 230–39.

Stohl, C. 1995. *Organizational communication: Connectedness in action.* Thousand Oaks, Calif.: Sage.

Stombler, M. 1994. "Buddies" or "Slutties": The collective sexual reputation of fraternity little sisters. *Gender and Society* 8 (3): 297–23.

Stombler, M., and P. Y. Martin. 1994. Bringing women in, keeping women down: Fraternity "little sister" organizations. *Journal of contemporary ethnography* 23 (2): 150–84.

Tanno, D. V. 2000. Names, narrative, and the evolution of ethnic identity. In A. González, M. Houston, and V. Chen (Eds.), *Our voices: Essays in culture, ethnicity, and communication* (pp. 25–30). Los Angeles, Calif.: Roxbury.

Thurston, K. 1994. Barriers to the self-definition of the Chicana: Gina Valdes and there are no madmen here. *Melus* 4: 61–73.

Ting-Toomey, S. 1988. Intercultural conflict styles: A face-negotiation theory. In Y. Y. Kim and W. B. Gudykunst (Eds.), *Theories in intercultural communication.* Newbury Park, Calif.: Sage.

Vasquez, M. J. T. 1982. Confronting barriers to the participation of Mexican-American women in higher education. *Hispanic Journal of Behavioral Sciences* 4 (2): 150–84.

Vento, A. C. 1998. *Mestizo: The history, culture and politics of the Mexican and the Chicano.* Lanham, Md.: University Press of American.

KEY TERMS

being different
Black Greek
communication
communicative practices
culture
difference
doing difference
doing identity
family
Greek letters
history

Latina Greek
Latino Greek
(re)constructing
respeto
Rush
"sellouts" or "*tio tacos*"
sisterhood
sorority
value systems
White Greek

REVIEW AND DISCUSSION QUESTIONS

1. How do symbolic representations manifest in the communicative practices of Latina Greek organizations?
2. Have your views of the Rush process changed since reading this study? If yes, in what way? If not, why not?
3. Does this study confirm or negate any stereotypes you may have had about Latina women, in particular of Latina sorority members?
4. Do you believe the stereotypes of White Greek organizations are warranted? Why or why not?
5. What are the commonalities and differences in the Latino concept of *respeto* and the Euro-American concept of respect?
6. What are the commonalities and differences in the Latino concept of family and the Euro-American concept of family?
7. Do you see any commonalities in the ways in which Latina Greek and White Greek organizations "do identity"? If so, what are they?
8. Do you believe that Greek organizations can ever be desegregated? How?

Communicating Deadhead Identity: Exploring Identity from a Cultural Communication Perspective

Natalie J. Dollar

A Deadhead explains it this way, "Garcia's writing partner Robert Hunter crafted his language at every level, both . . . at the level of the sounds of the language itself and also he was able to build these lessons into his music that sometimes would be floating through your head for twenty years before it yields its treasures of wisdom to you."

—Deadhead, radio call-in show, 8/9/95

Many students enter cultural and intercultural communication courses expecting to study communication among and between members of national, ethnic, and racial cultures. Although these expectations are generally met, some course readings expand the students' understanding of cultural and intercultural communication to include interactions among and between members of speech communities, or groups of persons sharing rules for the use and interpretation of speech, and rules for one or more linguistic varieties (Hymes 1972). Studies of speech communities contribute to our understanding of intercultural communication by examining cultural groups differentiated by their particular **ways of communicating**, thus emphasizing communication codes as a means for drawing cultural boundaries. Sometimes this emphasis correlates with national, ethnic, and racial boundaries (see Carbaugh 1998, 1999; Fitch 1998; Fong 2000; Philipsen 1998 for instance), whereas other times it correlates with boundaries defined otherwise, such as by shared Vietnam veteran experiences (Braithwaite 1997), physical abilities (Braithwaite and Braithwaite 2000), codes of rationality versus spirituality (Coutu 2000), legal housing status (Dollar 2000b; Dollar and Zimmers 1998) and organizational ideologies (Ruud 2000). This study contributes to this research line by examining the communication of Deadhead (DH) cultural identity, an identity that is sometimes stigmatized, as well as inaccurately ascribed to and by nonmembers in intercultural contexts.

Deadheads are devout fans of the **Grateful Dead (GD),** a rock and roll band that released their first album in 1967 and disbanded in 1995 after the death of lead guitarist, singer, and songwriter Jerry Garcia. Their fans vary along two meaningful continua; the first concerns "going to shows" (i.e., GD concerts) and the second concerns acceptance of the Deadhead worldview. At one end of the first continuum are "tour heads," the GD concert-goers who traveled from city to city, sometimes internationally, following the GD. Today, many tour heads continue to follow "family bands," including but not limited to former GD band members' current bands, such as Ratdog and Phil and Friends, and The Dead. At the opposite end of the first continuum are self-identified DHs who never actually saw the GD in concert. Most DHs fall somewhere between these endpoints.

At one end of the second continuum are Deadheads who share a worldview that, according to Sardiello (1994), incorporates "elements of humanist philosophy and Eastern religious doctrines" (p. 127). Some DHs described their worldview to me in terms of an "orientation to the present moment" and an emphasis on "freedom," values Wieder and Zimmerman (1974, 1976) discovered in their study of the 1960s and 1970s counterculture movement. At the opposite end are DHs who recognize this worldview but do not accept it, whereas many DHs accept the worldview to varying degrees. One's position along both continua can change.

Many people, Deadheads and others, attended Grateful Dead concerts, referred to as "shows" by DHs. The GD ranked among the highest grossing tours in the world, averaging $50 to $75 million in ticket sales while rarely charging more than $30 a ticket (Hill and Rifkin 1999, p. 139). The band and its followers are part of musical history, evidenced by the numerous popular and scholarly books, chapters, and articles documenting this history (see Dodd and Weiner 1997 for a comprehensive bibliography). The GD and DHs have influenced United States popular culture, musical industry, and economy. Grateful Dead Productions, the company founded by band members, was built on a business model "that flew in the face of conventional music industry wisdom" (p. 132) yet became "a highly profitable, debt-free, privately held 34-year old company" (p. 133). *Entrepreneur* magazine reported Grateful Dead Productions' revenues at $20 million while noting the "60 million that all Grateful Dead items generate each year for the band, the record companies, and outside licenses" (p. 134).

Persons from a wide variety of economic, educational, and professional backgrounds are Deadheads; teachers, lawyers, construction laborers, mail persons, astronomers, maintenance persons, senators, service providers, and students. Many people have no idea they know a DH, while others are clearly aware although are not themselves DHs. Whereas the phrase, "we are everywhere," is a favorite among DHs, being identified as a DH is not always a desired outcome due to the stereotype held by some nonmembers outside the DH culture.

How do Deadheads communicate cultural identity when interacting with other DHs? More specifically, this chapter explores **membering**, a concept that refers to instances of participants' communication that (1) is interpreted by members to be communicating like a member and (2) "gives off" to self the impression that one is communicating like a member (Philipsen 1989, p. 82). My exploration of DH membering is informed by a **cultural communication perspective of identity** (Carbaugh 1988, 1990; Hymes 1962, 1972; Katriel 1991; Philipsen 1987, 1989, 1992, 1997; Pratt 1998; Wieder and Pratt 1990), a growing body of scholarly research concerning the Deadhead speech community (Adams and Sardiello 2000; Dodd and Weiner 1997; Dollar 1989, 1991, 1999a, 1999b; Dollar, Morgan, and Crabtree 1997; Pearson 1987; Reist 1997; Roth 1998; Sardiello 1994; Weiner 1999), and my participation and membership in the DH speech community. Using Hymes's (1972) framework for exploring communication in a cultural context, this chapter builds on an earlier study (Dollar 2000a) by asking: What are some of the **cultural communication resources** DHs call upon when membering self as a DH? And how do DHs employ these communication resources in the process of membering?

Communicating Cultural Identity: An Interpretive Framework

How do members of speech communities communicate cultural identity? Hymes (1962, 1972) proposed the **ethnography of speaking** as a methodological and theoretical perspective for exploring and understanding speaking in a cultural context. Central to this approach is the concept of a **speech community**, which refers to a "community sharing rules for the conduct and interpretation of speech, and rules for the interpretation of at least one linguistic variety" (Hymes 1972, p. 54). Members of speech communities share a **speech code** or "system of socially constructed symbols and meanings, premises, and rules, pertaining to communicative conduct" (Philipsen 1997, p. 126). *Speech* as used by Hymes and throughout this chapter is a surrogate for all forms of communication.

English is the linguistic variety shared by most, but not all Deadheads. English is the language of Grateful Dead music and these lyrics, according to DHs, are important elements in their speech code. Knowing English, however, is not sufficient for communicating like a DH. Members of speech communities share a speech code and a **linguistic code**. It is one thing to understand the rules of grammar and syntax, and another to be able to use a language socially and meaningfully within a speech community. Many readers will understand this distinction by reflecting on their process of learning a second language. Many are able to read and translate the newly learned language but encounter problems using it in social situations, such as asking for directions or mediating conflict.

Members of speech communities share a culture that both informs and is informed by the speech code. Both systems, the speech code and culture, influence one another. **Culture** refers to "a socially constructed and historically transmitted system of symbols and their meanings, premises and rules" (Philipsen 1992, p. 7). Borrowing from and extending Geertz's (1973) definition of culture, Philipsen argues that culture is socially constructed through interaction. As members communicate they enact, reinforce, negotiate, and challenge their cultural system. Culture is not random and chaotic but organized into a system, into patterns. **Cultural symbols**, what Geertz calls "vehicles for conception" (p. 91), are used by members to communicate. The meanings of such symbols are situated within the **cultural history** and patterns. Deadheads, for instance, greet one another with the phrase "hey now." Although this phrase consists of symbols recognizable to many non-Deadhead speakers, among DHs it has "become a coded 'hello' that marks group membership, communicating that the member is truly 'on the bus' [a DH]" (Roth 1998, p. 66). For members this greeting is heard in the context of a song played but not written by the Grateful Dead. It is part of DH folklore (Roth 1998). Nonmembers may hear the symbols to be a form of greeting, but they do not hear the greeting in the context of the DH community history. For DHs the greeting resonates of folk ways and calls forth an emotional response arising from participation in the DH community.

Cultural symbols can be reconstructed, and new symbols emerge over time. Changes, however, occur slowly as they take place within a system grounded in cultural history, assumptions, and premises. Deadheads rely on a mythical model incorporating "self-fulfillment and enlightenment, and values that recognize human potential and creativity" (Sardiello 1994, p. 127). In addition, DHs believe in an "interconnectedness of the Universe" (Reist 1997) and emphasize **"communitas"** or the special connections arising from relating to others outside the dominant social structure, "spirituality," and "protection of environmental and human rights" (Dollar 1989). Cultural members rely on **cultural premises** and **rules** to guide their behavior, including their communication. A small but growing body of research contributes to our understanding of the rules for communicating like a DH (Dollar 1989, 1991, 1999a, 1999b; Pearson 1987; Reist 1997; Roth 1998; Sardiello 1994; Shenk and Silberman 1994). Culturally defined **speech situations,** such as the show (Dollar 1999b), and **speech events,** such as "show talk" (Dollar 1999a, 1999b, 2000a), for instance, are key components for understanding the premises and rules for communicating like a DH.

It should be clear from this discussion that culture is not a place, a location, or a group of people. Culture is a system that communities of persons share and call upon in their daily lives. By "share," I do not mean to imply total agreement. Culture is organized diversity (Hymes 1972). A **cultural system** is composed of differences within an acceptable range, organized but not homogenous. Consider the national culture you share with other persons, and you will quickly recognize examples of organized diversity. Diversity, although unnoticed by nonmembers, is part of the Deadhead culture and was expressed in the stories DHs told me of the different types of "Heads" they have met and known, their one commonality being a love for Grateful Dead music.

Culture can be shared by members of many types of groups, including but not limited to groups organized around ethnicity, sex and gender, profession or employment, geographical area, and physical ability and disability (Collier 2000). Some cultural boundaries are defined in terms of a speech code; these cultures are shared by members of speech communities. It is important to note that cultural boundaries are drawn in many ways, only one of which is in terms of speech codes. In this chapter the focus is on Deadheads as members of a speech community. As such, the consideration of DH culture is limited to those aspects revealed in DHs' ways of speaking.

Philipsen (1992) posits that "knowledge of, and ability to participate in, a particular community's spoken life are not only resources for information transmission but are resources for communal identification, and communal being, as well" (14). In this sense, cultural identification is an interactive accomplishment. Carbaugh (1988) argues that **cultural communication** is deeply felt, commonly intelligible, and widely accessible. In other words, cultural communication calls forth an ethos grounded in emotion and experience, its meaning is dependent on the folk logic shared by members, and members understand how and when to use the communication if they choose to do so.

Consider show talk, an instance of Deadhead cultural communication that involves communication about Grateful Dead and family band concerts and related community-relevant topics (Dollar 1991, 1999a, 1999b). This **cultural communication ritual** is widely accessible as a means of sharing DHs' individualized accounts of culturally meaningful themes, such as "when I got on the bus" or "my first show." In addition, show talk is widely accessible as a means for building connections with other DHs. Given that any DH with access to the community folk logic can participate, and that an established interpersonal relationship is not a requirement for participation, many DHs report that show talk is a meaningful way to meet "family members." Although the words used in show talk can be translated by nonmembers, the symbols are not commonly intelligible outside the context of the DH speech community, its history, and the actual topics being discussed. For nonmembers the symbols do not resonate with DH folk ways, whereas for DHs show talk is deeply felt as a means of enacting, negotiating, and affirming key symbols within their speech code, namely "show," "GD music," and "Deadhead." In these ways, instances of show talk are considered instances of cultural communication and a means for membering self as a DH.

Deadheads as a Speech Community

Since the August 9, 1995, death of Jerry Garcia, the Deadhead speech community has changed, and DHs are quick to point out that this community is always evolving. Nevertheless, music has remained the focus. Earlier explorations of communicating DH identity revealed that information about Grateful Dead music, shows, history, and legacy continue to be resources DHs call upon when communicating like a DH (Dollar 1991, 1999a, 1999b, 2000a; Dollar, Morgan, and Crabtree 1997).

In the early development of this speech community, Deadheads were dependent on face-to-face speech situations, such as shows and "family gatherings." With the Grateful Dead's 1971 initiation of a DH mailing list, the DH speech community incorporated a new channel for communicating, namely print. Soon there was a growing body of popular publications (see Dodd and Weiner 1997, for a comprehensive bibliography) that DHs embraced as cultural communication resources within their speech community. As the community expanded to include new channels for communicating, it grew to include more members. The most recent growth was spawned by the Internet, a channel some believe DHs pioneered (Rheingold 1993). In my research, many DHs reported that the Internet is critical to their expression of cultural identity, serving as a type of family gathering where Deadheads can interact on a daily basis. Some of these DHs suggested that this interaction may have gained greater importance among DHs since the death of Jerry Garcia and the end of GD shows as a focal place to gather and participate in the speech community.

The Deadhead speech community can be further understood by exploring nonverbal elements of cultural communication, the "pre-show" communication event, and Grateful Dead lyrics as cultural communication resources. Furthermore, an intercultural communication problematic faced by many DH speakers is the potential of negative stereotyping by nonmembers. The following pages illustrate how a consideration of "membering" contributes to our understanding of communicating cultural identity in both intercultural and cultural communicative encounters.

Communicating Like a Deadhead

My observations reveal that a common complaint among Deadheads is that nonmembers "think anyone who wears tie-dye, Birkenstocks, or batik [dyed fabric] is a DH." Not always, but on many occasions nonmembers inaccurately ascribe cultural membership to nonmembers; they identify another as being a DH when that person is not. In addition, cultural identification often goes undetected, unnoticed by nonmembers who do not have access to the Deadhead folk logic informing the use and interpretation of members' communication code. Without access to the DH speech code and culture, two systems in which DH communication is historically grounded, nonmembers are at a disadvantage for recognizing and understanding the communicative accomplishment of DH cultural identification. With regard to communicating DH identity, nonverbal communication can be particularly problematic.

Deadhead Nonverbal and Verbal Cultural Communication

Many nonmembers identify DHs through dress and appearance. Whereas many DHs wear tie-dye, batik clothing, and Birkenstocks, many DHs do not. With regard to DH nonverbal communication and membering, two points are worthy of comment. First, this type of clothing was once much more difficult to purchase. One had to buy from importers and artists as opposed to department stores. A Grateful Dead show was one place these items were readily available. Part of a show is the marketplace emerging at or near the concert venue, what some DHs refer to as "Jerry world" and "Shakedown Street." Although much smaller than those on GD tours, this area is still part of "family band shows." In this area, DHs buy and trade many cultural artifacts including clothing, art, food, and car decals. Over time, many of these items began to be retailed and made available to the general public, not only to DHs at Dead shows. Record and CD stores, for instance, began to carry GD car decals and sew-on patches, such as the popular "steal your face" skull, most often in red, white, and blue containing a lightning bolt, or the "dancing bears" sticker featuring four different colored dancing bears. With this wider accessibility some members of the general public have purchased various items simply because they liked the art or the item. The colored dancing bear symbol has been co-opted by a college sorority and is displayed on members' cars. Ironically, although intending no reference to the GD or DHs, this group uses the dancing bears as a symbol of membership in their sorority.

Today department stores carry what Deadheads refer to as "fake tie-dyes." To DHs these mass produced, made-to-resemble-tie-dye T-shirts look nothing like the artistic creations proudly donned by many youth of the late 1960s and early 1970s, as well as by some DHs then and now. Tie-dyes are individually created, no two are alike, and each is an artistic accomplishment. Nevertheless, these and other Dead-associated nonverbal symbols have become desirable goods outside the DH speech community. As such, within the DH speech community, it is known that dress, appearance, and other nonverbal symbols alone do not identify one as a DH.

A second point relevant to understanding Deadheads' nonverbal and cultural communication concerns the stigma associated with being a DH. Not all nonmembers associate a stigma with this cultural identity, but many do. The common references to drugs and the Grateful Dead scene has created an **identification predicament** for DHs: Do I display my identity by putting GD stickers and decals on my car or by wearing GD tour shirts and risk the negative consequences of the stigma? Many DHs reported this self-initiated identification leads to harassment, or at least suspicion by nonmembers, particularly law enforcement. The negative **stereotype** and attached stigma have the potential to hinder employment opportunities, development of interpersonal relations, and other communicative encounters with non-DHs. For example, an employer may hold a negative stereotype of Deadheads as "'pothead[s]' (person who regularly smokes marijuana)" and laid-back hippies. Because of these consequences, many conceal their DH identity, refusing to wear any Dead-associated clothing or to display Dead symbolism on their belongings (e.g., car decals, backpack sew-on-patches).

This is not to say that Deadheads avoid using nonverbal communication to enact and affirm shared identity, to member self (identify one's self as a member). When DHs interpret one another's use of nonverbal symbols to be deeply felt, commonly intelligible, and widely accessible as ways for communicating like a DH, the nonverbal symbols are interpreted as instances of membering. Sardiello (1994) argues that during interaction at shows, DHs use three symbols—the "steal your face" skull, the "skeleton and roses," and tie-dye—to reinforce and maintain the following aspects of their collective system of belief:

> elements of humanist philosophy and Eastern religious doctrines, resulting in a system of belief that combines values associated with self-fulfillment and enlightenment, and values that recognize human potential and creativity to form an encompassing worldview. (p. 127)

In his ethnographic study, Sardiello (1994) found that the steal your face symbol is used to convey unity, the balance of dualistically opposed forces, a belief associated with the Chinese philosophy of yin and yang (p. 125). For some DHs, the steal your face symbol is a metaphor for stripping persons of "structured social distinctions" resulting in unification of diverse persons (p. 125). The skeleton and roses communicate love (p. 126) and the tie-dye the support of "individual expressions and creative invention while conforming to a recognizable form" (p. 126).

Wieder and Pratt (1990) and Pratt (1998) argue that speaking and communicating like an Indian is a constituent feature of being a "real Indian"; being a real Indian means communicating like a real Indian. For many Deadheads this is the case as well. For these DHs, speaking like a DH is a constituent feature of being a DH. When DHs speak in a manner that other DHs hear to be consistent with the deeply felt meanings behind the Grateful Dead and DH iconography they display, the nonverbal symbols used by the communicators are interpreted by DHs as instances of cultural communication, as instances of membering.

Communicating Like a Deadhead

"Show" is an important cultural symbol, possibly the most celebrated symbol in Deadheads' speech code (Dollar 1991, 1999a, 1999b, 2000a). For DHs a Dead show was several things, but for many it was the most celebrated place for expressing and affirming cultural identity. While writing this chapter, I received the following e-mail from a "family member."

> I love the description of DSO [band] and will definitely take any opportunity that comes my way to see them. I had my first annual pang last weekend when the weather was balmy and you could feel summer approaching in the air. This always reminds me of summer tour coming up and time to get mail order going. Then I was telling [first name deleted] about your description of DSO and we had Dylan on the stereo and it all just melted inside me. My annual cry that there are no more Dead shows, and the loss of this part of my identity, or at least the preferred expression of it. Anyway, it was a good release. (Deadhead, e-mail correspondence to author, 3/21/00)

Her e-mail focuses on several aspects of the deeply felt dimensions of show as a resource for DH cultural communication. First, she comments on "summer tour," part of the "world according to shows" (Shenk and Silberman 1994) or the aspect of DH folk logic arising from experiences at Grateful Dead shows and touring. For her, spring calls forth the experience of preparing for summer tour and mail ordering for show tickets. The pre-show speech event, discussed in the following pages, is another resource for communicating DH identity. Second, she addresses a dilemma experienced by many DHs today, the "annual pang" or painful emotion experienced when recognizing the loss of GD shows as "the preferred expression of" DH identity. Attending and participating in a GD show was and is not the only way to express and communicate DH identity, but for many, it was the preferred way. Although it is not the purpose of this chapter to answer why it was the preferred way, it has to do with the notion of a Dead show as a cultural communication ritual. It was a **communication event,** enacted and performed according to cultural norms, through which members paid homage to two symbols featured in much DH communication, namely the music of the GD and the DH identity (Dollar 1991, 1999a).

Much of the study's communication with Deadheads focuses on shows, past and future. In the process of writing this essay I received a phone call from a friend who initiated some DH cultural communication with the comment, "Be sure and let me know if they announce the Phil and Dylan show. I definitely want to go with you." I knew she was referring to the Phil and Friends and Bob Dylan show rumored to be scheduled for the Gorge, an amphitheater and camping venue in eastern Washington. Phil refers to Phil Lesh, the bassist for the GD. In the last few years he has toured as Phil and Friends, bringing together a variety of musicians. The venue, the Gorge, is a favorite because of its natural beauty and the fact that the owners allow camping for concerts, one of the few venues to do so these days. Once my friend mentioned the rumored show our talk touched on several culturally relevant themes—the musicians, camping with family members, time away from work, and mail ordering tickets.

When I first "got on the bus," I quickly learned that the show as a speech situation began or begins not at the actual concert but months in advance. The Grateful Dead followed loosely organized touring schedules, as indicated by reference to "summer tour" in the e-mail example above. Before the days of the Internet, members anxiously called the official hotlines, east and west coast, to check their hunches for tour announcements and particular venue dates so as not to miss a deadline for mail ordering show tickets. Now many DHs visit the official web site (www.dead.net) for this information or read an e-mail announcement sent to them as subscribers of the GDTSTOO list managed by GD Ticket Sales. Once an announcement is received for a tour, show, or set of shows members plan to attend, DHs engage in the second phase of this culturally meaningful speech event, "planning the show." Immediately, talk and e-mail begins—Who is mail ordering for us? Who is driving to the shows or will we fly? Where will we stay? Camp, friends' house, or hotel? How many shows are we going to see? What venues? Who else is coming?

This pre-show ritual of checking the hotline or web site, planning the trip to shows, and ordering tickets constitutes the pre-show speech event. A deeply felt ethos exists among members who communicate in this cultural manner. While nonmembers have access to these communicative resources (e.g., hotline, web site), they generally do not use them to participate in this pre-show speech event. For nonmembers, these communicative resources are not widely accessible for planning "to see some shows," a speech event with a history of over thirty years in the DH community. Nonmembers can translate the words, even understand the content of the statements. They cannot, however, hear them communicated within the historically grounded system available to DHs; the interaction is not commonly intelligible as DH cultural communication. For Deadheads, this pre-show communication is heard as instances of membering, instances of communication in which participants hear self and others to be communicating like a DH. In the following section, DHs' use of GD lyrics to accomplish membering, to enact and affirm cultural identity, is discussed.

Grateful Dead Music and Cultural Communication

"The Dead seemed to be able to play a musical language that could speak to different generations and different people" (Deadhead, radio call-in show, 8/9/95). This statement, like so many reported to me by DHs, calls attention to the Grateful Dead's music and its ability to speak to DHs. Another similarity between this statement and many others shared with me is the claim that the Dead's lyrics spoke to different generations. When talking with DHs about music as communication, many described a particular feature they recognize in GD lyrics: The meaning reveals itself over time as it becomes relevant to one's life experiences.

A Deadhead explains it this way, "Garcia's writing partner Robert Hunter . . . crafted his language at every level, both . . . at the level of the sounds of the language itself and also he was able to build these lessons into his music that sometimes would be floating through your head for twenty years before it yields its treasures of wisdom to you" (Deadhead, radio call-in show, 8/9/95). Extending this idea, another DH comments, "they [the lyrics] were not terribly specific, it was stuff you had to sort of think along with and bring your own experiences to appreciate and . . . as [first name of other DH deleted] said, a lot of times it would be years after your first encounter with something, you'd get a whole new take on it" (Deadhead, radio call-in show, 8/9/95).

Members of speech communities share **cultural communication myths**, stories thematizing community values, personae, and ways of living (Philipsen 1987). Members call on these myths to tell their individualized accounts of communal life. One myth told to me many times, and experienced for myself, thematizes those moments when GD lyrics pop into one's head, seemingly out of nowhere, forging sense and understanding of something in one's life. Something that was unclear before this moment is now intelligible in a culturally meaningful way. Whereas some DHs did not initiate talk about this way of speaking, not one denied having heard other DHs tell their individualized versions of this DH myth, and most offered personal examples once the topic had been initiated. In other words, this way of speaking is widely accessible among DHs.

When Deadheads share stories thematizing the experience that "once in a while you get shown the light in the strangest of places if you look at it right" (Hunter 1990, p. 197), they create and affirm shared identity. For these Deadheads, the stories are deeply felt as one source of evidence for the importance of GD music in their daily lives. The stories are commonly intelligible as unique versions of a community-relevant story line. Among DHs their cultural stories are also intelligible as acts of membering. That DHs choose to tell their personalized accounts of this community theme suggests that particular cultural communication myths are widely accessible within the DH speech community. When DHs partake in their way of speaking about GD music, they realize their use of cultural communication that enacts and affirms shared identity. Thus, they are solidifying their membership.

Conclusion

This chapter discussed and examined Deadheads' situated use of their communication code to enact and affirm shared identity. The discussion emphasized the complexity of communicating **cultural identity** in intercultural contexts defined by membership in different speech communities. The data suggested that interactions tend to involve Deadheads communicating with either members of another musical speech community, such as popular music and heavy metal communities, or members of another U.S. American speech community, such as street-oriented youth or nacirema (Philipsen, 1989, 1992, 1997). When interactions concern diverse ways of communicating like a U.S. American, the interlocutors' communication resonates of "American" folk ways yet expresses distinct and often incompatible ways of communicating like a U.S. American.

Studies of these types of speech communities, musical and distinct U.S. American, can be compared and contrasted in cross-cultural analyses to discover similarities and differences in communicating cultural identity. Although Philipsen (1989, 1992) provides a cross-cultural analysis of U.S. American speech communities, more studies are needed to further our understanding of domestic intercultural interactions within the United States.

References

Adams, R. G., and R. Sardiello (Eds.). 2000. *Deadhead social science: You ain't gonna learn what you don't want to know.* Walnut Creek, Calif.: AltaMira Press.

Braithwaite, C. A. 1997. "Were you there?" A ritual of legitimacy among Vietnam veterans. *Western Journal of Communication* 61: 423–47.

Braithwaite, D. O., and C. A. Braithwaite. 2000. Understanding communication of persons with disabilities as cultural communication. In L. A. Samovar and R. E. Porter (Eds.), *Intercultural communication: A reader* (pp. 136–45). Belmont, Calif.: Wadsworth.

Carbaugh, D. 1988. Comments on "culture" in communication inquiry. *Communication Reports* 1: 38–41.

——— (Ed.). 1990. *Cultural communication and intercultural contact.* Hillsdale, N.J.: Lawrence Erlbaum.

———. 1998. "I can't do that!" but I "can actually see around corners": American Indian students and the study of public "communication." In J. N. Martin, T. K. Nakayama, and L. A. Flores (Eds.), *Readings in cultural contexts* (pp. 160–71). Mountain View, Calif.: Mayfield.

———. 1999. "Just listen": "Listening" and landscape among the Blackfeet. *Western Journal of Communication* 63 (3): 250–70.

Collier, M. J. 2000. Understanding cultural identities in intercultural communication: A ten-step inventory. In L. A. Samovar and R. E. Porter (Eds.), *Intercultural communication: A reader* (9th ed., pp. 16–33). Belmont, Calif.: Wadsworth.

Coutu, L. M. 2000. Communication codes of rationality and spirituality in the discourse of and about Robert S. McNamara's *In Retrospect. Research on Language and Social Interaction* 33 (2): 179–211.

Dodd, D. G., and R. G. Weiner. 1997. *The Grateful Dead and the Deadheads: An annotated bibliography.* Westport, Conn.: Greenwood.

Dollar, N. J. 1989. On tour with the Dead: A look into the lives of Deadheads. Paper presented at the annual meeting of the Southern Anthropology Association, Memphis, Tenn., April.

———. 1991. The cultural function of Deadheads' ways of speaking. Paper presented at the annual meeting of the Western Speech Communication Association, Phoenix, Ariz., February.

———. 1999a. Show talk: Cultural communication within one U.S. American speech community, Deadheads. *Journal of the Northwest Communication Association* 27: 101–20.

———. 1999b. Understanding "show" as a Deadhead speech situation. In R. Weiner (Ed.), *Perspectives on the Grateful Dead: Critical Writings* (pp. 116–29). Westport, Conn.: Greenwood.

———. 2000a. Deadheads and the loss of Jerry Garcia: Communicating identity during community transition. Paper presented at the annual meeting of the Western States Communication Association, Sacramento, Calif., February.

———. 2000b. Language diversity within the United States: Understanding the houseless youths' code for speaking. In L. A. Samovar and R. E. Porter (Eds.), *Intercultural communication: A reader* (pp. 230–38). Belmont, Calif.: Wadsworth.

Dollar, N. J., E. Morgan, and R. D. Crabtree. 1997. Communicating like a Deadhead: A cultural analysis of place formulations. Paper presented at the annual meeting of the Western Speech Communication Association, Monterey, Calif., February.

Dollar, N. J., and B. G. Zimmers. 1998. Social identity and communicative boundaries: An analysis of youth and young adult street speakers in a U.S. American community. *Communication Research* 25 (6): 596–617.

Fitch, K. L. 1998. A ritual for attempting leave-taking in Columbia. In J. N. Martin, T. K. Nakayama, and L. A. Flores (Eds.), *Readings in cultural contexts* (pp. 179–85). Mountain View, Calif.: Mayfield.

Fong, M. 2000. The crossroads of language and culture. In L. A. Samovar and R. E. Porter (Eds.), *Intercultural communication: A reader* (pp. 211–16). Belmont, Calif.: Wadsworth.

Geertz, C. 1973. *The interpretation of cultures: Selected essays.* New York: Basic Books.

Hill, S., and G. Rifkin. 1999. Listen to the band. *Entrepreneur* 27 (6) (June): 132–41.

Hunter, R. 1990. *A box of rain.* New York: Viking Penguin.

Hymes, D. 1962. The ethnography of speaking. In T. Gladwin and W. Sturtevant (Eds.), *Anthropology and human behavior* (pp. 13–53). Washington, D.C.: Anthropological Society of Washington.

———. 1972. Models of the interaction of language and social life. In J. Gumperz and D. Hymes (Eds.), *Directions in sociolinguistics: The ethnography of communication* (pp. 35–71). New York: Holt, Rinehart and Winston.

Katriel, T. 1991. *Communal web: Communication and culture in contemporary Israel.* Albany: State University of New York Press.

Pearson, A. 1987. The Grateful Dead phenomenon: An ethnomethodological approach. *Youth and Society* 18: 418–32.

Philipsen, G. 1987. Prospects for cultural communication. In L. Kincaid (Ed.), *Communication theory from eastern and western perspectives.* New York: Academic Press.

———. 1989. Speech and the communal function in four cultures. In S. Ting-Toomey and F. Korzenny (Eds.), *Language, communication, and culture: Current directions* (pp. 79–92). Newbury Park, Calif.: Sage.

———. 1992. *Speaking culturally: Explorations in social communication.* Albany: State University of New York Press.

———. 1997. A theory of speech codes. In T. L. Albrecht and G. Philipsen (Eds.), *Developing communication theories* (pp. 119–56). Albany: State University of New York Press.

———. 1998. Places for speaking in Teamsterville. In J. N. Martin, T. K. Nakayama, and L.A. Flores (Eds.), *Readings in cultural contexts* (pp. 217–25). Mountain View, Calif.: Mayfield.

Pratt, S. B. 1998. Razzing: Ritualized uses of humor as a form of identification among American Indians. In D. V. Tanno and A. Gonzalez (Eds.), *Communication and identity across cultures* (pp. 56–79). Thousand Oaks, Calif.: Sage.

Reist, N. 1997. Counting stars by candlelight: An analysis of the mythic appeal of the Grateful Dead. *Journal of Popular Culture* 30: 183–209.

Rheingold, H. 1993. *The virtual community: Homesteading on the electronic frontier.* New York: Addison Wesley.

Roth, L. 1998. The music never stopped: Roots of the Grateful Dead sound recordings review essay. *Journal of American Folklore* 111: 63–68.

Ruud, G. 2000. The symphony: Organizational discourse and the symbolic tensions between artistic and business ideologies. *Journal of Applied Communication Research* 28 (2): 117–43.

Sardiello, R. 1994. Secular rituals in popular culture: A case for Grateful Dead concerts and Dead Head identity. In J. Epstein (Ed.), *Adolescents and their music: If it's too loud, you're too old* (pp. 115–39). New York: Garland.

Shenk, D., and S. Silberman. 1994. *Skeleton key: Dictionary for Deadheads.* New York: Doubleday.

Weiner, R. G. 1999. *Perspectives on the Grateful Dead.* Westport, Conn.: Greenwood.

Wieder, D. L., and S. Pratt. 1990. On being a recognizable Indian among Indians. In D. Carbaugh (Ed.), *Cultural communication and intercultural contact* (pp. 45–64). Hillsdale, N.J.: Lawrence Erlbaum.

Wieder, D. L., and D. H. Zimmerman. 1974. Generational experience and the development of freak culture. *Journal of Social Issues* 30: 137–61.

———. 1976. Becoming a freak: Pathways into the counter-culture. *Youth and Society* 7: 311–44.

KEY TERMS

communication event	culture
communitas	Deadheads (DH)
cultural communication	ethnography of speaking
cultural communication myths	Grateful Dead (GD)
cultural communication perspective of identity	identification predicament
	linguistic code
cultural communication resource	membering
cultural communication ritual	nonverbal
cultural history	speech code
cultural identity	speech communities
cultural premises	speech events
cultural rules	speech situation
cultural symbols	stereotype
cultural system	ways of communicating

REVIEW AND DISCUSSION QUESTIONS

1. Explain the conceptual definition of *culture* advanced in this chapter.
2. How does the study of speech communities advance our understanding of intercultural communication?
3. Define the following concepts: *membering, speech code,* and *cultural communication.*
4. How do these concepts provide an interpretive framework for studying cultural identification?
5. Explain the claim: Speaking like a Deadhead is a constituent feature of being a Deadhead.
6. Compare and contrast the cultural communication perspective with other perspectives for studying the communication of cultural identity.

"I Want You to Talk for Me": An Ethnography of Communication of the Osage Indian

Steven B. Pratt and Merry C. Buchanan

LEARNING OBJECTIVES

After reading this chapter, students will be able to:

- understand how American Indian public speaking differs from European American public speaking;
- describe the ethnography of communication;
- differentiate the etic and emic perspectives of communication research; and
- explain the significance of cultural competency to Osages.

My aunt comes today and says that she danced on this song and it has brought back memories for her. These are good memories of a time when we were gathered here in this place. She says she is remembering this man whose song was just sung. When he was here we were all together and we came together in a good way and we had many happy experiences in this place. She also says that her sons were with her during this time and today for the first time in many years she has all her sons here again. They're all together and she is thankful for that. Those are her thoughts today and she has asked me to explain that to you. She has a few gifts that she wants to share in honor of this song.

Today, most people have a preconceived notion of the lifestyle and history of the American Indian. For many, this preconceived image of the Indian is the homogeneous picture depicted in books and movies of the "old west" (Rollins and O'Connor 1998; Strickland 1997). The American Indian has been portrayed as uncommunicative, speaking only in monosyllables, unemotional, and stoic—primarily because of a seeming reluctance to speak openly among others. Conversely, in contrast to the stereotype, American Indians are adept in the art of ceremonial or impromptu speaking within most any context, formal or informal, providing an arena for Indian oratory.

The cultural phenomenon of European American "public speaking" differs markedly from what constitutes American Indian "public speaking." Osage public oratory diverges from European American practices in that all culturally competent Osage tribal members are not properly allowed to speak for themselves. Instead, they are required to call upon an elder male to speak for them. Thus, in the context of Osage public speaking, it is considered inappropriate behavior for just anyone to speak out. Males of a certain age and status are the sole speakers at most Osage public functions. Specific, albeit implicit, speaking rules must be followed for one to be considered a culturally competent Osage. Whereas with practice and audience acceptance, anyone in the European American culture can be considered as a competent public speaker, this is not so for the Osage. Of utmost significance to the Osage identity is the concept of competence. Collier and Thomas (1988) note the significance of cultural competence, integral to the Osages: "Cultural competence is recursive with cultural **identity;** a person is a core member of a culture to the extent that he or she coherently articulates and understands symbols and follows norms" (p. 105).

Ethnography of Communication

The methodological grounding for the present study is the **"ethnography of communication"** (EC) as a specified research program (Hymes 1962, 1972; Philipsen and Carbaugh 1986). Following the EC tradition (Carbaugh 1988/1989), this study exemplifies an EC by fulfilling four defining standards: (a) explicating a prevalent practice of **Osage** communication and using the Hymesian specialized lexicon; (b) investigating communication on the cultural level and examining the patterned use of talk "from the native's point of view" (Geertz 1973); (c) using extant ethnographies to acquire insight into the distinguishing characteristics of the Osage case and as a foundation for cross-cultural comparison; and (d) researching Osage discourse *in situ*, with the first author positioned as a **participant-observer** and using intensive, unstructured interviewing techniques. Interviews were conducted with tribal elders and were recorded on field notes while concomitantly the authors received advice on how to appropriately speak for another. Whereas most of the data arises from the first author's cultural expertise and recounted experiences as a traditional leader, some of the material was elicited by the second author and D. Lawrence Wieder, who both treated the first author as an informant. Data organization included gathering reports, transcribing interviews, and utilizing Hymes's (1962, 1964, 1972) descriptive theory as a general framework for the contexts and components of ways of speaking.

The current study employs an integrative methodological approach in that it utilizes both the etic and **emic perspectives.** As Hofstede (1994) notes, "An emic point of view is taken from within a culture, usually the author's own. An etic point of view is a 'view from the bridge,' comparing different cultures according to criteria supposed to apply to all of them" (pp. xi–xii). Hymes's (1972, 1974) descriptive ethnography of communication serves to guide and theoretically ground this research in an etic manner. By applying Hymes's (1972, 1974) concepts of **speech community,** setting, events, participants, acts, and ways of speaking, the etic method is employed. Reinforcing and further validating the **etic perspective**, data collected from the first author (a culturally competent Osage) and additional culturally competent Osage informants provides complementary support for the emic perspective.

The Osage Speech Community and Setting

The Osage Nation reservation is located in northeastern Oklahoma and is composed of three tribal bands or districts: Hominy (Zon-zo-li), Pawhuska (Wa-xa-xo-li), and Greyhorse (Pa-tso-li), with each district situated approximately twenty miles apart. The area provides opportunity for the over two thousand tribal members who reside in the reservation vicinity to meet with some frequency when speech situations occur. Members of the three districts share some type of familial or quasi-familial relationship (explicated in Pratt 1985). Ceremonial or social events are frequently held in each district with members from their respective districts and other districts being "called upon" to attend. Each district has a permanent structure that is used primarily for the purpose of the I-lon-shka (ceremonial dance) that is held annually by each district for four days in June. Additionally, community buildings are located at each district that are used for dinners, dances, and types of traditional game playing (e.g., hand game).

Speech community members are defined as tribal and nontribal members who reside on or live in close proximity to the reservation and who share "knowledge of the rules for the conduct and interpretation of speech" (Hymes 1974, p. 51). Although there are many Osages who do not reside on the reservation, the **speech event** (e.g., ceremonies) must appropriately occur in this area. In order for the event to be considered "real," it must occur at "home"—as most tribal members who reside in urban areas or other states refer to the reservation area.

Social Units

Speech Events

Hymes (1972) defines the **speech situation** as "activities which are in some recognizable way bounded or integral" (p. 56). Almost any occasion, whether formal or informal, may provide an arena for Osage public speaking. However, this study focuses primarily upon three events that are pre-planned: honor dinners (feasts), the I-lon-shka, and namings. **Honor dinners** are usually communitywide feasts prepared and hosted by a family in honor of some member who has received an honor or has completed a task (e.g., home on leave from military duty or graduating from college). Dinners are also used for making formal announcements such as when a family is going to put their son into the I-lon-shka. They will host a dinner and invite relatives to inform them of their intentions. The **I-lon-shka** is a four-day ceremonial war dance of the Osage men and serves as the primary focus of cultural

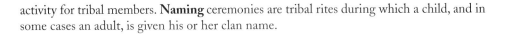

activity for tribal members. **Naming** ceremonies are tribal rites during which a child, and in some cases an adult, is given his or her clan name.

Participants

When Osages gather for a specific formal event such as an *honor dinner* or *naming ceremony,* only the **elder** member of the tribe or a male relative who has specifically been called upon by the host family speaks to those in attendance. In maintaining the public communication ethic, young men and most women, with certain exceptions, are prohibited from speaking for themselves and for others. However, in some isolated instances, a woman may be given the right to speak by the elders. One such exception occurs during discussions of ceremonial procedure, for example, how a certain ritual is to be enacted. For instance, at the Hominy district, two elder full-blood women will often offer advice during plenary meetings for the I-lon-shka, but in formal ceremonial occasions, both will have a male speak for them.

A naive listener might ask, "Why do only a few elder males speak for members of the tribe?" The practice of only elder males speaking follows the traditional social and political structure of the Osage tribe. Prior to the current political process of electing tribal officials, the Osages lived in bands (smaller clan units of the tribe) that were led by a hereditary chief. The chief was always a male and was born into this position much like members of the British monarchy. Among the duties associated with the chief's role were the responsibility to make decisions for the welfare of the band and to speak for the members on occasions of interaction with other bands, other tribes, or the federal government. Further, the chief would act as a teacher whose duty was to pass on the oral history and normative behaviors of the tribe.

In the late 1800s, the federal government changed the political structure of the tribe and ceased to recognize the hereditary chiefs (Bailey, Kennedy, and Cohen 1998). Instead, the federal government imposed a puppet regime of elected officials that were pejoratively referred to as mixed-bloods, that is, those possessing minimal blood quantum, by the full-blood members of the tribe. Although the elected chief and council began speaking for tribal members in dealings with the federal government, the hereditary chiefs still maintained their previous status and spoke for tribal members on cultural matters. With the passing of the era of the hereditary chieftains, the male heads of the extended families took on the role that the chiefs previously occupied. Therefore, the men who speak today are the "leaders" or "chiefs" of particular family groups. Although women are prohibited from openly speaking, this is not to suggest that women are not an important agent of socialization for both females and males. In fact, women are often sought out for advice and do serve as equals and superordinates, and the elder women are placed in positions of high honor as are the elder men.

Although one must be an Osage elder to be considered proficient to speak for others in most situations, age alone does not qualify one as a culturally competent speaker. A man can be considered elderly but his age alone would not automatically qualify him to speak for others. In addition to being past mid-life, the competent speaker must not only comport himself in the appropriate manner, but he must also establish his competency to speak of cultural matters. His knowledge of Osage ways neither comes from his own experiences, nor does it come from what he has read, studied, or what academic degrees he possesses.

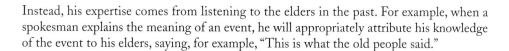

Instead, his expertise comes from listening to the elders in the past. For example, when a spokesman explains the meaning of an event, he will appropriately attribute his knowledge of the event to his elders, saying, for example, "This is what the old people said."

Speech Acts

Speech acts may include message content, form, sequences, dimensions, and types of illocutionary force (Carbaugh 1995). In this section, five unique and particular speech acts inherent within the context of Osage "public speaking" are examined. These include: *addressing, recognizing, give away, paying,* and *being called upon.*

Addressing

In almost all formal speech situations the spokesman begins by **addressing** those in attendance, offers a prayer, and explains the reason that everyone has been invited or called upon to attend the event and perhaps why he has been asked to speak. To the Osages, the act of *addressing (wa-hoi)* refers to publicly acknowledging the presence of the elder members of the tribe, each by name, and is intended as an overt sign of respect for the elders. Only the elders, both male and female, and some middle-aged principals (those who hold some type of ceremonial position) will be addressed. Additionally, the relationship between the speaker and the elders will be expressed. For example, one would begin speaking for another in the following manner: "I'd like to acknowledge our elders present today. Wi-tsi-koh Joe, Win-tse-ki Harry, Win-tse-ki Preston, I-koh Margaret, I-non-ton Mary, I-non Lottie, Wi-zhin Charles, Wi-zhin Mike. The family here has asked me to say a few words for them today."

After the elders have been addressed, the speaker then explains to the people what it is that he has been asked to say. The speaker will attempt to explain as closely as possible the thoughts and feelings of the requesters while at the same time trying not to put his own thoughts into the speech. A typical speech that was given during the I-lon-shka follows:

> My aunt comes today and says that she danced on this song and it has brought back memories for her. These are good memories of a time when we were gathered here in this place. She says she is remembering this man whose song was just sung. When he was here we were all together and we came together in a good way and we had many happy experiences in this place. She also says that her sons were with her during this time and today for the first time in many years she has all her sons here again. They're all together and she is thankful for that. Those are her thoughts today and she has asked me to explain that to you. She has a few gifts that she wants to share in honor of this song.

To the naive observer, the preceding speech might appear to be somewhat confusing with the main point being hard to identify. However, to the culturally competent Osage, the message is very clear. To fully understand the message, one must have knowledge of the situation, that is, one must know what has occurred and why. The woman whose thoughts were expressed is a full-blood elder member of the tribe. The song she is referring to was sung for a former Drum Keeper of the I-lon-shka. The time referred to was when this man had the drum (a ceremonial duty bestowed upon a young boy and his family) approximately twenty-five years ago. Her point was that although this man had died many years before, the feeling that was created by his presence many years ago still continues today. By hearing this song she was reminded of him and the people whom he had brought together. Her family was intact at that time, that is, her children were still living at home. Today, her sons are grown, have their own families, and have moved to other cities, but they all gathered to participate in the ceremonial dance just as they have for the past twenty-five years. During the speech no direct mention is made of the man's death, of his past ceremonial position, of his life, or the reason he had a song made. It is the culturally competent member's responsibility to know this information.

In this type of speech event, background information and explicit verbal codes are purposely omitted. Message interpretation among the Osage is contextually bound or "high context" (Hall 1976). The speaker assumes that the culturally competent listener possesses the knowledge required to interpret the message. Most of the topical areas are implied, and without shared cultural knowledge, the receiver would be incognizant of the subject. Therefore, only a "real" Osage would fully comprehend the message. Trudgill, Labov, and Fasold (1979) note that "An analysis of what speakers say and more particularly, what they do not say, can be indicative of the unstated, shared assumptions of particular social groups" (p. vii).

If the naive listener were to inquire about the purpose of the speech, he or she would be suspected of being culturally incompetent, as the culturally competent listener would not have occasion to ask this of others. This is one form—exhibiting appropriate listening skills—in which the cultural expertise of a person is demonstrated. A tribal elder explained that people are expected to know why they gather for a specific event and should know the purpose, rules of behavior, and expectations of those involved. Knowledge of a speech event is a criterion in one's acceptance as a culturally competent member. An informal rule of acceptance can be best summarized in the words of an elder who stated: "If you have to ask, then you are not one of us and if you want to be one of us, this is the type of information that you must know. You're supposed to have teaching." For example, after the first author began speaking for others, the only formal instruction received was from an elder uncle:

> Now that you have started speaking for others always remember two things; you never talk about yourself and you never talk about your family. You have been called upon to speak for someone else, always say what you have been asked to speak and nothing more.

The Osage culture is an oral culture and thus the manner in which the culture survives is through members sharing it verbally with other members and potential members. It would seem to the outsider that an oral culture would welcome potential members asking questions about observed events rather than doubting **cultural competency** by such an act. However, to the traditional Osage, knowledge is acquired by unobtrusively observing an event over an extended time span. Condon (1995), in his discussion of semantics and communication, found this approach preferable among cultures in which value is not placed upon putting everything into words: "The culture may teach its members that it is best to understand without having to be told, that it is better to learn through observation and sensing the environment, rather than learning through verbal teaching" (p. 143). For the traditional Osage, cultural competency is not acquired through the Western cognitive style of question and answer, but through patiently observing and sensing the environment.

Give-away

A **give-away** almost always occurs immediately following the speech event. *Give-away* refers to the act of the person or persons who have had their words expressed and they openly give gifts to selected individuals. Items that can be given away vary—one dollar, Pendleton blankets, groceries, ceremonial clothing, beef, and maybe even a horse—depending upon the feelings and finances of the people involved.

Recognizing

To *give-away* to an individual is to recognize that person publicly. For an Osage, to *recognize* an individual is to publicly honor him or her; that is, to bring attention to some act that the person has performed such as graduating from college, serving in the armed forces, providing assistance in a time of need, or simply to **recognize** someone who has been away from the reservation and has recently returned. It is unseemly for an Osage to speak openly of his or her own achievements. However, it is not improper for other Osages to speak of and make public the accomplishments of friends and family members.

Paying

Moreover, the *give-away* is also used to *pay* for the time that the person has taken with their speech. To *pay* does not denote that there is a fee for engaging in the speech event. For the Osages, the concept of **paying** refers to the notion that by engaging in the speech event they are imposing upon the time of the people who are gathered and the act is utilized as an overt means of gratitude. Following the *give-away* the spokesman will express gratitude to the people for their time: "The family wants me to thank you for taking this time. They realize that it's been a long day but this is something that they wanted to take care of."

Once the speech and the subsequent *give-away* is completed, all parties leave the center. There is no immediate feedback following the completion of the speech event, such as applause or comments telling the people that their message was received or how it was received. There is simply silence, a quiet form of acceptance, in contrast to a typical Western speech where applause by the audience is almost always exhibited, designating the end of the speech (Atkinson 1984). Further, if one were to applaud a speech at an Osage event, then he or she would be unfavorably sanctioned for exhibiting deviant behavior.

Being Called Upon

To **be called upon** refers to members of the community, specifically the elders, who have been invited to tacitly witness the event. In addition to witnessing the event, those who are *called upon* tend to validate or authenticate the ceremonial event. These events must adhere strictly to normative structure; therefore, those who witness these events can verbally validate to others that the act was carried out properly. Conversely, if the event is not properly enacted, then those in attendance will not validate the event to others.

If any of the others in attendance, during the course of the event, have a message that they want conveyed to those present, the appropriate procedure is to ask the designated spokesman, or an elder (usually a male relative, such as a grandfather, uncle, or a close family friend) to speak for them.

Ways of Speaking

Talking for another is a complicated process that is governed by an implicit set of rules. The culturally competent Osage adheres to particular norms of interaction and interpretation in **ways of speaking.** Rather than behavioral standards (Kolb 1964), norms are instead contextual prescriptions that apply to a particular social group in a specific situation (Collier and Thomas 1988; Hymes 1972; Shimanoff 1980). The "fluent speaker" must know and employ the rules and structure of the Osage speaking style; that is:

> (a) how to properly secure the attention of the audience and how to address the audience members; (b) what background information is considered high context and should be omitted; and (c) appropriately signal audience members that the speech is over, as well as the relationships among speech acts, and styles, on the one hand, and personal abilities, and attitudes, on the other. (Hymes 1974, p. 45)

In essence, this exemplifies the Osage "ways of speaking."

Topics of Talk

A person requesting someone to talk for him or her must have a purpose that is in keeping with the range of acceptable topics according to the context in which the speaking will occur. Acceptable topics are both associated with, and dependent upon, the speech situation. For example, if the occasion is one in which people are asked to witness a ceremonial act, such as a naming ceremony, the appropriate message would be one that describes the event, and discusses the relationship among the people in attendance and the background of the person involved in the rite. Additionally, the speaker expresses the host family's gratitude for the attendance of the witnesses, and almost always the relationship between the Osages and God (Wa-Kon-Ta).

It is inappropriate *to get up* and have someone talk for you for no apparent reason other than everyone else is doing it. *To get up* refers to the act of the person making a speaking request approaching the speaker (who is standing in full view of the people gathered—who are almost always seated in a circular or rectangular shape) and positioning one's self so that all in attendance can see. This act denotes that a message is about to be delivered and signals the listeners to become attentive. A person must know what it is he or she is doing, that is, what the meaning of the event is, and have a sincere message about these activities. Many contemporary or culturally incompetent Osages do not know the meaning of the events in which speaking occurs. Therefore, they will often request that an inappropriate message be presented. This is considered improper to the Osages who believe that, to a certain extent, you are imposing upon those in attendance. As one elder explained: "You should be sincere about what you are doing and be respectful of people's feelings and the time that you are taking."

The inappropriateness of a message and an individual's lack of cultural expertise in understanding the speech event is shown in an event that occurred during the Osage ceremonial dances in which the first author was a participant. It had been a long mid-June afternoon and about six hours of singing, dancing, and oration were coming to an end. During the course of the day, the men who are participating in the ceremonial are not allowed to leave the arena or dance ground once they enter. They are clad in ceremonial attire made of wool tradecloth or buckskin; the temperature is usually in the high nineties to one hundred degrees; and they are seated upon wooden benches. A middle-aged woman from the Ponca tribe *got up* on the last song and asked the *head committeeman* to *speak for her*. Her message was that she wanted to give away to the "O" people. She stated that the "O" people had been doing a good job and that she was appreciative of their efforts and wanted to recognize them by letting the people know who they were and what they had done.

Now this in itself is not offensive; in fact, this is primarily the type of message that would generally be conveyed. However, the insult came from the fact that the "O" people she was referring to were the people who keep the bathrooms clean and stock them with "O" paper, that is, toilet tissue. The expression "O" is a slang word common among the Osage people and is a euphemism for the Osage word *o-zheh-tsi*. The literal meaning of *o-zheh-tsi* is "shit house." Understandably, this speech was interpreted by the traditional elder Osages as a farcical interpretation of the tradition of Indian speaking and as an insult to the people who sat there all day during this particular ceremony. Rather than respecting those in attendance, this specific speech act was considered offensive. According to the elders, this was the first time that the "shit house" personnel were ever recognized during a ceremonial activity. To say the least, this speech was not well received and many were insulted. Moreover, the credibility of the speaker was suspect for taking the people's time with this type of speech, as evidenced by the comment of an elder who stated: "Why in the world would . . . ever say something like that? He should have known better than to say that for her."

Spokesman's Responsibilities

Talking for another person is a difficult process to engage in even for the person who has spoken for others for many years. It is complex in that it requires an excellent memory because the spokesman must be able to accurately recount the thoughts of other people. When a requester is explaining what they want the spokesman to relate, the appropriate behavior for the spokesman is to simply sit, avoid eye contact, and let the person talk. The spokesman seldom provides feedback in the sense that he does not ask questions for clarification and is rarely afforded the luxury of asking for reiteration. It is the spokesman's role to listen attentively, for he must recount exactly what someone has told him although he has only heard this information one time. Often when a requester is disclosing to the spokesman his or her thoughts and feelings, he or she may become very emotional, which further confounds full comprehension of the message. The proficient spokesman is required to "fill in the gaps" in the speech. That is, if the requester has excluded some information (e.g., family background), then it is the spokesman's responsibility to know his or her background. If the spokesman is not familiar with the requester's background, then he asks someone who knows and subsequently incorporates this information into his speech. He must place this information into a manageable unit and then think about how he can best express the thoughts of others. He does this without the amenity of note cards or other types of written

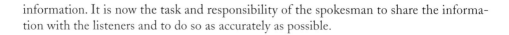

information. It is now the task and responsibility of the spokesman to share the information with the listeners and to do so as accurately as possible.

Conclusion and Implications

Using Hymes's (1972) descriptive taxonomy, the current study characterizes the communicative phenomena of Osage public speaking. Because communication orders social life, identities and social relations are accomplished interactionally (Carbaugh 1995). As Griswold (1994) notes, identity, or a sense of self, "is produced through interaction with others and requires confirmation from others" (p. 55). The communal function of a speech community and how people constitute communal identities with their communication is the focus of this ethnography of the Osage practice of "I want you to talk for me."

The present study possesses similarities to Philipsen's (1975, 1976) Teamsterville EC accounts in which he delineates what it is to "be a man" in Chicago's Teamsterville community. Characteristically, Philipsen's (1975, 1976, 1986, 1992) ethnographic studies demonstrate that to "be a man" in Teamsterville, one prefers to hit rather than talk; one chooses to remain silent rather than talk; and one favors the use of an intermediary to exert power rather than talk. Philipsen (1992) contends that these choices are components of a community's method of communication, rather than personality or psychological characteristics. Similarly, what it is to "be a culturally competent Osage" is demonstrated through one's knowledge and correct use of speaking for another, how to properly ask someone to speak for you, what topics are acceptable, and how to properly listen. Communicating what it is to be a real Osage is accomplished through observing and enacting appropriate communicative behaviors. When an Osage speaks in public speaking situations, it is within the boundaries of tacit sociocultural constraints.

If an at-risk culture, such as the Osage with only six fluent speakers, is to survive, then it is critical that the basic elements of the culture, e.g., language usage and values, be retained and passed on for future generations (Pratt and Buchanan 2000). Books, ethnologies, artworks, music, and other forms of written information are common methods utilized in preserving cultural elements. However, for an oral culture such as the Osage, even if such materials existed it would be inappropriate to learn from such sources, let alone write down such matters. For the elders of the Osage tribe, it is their responsibility to teach the culture through enacting appropriate behaviors such as how to *talk for another* or through tacitly teaching what is appropriate and inappropriate communicative behavior through simply engaging in day-to-day conversation. The basis of Osage cognition, as an elder explained, is through listening to the elders talk, by observing their behaviors, and finally by participating in the event:

> You can't learn these things [Osage culture] from a book. You have to be a part of it and you have to participate. This one woman wrote a book about the I-lon-shka but she doesn't know what she is talking about. You can't pick that book up and know about our ways. You have to be here and you have to watch what is going on and then after awhile you start participating.

Therefore, the culture must rely upon the accurate presentation of the culture being exhibited for neophyte members who then become responsible for the retention, preservation, and transmission of the culture. Events can be observed and enacted, but the meaning of an event requires the person possessing cultural expertise to properly interpret the act implicitly as well as explicitly. Cultural preservation lies in the appropriate teaching of communicative behaviors. Cultural competency is a necessary component of the accurate transmission of Osage ways of speaking. Additionally, as a direct defining aspect of culture, language serves a functional role (Scollon and Wong Scollon 1995) and in this case, language is used to establish identity. For the Osages, one form in which the basic elements of the culture are preserved is through enacting, observing, and participating in speech events.

Note

This chapter evolved and was further developed from a portion of the previously published article, S. Pratt and D. L. Wieder 1993 (The case of *saying a few words* and *talking for another* among the Osage people: "Public speaking" as an object of ethnography, *Research on Language and Social Interaction* 26: 353–408).

References

Atkinson, J. M. 1984. Public speaking and audience responses: Some techniques for inviting applause. In J. M. Atkinson and J. Heritage (Eds.), *Structures of social action: Studies in conversation analysis* (pp. 370–409). Cambridge: Cambridge University Press.

Bailey, T. A., D. M. Kennedy, and L. Cohen. 1998. *American pageant: A history of the republic*. New York: Houghton Mifflin.

Carbaugh, D. 1988/1989. Deep agony: "Self" vs. "society" in Donahue discourse. *Research on Language and Social Interaction* 22: 179–212.

———. 1995. The ethnographic communication theory of Philipsen and associates. In D. P. Cushman and B. Kovacic (Eds.), *Watershed research traditions in human communication theory* (pp. 269–97). New York: State University of New York Press.

Collier, M. J., and M. Thomas. 1988. Cultural identity: An interpretive perspective. In Y. Y. Kim and W. B. Gudykunst (Eds.), *Theories in intercultural communication* (pp. 99–120). Newbury Park, Calif.: Sage.

Condon, J. C. 1995. *Semantics and communication* (3rd ed.). New York: Macmillan.

Geertz, C. 1973. *The interpretation of cultures*. New York: Basic Books.

Griswold, W. 1994. *Cultures and societies in a changing world*. Thousand Oaks, Calif.: Pine Forge Press.

Hall, E. T. 1976. *Beyond culture*. New York: Doubleday.

Hofstede, G. 1994. Foreword. In U. Kim, H. C. Triandis, C. Kagitcibasi, S. Choi, and G. Yoon (Eds.), *Individualism and collectivism: Theory, method, and applications* (pp. ix–xiii). Thousand Oaks, Calif.: Sage.

Hymes, D. 1962. The ethnography of speaking. In T. Gladwin and W. Sturtevant (Eds.), *Anthropology and human behavior* (pp. 13–53). Washington, D.C.: Anthropological Society of Washington.

———. 1972. Models of the interaction of language and social life. In J. J. Gumperz and D. Hymes (Eds.), *Directions in sociolinguistics: The ethnography of communication* (pp. 35–71). New York: Holt, Rinehart and Winston.

———. 1974. *Foundations in sociolinguistics*. Philadelphia: University of Pennsylvania Press.

Kolb, W. L. 1964. Norm. In J. Gould and W. Kolb (Eds.), *Dictionary of the social sciences* (pp. 472–73). New York: Free Press of Glencoe.

Philipsen, G. 1975. Speaking "like a man" in Teamsterville: Culture patterns of role enactment in an urban neighborhood. *Quarterly Journal of Speech* 61: 13–22.

———. 1976. Places for speaking in Teamsterville. *Quarterly Journal of Speech* 62: 15–25.

———. 1986. Mayor Daley's council speech: A cultural analysis. *Quarterly Journal of Speech* 72: 247–60.

———. 1992. *Speaking culturally: Explorations in social communication*. Albany: State University of New York Press.

Philipsen, G., and D. Carbaugh. 1986. A bibliography of fieldwork in the ethnography of communication. *Language in Society* 15: 387–98.

Pratt, S. B. 1985. Being an Indian among Indians. Unpublished doctoral dissertation, University of Oklahoma, Norman.

Pratt, S. B., and M. C. Buchanan. 2000. *Wa-Zha-Zhe I-E:* Notions on a dying ancestral language. In A. Gonzalez, M. Houston, and V. Chen (Eds.), *Our voices: Essays in culture, ethnicity, and communication* (3rd ed., pp. 155–63). Los Angeles, Calif.: Roxbury.

Pratt, S. B., and D. L. Wieder. 1993. The case of *saying a few words* and *talking for another* among the Osage people: "Public speaking" as an object of ethnography. *Research on Language and Social Interaction* 26: 353–408.

Rollins, P. C., and J. E. O'Connor (Eds.). 1998. *Hollywood's Indian: The portrayal of the Native American in film*. Lexington: University Press of Kentucky.

Scollon, R., and S. Wong Scollon. 1995. *Intercultural communication: A discourse approach*. Oxford: Blackwell.

Shimanoff, S. 1980. *Communication rules: Theory and research*. Beverly Hills, Calif.: Sage.

Strickland, R. 1997. Coyote goes Hollywood. Available at www.nativepeoples.com/np_features/ ...7_fall_article/coyote_hollywood_cont.html.

Triandis, H. C. 1972. *The analysis of subjective culture*. New York: John Wiley.

———. 1994. Theoretical and methodological approaches to the study of collectivism and individualism. In U. Kim, H. C. Triandis, C. Kagitcibasi, S. Choi, and G. Yoon (Eds.), *Individualism and collectivism: Theory, method, and applications* (pp. 41–51). Thousand Oaks, Calif.: Sage.

Trudgill, P., W. Labov, and R. Fasold. 1979. Editors' preface: Language in society series (pp. vii–ix). In H. Giles and R. St. Clair (Eds.), *Language and social psychology*. Baltimore: University Park Press.

Wieder, L., and S. Pratt. 1990. On being a recognizable Indian among Indians. In D. Carbaugh (Ed.), *Cultural communication and intercultural contact* (pp. 45–64). Hillsdale, N.J.: Lawrence Erlbaum.

KEY TERMS

addressing	naming
being called upon	Osage
cultural competency	participant-observer
elder	paying
emic perspective	recognizing
ethnography of communication (EC)	speech act
etic perspective	speech community
give-away	speech event
honor dinner	speech situation
identity	talking for another
I-lon-shka	ways of speaking

REVIEW AND DISCUSSION QUESTIONS

1. In what ways does American Indian public speaking differ from European American public speaking?
2. Explain Collier and Thomas's (1998) statement: "Cultural competence is recursive with cultural identity." How does this statement apply to Osages?
3. List three components of a study utilizing the ethnography of communication (EC).
4. Compare and contrast the etic and emic perspectives.
5. Define *speech event* and provide an example of an Osage speech event.
6. Describe two Osage *speech acts*.
7. How does the traditional Osage attain cultural competency?
8. Explain the Osage spokesman's responsibilities in the process of "talking for another."

Building a Shared Future across the Divide: Identity and Conflict in Cyprus

Benjamin J. Broome

LEARNING OBJECTIVES

After reading this chapter, students will be able to:

- understand the complex relationship between identity issues and ethnic conflict;
- examine a case study of the Cyprus conflict that illustrates how identity both pushes people apart and ties them together in an interdependent manner;
- appreciate what lies "behind the scenes" of the daily televised images we receive of war and violence between ethnic groups; and
- understand the processes that are required for positive change in conflict situations.

When I first arrived in Cyprus to start my residency as Fulbright scholar in conflict resolution, it was the commonalities between the two main ethnic groups that stood out to me. With few apparent differences in physical features, a similar accent and rhythm of speech, a shared cuisine, and stylish Western dress, it wasn't always easy to distinguish between Greek Cypriots and Turkish Cypriots. Their high level of education, cosmopolitan outlook, and knowledge of world affairs led me to an initial impression that the Cyprus conflict was simply a case where people who had much in common had been forced apart by outside forces. It wasn't long, however, before my idealistic notions of peace and harmony gained a few rough

275

edges. As I traveled back and forth between the two sides of the buffer zone, I began to take notice of the many facets of life that differentiated the two communities—disparity in level of economic development, subtle variations in communication style, incongruent views of Cypriot history, different religious beliefs, and contrasting opinions about how to settle the conflict. Soon I realized that the similarities I had observed initially and the common culture I had experienced during my first days in Cyprus were overshadowed by a deeper schism that was extremely difficult to bridge. The two communities lived only meters apart, but the thin Green Line between them separated people who inhabited vastly different worlds. Although it required just minutes for me to walk across the U.N. controlled area between the north and south of the island, the psychological distance that I traveled was much further. Suddenly, the task before me looked quite daunting.

—Benjamin Broome

Every day our news is filled with reports of war and conflict—"Tamil Tigers attack Sri Lankan police station"; "Kashmir fighting intensifies"; "Israeli soldiers and Palestinians clash"; "Macedonian army unit launches offensive against Albanian rebels"; "Philippine army chases rebel kidnappers"; "Sierra Leone guerrillas continue fighting in spite of peace accord"; "Algerian fundamentalist groups attack civilians"—the list seems never ending. Our minds are filled with images of bombings, human carnage, destroyed homes and villages, mothers and children crying, refugees living in miserable conditions. It seems that everywhere there is hatred, prejudice, intolerance, fanaticism, and revenge. The phrasing of war becomes part of our vocabulary—*ethnic cleansing, collateral damage, scorched earth, buffer zone, warlords,* and *partition.*

Is there any hope that **ethnic groups** can live together in peace? Is it possible for different religious groups to co-exist? Can people overcome a history of bitterness? To answer these questions we must ask ourselves what drives such conflicts. Is it primarily a matter of political positioning, thirst for military dominance, struggle for economic advantage, quest for control of oil and other resources, or geopolitical maneuvering by the big powers? Or is there something deeper, more human, lurking behind the scenes?

Although we must recognize the immediate and direct impacts of the more "visible" factors such as those listed above, I believe that the hidden element in many conflicts, especially those involving different ethnic groups, is **identity** concerns. How do the different groups see themselves? What images do they hold of the other? How do these differences in self-perceptions and views of the other clash? How do they help create different views about the future? How is each group's view of itself threatened by the other? Can the conflict itself become essential to how groups see themselves? I'm convinced that these and related questions lie at the core of most ethnic conflicts.

These identity issues impact the conflict situations in several ways. The **conflict** itself is likely to revolve around differences in how each party perceives itself, especially vis-à-vis the other. These differences in perceptions may have led to the conflict in the first place, and they usually exacerbate the separation and make reconciliation nearly impossible. Trust is shattered, accusations fly, wounds fester, hope is lost. If they have lived in close proximity in the past, each party's definition of themselves includes the relationship they had together. Separation tears apart this collective identity and requires a redefinition of one's self. In order for suitable agreements to be reached between the conflicting parties, these identity issues must be addressed.[1]

Since 1995, I have worked with various groups on the eastern Mediterranean island of **Cyprus**, where the two primary ethnic communities have been separated by war for more than three decades. [2] In this chapter, I share some of my experiences and observations from working as **facilitator** with groups of ordinary citizens on the island who were involved in seminars, workshops, training programs, and other projects that I helped organize. I focus on the role played by identity issues in the development and maintenance of the conflict. First, I provide a brief description of the situation in Cyprus. Next, I describe the **context** within which the work I was involved with took place. This is followed by an examination of identity issues in Cyprus, with a discussion of how identity concerns are related to the conflict. Finally, I discuss applications of my analysis to the larger context of intercultural communication.

Background of the Cyprus Conflict

Cyprus is a small island in the eastern Mediterranean, located only forty miles (at its closest point) from the Anatolian coast of Turkey, about sixty miles from the coast of Syria, and approximately ninety miles from Lebanon. From east to west at its longest point, the island is about two hundred miles in length, and at its widest section it is about fifty miles from north to south. It has two mountain ranges that run from east to west, with a broad valley between. Cyprus has a history of human settlements that date back over eight thousand years. Greek language and culture were introduced on the island from about 1500 B.C.E., and when Ottoman rule began in 1571 A.D. nearly all the inhabitants were Greek-speaking Orthodox Christians. With the Ottomans came Turkish-speaking people, and Islam was introduced to Cyprus. Today, Greek Cypriots make up approximately 80 percent of the population, and Turkish Cypriots comprise less than 20 percent of the island's inhabitants. There are also Marionites and Armenians, along with a sizable number of "guest workers" from the Philippines and Sri Lanka (in the south), and Anatolia (in the north).

The roots of the current conflict can be traced to the 1950s, when the Greek Cypriots were fighting a guerrilla war against the British colonial rulers in order to achieve "enosis" or unification with mainland Greece. The Greek Cypriot struggle for enosis gave rise to the Turkish Cypriot call for "taxism," or division of the island into two geographical areas, with each ethnic group controlling one of the areas. When Cyprus achieved independence from Britain in 1960, an "arranged marriage" occurred between the **Greek Cypriots** and **Turkish Cypriots**, who became partners under a constitution that neither had any say in creating. The arrangement lasted only three years before breaking down, and fighting that occurred at the end of 1963 led to the division of the capital and the withdrawal of Turkish Cypriots into protected enclaves scattered throughout the island. United Nations troops were brought in to patrol a buffer zone that was created to separate the two communities in the capital, Nicosia.

In 1974, the Greek junta in Athens, whose officers were running the Greek Cypriot National Guard, worked with a faction of Greek Cypriots to overthrow the elected government and install as president Nicos Sampson, a person known to the Turkish Cypriots as a terrorist and murderer. This set the stage for intervention by Turkey, whose military forces quickly overran the northern third of the island. Many Greek Cypriots were killed or captured in the resulting battles, and over one-third of the population became refugees as they fled the advancing Turkish army. They lost their homes and businesses overnight, leaving behind their possessions and their ancestral lands. After **negotiations** created a cease-fire, the Turkish Cypriots in the south were transferred to the north, thus creating two ethnically "pure" geographical zones, accomplishing the Turkish aim of taxism. The Greek Cypriot coup lasted only a few weeks before international pressure led to the restoration of the democratically elected leaders, but the damage that had been done was irreversible. A buffer zone was created between the two sides, and additional United Nations troops were brought in to patrol this line of separation, which now stretched across the entire island, from west to east. The Greek Cypriot–led government in the south received international recognition as the legitimate government of the island, while the Turkish-controlled area became an unrecognized breakaway entity. Although U.N. resolutions have called for the withdrawal of Turkish troops from the island, today the line stands firm, with 40,000 Turkish troops on one side and 12,000 Greek Cypriot forces on the other. Only a few clashes along the buffer zone have occurred since the cease-fire was arranged in 1974, but both sides are heavily armed, and tensions remain high.

Despite years of negotiations to end the conflict, the situation stands much as it was in 1974, with the island divided and the people cut off from contact with one another. Despite the low number of incidents of intercommunal violence since the cease-fire was declared, people live in constant fear of another war. The overall situation is unstable, and the international community is engaged in ongoing efforts to bring about an agreement that is acceptable to both sides. Currently, the Republic of Cyprus (the Greek-Cypriot led government) is in the final stages of negotiations to enter the European Union during the next round of enlargement, and every attempt is being made to reach a settlement prior to accession so that the Greek Cypriots and Turkish Cypriots can enter this political entity together. Otherwise, it is likely that the current de facto partition will become permanent, and the possibility for a stable situation will have been lost for decades to come.[3]

Context for Analysis

The observations, analysis, and conclusions in this essay are grounded in several years of living and work experience in Cyprus, where I resided as Senior Fulbright Scholar for over two years, and in the eastern Mediterranean region, where I have been involved in numerous projects over the past twenty years.[4] I make no claim of objectivity or even of detached scholarly observation. The people of Cyprus are my family and friends, and the shape of their future matters a great deal to me. My own identity as a professional is strongly tied to the situation in Cyprus, and I am sure that the conclusions I reach are different from those that might come from a more disinterested **third party**.[5]

At the same time, I am constantly aware that I am an outsider to the Cyprus conflict. I did not live through the experiences that separated the people of Cyprus; I have not lost my property in the battles and wars that took place; I have not been a refugee; and it is unlikely that I will suffer the direct consequences of future clashes that could occur if satisfactory agreements are not reached soon. I have an allegiance to the individuals and groups with which I work, but the consequences of success or failure will never be the same for me as it will be for the people of Cyprus. My status as an "insider-outsider" allows me to play a special role in the conflict, but it does not give me a special lock on the "truth." At a minimum, it allows me to see the truth in the perspectives of both parties, and at a maximum it allows me to participate in and serve as facilitator for discussions that might help bring the two sides closer together.

I draw my analysis from a series of seminars that I facilitated with Greek Cypriots and Turkish Cypriots during the past eight years. These seminars involved a wide range of individuals from various sectors of Cypriot society—educators, businesspersons, professionals such as lawyers and psychologists, civil servants, diplomats, political figures, and university students. In some of these seminars, the issue of identity was the primary topic of discussion, and the participants had the opportunity to examine their perceptions of self and other in a rich and meaningful way. I also draw upon data from other workshops where identity issues were embedded in the discussion, even though they were not the focus of the activity. Finally, I incorporate information from numerous discussions I have had with individuals and groups in Cyprus while visiting in their homes, sharing dinner at a taverna, traveling together, or planning and debriefing workshops and other meetings.

The data from which I base my analysis are not the result of a traditional scientific study in which a broad cross section of individuals were surveyed or interviewed systematically. The ideas discussed here came from intensive group **dialogue** sessions, in which participants generated and clarified ideas, struggled to understand one another, and dealt constantly with the strain of separation and the weight of historical events. They confronted the differences in perceptions that divided them, and they sought ways to overcome obstacles to their coexistence. The discussions were always emotional and engaging—there were no detached, objective, academic debates. The participants were facing a conflict that had torn apart the fabric of their previous existence together, and they were dealing with issues that were vital to their future.

As a scholar, my primary purpose was not to conduct academic research about identity—rather, it was to act as a third-party facilitator of dialogue in **peace-building** groups that were seeking to understand one another better and to find ways of working together productively. My analysis is an ex-post-facto examination of results from these discussions. It is important to keep in mind that the data are contextualized within an intergroup instead of the more common individual framework. Discussions took place within group settings, and they were always focused on some aspect of the Cyprus conflict. So participants constantly had in front of them the other community, even when the other was not physically present. The purpose was not to get an overall sense of how individuals in Cyprus see themselves but to discuss how members of the two ethnic groups see themselves and each other vis-à-vis the conflict, especially in light of the need to build a culture of peace on the island.

Identity Issues in Cyprus

In some ways, identity issues in Cyprus appear to be relatively straightforward. There are two well-defined geographical zones, each populated and administered primarily by a single ethnic group. Each community uses a consistent label for itself—Turkish Cypriots in the north and Greek Cypriots in the south. The Turkish Cypriots are Turkish-speaking, think of themselves as secular **Muslims,** take pride in their Ottoman heritage, and consider themselves European in outlook and orientation. The Greek Cypriots are Greek-speaking, belong to the **Orthodox Christian** church, take pride in being part of the Hellenic world, and orient themselves toward Europe and the West. To an outsider, it may be easy to see the Turkish Cypriots simply as part of Turkey and the Greek Cypriots as an extension of Greece—merely two "outposts" of their respective motherlands.

The reality in Cyprus, however, is much more complicated. The multifaceted nature of Cypriot identities and their influence on the conflict emerged during the workshops that I facilitated with citizen peace groups. In most of these workshops, discussion was guided by two questions, one posed for the purpose of generating and clarifying ideas and the other for exploring the relationships among the ideas. In each group we were trying to create an influence structure that represented the system of issues surrounding the topic of our discussion. In the core group with which I first worked, we explored initially the obstacles to peace-building efforts in Cyprus, followed by goals for the group's peace-building activities. In other groups we examined issues facing the youth of Cyprus, barriers to increased cooperation among young business leaders, factors that led to pain and suffering in Cyprus, obstacles to cooperation among citizen peace groups in the region, and other topics. In none of these workshops was identity the primary topic, but in every case there were identity issues that became part of the influence structure.[6]

In addition to these workshops, I also facilitated several seminars that posed specific questions about identity. For example, we often addressed questions related to perceptions of the "other," perceptions of self, and perceptions of how the other sees you. In one of these workshops, we spent nearly six weeks exploring how participants see themselves, within their own society and vis-à-vis one another. The main purpose of this particular seminar was to explore how identity issues affect the Cyprus conflict. In the initial stages of their discussion, the participants in this group generated specific responses to the question: "What feelings and beliefs are associated with my identity as a Turkish or Greek Cypriot?" The Greek Cypriots generated eighty-eight statements about their own identity, and the Turkish Cypriots generated seventy-four statements. As part of our discussion, we explored the major themes that ran through these statements, categorizing the responses under six headings (see table 18.1). In the following section I explore each of these themes in greater detail. Most of the information is taken from the identity seminars, but it is augmented by discussions from the other workshops described above, as well as from recent seminars concerned about rapprochement in the region.

Before continuing, it is important to point out that there is a great deal of variety within each community, and although these intragroup differences are often overshadowed by their allegiance to the "national cause," it is important to recognize that neither group can be treated as a monolithic whole. This diversity, which is reflected in the large number of political parties (four to five) in each community (none of which receives an outright majority of votes in most elections), was also evident in our workshops. Sometimes the most contentious discussions took place between members of the same community rather than across ethnic lines. Thus, the descriptions I present below must be understood as general patterns that emerged from the discussions during our seminars. It is inappropriate and misleading to see individual Greek Cypriots or Turkish Cypriots as embodying all or even most of the characteristics presented in the following sections. Nevertheless, within each group there was a consensus that the beliefs and feelings we discussed are representative of the general population and are reliable guides to how people see themselves.

TABLE 18.1 COMPARISON OF IDENTITY PERSPECTIVES IN CYPRUS	
Turkish Cypriots	*Greek Cypriots*

Connection to Motherland

• Pride associated with Ottoman Heritage, Turkish language, Muslim religion • Increasing uneasiness about the degree of influence exerted by Turkey over internal affairs	• Carrier of Hellenic civilization, member of Greek community, part of Orthodox religion, pride in contributions to Western civilization • Confusion about relation between Greek and Cypriot heritage, distrust of Greek intentions toward Cyprus

Attachment to Cyprus

• Connection to the soil, pride in richness of culture, Cypriot dialect • Distinction from people of Turkey	• Connection with whole of island, attachment to place of birth, pride in 8,000 years of Cypriot history, Cypriot dialect • Distinction from people of Greece

Burden of Cyprus Conflict

• Suffering through many troubles, difficult to survive as a Turkish Cypriot, suppressed economic potential • Sandwiched between Turkey and Greek Cypriots, helpless, victims of situation	• Sense of incompleteness, lack of freedom to move in "my island," bitter about past • Always compromising, victims of international forces, weak position, strength to survive

Relation to Other Community

• Treated as minority, separated by language & religion, sense of insecurity • Desire for dialogue, willingness to make peace	• Fractured by separation • Search for similarities, desire for unification

Cultural Characteristics

• Close family ties, strong sense of neighborhood, emphasis on social events • Passivity in dealing with difficult situations, tolerant of others	• Close family ties, strong sense of neighborhood, emphasis on social events • Peace loving, compassionate, sentimental, hard working

Connection to International Community

• Identification with Europe, cosmopolitan, insufficiently aware of international issues • Misunderstood by international community	• Identification with Europe, emphasis on international law and rights, self-assured on world stage • Suspicious of other cultures, blame international community for problems

Connection to Motherland

The category that emerged as the dominant theme for both groups (in terms of associated strength of category, not number of items) was the connection they felt to what they describe as their motherlands, Turkey and Greece. For the Turkish Cypriots, this connection was relatively straightforward. They saw themselves as part of a larger Turkish population that lived not only in Turkey but also in many other countries of the region. The Turkish language was an important part of their self-definition, and they found great meaning in the poetry and literature of the Turkish language. They took pride in being descendants of the Ottomans, whose empire they perceived as the most tolerant and multicultural in the world's history, providing some of the progressive ideas that are found in many modern nations, especially those that incorporate many cultures within their borders. Turkish Cypriots considered themselves secular Muslims, celebrating the Islamic holy days and attending to the primary rituals, such as marriage and death ceremonies, but not participating actively in worship services or following the more conservative practices related to clothing, daily prayer, attending the services of the mosque, and so on. For the most part, they felt strongly aligned with the institutions and cultural life of Turkey, and they took comfort from being so close to the people from whom they descended and the land from which their forefathers emigrated nearly four hundred years earlier. As is clearer in later sections of this essay, Turkish Cypriots also differentiated themselves from the mainlanders, especially from the religiously conservative Anatolian settlers who have come to Cyprus more recently, but their strong connection to Turkey was undisputed.

For the Greek Cypriots, the connection they felt to their motherland was more complicated. Clearly, they saw themselves as part of Greek culture, as belonging to the larger Greek community, and as part of Greek history. They felt power in the expressiveness of the Greek language, the richness of its vocabulary, and the many poets and writers who used the language with skill and beauty to create works recognized by the world community. They took great pride in the accomplishments and contributions of the Hellenes, who are considered as providing the basis of Western democracy, philosophy, science, medicine, psychology, literature, and arts. The Orthodox Christian religion was an important aspect of Greek Cypriots' identity, providing celebrations, feast days, rituals of birth, marriage, and death, but no one described themselves as religious and few believed the Church held much influence over their daily lives. Unlike the Turkish Cypriots, however, they did not feel close to the daily life and institutions of their Greek kin, and to some extent they even felt a dislike of the Greeks, discussing how they often felt treated by them as second-class citizens. Even though they took some comfort from the promises of the Greek government to provide protection from outside threats, they did not believe the Greeks could (or would) deliver when the need arose. On the one hand, they felt a need for support and security arrangements with Greece. At the same time they were suspicious about the intentions and goodwill of Greece toward Cyprus, viewing Greece as directly responsible for much of the pain and frustration of the island. Finally, they expressed uncertainty about how much of their heritage was Greek and how much was due to the numerous influences from other rulers of Cyprus. Overall, despite several misgivings and confusions, the Greek Cypriots recognized their ties to the mainland and felt pride in their Greek heritage.

The difference in the Greek Cypriot feelings toward Greece, compared to the Turkish Cypriot feelings toward Turkey, can be explained partially by the different historical circumstances each face. The Greek influence in Cyprus goes back over three thousand years, to the time of the first Greek settlers who came to Cyprus after the Trojan wars described by Homer, while the Turkish presence in Cyprus started over four hundred years ago with the Ottoman conquest of the island. While the period of Turkish influence has been relatively uninterrupted, except for the British colonial period, the Greek impact on Cyprus lies within several other layers of conquest, including Phoenician, Assyrian, Egyptian, Roman, Byzantine, Lusignian, Venetian, Ottoman, and British. Although the language and mythology remained predominately Greek, these periods have left their mark as well. Many Greek Cypriots will point to the "unbroken chain of Greek heritage," but it is not a very convincing argument, even to the Greek Cypriots themselves. In addition, the distance to the motherland is greater for the Greek Cypriots than for the Turkish Cypriots (it is five hundred miles to Athens, while it is only forty miles to the Turkish coast), and besides the practical difficulties of maintaining a close relationship with a faraway neighbor, such physical distance also creates psychological distance. Another factor is the ratio of Turkish Cypriots (120,000 total population) to mainland Turks (65 million inhabitants) compared to the Greek Cypriots' (650,000) relation to the inhabitants of Greece (10 million). The Greek Cypriots do not feel overwhelmed by the size of the Greek population, so it is not difficult for them to feel and act independently of Greece, while the Turkish Cypriots feel more constrained in the face of the large population of Turkey. Finally, the Greek role in the 1974 coup that led to the Turkish intervention is openly acknowledged, and Greek Cypriots quickly condemn both this intervention in their internal affairs and the lack of Greek help in their attempt to defend themselves against the Turkish forces. By contrast, the Turkish Cypriots express gratitude to Turkey for their intervention in 1974, viewing this as an act of "salvation" for their community.

Attachment to Cyprus

In addition to the strong ties both communities feel toward their mother countries, both Turkish Cypriots and Greek Cypriots also expressed deep attachment to the island of Cyprus. The Turkish Cypriots emphasized their love for the island, their roots in the soil, their emotional attachment to the landscape and its smells, colors, sounds, and cooling winds of summer evenings. They discussed the uniqueness of their Cypriot dialect, cuisine, and many cultural traditions. They also took pride in having a separate identity from their Turkish kin, speaking about their secularism and dislike for anything too religious.

Similarly, the Greek Cypriots discussed at length their feelings of belonging to the land of the island, the human and natural aspects of the Cypriot landscape, and the emotional ties they feel to the mountains and the sea, the smell and colors of the sun and the air. They also emphasized the Cypriot dialect, in their case tracing it back to the times of Homeric Greek, emphasizing, as did the Turkish Cypriots, ways in which their culture differs from that of the mainland Greeks. Unlike the Turkish Cypriots, they pointed to the eight-thousand-year history of human settlement on Cyprus, recognizing that monuments were built by their ancestors prior to Greek influence. They also emphasized the international recognition given to their government and the fact that Cyprus was an independent state, allowing Cyprus to play a role on the world stage. Also unlike the Turkish Cypriots, they talked about their unwillingness to leave the island, even when conditions are bad and the future grim. Finally, the Greek Cypriots stressed their connection with the whole of the island, and they gave special importance to the place (village and setting) of their birth.

Beyond these differences, both Greek Cypriots and Turkish Cypriots expressed very similar feelings of affection for their homeland. For both, it reflects the meaning they give to the *Cypriot* part of their name. However, the differences that emerged between the Turkish Cypriot and Greek Cypriot views are not insignificant. The latter's attention to the eight-thousand-year history of the island is no accident—they have been taught in their history that they are the original inhabitants of the island and that the Turkish Cypriots are relative newcomers. The attention to international recognition is another part of the political nature of Greek Cypriot identity—they derive part of their legitimacy from this legal status as the official representatives of Cyprus, and an important part of the way they see themselves has to do with this status. Finally, the emphasis Greek Cypriots gave to their connection with the whole of the island is quite different from the Turkish Cypriot views. The Greek Cypriot official position is that every Cypriot must have free access to the whole of the island, and this political message has been hammered into the consciousness of every Greek Cypriot from birth. For many of them, the village of their birth (or the village of their parents) lies in Turkish Cypriot–controlled territory, and giving attention to a specific location is a way of keeping alive the political hope that one day they will have access to these places. For the Turkish Cypriots, although they may miss the place of their birth (if their home was formerly in the south), and nearly all of them want to visit places in the south that used to be important to them, few Turkish Cypriots express a desire to live again in those places. These differences between the two communities are major driving forces in the conflict, and they represent issues that are very difficult to resolve.

Burden of the Cyprus Conflict

Very few Greek Cypriots or Turkish Cypriots have known a period without the Cyprus conflict. It has been at the forefront of their lives since the 1950s, and today it is a pervasive force that overlies much of their existence. Both groups have suffered physically and both now suffer psychologically. Although the Cyprus conflict impacts strongly on the identity of both Greek Cypriots and Turkish Cypriots, it does so in different ways. For the Turkish Cypriots, an important part of their identity is the struggle to survive as a community. They see themselves as having endured a great deal of suffering over the years at the hands of the Greek Cypriots, and they are constantly reminded of the events that caused this suffering. They hold within themselves a feeling that they are victims of grave injustice, that they have been persecuted by many forces. Turkish Cypriots believe strongly that their community deserves better, both in term of recognition as a community and in economic opportunities.

For the Greek Cypriots, identity is also tied to struggle, but their fight is for justice that will address the wrongs committed against them in the past. They see themselves as suffering, but the cause of their troubles is primarily Turkey and the international community, not the Turkish Cypriots. They feel divided, incomplete, and without freedom (to move freely and settle within Cyprus). There is a lot of bitterness about the past and uncertainty about the future. They see themselves as constantly compromising in the interest of peace, putting themselves in a weak position at the bargaining table.

Despite the similarities at one level, the differences in Greek Cypriot and Turkish Cypriot views of themselves vis-à-vis the Cyprus conflict are one of the primary forces that keep the conflict alive. The Turkish Cypriots' struggle to survive as a community is pitted against the Greek Cypriots' struggle to exercise their individual rights. The Turkish Cypriot feelings toward the Greek Cypriots for the suffering they caused is ignored by the Greek Cypriots in their emphasis on outside forces (primarily Turkey) as the cause of suffering in Cyprus. The constraints that the Turkish Cypriots feel because of their international isolation are incompatible with the Greek Cypriot belief that they have to be constantly alert to the danger of the world community accepting the status quo as the starting point for a solution, leaving them in an even weaker position. In the meantime, there is a general "heaviness," caused by the existence of the unresolved conflict, which pervades the psychological and social well-being of all Cypriots and their views of themselves.

Relation to the Other Community

The Greek Cypriots and Turkish Cypriots have lived together on the same small island for over four hundred years, and the ties they have with one another form a crucial backbone of their identity. For the Turkish Cypriots, there is a clear awareness of the ways in which language and religion separate them from the Greek Cypriots. There was some discussion about the existence of an inferiority complex, brought about by so many years of being dominated economically, politically, and culturally. Turkish Cypriots expressed a feeling of insecurity toward Greek Cypriots, feeling threatened by the larger community, and they saw a need to protect themselves from the prejudice and abuse that used to happen daily. There was a strong dislike of being treated today as a minority by the Greek Cypriots. At the same time, there was a strong desire to have more dialogue, to directly communicate and engage in trade, and to find ways to live peacefully side by side.

The Greek Cypriots emphasized their similarities with Turkish Cypriots, along with an explicit recognition that they seldom thought about differences. They expressed a desire to coexist with the Turkish Cypriots, to live together with their neighbors in peace. There was a strong dislike for any form of artificial separation between the two communities, and they saw themselves as constantly fighting for individual rights, both their own and their neighbors'.

It was clear that neither of the communities feels "complete" without the other, but this seemed truer for the Greek Cypriots than for the Turkish Cypriots. Because of their minority status (numerically, economically, and politically), the Turkish Cypriots had always been aware of their differences with the Greek Cypriots, and they had long taken these dissimilarities as a matter of fact. For the Greek Cypriots, however, who were the ruling majority for much of the twentieth century, the differences between themselves and the Turkish Cypriots have been more or less overlooked and ignored. In many ways, the basic difference in how each group sees themselves vis-à-vis the other fuels the conflict, leading to incompatible positions about how the two communities should relate to one another. The Greek Cypriots' insistence on "living together" on the island is in direct opposition to the Turkish Cypriot assertion that the only future for Cyprus is an arrangement with appropriate safeguards that allows the two neighbors to live securely and peacefully side by side.

Cultural Characteristics

In spite of speaking different languages, following different religions, and holding such different views of history and the current situation, Greek Cypriots and Turkish Cypriots share many common cultural characteristics. In each community, individuals define themselves within the context of family ties, and personal identity is closely linked to parents, siblings, and relatives. Neighborhood is also important, and the character and history of the place where they reside helps determine how they see themselves. Emphasis is given in both communities to helping neighbors and others in need. At the same time, people are curious about the affairs of their neighbors, and both sides said there is a tendency to talk about others "behind their back." For both groups, much of life revolves around social activities, and food is a central feature of social gatherings. Although there are a few differences in the cuisine of each side, for the most part the diet is the same, and everyone will point quickly to their favorite Cypriot foods such as *halloumi* (a special cheese) and *souvla* (a grilled meat). In each community, people see themselves as friendly to others, hospitable to guests, and eager to learn about others.

Music, dance, and art are integral parts of social life among both Greek Cypriots and Turkish Cypriots, and they tend to have the same or similar dance costumes, instruments, melodies, and forms of artistic expression. Each group pointed to their love of *tsifteteli,* a popular dance and music that has origins in the Middle East. Both groups discussed their tendency to treat time in a somewhat casual manner, especially their habits of being late for events and doing things "at the last minute." There are many common nonverbal expressions, quite a few shared words and phrases, and numerous communication habits that are identical—both groups pointed out that several people are usually talking together at the same time in social conversations (and other settings) and that most social visits end with a long conversation at the gate, even if it is already very late at night (something I experienced myself many times!). Finally, Greek Cypriots and Turkish Cypriots both value humor, placing emphasis on telling jokes, and they consider themselves to have a good sense of humor toward events and toward other people.

The primary cultural characteristics that separate the two sides relate to activity orientation and emotional expression. The Turkish Cypriots saw themselves as somewhat passive in responding to external events, and they considered themselves as having a relaxed approach to life. They talked about their ability to "forgive and forget" wrongdoings against them. While they considered themselves emotional, they are careful about publicly displaying their emotions too strongly. The Greek Cypriots, on the other hand, saw themselves as taking a more proactive approach to situations, as impatient, and as future oriented. They see themselves as sentimental, quick tempered, and emotionally expressive. They have trouble letting go of past wrongs that others have done against them, and they feel bitter about the way they have been treated by the outside world. These differences in approach to action and in expression of emotion have created many misunderstandings when Greek Cypriots and Turkish Cypriots attempt to work together.

Connection to International Community

Although neither Turkish Cypriots nor Greek Cypriots generated many individual items about how they see themselves in relation to the rest of the world, the similarities and differences in their views are central aspects of the Cyprus conflict. One consistent component of both groups' view of self is their European orientation. Despite the location of Cyprus in the eastern Mediterranean, near countries such as Syria, Lebanon, Israel, Egypt, and other Middle Eastern countries, the Cypriots clearly locate themselves as part of the Western world. There is actually a physical connection to the West—two large British sovereign military bases are located in Greek Cypriot–controlled territory. In addition, Greek Cypriots receive over two million tourists every year, most of them British and northern Europeans. Even the Turkish Cypriots, who are Muslim by religion, turn away from the Arab world and toward Europe. While there is some acknowledgment of Middle Eastern influences on their culture, Cypriots are vigorous in defending their Western lifestyle and ways of thinking, as well as their political connections to Europe, Britain, and the United States. This probably comes from several factors—the many years they were a British colony, the large number of Cypriots living currently in Europe (especially London) and the United States, the fact that many students have studied abroad, and the current accession process of Cyprus's entry into the European Union.[7]

Beyond the similarities, however, the type of connection each community maintains with the Western world is quite different. The Turkish Cypriots feel frustrated by their inability to make the rest of the world understand their situation. They don't easily trust the West to deal with them fairly, since it has a history of prejudice toward Islam. They can't understand why the international community refuses to recognize their political legitimacy and fails to acknowledge the reality of the division of Cyprus. The Greek Cypriots, although their standard of living is not very different from those found in most European and U.S. cities, have tended to maintain a nonaligned position toward the West. While they rely on the United States and Europe for political support and economic trade, they are suspicious of the intentions of the West, particularly those of the United States, which they perceive as favoring Turkey.

Identity and Interdependence in the Cyprus Conflict

While one must be careful in drawing analogies between vastly different situations, the Cyprus conflict has many characteristics of a married couple seeking legal divorce. When such separation occurs between married partners in contemporary Western societies, it is usually difficult and almost always painful, but it can allow each person to go her or his own way, finding new opportunities and building a new life. It is not so easy, however, to just walk away from a marriage and begin anew, because the divorce situation is complicated by the interdependence that exists between the marriage partners. Often children are involved and both parents want custody, or the couple lives in a small town and neither can move away easily, or both work for the same organization and cannot change jobs effortlessly. Additionally, they may own joint property, such as the house they built together, or they may have established an estate that cannot be easily broken into separate pieces and divided between the two sides. Quite often, one of the parties is in a stronger position economically (e.g., one spouse may have a full-time salary while the other has never had a full-time job outside the home, leaving this person with few opportunities for gainful employment). It is not unusual for the separation to be initiated by one of the parties against the wishes of the other, with the aggrieved party denying the difficulties that led to the breakup and at the same time harboring illusions of bringing the marriage back together "like it was before." The situation is sometimes exacerbated by the parents of the couple, especially if these different sets of parents don't get along with each other. In most situations friends or colleagues of the couple

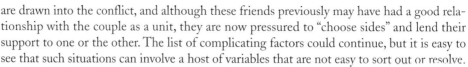

are drawn into the conflict, and although these friends previously may have had a good relationship with the couple as a unit, they are now pressured to "choose sides" and lend their support to one or the other. The list of complicating factors could continue, but it is easy to see that such situations can involve a host of variables that are not easy to sort out or resolve.

In the case of Cyprus, the situation is complicated by many factors similar to the ones listed above. After a short **partnership** in governing the island, disagreements and difficulties led to fighting, and an initial cease-fire has turned into a de facto separation. Intercommunal violence has ceased, but no agreement has been reached on matters that divide the parties—who will control which territory on the island, how the parties will share power and responsibility in matters that concern everyone, what guarantees will be put in place for security, how the weaker party will be protected from economic and cultural domination by the stronger side. The Greek Cypriots want to turn back the clock to recreate the situation before the war, when they were the dominant group, while the Turkish Cypriots insist that the separation is final—at last they can build their own institutions without the interference of the Greek Cypriots. The motherlands of the two communities are traditional enemies, and although they promise to "protect" the respective communities from aggression by the other, Cyprus suffers continuously from their interference in its internal affairs. External parties, such as the United States, Britain, and the European Union, are trying to help broker an agreement, but each side feels that the other is favored.

Like the married couple seeking a legal divorce, the two communities of Cyprus find themselves in a position of **interdependence**. Identity issues divide them but also tie them to each other. The conflict has become an integral part of both individual and community identity. Because war and forced division, rather than a natural process of relocation over time, created the geographical zones in which the two communities of Cyprus live, the conflict is an unsettled presence that permeates society. It is nearly impossible to carry on a conversation for any length of time (on almost any topic) with either a Greek Cypriot or Turkish Cypriot without the conflict entering the discussion.

The dominance of the conflict in the individual and collective psyche affects the society in an interesting manner—it serves to heighten or even strengthen individuals' sense of self-importance. The international community has devoted much attention to Cyprus, and it is doubtful that this small island would have received such interest from the world community if the conflict did not exist. It is not uncommon to hear Cypriots (of both communities) say (only half-jokingly) that Cyprus is the center of the world, but this perception would be more difficult to maintain without the existence of a conflict that receives constant notice from Europe and the United States. The news media in Cyprus give daily headline coverage to even the most insignificant statements by special envoys, ambassadors, politicians, and almost any other outsider who mentions Cyprus in the text of their remarks. It is ironic that outside Cyprus few people know anything about the conflict (or even where Cyprus is located), while in Cyprus one gets easily the impression that the world's attention is focused on the most recent developments about the Cyprus conflict.

At the same time, the crucial role played by the Cyprus conflict creates many problems in the everyday life of Cypriots in both communities. The psychological burden is great, and most people suffer emotionally a great deal from the unresolved feelings associated with the 1974 events and from the fear that war will come again. Uncertainty, anxiety, insecurity, and pessimism abound in Cyprus, and these negative feelings affect family life, worker productivity, and political decisions about economic, environmental, educational, and almost all other issues. The attention given to the conflict also allows Cypriots to avoid or ignore many of the social problems that face their society. Domestic violence, mental depression, treatment of foreign guest workers, environmental problems, and other concerns can be easily shoved aside by politicians who use the "national cause" as an excuse to focus on other issues.

Finally, identity concerns help keep the conflict alive in Cyprus. Differences in how the two communities define themselves make it very difficult for the conflict to be resolved. Like marital separations, which seldom end harmoniously, each side in Cyprus blames the other for the breakup, trust has disappeared from the relationship, tension is high, and communication with one another has broken off. Although many attempts have been made to reestablish the relationship, there seems to be little hope for the "marriage" resuming, certainly not in its previous form. However, there is hope that the two sides can work out an amicable agreement that allows them to share the island without constant tension, fear, and the psychological burden of a failed partnership.

Perhaps it is only natural that two ethnic groups with different languages, different religions, and different cultural heritage would have difficulty living together. However, a partnership, even if it is an arranged "marriage," cannot simply end with both parties going their separate ways, especially when they have over four hundred years of shared history and live on a small island near feuding "parents." Reaching agreement about a shared future will not be easy, but the issues of language, religion, and heritage are not the main stumbling blocks in this endeavor. The following section examines how ethnic conflicts can be managed more productively and how identity issues can interfere with this process.

Keys to Constructive Management of Ethnic Conflicts: The Role of Identity

Fortunately, most of us (in Western societies) do not have to face violent conflicts and deadly war. However, intercultural relationships are the norm rather than the exception in our society, and conflicts lead to a variety of difficulties, resulting in a breakdown of communication and often leading to a breakup of the relationship. Conflict can be managed productively only if both parties take specific steps toward resolving the issues that separate them from one another. The past must be confronted honestly and dealt with productively, but the focus must turn to the future of the relationship. Unfortunately, identity issues can make this shift difficult, if not impossible. If people feel that their identity is under siege, if they feel insecure, if they don't feel acknowledged and respected, if they feel wronged—they will become defensive, accusatory, and provocative, preventing the very actions that are necessary to look ahead. On the other hand, if threat can be removed, if respect can be demonstrated, and if confidence can be built, the relationship can be redefined and the two sides can learn to work together cooperatively.

The following are critical elements in the resolution of conflict, and all of them can be affected, both negatively and positively, by identity concerns:

1. Both parties must assume "co-responsibility" for the conflict. Rarely can difficulties in a relationship be "blamed" on one side or the other. In almost all cases, both have contributed to the difficulties, and until each party acknowledges the pain they

have brought to the other and the role they have played in escalating the tension, it will be impossible to reach a satisfactory agreement to resolve the conflict. Identity issues stand squarely in the path of such acknowledgment, especially when each side feels threatened by the other. Nothing leads to defensiveness faster than attack, and when identities are assaulted, the search for blame is heightened. However, if parties are able to publicly recognize their "mistakes" and take responsibility for past actions, threat will be reduced to each side's identity, making it much easier to approach the conflict in a positive manner.

2. The focus must be on the future. The past can never be ignored, even though it may be painful to discuss and difficult to acknowledge, but it is counterproductive to dwell exclusively on the past. Life takes place in the future, and until the parties are willing to discuss what lies ahead, they will never be able to go there creatively. Identity conflicts tend to be locked in the past, blocking the ability of groups to envision a future they could share. Entombed in a poisoned past, parties are unable to look beyond a period that no longer exists. Once they direct their thinking toward how their relationship will look now that they are no longer in a "marriage," opponents will be able to redefine themselves and the way in which they will work together under new arrangements.

3. A working partnership must be formed. A relationship will never be the same as it was in the past, but it can never be discarded completely, as if it never existed. Two parties who have ended the formal partnership they once shared must establish a new partnership, based on new principles. Even if this new relationship entails separate living arrangements, they will need to find a way to deal with matters that concern the two of them. Threats to identity make it very difficult to share with anyone, especially with the enemy. The natural tendency is to protect one's hard-earned rights, to keep the other away, to prevent encroachment on one's territory, or to push for access to what is "rightfully" yours. Demands and denials rule the day, and tension remains high. When the two sides start thinking seriously about how they will co-exist, how they will share what cannot be divided, and how they will work together to take care of tasks that must be co-administered, then they will be moving toward a workable agreement.

4. The complexity of the situation must be acknowledged. Conflicts are never simple, yet they almost always get framed in "either-or," "us-them," or "right-wrong" terms. "Our side" is justified in its actions and the other side is obstructing progress. Additionally, there is a tendency to view the other community as homogeneous and to portray them in strictly negative terms. Yet the other is never an undifferentiated entity, and neither is everyone on one's own side all of the same opinion. Identity issues make it difficult to recognize the variety that exists among the "enemy" or within one's own community. When one's definition of self is under attack, the impulse is to rally around a single cause and to portray the other as a uniform evil. Under such conditions, common interests cannot be discovered, and joint actions will never be taken. On the other hand, if each side can begin to see the other in differentiated terms, and if both of them can identify the multiplicity of factors that complicate the situation, they will be able to confront the conflict in much more realistic and practical terms.

5. Risks must be taken to make positive moves. Parties in conflict often remain in a stalemate because each is waiting for the other to make the first positive move.

Sometimes both sides are afraid that if they take the first step, the other will take advantage of them. Yet stalemates require action before they can be broken. Identity concerns can preclude the willingness to take a risk, to offer something that will affect the situation in a helpful way. Insecurity leads to inaction, and there is no way to move forward. The future can never be certain, and the consequences of one's actions are never predetermined, but unless one or both parties are able to take steps that offer something useful to the other, both will remain mired in a quicksand that continues to pull them downward. Taking risks can lead to unintended consequences, and sometimes can even be dangerous, but if either or both sides are willing to "step out on a limb," they break the deadlock and encourage other beneficial moves.

6. Trust must be built. No partnership can exist without **trust**. Suspicions, misgivings, and skepticism make it impossible to work together or live together peacefully. Identity concerns inhibit the development of trust, making it far less likely that parties in conflict can remove the protective shields they have built up around them. Although it may never be easy to reach a state of complete confidence in the other, it is essential to recognize, acknowledge, and respect each other's view of self. If parties are able to deal with identity matters in a positive way, they can start to tear down some of the fences that have kept them apart.

7. Security must be established. Fear is one of the primary driving forces behind defensiveness. Insecurity leads to anxiety, apprehension, and fear. If a group feels threatened, it will retreat from the other and build protective walls. Whether the threat comes from physical violence, political control, economic domination, or loss of cultural traditions, the reaction is the same. In order for a relationship to work productively, the fear of such possibilities must be removed.

8. Wounds must be healed. War injures people, and it leaves scars. Sometimes the wounds caused by conflicts never heal, particularly when people are pulled apart against their will. The injuries, the scars, and the open wounds become part of the identity of the victims, and they result in bitterness toward the other that cannot go away on its own. Often only reconciliation can remove the pain of the past. Identity problems can prevent people from coming together to share their pain, to discuss their suffering, to overcome their hatreds. If the animosity toward the other can be purged from one's identity, it is likely that the damage from conflict can be repaired, providing an opportunity to frame the other as a fellow human being who has also suffered long enough.

The people of Cyprus, after decades of separation, are at a crossroads. The generation that planted the seeds of discord has never managed to take the steps that can lead toward positive redefinition of the relationship. As a result, progress is frozen, and the future is on hold. During the past few years, several citizen-level peace-building groups have been formed, some of them facilitated by third parties, that hold promise for the future. A large number of people in both communities have started reaching out to the other side in an effort to develop trust that can lead to true partnerships. In their meetings, they have taken many of the steps outlined above, and for these individuals and groups, a new identity of "peace builder" is emerging. This identity, which is more positive, more realistic about the past, more forward-looking, and more aware of the interdependence between communities, is helping to build trust and heal wounds.[8] Still, the challenges are many, and time is running out. One hopes it will be possible soon to describe the identity of "peace builder" in more specific terms, and if sufficient numbers in each community can reconcile their differences and redefine their collective relationship, the people of Cyprus will be on their way to negotiating an agreement that will allow them to lead productive lives, both separately and in cooperation with one another in those areas where their interdependence binds them together.

Notes

1. In the social sciences, identity has been an important construct since George Herbert Mead's *Mind, Self, and Society* (1934). In recent years, the study of identity has assumed greater importance in intercultural communication, as evidenced by the publication of the current volume of essays. For a recent discussion of identity in various cultural contexts, see Tanno and Gonzalez (1998). Personal narratives about identity issues are also discussed in Gonzalez, Houston, and Chen (2000). Collier (1998) provides a good overview of various approaches to studying identity issues.

2. From 1994 to 1996 I held the position of Senior Fulbright Scholar in Cyprus, where I offered workshops, seminars, and training in conflict resolution, intergroup relations, and intercultural communication to bicommunal groups of Greek Cypriots and Turkish Cypriots who were involved in peace-building efforts on the island.

3. For a history of the Cyprus conflict, see Attalides (1979), Hitchens (1997), Koumoulides (1986), Markides (1977), O'Malley and Craig (1999), and Stearns (1992). Recent social and psychological perspectives are contained in a volume edited by Calotychos (1998). For perspectives of the two political leaders, see Denktash (1982) and Clerides (1989). Prospects for a solution are discussed by Joseph (1997), Theophanous (1996), Richmond (1998), Bahcheli and Riziopoulos (1996), and Anastasiou (2000). For various perspectives on the people and culture of Cyprus, see Durrell (1957), Thubron (1975), Burch (1990), and Pierides (1998). Anastasiou (2000) looks at nationalism and conflict in Cyprus. For a summary of the perspectives of each community in Cyprus, see Broome (1998a).

4. Since 1980, when I held a teaching position at the American College of Greece, I have been involved with various projects in the eastern Mediterranean, primarily concerning Greece, Cyprus, and Greek-Turkish relations.

5. For an overview of various approaches to third-party facilitation in conflict resolution settings, see Fisher (1997).

6. These workshops were conducted using a process called "Interactive Management (IM)," which was developed specifically for helping groups work through complex issues. For more information about IM and for a detailed description of the IM sessions in Cyprus see Broome (1997 and 1998c), and Broome (2001).

7. The Greek-Cypriot controlled Republic of Cyprus is currently engaged with the European Union in negotiations that are scheduled to result in full membership for Cyprus in the near future. These negotiations are taking place without the participation of the Turkish Cypriots, who have declined to join the talks. The hope is that an agreement will be reached about the Cyprus conflict prior to the entry date, and the whole of the island will become a member. The European Union has agreed that, if a political solution to the Cyprus conflict is not reached, the Republic of Cyprus will enter without the Turkish Cypriots. Many fear that this situation will permanently divide the island, erasing any hope of reconciliation and creating an even more unstable situation there.

8. See Broome (1998b and 1999) for a description of conflict resolution activities in Cyprus. Diamond and Fisher (1995) examine the important work of the Institute for Multi-Track Diplomacy. Hadjipavlou-Trigeorgis (1993) provides an inside look at track two diplomacy in Cyprus.

References

Anastasiou, H. 2000. Negotiating the solution to the Cyprus problem: From impasse to post-Helsinki hope. *The Cyprus Review* 12 (1): 11–33.

Attalides, M. A. 1979. *Cyprus: Nationalism and international politics*. Edinburgh, U.K.: Q Press.

Bahcheli, T., and N. X. Riziopoulos. 1996/1997. The Cyprus impasse: What next? *World Policy Journal* (winter): 27–39.

Broome, B. J. 2001. Participatory planning and design in a protracted conflict situation: Applications with citizen peace-building groups in Cyprus. *Systems Research and Behavioral Science* 18: 1–9.

———. 1999. Inter-communal contacts help build links for the future of Cyprus. *Washington Report on Middle East Affairs* 18 (6): 69–71.

———. 1998a. Views from the other side: Perspectives on the Cyprus conflict. In J. Martin, T. Nakayama, and L. Flores (Eds.), *Readings in cultural contexts*. Mountain View, Calif.: Mayfield Publishers.

———. 1998b. Overview of conflict resolution activities in Cyprus: Their contribution to the peace process. *The Cyprus Review* 10 (1): 47–66.

———. 1998c. Designing citizen based peace-building efforts in Cyprus: Interactive Management workshops with Greek Cypriots and Turkish Cypriots. In Alexander Woodcock and David Davis (Eds.), *Analysis for peace operations*, pp. 33–58. Lester B. Pearson Canadian International Peacekeeping Training Centre. Cornwallis Park, Nova Scotia: Canadian Peacekeeping Press.

———. 1997. Designing a collective approach to peace: Interactive design and problem-solving workshops with Greek Cypriot and Turkish Cypriot communities in Cyprus. *International Negotiation* 2 (3): 381–407.

Burch, O. 1990. *The infidel sea: Travels in north Cyprus*. Southampton, U.K.: Ashford, Buchan and Enright.

Calotychos, V. (Ed.). 1998. *Cyprus and its people: Nation, identity, and experience in an unimaginable community, 1955–1997*. Boulder, Colo.: Westview.

Clerides, G. 1989. *Cyprus: My deposition*. Nicosia: Alithia Publishing.

Collier, M. J. 1998. Researching cultural identity: Reconciling interpretive and postcolonial perspectives. In D. V. Tanno and A. Gonzalez (Eds.), *Communication and identity across cultures* (pp. 122–47). Thousand Oaks, Calif.: Sage.

Denktash, R. R. 1982. *The Cyprus triangle*. London: Allen and Unwin.

Diamond, L., and R. J. Fisher. 1995. Integrating conflict resolution training and consultation: A Cyprus example. *Negotiation Journal* 11: 287–301.

Durrell, L. 1957. *Bitter lemons*. Boston: Faber and Faber.

Fisher, R. J. 1997. *Interactive conflict resolution*. Syracuse, N.Y.: Syracuse University Press.

Gonzalez, A., M. Houston, and V. Chen (Eds.). 2000. *Our voices: Essays in culture, ethnicity and communication*. 3rd ed. Los Angeles: Roxbury.

Hadjipavlou-Trigeorgis, M. 1993. Unofficial inter-communal contacts and their contribution to peace-building in conflict societies: The case of Cyprus. *The Cyprus Review* 5 (2): 68–87.

Hitchens, C. 1997. *Hostage to history: Cyprus from the Ottomans to Kissinger*. London: Verso Books.

Joseph, J. S. 1997. *Cyprus: Ethnic conflict and international politics*. London: McMillian Press.

Koumoulides, J. T. A. (Ed.). 1986. *Cyprus in transition: 1960–1985*. London: Trigraph.

Markides, K. C. 1977. *The rise and fall of the Cyprus Republic*. New Haven, Conn.: Yale University Press.

Mead, G. H. 1934. *Mind, self, and society*. Chicago: University of Chicago Press.

O'Malley, B., and I. Craig. 1999. *The Cyprus conspiracy: America, espionage and the Turkish invasion*. New York: St. Martin's Press.

Pierides, G. P. 1998. *Tetralogy of the times: Stories of Cyprus*. Translated from the Greek by D. E. Martin and S. G. Stavrou. Minneapolis, Minn.: Nostos Books.

Richmond, O. 1998. *Mediating in Cyprus: The Cypriot communities and the U.N.* Portland, Ore.: Frank Cass.

Stearns, M. 1992. *Entangled allies: U.S. policy toward Greece, Turkey, and Cyprus.* New York: Council on Foreign Relations Press.

Tanno, D. V., and A. Gonzalez. 1998. *Communication and identity across cultures.* Thousand Oaks, Calif.: Sage.

Theophanous, A. 1996. *The political economy of a federal Cyprus.* Nicosia: Intercollege Press.

Thubron, C. 1975. *Journey into Cyprus.* Middlesex, England: Penguin Books.

KEY TERMS

conflict	Muslim
context	negotiation
Cyprus	Orthodox Christian
dialogue	partnership
ethnic group	peace building
facilitator	third party
Greek Cypriot	trust
identity	Turkish Cypriot
interdependence	

REVIEW AND DISCUSSION QUESTIONS

1. Why is it necessary to examine identity concerns in order to understand ethnic conflict?
2. How are the identities of ethnic groups interdependent?
3. Is the Cyprus conflict similar to any of your own experiences? What do you think it would be like to live in a country torn apart by war and conflict? How would you handle the experience of becoming a refugee?
4. Do you think it is appropriate to compare ethnic conflict to the process of marital separation and divorce? In what ways are these two phenomena similar to and different from one another?
5. Is there any hope for different ethnic groups to live together in peace? What will it take for this to happen?

Negotiating Cultural Identities and the Sense of Belonging

PART V CONSISTS of four chapters that illuminate how individuals in various groups negotiate their cultural identities and sense of belonging. These cultural groups include: Franco Americans, Mexican Americans, African Americans, and Asian Americans.

Kristin M. Langellier examines Franco Americans as an example of White ethnic identity. She describes various strategies for communicating Franco American identity: bilingual issues and options, rules for speaking in the home and workplace, gestures and cross-cultural miscommunication, the kinwork of women in the family and community, and online innovations of identity. Her chapter concludes by invoking a more complicated story of White ethnicity, one that incorporates issues of power and the differences of race, region, religion, class, gender, and sexuality.

Lisa Bradford, Nancy A. Burrell, and Edward A. Mabry explore the negotiation of cultural identity in intercultural interactions through the experiences of three Latino college students. Specifically, these examples suggest that individuals employ communication strategies to achieve a sense of belonging in their marginalized social worlds. The double-binding role of belonging in the negotiation of cultural identities is addressed. The concept of intercultural identities is introduced as a way to offset the exclusionary aspects of the "dark side" of belonging.

Bryant K. Alexander reveals five themes that emerged in the discovery phase of data processing: (1) Cultural Languaging, (2) Sociocultural Responsibility, (3) Recognition,

Association, and Affiliation, (4) Expectations and Denials, and (5) Authority and Challenge. His research serves as a bridge to understanding the sociocultural and political issues that intervene in the classroom between Black male teachers and Black male students.

Rueyling Chuang aims to describe the lived experience of Asian Americans and to investigate the extent to which Asian Americans' bicultural background influences their double consciousness. Her chapter provides a situated understanding of Asian Americans' *lifeworld*. Several themes emerged through her interviews and analysis of Asian Americans' ethnic and cultural identity: (1) Mixture/Difference/Balance; (2) Clash and Struggle; (3) Misperception—Being Mistaken for Other Co-Cultural Groups; (4) "Outsider . . . Where Are You From?"; (5) Crossing the Border—Where Is Home?; (6) Belonging and Exclusion; (7) Americans as "White"; and (8) Self-Identity and Self-Pride.

"Where I Come from Is Where I Want to Be": Communicating Franco American Ethnicity

KRISTIN M. LANGELLIER

LEARNING OBJECTIVES

After reading this chapter, students will be able to:

- understand the history and communication practices of Franco Americans as an example of White ethnicity;

- realize the significance of context in understanding communication practices that distinguish among American ethnicities and within ethnicities in different regions of the United States;

- recognize ethnic identity as a site of communicative action and negotiation rather than an individual's self expression: an ongoing, everyday, active, strategic, multileveled, and dispersed process of social interaction with the dominant culture and other ethnic groups;

- discuss the point that communicating ethnicity expresses and engages in power interests and negotiations; and

- explain the complex relations among ethnicity and race, language, class, region, religion, gender, and sexual orientation, and other social markers of difference.

> *When I took my first university position in Orono, Maine, more than fourteen hundred miles from where I was raised, I could not have predicted it would lead me home, nor that I would participate in building a Franco American Studies program at the University of Maine (Langellier 1996). Through the back roads of French Maine—the St. John Valley, Lewiston, Waterville, Old Town—I wound my way back to the French Midwest of Kankakee, Bourbonnais, and St. Anne, Illinois. I noticed first that people in Maine didn't have trouble with my French last name; and I recognized right away numerous French names among my students, many the very same names from home. I learned the French Fact in Maine: at one-third of its population, French descendants are the largest ethnic minority in the state. I soon noticed, too, that many of my students, like me, are first-generation college. I had often felt different, and so I strived, as a college student and then as a college teacher, to transcend my provincial background, presuming that the more "professorial" I became, the less others would discern my working class, tenant-farming, first-generation-college family of ten children, and—I now was beginning to understand—my Franco American ethnicity.*

> —Kristin Langellier

White Ethnicity and Franco Americans

Where I come from is where I want to be. I used to want to be from someplace else. More white. I am a Franco American girl growing up in a French-Canadian neighborhood. Un p'tit Canada. (Robbins 1997, p. 60)

The study of communicating **ethnicity** begins at home, with "us," with "where I come from." Recent scholarship on difference—cultural, racial, ethnic, class, gendered, sexual, and so on—argues for situated knowledge from "somewhere in particular" in distinction from the "conquering gaze from nowhere" (Haraway 1988). Situated knowledge about communication cannot only encounter the *other elsewhere* in order to reflect *ourselves at home;* it involves being situated, engaged, and accountable *wherever one is.* In Maine it is a commonplace, for some a lament, that we are not diverse, that we are all "White." We look out over our classrooms and see mostly White students. Indeed, in the most recent census, Maine surpassed Vermont as the "Whitest" state in the United States.

But statistics can mask as much as they uncover. In the racialized and racist U.S. **context,** ethnicity codes race, and **race** is sometimes narrowly coded as a Black and White issue only, while we know in reality it is not. We are all called upon as scholars, students, and citizens to struggle with and against the legacies of slavery and Native American genocide. But we also need to examine ethnicity beyond its meaning as not-Black. To think of ethnicity as monolithic or universal or self-evident homogenizes and dilutes Whiteness—it's all white milk, and skim at that—at the same time that it removes the communication of ethnicity from the formative contexts of history, economics, and region. Not only do Black and White invoke shades of gray and other colors, but Whiteness itself is also historical, multiple, and relational. Spanish can mean White or non-White, depending upon the context; the Irish became White in the United States (Ignatiev 1995); and a Franco American may have wished to be "more White," as the quotation cited above suggests.

The topic of **communicating ethnicity** opens a way to ask: what is a Franco American, and why should anyone, even Franco Americans, care? This chapter examines the Franco American culture as an example of White ethnic identity. Opening up a Franco American space extends the opportunity to other White ethnic groups to explore where they come from and where they want to be. This ethnic space is precisely not the place of individual expression but the social, cultural, and political space of communicative action and interaction. This chapter proceeds in three steps. I first place Franco American identity in history in order to tell an untold story of these people in America. Given their particular historical situation, I next explore several specific aspects of communicating Franco American ethnicity. Finally, I offer arguments for why studying **White ethnicity** may erase race and harbor **racism**. I argue for an analysis of White ethnicity that incorporates issues of power and differences of race, **region, religion, class, gender,** and sexuality.

Historicizing Franco American Ethnicity

Throughout this chapter, I incorporate narratives of personal experience and observations of French culture in Maine, such as this episode:

> A scene in an elementary school classroom in Maine: "Raise your hand if you are Franco American." No response. Second try: "Who has French names in their family?" A couple of reluctant takers. "How many in here have a *mémère* [grandmother]?" Ah, the hands go up.

The French presence in Maine has produced both pride and shame. If students in Maine are unsure about what a Franco American is and, when they know, are unwilling to publicly claim their identity, others outside the Northeast may be even more puzzled. Where would one learn about Franco American history? One of the most used and respected high school history textbooks, *The American Pageant,* devotes just two of its five hundred pages to the French in North America; these two pages are not a part of the general discussion but one of the "special essays" added to the ninth edition to focus on the "diverse ethnic and racial groups that compose our strikingly pluralistic society" (Bailey and Kennedy 1991, p. viii). Although foreign language study increasingly integrates the diversity of the **French** global diaspora—*la Francophonie* that includes, among other places, Canada, parts of Africa and the Caribbean, and Vietnam—it rarely mentions the United States or it narrows its U.S. spotlight to Cajun Louisiana.

If *Franco American* conjures up any images in the public mind at all, they may be of canned spaghetti; or of the cartoon womanizing skunk "Peppi le Pew" with his broken English and outrageous French accent. Or the references to "Canucks" by Thornton Wilder in *Our Town* and by John Steinbeck in *Travels with Charley.* Or perhaps the epithets of "Frenchy" or "Frog," the latter term imported from Europe by U.S. soldiers after World War I; or the Northeast version of the ethnic joke, "how many Frenchmen does it take . . . ?" (Doty 1995). In Maine, one might hear about a worker that "he did it like a Frenchman," or from a student that "Oh, I'm French sometimes"—not to summon the sexiness, sophistication, and glamour of Paris, France, but to insult someone or to signal an error or incompetence. More positively, some may know that Henry Wadsworth Longfellow's *Evangeline* is a story of the French Acadians deported from Nova Scotia; or that Jack Kerouac *(On the Road)*, award-winning Annie Proulx *(The Shipping News)*, and Grace Metalious are Franco American writers. Metalious, author of *Peyton Place* and three other novels, had the French Canadian name of de Repentigny.

Franco Americans are unique in maintaining ethnic status for nearly four hundred years in two countries, the United States and Canada—seemingly without the mark of racial stigma. The first major non-English-speaking population in the Northeast, French Canadians accounted for one in five New Englanders by 1900, and French descendants number seven million today. As unmeltable ethnics with **bilingual** and bicultural communities surviving today, Franco Americans defy the straight-line theory of irreversible ethnic decline and **assimilation.** U.S. boundaries with French-speaking Canada form a Northeast borderlands parallel to the Southwest borderlands (Anzaldua 1987) with its Spanish-speaking peoples. Yet the Franco American story is not familiar enough to be popularized; not exotic enough to be marketed (with the possible exception of Cajun food and music); not studied enough to be anthologized. "Silenced, forgotten, lost, sold, abandoned, translated into English, absorbed, deported, or conquered, still often poor or working class, keeping to ourselves, staying out of sight, on the move. And ashamed of ourselves" (Bérubé 1997, p. 47). What is the Franco American story?

> I never knew I was French until I moved to Maine. "You've got to be French," people kept telling me, and I am, on both sides, via Quebec and farther back from France. But it would take me years to unravel the tangle of meanings for being Franco American and to connect the dots among French migrations just inside the U.S.: Woonsocket, R.I., Manchester, N.H., Lowell, Mass., Madawaska, Me., Lafayette, La., Frenchtown, Mt., Cohoes, N.Y.; Hollywood, Fla., Ste. Genevieve, Mo., Kankakee, Ill. Being French in the Northeast and being French in the Midwest differ, depending on the specifics of history and economics. What I knew about the French in the Midwest cast them as intrepid explorers and the founding fathers of Detroit, Joliet, Marquette, LaSalle, St. Louis. Later French Canadian immigrants started farms and businesses. The Midwest had French Catholic parishes like my mother attended as a child near Kankakee, Illinois, but it lacked the bilingual parochial schools of the Northeast. Compared to the Northeast, assimilation was more rapid and complete in the Midwest, where, except for names, the French today are quite invisible. Being French Huguenot in Atlanta has distinctive meanings; and the French on the West coast may garner prestige—because they are not Spanish-speaking. Not so for Maine where "French" is a pejorative term.

Identity construction is a reciprocal process of communication that sets boundaries and distinguishes "us" and "them"— not just as difference but as hierarchy: "us" over "them" or vice versa (Nakayama and Martin 1999). Neither "just words" or "mere rhetoric," language is action in the world, the critical behaviors and meanings that constitute who we are in relation to others. Formulated within historical, social, and economic relations, identity construction is always political: who gets to say who and what we are? To understand the meanings of being Franco American, we must trace a brief history as context for the communication of this ethnicity.

French history in North America is a story of explorations, expulsions, and migrations. The French migrated in two waves, first to New France as explorers in eastern Canada as early as 1604; and later west and south as fur traders, and particularly as workers to the industrializing Northeast. The defeat and colonization of the French by the British in 1713 and 1760 *(La Conquête)* was accompanied by the deportation of the Acadians *(Le Grand Dérangement),* expelling them at bayonet point from Nova Scotia by 1763, many to settle in the bayous of Louisiana. Under British rule, the French elite fled Canada for France, leaving New France to peasants and Roman Catholic priests. The British closed off immigration from France, effectively isolating the North American French from their mother country and mother tongue.

Because of economic pressures—depressions, indebtedness, and a decline in farming—French Canadians from Quebec streamed into the U.S. Northeast between 1865 and 1930, enticed especially by agents recruiting cheap manual labor for the rapidly growing textile industry, paper mills, machine shops, and shoe factories. With **women** and children joining the men at work, French Canadian families hoped to quickly earn enough money to return to Quebec, although many stayed to become permanent residents. In competition with English, Scotch, Irish, Italian, Portuguese, Polish, and Greek immigrants, the French Canadians were considered to be desirable workers, and by 1900, Franco Americans in the cotton industry surpassed all other ethnic groups in number and percentage (Roby 1996).

On both sides of the U.S.-Canadian border established in 1875, French ethnic culture was promoted as *la survivance,* the passionate and valiant effort to maintain French Canadian identity even while becoming Franco American. *La survivance* focused on the trinity of French language, large families, and strict allegiance to the Catholic Church. French women bore a particular, indeed literal, burden for *la survivance:* to produce numerous children to combat the dwindling numbers of French within the swelling sea of British. Known as "the revenge of the cradles" *(revenches des berceaux),* large French Catholic families—more than ten children was not unusual—doubled the population every two decades from the eighteenth to the twentieth centuries (Chodos and Hamovitch 1991, p. 14). Enforced through Church hegemony and supported by pronatal social policies, such "heroic fecundity" mythologized motherhood within French Canadian and Franco American cultures.

Church power migrated to the Northeast to secure French identity through its hold on education, the system of some two hundred **parochial schools** unifying language, faith, and customs. With parish churches, these bilingual schools anchored *les p'tits Canadas,* the neighborhoods with French language newspapers, ethnic organizations, social clubs, hospitals, hospices, and orphanages. Reproducing rural villages in urban settings created a diverse class structure and the structural bases that successfully resisted assimilation. Proximity to French Canada also advanced and maintained ethnic identity, distinguishing the French from other White ethnics more distant from their mother countries, as they crossed the borders to visit their old homes. The French called the Northeast *Quebec d'en Bas* (Quebec Down Below).

In the mutual construction of ethnic identity, the internal cohesion of the French was reinforced by external hostilities. Conflict in colonial Canada emerged from contrasting cultural norms: French Canadians spoke French, were Catholics, and belonged to an agrarian economic system; the British spoke English, were Protestants, and developed a progressive industrialized society. Conflict persists today in the political movement for an equal and independent French Quebec. Ethnic frictions likewise arose in the United States, particularly as class conflict when French workers were pitted against other White immigrants for jobs. The French refusal to assimilate was met with challenges to their whiteness. The French were characterized in an 1881 Massachusetts labor report as "the Chinese of the East" *(les chinois de l'est)* because of their alleged passivity and anti-union sentiments (Doty 1995, p. 87). Within the White ethnic hierarchy in the Northeast, Franco Americans were at the bottom. One 1918–1919 study, for example, ranked Franco Americans seventh among ethnic groups, far behind first-ranked "Native White Americans" but ahead of tenth-ranked "Negroes" (Doty 1995, p. 89); and in 1964 another study ranked the French the lowest of White ethnics with only Blacks below (Secord and Backman 1964, p. 570). Intercultural conflict submitted Franco Americans to one hundred years of discrimination, including ethnic slurs and jokes, hostility to the French language, and anti-**Catholicism**. French Catholics—along with Jews—were the target of cross-burnings and rallies by a flourishing Ku Klux Klan in Maine, numbering 150,141 members in 1925, a trauma that older Franco Americans have not forgotten (Doty 1995).

The restricting of **immigration** in the 1920s arrested the north-to-south-to-north border crossings. The east-to-west **migrations** that followed resulted in the present-day connect-the-dots geography of Franco Americans. Today in the Northeast, Franco Americans are described as a "quiet presence." They are changing but not disappearing. Like the term *Asian American,* the term *Franco American* is a usable fiction, designed to make a political statement about an identity oppositional to British/English/Anglo dominance and to other ethnic groups. The term precedes and succeeds the ethnic revival of the 1970s, although it gained strength from that historical moment. It also borrowed from the civil rights and Black power movements by reclaiming the derogatory term *Frog,* similar to redefining *Black* as beautiful (Peterson 1991). Franco Americans have not achieved a powerful political presence comparable to French Quebec, but as recently as 1999 they thwarted an English-only bill in Maine.

Because many structures of *la survivance* have now faded, how do we make sense of Franco American ethnicity today? *La survivance* privileges language and religion—both of which continue to inform ethnicity—but it misses everyday communication and the cultural performance of identity. "Individuals frame and reframe their ethnic experiences from day to day, as they accept, reject, and modify prevalent ethnic ideologies" (di Leonardo 1984, p. 191). In this active, strategic, multileveled, and dispersed process, people perform their culture in social interaction with the dominant culture and other ethnic groups. This view of ethnicity as communication dispels the myth of ethnic identity as singular, pure, unchanging, and traditional. No one or combination of characteristics—French language, Roman Catholic religion, large family, working class—defines the varieties of Franco American ethnicity as they strategically adapt their communication to changing conditions and relations (Peterson 1994).

Communicating Franco American Ethnicity

My grandparents on both sides were bilingual; my parents understood but did not speak French; and my little French is from school. So by my generation only a few French expressions remained in my family, most notably "ferme ta bouche" (shut your mouth). Family rules forbade saying "shut up" but permitted this French equivalent. It lingers among the grandchildren today, witness to our French roots and an expletive that does not incur Grandma's reprimand. I recently recovered a bit more family French when I stopped by a Franco American colleague's office for a little "visite." Because he had his back to the door and I didn't want to startle him, I verbalized "knock-knock" and gestured it in the air. "Is there French for knock-knock?" I asked. He replied "coin-coin," and I was immediately transported to a head-knocking-gentle-game we played with all our babies, and I with mine. What I had always thought were nonsense syllables are French.

Boscia-Mulé (1999) argues that "ethnicity, then, is far from a primordial force existing within the individual, apart from his [sic] own awareness and control. Neither is it an external reality that the individual passively and inevitably loses through assimilation. It is, instead, expression and function of **power** interests and negotiations" (p. 23). This conception of ethnicity suggests how Franco Americans continue to reinvent themselves today in a variety of communication practices.

Speaking in Tongues/*Langues*

Franco Americans speak in tongues, the plurality of languages and dialects reflecting varieties of Franco American experience. The French language issue in the Northeast is tender and tendentious. The pride in being bilingual was undermined both by outright hostility and by knowledge that those around them viewed North American French as substandard to "Parisian" French, *le francais de France*. Remarkably, bilingual speakers persist after several generations, but many Franco Americans have lost their French, an aching loss that Kim Chase (1998) depicts through a daughter who never learned her mother's French: "*Ça fait mal partout*. I know that's how you say it because those were my mother's last words to me. She could speak no English in the last days of her illness, and when I asked her where she felt the pain, she whispered, '*Partout. Ça fait mal partout.*' Ma tante Estelle turned to me and said, 'Everywhere. It hurts everywhere'" (p. 114).

In the context of assimilation, public schools threatened the Franco American family and community. From the 1920s to 1976, a language law in Maine suppressed French. Stories abound about being punished on the school grounds for speaking French, as Anglo children accumulated rewards for tattling. Classrooms might be divided into two groups: those who spoke "good," "real," or "right" French from those who spoke "slang," "kitchen," or "wrong" French. Public school teachers admonished French children to "speak White," a racist form of ethnic shaming that drew on the promise of White privilege because of their European ancestry (and despite their Native American ancestors) (Bérubé 1997, p. 49). Bilingual children were mocked for their French accents ("mudder" and "fadder"; "tree" for "three"); and as recently as fifteen years ago, young children were placed in speech therapy to "correct" their accents. Rhea Côté Robbins (1997) writes about "the wound of being French *avec les americhaines* all around you—being tough in *Franglais*—speech and **body language** dead giveaways" (p. 17); Jack Kerouac writes with regret about hiding his French and "Englishing myself" *(me faire un Anglais)* (Doty 1995, p. 92).

Allen Bérubé (1997) describes how the history of working-class Francos trying to survive in a fiercely Anglo North America resonates with the emotional history of **homosexuals** trying to survive in a fiercely heterosexual world. He writes, "It's difficult for me to say the word *mé-mère* in public. It was a private Franco-American family word spoken only at home, not found in French dictionaries, that we always translated as 'grandmother' when speaking to outsiders. It was one of a small category of words so charged with power they had to be said in hushed tones, with shame or reverence, or never at all" (p. 50). Growing up Franco but ashamed to speak French gave Bérubé practice in not saying the word so often on the tip of his tongue: *homosexual*. He powerfully and proudly weaves together the strands of his life story—his Franco American ethnicity, working-class roots, and **homosexuality**—to understand the larger historical processes that shape language, sexual desire, intellectuality, and communication. Like many other Franco Americans, he embraces his French roots by communicating in both English and North American French.

Rules for Speaking Franco American

Whether speaking varieties of French, English, or Franglais, speakers must coordinate their speech with others in interpersonal and ritual encounters. Bilingual speakers tend to rank speech events in terms of intimacy and formality. They use English, the dominant language, in all but the most informal situations, reserving French for the most intimate spaces of the bathroom and bedroom. But the kitchen is the Franco American's "room of one's own" (DeRoche 1996). Dufresne (1996) writes that "the first stories I heard, I heard around my *mémère*'s kitchen, and in them I heard the voice of the neighborhood. And what I felt immediately was that stories increase your love for the world" (p. 662). This rule for speaking indicates how, in different speech events, Franco Americans strategically communicate ethnicity and the kinds of speech they value, especially the personal, communal, and storied.

In more formal situations of status differences, particularly outside the neighborhood, Franco Americans may interact within a "rhetoric of connections" (Philipsen 1975). Rather than speaking directly to a superior, a Franco American may go through an intermediary—a priest, politician, union steward, or simply a friend—to negotiate matters of employment, law, social welfare, healthcare, and the sacred. The hegemony and hierarchy of the Catholic Church in Franco American history may also contribute to rules for speaking Franco American. Verba et al. (1995) find that religion has a strong institutional effect on political participation, that is, that Catholics are less active and less likely to practice civic skills than are Protestants. Protestants have more opportunities for civic skill development than do Catholics due to their smaller congregations, greater lay participation in the liturgy, and investment of authority in the congregation rather than in church hierarchy. Despite the Maine French Fact, there has never been a Franco American governor or U.S. senator or representative, and until recently no Franco American bishop, even though 70 percent of Maine Catholics are of French ancestry. By the concept of the intermediary in their dealings with authority and power, cultural speakers such as Franco Americans "know their place" and negotiate their place in the social hierarchy.

Cross-cultural Miscommunication

When rules for speaking differ between groups, cross-cultural miscommunication may result. The defiant female narrator of *Wednesday's Child* (1997), by Rhea Côté Robbins, describes a situation where the meaning of a given behavior, "leaning," is misunderstood: "Rumor has it we give out sex for free. Like candy. We have a reputation of being uninhibited. We have body language, but what we Franco American girls are saying isn't what the Colby [College] boys and '*les Anglais*' are hearing. Things get confused" (p. 60). Robbins describes how French women in Waterville, Maine, lean on lampposts when they talk to men. "Leaning is sex standing up, but leaning is a casualness of posture, too. I lean because I am tired. Women who lean are inviting with their bodies to do some other kinds of leaning. We French girls can lean and not mean what the leaning says" (p. 60). This brief example suggests the multiple meanings for "leaning" ("things get confused"), the strategic nature of communicating ethnicity (leaning-with-intent), and audience misunderstanding ("what '*les Anglais*' are hearing").

This example of body language shows ethnicity to be communicated gesturally as well as in spoken language, and it additionally signals the significance of **gender** and class in cross-cultural communication. Robbins clarifies that for the Colby College men, French women are "playthings," not women to fall in love with and marry. For Franco Americans, Colby College, an Ivy League school, is the place they work as cooks, janitors, and secretaries. "Rarely do Franco American children attend Colby College. Although children of workers can attend for free. Few choose to stoop to that level of social climbing. Who would talk to them when they came back from that foreign land, and while there, who would understand them?" (pp. 49–50). Robbins suggests the distrust of educated talk among Franco Americans, a class divide and cultural gap that may result in miscommunication and alienation.

Kinwork as Gendered Communication

> I am troubled by the image of the traditional ethnic woman and the patriarchal ethnic family, in the Franco case the mythologized mother with lots of kids, little education, and relentless labor. As the fifth of 10 children, the historical "revenge of the cradles" hit close to home with a contemporary thud. In my lifetime I have been alternately proud of and somewhat embarrassed by the size of my family. In the days before Maine, I attributed our fecundity solely to Roman Catholicism, but I now consider it within Franco American history. I learned early in life to plead homework to get out of house-work that my brothers escaped by gender. Sometimes my feminism and Franco American studies seem on a collision course. How do I tell my mother's and grand-mother's stories without turning them into myths or martyrs? Can we tell our Franco American family stories without evoking nostalgia for a less assimilated family, more stable gender roles, less complicated times?

Ethnic groups occupy an intermediate space between the family and the nation; and ethnic women in particular guarantee ethnicity as they produce cultural foods, religious rituals, holiday traditions, and family storytelling (Fine and Speer 1992). As the most folk of the folk, the traditional working class ethnic mother embodies the gender stereotypes and patriarchal structures of family ethnicity, for example, the Jewish mother, the Black granny, the Italian Mama, and the Franco American *mémère*. In her study of contemporary Italian Americans, Micaela di Leonardo (1984) conceptualizes **kinwork** as a term for the invisible and creative labor performed by ethnic women to knit households together. Kinwork is the communication work of rites and rituals between households to maintain family, community, and work ties, for example, birthday parties, holiday activities, communal meals, and festivals. In kinwork ethnic families perform their identities for themselves and for others—other kin, community, or mass media. The responsibility of ethnic women, regardless of individual class membership, kinwork also forms women's base of power and communication expertise.

Among Franco Americans, kinwork features the expressivity and sociality of the rituals of everyday life: talking, joking, laughing, playing cards, eating, and drinking. The visits, cards and letters, presents, phone calls, and e-mails; organization for holiday gatherings; services, food, goods, and money exchanged in ordinary and crisis times for families and communities—all the work of kin—are organized and facilitated primarily by women. Leisure time for Franco American women is illusive, and even "free" time is expected to be family time spent talking or otherwise interacting with the family group. Reading or writing may be discouraged as too private, individualistic, and unproductive (Lanza 1994). Vacation time is less often a nuclear family trip to the Grand Canyon, San Francisco, or Disney World than a visit to other family. Kinwork crosses households, and my mother describes how her mother hosted one dinner after another for relatives throughout the year. The legacy of food and visiting survives today, embodied in the Cousins Club. The cousins of the club—no boys allowed—are women related through their mothers, the Bouchard sisters. They have been meeting continuously each month since 1961. In the early years they rotated among their homes for a meal and card-playing, but more recently they go to a restaurant and then adjourn to a cousin's home for some 500, a version of euchre, but mostly for fun and talk.

Perhaps the defining ritual of Franco American culture has been the extended family's Sunday-after-Mass visit to *mémère*, with its storytelling, music, and meal (Dufresne 1996). The *mémère* embodies the traditional ethnic woman, a privileged icon, a compelling and centralizing figure in Franco American kinship, and a locus of power. She is the keeper of family and folk memory, and she is mythologized in cultural stories. The first anthology of Franco American women's writings (Robbins, Petrie, Langellier, and Slott 1995) catalogs *mémère* stories. Although these narratives appear on the surface to serve nostalgia and the conservative political idealization of the traditional ethnic female, they simultaneously unveil a complex negotiation between grandmother and granddaughter about changing gender roles. In "A Tribute to Pheobe," for example, Kimberly J. Cook (Robbins et al. 1995, p. 66) honors the hard work, suffering, and sacrifices of her maternal grandmother. She writes that "I was constantly in touch with the reality of being the youngest of the youngest of 18 children," but also that "As my feminist consciousness grew, so did my realization that if these strong women had not suffered the oppression of the Catholic patriarchy, I would not exist today." Her poignant tribute to Pheobe is situated as a dialogue with feminism within the context of changing social opportunities for women.

Kinwork can help us understand the seeming contradiction of Franco American culture as simultaneously patriarchal and matriarchal by redefining women's communicative power. The idealized ethnic family situates Franco American women, the *mamans* and the *mémères*, at the center of the family with considerable performative power. This view of their power is constrained, however, to the extent that it is contingent upon its conformity to patriarchal interests and the women's performance as traditional wives and mothers. Boscia-Mulé (1999) notes that ethnic men can enact a private traditionalism and a social individualism without conflict, but because of the burden of kinwork, ethnic women cannot so easily engage in expressive freedom and personal interests. Kinwork thus embraces both the responsibility of ethnic women to maintain the idealized family and their strategic responses to this burden. Franco American women may use traditionalism as a resource to further women's own interests, as when the Cousins Club provides opportunities for bonding, talk, and fun; or they may resist traditional gender norms, as we see below.

Innovating Ethnicity Electronically

The Franco American Women's Institute (FAWI), established in 1997, shows the ongoing negotiation of ethnic identity within a feminist vision to become visible after generations of being unseen, and to become vocal after generations of being unheard. The "first and only Institute of its kind to exist that is solely dedicated to the promotion, advocacy, research, and archiving of Franco American women," FAWI's website includes an e-zine, a slide show of Franco American women writers, numerous links to related sites, and English/French options. FAWI is described as "a NET designed to capture, catch, and free the diversity of expression of the women, their *mamans* and *maman's mamans*. Daughters, too. Because daughters are the best insurance for the future." The institute emphasizes diversity and inclusivity in terms of race/ethnicity (e.g., Québécois, Acadian, Métis, and Mixed Blood) and lifestyle (e.g., community women, academic women, women of faith, women of skepticism, women of the seam, women of sensuality, women who farm). Their mission is both to archive their heritage and to move into the next millennium as "an alive, present, and accounted for cultural group of women." Their strategic adaptation to changing social and technological conditions creates a virtual community of culture and kin to gather, document, write, and speak about the many ways to be a Franco American woman today.

> I heard a Black feminist scholar talk about her fieldwork on grannies and midwives. When a midwife challenged her project, she confessed that "the indigenous researcher is not a homegirl." Nor am I exactly one of them, the Franco Americans from Maine. Education, a professorship, and mobility grant me privileges many Franco Americans do not enjoy. When I collaborate with community people on Franco American studies, I can call on a flexible work schedule (versus a half-hour lunch), travel budget, conference contacts, publication outlets, and the credentials to teach a class on Franco American communication—which they cannot. As a middle-class "outsider," I can also more easily distance myself from such local remarks as "they got an education so they don't know us anymore." My friend Lanette, a part-time secretary for the university for many years, writes about classism and taking college classes (Robbins et al. 1995, p. 118). She lists the costs that some incurred in getting an education and leaving the neighborhood: changing their names, leaving their religion, moving away from their families, and taking on more materialistic values. She concludes, "I suspect that's why I never got a college education. I never had enough self-esteem to turn my back on all that. I still find it difficult to explain to my family why I'm taking classes." How can Lanette migrate with her ethnic working-class roots to the university? How can I travel as working class and Franco American within the university? How can we bridge the class divide that education may create?

Why Communicating Ethnicity Is Not Enough

Like many other labels, the term *Franco American* is a cultural and a political identity. The ethnic renaissance of the 1960s and 1970s instilled pride in heritage for many White ethnics, a project important to Franco Americans in order to combat cultural shame inflicted by Northeast history and economics. White ethnicity, however, may harbor racism. Lillian Rubin (1994) identifies a new immigration story that goes like this: "we came, we suffered, we conquered" —without a single reference to race—and "it just happens that [we're] all white" (p. 192). Waters's (1990) study of White, middle class, suburban Roman Catholic ethnics (Italians, Poles, and Irish) defines this new ethnicity as a symbolic identification with ancestry, enacted situationally, most often in leisure time activities, such as family celebrations and St. Patrick's Day. Evoked by personal choice, the new ethnicity influences one's life only if and when one *wants* it to. Waters concludes that such ethnicity is an *option* exercised voluntarily and individually for its pleasures, significantly without social costs. The **ethnic option** fulfills the specifically American quest for community and individuality.

From a communication perspective, however, the ethnic option is problematic for several reasons. First, White ethnicity is conceptualized in pure, primordialist terms, as an authentic or genuine ethnic essence, such as being Black or Chicano or French. This view of ethnicity is static and singular, outside the context of particular historical, **regional**, social, and economic relations in which it is communicated. Second, the ethnic option is conceptualized in individual rather than collective terms, a personal choice in isolation from a social group, with meanings self- rather than other-defined. The ethnic option ignores how identity is socially constructed in a relational and reciprocal process, in the formative context of specific **language** and communication practices. Third, the ethnic option assumes that all ethnicities are equal, interchangeable, and positive.

Ethnicity is a one-way street in which one "old" identity is exchanged for a "new," better one (Wellman 1996). What does it mean, for example, to argue that in coming to America to escape racism, the Jews "opted to be white" (Kaye/Kantrowitz 1996)? And do all ethnics desire assimilation, social mobility, and dominance? Finally, the ethnic option erroneously conflates ethnicity and race because the option operates for *White* Americans but not people of color, whether they are indigenous Native Americans, Africans imported under slavery, or recent Asian or Latino immigrants whose differences are still marked— often visibly—and material. Waters (1990) explains that, "if your own ethnicity is a voluntaristic personal matter, it is sometimes difficult to understand that race or ethnicity for others is influenced by social and political components" (p. 164).

Moreover, the case of communicating ethnicity described here shows how the Franco American narrative challenges the new immigration story. Given their particular contexts, one can discern how Franco Americans strategically communicate in response to racialized labeling, within specific geographies, with linguistic variety, through class migrations, in changing religious circumstances, and using traditional gender roles as both a resource and site of resistance. The Franco American story asks us to think carefully through both the similarities and differences between race and ethnicity, and to further complicate White ethnicity in terms of multiple constraints on communication, such as class, gender, region, and religion. I suggest the intercultural implications of this study call for a more complex story of communicating (White) ethnicity.

1. *Communicating ethnicity is not enough if it erases the difference of race.* Franco American identity emerged in resistance to Anglo assimilation. At the same time, the racializing of Franco Americans as "less White" provides a context for understanding Robbins's sometime desire to be "more White." Notably, however, she does not wish to be darker. Franco Americans undoubtedly benefit from White skin privilege, even when Whiteness has not guaranteed social power and mobility. This **privilege** requires much more analysis (Nakayama and Martin 1999) because race is always in play, whether or not one recognizes it. When is race deployed in ethnic communication, and when is it downplayed?

2. *Communicating ethnicity is not enough when it omits the geography of difference.* Postcolonial theory rejects the binarism of colonizer and colonized because there are few pure oppressors or pure victims. With England and Spain, France colonized the New World and Native Americans. Yet in both Canada and the United States, the French were arguably colonized by British and Anglo control and culture. French experience cannot be universalized, and Franco American identity must be situated so that particular geographies can emerge, such as the Northeast **borderlands** with its specific history, economies, and education systems. Wellman (1996, p. 38) cautions, however, that "it is one thing to choose to recognize the ways one inhabits the 'borderlands' and it is quite another to theorize a consciousness in the name of survival." Again, the benefits of privilege must be considered. Furthermore, regional differences and the complex relations of Franco Americans with other racial and ethnic groups, such as Native Americans in the Northeast and Midwest, must be examined.

3. *Communicating ethnicity is not enough when the relations of class are not made explicit.* Although they are "White ethnics," the racialized marking of Franco Americans reveals how malleable and changeable "race" is, as well as its profound connections to social class. The variety of forms of historical discrimination experienced by Franco Americans (linguistic hostility, religious persecution, ethnic slurs, racialized discourse, and sexist practices) have been frequently played out in class conflict and job competition. Contemporary communication practices are also informed and constrained by class relations; for example, Franco Americans' strategic use of bilingualism, intermediaries, and body language in social interactions, and their ambivalent relationship to education. More analysis is required to examine class differences and migrations and to complicate the stereotype of the working-class immigrant experience.

4. *Communicating ethnicity is not enough when it obscures the workings of gender, **sexism**, and **heterosexism**.* The kinwork of Franco American women is instructive because ethnic identity is popularly assumed to mean adherence to tradition, and tradition encodes the ideal patriarchal family. Di Leonardo (1984) concludes that, "In fact, ethnicity itself is seen to belong to men: they arrogate to themselves (and identify with) those ethnic characteristics maintained by women to whom they are

connected. A woman, in this ideological frame, is properly ethnic when she pro-vides the nurturing, symbolically laden environment for which ethnic men can take credit" (p. 221). The fusion of ethnic chauvinism and sexual chauvinism reproduces limiting gender roles and communication rules for women *and* for men. It also masks the varieties of feminisms within Franco American ethnicity; for example, electronic innovations of ethnic identity. The significance of gender and sexuality invites a more nuanced analysis of communicating ethnicity, including the experiences of **gay and lesbian** ethnics.

5. *Finally, communicating ethnicity is not enough if religion is not examined more closely.* Unlike in the American South, the Ku Klux Klan in the Northeast targeted Jews and Roman Catholic French. Additionally, the American Catholic Church hierar-chy privileged the Irish among White ethnics. In the U.S. context, *Christian* serves as the unmarked term for religion, a term in need of marking within a culture of multiple religions (Jewish, Muslim, Buddhist, and so on) and of more precision among and within Christian religions in order to understand its effects on commu-nication practices.

> "Where I come from is where I want to be." Recently I wrote my mother's and grandmother's Franco American stories. More than any of my academic publi-cations, this writing has connected me with the Franco American community and students in Maine. Black cultural critic bell hooks writes that "the most powerful resource any of us can have as we study and teach in university settings is full understanding and appreciation of the richness, beauty, and primacy of our familial and community backgrounds" (1989, p. 133). Even more so, this was writing that my family could read. It brings me closer to home, it closes the class divide between education and Franco American lives, and it draws com-munication studies more deeply into the complexities of White ethnic identity.

References

Anzaldua, G. 1987. *Borderlands/la frontera: The new mestiza*. San Francisco: Aunt Lute.

Bailey, T. A., and D. M. Kennedy. 1991. *The American experience: A history of a republic*. Vol. 1 (9th ed.). Lexington, Ky.: D. C. Heath.

Bérubé, A. 1997. Intellectual desire. In S. Raffo (Ed.), *Queerly classed* (pp. 43–66). Boston: South End Press.

Boscia-Mulé, P. 1999. *Authentic ethnicities: The interaction of ideology, gender, power, and class in Italian-American experience*. Westport, Conn.: Greenwood.

Chase, K. 1998. Ça fait mal partout. *South End* 1 (1): 110–14.

Chodos, R., and E. Hamovitch. 1991. *Quebec and the American dream*. Toronto: Between the Lines.

Cook, K. J. 1995. A tribute to Pheobe. In R. C. Robbins, L. L. Petrie, K. M. Langellier, and K. Slott (Eds.), I am Franco American and proud of it/Je suis Franco Américaine et fière de l'être (p. 66). Unpublished manuscript, University of Maine, Orono.

DeRoche, C. 1996. "I learned things today that I never knew before": Oral history at the kitchen table. *Oral History Review* 23 (2): 45–61.

di Leonardo, M. 1984. *The varieties of ethnic experience: Kinship, class, and gender among California Italian Americans*. Ithaca, N.Y.: Cornell University Press.

Doty, S. 1995. How many Frenchman does it take to . . .? *Thought and Action: The NEA Higher Education Journal* 11 (2): 85–104.

Dufresne, J. 1996. Telling stories in *mémère's* kitchen. In C. Quintal (Ed.), *Steeples and smokestacks: A collection of essays on the Franco American experience in New England* (pp. 660–69). Worcester, Mass.: Editions de l'Institut Francais.

Fine, E. C., and J. H. Speer (Eds.). 1992. *Performance, culture, and identity*. Westport, Conn.: Praeger.

Franco American Women's Institute. Http://members.aol.com/FAWI2000/index.html.

Haraway, D. 1988. Situated knowledges: The science question in feminism and the privilege of partial perspective. *Feminist Review* 14: 575–99.

hooks, b. 1989. *Talking back: Thinking feminist, thinking Black*. Boston: South End Press.

Ignatiev, N. 1995. *How the Irish became White*. New York: Routledge.

Kaye/Kantrovich, M. 1996. Jews in the U.S.: The rising costs of whiteness. In B. Thompson and S. Tyagi (Eds.), *Names we call home: Autobiography on racial identity* (pp. 121–38). New York: Routledge.

Langellier, K. M. 1996. Responding to ethnicity: Franco American studies in Maine. In H. Barthel (Ed.), *Logon didonai: Gespräch und Verantwortung [festschrift für Hellmut Geissner]* (pp. 93–100). Marz: Voraussichtlicher Erscheinungstemim.

Langellier, K. M., and E. E. Peterson. 1999. Voicing identity: The case of Franco-American women in Maine. In E. Slembek (Ed.), *The voice of the voiceless* (pp. 135–45). St. Inglebert: Röhrig Universitätsverlag.

Lanza, C. D. 1994. "Always on the brink of disappearing": Women, ethnicity, class, and autobiography. *Frontiers* XV (2): 51–68.

Nakayama, T. K., and J. N. Martin (Eds.). 1999. *Whiteness: The social communication of identity*. Thousand Oaks, Calif.: Sage.

Peterson, E. E. 1991. Dial 581-FROG: The struggle over self-naming by Franco Americans in Maine. In E. Slembek (Ed.), *Culture and communication* (pp. 185–93). Frankfurt am Main: Verlag fur Interculturelle Kommunikation.

———. 1994. Diversity and Franco-American identity politics. *Maine Historical Society Quarterly* 34: 58–67.

Philipsen, G. 1975. Speaking "like a man" in Teamsterville: Cultural patterns of role enactment in an urban neighborhood. *Quarterly Journal of Speech* 61: 13–22.

Robbins, R. C. 1997. *Wednesday's child*. Brunswick: Maine Writers and Publishers Alliance.

Robbins, R. C., L. L. Petrie, K. M. Langellier, and K. Slott (Eds.). 1995. I am Franco American and proud of it/Je suis Franco Américaine et fière de l'être. Unpublished manuscript, University of Maine, Orono.

Roby, Y. 1996. A portrait of the female Franco-American worker (1865–1930). In C. Quintal (Ed.), *Steeples and smokestacks: A collection of essays on the Franco American experience in New England* (pp. 544–63). Worcester, Mass.: Editions de l'Institut Francais.

Rubin, L. B. 1994. *Families on the faultline: America's working class speaks about the family, the economy, race, and ethnicity*. New York: HarperCollins.

Secord, P., and C. Backman. 1964. *Social psychology*. New York: McGraw-Hill.

Verba, S., K. L. Scholzman, and H. E. Brady (Eds.). 1995. *Voice and equality: Civic voluntarism in American politics*. Cambridge, Mass.: Harvard University Press.

Waters, M. C. 1990. *Ethnic options: Choosing identities in America*. Berkeley: University of California Press.

Wellman, D. 1996. Red and Black in White America: Discovering cross-border identities and other subversive activities. In B. Thompson and S. Tyagi (Eds.), *Names we call home: Autobiography on racial identity* (pp. 29–42). New York: Routledge.

KEY TERMS

assimilation

bilingual (ism)

body language

borderlands

Catholic(ism)

class

context

ethnic option

ethnicity (communicating ethnicity)

Franco Americans

French

gay and lesbian

gender (gendered communication)

heterosexism

homosexual (homosexuality)

kinwork

language

migration (immigration)

parochial schools

power

privilege

race

racism

region (regional)

religion

sexism

White ethnicity

women

REVIEW AND DISCUSSION QUESTIONS

1. Many European Americans feel that they don't have a culture or ethnicity; only "others" have a cultural identity. How might the Franco American story contribute to rethinking this concept of *American?* How are Franco American communication practices similar to and different from other (White) ethnic groups?

2. How were Franco Americans racialized as "not White" or "less White"? How does the Franco American story show that race and ethnicity are social constructions? How does the "new immigration story" by White ethnic groups erase race or harbor racism?

3. How does the chapter suggest we examine White ethnicity more closely and complexly? Consider how language, class, gender, region, religion, sexual orientation, and other differences shape communication and miscommunication.

4. What is the *ethnic option?* Why is it a useful concept? How is it problematic?

5. How are the Northeast borderlands similar to and different from the Southwest borderlands?

6. Why is it important to consider varieties of White ethnic experiences?

7. Discuss examples of the power of communication in identity and community formation. How have Franco Americans maintained communities over time? Other ethnic groups? How is cultural identity performed in personal narrative and family stories?

Negotiating Cultural Identity: Strategies for Belonging

LISA BRADFORD, NANCY A. BURRELL, AND EDWARD A. MABRY

LEARNING OBJECTIVES

After reading this chapter, students will be able to:

- understand the definition and functions of cultural identity;
- recognize the relationship between cultural identity and communication;
- describe the importance of "belonging" to cultural identity;
- visualize how cultural identity is negotiated; and
- identify common Latino cultural values.

Is who I think I am who you think I am? How is what I think you said influenced by who we think we are? Who will we think we are after we have communicated on the basis of who we thought we were?

Through social interactions, people accumulate meanings or identities that are essential for understanding themselves (Stephan 1992). Communication scholars have long been intrigued with the process of how individual identities are negotiated and how they affect communicative interaction, particularly when the individuals communicating represent different cultural groups. This chapter explores the negotiation of cultural identity in intercultural interactions by examining the cultural identity negotiation experiences of three Latino college students. Specifically, their experiences underscore the importance of achieving a sense of belonging during the negotiation of cultural identity and how specific communication strategies are employed to this end.

Cultural Identities

Our cultural identities influence our self-concepts and function to organize and interpret our interactions with others (Lustig and Koester 1999). Using Kim's (1996) inclusive approach, **cultural identity** here is viewed as "interchangeable with other terms commonly used in both international and domestic contexts such as national, ethnic, ethnolinguistic, and racial identity, or more generic concepts such as social and group identity" (p. 349). Hence, culture can be broadly defined to include the influences of a variety of domestic and international groups. Consistent with Adler (1998), we see cultural identity as one's **perception of one's self** that "incorporates the world view, value system, attitudes, and beliefs of a group with which such elements are shared" (p. 230). Further, cultural identities may be both a product of a person's identity with national origin (i.e., United States) and also ethnic background (i.e., Latino). This is significant in understanding why Latinos from the United States may have different cultural identities than Latinos from Panama or other countries.

There is an interdependent relationship between one's identity and communication (Martin and Nakayama 2000). Mead's (1934) theory of **symbolic interactionism** explains that only through the process of communicating with others, using verbal and nonverbal symbols, can identity formation occur (Wood 1997). Further, Mead's concept of the **"looking-glass self"** suggests that our perceptions of how other people see us have a great influence on how we see ourselves. A meta-analysis of past research on the relationship between individuals' (primarily African Americans and European Americans) feelings about their racial group orientations and their self-esteem found that when people feel negatively about their racial groups they may have less positive self-esteem (Allen, Howard, and Grimes 1997).[1] In other words, if people from one ethnic/racial group are given negative feedback (i.e., racial/ethnic jokes, derogatory labels, discriminatory treatment) about their membership in that group, this may negatively impact their self-esteem, especially when there are few or no competing sources of positive feedback. In short, "We learn to see ourselves in terms of the labels others apply to us" (p. 128). Mead also concluded that others' perceptions could become **"self-fulfilling prophecies"** to the extent that people may live up to the implications of the labels imposed on them by others.

Symbolic interactionists suggest there are two types of "others," "particular others" and "the generalized other" (Wood 1997). **Particular others** are individuals who are significant to us (i.e., family, friends, romantic partners, coworkers) while the **generalized other** reflects the perspective of our social groups (i.e., communities, cultures, societies). Our self-perceptions are a composite of the feedback we receive from both of these others. Others' perceptions contribute to how we make meaning of ourselves, others, our experiences, and our subsequent behavior. Accordingly, our cultural identities are negotiated through our communicative interactions, both influencing and being influenced by those interactions.

Negotiating Cultural Identities

Cultural identities are more than just collections of cultural values, attitudes, beliefs, and norms. Cultural identities also include emotional evaluations of others' perceptions of our cultural groups. During communicative interactions, individuals may apply various communicative strategies to negotiate cultural identities that are positive and fulfill social needs.

Cultural identity negotiations may become particularly intense during intercultural interactions and **cultural adjustments.** During these experiences, communicators frequently encounter feedback that motivates them to renegotiate their cultural identities. "Even in the briefest encounter with people whose cultural backgrounds differ from your own, your sense of who you are at that instant may well be altered, at least in some small ways" (Lustig and Koester 1999, p. 143). This process leaves some individuals feeling a host of unpleasant emotions. One of this chapter's authors depicts the emotional challenges experienced during the cultural adaptation process in the poem, "Caught."

> I'm caught in a place that's gone crazy—
> Got two worlds pulling and tugging me.
> Do I choose one and leave one behind?
> When I'm done will I like who I find?

These lines reflect the tension and isolation immigrants may feel as they try to renegotiate their cultural identities (e.g., Am I Mexican, American, Latino, Mexican American—who am I and where do I belong?).

Cultural Identity Negotiation and Belonging

During intercultural (both domestic and international) interactions, individuals may feel isolated or marginalized when they perceive a lack of acceptance or negative feedback about their cultural identities from particular others or the generalized other. For example, recent immigrants may feel marginalized if dominant culture friends make negative comments about their cultures or when they see negative portrayals of cultural members by the media. Feelings of isolation or marginalization frequently lead to psychological stress because they evidence the absence of a basic human need—"belonging" (Maslow 1968). **Belonging** is a perception that one is relationally connected to other significant human beings or social groups. When people feel they are recognized, accepted, and belong to groups of others, they experience more positive feelings about themselves (Collier and Thomas 1988; Kich 1992). Further, when minority youth feel positively about their own ethnic identities, they tend to display higher self-esteem. However, "those who feel alienated do not. Esteem, therefore, is related to the sense of belonging, and not to race or ethnicity *per se*" (Fuhrmann 1990, p. 340).

The relationship between belonging and cultural identity is illustrated in Arce's (1982) description of **ethnic identity** as providing individuals with "a sense of historical continuity to life, a continuity based on preconscious recognition of traditionally held patterns of thinking, feeling, and behaving that is the cornerstone of a sense of belonging" (pp. 137–38).

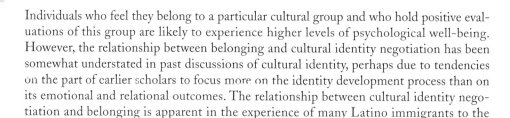

Individuals who feel they belong to a particular cultural group and who hold positive evaluations of this group are likely to experience higher levels of psychological well-being. However, the relationship between belonging and cultural identity negotiation has been somewhat understated in past discussions of cultural identity, perhaps due to tendencies on the part of earlier scholars to focus more on the identity development process than on its emotional and relational outcomes. The relationship between cultural identity negotiation and belonging is apparent in the experience of many Latino immigrants to the United States.

Latinos in the United States

The term **Latino** generally refers to anyone born in a Latin American nation (Hurtado 1995). A 1996 census report projected that during the next ten years, Latinos were expected to emerge as the largest ethnic group in the United States (U.S. Bureau of the Census 1996). The increase in the Latino population is largely due to high rates of immigration (Ortiz 1995). Although Latinos have been present in the United States since the beginning of its colonization (Marín and Marín 1991), they still face many political and cultural challenges, including how to successfully negotiate their cultural identities in a non-Latino dominant culture. "The question of identity, both in the majority society and in their community, is much on the minds of the Latino community" (Roy 1997, p. 1).

Several social conditions contribute to this challenge. Most Latino immigrants have settled in neighborhoods where U.S.-born Latinos or older immigrants live, which has led to a state of cultural flux. "Family patterns, cultural practices and values, and socioeconomic integration are in a state of transition for Latinos as a whole" (Hurtado 1995, p. 41). Language fluency affects Latino cultural identity negotiation. Latinos with poor English skills have difficulty achieving a sense of belonging among English-speaking Latinos and non-Latinos. In contrast, non-Spanish-speaking Latinos may also find they are not accepted as "Latino" by Spanish-speaking Latinos.

Education levels (Rogler, Cooney, and Ortiz 1980), age upon arrival in the United States (Hurtado 1995), perpetuation of stereotypes by the mass media (Ríos 2000), and negative interactions with non-Latinos also influence Latino cultural identities. Negative or incorrect stereotypes, misunderstandings due to language and cultural differences, and an overall ignorance of how differences in cultural values and norms affect perceptions of cultural members have frequently resulted in the **marginalization** of Latinos by non-Latinos.

Further, Latinos are frequently perceived as a homogeneous group. This is an antiquated and overly simplistic perception (Marín and Marín 1991) that fails to recognize the diversity of experiences among Latinos who are from different national origins and ethnic and socioeconomic backgrounds. Ignorance of heterogeneity among Latinos leads to misunderstandings, particularly among non-Latinos. Despite the diversity among Latinos, they do share a few common values that serve to both distinguish and separate Latinos as a group from non-Latinos, regardless of national origin. These include: familialism, collectivism, *simpatía*, power distance, gender roles *(machismo)*, personal space, and time orientation (Marín and Marín 1991). What follows is a brief discussion of the Latino values of familialism, collectivism, *simpatía*, and power distance, which provides cultural background for examining the Latino student examples.

Familialism

Latinos as a group[2] tend to report very strong identification with, high commitment to, and attachment to their nuclear and extended families (Hurtado 1995; Marín and Marín 1991). Gangotena (2000) notes that the Latino **familialism** and the European American notion of family reflect different assumptions about how family is defined and what it does for its members. Further, Latino families stress interdependence among family members across generations and value time for family interaction (including the importance of conversation, touch, affection, and greeting rituals). In contrast, European Americans emphasize individualism and more restricted communication and touch. These differences have contributed to non-Latino misunderstandings about the degree to which the Latino family can impact identity formation, use of time, loyalties, decision making, and family communication styles.

Collectivism

Latinos, in general, possess high degrees of **collectivism** (Hofstede 1984). They value group harmony and conformity and are more willing to sacrifice for the good of the group. They tend to value group loyalty, use less direct communication strategies, and choose less assertive or avoidance styles during conflict (Martin and Nakayama 2000). Their communication style preferences are frequently juxtaposed with the communication styles of European Americans who tend to value individualism (Hofstede 1984). Misperceptions resulting from these differences have frequently led to negative intercultural interactions and subsequent poor relationships between Latinos and European Americans.

Simpatía

Simpatía is derived from collectivism and refers to "a permanent personal quality where an individual is perceived as likeable, attractive, fun to be with, and easy-going" (Triandis, Lisansky, Marín, and Betancourt 1984, p. 1363). Individuals who possess this quality show empathy toward and respect for others and avoid criticizing, insulting, or fighting. Further, they also tend to show more concern about social protocols and protecting the other's face during interpersonal interactions.

Power Distance

Hofstede (1984) found that Latinos report high levels of **power distance,** implying a tendency to display deference to powerful individuals and groups in their societies. High value is placed on showing respect for and obedience to authority. Individuals with specific professional roles (i.e., mayors, doctors, lawyers, professors) and older individuals are held in high esteem, and one is expected to listen to and obey them. Intercultural interactions between Latinos and European Americans in the United States are sometimes frustrated because European Americans tend to report lower levels of power distance. European Americans frequently seem rude because they violate Latino expectations for when and how to show respect.

Value differences frequently contribute to misunderstandings between Latinos and non-Latinos in the United States, which lead to negative stereotyping and negative feedback from non-Latino particular others and the generalized other. Ultimately, these misunderstandings contribute to the feelings of displacement and marginalization that many Latinos experience.

The following three case studies reflect the personal and cultural tensions experienced by three Latino students as they negotiated cultural identities and tried to find a sense of belonging among their Latino and non-Latino peers.

Case Studies

The three redactive case studies[3] report experiences of three young Latinos[4] who faced different cultural negotiation challenges and how they used specific communication strategies to negotiate their cultural identities. Each case illustrates how the need to feel some sense of belonging appeared to motivate the communicative strategies employed.

Mária

I am a second-generation Mexican American. My grandparents were born in Mexico and immigrated to Texas. My parents moved to the Midwest from Texas before I was born, and our family has had little contact with any of the family residing in Mexico. Because I was born and raised in the Midwest, my cultural experiences differed from both my parents' and those that my siblings had while they were raised in Texas. Contrary to my siblings, my skin is lighter and I am not a fluent speaker of Spanish (though I understand it). I speak English without an accent. My parents instilled in me a knowledge of my heritage and an appreciation for traditional Mexican foods and customs. However, my inability to speak Spanish continues to set me apart from other Latinos. I plan to learn Spanish in the future.

I attended a predominantly White parochial school. I was well-liked by peers and had friends from various social groups. My light skin and unaccented English may have helped me to fit in with my peers. While I noticed some cultural differences such as the tacos and beans my mother packed for my lunch instead of peanut butter and jelly sandwiches like others brought, and how students mispronounced my name; I took pride in my culture and explaining how I was different from the other students.

Since our family was the only Mexican family in the neighborhood, we did experience some prejudice from other families that would not let their children play with me. My parents said I should not worry about this and that if I continued to be polite to them, they would eventually come around. Most of my friends were intrigued by my cultural differences.

When I entered high school, I began to experience some problems with people's perceptions of me. Prior to high school I had not had much contact with other Latinos outside of my family members. In high school, there was a group of Latino girls who said I was "White washed." These Latino girls spoke Spanish and had grown up in a predominantly Latino community. Their style of dress, behavior and speech patterns differed from the other students. However, they were a well-respected group because they looked out for one another, which is a traditional characteristic of Latino culture. Predictably, they would not have accepted me into their group, but I became friends with a girl from Mexico who was part of the group. Because of this friendship, I was eventually accepted by the rest of the girls.

I experienced difficulties again when I married my Caucasian husband. Some Latino friends quit speaking to me. They said I needed to educate myself about my race and that I was losing touch with my ethnicity. My true friends and family took the time to get to know my husband, and then they accepted him.

Initially, Mária faced few challenges in negotiating her cultural identity because her particular others (i.e., her classmates and parents) gave her positive feedback about her ethnic background, and she belonged to a supportive peer group. Positive feedback from her particular others offset her neighbors' negative evaluations of her ethnicity. Given the high value placed on the family by Latinos, it is not surprising that feedback from Mária's family carried more weight than her neighbors' feedback. Mária also felt comfortable identifying herself as Latino American and perceived few differences between herself and her non-Latino friends because she felt they accepted her for who she was.

Mária's cultural identity challenges began in high school when she was rejected by her Latino particular others. They did not feel she was Latino "enough" to belong to their group. Perhaps the fact that she did not speak Spanish contributed to their perception that Mária was "White washed." Regardless, their negative feedback about her cultural identity left her feeling marginalized. Mária was frustrated because although she *felt* Latino and others had identified her as a Latina, these peers would not accept her as a Latina.

Whether intentionally applied or not, the strategy that allowed Mária to gain her Latino peers' acceptance was her use of an intermediary. Her Mexican friend bridged the perceived cultural gap between Mária and the other girls. Intermediaries are commonly used by out-group members to gain entrance into the groups they desire to affiliate with, particularly by members of collectivistic cultures.

Mária's Latino cultural identity was again challenged when she married her Caucasian husband. Some of Mária's Latino friends perceived her marriage as an attempt to reject her Latino heritage, and they in turn rejected her. Mária used a different strategy in this situation. Rather than choosing a strategy designed to build her relationship with these particular others, Mária chose to redefine who her particular others were. She redefined her particular others as those family and friends who had taken the time to get to know and accept her husband. Choosing the less assertive strategy of redefining her particular others, rather than confronting her former friends assertively, is consistent with the Latino value of *simpatía*.

For Mária, major junctures for renegotiating her cultural identity came when she received negative feedback from particular others (important peers). Negative feedback from parents of the non-Latino children in her neighborhood had little effect on her cultural identity because they were not perceived as particular others. At that point in her life, her belonging needs were satisfied by her relationships with her school friends and her parents.

However, the negative feedback she received from her Latino high school peers did have an impact on her sense of identity. During adolescence, peers can become powerful particular others. As Fuhrmann (1990) notes, "Success in the adolescent world is most often defined in terms of popularity—the acceptance by peers and ease in making friends that enhances one's power in the peer group" (p. 121). Years later, although the negative feedback from significant Latino friends about her marriage concerned her, Mária was less motivated to gain their approval, because she had different criteria for selecting her particular others. As a result, she redefined her group of particular others to exclude those who opposed her marriage. Both of the communication strategies Mária reports using to negotiate her cultural identity were motivated by her desire to belong to groups of particular others who provided positive feedback about her cultural identity.

Michael

I was born and raised in the Midwest after my parents moved from Texas. I am a second-generation Mexican American. My parents spoke poor English and primarily used Spanish. My father had a third grade education, and my mother had no formal education. I spoke Spanish until I turned three, but once I entered school, I quickly assimilated and lost my Spanish. I went to a public school that had predominantly White students with a small percentage of Latino and African American students. I noticed immediately I was different from the other students because my parents did not speak English. My dark skin and accent made me an easy target for the other kids to tease. I remember seeing negative portrayals of Latinos in the media and wondered why my family was not more like the Cleavers in Leave it to Beaver.

I began to feel Latinos were inferior to Whites. I shocked my parents by cutting all the curls out of my hair and insisted on wearing it short at all times, so I could be more like the White kids. In high school I decided to date only White girls because I thought it might give me more status. Parent-teacher conferences were particularly difficult for me because my parents could not speak English. I spent minimal time on my homework because my parents were not educated enough to help me with it, and I was too embarrassed to ask for the teacher's help. I lied to get out of uncomfortable school situations. I graduated from high school at a seventh grade reading level.

Then I spent many years trying to be someone I was not. The negative experiences and interactions from my childhood caused me to deny my Latino ethnicity. Finally, when I was older, my aunt encouraged me to learn Spanish and experience my culture. I took a trip to Mexico and fell in love with my ethnic background. I now embrace my cultural differences as something that makes me unique. I am now an active member of my Latino community and write for the Latino community newspaper. I will soon have a college degree and hope to serve as a role model for young Latinos.

In contrast to Mária, Michael internalized the belief that Latinos were inferior to White peers as a child. Negative cultural feedback from the generalized other, communicated through media representations, combined with negative feedback from particular others, seems to have had a profoundly negative effect on Michael's perceptions of himself as a Latino. Michael's account does not suggest that his family was able to mediate that negative feedback. Perhaps they were experiencing their own identity challenges, or Michael may have been so ashamed of their struggles with English that he did not give their feedback as much credibility as feedback from peers and the media. Michael's experience illustrates another role language may play in the negotiation of identity.

Feeling that Latinos were inferior to White people fueled Michael's desire to disassociate from his Latino ethnic background and associate with White peers. He strategically adopted behaviors that communicated his desire to belong in his White peer group (i.e., changing his appearance, lying, dating only White girls). Michael, like Mária, tried to use intermediaries (White girlfriends) to help negotiate peer group membership.

The Latino value of high power distance may help explain Michael's decision to hide the difficulties he was having with his schoolwork and the lack of academic support he had at home. He may have felt uncomfortable approaching his higher status teachers for help because the perceived social distance between himself and them seemed too great. On the other hand, Michael may have avoided talking to his parents and his teachers about his problems because he did not want his parents to look or feel badly about their lack of English language skills. This behavior would have been consistent with collectivism. In collectivistic cultures, it is most important to preserve face for members of the in-group even at the expense of one's own face (Triandis 1995). Family is generally considered the most important Latino in-group (Hofstede 1984).

Michael continued to deny his Latino background until his aunt encouraged him to try to reconnect with his Latino heritage. Taking his aunt's advice seriously, Michael began to learn Spanish, study Latino history, and even traveled to Mexico. The influence of extended family members, especially older family members, is very significant in the Latino culture. The strength of this influence can be explained by familialism and power distance. In Latino families children are taught not only to listen to their parents, but to respect and listen to all their extended family members. Extended family members influence decision making and have an active part in the lives of family members. Children are taught that they must show deference and respect to family members, especially those who are older than they are.

Although Michael studied Latino history and learned Spanish, by his own account he "fell in love" with his ethnicity while he was in Mexico. The trip gave Michael positive feedback about his Latino background. Being in Mexico provided Michael a sense of connectedness to the history and people of Mexico that gave him a sense of belonging he had not previously experienced as a Latino. This connection was especially inspired by the acceptance he felt from his Latino peers in Mexico. His experiences in Mexico motivated his desire to affiliate with his Latino community at home. When Michael returned home, he changed behaviors that had disassociated him from this group and became actively involved in the Latino community.

While the angst of many high school adolescents—the need for peer group membership and acceptance—initially disassociated Michael from his Latino heritage, over time he reconnected with his culture as a result of his trip to Mexico. Perhaps the opportunity to learn about his culture in a context where Latinos were empowered gave Michael the motivation to reexamine the feedback of the generalized other in the United States. Regardless, Michael came home feeling that being Latino was something to be proud of.

Edward

I am a first-generation light-skinned Puerto Rican American. My parents moved to New Jersey from Puerto Rico. During the early part of my childhood, I grew up in a Latino, predominantly Puerto Rican community. People there expressed pride in their ethnicity by displaying Puerto Rican flags in their windows. I attended a public school with an ethnically mixed, rather than predominantly White student body. Both of my parents speak Spanish, and although I can understand Spanish, I did not take learning it seriously. When I was eight years old, my family moved to a mainly White neighborhood in the Midwest. Our family was the only Puerto Rican family in the neighborhood.

Suddenly I had to deal with discrimination that I had never experienced before. Although I am a lighter skinned Puerto Rican, kids teased me for having darker skin. They also teased me about my accent and made fun of the way my parents spoke. Even though I realized that the other kids had negative ideas about Latinos, I did not let it bother me because I had Latino friends that were dealing with the same challenges.

Some time after high school, I took a job on a farm. This was during the migrant farm worker's movement led by Caesar Chavez. Even though I was Latino and a farm worker, I was not Mexican, not a migrant worker, and I did not speak Spanish. These differences kept the Latino farm workers from accepting me as one of them.

Edward initially received positive feedback about being Latino from his primarily Latino particular others who were proud of their Latino ethnicity. Until he was eight years old, he had had little exposure to negative feedback about his culture. Then, when he moved to the Midwest and began to communicate with predominately White peers, he found that they viewed him as different and in some cases evaluated those differences very negatively. He experienced discrimination that prevented him from achieving a sense of belonging among his White peers.

Unlike Michael, Edward chose not to change his behaviors or adopt other strategies to encourage the acceptance of his White peers because his need to belong in their group was not as high as Michael's. Edward had a group of Latino friends who were bound together by their common heritage and the discrimination they were subjected to. Edward felt less negative about being Latino than Michael, because he belonged to this group of Latino peers. Edward's Latino friends constituted his particular others, and so he gave more credence to their positive feedback about his Latino identity than the negative feedback from his White peers.

Edward faced greater challenges in negotiating his cultural identity among his migrant worker peers after high school. They did not accept him because he did not speak Spanish and was not a migrant worker. This was frustrating to Edward, who saw the migrant workers as part of his Latino particular others. However, they did not feel like he was one of them because he could not relate to their experience. In cultures where members value collectivism, the boundaries between in-group and out-group members are frequently more difficult to penetrate than in cultures where members value individualism (Triandis 1995). Edward did not have an intermediary who could help him gain membership among the migrant workers, so he was unsuccessful in achieving their acceptance. He did not report finding a successful strategy for achieving a sense of belonging in this group.

Cultural Negotiation Strategies

In these three examples, it is clear that even when individuals share similar national and ethnic backgrounds, there may be cultural differences that prevent some individuals from gaining acceptance by members of their national and ethnic peer groups. Both Mária and Edward experienced rejection by groups of individuals whom they felt shared their own cultural backgrounds. Mária was negatively labeled by the Latino girls at her high school, and Edward was rejected by the migrant workers he associated with. The desire to belong in peer groups influenced how these three Latino students negotiated their cultural identities and their strategy choices. When negative feedback came from particular others, they attempted to gain group acceptance through one of three strategies. They either changed themselves to look and behave more like their significant others (e.g., cutting hair), relied on intermediaries (e.g., White girlfriends), or redefined their group of particular others (e.g., Mária's redefining her group of friends).

The lack of acceptance by others posed less threat to the students' cultural identities when they were disinterested in belonging to the group or when the members of the group did not have particular other status. Related to the Latino values of collectivism and familialism, family members and friends were frequently able to offset the negative feedback of the generalized other or played the role of intermediaries by facilitating group memberships. In the case of Mária and Edward, parents and friends mediated the negative feedback of neighbors and peers. In the case of Michael, the Mexican peer group he established in Mexico motivated him to reevaluate his cultural identity and reconnect with his Latino cultural identity.

Consistent with these examples, Hall (1990) argues that cultural identity is not an "already accomplished fact," rather it is a "production." Cultural identities shift as a result of the feedback received during communicative interactions. Hall notes that cultural identity "is a matter of 'becoming' as well as of 'being'" (p. 225). Our examples suggest that the negotiation of cultural identities is also a matter of belonging—to the degree that an individual's desire to belong to a significant group motivates the implementation of cultural identity negotiation strategies. The accounts by Mária, Michael, and Edward suggest that these strategies might include: aligning one's behaviors and appearance with the desired group, relying on or seeking out intermediaries who can facilitate one's acceptance by the group, or redefining who one's particular others are. However, it is also important to understand the dynamic tension attached to the notion of "belonging" (Adler 1982; Carnes 1995; Kim 1996, 2000).

The Tension of Belonging

The notion of belonging results in a "double-binding conundrum" for identity negotiation. There are a variety of good reasons for belonging to groups including: strength in numbers, teamwork and distribution of labor; self-esteem; pride; personal support; and resources for learning (Carnes 1995). The desire to belong to cultural groups may motivate individuals to use a variety of strategies similar to those found in the examples of Mária, Michael, and Edward. However, as Kim (1996) contends, "belonging" may have a "dark side" for intercultural communicators.

The limitations associated with belonging in a particular group include: possible rejection of out-group members, conformity, minimization of personal responsibility for group actions, and subjection to peer pressure (Carnes 1995). Once individuals feel like part of a group, the group's boundaries may be perceived as immutable or inflexible. When group boundaries are perceived to have these characteristics, they may become impermeable to others and members may be unresponsive to contextual changes. Hence, the tension of belonging is balanced between inclusion versus exclusion. Being included in a particular group can come at the expense of excluding others. Some scholars, in recognition of this tension, have suggested that individuals should focus their attention on developing intercultural or multicultural identities rather than specific cultural identities (Adler 1982, 1998; Kim 2000).

Adler (1982) argues that the identity of an intercultural or multicultural person should be based "not on belongingness, which implies either owning or being owned by culture, but on a style of self consciousness that is capable of negotiating ever new formations of reality" (p. 391). Hence, an intercultural identity has boundaries that are more fluid and responsive to change. Individuals who have developed intercultural identities would in a sense "live on the boundary," perceiving their cultural identities not as end states but as dynamic and evolving components of their intercultural identities. As such, Adler (1982) would be less excited about Mária, Michael, and Edward's success in negotiating their Latino cultural identities

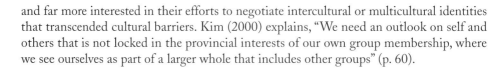

and far more interested in their efforts to negotiate intercultural or multicultural identities that transcended cultural barriers. Kim (2000) explains, "We need an outlook on self and others that is not locked in the provincial interests of our own group membership, where we see ourselves as part of a larger whole that includes other groups" (p. 60).

Conclusion

Particular others play a key role in determining how we balance the feedback we receive about our cultural groups from the generalized other. Cultural identity negotiation is facilitated when feedback from the generalized other and particular others converges. Cultural identity negotiation is challenged when feedback from the generalized other and particular others diverges. However, these three examples suggest that when the feedback diverges, feedback from particular others may be perceived as more salient and may mediate the feedback of the generalized other. Further, our motivation to belong to a group of particular others may motivate the use of specific identity negotiation strategies such as those used by Mária, Michael, and Edward.

The intercultural or multicultural identity perspective of belonging does not negate the importance of belonging as a motivator for the strategies. Rather it is cautionary, alerting us that we should avoid viewing cultural group membership myopically and should recognize the importance of adopting a broader perspective on how we view our cultural identities within the larger context of our multicultural world.

Part of adopting an intercultural identity is understanding the concept of the "looking-glass self" and recognizing the powerful role that each human being plays in providing feedback to others about their cultural identities. Instead of viewing our memberships in cultural groups from an exclusionary perspective, we need to adopt responsibility for participating in the more inclusive perspective is described in the poem, "Our Town," by one of the authors of this chapter.

> Yesterday I moved into your town.
> Rich, poor, old, young, white or black or brown
> Some folks ignored me or did me wrong.
> You called me friend, and now I belong—
>   In our town!

If greater numbers of people adopted intercultural or multicultural identities, fewer people would experience the isolation and marginalization felt by Mária, Michael, and Edward. Particular others and the generalized other would focus on deleting group boundaries and communicating positive feedback about the attributes that make us different from one another. Then people would begin to experience a sense of belonging that transcends cultural and national boundaries.

Notes

1. There have been mixed results in past research regarding the relationship between self-esteem and racial group orientations. The Allen et al. (1997) meta-analysis found a slight positive relationship between self-esteem and racial group orientation. However, they agree with other authors that exposure to negative messages about one's racial group does not necessarily cause a person to develop

poor self-esteem, particularly when other factors mediate the negative impact of the message. Some factors that may mediate the impact of negative racial group messages include having powerful mentors and role models from one's culture and exposure to racial group histories and contributions.

2. Members of the same culture tend to share cultural values. However, not every member of a culture will share these values. For example, in cultures where most people tend to hold a high value for collectivism, there may be some cultural members who value individualism more than collectivism. As such, one should recognize the values ascribed to the Latino culture as general tendencies in the Latino population and avoid stereotyping every Latino as collectivistic.

3. The three redactive case studies used in this chapter come from reanalyzing field notes taken during interviews with Latino students as part of a larger study reported in Burrell, Diaz, and Bradford (1996a, 1996b). The case studies are presented in first person to distinguish them from the text and to give power to the voice of each interviewee.

4. The names of the interviewees have been changed to protect the identity of the interviewees.

References

Adler, P. 1982. Beyond cultural identity: Reflections on cultural and multicultural men. In L. A. Samovar and R. A. Porter (Eds.), *Intercultural communication: A reader* (3rd ed., pp. 389–408). Belmont, Calif.: Wadsworth.

———.1998. Beyond cultural identity: Reflections on multiculturalism. In M. J. Bennett (Ed.), *Basic concepts of intercultural communication* (pp. 225–45). Yarmouth, Me.: Intercultural Press.

Allen, M., L. Howard, and D. Grimes. 1997. Racial group orientation and self-concept: Examining the relationship using meta-analysis. *The Howard Journal of Communications* 8 (4): 371–86.

Arce, A. A. 1982. Discussion: Cultural aspects of mental health care for Hispanic Americans. In A. Gaw (Ed.), *Cross-cultural psychiatry* (pp. 137–48). Boston: PSG.

Burrell, N. A., A. Diaz, and L. Bradford. 1996a. The developmental stages of ethnic and bicultural identity: A conceptual model. Paper presented at the meeting of the Western Speech Communication Association, Intercultural Division, Pasadena, Calif., February.

———. 1996b. Searching for a cultural identity: An application of symbolic interactionism. Paper presented at the meeting of the National Communication Association, Family Communication Division, San Diego, Calif., November.

Carnes, J. 1995. *Us and them: A history of intolerance in America.* Montgomery, Ala.: Southern Poverty Law Center.

Collier, M. J., and M. Thomas. 1988. Cultural identity: An interpretive perspective. In Y. Y. Kim and W. B. Gudykunst (Eds.), *Theories in intercultural communication* (pp. 99–122). Newbury Park, Calif.: Sage.

Furhmann, B. S. 1990. *Adolescence, adolescents.* Glenview, Ill.: Scott, Foresman/Little, Brown Higher Education.

Gangotena, M. 2000. The rhetoric of *la familia* among Mexican Americans. In A. González, M. Houston, and V. Chen (Eds.), *Our voices: Essays in culture, ethnicity, and communication* (3rd ed., pp. 72–83). Los Angeles, Calif.: Roxbury.

Hall, S. 1990. Cultural identity and diaspora. In J. Rutherford (Ed.), *Identity: Community, culture, difference* (pp. 222–37). London, U.K.: Lawrence and Wishart.

Hofstede, G. 1984. *Culture's consequences.* Beverly Hills, Calif.: Sage.

Hurtado, A. 1995. Variations, combinations, and evolutions: Latino families in the United States. In R. E. Zambrana (Ed.), *Understanding Latino Families: Scholarship, policy, and practice* (pp. 40–61). Thousand Oaks, Calif.: Sage.

Kich, G. 1992. The developmental process of asserting a biracial bicultural identity. In M. P. P. Root (Ed.), *Racially mixed people in America* (pp. 304–17). Newbury Park, Calif.: Sage.

Kim, Y. Y. 1996. Identity development: From cultural to intercultural. In H. B. Mokros (Ed.), *Interaction and identity: Information and behavior* (pp. 347–69). New Brunswick, N.J.: Transaction.

———. 2000. On becoming intercultural. In M. W. Lustig and J. Koester (Eds.), *Among us: Essays on identity, belonging, and intercultural competence* (pp. 59–67). New York: Addison Wesley Longman.

Lee, E. 1995. Immigrant youth. *Journal of Undergraduate Research* 2 (1).

Lustig, M. W., and J. Koester. 1999. *Intercultural competence: Interpersonal communication across cultures.* New York: Longman.

Marín, G., and B. V. Marín. 1991. *Research with Hispanic Populations.* Newbury Park, Calif.: Sage.

Markham, E. 1936. Outwitted. In H. Fellman (Ed.), *The best loved poems of the American people* (p. 67). Garden City, N.Y.: Garden City Publishing.

Martin, J. N., and T. K. Nakayama. 2000. *Intercultural communication in contexts* (2nd ed). Mountain View, Calif.: Mayfield.

Maslow, A. H. 1968. *Toward a psychology of being* (2nd ed.). Princeton, N.J.: Van Nostrand.

Mead, G. H. 1934. *Mind, self, and society.* Chicago: University of Chicago Press.

Ortiz, V. 1995. The diversity of Latino families. In R. E. Zambrana (Ed.), *Understanding Latino families: Scholarship, policy, and practice* (pp. 18–39). Thousand Oaks, Calif.: Sage.

Ríos, D. I. 2000. Latina/o experiences with mediated communication. In A. González, M. Houston, and V. Chen (Eds.), *Our voices: Essays in culture, ethnicity, and communication* (3rd ed., pp. 105–12). Los Angeles, Calif.: Roxbury.

Rogler, L. H., R. S. Cooney, and V. Ortiz. 1980. Intergenerational change in ethnic identity in the Puerto Rican family. *International Migration Review* 14: 193–214.

Roy, D. L. 1997. Strangers in a native land: A labyrinthine map of Latino identity. Unpublished master's thesis, University of Kansas, Lawrence.

Stephen, C. W. 1992. Mixed heritage individuals: Ethnic identity and trait characteristics. In M. P. P. Root (Ed.), *Racially mixed people in America* (pp. 50–63). Newbury Park, Calif.: Sage.

Triandis, H. C. 1995. *Individualism and collectivism.* Boulder, Colo.: Westview.

Triandis, H. C., J. Lisansky, G. Marín, and H. Betancourt. 1984. *Simpatía* as a cultural script of Hispanics. *Journal of Personality and Social Psychology* 47: 1363–75.

U.S. Bureau of the Census. 1996. *Resident population of the United States: Middle series projections.* March. Washington, D.C.: Government Printing Office.

Wood, J. T. 1997. *Communication theories in action: An introduction.* Belmont, Calif.: Wadsworth.

KEY TERMS

belonging	looking-glass self
collectivism	marginalization
cultural adjustments	particular others
cultural identity	perception of one's self
cultural identity negotiations	power distance
ethnic identity	self-fulfilling prophecies
familialism	*simpatía*
generalized other	symbolic interactionism
Latino	

REVIEW AND DISCUSSION QUESTIONS

1. What is *cultural identity?* What does your cultural identity mean to you?
2. How does your "looking-glass self" affect your sense of cultural identity?
3. What is the relationship between belonging and cultural identity?
4. Reflect on your own experience, and discuss the extent to which you can relate to the common values of Latino culture.
5. The authors use case studies to illustrate Latinos' cultural identity. What are the similarities among these case studies and what do they imply?

Negotiating Cultural Identity in the Classroom

BRYANT K. ALEXANDER

LEARNING OBJECTIVES

After reading this chapter, students will be able to:

- comprehend that in spite of the specificity of this study, culture always intervenes in the educational process regardless of specified racial or ethnic distinctions or similarities;
- identify key features of Black discourse and observe that through language people not only share meaning, but establish relational connections;
- recognize that language is an agent of culture;
- understand how cultural background affects attitudes, beliefs, and values about education; and
- recognize that shared racial and gender categorization does not ensure equal bonds of affinity.

There are times when my Black male students ask me to repeat something that I have said in class. Often this is not because they didn't hear me the first time, but often I suspect that they want me to translate it in different terms. This could be considered paraphrasing, but I suspect that they want me to sort of re-code my message in Black English or at least with cultural references that they can relate to. This is not a problem when I think that it is sincere, but sometimes it comes as a sort of challenge to see if I can "talk the talk."

This chapter reflects and chronicles how (some) Black male teachers describe and make sense of their own **cultural negotiations** with Black male students. In this study, the specific notion of "cultural identity" is grounded in the idea that communities create symbols, expressions, and manners that when shared help to establish and negotiate intracultural relations. The classroom of the predominately White university serves as a backdrop in which, through **ethnographic interviews,** participants narrate their lived experiences. **Ethnography** is both a process and a product of describing culture. In *The Ethnographic Interview,* Spradley (1979) says that "[t]he essential core of this activity aims to understand another way of life from the native point of view" (p. iii).

This study focuses on the educational interactions between Black male teachers and students. This exclusive focus is important because of the language of crisis that is used to describe Black men. Black men are described as an "endangered species" (Gibbs 1988), "at risk" (American Council on Education 1988) and "living in a crisis situation" (Wiley 1990). This type of research seeks to serve as a bridge to understanding the sociocultural and political issues that intervene in the classroom between Black male teachers and Black male students. The research also adds to the growing body of educational research, which seeks to understand how culture intervenes at all levels of education.

The five Black male teachers interviewed for this study were representative of the eight Black male classroom teachers at the university. During each of the interviews open-ended questions were asked. Each interview was recorded. The recordings were later transcribed for analysis. Five cultural themes emerged during the discovery phase of data analysis. Spradley defines a cultural theme as "any cognitive principle, tacit to explicit, recurrent in a number of domains and serving as a relationship among subsystems of cultural meanings" (p. 186). This chapter is organized around the five themes that emerged in the discovery phase of data processing: (1) cultural languaging; (2) sociocultural responsibility; (3) recognition, association, and affiliation; (4) expectations and denials; and (5) authority and challenge.

Cultural Languaging

Many of the Black male teachers suggested that through specified features of **Black discourse,** broadly described here as *cultural languaging,* Black male teachers and students in general are able to make what Stewart (1995) calls "articulate contact." The notion of *cultural languaging* is an apt description of the active process of language. Language not only shares meaning but establishes relational connections by invoking culturally specific patterns of discourse—which may include specified jargon, cultural references, and ritualistic patterns of delivery and narrative construction. In *Black Language: The Research Dimension,* Taylor (1974) offers a definition of language that indicates cultural specificity:

> Language may be viewed as the collection of verbal symbols and rules used by individuals in a specified society to represent the concepts dictated by their world. In this definition, we see that language is a code which, as a structural system, is inextricably linked to and indeed dependent on both psychological (cognitive) and sociocultural controls. From this framework, **black language,** at least that produced in the United States, can be defined as the collection of lexical items transmitted by means

of phonological, syntactic, and supra-segmental systems used by black Americans to represent the conceptual systems underlying what might be loosely called "black culture." (pp. 146–47)

Taylor's definition underscores the notion of language as an agent of culture. The phrase *cultural languaging* used by Abram (participant 1) thus captures the performative nature of culture itself but marks it in linguistic terms. The phrase *articulate contact* also assumes a double meaning of both the act of using language as a tool of communication and the quality and specificity of that language used within a given speech community. Key features of Black discourse such as **code-switching**, signifying, and **call and response** were alluded to in the conversations as elements of cultural languaging.

Code-switching is often associated with bilingual communities in which speakers "alternate from one language to the other out of communicational convenience or preference" (Conklin and Lourie 1993, p. 161). Echoing Darder (1991), minority students enter the classroom with "bicultural identities" in which they negotiate their own cultural language with the standard language of the educational context, as a means of maintaining their **cultural identity** (p. xvi–xvii). In any speech community members distinguish nonmembers simply by the outsider's manner of expression (Conklin and Lourie 1993, p. 114). Joseph references code-switching when he talks about Black male students asking him to repeat lecture content. Joseph (participant 2):

> There are times when my Black male students ask me to repeat something that I have said in class. Often this is not because they didn't hear me the first time, but often I suspect that they want me to translate it in different terms. This could be considered paraphrasing, but I suspect that they want me to sort of re-code my message in Black English or at least with cultural references that they can relate to. This is not a problem when I think that it is sincere, but sometimes it comes as a sort of challenge to see if I can "talk the talk."

Alternating codes between Standard American English and Black English **Vernacular** with the Black teacher, or in the community of other cultural members, functions to communicate social information, to define and maintain social roles, and to establish cultural membership. Joseph's reference to a linguistic challenge by his Black male students—to "talk the talk"—suggests that code-switching is also used as a performative display of cultural membership. Smitherman (1994) defines "talk that talk" as the ability "to use the forms of African American Verbal Tradition in an intense, creative, dynamic, energetic style" (p. 221). This reference draws upon a connection between code-switching and signifying.

In *The Signifying Monkey*, Gates (1988) variously describes signifying as "a double-voice discourse" (pp. 50–51), "a rhetorical mode" (pp. 77–78), a form of "ritual insult" (pp. 85–86), and "indirect discourse" (p. 208). His referencing of Mitchell-Kernan's (1973) definition of *third-party signifying* and *metaphorical signifying* seems to capture the complexity of these multiple descriptives:

> In the metaphorical type of *signifying,* the speaker attempts to transmit his message indirectly and it is only by virtue of the hearer's defining the utterance as *signifying* that

the speaker's intent (to convey a particular message) is realized. In third-party signifying, the speaker may realize his aim only when the converse is true, that is, if the addressee fails to recognize the speech act as *signifying*. [Original emphasis] (Gates 1988, p. 85)

Signifying is popularly referred to as a game of verbal dueling, but it is also a coded language of misdirection.

In his interview Joseph alluded to a simple form of signifying that he uses. "Sometimes [students] enter class 20–30 minutes late and without missing a beat I say, 'You sho got to class early this morning. We're mighty happy that you decided to grace us with your appearance.' They usually smile embarrassingly and take their seat. Others who picked up on the signifying laugh and might tease them further." Smitherman (1977) would suggest that Joseph's simple form of signification has the intent "to put somebody in check, that is, make them think about [and], one hopes, correct their behavior" (pp. 120–21). The signifying in this phrase happens in the ironic indirection of language—"early" meaning "late," "happy" meaning "upset," and a *warm greeting* versus a *blatant admonishment*. Abram referred to his practice of signifying in the classroom as ***playful teasing***.

> Yet while it might appear to externalized sources, that there is a kind of free for all going on, there is an incredible amount of respect because, we would call it playful teasing. And that takes place too—I'll talk about anybody in class. I just talk about you sitting there. I'm gonna talk about you, now depending on how well you are culturally conditioned or deconstructed, you may feel that's really uncomfortable or, you are going to really engage in it, but when it's honest, students pick up on it. (Abram)

Abram speaks from a position of a veteran teacher reflecting on positive teaching experiences. His experiences and methods are valuable in understanding the multiple tools that Black male teachers use in negotiating culture in the classroom. He talks about how the technique of signifying and what he also calls "playful teasing" serve as teaching tools. He suggests that, as a Black male teacher, he uses this common form of cultural languaging to facilitate student learning and more specifically his relational dynamics with Black male students. "And then when you shift from the playful to the very serious they follow that and they take you seriously. Now that is all of those cultural ways of interacting. That is what Grandpapas do and what daddies do and uncles do" (Abram 1998). Abram's explication of this technique alludes to a form of narrative pedagogical discourse that is often used by the elders of cultural communities. Lessons are embedded within narratives, myths, fables, or allusion to specified characters and situations. The unfolding of the narrative reveals the text as a lesson in morals, ethics, and values.

The performative strategy *call and response* refers to a pattern of active participation that is the cornerstone of Black discourse. In *Talkin' and Testifyin'*, Smitherman (1977) offers a description of the practice. "The African-derived communication process of call-response may be briefly defined as follows: spontaneous verbal and non-verbal interaction between speakers and listeners in which all of the speaker's statement ('calls') are punctuated by expressions ('responses') from the listener" (p. 104). Joseph's comments offers a practical classroom example:

> Black students sometimes engage a sort of call and response in class. While I am talking they seem to be talking back at me. Sometimes in a mumbling under their breath sort of way and other times they are quite loud. Most often their comments are supportive and encouraging. Other times they are challenging, but I understand where that's coming from and I support it. (Joseph)

The practice of call and response is usually linked to the traditional Black church and reflects the interactive and spiritual relationship between the preacher and the congregation. The spiritual is not exclusively linked with the religious. In the classroom this may manifest itself as an invocation of the "spirit"—the fever of learning and knowledge.

Sociocultural Responsibility

Black teachers, in conversation, articulated a **sociocultural responsibility** to Black students in general. The responsibility was constructed as accountability for the care and welfare of Black male students. The Black community often has expectations of the Black teacher as focused on nurturing and educating with an understanding of the issues facing the Black community. In "Ethnicity, Instructional Communication and Classroom System," Collier and Powell (1990) echo this notion. They say, "cultural background affects attitude, beliefs and values about education, ideas about how classes ought to be conducted, how students and teachers ought to interact, and what types of relationships are appropriate for students and teachers" (p. 334).

Much of the talk in the interviews centered not only on the visible presence of Black men in the predominately White university and the need to support each other, but on historical inequities and inefficiencies in the lives of Black men and the Black community. Abram offered an overarching sense of how these issues affect his relationships with Black male students.

> I really am convinced that young Black men have no one to whom they are obligated. . . . That is critical to me. There are so many young Black males who are cultural orphans and therefore there is nobody there who says, "You now have my name, you better not disgrace it in the streets." Because for too many of them their fathers have already disgraced their own names and have not handed them on to their sons—or they have so disrespected the relationship that the son is dishonoring the name publicly. . . . I have to teach them to become socialized on the street. I absolutely have to. That's what daddies do. Mama worries about whether or not your underwear is clean. Daddy has to worry about where you taking it off. (Abram)

Abram claims a parental positionality as teacher: *in loco parentis*. Ultimately, he claims a role in the lives of his Black male students in which their academic and social behavior in the university becomes a reflection of his own presence and what he has taught them.

Malcolm (participant 3) outlines a similar notion of sociocultural responsibility. In his response he offers a shifting focus of responsibility from the specified relationship of the teacher and student to the responsibility that a student has to the larger Black community. He links the pedagogical site with the sociocultural imperative that education should remedy the ills of the past and can remedy the ailments of flailing Black communities:

> I think that a lot of Black male students are starting to recognize their unique posi-
> tion within higher education. I am not going to attribute it to one single event—like
> the Million Man March, or one person like a Colin Powell or a Louis Farrakhan, or
> Jesse Jackson. I think that young Black men in colleges and universities are starting
> to realize that if the problems in their communities and in their lives are to be
> solved—they are the ones who are going to have to do it. Many of them that I know
> are heavily into what they are doing—yeah they go out and have a good time—this
> is college, but I have seen a lot of Black men put their nose to the grindstone. I don't
> see them offering many excuses because they know that their own personal survival
> is at stake. (Malcolm)

Within his response Malcolm speaks to the reciprocity of responsibility of young Black men to their communities. He also alludes to how he is positioned, as a Black male teacher, in making that realization known. Joseph strengthens this notion by saying: "As a Black male teacher I think that it is ultimately my responsibility to offer the young Black men in my class a reality check. It was certainly done for me in my own education, both in the Black community and by Black male teachers in the predominately White institutions that I attended." Like Abram and Malcolm, he articulates an internal mandate that is centered in his lived experience within the Black community. If young Black men do not acknowledge their responsibilities to achieve, then ultimately it is the mandate of the Black male teacher to reinforce this understanding.

James (participant 4) mentions the special needs of Black male students when he uses the metaphor of wearing many hats, in order to address these varied needs and desires. He specifies his response particularly to Black male students:

> I think that when you are dealing with Black male students you have to be prepared to
> wear many hats. Black male students also understandably and justifiably come in with
> a lot more needs—and sometimes White students, because they may have been privi-
> leged, are sometimes very naive to certain issues of Black male students. Black male
> students have an acute sensitivity of their inadequacies, because they have been trained
> to learn to carry the burden. (James)

Black male students carry within their life scripts the socially constructed **at-risk** status of their academic potential and social worth. With public reports like *The Bell Curve*
(Hernstein and Murray 1994), the understanding of at-risk status conflates issues of access,
opportunity, class, and intellect into issues of race and potential. This is further complicated
by the publicly pathologized trope of the Black male. For the Black male student within the
predominately White university, self-doubt is compounded by a sense of isolation.

Recognition, Association, and Affiliation

Each of the Black male teachers I interviewed suggested that his orientation to Black male
students is different from his orientation to White students. This was primarily based in a
broad collectivizing notion of the varying cultural traditions that link and describe the Black
male's lived experiences. Malcolm's initial thoughts on this issue can be used to ground the
nature and purpose of this associative relationship:

> I may have a [Black male] student in my class who is from the South Side or West Side of Chicago. I am from the rural south. There are different things that we bring to the table. My students may listen to house music. I listen to Jazz, but the one common tie that we know that we have is that we know that we [are Black people who] like Black music. . . . We know that in our lives there is very strong stress on family and on being with friends and kicking it. Kicking it in different ways, but we kick it nonetheless. They know that when I am not in the classroom or at this desk—they know that I am somewhere—either in Chicago or St. Louis, Nashville or Memphis, having a good time. They know this and they respect it. (Malcolm)

He describes the regional differences between Black men as negotiated through an emphasis on the common threads of race and culture grounded in a shared appreciation of Black musical traditions. He suggests that their validation of these practices and beliefs gains him respect and potentially facilitates their teacher-student relationship.

It is within the very broad strokes of racial and gendered experiences that Black male teachers articulate a desire and a need to establish **recognition,** association, and affiliative bonds with Black male students within the predominately White university. They expressed these both as student-based needs, and as an extension of their social-cultural responsibility as Black male teachers. The three concepts of recognition, association, and **affiliation** are similar as relational concepts, but I would suggest that recognition and association are steps toward affiliation**,** which inevitably is an attempt to gain rewards and benefits such as respect. These three concepts are not unproblematic, for as relational concepts they are based in a socially constructed standard of cultural performance in which variation is often accompanied by social sanctions.

Recognition is the identification of sameness or familiarity. It may occur when Black male students enter the classroom and recognize that the teacher is another Black man. Yet, recognition is based in two orientations—either to confirm or disconfirm familiarity. These two phases might be constructed as a *physical assessment* and a *performative assessment.* The aspect of physical assessment includes the perceived ability to identify race, which is "supposedly distinguishable by inherited and invariable characteristics" (O'Sullivan, Hartley, Saunder, Montgomery, and Fiske 1994, p. 255). Inevitably these traits are reduced to variable features such as skin color, hair texture, body type, and facial features like eye color and nose and lip thickness. Certainly these are reductive, if not essentializing in nature, but that does not negate them as commonly used identifiers of race (Berry, Poortinga, Seagall, and Dasen 1992). Performative assessment, as the second phase in recognition, is the identification of a delimiting list of predetermined cultural behavioral patterns, some of which might be based in walk, talk, performative "cool," and the use of specified cultural references. The previous discussion of cultural languaging offers some of these performative features.

In his response Joseph offers a frame of the perceived desires that accompany his first contact with some Black male students. For him, the full and immediate benefits of recognition are not always possible—or at least, not unproblematic.

> Black male students walk into the class sometimes and see me. When they see that I am Black, they seem to relax. At first I perceive that as a good thing. Then I come to realize that they have relaxed themselves into complacency—excessive absences, lack of responsiveness and participation, poor test scores. I think that their assumption is

that because I am Black, that they can now sleep through the class and the "brother" is still going to give them an A. It is in those moments that I begin to question the relative benefits of them having a Black male teacher, but not for long. I see it as an unhappy, but necessary burden to enlighten these young brothers about what it means to be a student and what it means to be a brother. (Joseph)

He later spoke about the sometimes impossibility of developing a friendship with these Black male students, because they perceive him as being *wrong:* "I find that with the young brothers who enter the class with that attitude that we can never get to a comfortable place with each other. They see me as being wrong, because I don't give them a free ride. And to a certain extent that is fine with me; they don't have to like me in order to learn from me" (Joseph).

Within most of the conversations I had with Black male teachers, they made an immediate move from identifying specified features of their relationships with Black male students, to articulating how those relational dynamics are then translated into pedagogical strategies and culturally relevant teaching. For them culturally relevant teaching means engaging the social exchange of knowledge in the classroom with an articulated understanding of how culture has influenced curriculum, teaching practices, and social indoctrination—as well as how cultural experience shapes expectation. It is, as Ladson-Billings (1995) has formally described, a critical "pedagogy that empowers students intellectually, socially, emotionally, and politically by using referents to impart knowledge, skills, and attitudes" (p. 18).

Like Joseph, James poignantly describes the tensions that exist between Black male teachers and Black male students. He expounds on the benefits of empathy while he strategizes on how finding common points of entry is a method to engage all students.

I think that within every relationship there is a common ground and there is a quake of difference that can become a point of conflict and also a moment of urgency. I think that the common ground when understood by both persons is an open door possibility for better communication in that relationship. I think that common ground when it is understood well is what should allow you, a moment of essentialism, to come in and talk to this Black male student and say, "We both know—in essence before we even talk. We know what's up. We understand what's coming down here." Then we start talking, in the middle of the conversation. (James)

James's response captures the serious complexities of Black male teacher-student relationships. The "quake of difference" that he refers to can certainly be the difference between a physical or racial assessment and the performative or cultural assessment. It can also refer to the regional or generational differences that Malcolm outlined in his response. What James suggests is that those "quakes of difference" can acknowledge their shared membership in a dominant racial group with differing cultural experiences. Yet, the "moment of essentialism" is those times when they assume certain knowledge based on their historical "field of experience" as Black men in the United States of America. In such cases acknowledged difference is overshadowed by perceived similarity.

Recognition enables association. Abram constructs the notion of ***intuitive interventions*** as an intense form of association between Black male teachers and Black male students. His notion of intuitive interventions is really recognition of behavioral shifts and the motivation to question the significance of those changes:

Intuitive interventions are built on family relationships. Many of our young people, especially the young Black men, are used to their Mama's doing that to them, but they are not used to men doing it. And I find myself very valuable as a teacher when I perform an intuitive intervention. "Come here, what's wrong? *Nothing's wrong.*" "Something's wrong, now sit down and tell me what's going on." *"Ain't nothing going on."* "Well how come you look like such and such." *"Well, here's what's happening."* You can see that happening in the classroom. (Abram)

Abram equates the notion of ***intuitive intervention*** with female intuition, or the intimate sense of knowing that mothers have for their children. He suggests that the close scrutiny of a mother for her child becomes a form of pedagogical identification. This is the technique used when the Black male teacher notices changes in the behavior of his Black male students. Intuitive intervention, as Abram constructs it, is grounded in intracultural communication in which the cultural performative knowledge of young Black men in the given situation is used to gain a sense of what is happening.

The process of recognition and association may lead to affiliation. Several different theoretical approaches seek to explain **group affiliation** that might reflect the varying logics used by the Black teachers interviewed. The psychodynamic perspective (Freud), the sociobiological perspective (Darwin), social-comparison theorists such as Leon Festinger, and the social exchange theory as articulated by Kelley and Thibaut are but a few (Forsyth 1983). Most of the responses given by the Black male teachers were grounded in these varying perspectives. They used psychological needs, sociocultural desire, information-seeking, and social exchange as undergirding logics. Each response echoed not only benefits—such as positive feelings, a sense of empathy, and respect—but also the costs such as additional time, personal challenge, and the rewards of focused intuitive interventions.

Expectations and Denials

Throughout the interviews with Black male teachers there was the notion that their relationships with Black male students are filled with expectations. Black male teachers expressed that these expectations are not only emergent or intrinsic to the sociocultural dynamic with Black male students, but they are sometimes formalized as mandates of the course and interspliced in the course syllabus. Other times they were socially negotiated in the development of the class. James describes his approach as the direct method.

Your syllabus has to do it, and what you say from day one at the beginning of the class, because you can't afford to wait until week five or week ten. It is important that people know exactly where you are coming from and that you have already established [the tone and focus of the course] and that there are no turn-abouts or twists. (James)

He literally uses the syllabus and the first meeting days of the class, as do many teachers, to articulate not only the course content and procedures, but the tone of the course. He suggests that this serves multiple purposes. First, it gives students a sense of the game plan by clearly establishing a direction of the course that will not be altered. Second, it informs students so that they can makes choices based upon their own desires and comforts.

James focuses on Black students to suggest that they bring in a set of expectations that are twofold. They expect, as do all students, to gain a certain knowledge or information from the course, but when encountering the Black male teacher they also have expectations about methods of teaching as well as the perspective of the Black male teacher on the subject matter and in response to their Black male presence:

> They are going to polarize you [the Black teacher]. They want to know from day one, "which one are you going to fall into." I think that it is important that you convey that, "I am not a sell out and that's for sure" and I would rather have them know that I am committed to culture. I do understand where I am coming from and I want them to be as committed to culture as I am. (James)

When James says, "I do understand where I am coming from," his talk has moved away from a discussion of course content to an articulation of cultural knowledge. In the Black community, "to know where you come from" is an expression that positions one's centrality in Black cultural traditions, to remembering one's roots and to using that history as a guiding impulse in one's daily life. Not to do so is to be "a sellout" (or "to be wrong"). James uses the syllabus and the first days of class to state his commitment to talking about embodying Black cultural traditions in ways that are meaningful and validating to both of their lived experiences, as teacher and as students.

Throughout Malcolm's and Abram's interviews they referenced these historical and community-generated desires as orienting impulses for their relationships with Black students in general and Black male students in particular. Nat (participant 5) also uses a Black cultural truism to first deconstruct the question, and then to construct his own response based on the same truism:

> Well, if you are getting at the question . . . talking about that old saying that all of the folks from my generation heard, when your parents said, that "as a Black person you had to be better. It's not good enough just to be good, as a Black person you have to be better." I certainly did hear that a lot from my folks. And I try not to impose that on my students because I think that—I have often felt that it was an unfair expectation put upon me. I understood the reason for it, but I think ultimately it is too easy for that to become more destructive than constructive . . . so I try not to do that. (Nat)

The parental logic that he refers to suggests that as a Black person, one enters any socially constructed and primarily White arena at a deficit, because of racial prejudice, which is often manifested as lowered expectations. This is also linked to lack of access, lack of resources, and lack of experience.

This parental safeguard crosses lines of cultural experience and class. The desire to have students "be better than" overprepares minority children and children of working-class parents for the social, cultural, and academic challenges that they will face. Yet, as Nat articulates his disdain for this practice, he also concedes his own desire to prepare and challenge his Black students in the same way:

> There is a part of me that always wants the kids to really shine—to distinguish themselves. Particularly, when I recognize in them the capability to do it. So, I suppose that

in a certain subtle way, I do. I really want them to succeed—by saying that I want them to shine, that means that they are going to distinguish themselves as being somewhat set apart from the norm. So yes, I guess I do expect a little bit more of Black students. I would hope that it's one of those situations where you have to expect more in order for them to do more—and it's not that you are setting up a scenario for their failure, by inflating the expectations, but yes I think that maybe, I do, to be perfectly honest. (Nat)

Nat's hesitance reflects a kind of tension between the challenge of the Black community, which he perceives as sometimes being "unfair," and his understanding of how it serves as motivation.

Among others, James reflects on a student's expectation of him to be a **cultural worker** in the classroom. In many ways his response identifies the nature of what most Black male students expect of him as a Black male teacher:

I remember that I had one class when I had one student that came to me after we had openly talked about his story in class. He came to me at the end of class and said, "Well I wished that you had been more aggressive about telling the White students something about culture here." I think that it was a valid point. I felt that what he was saying to me is that "because you are a Black instructor, that should also be your role in discussing these issues." (James)

His student wanted him to be "more aggressive" on issues of culture. For students, being a cultural worker might mean that Black (male) teachers are expected to be actively engaged in the critical reading of culture in ways that not only validate the historically oppressed but also unearth systems of oppression that operate on multiple and various levels even in the classroom.

Authority and Challenge as Relational Elements

Most of the Black male teachers made references to points of conflict and tension with young Black men in the classroom. This tension was described as a challenge of teacher authority or as playing a "race card" in which the teacher is challenged on their racial or political ideology. Malcolm has alluded to a form of tough love that he has to practice with Black male students who enter his class "lazy, lackadaisical," assuming some privilege with the Black male teacher. James also spoke about the need for Black male teachers to be cultural workers. Abram further defines this behavior not as assumed privilege, but as a challenge and test of authority that is intrinsic to the maturing young male in any society:

I have seen almost inevitably, a confrontation in which testing takes place by the late adolescent towards himself and the Black male teacher. That happens in the classroom when they stop turning in their work. That happens in the classroom when they start sitting in the back with gansta posses. That happens when they start coming into the class late or not showing up. (Abram)

Abram's observation may be typical descriptions of the performative displays of any young student in the classroom with any teacher. Yet, the difference that he articulates is in the perceived intention of the student. The young Black male student performs what McLaren (1985) and Aronowitz and Giroux (1991) might discuss as resistance.

The typical construction of **resistance** in **critical pedagogy** suggests that students are denying the educational system in which their lived experience is not reflected. Their behavior can be constructed as a form of negative resistance characterized by rejection and the ensuing problematic outcomes—conflict, absenteeism, failure, dropping out, and so on. Abram suggests that the Black male student is not performing resistance to a lack of inclusion, for through the process of recognition, association, and affiliation with the Black male teacher, he has already established some degree of affirmation of his racial and cultural experience in the classroom. The performance of resistance by the Black male student may be a ritualized performance in which he seeks a form of intracultural acknowledgment, which would further the affiliative bond with the Black male teacher. The challenge is a test of caring:

> That is a very cultural thing—more so with men than women. And when that confrontation happens I have had to sometimes say—"you are not welcome right now at my table. You are not welcome in my house. Your behavior is not up to what it should be; therefore change it before you come back." That is a major issue and the more difficult the relationship of a young man to his biological father—the more likely that confrontation is going to be big time—because they are, as most adolescents, looking for some consistency. Once that confrontation has occurred and has been successfully negotiated, academic performance goes up. I have seen it. I have had those confrontations and then two years later they are applying for graduate school. (Abram)

Abram's response to students' challenges operates on multiple levels. First, he once again invokes a familial, if not biblical reference, of not being "welcome to the table" or "in my house." Second, his response also calls into question cultural performative etiquette of adult-child relationships, in terms of respecting elders, as well as the performative etiquette of the classroom.

This response resonates with the concept of **emergent culture.** Emergent culture refers to how cultural norms are negotiated and established within a given context. Within the classroom there is an emergent culture in which teachers and students negotiate the norms and standards of that given context. This culture may be in alignment with the already existing policies and procedures of the educational system. However, it may also refer to the emergent culture of Black male teachers negotiating and outlining performative behaviors in the classroom: what will and will not be allowed, or what will and will not be sanctioned. Abram's response to student challenge is a move toward further establishing the culture of the classroom. This may address what James referred to as the test of **authenticity**, which takes place in the classroom between Black male teachers and Black male students:

> Authentic would be a word that I would use. Authenticity based on integrity or at least perceived integrity, and obviously I think that perceived integrity should be real integrity. By integrity a person communicating with you has to believe that what you say comes from the heart—that you care about it, that you have a vested interest in it, that you have something more at stake than just your own personal interest—or at least that your personal interest is also them. I think that has to be perceived on a consistent level at all times, almost without fail—because the minute that you fail or slip out of it, it deconstructs the whole thing and complicates your whole image, your whole being. (James)

In this way James supports Abram's notion that Black male students challenge and perform resistance as a means of gaining ground, of gaining a deeper understanding of the Black male teacher. They seek to gain an understanding of the authentic character of the Black male teacher and that is perceived as coming through in moments of strife and challenge. Authenticity is not defined in this case as "to be real or Afrocentric" as it has been in the struggle of many Black intellectuals when relating back to the Black community (Banks 1996). The "real" in authenticity is related to sincerity and consistency of caring. It is within these complicated negotiations of authority, challenge, and authenticity as relational elements between Black males that Black male teachers attempt to address both the content of the course and the needs of their students.

Negotiation, as it has been constructed in this study, is not necessarily the result of conflict, but it stems from the awareness of cultural similarities in a nontraditional cultural space. This negotiation includes awareness, acknowledgment, accommodation, and assurance of the significance and value of difference and shared experiences. Ultimately, the Black male teachers interviewed for this study articulated an active process and awareness of the negotiation of cultural identity in the classroom with Black male students.

Intercultural Implications

The core concern of *intercultural communication* is a close examination of the elements of culture that most influence communication when members of two different cultures encounter each other. While this study focuses on what is presumed to be intracultural communication, it allows a focus on the following implications in intercultural contexts. First, we must examine in further detail more expansive notions of *culture* that extend beyond the presumption of shared race and ethnicity. Next, the definitional assumption of intracultural communication should be explored. The issues expressed in this chapter both confirm and test notions of difference within culture (Sitaram and Cogdell 1976). Third, the five categories that structured this essay can also be used as emergent themes in exploring communication in intercultural contexts. A further implication: the classroom is always a cultural arena. Last, culturally relevant teaching is a challenge for all teachers. The classroom is always and already a cultural site in which multiple and varying cultures negotiate ideas and their specified ways of being in the world.

Note

This chapter is an excerpt from a much longer work in which Black male teachers and Black male students were both interviewed. Permission to copy this chapter should be sought from the publisher. Additional information related to this project could be addressed to the author at *abryant@calstatela.edu*

References

American Council on Education, Commission of the State. 1988. *One-third of a nation: A report of the commission on minority participation in education and American life.* Applied Social Research Methods, Series 20. Newbury Park, Calif.: Sage.

Aronowitz, S., and H. Giroux. 1991. *Postmodern education: Politics, culture and social criticism.* Minneapolis: University of Minnesota Press.

Banks, W. W. 1996. *Black intellectuals.* New York: W. W. Norton.

Berry, J. W., L. H. Poortinga, M. H. Seagall, and P. R. Dasen. 1992. *Cross-cultural psychology: Research and applications*. New York: Cambridge University Press.

Collier, M. J., and R. G. Powell. 1990. Ethnicity, instructional communication and classroom systems. *Communication Quarterly* 38: 334–49.

Conklin, N. F., and M. A. Louire. 1993. *A host of tongues: Language communities in the United States*. New York: Free Press.

Darder, A. 1991. *Culture and power in the classroom: A critical foundation for bicultural education*. New York: Bergin and Garvey.

Forsyth, D. 1983. *An introduction to group dynamics*. Monterey, Calif.: Brooks/Cole Publishing.

Gates, H. L. 1988. *The signifying monkey: A theory of African-American literary criticism*. New York: Oxford University Press.

Gibbs, J. T. (Ed.). 1988. *Young, Black and male in America: An endangered species*. Dover, Mass.: Auburn House.

Hernstein, R. J., and C. Murray. 1994. *The Bell curve: Intelligence and class in American life*. New York: Free Press.

Ladson-Billings, G. 1995. Toward a theory of culturally relevant pedagogy. *American Educational Research Journal* 32 (3): 159–65.

McLaren, P. 1985. The ritual dimensions of resistance: Clowning and symbolic inversion. *Journal of Education* 167 (2): 84–97.

O'Sullivan, T., J. Hartley, D. Saunder, M. Montgomery, and J. Fiske. 1994. *Key concepts in communication and cultural studies*. New York: Routledge.

Sitaram, K. S., and R. T. Cogdell. 1976. *Foundations of intercultural communication*. Columbus, Ohio: Merrill.

Smitherman, G. 1977. *Talkin' and testifyin*. Boston: Houghton Mifflin.

———. 1994. *Black talk: Words and phrases from the hood to the amen corner*. Boston: Houghton Mifflin.

Spradley, J. P. 1979. *The Ethnographic interview*. New York: Holt, Rinehart and Winston.

Stewart, J. 1995. *Language as articulate contact: A post-semiotic account of the nature of language*. New York: State University of New York Press.

Taylor, O. L. 1974. Black language: The research dimension. In J. L. Daniel (Ed.), *Black communication: Dimensions of research and instruction* (pp. 145–59). New York: SCA.

KEY TERMS

affiliation	ethnographic interview
at-risk	ethnography
authenticity	group affiliation
Black discourse	in loco parentis
Black language	intuitive intervention
call and response	performative assessment
code-switching	physical assessment
critical pedagogy	playful teasing
cultural identity	recognition
cultural languaging	resistance
cultural negotiations	sociocultural responsibility
cultural worker	vernacular
emergent culture	

REVIEW AND DISCUSSION QUESTIONS

1. To what degree does the shared dominant culture of these Black male teachers and their Black male students, separated by issues of hierarchy, power, dominance, geographical origin, and familial ties, signify similar issues that would be faced in an intercultural context?

2. How would you apply the five themes that emerged through the interviews to your understanding of intercultural communication?

3. To what degree do you see schools and the process of education as a negotiation of culture and cultural knowledge?

4. How would you define the notion of *cultural knowledge?*

5. How would you define the notion of *culturally relevant teaching* as applied across borders of race and ethnicity?

6. What is the relationship between the notion of *culturally relevant teaching* and the concept of *emergent culture?*

"Perpetual Foreigner": In Search of Asian Americans' Identity and Otherness

Rueyling Chuang

LEARNING OBJECTIVES

After reading this chapter, students will be able to

- understand that cultural identity is multifaceted and multidimensional;
- explain Asian Americans' fluid cultural identity and double consciousness;
- describe Asian Americans' struggle to cross cultural boundaries and their feelings of otherness; and
- identify some of the common problems Asian Americans face, such as trying to balance American and Asian cultures.

There was one example . . . when I was working in a Chinese restaurant. Every once in a while, they [the customers] would speak like, "I n-e-e-d s-o-m-e w-a-t-e-r." I tried really hard not to be rude. I said, "I speak English; do you know what I mean?" and they will say "Oh, oh, sorry," you know. They assume that because I am working at a Chinese restaurant, I am just a "fresh off-the-boat" kind of person. They talk slowly, and appear shocked when I reply that I can speak English.

—Interviewee

> *The question in this research is one of identity: Who am I perceived to be when I com-municate with others? What does it mean to be a "perpetual foreigner" in one's native country? My identity is very much tied to the ways in which others speak to me and the ways in which society represents my interests.*
>
> —Thomas Nakayama (2000, p. 14)

Nakayama's quote exemplifies Asian American identity and **double consciousness.** A brief examination of current intercultural communication identity studies indicates that most researchers do not go beyond theoretical discussion (e.g., Gudykunst and Ting-Toomey 1988; Ting-Toomey 1989); indeed, little empirical research has been conducted in this area. Moreover, the few published empirical studies dealing with Asian American identity tend to be quantitative in nature or emphasize ethnic group comparisons (e.g., Porter and Washington 1993). Although they might present an overall general picture of Asian American identity, these studies tend to be monolithic and imply a monolithic reality. The literature does not manifest an empathic understanding of the identity of Asian Americans.

The notion of dichotomy is a prevalent theme in most intercultural communication comparison literature. Hall's (1966, 1976) high context (Asian) versus low context (North American) culture and Hofstede's (1984) individualistic/collectivistic cultures schema exemplify this dualism. Altman and Gauvain's (1981) explanation of this (cultural) identity-communality dialectic reflects the dualistic dimension of individualism-collectivism and power distance (i.e., Eastern culture tends to produce a greater power distance, while Western culture has less power distance). However, this polarization of Eastern and Western culture might not explain how Asian Americans communicate and how they identify themselves in this culturally and demographically diverse society. As Collier and Thomas (1988) state, **cultural identity** is a dynamic, fluid process assumed *a priori* to have "scope, salience, and intensity" (p. 116). They argue that it is oversimplifying to say it is based on nationality.

In addition, in the past ten years most (mainstream) intercultural communication textbooks (e.g., Lustig and Koester 1993; Samovar and Porter 1997) seem to emphasize comparing and contrasting cultural variables. Asian American voices either do not receive much attention in textbooks, or there are only a few token pages that relate to Asian Americans. It is quite problematic to assume that the discussion of, say, Asians' accultural/encultural process can be applied to Asian Americans. Asian Americans' *lifeworld (lebenswelt)* tends to be **rhizomatic** or on the borderline; they do not project themselves as Asians nor do they perceive themselves to be part of the White mainstream culture. Even when the literature does discuss Asian Americans, it tends to be fictional (e.g., Kingston 1976; Tan 1989) or mentioned in self-reflexive, essay-type articles (e.g., Chen 2000; Nakayama 2000). More qualitative empirical research that enlightens our empathic understanding of Asian Americans' *lifeworld* warrants the attention of intercultural communication researchers. The crux of this chapter, then, is to describe Asian Americans' lived experience and their *lifeworld.*

Asian Americans' Cultural Identity

According to Resnick (1990), **misperception**s of Asian Americans identified by non-Asian survey takers include the idea that Asians tend to be "passive or unassertive" and "inscrutable."

It is assumed that all Asians "are of a common culture, having a uniform ethnicity" (p. 24). The passive or submissive Asian stereotype is a dominant theme in American mainstream society's portrayal of Asian (American) women (see, for example, Hagedorn 1994; Ling 1989).

Resnick (1990) also found that the most prevalent core values of (Eastern) Asian Americans (i.e., Chinese, Japanese, Koreans, Filipinos) are in "strong support of and loyalty to the family, great emphasis on achievement (especially academic) and emphasis on a strong work ethic. Other core cultural values shared by Asian Americans include compliance with parental expectations; cultural identity; obedience and respect for authority; and respect for elders" (p. 25).

Resnick's survey is one of the few studies that attempts to increase our understanding of Asian Americans and to compare how Asian Americans perceive themselves as well as how non-Asians see Asian Americans. However, Resnick's study also exemplifies the tendency to lump Asians and Asian Americans together (see also, for example, Fernandez 1991). Resnick's findings suggest that "Asians are more Asian than American"; the findings above indicate that Asian Americans emphasize "obedience and respect for authority" (p. 25). One wonders whether an Asian American who grew up in the states would regard himself or herself as "obedient" or as more Asian than American, as presented by Resnick.

Resnick's study exemplifies the conflation of Asian and Asian American. As Nakayama (2000) states, the "conflation of Asian [American] differences" and "orientalism" is deeply rooted in American cultural traditions. The American mass media (e.g., films) and society in general often overlook the dissimilarities among Asian American ethnicities.

Strangers

Nakagawa (1995) writes that two of the prevalent themes in the literature dealing with Asian Americans are the "stranger" and "migration" metaphors. The notion of Asian Americans as (perpetual) **strangers** (see, for example, Takaki's [1989] *Strangers from a Different Shore: A History of Asian Americans*), underscores the central role of **Eurocentricity** and the Asian American as "the other" in U.S. society. The migration metaphor signifies the state of **dis-/belonging:** there is no place for Asian Americans to call home.

Kazmi (1994) contends that the immigrant population in recent years has become very different from the European immigrant population of the eighteenth-century colonial era in terms of race, culture, and language. Thus, an immigrant (non-European) is perceived as a person who cannot "be easily assimilated" and who remains "a perpetual stranger" (p. 66). This perpetual stranger disturbs our way of life not because he or she will destroy it in a physical sense; rather, he or she disturbs "our" (i.e., Euro-Americans') tranquility just by proximity, by living next to us and working next to us. Coincidentally, Williams's book, *Strangers Next Door* (1964), indicates that people of color (e.g., Black or other minority members) are perceived as the strangers who are living close to us ("us" meaning White European Americans).

In accord with Kazmi's notion of the perpetual stranger, Chan (1991) describes Asian immigrant's *Erfarung* (lived experience) in the United States as that of **"perpetual foreigners."** Asian immigrants can never be completely absorbed into the American mainstream society because of their non-White (or non-European) origins and distinct physical attributes. In a similar vein, Wei (1993) found that the question Asian Americans are most often asked is, "Where are you really from?" The question itself suggests that Asian Americans are strangers in the states (see also Aguilar-San Juan 1994). It is as though "European Americans seldom accept an American locality" for an answer (p. 44). Wei further explains that although Asian Americans feel and behave like Americans and share American cultural values and social norms, most of their "fellow countrymen" perceive them "as unwelcome foreigners." Asian Americans are "excluded by mainstream society, they were in American culture, but not of it" (p. 45). Wei's statement clearly represents the sense of **otherness** and the sense of the perpetual stranger/foreigner that the Asian American might feel toward himself or herself.

Intergenerational Conflicts

Chen (2000) contends that Chinese American women experience a double exclusion, both from mainstream American **hegemonic** culture because of their race, gender, and ethnic heritage, and from their (first-generation) Asian communities due to the clash between their Americanization and traditional Chinese values and norms. Chen also suggests that the intergenerational conflicts between the American-born Chinese and their first-generation immigrant parents "are incommensurate" and "there is no shared discourse" in which the conflicting outlooks of life can be discussed (p. 9, see also Chen 1992). Chen's explanation can apply to other (second-generation) Asian Americans, be they Filipinos, Japanese Americans, or others.

Double Consciousness and Identity

Recently, Asian American communication scholars have employed W. E. B. DuBois's double consciousness concept to scrutinize ethnic identity in their own bicultural *lebenswelt* (Chen 2000; Ling 1989; Nakayama 2000) and the discourse produced by Asian Americans (e.g., Maxine Hong Kingston's [1976] "most widely studied work in American literature on college campuses" [Chen 2000, p. 3]—*The Woman Warrior*). DuBois (1989) argued that Blackness and Black consciousness were significant components of Black reality—they were the essence of being Black in America. DuBois defined double consciousness as the myopia of a dual or bipolar consciousness or identity, which produces a fundamental alienation in Black people; double consciousness causes Black people (and, one could claim, members of any minority group) to view themselves both through their own eyes and through the eyes of others. This self-consciousness of **alienation** is problematic because it embodies both self-disregard and self-liberation. The result is a self in search of its own identity and fulfillment through the presence of the other.

To DuBois, double consciousness not only accounts for the double bind and ethnic identity of African Americans, it can also be extended to other minority groups (e.g., Chinese immigrants). Ling (1989) writes that American society maintains its White male hegemony by devaluing those who are "the others" (e.g., women, non-White ethnic groups, physically challenged people, people with a different sexual orientation). Ling argues that minorities develop a "double consciousness" or positive awareness of themselves and an awareness of the negative perceptions that the hegemonic society has of them.

To Chen (2000), the identity of Asian Americans is not an "either/or choice, but a both/and transformation, a new kind of integration or sometimes a lack of integration, of two cultural lifeworlds" (p. 8). Chen asserts that although Asian Americans might "look like" Asians, they differ from Asians in their thinking. Chen used metaphors such as "**double vision**" (p. 8) and "double bind" (p. 10) to describe **bicultural** people's, such as Chinese Americans', paradoxical lived experience and ambiguous cultural identity. Chen's (2000) illustration of double vision for bicultural individuals coincides with DuBois's double consciousness. Both concepts can be used to gain situated understanding *(verstehen)* with respect to multiple cultural insights and bicultural identity. They help to construct meanings and increase awareness of the plurality of our cultural interpretations and practices.

DuBois's double consciousness and Chen's explanation of Asian/Chinese Americans' double vision lived experience illustrate how the dualities of low context/high context and individualism/collectivism fail to contribute to an understanding of people who are trapped in two cultures. Cross-cultural theorists (e.g., Samovar and Porter 1997; Ting-Toomey 1989) proceed from a definition of U.S. culture (North American culture or Western culture) as low-context and individualistic in nature, whereas Asians (e.g., Chinese culture or Eastern culture) are on the other end of the spectrum—high-context and collectivistic in nature. It is important to ask: Which ethnic groups in the United States are we talking about? Who are the Northern Americans?

The sense of identity within the Asian American community is another important issue. While Asian Americans' physical attributes remain similar, they do not share the same lived experiences and identities. One wonders whether an Asian American who grew up in the United States and speaks English exclusively and a "new" Asian immigrant who can barely speak English are able to communicate with each other, and to what extent they can identify with each other. On American college campuses, one frequently finds that students from various Asian countries and Asian Americans who grew up in the United States retain social communication practices that create barriers working against their ability to act together.

Nakayama (2000) describes the dis/orientation in Asian/Asian American ethnic groups as a dialectical process. He contends that Asian Americans are as diverse as Asians, and rejects the notion of "orientals" and how they are often categorized as "other" in U.S. culture (p. 13). Nakayama argues that differences in the lived world of Asian Americans in many regions of the United States are often overlooked. In response to the perception of Asians-in-America as "perpetual foreigners" (Chan 1991, p. 187), Nakayama poses the question: What is the Asian American's identity? What does it mean to be a "perpetual foreigner" (due to physical attributes) in one's own native country? These compelling questions have not been addressed in most of the mainstream and hegemonic intercultural studies of the past decade, whether researchers employed the positivistic/covering law approach, the humanistic/rule-grounded approach, or systems theory.

Participants

This study invites Asian Americans to freely discuss their lived experiences in group and individual interviews. The group and individual interviews seek to probe the epiphany of Asian Americans' lived experiences through their narratives (i.e., storytelling). The study seeks to understand and provide an explanation of how Asian Americans project themselves (e.g., being marginalized citizens in the United States) and in what manner they perceive how people from the hegemonic culture see them. Through their reflexive anecdotal illumination, the essence of double consciousness unfolds.

Eleven Asian Americans participated in this study. Although all of the participants are Asian American, each comes from a different family background and has his or her own distinct lifeworld: three participants are Filipino Americans; two Korean Americans; three are biracial (one is of Japanese and Euro-American descent, another of Pakistani and Filipino descent, and still another of Korean and Norwegian descent); two are Taiwanese/Chinese American (one was born in the states, the other came to the United States when he was fourteen years old); another respondent is a third-generation Japanese American who grew up in Hawaii. These eleven respondents were purposely selected because of the diversity of their family heritage and backgrounds, to better explore the extent to which their lifeworlds and identities emerge.

Results of Thematization

Several recurring themes emerged from focus group and individual interviews (which lasted at least fifty minutes each). Although the transcripts are organized according to different themes, it is important to note that these themes are not mutually exclusive. They intertwine with each other and are mutually related. For example, feelings of mixture, of being in-between and different are interrelated. One caveat is that there is an enormous gray area among the themes. One cannot use a cookie cutter to arbitrarily differentiate each theme. The themes are not ordered according to the frequency of their mention, nor according to some sense of importance ascribed to them by the researcher; rather, order is based on connections made in the interviews. Long quotes are cited as thick description(s) of these Asian Americans' multifaceted lived experiences.

Theme 1: Mixture/Difference/Balance

As mentioned above, certain themes are interconnected. Thus, to classify them into different categories may prove unfeasible. The sense of being **different,** and being balanced between two different cultures, is a prevalent theme apparent in every interview. As one of the participants said:

> I realize I am different, I am not going to be like them. It is like a mixture growing up as a Japanese Buddhist who is also an American. I grew up as a Japanese. In a way, I have a strong sense of deferring to a man. For many years I rebelled, but [now I see] a balancing act, negotiation, between the traditional Japanese value of the individualist twentieth century of the [American] gender role.

How Asian Americans perceive themselves can change as time goes on. One participant describes how she perceived herself when she was young:

> When I was younger, I wished so much that I could look much more Japanese. When I was thirteen, I wished that I would look White. I wanted to be one or the other. Uh, now I am, like, looking different.

A similar self-denial and self-acceptance was described by another participant, who is also a biracial child:

> When I was younger, but not because of the environment, I never liked my name, never liked the way I looked—I was thinking about getting a nose job [laugh], but now I don't really care, I did not want to be different. . . . or my mom always packed a lunch with Filipino food and it smelled and other kids' lunch did not.

However, balancing two different cultural heritages does not necessarily cause confusion. As one of the participants stated:

> I don't remember, I don't even remember. I just grew up speaking English. My parents are basically a mixture, ya, a mixture. I am never confused or have trouble.

Asian Americans' growing-up experience can also be represented by another participant, who recalled that when she was in the first grade, the teacher told her mother to have her discontinue her [once a week] Japanese lessons and,

> on top of that, I had to go to speech classes, because they said that I had an accent. I couldn't pronounce "r" and "l" correctly, um, that was much more destructive for me. I would have been much more adjusted growing up if I had been able to speak both Japanese and English. They said it's gonna be confusing, but I don't think that at all.

It is also important to note that Asian Americans' identity is fluid, rather than static. One participant talked about her mixed identity and her growing up experience as a third-generation Asian American and her identity being situational:

> [My identity is like a] hybridization, having mixed identity, layers, like my identity is fluid. Depending on the context, it can be Japanese . . . or your identity is contextual—fluidity and the idea of identity being contextual.

A similar example of "code" switching or situational self-presentation by Asian Americans can be found in the following quote from another participant:

> Especially when I am with Chinese friends, they would treat me like an American and sometimes when I am with Americans, I would act like a Taiwanese . . . maybe, uh, different from how an average American would act. I would act differently in different situations. Because of this mixture, I would be perceived as different from their point of view.

Theme 2: Clash and Struggle

Living in two distinct although not mutually exclusive cultures can sometimes create problems, as one of the participants reported:

I don't think I've found my balance. There is a "clash" because when I grow up in Taiwan, I already have this sort of ideas and assumptions, even some of the ideas have disappeared, but there are some fundamental ideas that are still there, they don't fit very well with the American culture. . . . my cousin [on the other hand], has no concept whatsoever [because he has no recollection of Taiwan]; for people in that case, because they identify themselves as Americans, there would not be a clash, because of the upbringing.

In a similar vein, being raised in the parents' family heritage can also influence how Asian Americans **struggle** and negotiate with their own identity.

Cultural differences, the bi-raciality, we have that too (between Pakistan and Philippines), . . . growing up, we have to struggle with that. In your heritage and your own environment . . . usually there is something common around me.

The struggle between the traditional first-generation immigrant and the Americanized second-generation Asian American can be best illustrated by the following statement:

My father is a strong religious Moslem, and he holds on so much to the culture and religion. . . . Like mixing with opposites, it's a taboo, it's hard for him to accept that, because you don't want to, in a way, become completely, totally "Americanized," so a lot has to do with that kind of struggle.

Theme 3: Misperception: Being Mistaken for Other Co-cultural Groups

A common experience Asian Americans encounter is being mistaken for belonging to a different co-cultural group. As one of the participants commented:

I think it's weird, if they notice like, if you are of Asian descent, they just assume that you are Chinese or Japanese or Korean. They just don't differentiate.

The fact that Asian Americans tend to be lumped together (negatively) was discussed by a participant who is a biracial child of Filipino and Middle Eastern parents and has been called "Chink," a racial slur that aims to label Chinese in a condescending way. This illustrates that people tend to assume that "if you are an Asian, then you must be a Chinese" regardless of how you look or what your family heritage is. The conflation of Asian Americans with other ethnic groups can be exemplified by mistaking Filipino Americans for Hispanics:

It's just like those instances, because Filipinos are of Hispanic descent, so a lot of time when I go to the store, people follow me. People don't really understand, because I am a person of color.

Sometimes, the conflation and misperception can occur among "the assumed same ethnic group." For example, oftentimes Asian Americans are mistaken for, or treated as, Asians.

Also, Asian Americans are often treated as international students on college campuses. One of the participants mentioned that "they [the White American students] are treating me as an international student and they don't even realize it."

Another story illustrates how Asian Americans' language proficiency can be discredited simply by how they look. One participant said:

> There was one example in point, when I was working in a Chinese restaurant. Every once in a while, they [the customers] would speak like, "I n-e-e-d s-o-m-e w-a-t-e-r." I tried really hard not to be rude. I said, "I speak English; do you know what I mean?" and they will just say "Oh, oh, sorry," you know. They assume that because I am working at a Chinese restaurant, I am "fresh off-the-boat." They talk slowly and appear shocked when I replied that I can speak English.

Another common experience shared by most Asian American participants is that people tend to be surprised at their American accent. It is as though their American accent is unexpected, while if one is a Euro-American, then one's American accent is automatically assumed. As one of the participants described her story:

> A couple of years ago, my cousin came to visit; we went to the Gap, and I remember the sales lady came up to me and said, "Your accent is so good."

Theme 4: "Outsider . . . Where Are You From?"

In addition to those times when an Asian American's American accent is unexpected, Asian Americans' nationality is often challenged. One of the participants mentioned that:

> I thought when I was growing up, it was like everyone in the school at one point would come up to me and say, "Where are you from?" And I thought that was because I was half and half. When I joined the AASA (Asian American Student Association), I realized that if you are Asian, if you look at all Asian, you are gonna be asked that at half quarter or whenever, as long as you look that way.

Although she mentioned that she doesn't "necessarily get offended," other Asian Americans tend to find "it's kind of annoying." In addition to the question "Where are you from?" which almost all the participants have been asked, the aforementioned participant pinpointed another question that implies the disenfranchisement of Asian Americans:

> I think the worst question is "When are you going back?" which I have been asked as well. I have never heard anyone from European descent being asked a question like that: "When are you going back?" Like, "When are you going back to Germany?"

Theme 5: Crossing the Border—Where Is Home?

Along with the questions "Where are you from?" and "When are you going back?" which Asian Americans are often asked, the notion of *home* warrants our attention. As a participant stated:

I guess I identify myself as a Chinese American. I do still have a lot of memories of Taiwan; I identify with them sometimes. I want to go back to Taiwan, but I can't. . . . Taiwanese call me American, and Americans perceive me as a Chinese. I don't see myself as an international student.

The assumption that an American should look a certain way is problematic. Moreover, how to place an Asian American seems quite confusing. As one participant said:

I think some of them do not know how to place me. There was a student from Japan at the BBQ. She thought I was part Japanese. I always get eyed strangely—they think I am not Japanese, they have problems placing me. A lot of Asian students are very surprised that I don't speak their language; they are just appalled in that I don't speak Japanese.

Theme 6: Sense of Belonging and Exclusion

Along with the confusion of placing an Asian American, the sense of **belonging** and **exclusion** merits attention. One participant said:

I think they probably think I am pretty friendly, but I don't think they perceive me as one of them. They probably don't think I am someone they can be friends with, like Black. They don't identify with me. They would never see me as one of them.

Another participant described how she came to the realization that she is a "Japanese American":

I never used the term *Japanese American* until I came here to the Mainland. It was not until I moved to the Mainland that I realized *American* as part of my cultural identity. I also realized that the stereotypical view of Americans is White, although I am an American and I grew up in the United States.

She further discussed her feeling of having been excluded from the American "mainstream" history and culture:

This past week I went to Philadelphia. It's a very historic city. There were seven or eight people, four of them White Americans. For some reason I couldn't share their history with them; I did not feel it; I could not pretend to. I could not hold the brick like others [White American students], or even listen at Independence Hall; even listening doesn't mean anything. It's an empty signifier; history is constructed, and it's not my history. The idea of America is constructed.

Theme 7: Americans Are "White"

Because of Asian Americans' physical attributes such as skin color, for example, their national identity is often mistaken. The assumption that if you are not White, then you are not an American, is a common theme that Asian Americans face.

[There are] a lot of Chinese students [on this campus], and few of them expect me to understand [their language]. There is another incident—I was with another student, a Chinese from China. Another woman came by and she said, "*Ni Hao Ma?*" (How are you) to me. She was really embarrassed [after she found out that I was not Chinese], because she assumed that I am from China. She did a piece on multiculturalism in America afterward, [because] it reminded her that you really can't tell [who is American].

This participant further mentioned that even well-educated people have similar (mis)perceptions that an American should be White. She talked about her professor who made a comment about Americans:

He assumed that I am really not American. Because I am not White, he made a comment about my background, and I told him, "You are making this comment that being American is being White and," I said further, "a lot of us aren't." After class, he apologized to me.

Theme 8: Self-Identity and Self-Pride

Asian Americans' **self-identity** and self-pride can be represented by the following statements from a participant:

I don't have really bad experiences (either), but there have been small problems, like name-calling or something like that. I have never let it get me down or anything like that. I have never been, uh, having problems, or felt ashamed about being Asian.

Another participant made clear how people think her reaction to their mistaking her cultural identity is "too sensitive":

I have a problem with people thinking that I am too sensitive, when I bring up things that happened like last week or so but also that happened before, that I think people are disrespecting me or disrespecting Asians. Then people tell me "Well, it's only a joke," or "You have to get over it," or something to that effect. I know there are a lot of people who still don't believe that there are prejudices against Asians and Asian Americans, but there definitely are. I hear jokes all the time that imply much disrespect. Also, people, especially a lot of White people, don't wanna hear that, and they think I am just complaining, because I want a special status for minorities. That has happened several times.

Discussion

This discussion is divided roughly into three parts, as responses to the three research questions posed above.

Asian Americans' Lifeworld

This chapter responds to Nakayama's compelling question: What does it mean to be a "perpetual foreigner" in one's native country? Asian Americans' lived experience of being constantly asked "Where are you from?" and "When are you going back?" exemplifies that Asian Americans are treated as others. The United States is perceived not to be their native country and people from the hegemonic society expect them to go back home. But the question is, where is home? Perhaps one participant's answer can best describe the Asian American lifeworld: "I have crossed so many borders that I can't go back anymore." The metaphor of crossing border(s) and migration can be applied to Asian Americans. Another Asian American's response is "I would like to go back to Taiwan, but I can't." Thus, Asian Americans' lifeworld remains on the borderline, rhizomatic. The old tradition was given to them by their parents and they received acculturation into American ways through their own growing-up experiences; the two have mingled. For example, the traditional Asian values of deferring to men or not messing around with the opposite sex have been contradicted by American gender roles. As a result, there is a prevalent notion of struggle and cultural clash in the Asian American lifeworld.

Further, some of the participants' experience of learning their parents' native language has been horrible. Even if they found it was not confusing for them to learn two languages, they were still forced to stop it so as to adopt standard English. This acculturation process, as intercultural communication scholars like to call it, does not necessarily have a positive result. In describing her experience when she was forced to learn Chinese, one participant said that she dropped out because "it was horrible"; yet, when she went back to her parents' home country, she was "practically mute the whole time, because [she] just couldn't really get around."

How Do Asian Americans Position Themselves in This Eurocentric Hegemonic Society?

The notion of Asian Americans' double consciousness (Chen 2000; Ling 1989) was prevalent throughout the interviews. The sense of how they see themselves and how they think people from the hegemonic culture perceive them can be represented by how they react to name calling (e.g., "Brown Child" and "Chink")—how they have tried to "never let it get [them] down." Frequently Asian Americans react to comments like "Your American accent is so good" in a sarcastic way, even going so far as to sneer, "I wonder if their own American accent is that good." In essence, these Asian Americans are proud of their heritage; yet they are also aware of the negative comments they may receive from people in the mainstream culture. For example, sometimes there is a rejection of the stereotype that Asian Americans are a "model minority" and "overachievers." Their awareness and rejection of the labels "coconut" (brown outside and White inside) and "banana" (yellow outside and White inside) that people use about Asian Americans also signifies how they position themselves. In addition, their annoyance with being mistaken for international students, Chinese, or Hispanic, or the misperception that "if you look Asian at all, then people are going to treat you the same way [regardless of whether or not you were born in the States]," exemplifies their sense of pride in being an American. Yet, they are also aware of the misconceptions that people tend to have of them: "If you are not White, then you are not an American."

Another important point to note is that the conflation of Asian American conforms to Nakayama's (2000) illumination of the dis-/orientation of Asian American identities. Asian Americans' different ethnicities and cultural identities support Espiritu's (1992) assertion that

Asian Americans are a "complex" and "changing population," and they are far from being "homogenous" (p. xi). Moreover, their rejection of being treated as strangers or labeled by the term *strangers* implies their denial of being treated as peripheral. The term *strangers* underscores a binary thinking of "us against them," and its use asserts that Asian Americans are not perceived to be part of the mainstream culture. Thus, themes like being different and sense of belonging and exclusion are the manifestation of Asian Americans' double consciousness.

What Can Best Describe Asian Americans' Lived Experience?

This chapter has discussed Asian Americans' lifeworld as rhizomatic but it does not necessarily claim that there is no balance in their lifeworld; rather, their lived experience is full of the **dialectical process** of mixture and **balance**. Because of this mixture and balance between two distinct cultures, and the awareness of otherness and of being treated as perpetual foreigners, Asian Americans have constructed their own worldview, which is complex and should not be oversimplified by traditional cultural identity research (e.g., Altman and Gauvain 1981). For example, the theorization of cultural identity according to the binary contraction of power distance ("Japanese" has larger power distance, while "Northern American" has less power distance) cannot be applied to Asian Americans, because their lived experience is a continuous balancing act of two different cultures.

Conclusion

This study incorporates a discussion of double consciousness and the literature pertaining to Asian/Asian Americans' lived experience and (cultural/ethnic) identity. Several themes emerged from the individual interviews and focus groups: mixture/difference/balance; clash and struggle; misperception—being mistaken for other co-cultural groups; "**outsider** . . . where are you from?"; **crossing the border**—where is home?; belonging and exclusion; Americans as "White"; and self-identity and self-pride. Asian Americans' communicative style is deemed different from Asians' (for example, Asians are seen as unassertive and indirect). As Collier and Thomas (1988) state, cultural identity is a fluid process; an arbitrary set of variability is oversimplifying. Thus, to apply the traditional constructs of intercultural communication research to Asian Americans' lived experience could potentially perpetuate stereotypes and misconceptions.

Future researchers might expand upon the findings of this study by inviting more participants from various socioeconomic backgrounds. In addition, the development of a truly comprehensive theoretical framework for the study of ethnic minority communication styles should account for Asian and Asian American patterns. Such a framework should not be monolithic in nature; while some aggregation is necessary in theory building, one should not overextend that approach by failing to allow for other-group differences.

Note

An earlier version of this chapter was presented at the annual convention of Central States Communication Association, Indianapolis, April 19–23, 1995.

References

Aguilar-San Juan, K. 1994. *The state of Asian America: Activism and resistance in 1990.* Boston: South End Press.

Altman, I., and M. Gauvain. 1981. A cross-cultural dialectic analysis of homes. In L. Liben, A. Patterson, and N. Newcombe (Eds.), *Spatial representation and behavior across the life span.* New York: Academic Press.

Chan, S. 1991. *Asian Americans: An interpretive history.* Boston: Twayne.

Chen, V. 1992. The construction of Chinese American women's identity. In L. F. Rakow (Ed.), *Women making meaning: New feminist directions in communication* (pp. 225–43). New York: Routledge, Chapman and Hall.

———. 2000. (De)hyphenated identity: The double voice in *The woman warrior*. In A. Gonzalez, M. Houston, and V. Chen (Eds.), *Our voices: Essays in culture, ethnicity, and communication* (pp. 3–12). Los Angeles, Calif.: Roxbury.

Collier, M. J., and M. Thomas. 1988. Cultural identity: An interpretive perspective. In Y. Y. Kim and W. B. Gudykunst (Eds.), *Theories in intercultural communication* (pp. 99–122). Newbury Park, Calif.: Sage.

DuBois, W. E. B. 1989. *The souls of Black folk.* New York: Penguin.

Espiritu, Y. L. 1992. *Asian American panethnicity: Bridging institutions and identities.* Philadelphia: Temple University Press.

Fernandez, J. P. 1991. *Managing a diverse work force: Regaining the competitive edge.* Lexington, Mass.: Lexington Books.

Gudykunst, W. B., and S. Ting-Toomey. 1988. *Culture and interpersonal communication.* Newbury Park, Calif.: Sage.

Hagedorn, J. 1994. Asian women in film: No joy, no luck. *Ms.* (January/February), pp. 74–79.

Hall, E. T. 1966. *The hidden dimension.* New York: Random House.

———. 1976. *Beyond culture.* Garden City, N.Y.: Doubleday.

Hofstede, G. 1984. *Culture's consequences: International differences in work-related values.* Beverly Hills, Calif.: Sage.

Kazmi, Y. 1994. Thinking multi-culturalism: Conversation or genealogy and its implication for education. *Philosophy and Social Criticism* 20 (3): 65–88.

Kingston, M. H. 1976. *The woman warrior: Memoirs of a girlhood among ghosts.* New York: Alfred A. Knopf. Reprint Vintage Books edition, 1977.

Ling, A. 1989. Chinamerican women writers: Four forerunners of Maxine Hong Kingston. In A. Jagger and S. Bordo (Eds.), *Gender/Body/Knowledge* (pp. 309–23). New Brunswick, N.J.: Rutgers University Press

Lustig, M. W., and J. Koester. 1993. *Intercultural competence: Interpersonal communication across cultures.* New York: Harper Collins.

Nakagawa, G. 1995. Asian American communication: The silent voices. Discussion presented at meeting of Western States Communication Association, Portland, Ore., February.

Nakayama, T. K. 1994. Show/down time: "Race," gender, sexuality, and popular culture. *Critical Studies in Mass Communication* 11 (2): 162–79.

———. 2000. Dis/orienting identities: Asian Americans, history, and intercultural communication. In A. Gonzales, M. Houston, and V. Chen (Eds.), *Our voices: Essays in culture, ethnicity, and communication* (3rd ed., pp. 13–28). Los Angeles, Calif.: Roxbury.

Porter, J. R., and R. E. Washington. 1993. Minority identity and self-esteem. *Annual Review of Sociology* 19: 139–61.

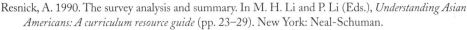

Resnick, A. 1990. The survey analysis and summary. In M. H. Li and P. Li (Eds.), *Understanding Asian Americans: A curriculum resource guide* (pp. 23–29). New York: Neal-Schuman.

Samovar, L. A., and R. E. Porter. 1997. *Intercultural communication: A reader* (8th ed.). Belmont, Calif.: Wadsworth.

Takaki, R. T. 1989. *Strangers from a different shore: A history of Asian Americans*. Boston: Little Brown and Company.

Tan, A. 1989. *The joy luck club*. New York: G. P. Putnam's Sons.

Ting-Toomey, S. 1989. Identity and interpersonal bonding. In M. K. Asante and W. B. Gudykunst (Eds.), *Handbook of international and intercultural communication* (pp. 351–73). Newbury Park, Calif.: Sage.

Wei, W. 1993. *The Asian American movement*. Philadelphia: Temple University Press.

Williams, R. M. 1964. *Strangers next door: Ethnic relations in American communities*. Englewood Cliffs, N.J.: Prentice-Hall.

KEY TERMS

alienation	exclusion
balance	hegemonic
belonging	lifeworld
bicultural	lived experience
crossing the border	misperception
cultural identity	otherness
dialectical process	outsider
different	perpetual foreigner
dis-/belonging	rhizomatic
double consciousness	self-identity
double vision	struggle
Eurocentricity	strangers

REVIEW AND DISCUSSION QUESTIONS

1. What does it mean to be a perpetual foreigner in one's own country?
2. How does the concept of *double consciousness* affect how we see ourselves? Discuss situations where double consciousness may relate to your own personal experience.
3. Discuss our social construction of *American*. What does it mean to be an American? What does it mean to be an Asian American?
4. Imagine you were an Asian American and people often asked you "Where are you from?" and "When are you going back?" and people treated you as if you did not understand English or as if you were fresh off the boat. What types of reactions might you experience?
5. What are the common experiences and communication problems that Asian Americans share, as indicated in this chapter?

Autoethnographies: Developing and Transforming Ethnic and Cultural Identities

IN THIS FINAL SECTION, two undergraduates share personal narratives of development and transformation of their cultural and ethnic identities through their cultural and intercultural interactions during childhood, teenage, and young adult years. Autoethnographies include a bicultural/ethnic identity (Chinese and Cambodian) and a multiethnic identity (African American, German, and Cuban).

Peter Chhuor writes about his ethnic and cultural identity struggles as a Chinese Cambodian in predominately Hispanic communities and then a Chinese community in Southern California. He recalls his sense of humiliation, confusion, and loneliness when some of his peers mistreated him to the point of questioning his ethnic/cultural identity. Peter Chhuor talks about his times of despair and his heights of liberation and acceptance of his bi-ethnic/cultural identities.

Jerry Pinkney describes his ethnic/cultural identity journey growing up in Germany and in various regions of the United States, including New Jersey, Texas, and California. He writes of his ethnic identity struggles and how people treated him and questioned and denied aspects of his multi-ethnic background as African American, German, and Cuban. It is a true and touching story that recalls his trials of mistreatment through harsh prejudicial words and fistfights with people who denied and ridiculed his multi-ethnic identity.

Through it all, however, Jerry Pinkney finds his true ethnic/cultural identity and knows where he belongs.

Both autoethnographers offer rich insights about their significant and meaningful cultural and intercultural interactions with people with whom they have crossed paths in the development and transformation of their ethnic and cultural identities. Through their struggles and challenges, they have finally arrived at a point where they have peace with who they are and a clear sense of their cultural and ethnic identities.

Personal Journey: My Struggle between Cambodian and Chinese Identities

Peter Chhuor

LEARNING OBJECTIVES

After reading this chapter, students will be able to:

- explain Phinney's three-part model of cultural identity development;
- discuss the content and relationship levels of ethnic and cultural identity;
- understand how language influences a person's ethnic and cultural identity; and
- recognize how an identity crisis is formulated in social interaction.

The kids at school always made fun of Asian people even though there were only a few around to make fun of. With not many Asians around, I was their chosen target of ridicule. They specifically had something against Chinese people. They would always use their fingers to slant their eyes and start mimicking what they thought a Chinese person sounded like by saying, "Ching, chong, ching, chong." They would always refer to me in a derogatory way as a "chino" or a "chinito" meaning, "little Chinese."

I am a son of immigrants who came to the United States from Cambodia. I was born in Los Angeles and have lived in and around Southern California all of my life. I am now twenty-one years old and I describe myself as a

Chinese Cambodian when I am asked to indicate my ethnic identity. In this chapter I give a brief history of my ancestors and how I came to call myself a Chinese Cambodian.

My maternal grandfather was born in Cambodia to my great-grandfather, who was a Chinese immigrant, and my great-grandmother, who was Cambodian. My maternal grandmother came to Cambodia from China around the time that the Japanese invaded China in World War II. My paternal grandfather was an ethnic Chinese who was born in Cambodia to Chinese immigrants. My paternal grandmother was an ethnic Chinese who lived in Cambodia. My grandparents have their roots in the Chiu Chow region of southern China and they speak Chiu Chow, which is a dialect of Chinese. In all, most of the Chinese who live in Cambodia are from the Chiu Chow area. Many of them moved to Cambodia for various reasons including fleeing famine, seeking better economic opportunity, and so forth. In this chapter I present some narratives about how my interactions with various people have influenced me in the development of my ethnic identity and how I came to call myself a Chinese Cambodian.

Developing My Ethnic Identity

Phinney's (1993) **model of cultural identity development** consists of three stages: **unexamined cultural identity,** cultural identity search, and cultural identity achievement. In my autoethnography, I essentially present four narrative themes on the development of my ethnic identity. From the first narrative theme through the fourth narrative theme, described below, I engaged in Phinney's second stage, **cultural identity search.** By the end of the fourth narrative theme, I had reached Phinney's third stage of ethnic identity development, that is, **cultural identity achievement.** My first narrative theme involves how language influenced my ethnic identity early in my life. Second are narratives on how my physical appearance identified me as a Chinese and not just Cambodian. Third, I offer narratives on how other people influenced me in the course of my life experiences to deny part of my own ethnic identity. Last, I bring to light narratives that lead up to my acceptance of my ethnic identity.

I'm Not a *Chino*, I Speak Cambodian

My parents immigrated, along with my two older brothers, from Cambodia in 1980 to Los Angeles, California, where I was born the following year. They immigrated to the United States because there was a genocide occurring in Cambodia around that time that was perpetrated by the Cambodian Communists who were called the Khmer Rouge.

My family was very poor and they had to move into many low-income neighborhoods. At one time my family had to live in a one-room apartment in a bad part of Hollywood. Later we moved to a city called Cudahy, which was a very poor neighborhood with the population consisting of mostly Mexican immigrants. I was six years old at the time and I cried because I had to move away from some of my friends.

In this new neighborhood of ours, I did not see one single White family or one single African American family. Almost everyone spoke Spanish. There was one Cambodian family who lived on my block. I played with them many times and became good friends with them, but they moved out soon after I had started to feel comfortable there. There was a

Vietnamese family who lived on the same block and I also became very good friends with them. I remember always hanging out with them and feeling a sense of comfort because they were also Asian. We would always team up and confront any Mexican kids who would taunt us in any way. I was comfortable with my life there until they moved out after a year and a half. After the two other Asian families moved out of the neighborhood, I started to feel alone and different around everyone. In school there were only two other Asians that I saw. I knew one of them pretty well and was friends with him. The other one pretty much ignored me and hung out with his Mexican friends. I did my best to make friends with the Mexican kids in my neighborhood, with some of them accepting me, while others totally rejected me because I looked too different from them.

The kids at school always made fun of Asian people even though there were only a few around to make fun of. With not many Asians around, I was their chosen target of ridicule. They specifically had something against Chinese people. They would always use their fingers to slant their eyes and start mimicking what they thought a Chinese person sounded like by saying, "Ching, chong, ching, chong."

The kids at school used **labels** and **names** that created a sense of exclusion. They would always refer to me in a derogatory way as a *chino* or a *chinito,* meaning "little Chinese." Some people who referred to me as a *chino* did not mean it in a derogatory way, but I still felt offended. Even though I knew that *chino* simply meant Chinese and it was a standard, proper Spanish word, I came to associate *chino* as a bad word. I was offended because I did not think of myself as a Chinese because I did not speak the language. I spoke Cambodian and that was how I identified myself at the time. The language that I spoke strongly influenced how I perceived my ethnic identity.

In the first chapter of this book, Fong states, "Difficulties arise when names and labels are used inappropriately in a social context or we feel they do not accurately describe who we are." For example, my brother and I were playing catch with a Mexican friend, who was a good friend of ours. We had known him for almost three years at the time, and he never taunted us in any way and was always nice to us. My brother and I always went to his house to hang out, play video games, and have fun. One day, after playing catch with him, his mother called him in because it was getting late. He said something in Spanish to her, and then I saw him point to me and my brother. He then referred to us as *chinos* when he talked to his mother. I was so angry when he used that word to describe us because we had mentioned to him several times that we were Cambodian and not Chinese. I know that he did not mean to demean us or taunt us in any way, but I was upset nonetheless. After he had used that word to describe us, I interrupted him to say we were Cambodian and we spoke this language and that we didn't speak Chinese. I felt hurt when he referred to us in this way not only because I thought that *chino* was a bad word but also because he was my friend. According to Collier (1997), another property of identities is the **content** and **relationship levels** of interpretation. My relationship with my good Mexican friend and his use of *chinos,* in reference to my brother and me, created confusion and anger within me. I had always associated the label *chino* to have a negative **connotation** because some kids in the past would use that term to label me, which made me feel like an outsider. So when my good Mexican friend referred to me as a *chino,* I felt confused because I thought it was inappropriate and disrespectful for a friend to call me a label that was inaccurate about my ethnic identity and that had a negative connotation to me.

I never understood why he kept calling me a *chino* because I had told him many times that I was Cambodian. When I asked him why he referred to us in that way, he told me that although he knew that I was Cambodian, he could not think of any other way to refer to us because he thought we looked Chinese. At the time, I never thought that I was Chinese, partly because I did not speak Chinese but instead spoke Cambodian. The fact that I spoke Cambodian, and not Chinese, made me think that I was only Cambodian and not both. **Language** played a large part at the time in confirming my ethnic identity. Many times, language is a distinguishing feature that may identify and reflect a person's ethnic identity, as stated earlier in this book.

Another example of how language strongly influenced my ethnic identity involved my cousin's parents, who are from Cambodia but are ethnically Chinese. In my cousin's household, the only Cambodian spoken is between his parents. But when my cousin speaks with his parents, he only speaks Chinese with them. He doesn't speak Cambodian, but he understands it. Although his parents are from Cambodia, my cousin sees no reason why he can't call himself Chinese and not Chinese Cambodian, since he only speaks Chinese and not Cambodian.

The constant taunting also made me feel ashamed of myself as an Asian person. I always thought to myself, why did I have to be different and what did I do to deserve this misery? I was embarrassed about the way I looked and wished that I was born looking like everyone else around me. I didn't want to be different. Instead I wanted to fit and blend in with everybody else in my community so I could get away from the everyday taunting and harassing that I got at school.

What Part of Me Looks Cambodian?

I learned more about my ethnic identity when my family moved to Monterey Park when I was about twelve years old. Monterey Park was a totally different neighborhood than Cudahy, which was where I had moved from. Instead of being completely devoid of Asians, it was almost a sea of Asian faces, most of them Chinese. I finally saw other people who looked like me and I felt that I was not different and didn't stand out anymore. I still felt a little strange, and I felt that I didn't fit in because I wasn't used to being around Asian people that often. I also felt alienated around the Chinese people because I did not speak their language and I felt that I was Cambodian.

One experience my mother described changed my view of my ethnic identity. She told me that she was in a Chinese supermarket one time buying groceries. She was waiting near the cashier counter while someone was bagging her groceries. Someone then approached her and asked her what she was, meaning her ethnicity. She said she was Cambodian. The man then said to her that she could not have been a Cambodian because she was too light-skinned to be one. My mom just laughed and explained to him that she was Chinese Cambodian, which meant that most of her heritage is Chinese, but she was born in Cambodia. I was curious about her experience and reflected on it.

This was the first time I thought I could also possibly be Chinese. I never knew that we were Chinese. My parents never told me about our heritage, only that they were from Cambodia, and the language we spoke was Cambodian. They never told me specifically that we were also Chinese. It was probably my inattention to the things that went on around me in the family. I was just a kid and didn't care about anything that went on in and around the household. The only thing I thought about was getting out of school to play video games or to play with my friends. I knew we celebrated Chinese New Year but I never really thought about it that much. My parents liked to go to Chinatown often and I went along with them frequently when I was younger, and we had some items that were Chinese in nature in our house. I came to find out later that both my parents also spoke Chinese. My father knew how to speak Mandarin and also the Chiu Chow dialect. My mother knew how to speak the Chiu Chow dialect. They never spoke Chinese around the house but I started to notice that when we went to Chinatown, they would always bargain with the vendors using Chinese rather than Cambodian. I started to become more aware and attentive toward everything that went on around me.

The reason that I had only identified myself as Cambodian was due partly to the fact that I did not speak Chinese but also because I was never around other Asians, specifically other Chinese and Cambodian people. When I looked at myself in the mirror, I thought to myself, "What part of me looks Cambodian and what part of me looks Chinese?" Being in a predominantly Mexican community most of my life prevented me from seeing other, different Asian people. I had an idea of what Chinese people looked like and I also had an idea of what Cambodian people looked like. But the thing was, I was never around these groups of people long enough to notice the difference. I was usually at home playing with my Mexican friends and rarely seeing someone similar to me.

You're Not Chinese, You're Not One of Us

When I lived in Monterey Park, the peers I socialized with in middle school were mostly Asians. It was absolutely a different experience from the time I lived in a predominately Mexican neighborhood. There were no more kids mocking me by slanting their eyes or speaking their ignorance by saying "Ching, chong, ching, chong." Although I did feel a little more comfortable in my new neighborhood, I still had some conflicts with some kids, who were my classmates, about my ethnic identity.

I had made friends with many other students in middle school and most of them were Asian just like I was. I got along with most of them fine and some of them became very good friends of mine. There was every kind of Asian nationality and I was very surprised, in a good way, by it. I had friends from many different Asian backgrounds, which included Japanese, Burmese, Chinese, and Korean. I got along with many of the kids in school except for these two Chinese kids from Hong Kong.

One time during recess, I was talking with my Burmese friend on the playground. The two kids from Hong Kong approached me from behind and just started to rudely interrupt us in the middle of our conversation. I had seen them before and just by looking at them from a distance, I could tell that I wasn't going to like them very much. I then asked them what they wanted of me because they completely ignored my friend and just looked directly at me when they were talking. One of them asked me where I lived. I was wondering to myself why he wanted to know. I then told him that I lived on a street called College View Drive, which was near the school. After hearing my response, they just started to laugh very loudly in my face. They then left my friend and me alone. I thought to myself about the reason why they laughed at me. I then started to realize that College View Drive was a street full of small apartments, which indicated that most of the people who lived there had a lower income. The two Chinese kids, on the other hand, lived up the hill in big houses that were in the price range of $350,000 and up. I realized that they had looked down upon me because my family was not as well off as they were. At first I thought this was the only reason they had mocked me but after another experience with them, my view changed on their reason for mocking me.

My classmates and I had just returned to school from a field trip to a harbor where we went sailing. During this trip, we had learned how to test the pH of the water and we even caught some marine life, which included various strange types of fishes, shellfish, crabs, and even a small shark. When we returned to school, I was walking down some stairs with all of my classmates. I was talking with some of my friends about the trip and how we had fun. I was minding my own business when suddenly the same two Chinese kids approached me. I did not really want to talk to them because I did not like them very much ever since the earlier incident.

When they looked at me, they looked like they were about to laugh at me, but they held back long enough to ask me a question. They asked me whether I spoke Chinese or not. I told them that I did not speak Chinese but that I spoke Cambodian instead. After I had answered them, the two of them started to speak to each other in Chinese, then they snickered a little bit, which eventually led to an outburst of laughter from them. After seeing them laughing, I told them that although my parents were from Cambodia, we were also ethnically Chinese. I was hoping that this would shut them up a little bit since I could say that I was also part of their ethnic group. Instead of my desired result, they burst into even louder laughter. I asked them why they were laughing at me. They told me that I was not Chinese and that I was not one of them. I said that I was Chinese, but they continued to deny my identification as part Chinese.

I kept thinking to myself, why were they laughing at me? My first thought was that they had identified me as a Cambodian and not one of them. They had known earlier that my parents were not from Hong Kong, China, or Taiwan. They knew that my parents were Cambodian because of an earlier presentation that I had to give in English class in which I identified my parent's country of origin. They had known but they wanted to have fun demeaning me to my face.

Then I thought, what was so funny about me being Cambodian? Fong states in the second chapter, "our **class identity** influences how we communicate toward others and how others perceive us based on our communication competence, our material possessions, and how we conduct ourselves." In responding to my questions and connecting it to class identity, I think the two Chinese boys had made fun of me because of my family's economic status. They saw themselves as being better than me as a person. They looked down on me because my parents were from a poor Southeast Asian country. Their families were from Hong Kong and they were wealthy. I knew they were wealthy because I had seen their enormous homes before.

They were racist against other Asian groups. Southeastern Asians tend to be poorer and have a different complexion than most East Asians. They saw me as being part of this group since Southeast Asia was where my parents were from and the language I spoke was Cambodian and not Chinese. Even though I knew I was mostly Chinese in terms of ancestry, I had this sense of inferiority to them in terms of ethnicity. I tried to include myself in their group when I responded back by saying that I was Chinese, but they continued to deny me the "privilege" of being one of them. They did not feel that I was worthy of being one of them because of the country of my parents' origin, the language I spoke, and my family's economic status.

After this incident, I felt very ashamed of myself. I was experiencing an **identity crisis.** As stated in part I of this book, when the **subjective** and the **objective identities** of a person contradict one another, a person is said to be suffering from an **identity crisis.** Moreover, a person denies one's ethnic identity. I kept thinking, why did I not know how to speak Chinese? I wanted so badly to become more Chinese, so I thought about going to Chinese school. I wanted to learn Chinese so I could be accepted among my Chinese peers. I even told my brother I wanted to learn Chinese because I wanted to fit in and I wanted those kids to stop taunting me. I began denying my Cambodian identity but I felt that I could not do so because it was the language that I spoke. Even though it was hard for me to deny my Cambodian identity, I tried very hard to **pass** as only Chinese. At this point in my life I was so afraid of ridicule that I stooped so low that I denied a part of me. This went on throughout high school until I went to college. At college I became wiser and at the same time I felt ashamed of myself. I was ashamed of myself because I had let other people cause me to not be true to myself.

My Dual Identity of Being Chinese Cambodian

I had many experiences in which my appearance instead of my language started to identify my ethnicity. In the beginning, language gave me my ethnic identity, as demonstrated when the two kids mocked me because I spoke Cambodian; therefore I was a Southeast Asian, therefore they thought I was not as good as they were. But as I went on to college, my appearance influenced my colleagues' perception of my ethnic identity. Many of them thought I was Chinese, which influenced my self-perception of my ethnic identity.

There were many small experiences in my life that confirmed the Chinese part of my ethnicity. Once I was sitting in class listening to my professor lecture about the geography of a certain country. I was sitting next to a Korean girl. We started talking a little bit and she then asked me what ethnicity I was. I told her that I was Chinese Cambodian. She then told me that I was right in saying that I was Chinese Cambodian. She said I was too light-skinned to be Cambodian and that I looked more Chinese.

Another experience that reinforced the Chinese part of me occurred during Chinese New Year. I was in my girlfriend's apartment for a Chinese New Year party. I was the only one there who did not speak Chinese, so I felt a little uncomfortable being around all of her friends. I just sat there most of the time watching television while everyone just talked and had a good time. One of her friends then mentioned to my girlfriend that it was strange to speak English to me. She said that it was strange because every time she looked at me, she saw a Chinese face and she wasn't used to speaking English to someone who looked Chinese. I started to feel from their responses that the only thing that would identify me as Cambodian would be the language that I spoke and the country my parents were from. I could have just denied that part of me and passed as a Chinese person, like my cousin I mentioned earlier. But I knew I had this dual identity that I must keep.

Another important experience for me reinforced my dual identity of being Chinese and Cambodian. It was the first day of class during the fall quarter of 2002. We had just come back from summer vacation and I was tired. My first class was Aikido, which is a Japanese martial art. I was looking around the class for some friendly faces when I saw this one Asian girl I had previously noticed. During class, the instructor told us to pair off so we could practice a technique that he had just finished showing us. I ended up pairing up with the Asian girl I had noticed earlier. We got along nicely and then I asked her what her name was. Her name was unfamiliar to me so I asked her what kind of name it was. She then told me that she was Cambodian. I was so surprised to hear that she was Cambodian because I seldom have met Cambodian people on campus. Then I spoke Cambodian to her and I felt a sense of closeness because we shared the same language. She was so shocked to hear that I could speak Cambodian. I asked her why she was so surprised. She responded, "When I first saw you in class, I just thought you were some Chinese guy." After she said that, I just laughed and explained to her that I was Chinese Cambodian. She, on the other hand, looked purely Cambodian. I started to find out the differences between our two identities. An example was how we referred to our aunts and uncles. When I was talking with her, I used what I thought was the Cambodian word for *aunt* and *uncle*. She then looked at me like I was crazy or something. I then thought to myself and remembered that my mom told me that the word we used for aunt and uncle was actually Chinese and not Cambodian. I laughed and explained it to her. She taught me the Cambodian word for aunt and uncle.

After meeting her, I could have decided to see myself as more Chinese than Cambodian, but I refuse to do that. I felt it was important to maintain my dual identity and to never deny one part of my ethnicity, because that is who I am; and I am not ashamed of it.

Conclusion

I feel complete as a person concerning my identity as a Chinese Cambodian and as an Asian American. As for my Asian American identity, I am very proud to be Asian. In the early phase of my life when I lived among Mexicans and Mexican Americans, I was always ashamed of myself being Asian because the people around my life made me feel that way. I felt that way through the constant taunting and harassing that followed me everywhere I went, from school to just walking around my neighborhood. I now look at myself in the mirror and instead of feeling that I look strange and different from everyone else, I feel that I like what I see. I am not conceited or anything, it is just that I have finally accepted myself. I am proud to be Asian and I don't want to be anything else.

When I associate with non-Asians, I feel that they think I am just another Asian person. I think that there are many people who feel that all Asians are all the same instead of knowing that there are differences between the many Asian cultures. Among other Asians, I have a feeling of a better connection, a better familiarity and comfort with them. Even though there are many different Asian cultures, I feel that I am closer to Asians than to other groups of people. It is important to know where you and your ancestors are from because it is *who you are.*

Note

I would like to thank Professor Mary Fong for her helpful suggestions in the writing of my autoethnography that originated in an Ethnography of Communication course.

References

Collier, M. J. 1997. Cultural identity and intercultural communication. In L. Samovar and R. Porter (Eds.), *Intercultural communication: A reader* (pp. 36–44). Belmont, Calif.: Wadsworth Publishing Co.

Phinney, J. S. 1993. A three-stage model of ethnic identity development in adolescence. In M. E. Bernal and G. Knight (Eds.), *Ethnic identity* (pp. 61–79). Albany: State University of New York Press.

KEY TERMS

class identity	model of cultural identity development
connotation	names
content level	objective identity
cultural identity achievement	pass
cultural identity search	relationship level
identity crisis	subjective identity
labels	unexamined cultural identity
language	

REVIEW AND DISCUSSION QUESTIONS

1. Explain Phinney's three-stage model of cultural identity development by referring to Chhuor's experiences.
2. Discuss Collier's content and relationship levels as aspects of cultural identity by making reference to Chhuor's experience with the term *chino* and his interactions with the two Chinese boys who were bullying him.
3. Discuss the power that language, labels, and names have in influencing a person's ethnic and cultural identity.
4. Define *identity crisis* and discuss how Chhuor developed a crisis with his ethnic and cultural identity.

A Little Bit Black, But Not All the Way

JERRY PINKNEY

LEARNING OBJECTIVES

After reading this chapter, students will be able to:

- identify avowal and ascription aspects of cultural identity;
- define and explain White privilege;
- understand how the self-fulfilling prophecy influences the fate of a person's success; and
- discuss the labels, names, negative stereotypes, and ethnocentric attitudes used to create barriers and mistreatment in cultural and intercultural interactions.

My German grandmother has always made little side comments about Black people or how I do not preserve my German heritage. My Black grandmother, I feel, does not appreciate nor love me as much as she would if I were fully Black. Anywhere I go, people are always categorizing me as the "half-breed." I don't feel it is right for me and other bi-racial people to have to prove their Blackness or Whiteness. In the past I have literally fought with people who didn't see me as Black enough or White enough. Nowadays I have come to realize that my race or skin color has nothing to do with who I am as a person. I am satisfied with just being me and don't feel the need to fight for my Blackness or Whiteness. I don't have to prove anything to anyone, as long as I am happy with myself.

—Desiree Pinkney

Growing up seems to be hard for everyone, even life itself seems to be hard. While growing up, one of the biggest challenges a person can face is finding out where they fit in with society. We are tackled with a barrage of questions, like *who am I? Where do I belong? Who do I fit in with? Why am I different?* All of these are questions we ask ourselves in our quest to find out where we fit in. I am no different. I discuss here the biggest problem: being labeled an "outcast" growing up.

I was born into a military family as both of my parents were in the United States Army. My family and I have lived in many places in the world such as Germany, Italy, France, Belgium, and the United States. In the United States, we have lived in New Jersey, Texas, and California. My sister (five years younger) and myself are the only two children in my family.

My mother is one-half German and one-half Caucasian American, as her father (also a soldier in the army) met her mother in her homeland of Germany. Many people refer to these two ethnicities as the same; however, if I were to ask my grandmother she would disagree. As for my father, he is African American, as are both of his parents. My younger sister came out looking predominately Caucasian; she has green eyes, pale skin, and brown hair. Myself, however, came out looking more African American than Caucasian. I have brown skin, brown eyes, and dark brown hair. It was not until I was the age of thirteen that I discovered that my father who raised me was not my biological father. My mother had informed me that I had another father and after talking with him I realized that I possessed yet another ethnicity, Cuban. My biological father informed me that he was one-half African American and one-half Cuban, his father being African American, and his mother an immigrant from Cuba.

Now comes my dilemma, being of multi-racial/ethnic background. I had a difficult time trying to fit in, let alone be accepted by my peers. The main issue my sister and I faced was determining which race we belonged to. It was and still is a constant struggle to be accepted by any of the races or ethnicities I belong to. I played the constant game of "monkey in the middle," as I have never been fully accepted by any of my ethnic groups. My constant uphill struggle has been a learning experience for me and has broadened my horizons in my search for identity and who I am as a person. My autoethnography includes four subsections relating to various aspects of my ethnicity and the final outcome of my dilemma. I also discuss my younger sister's feelings toward racial acceptance to give even more insight from the point of view of a biracial child. My autoethnography covers my own personal experiences dealing with the issue of race. I discuss the problems I faced being accepted by African Americans, Caucasians, and later Hispanic Americans.

Let me start with a quote from my younger sister on her feelings of being accepted by society.

A lot of times in my life I've had to deal with racial issues that I have no control over. I grew up in a world where I wasn't Black enough for the Blacks nor was I White enough for the Whites. I've constantly had to prove my Blackness to people and I'm just plain tired. I feel I get the worst end of it as my skin tone is hundreds of shades lighter than most African Americans and twenty shades darker than most Caucasians. My German grandmother has always made little side comments about Black people or how I do not preserve my German heritage. My Black grandmother, I feel, does not appreciate nor love me as much as she would if I were fully Black. Anywhere I go people are always categorizing me as the "half-breed." I don't feel it is right for myself and other biracial people to have to prove their Blackness or Whiteness. In the past I have literally fought with people who didn't see me as Black enough or White enough. Nowadays I have come to realize that my race or skin color has nothing to do with who I am as a person. I am satisfied with just being me and do not feel the need to fight for my Blackness or Whiteness. I don't have to prove anything to anyone, as long as I am happy with myself. That is fine with me.

My sister's testimonial epitomizes how I feel, as well as how many other biracial people feel. It took a while, but in the end I have realized how to be happy with myself as a person, not only in terms of a race or ethnicity.

Throughout this autoethnography, the concepts of **avowal** and **ascription** processes of cultural identity are apparent, particularly in my cultural and intercultural interactions. According to Collier (1997), avowal involves the presentation of self in communicating the "who I am" to others. She also explains that ascription is what others perceive and communicate about what they think another person's identity is, such as making attributions and stereotypes about a person.

Realization that I Am Not the Same as Everyone

I first realized ethnic differences among people in my early experiences in Germany. I attended an all-German-speaking kindergarten because my mother wanted me to learn the German language. I first had to deal with the experience of understanding my classmates. After the frustrating ordeal of learning German I came to realize that the kids still did not like me. I assumed that if I learned the language, my peers would play with me. But I was mistaken. My classmates were all Caucasian and would not play with me because of my skin complexion. I soon learned about the "nigger" word as even Germans used it. I remember it distinctly. I was on the school playground. I walked over to a group of male classmates who were playing on the jungle gym. They were playing tag and I asked if I could play:

> "*Kann ich mit dir spielen?*" (Can I play with you?)
> "*Nein, du kannst nicht mit mir spielen.*" (No you can't play with us.)
> "*Bitte kann ich spielen, ich bin gut.*" (Please, I'm good at tag.)
> "*Nein, wir sind alle weiss, und du bist ein nigger.*" (No, because we're White and you're a nigger.)

I did not know what the word *nigger* meant, but seeing all the boys laugh at me told me it was an insult. I immediately began to fight all of them that day and many days that followed. When my parents asked me why I was fighting I would reply, "They were making fun of me." It's funny that I did not realize what my classmates were calling me until I later moved to the United States.

It was not until I attended an American kindergarten in Texas that it was clear that I was of a different race than everybody else. I was in class waiting for my parents to pick me up when my mom walked in. All of my so-called friends started laughing at me (they were all African American). I asked what they were laughing at and one replied, "Your mom is White, why is she White?" I naively replied, "Because my dad is Black." I went home and asked my parents why my friends were laughing at me and it was then they explained to me what race was. They also explained their racial and ethnic differences and I thought nothing more of it. I was a good fighter so the laughter and jokes from my friends soon stopped, but the teasing picked up from time to time. My parents' ethnic differences did not bother me much, and I did not see anything wrong with them. I did not even care about the jokes my friends made about me.

One day, however, on the playground, fitting in became my newest and most formidable problem. I wanted to play with my friends but they would not let me. They said I was not like them and I was not allowed to play with them. I shrugged them off and tried to play with other classmates, but they would not play with me either. I thought nothing of it, until I tried to walk home with one of my African American friends and his big brother. I remember he told me I could not walk with them because I was different. I asked him why and he replied, "Because your mom is a honky and your daddy is Black. It's wrong for them to be married because they're different." Angrily and with protest, I told him he was wrong and attempted to fight him but he was a lot older than me and he beat me up. I then realized that fitting in was going to be a problem for me for the rest of my life.

Only a Little Bit Black, Not All the Way

With physical traits that resemble African Americans more than Caucasians, I felt that I was Black. I had the physical attributes that Caucasians and other races considered Black. My father was Black, and I looked like him in terms of skin complexion, eye color, and hair type. Like every other boy, I wanted to be like my father. My father was Black and I wanted to be Black too. I even found myself liking society's stereotypes of African Americans. I enjoyed rap and R&B music. I liked using popular African American slang, and I even had the hairstyles that were popular with African Americans. I had a Jerry-Curl, a high top, a gumby, a step, a ramp, and even an Afro (all different African American hairstyles). Regardless of how I felt, peers constantly let me know that I was not fully Black and always "corrected" me. Growing up, most of my friends were of African American descent. I socialized with people who looked like me because I felt that I fit in better with them. As a young child in the early 1980s, many of my African American friends were very accepting of me.

However, my problems began once my friends would discover that my mother was Caucasian. I would always have a false sense of hope that I would be accepted and respected, until my friends were reminded that I was biracial. Whenever ethnic issues came up, I was constantly reminded that I would not understand. My peers and the various people I came across also used **labels** and **names** to exclude me and to make me feel "less than" them. Negative names and labels used toward another for the intent to exclude also display an ethnocentric view of the other. **Ethnocentrism** is a person's disposition that one is better or superior than another person or ethnic/cultural group. One example occurred while I was on a field trip in Germany and a snack vendor told my friend, "hurry up nigger." My friend became upset and stormed off as I followed behind him. I tried to express my anger as well and my friend looked at me and said, "What are you mad about, you're not Black anyways." Another example was during the Rodney King incident, as many of my peers were upset by it. There would be debates about the issue and counselors would even have open discussions about it with us. I would often try to display how angry I was and state my opinion, but I was often cut off with the reply of, "What are you talking about zebra, you don't understand, you ain't Black." Statements like these often discouraged me as I came to realize that I would never fully gain acceptance in the African American society by my peers. My lighter skin tone was also a barrier, as many African Americans would ask me, "What are you mixed with?" I would reply, "How do you know I'm mixed?" Their reply would be, "Because you're definitely not Black." Statements like this have often hurt my feelings, as I would feel like I was some sort of a "freak" or deviant. Not only was I not accepted by African Americans, I was also called a barrage of names that stuck with me throughout life.

By sixth grade it was obvious that I was biracial as I looked it and expressed it to my peers. My friends and other classmates started to call me "Zebra" in reference to its Black and White stripes and my parents being Black and White. As much as I hated my new nickname, I acknowledged it. I felt that if I let people call me this, they would accept me. I was mistaken, as it was only a means to degrade me and make fun of me. Another name that the same people called me was "wigger," which means White "nigger." The irony of this name is that as much as African Americans hate to be called a "nigger," they deemed it okay to call me one in another form. This one hurt me the most and often caused me to get into fights. When I went to junior college and played football, I was called "yella," in reference to my lighter skin tone, by my teammates. I was never given the respect of being called by my name; from the first day of practice to the last day, that was my name. It hurt me to discover that many of my teammates did not know my real name until the banquet at the end of the season.

While attending college in Alabama, a place where I had assumed racial tension was gone, I was given the labels of "light-skinned" and even worse, "Black-ass-White-boy." I even got my jaw dislocated as many African American students jumped me because I was of light complexion. This incident hurt me the most as I thought being half Black would be enough to gain acceptance at least in Alabama. Besides the constant name calling, I also noticed that I was not always welcome in the inner circle of my so-called friends.

I remember when I first moved to Barstow, California, and I thought I had made some new African American friends. I tried to talk to my "new friends" and was met with statements like, "What are you doing here, this is for *real* niggas only." Or when I was allowed to hang out they would say, "I feel sorry for you, White people are crazy." I was often made to feel insecure about myself, as when I came up with ideas, my friends would reply, "That must be the White in you talking." People of other ethnicities and races would also remind me that I was not fully Black. On numerous accounts I have been told, "You're not really Black though." When I was dating my first girlfriend in the fifth grade, I met her mother, and she said to me, "I don't like my daughter having a Black boyfriend. But you're not really Black though, so it's okay."

Throughout my schooling, there were times when I was the beneficiary of **"White privilege"** because the Caucasian teacher saw that I was not completely Black, but was a light-skinned Black. White privilege refers to receiving benefits because you are perceived to have characteristics of being White, and other ethnic persons are not given the same or similar privileges or benefits in the same or similar situations. For example, in grade school I had problems with multiplying numbers by the number nine and had failed my multiplication test twice. My Black friend Tito had failed twice also. I remember my teacher telling me to keep trying and practicing and then seconds later scolding Tito and telling him that he was ignorant and did not belong in that class.

Another example in which I received better treatment was in the fifth grade. Many other students had issues with homework. Many of my classmates as well as myself would always stuff our homework in our desks. After a month we would have the sloppiest, most crammed desks you could think of. My teacher called my parents and asked them to bring me to class to clean my desk and complete all of my homework before the quarter ended. I also noticed that my White classmates who shared my problem would be there with their parents but I never noticed any of my Black classmates. I would later ask my Black classmates if the teacher had called them and they would reply, "Nope." Many of them failed to pass to the next grade, as they were not given the same opportunity as I was. To this day I feel that I was given that opportunity to complete my homework because my teacher viewed me as not fully Black. The differences in how teachers treated the Caucasian and Black students demonstrated a teacher's **self-fulfilling prophecy**. Influential significant people such as parents, older siblings, relatives, teachers, and so on are in positions to treat (verbally and nonverbally) another person who has less power and to guide and make decisions that will determine the success or failure of an individual.

In high school a teacher told me, "You've got it better than them (Blacks), because you're only half." I felt hurt as I wanted to be accepted by African Americans. This White teacher even acknowledged that I "wasn't Black enough." I have received special treatment because of my lack of "Blackness." To this day, I have noticed that Caucasians and people of other races who associate with me treat me differently than they treat other African Americans. I am treated better than other African Americans due to others (predominately Caucasians) not viewing me as all the way Black. I have noticed it from grade school all the way through high school and even in college. There have been many occasions when a professor has talked to me in a nicer tone or treated me with more respect than other African American classmates are treated.

"You're Not Cuban, Only Black"

At the age of thirteen I discovered that I had Cuban roots from my biological father's side. I am careful to use the term *biological father* as he is only that and did not raise me. After discovering this, this has answered many questions I had, such as, why do people always ask me "Are you Puerto Rican?" or "Do you have some form of Hispanic in you?" I was always confused by my appearance. As I grew older I started to look less African American and more Hispanic. I accepted the fact that I was also mixed with Cuban and when asked if I possessed any Hispanic roots, I proudly stated, "Yes, I'm part Cuban." I thought that I would gain acceptance from Hispanics but was surely wrong. For one, I live in Barstow, California, where racial tension between Mexican and Black gangs is thick. A killing or drive-by shooting occurred at least every other weekend. The gang tension spread so that Mexicans in general hated Blacks and vice versa. I would tell Mexicans from my town that I had Cuban in me but was often disrespected and told I was only Black. I remember one occasion when a few guys from the Mexican gang asked me if I was in the African American gang and I replied, "No!" They then asked me what ethnicity I was and I told them my ethnicities and they laughed and told me, "You're not Cuban, you are Black. So leave before we fuck you up, *miate* (Spanish for *nigger*)."

When I attempted to date a Mexican girl I was faced with adversity. Her Mexican friends would give her a hard time and call her a "nigger lover." Her family, relatives, and friends had **negative stereotypes** of me that were hurtful to the both of us. They did not care that I had Cuban in my blood; they only saw me as Black. Her parents were no better. I tried to meet them and they refused. Oftentimes, the girls I was interested in were told by their parents that they were not allowed to date me anymore. Their parents would tell them that dating a Black guy was embarrassing to the family and to leave me alone. They did not care that I was part Cuban. All they saw was another stereotypical Black guy. They (Mexican parents) would say that I was a "thug" or a drug dealer, or they would say that I was ignorant like all the other Blacks and that I would hit her. My heart was broken on many occasions because Mexican parents disapproved of their daughter dating a Black, not a Cuban but only a Black guy.

I also had difficulties with my ex-girlfriend's family who are of Mexican descent. She invited me to meet her family during Thanksgiving. Her family was nice to me while I was there but as soon as I left "all hell broke loose." She told me that her parents began to yell obscenities at her and that her sisters and cousins talked negatively toward her. She said she argued with them for at least an hour until she informed them of my Cuban ethnicity. It was like morning to night how their attitude changed toward me. Her mother, also part Cuban, became pleased. She stated to her daughter, "Well okay, I guess I can ignore the fact that he's Black and see him as Cuban."

My fiancée is of Mexican descent and it was definitely a challenge to get her family to accept me. When we first started dating I was only allowed to meet her mother and father. Her father was a Christian man and was very accepting of me and did not see me as Black or Cuban. He saw me as a person. Her mother, on the other hand, hated the fact that her daughter was dating a Black man. She did not care that my dad was half Cuban or not. Her mother was only willing to see me as a negative stereotype of a Black man. Leslie (my fiancée) would tell me how her mother would talk bad about Black people and me in general. She would say that I was ignorant and a nobody, even though she did not know me. She would tell Leslie that her aunts and uncles disapproved of her dating me. She even tried to scare Leslie into ending our relationship by bringing up the issue of her grandmother's health. She would say things like, "You know if your grandmother finds out she's going to have a heart attack and die because of you." When nothing worked, her mother had to accept the fact that she was dating me. Her mother finally got to know "Jerry" and not the Black guy that was dating her daughter. She was able to realize that I have a good head on my shoulders and was heading in the right direction. Her family was able to realize this, but it took longer than it should have because they would not meet me right away. Her grandmother likes me but still makes little comments such as, "Jerry's a nice guy, but he's a little dark though." This obviously displays that she does not respect the fact that I am Cuban, but only Black. One Mexican family accepted me, and it was because they chose to ignore the fact that I was Black.

"Definitely You're Not White"

Not only have I been faced with the problem of not being accepted as an African American by Blacks, but I have also faced the problem of not being accepted by Caucasians. Although I am not as dark as other African Americans, my skin tone is still dark and if forced to categorize me, Whites would say that I am Black. My whole life I have felt that some White people I knew have viewed me as somewhat better than most Blacks, but not equal to Whites. For example, in Texas at a barbecue for my dad's army unit, I was told I am not equal to Whites. It was a hot day, and a White friend of my mother's had some bottles of water. One Black kid had asked for a water bottle and she told him to drink from the water fountain. I later asked her for a bottle and she replied, "Yes" and gave me a different bottle than the White kids. I asked why it was different and she told me, "You can have a bottle of water, but not the same as us." I asked, "Why?" and she replied, "Because you ain't really a nigger, but you sure as hell ain't as White as us." I later told my mother of the incident and their friendship ended shortly afterward.

In all the places I have lived or visited, I have been called a "nigger." In Germany I was called a "nigger" in kindergarten and had no idea what it meant. When I went back to Germany in the third grade, I had to deal with White American kids calling me a "nigger" and also German kids calling me a "nigger." The German kids calling me a "nigger" hurt the most as many of them were my friends and all of a sudden they disliked me because their parents had told them I was a "nigger." I felt betrayed and grew to hate them as I engaged in picking fights with German kids as much as possible. In Texas, California, Utah, Alabama, and even Colorado, I have been called a "nigger."

One time during spring break while driving home through Utah, a few of my friends and I got pulled over. The officer had no reason to pull us over and did anyway. His reason for pulling us over was that I was the only Black guy in the car. He ordered only me out of the car and asked me irrelevant questions like, "Are you in one of those Black gangs boy?" and "Do you have any tattoos?" I tried to explain that my mother was Caucasian and he abruptly interrupted me saying, "Your momma may be White and confused [referring to her interracial marriage], but you're still a nigger to me." I cannot describe the rage and hatred I felt toward that man as he insulted me.

I also feel that many of the White people I have come in contact with have negative stereotypes of Blacks. I have felt this on numerous occasions throughout my life. For instance, there is the stereotype that Black people steal. When I go into a store, I am constantly looked at and followed around by the sales associate to make sure I do not try to steal anything. This annoys me deeply as African Americans are always stereotyped as crooks and thieves. I was working at a Tommy Hilfiger store and was told to watch Black people when they came in because they like to steal. My manager specifically told me that my people (referring to Blacks) have a problem with paying for the items they want. When I am walking on the street, especially in the evenings, women clutch their purses tighter when I walk by and if I am with a group of my Black friends, people will break their necks to cross the street or get out of the way. This portrays the stereotypes of Blacks as hoodlums, gangsters, or purse snatchers.

There is also the stereotype that Black people are uneducated and ignorant. I have been a victim of this throughout my career as a college student. When professors have explained something and then asked whether everyone understood, they looked directly at me or other

African Americans in the class as if we do not have the cognitive skills to grasp their concepts. I faced more stereotypes of being ignorant while attending Colorado State University, which has 25,000 students. Eight percent of the school population was Black. In Colorado, nobody cared that I was half-White. I was seen as only being Black. I had to live with people's assumption that I got into college as an athlete, and not on academic merit. While attending study groups, other students would go over the lessons with me slowly, assuming that I was not educated enough to understand. I remember one time a male Caucasian student tried to go over the lesson using stereotypical Black slang. I also faced being stereotyped as ignorant and lazy while working on group projects. One girl said to me, "You better pick up your end of the slack. We both know how you people are lazy."

Comments like these were factors that made me realize that I was definitely not White according to Caucasians. For example, my German grandmother tells me how much she loves me, but when her friends come over to her home, she hides the pictures of my dad and me. She hides our pictures because she does not want her White German friends to talk bad about her. I realize no matter how White my mother is, I will never be seen as White or even accepted as a White person. For instance, my friend and I were leaving a nightclub in Las Vegas, Nevada. I was driving with only one headlight working, but I thought nothing of it since it was 5 A.M. and the sun was rising. We passed a police car that made a sudden U-turn and turned on its flashing lights. We pulled over to get out of the way, and to our surprise, we were being pulled over. The police officer drew his gun and yelled for us to get out of the car and lie on the ground face first. After being handcuffed I asked, "What's wrong?" The cop replied, "Your headlight is out." I then asked, "Why all of the drama with the cuffs and the lights?" The cop answered, "You can never be too careful with you guys (Black people)." After about two hours of harassment, the police officer finally dismissed us with only a "fix it" ticket. I feel that if I were a White man, this never would have happened to me. I was only pulled over due to "invisible" racial profiling. On many occasions, Whites have treated me unfairly, and I feel that I am seen as an unequal. Granted, I may have White friends, but I wonder if they see me as an equal?

Where Do I Fit In?

Growing up and not being fully accepted by any of my ethnic groups, I have often asked myself, "Where do I fit in?" It took many struggles, fistfights, and years of being ridiculed and ostracized to realize where I fit in. It's like the phrase, "It ain't where you're at. It's who you are." Nowadays I don't allow myself to get caught up in race or ethnicity. I have learned that your race or skin color does not matter, but the person you are is what matters. I have learned to be proud of the person I am. I am happy with who I am, and that's Jerry Jerome Mays; soon to be Jerry J. Pinkney (after I change my last name to my nonbiological father's name).[1] I am smart and educated. I'm sincere and honest. I am multiracial/ethnic and proud. I'm mature and good-looking. And I am a child of God. I do not need to be anything else because I will fit in where I fit in.

I have friends of all ethnicities who do not care about my race, and vice versa. If I spent my whole life trying to fit in with one specific race, I would never completely fit in. I feel that if you do not like me because of whatever race you want to classify me as, then you're the ignorant one. As for fighting, I'm done with that too, because that just feeds a person's ignorance as well as validates their stereotype of me as Black person. I feel that if you do not like who I am, then, "Oh well!" My true friends like me for being Jerry, not for being Black, White, German, or Cuban. They like me for me, and not because of my race or ethnicity. As for my Mexican fiancée, she has never seen me as Black. She has always seen me as a true person and a guy with a lot of potential.

In conclusion, I say be proud of your ethnicity and who you are, but not so much that you let your race determine who you are in society. Besides, as culturally diverse as America is, nobody is one pure race and no race is better than another—at least that is how it should be. Do not get all caught up in race as it will lead you to an infinite uphill struggle through life. Accept who you are. Be proud of who you are. And live life to the fullest and enjoy it.

Notes

I would like to thank Professor Mary Fong for her helpful suggestions in the writing of my autoethnography that originated in an Ethnography of Communication class.

1. Jerry's last name has officially been changed since the writing of this chapter.

Reference

Collier, M. J. 1997. Cultural identity and intercultural communication. In L. Samovar and R. Porter (Eds.), *Intercultural communication: A reader* (pp. 36–44). Belmont, Calif.: Wadsworth.

KEY TERMS	
ascription	names
avowal	negative stereotypes
ethnocentrism	self-fulfilling prophecy
labels	White privilege

REVIEW AND DISCUSSION QUESTIONS

1. Define *ascription* and *avowal* aspects of cultural identity and explain how these concepts apply to Jerry Pinkney's development and transformation of his cultural/ethnic identity in his autoethnography.
2. Define and discuss how the use of labels, names, negative stereotypes, and ethnocentrism are barriers to intercultural interactions.
3. Explain what White privilege is and discuss what your experiences are.
4. Define and explain how the self-fulfilling prophecy influences the fate of a person's success.

Index

About the Contributors

Fay Yokomizo Akindes (Ph.D., Ohio University) is an associate professor of communication at the University of Wisconsin-Parkside. Her research problematizes communication, culture, and identity in Hawai'i and the United States, and appears in *Diegesis, Discourse,* and *Qualitative Inquiry*. Her doctoral dissertation, "Hawaiian-Music Radio as Diasporic Habitus," was awarded Outstanding Dissertation of 1999 by the National Communication Association's International and Intercultural Communication Division. She is currently developing her dissertation into a book.

Bryant K. Alexander, (Ph.D., Southern Illinois, Carbondale) is an associate professor of performance and pedagogical studies in the Department of Communication Studies at California State University, Los Angeles. His research is grounded in the social and performative construction of identity as related to issues of race, culture, and gender—often placing these concerns within the broad context of education, schooling, and specifically in the classroom. His published essays have appeared in a wide variety of scholarly journals including: *Qualitative Inquiry, Cultural Studies /Critical Methodologies, Theatre Annual, Theatre Topics, Callaloo, Text and Performance Quarterly, Anthropology & Education,* and others. He has entries in a series of books and proceedings including: *The Image of the Outsider; Beacon Best 2000: Best Writing of Men and Women of All Colors; Communication, Race, and Family; The Future of Performance Studies,* and others. Bryant is the co-editor of the upcoming book *Performing Education: Pedagogy, Identity, and Reform* (Erlbaum).

Timothy J. Anderson (B.A., Seattle Pacific University) is a writer, truck driver, and horseman. Currently he is a graduate of Lutheran Bible Institute of Seattle (now Trinity College). He has sixteen years of over-the-road trucking experience throughout North America. Anderson's essays have appeared in several local and trade magazines including *Guide Magazine* and *Frontiers*. Interviews of Anderson have appeared in *The Advocate, Overdrive,* and *Truck News*.

Curtiss L. Bailey (B.A., University of New Mexico) is a lieutenant junior grade in the United States Navy. He is presently a surface warfare officer on the USS *Gladiator*. He majored in political science and minored in sociology during his undergraduate studies.

Lisa Bradford (Ph.D., Arizona State University) is currently working as an independent researcher and part-time teacher in Germantown, Wisconsin. Her previous research focused on issues related to intercultural competence in interpersonal communication interactions. Recently she has shifted her research to address issues related to how culture and cultural transitions affect a person's experience with health care services and providers.

Benjamin J. Broome (Ph.D., University of Kansas) is a professor in the Hugh Downs School of Human Communication at Arizona State University. His teaching and scholarship focuses on intercultural communication, conflict resolution, and group facilitation. His publications appear in numerous international journals, and his book *Exploring the Greek Mosaic* received the Distinguished Scholarship Award from the International and Intercultural Communication Division of the National Communication Association. He held the position of Senior Fulbright Scholar in Cyprus from 1994 to 1996, and he continues to work actively with various peace-building groups in the eastern Mediterranean.

Merry C. Buchanan (Ph.D., University of Central Oklahoma) is an assistant professor of corporate communication at the University of Central Oklahoma. Her research emphases are in interpersonal, intercultural, and organizational communication. Dr. Buchanan recently co-authored an article published in *Health Communication* (2002) and won the award for Top Four Paper in the Family Division at the 2002 National Communication Association Convention.

Nancy A. Burrell (Ph.D., Michigan State University) is a professor of communication at the University of Wisconsin-Milwaukee, is both a researcher and practitioner. Her research centers on managing interpersonal conflict in family, organizational, and educational settings. She has edited several books focused on issues in interpersonal communication, classroom instruction, and media effects that synthesize quantitative research through meta-analysis. Recognizing that alternative dispute resolution processes are effective, Professor Burrell is director of the Mediation Center at UWM and administers the Graduate Certificate in Mediation and Negotiation. She helps to design and evaluate mediation programs for school systems, small businesses, and nonprofit organizations. She has presented conflict management seminars and workshops to corporations, small businesses, and nonprofits for the past fifteen years. She mediates for the U.S. Postal Service and the Department of Justice.

Peter Chhuor is an undergraduate student majoring in communication studies at the California State University, San Bernardino.

Rueyling Chuang (Ph.D., Ohio University) is an assistant professor in the Department of Communication Studies at California State University, San Bernardino. Her research interests include intercultural communication, interpersonal communication, cultural diversity, multiculturalism, language and communication, Chinese communication, and conflict resolution. Her work has appeared in *Civic Discourse, Civil Society and the Chinese World, Free Speech Yearbook, Communication and Global Society, Chinese Conflict Management, and Resolutions, Gazette: The International Journal for Communication Studies,* and the *Southern Communication Journal.*

Natalie J. Dollar (Ph.D., University of Washington) is an associate professor of speech communication at Oregon State University-Cascades. Dollar's research focuses on communication, identity, and culture. Much of her published research has focused on Deadheads, street-oriented youth, and the ethnography of communication. She is most interested in studying marginalized speech communities. Her current research projects include a study of U.S. media's movement from the drug culture to drug wars, parenting our grandchildren, and dialogue within the community. Dollar teaches a variety of courses, some of which are ethnographic methods, cultural codes of communication, intercultural communication, and communication theory.

Mary Fong (Ph.D., University of Washington) is an associate professor in the Communication Studies Department at the California State University, San Bernardino. Her areas of teaching and research are cultural and intercultural communication, ethnography of communication, and instructional communication. Three of her conference papers have been presented in divisional Top Three panels at national and regional conventions. She has published in the *Howard Journal of Communication, Journal of Pragmatics, Intercultural Communication Studies, Intercultural Communication: A Reader, Our Voices, Intercultural Encounters,* and others.

Susan Hafen (Ph.D., Ohio University) is an associate professor at Weber State University. In the fifteen years between those two graduate degrees, Hafen worked in the business world as a trainer and human resource manager for Kimberly Clark Corporation in Utah, Mobil Oil in Wyoming, and Potomac Electric Power Company in Washington, D.C. Prior to her business world experience, she taught marketing in high school, certified as a school counselor, and worked as a vocational curriculum specialist. Hafen's eclectic research interests include diversity training, organizational gossip, animal-human semiotics, ethnography, and feminist criticism.

Kristin M. Langellier (Ph.D., Southern Illinois University) is a professor of communication at the University of Maine where she teaches performance studies, narrative studies, and communication theory. She is also a participating faculty member in Women's Studies and Franco American Studies. A former editor of *Text and Performance Quarterly,* she is co-author (with Eric E. Peterson) of *Storytelling in Daily Life: Performing Narrative.* Her numerous publications include research on Franco American family storytelling, personal narrative performance, breast cancer storytelling, and quiltmaking culture.

Wendy Leeds-Hurwitz (Ph.D., University of Pennsylvania) is a professor of communication at the University of Wisconsin-Parkside. Her major areas of expertise are language and social interaction, intercultural communication, and communication theory. She has published articles in such journals as *Communication Theory*, *Research on Language and Social Interaction*, and *Quarterly Journal of Speech*. Major publications include the books *Communication in Everyday Life*, *Semiotics and Communication*, *Wedding as Text*, and the edited collection, *Social Approaches to Communication*.

Edward A. Mabry (Ph.D., Bowling Green State University) is an associate professor of communication, University of Wisconsin-Milwaukee. His research and teaching focuses on group and organizational communication from a social systems perspective with an emphasis on mediated communication. Recent publications include: "Ambiguous Self-Identification and Sincere Communication in CMC," in L. Anolli, R. Ciceri, and G. Riva (Eds.), *Say Not to Say: New Perspectives on Miscommunication* (2002); "Group Communication and Technology: Rethinking the Role of Communication Modality in Group Work and Performance," in L. R. Frey (Ed.), *New Directions in Group Communication* (2002); "The Systems Metaphor in Group Communication," in L. R. Frey, with D. S. Gouran, and M. S. Poole (Eds.), *The Handbook of Group Communication Theory & Research* (1999).

Keturah McEwen (M.A., University of Phoenix) received a degree in organization management. She also received her B.A. in communication studies at the California State University, San Bernardino.

S. Lily Mendoza (Ph. D., Arizona State University) is an assistant professor in culture and communication at the University of Denver. She is the author of *Between the Homeland and the Diaspora: The Politics of Theorizing Filipino and Filipino American Identities* (2002). Her research interests include identity and cultural politics, cultural translation, nationhood, indigenization, transnationalism, and the politics and dynamics of cross-cultural theorizing.

John Oetzel (Ph.D., University of Iowa) is an associate professor in the Department of Communication and Journalism at the University of New Mexico. He teaches courses in intercultural, group, and organizational communication, as well as research methods. His research interests focus on the impact of culture on conflict communication in work groups, organizations, and health settings. His work has appeared in journals such as *Human Communication Research*, *Communication Monographs*, and the *International Journal of Intercultural Relations*. He is co-author (with Stella Ting-Toomey) of *Managing Intercultural Communication Effectively* (2001).

Jerry Pinkney is an undergraduate student majoring in communication studies at the California State University, San Bernardino. He enjoys hip-hop music and dance, and writes poetry and narratives.

Margarita Refugia Olivas (Ph.D., University of Colorado, Boulder) is a part-time lecturer at the California State University, Northridge, in the Communication Studies Department and the Chicana/o Studies Department. Her current research is the Greek system, particularly

Latina sororities, for the past ten years. Her field of study is organizational communication/intercultural communication.

Steven B. Pratt (Ph.D., University of Oklahoma) is a professor in the Department of Communication at the University of Central Oklahoma. His research interests focus on cultural identification and social interaction, with an emphasis on identifying American Indian communicative behaviors. He serves as a traditional and ceremonial leader of the Osage Nation and works extensively with the revitalization of the Osage language.

Anjali Ram (Ph.D., Ohio University) is an assistant professor of communications at Roger Williams University, Bristol, Rhode Island. She studies the immigrant identity, gender issues, and popular culture particularly in relation to the Asian Indian diaspora. Her publications have appeared in journals such as *Women's Studies in Communication, Human Development*, and *Culture and Psychology* and the edited volume *Mediated Women*.

Debra-L Sequeira (Ph.D., University of Washington) is a professor of communication and associate dean of the College of Arts and Sciences at Seattle Pacific University. She has published nationally and internationally in communication and language studies. Her current research focus is in culture and religion.

Robert Westerfelhaus (Ph.D., Ohio University) is an assistant professor at the College of Charleston (Charleston, South Carolina). His research applies rhetorical and semiotic theories to communication issues related to culture, religion, and human sexuality. In 2000, he earned the Religious Communication Association's Dissertation of the Year Award. He has presented over thirty competitively chosen conference papers (five of which were top ranked). He has published articles in *Critical Studies in Media Communication, Communication Quarterly*, and the *Journal of Communication Inquiry*. Forthcoming publications include a book chapter in the second edition of the popular text, *Critical Approaches to Television*. In addition to his numerous academic publications, he is also a frequent contributor to various newspapers.

Gust A. Yep (Ph.D., University of Southern California) is a professor of speech and communication studies and human sexuality studies at San Francisco State University. His research has been published in numerous interdisciplinary journals and anthologies. Most recently, he co-authored a book entitled *Disclosure of HIV Status in Interpersonal Relationships: A Sourcebook for Researchers and Practitioners* (2003) and guest edited a special issue of the *Journal of Homosexuality*, which will also be simultaneously released as a book in Haworth's Gay and Lesbian Studies Series, entitled *Queer Theory and Communication: From Disciplining Queers to Queering the Discipline(s)* (2003). Dr. Yep has received a number of research grants and several teaching and community service awards. In 1999, he was the universitywide San Francisco State University nominee for the Carnegie Foundation U.S. Professors of the Year Award.